AF478853

Klee and America

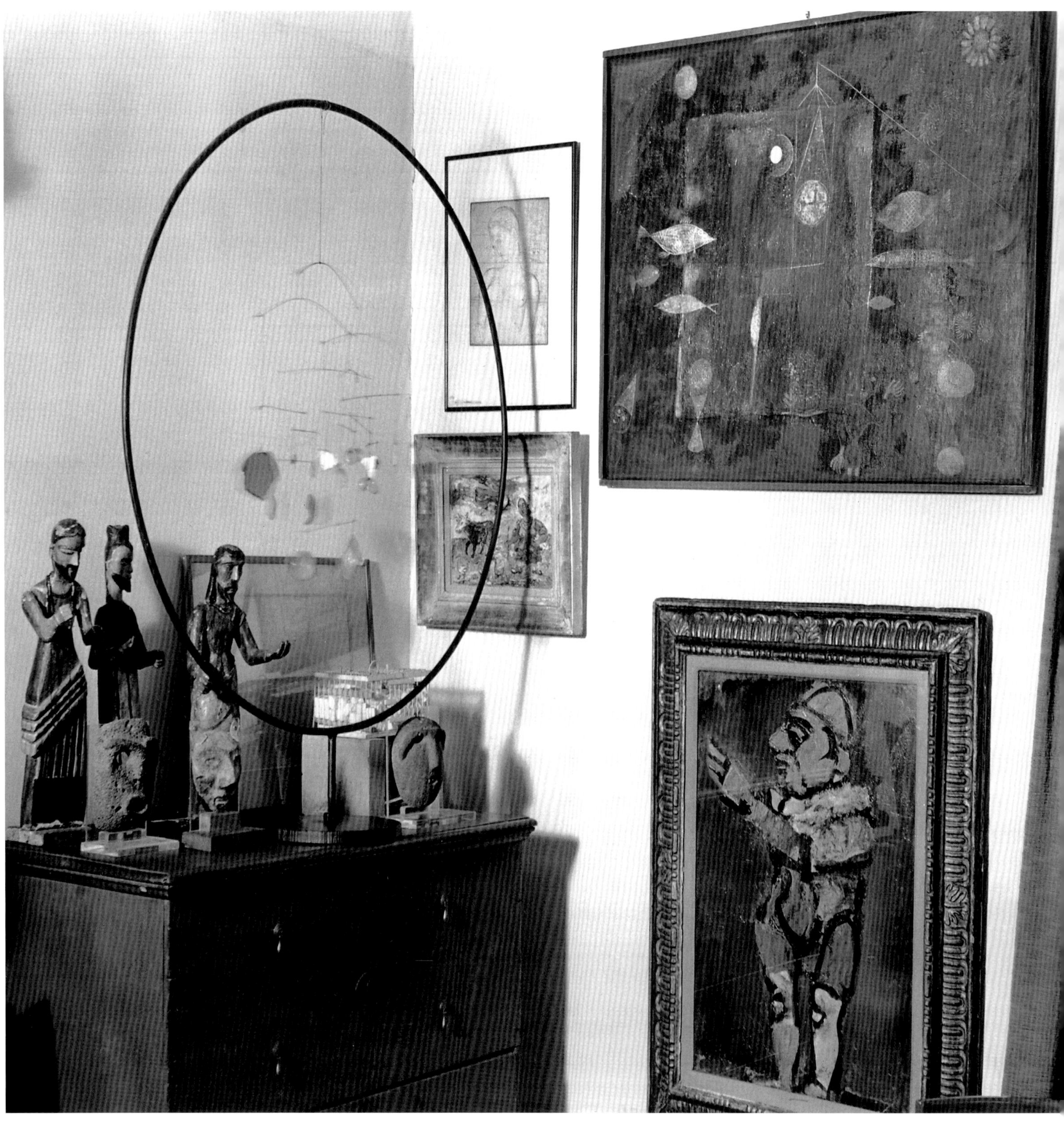

Klee and America

Edited by

Josef Helfenstein and Elizabeth Hutton Turner

With contributions by

Jenny Anger, Vivian Endicott Barnett,

Michael Baumgartner, Bradford Epley, Christa Haiml,

Charles W. Haxthausen, Josef Helfenstein,

Osamu Okuda, Elizabeth Hutton Turner

Published by

THE MENIL COLLECTION

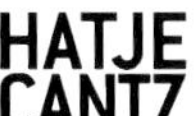
HATJE CANTZ

Published on the occasion of the exhibition
"Klee and America"
Organized by The Menil Collection
Curated by Josef Helfenstein

Neue Galerie New York
March 10–May 22, 2006

The Phillips Collection, Washington, D.C.
June 16–September 10, 2006

The Menil Collection, Houston
October 6, 2006–January 14, 2007

"Klee and America" is sponsored nationally by Altria Group, Inc.

The exhibition is also generously supported by Mary Lawrence Porter; National Endowment for the Arts; The Brown Foundation, Inc. of Houston; Marion Barthelme and Jeff Fort; Nancy B. Negley; The Eleanor and Frank Freed Foundation; Karol Kreymer and Robert J. Card, M.D., in memory of Edward B. Mayo; Sotheby's; Susan Vaughan Foundation, Inc.; and Clare F. Sprunt; with additional support from Fayez Sarofim & Co.; The Wortham Foundation; and the City of Houston.

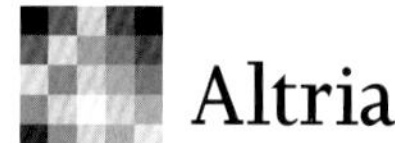 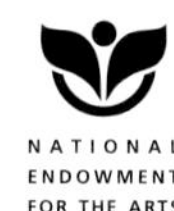

Front cover: *Jugendlicher Schauspieler=Maske [Youth Actor's Mask]* (detail), 1924.252. The Museum of Modern Art, New York, The Sidney and Harriet Janis Collection, 616.67 (see pl. 28).

Back cover (trade edition): Paul Klee in Bern, Switzerland, 1911 (see fig.1).

Frontispiece: View of Louise and Walter Arensbergs' residence, Los Angeles, 1945 (see fig. 55).

Published by
Hatje Cantz Verlag
Senefelderstrasse 12
73760 Ostfildern-Ruit, Germany
Tel. +49 711 4405-0   Fax +49 711 4405-220
www.hatjecantz.com

Hatje Cantz books are available internationally at selected bookstores and from distribution partners world wide. Distribution information is included on page 315 of this catalog.

Printed in Germany

ISBN 3-7757-1723-4 (trade edition, hardcover)
ISBN 0-939594-62-5 (museum edition, softcover; available only from the museum)
LCCN 2005937548

Contents

Intimate yet daring, abstract yet masterful, Paul Klee's reach and output were vast. His paintings and works on paper have great appeal and depict subjects ripe with symbolism and objects rendered in simple yet complex ways. Klee looked to the spontaneity of children, whose fertile imaginations guided him to create works with mysterious, dreamlike references that strip away the artifice from recognizable forms and objects.

Klee's first exhibition in America took place in 1921 at the Société Anonyme in New York City. It was an event that introduced Americans to the work of an artist who would become one of the most recognizable and admired twentieth-century modernist painters. Eighty-five years after that inaugural exhibition, Klee's work will be seen again in "Klee and America," an exhibition that brings to light Klee's influential relationship with the American art community of the mid-twentieth century.

Altria Group, Inc. is proud to sponsor "Klee and America." This exhibition is one of many projects that we have supported over fifty years that highlight the artistic achievements of the innovative, pioneering artists of the last century. Our program was founded on a belief in the value that creativity plays in defining our culture, ourselves, and our histories. With his unique vision and style, Klee symbolizes the important role of the visionary artist in society and the durability of that work over generations.

Jennifer P. Goodale
Vice President, Contributions
Altria Corporate Services, Inc.
Altria Group, Inc.

Lenders to the Exhibition

Albright-Knox Art Gallery, Buffalo, New York

The Art Institute of Chicago

The Arts Club of Chicago

The Baltimore Museum of Art, Maryland

Calder Foundation, New York

The Carl Djerassi Trust, San Francisco

Colby College Museum of Art, Waterville, Maine

Columbus Museum of Art, Ohio

The Denver Art Museum

The Detroit Institute of Arts

Frelinghuysen Morris Foundation, Lenox, Massachusetts

Galerie Jan Krugier, Ditesheim & Cie, Geneva

Hope Dempsey Hungerford

Collection Maria and Conrad Janis, Los Angeles

M. R. Lowe

Marion Koogler McNay Art Museum, San Antonio

The Menil Collection, Houston

The Metropolitan Museum of Art, New York

Museum of Art, Rhode Island School of Design, Providence

The Museum of Fine Arts, Houston

The Museum of Modern Art, New York

National Gallery of Canada, Ottawa

Neue Galerie New York

Norton Simon Museum, Pasadena, California

The Old Jail Art Center, Albany, Texas

Philadelphia Museum of Art

The Phillips Collection, Washington, D.C.

The Picker Art Gallery, Colgate University, Hamilton, New York

The Pierpont Morgan Library, New York

Private Collection, Los Angeles

Private Collection, New York

Private Collection, Pennsylvania

Private Collection, St. Louis, Missouri

Juan Rafael Coronel Rivera

Sabarsky Gallery, New York

The Saint Louis Art Museum

San Francisco Museum of Modern Art

Smith College Museum of Art, Northampton, Massachusetts

Solomon R. Guggenheim Museum, New York

Collection of Michael and Judy Steinhardt, New York

Tobin Foundation for Theatre Arts, San Antonio

Worthington Collection, Chicago

Yale University Art Gallery, New Haven, Connecticut

Preface

"Klee and America," organized by The Menil Collection, is the first large-scale exhibition of Klee's work to take place in the United States in almost two decades. Yet, despite Klee's low profile with American audiences in recent years, the work of the German-born artist has enjoyed a long and complex history of enthusiastic reception in the United States, especially during the 1930s and 1940s. By the early 1920s Klee was one of the leading figures within the European modernist movement, often mentioned alongside Picasso and Matisse. Over the next few decades his acclaim in Europe was quickly paralleled in the United States, where both private collectors and major museums sought out his works with increased passion. Why were American collectors first attracted to Klee's art? How did the political and economic upheavals in Europe prior to and during World War II affect Klee's reputation? What sort of legacy did Klee leave for American artists of the mid-twentieth century? This exhibition and book offer an in-depth exploration of these questions.

The concept for "Klee and America" began over a decade ago with the extensive research carried out by the Klee Foundation in Bern, Switzerland, for the ongoing nine-volume Paul Klee catalogue raisonné project. As the material for each work's provenance was compiled, it became increasingly clear that many of Klee's finest works had fascinating histories in America and remained there in prominent collections.

The narrative of Klee's success in America forms around several critical collectors, museum directors, curators, and gallery dealers. Notable among the earliest American collectors of the works of Paul Klee was Katherine Dreier, a wealthy and diligent supporter of contemporary art. With artists Marcel Duchamp and Man Ray, she founded the Société Anonyme in 1920, an association that sponsored the exhibitions of pioneering abstract art in which Klee's paintings were first shown to the American public. Klee's reputation in New York grew as art historians and dealers, including William Valentiner, Galka Scheyer, and J.B. Neumann, promoted his work. Other significant collectors, including Arthur Jerome Eddy from Chicago, Albert C. Barnes from Pennsylvania, and Duncan Phillips from Washington, D.C., also began to acquire Klee's art as they traveled abroad. In Los Angeles, Walter and Louise Arensberg began a collection of Klee's paintings that would be second only to that of Katherine Dreier.

Throughout the 1930s and 1940s, Klee's art was pursued in the United States with increasing vigor. American collectors demanded greater numbers of his works and sought out increasingly important watercolors and paintings. In Germany, however, Klee's works were targeted in Hitler's campaign against Entartete Kunst (Degenerate Art), and the market for Klee's art collapsed in 1933. To escape the censorship of the National Socialists, the vast majority of Germany's most prominent artists and art dealers sought refuge elsewhere in Europe and in the United States. Klee, who was removed from his teaching post in Düsseldorf in 1933, moved to Switzerland, his childhood home, but continued to be represented by a number of German-Jewish art dealers who immigrated to the United States. For American audiences, Klee's significance became fully pronounced shortly before and during the World War II period as pivotal works were added to the collections of The Museum of Modern Art, the Solomon R. Guggenheim Museum in New York, and later to The Art Institute of Chicago.

The current exhibition and catalogue draw together an impressive group of Klee's works, loaned both from major American museums and from private collections that are rarely, if ever, seen by the public. We have carefully selected each work for its American provenance; owners have included prominent architects Walter

Gropius and Philip Johnson; author Ernest Hemingway; and artists Alexander Calder, Mark Tobey, and Andy Warhol, not to mention the critical collectors and dealers listed above.

We are pleased to offer "Klee and America" at three unique American venues, each of which provides a different context for Klee's work. The Neue Galerie's dedication to German art continues to highlight an important segment of modern art that has often been overlooked in the United States. The late Serge Sabarsky's commitment and expertise as a dealer accompanied by Ronald S. Lauder's passion as a collector continue the legacy of critical dealers and collectors that helped make Klee's work visible in America.

The long history of the Phillips Collection reminds us of the dedication of early collectors of Klee, including its founder Duncan Phillips, whose intimate "Klee Room" influenced a generation of visitors to the museum. Dominique and John de Menil not only acquired a substantial group of Klee's paintings and drawings in the 1950s and 1960s, but simultaneously worked to show his art to the people of Texas, especially through exhibitions like the one they organized at the Museum of Fine Arts, Houston in 1960, "Paul Klee." We hope that "Klee and America" will provide the opportunity for viewers in the United States to once again experience the power of this enigmatic and enduring artist.

Josef Helfenstein
Director, The Menil Collection, Houston

Renée Price
Director, Neue Galerie New York

Jay Gates
Director, The Phillips Collection,
Washington, D.C.

Acknowledgments

An exhibition of this scope is impossible without the support, assistance, and hard work of many people. My profound thanks go to the many institutions and private collectors listed on page 9 who generously made their works available for this exhibition. I was also fortunate to have the knowledgeable advice and support of Stefan Frey at the Paul Klee Estate and Michael Baumgartner, Fabienne Eggelhöffer, Heidi Frautschi, Edith Heinimann, Christine Hopfengart, Osamu Okuda, and Eva Wiederkehr at the Zentrum Paul Klee, Bern, Switzerland.

I am delighted to have Renée Price at the Neue Galerie New York, and Jay Gates at The Phillips Collection, Washington, D.C., join The Menil Collection in hosting this exhibition. My thanks go out to Deputy Director Scott Gutterman and Registrar Sefa Seglam at the Neue Galerie and Chief Curator Eliza Rathbone, Associate Curator Elsa Smithgall, and Registrar Chris Ketcham at The Phillips Collection for their hard work coordinating the exhibition at their ends. I also send my sincere thanks to the colleagues who contributed essays for this catalogue: Jenny Anger, Vivian Endicott Barnett, Michael Baumgartner, Bradford Epley, Christa Haiml, Charles W. Haxthausen, and Osamu Okuda. Elizabeth Hutton Turner deserves special recognition not only for the contribution of her superb essay, but also for her assistance as co-editor of the catalogue.

First, at The Menil Collection, my thanks go to Louisa Stude Sarofim, President, and the entire Board of Trustees, who gave me their unconditional support. This exhibition was possible only through the hard work of the Menil's staff, who were instrumental in bringing this important project to Houston. I also owe a sincere debt of gratitude to Curatorial Assistant Sarah Eckhardt, who assisted in all aspects of the exhibition and catalogue from the earliest stages; Curatorial Assistant Clare Elliott, whose efforts were also critical in coordinating the exhibition catalogue; and Chief Curator Matthew Drutt, who provided staff and valuable input on the logistics of the exhibition. Registrar Anne Adams and Assistant Registrar Judy Kwon, arranged the safe transport and handling of the works at the Menil. Bear Parham, Tom Walsh, and Peter Bernal in Art Services ensured the careful and thoughtful installation of the exhibition. Brooke Stroud and Tony Martinez in Exhibitions and Public Programs provided the groundwork for a beautifully designed presentation and provided excellent programming to accompany the exhibition. Steve McConathy and the Building and Security staff worked diligently to safeguard and protect the exhibition, from the time they built the first wall, and Will Taylor and his staff in Planning and Advancement assured that there would be the financial support to get those walls built, as well as making sure the public was well aware of the exhibition's generous patrons. Elizabeth Lunning and the entire Conservation staff provided valuable care for these delicate treasures. Laureen Schipsi, Manager of Publications, provided important assistance with the editing and distribution of this book. Other colleagues at the Menil who contributed to catalogue research in invaluable ways include Geraldine Aramanda, Archivist; Susan Braeuer, Project Curatorial Assistant; Stephanie Capps, Assistant Librarian; Joanna Cook, Manager of Rights and Reproductions; Phil Heagy, Librarian; Mary Kadish, Collections Registrar; Kristina Van Dyke, Associate Curator of Collections; and interns Stephanie Hunter and Anne Kemper. Last but not least, I'd like to thank my assistant, Kristin Schwartz-Lauster, for her invaluable assistance and good humor.

Don Quaintance is to be applauded for his sensitive attention to the design of the catalogue, aided by Elizabeth Frizzell. Special thanks are also due to Polly Koch for her skillful editing of the texts and to Russell Stockman for his expert translations. I am delighted to be working again with Hatje Cantz and would like to extend special thanks to publisher Markus Hartmann for his support of this project and to Britta Nething for production assistance.

Valuable research assistance was provided by the following people: Stephanie D'Alessandro at the Art Institute of Chicago; Susan K. Anderson at the Philadelphia Museum of Art Archives;

Julie Bakke at The Museum of Fine Arts, Houston; Andrea Clark at the Norton Simon Museum, Pasadena, California; Susan Davidson at the Solomon R. Guggenheim Museum, New York; Thomas D. Grischkowsky and Kathleen Tunney at The Museum of Modern Art, New York; Harald Krejci and Valentina Sonzogni at the Austrian Frederick and Lillian Kieslcr Private Foundation, Vienna; Sarah Noreika at the Barnes Foundation, Merion, Pennsylvania; and Hector Olea, Houston.

Finally, no exhibition of this scale is possible without the generous support of sponsors. My sincere gratitude goes to Altria Group, Inc. for their national sponsorship of this exhibition. I also wish to thank the following supporters for their generous contributions: Mary Lawrence Porter; National Endowment for the Arts; The Brown Foundation, Inc. of Houston; Marion Barthelme and Jeff Fort; Nancy B. Negley; The Eleanor and Frank Freed Foundation; Karol Kreymer and Robert J. Card, M.D., in memory of Edward B. Mayo; Sotheby's; Susan Vaughan Foundation, Inc.; and Clare F. Sprunt; with additional support from Fayez Sarofim & Co.; The Wortham Foundation; and the City of Houston.

Josef Helfenstein
Director, The Menil Collection, Houston

Introduction

The subject of "Klee and America" is at once unlikely and provocative. What was America to Paul Klee? Paul Klee never harbored any fantasies of "Amerika." Unlike Picasso, he was not entranced by American popular culture—never dreamed of the land of cowboys and skyscrapers. A single comment regarding a performance of Loie Fuller and a single rendering of Josephine Baker are the only known instances of "American icons" drifting into his psyche. Unlike Miró who desperately wanted to see America, Paul Klee himself was never curious, never wanted to set foot in the New World. Klee, or rather his works, came to America by way of emissaries. Initially, America's first generation of modernists like the painter Albert Bloch and collector Arthur Jerome Eddy traveled to Munich to pursue Kandinsky and the Blaue Reiter, but soon discovered the distinctiveness of Paul Klee highly esteemed by his colleagues. For the better part of the next two decades, it remained for American artists, collectors, and students following familiar patterns of travel and study abroad to beat a path to Klee's door in Munich and to the Bauhaus in Weimar and later in Dessau. Throughout the twenties Klee's works criss-crossed the Atlantic and the American continent with great frequency, thanks primarily to the efforts of Galka Scheyer in California and Katherine Dreier and J. B. Neumann in New York.

Though Klee might have gained a foothold through exhibition and promotion—particularly through the campaigning of both Scheyer and Dreier to educate the general public about personal expression and modern art—Klee's art remained without critical discourse or context in this country until the late 1920s. Whereas in Paris, Klee was already celebrated as one of the fathers of Dada and Surrealism, in America he was described by critic Henry McBride in 1924 for the readers of the *New York Herald* as "that strange meteor from Switzerland." By the late 1920s, only two major

private collectors of Klee (Dreier and Scheyer) existed in the United States. If asked in January 1930, Klee would have predicted with good reason, given the recent publication of René Crevel's monograph in France and the accession of his works into many German museums, including the Nationalgalerie, Berlin, that the future of his success lay in Europe. By 1933, however, with the rise of Hitler's National Socialist regime and the suspension of Klee from the Düsseldorf Academy, it became clear that only a breakthrough in the New World could salvage Klee's career. With the arrival of exiled Bauhaus artists and Surrealists as well as dealers Karl Nierendorf and Curt Valentin in the late 1930s, America ultimately provided both a great market for Klee's work as well as an important forum for his message.

What was Klee to America? More so than any other modern master, the fortunes of Paul Klee parallel America's coming of age in the modern world. Diego Rivera easily recognized an analogous sensibility at once ancient and childlike that united Klee with the New World. Perhaps it was Klee's lack of a single style or the sheer range of his experiments that made him so compelling, as Marcel Duchamp once suggested. Certainly Klee appealed to young Americans wanting to free themselves from the limitations of geometric abstraction and Surrealist narrative. Without doubt Klee's cryptic marks—his solutions and suggestions concerning almost every type of composition and every formal problem imaginable—had a liberating influence upon the Abstract Expressionist generation of the 1940s and 1950s. Ultimately this was the moment when the audience was with Klee; when they also dared to dream of a universal language of art, in Klee's words, "a work of really great breadth."

What of the legacy of Klee? According to the Klee Foundation, over ten percent of the artist's complete output—approximately 1,150 works—is held in collections in the United States, yet his influence in this country has never fully been investigated. On the occasion of Klee's 1987 Retrospective at The Museum of Modern Art, New York, critic John Russell suggested that the scale of Klee's cabinet-sized pictures in American museums belied the artist's monumental impact upon modernism in this country. It was, in his opinion, ultimately the perception of the "little work, little man syndrome" that distracted from the consideration of Klee's highly original form and content. Russell observed, however, that Klee's influence was so pervasive that it would be difficult to pass a day in the city and not be reminded of Klee and his manner of signifying bodies and faces, his floating arrows and initials, and his shorthand architectures. Today, nearly twenty years after the MoMA show, in a similar retrospective moment for Klee, The Menil Collection seeks to explore the reasons for Klee's prominence in America—by assembling a team of scholars to document and analyze the American exhibition, reception, and pedagogy of Klee—and thereby restore an influential but often overlooked chapter to the history of modern art.

Josef Helfenstein and Elizabeth Hutton Turner

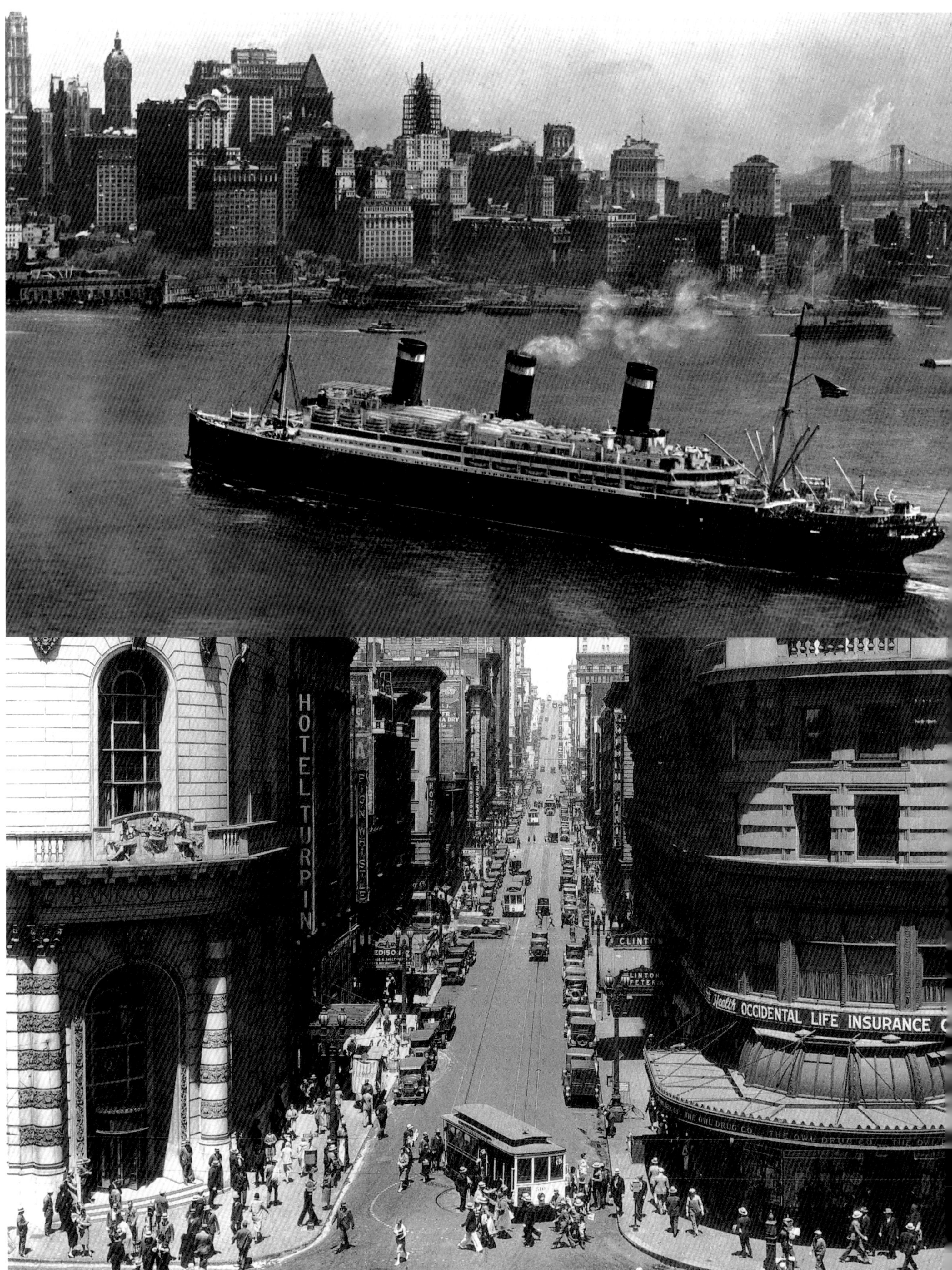

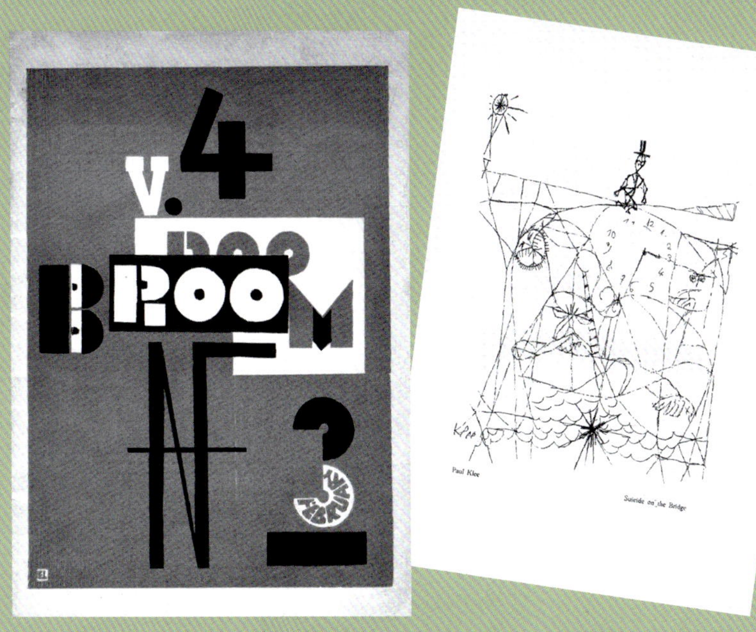
v.4
nos.?
BROOM
N.?
3
Paul Klee
Suicide on the Bridge

The Beginnings:
Paul Klee and America before 1920

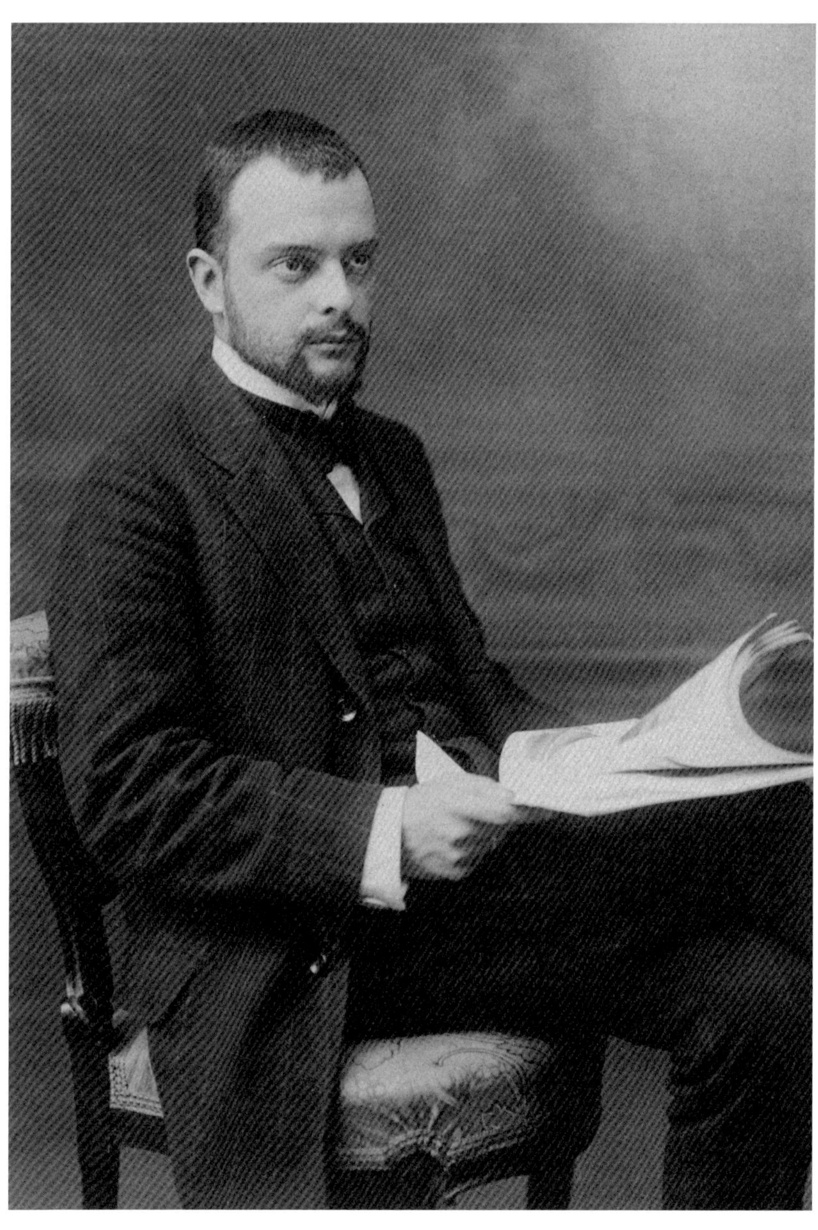

n January 1914 Paul Klee sent twenty-five watercolors by American Express to the well-known American collector Arthur Jerome Eddy, a legal advisor on cartel issues and a partner in a Chicago law firm (fig. 2).[1] He pinned high hopes on the shipment. In contrast to his fellow artists Vasily Kandinsky and Franz Marc—the organizers of the Blaue Reiter exhibition, whose paintings were distinguished by their expressive colors and formal daring—Klee's idiosyncratic drawings, many of them only postcard size, had as yet excited little interest on the part of collectors of contemporary art, meeting with slight notice or even rejection from the art press.

Klee had studied art on his own for four years while living at his parents' house in Bern, Switzerland. Then in late November 1906 he had moved with his wife, Lily, to Munich, where he tried to find a foothold—at first with little success—in the local art world. As late as 1911, Klee's friend Hans Bloesch, editor of *Die Alpen*, a Swiss cultural monthly in Bern, still found it necessary to challenge the public's lack of understanding of Klee (fig. 1). He wrote that the response to Klee's art "has always been a cautious silence on the part of the critics and helpless mystification on the part of the public, which after the initial shock, in its hunger for making aesthetic judgments, has turned either scornfully or dismissively toward more familiar grazing spots…. What Paul Klee is striving to do is to express in art his own subjective way of seeing; his is an honest search for the appropriate means of expression for such seeing and feeling."[2]

By the end of 1913, despite repeated efforts, Klee had captured the interest of only a single well-known collector, the Blaue Reiter patron Bernhard Koehler, to whom he sold nine works. And it was only recently that he had begun making a few straggling sales from the exhibitions mounted by gallery owners Hans Goltz in Munich and Herwarth Walden in Berlin. Given this situation, the fact that a high-profile collector like Eddy had expressed interest in Klee's work seemed promising indeed. Eddy had begun collecting art in 1884 at the age of twenty-five, had commissioned portraits of himself from Auguste Rodin and James McNeill Whistler (fig. 3), and had caused a stir in Munich's avant-garde circles in 1912 with his great enthusiasm for the work of Kandinsky.[3] The large shipment that immediately went to Eddy was part of Klee's strategy of demonstrating the diversity of his offerings and thereby stimulating the buyer's interest.

Germany—Mecca for Nineteenth-Century American Artists

A full two years earlier, Klee had made the following interesting observation in *Die Alpen* regarding the importance of American collectors to the Munich art market: "Munich has seen a number of inroads made on its reputation as a fine art center, mainly as a result of the broad dissemination of French Impressionism. Evidence

Page 16
USS Leviathan steams into New York City harbor, 1925.

Cablecar turnabout, Powell at Market Streets, San Francisco, c. 1925.

Page 17
Cover and page 171 of *Broom* 4, no. 3 (February 1923). Klee's *Selbstmörder auf der Brücke [Suicide on the Bridge]* (1913.100) is reproduced.

Fig. 1
Paul Klee in Bern, Switzerland, 1911.

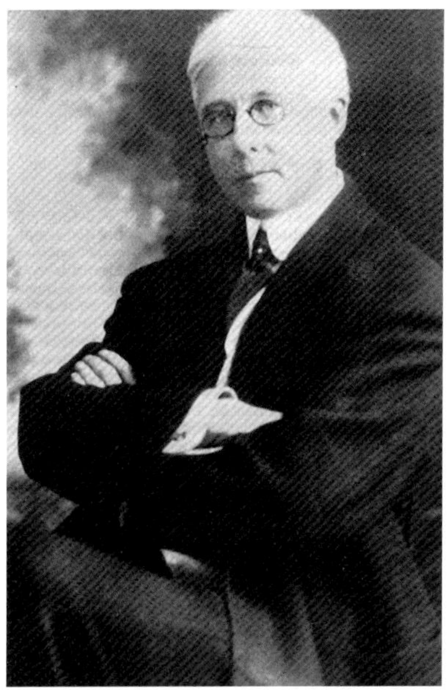

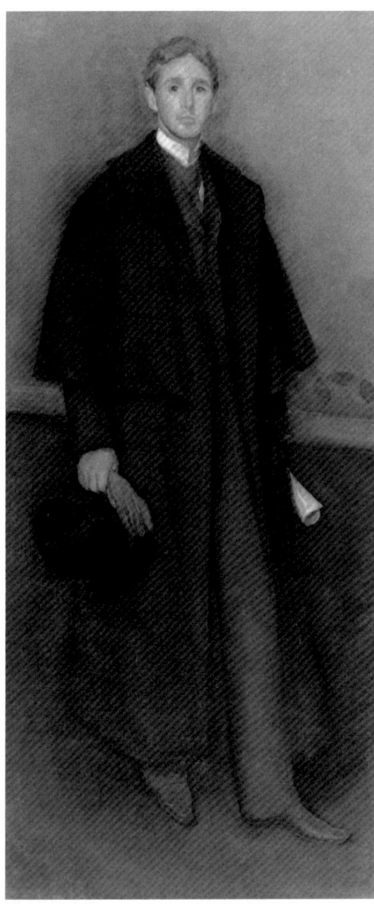

of this is the ominous fact that it is now Germany that is primarily involved in the local market and no longer America as before."[4] Klee's statement suggests that things had once been better in large part because American artists and collectors had enlivened the local scene. Until the 1890s, when Impressionism began to draw their attention to Paris, Munich had been the chief focus of their interest.

It was not the first city in Germany to attract American artists. In the mid nineteenth century, an art center had developed in Düsseldorf around an academy whose faculty enjoyed an outstanding reputation.[5] The most important outlet for this school of painters was New York's Düsseldorf Gallery, which dominated the city's art market at that time—it was there that the young Henry James developed his artistic tastes.[6] But in the second half of the century, Düsseldorf's position as a magnet for American artists and collectors was taken over by Munich. Between 1870 and 1900, nearly five hundred American painters and sculptors (roughly a third of them of German ancestry) came to the Bavarian capital for brief or extended stays, studying either at the academy or privately.[7] Some American painters grouped themselves around their countryman Franz Duveneck, adopting his free painting style and developing an expressive, imaginative form of landscape painting (they came to be known as the "Duveneck Boys"). Others made their way to the Bavarian village of Polling, which became an American artists' colony dominated by J. Frank Currier.[8]

Klee first went to Munich in 1898 to study in the private painting class of Heinrich Knirr and with Franz von Stuck at the academy. At that time a number of Americans were still studying there, even though the American art world had largely shifted its attention to Paris. One of Klee's fellow students in Knirr's class was an American by the name of David Karfunkle, who was later active in New York as a painter.[9]

German Avant-Garde in Early Twentieth-Century America

Because of the shift of interest from Munich to Paris in the closing years of the nineteenth century, the art of Germany's early twentieth-century avant-garde was slow to find admirers in the United States. Movements like the Secession, to say nothing of such avant-garde groups as Die Brücke or Der Blaue Reiter, made their impact there considerably later than they had in Europe.[10] Instead American notions of the European avant-garde were mainly influenced by

Fig. 2
Arthur Jerome Eddy, n.d.

Fig. 3
James McNeill Whistler, *Arrangement in Flesh Colour and Brown: Portrait of Arthur Jerome Eddy*, 1894. Oil on canvas, 81⅞ x 36¼ inches (210 x 93 cm). Art Institute of Chicago, Arthur Jerome Eddy Memorial Collection, 1931.501.

French modernism. All the more remarkable, then, was the "Exhibition of Contemporary German Graphic Art" assembled by the German art dealer and critic Martin Birnbaum on the model of the Berlin Secession's "Black–White" exhibitions. He presented the exhibition at the New York branch of the Berlin Photographic Company in the winter of 1912–13. The core of his selection of 370 works was made up of pieces by such artists as Max Klinger, Käthe Kollwitz, Max Liebermann, and Heinrich Vogler, but there were also works by Marc, Kandinsky, Lyonel Feininger, Wilhelm Lehmbruck, Moritz Melzer, Emil Nolde, and Max Pechstein, to name only the most prominent, all of them exhibiting for the first time in America.[11]

However limited it was, Birnbaum's view of the essence of German art—in his foreword to the catalogue, he insisted that "Germany's artistic genius has always been distinctly graphic"[12]—was in accord with contemporary thinking. Birnbaum's annual trips to Europe took him to Germany, Austro-Hungary, and Scandinavia rather than Paris, and despite his narrow focus, he proved to be a profound connoisseur and admirer of contemporary German art movements. This was in contrast to Walt Kuhn, the organizer of the Armory Show that opened in New York a few months later in February 1913. Kuhn showed little interest in current developments in Germany, and except for Kandinsky's legendary *Improvisation No. 27* (1912), he paid no notice to the German avant-garde. Birnbaum's show had already included Kandinsky, exhibiting the artist's color lithograph *Composition No. 4* (1911), which had been reproduced in the *Der Blaue Reiter* almanac. In his memoirs Birnbaum rightly emphasized his trailblazing role: "The Armory Show, a turning point in the development of American art, had not yet familiarized us with the work of these [German artists], who are now enthusiastically accepted but were then treated like Anarchists."[13]

Eddy and Klee

The exhibition at the Berlin Photographic Company definitely piqued the interest of people like photographer Alfred Stieglitz, whose Galerie 291 was just around the corner.[14] But Eddy's first exposure to the German avant-garde was paradoxically through the Armory Show.[15] Although the twenty-five works Eddy bought at that exhibition were almost exclusively French, it was Kandinsky's *Improvisation No. 27*—bought by Stieglitz—that most impressed him. As a result, he called on Kandinsky in Munich that same year and returned to America with eighteen of the artist's works.[16] Through his interest in Kandinsky and Marc, Eddy also became acquainted with Klee, whose work he might have seen in the second group show of the Munich gallery Neue Kunst Hans Goltz and whom he possibly even met in Munich.[17]

Soon after Eddy's return to Chicago, Klee's American Express shipment arrived. The range of the work astonished Eddy. Klee had deliberately larded his selection with color or tonal watercolors, assuming that they would appeal to the collector more than drawings. And Eddy appeared to confirm those suspicions, writing to Klee: "I have never bought either etchings or small drawings, because I cannot afford to buy all forms of art, so I confine myself almost exclusively to paintings."[18] Despite this reservation, Eddy asked the artist to send him a number of black-and-white works as well, a request that Klee complied with by return mail. After tough negotiations, which tell us something of the two protagonists' highly developed business sense, Klee and Eddy finally agreed on the purchase of six works for a total of 400 marks (fig. 4).[19] In his choices Eddy was intent on securing a representative overview of Klee's work from the previous years.[20] His selection included the important *Steinhauer II (getont) [Stonecutters II (tinted)]* (1910.74), the only work of Klee's that had been reproduced in the *Der Blaue Reiter* almanac, which gave it a certain documentary value.

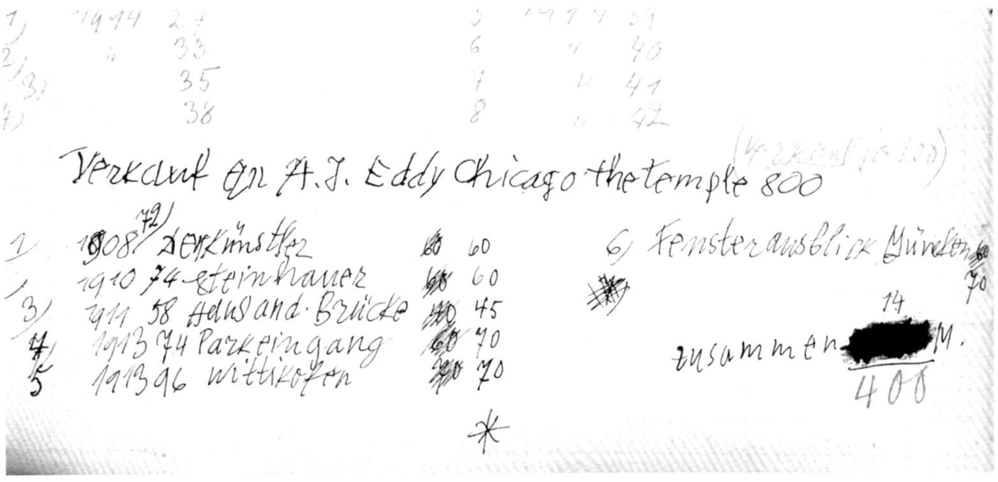

Fig. 4
Paul Klee's entry regarding sales to Arthur Jerome Eddy, œuvre catalogue, Katalog A 1 1883–1918.

"Cubists and Post-Impressionism"

In his epoch-making book *Cubists and Post-Impressionism* (1914), Eddy devoted a full four pages to Klee's work in the chapter "The New Art in Munich," as much space as he allotted to Gabriele Münter or Marianne von Werefkin—a clear judgment of Klee's high value for him.[21] By comparison, he gave Marc and Alexei Jawlensky a page each, whereas Kandinsky, Eddy's favorite, received a full twenty-four.[22]

Of Klee, Eddy wrote: "There is another and almost unknown artist, P. Klee, who is very highly esteemed by the most advanced men. There is certainly an exquisite refinement to his line; it is so alive it scintillates."[23] Eddy definitely tagged Klee, whose artistic importance he found difficult to assess, as a draftsman rather than a painter. Furthermore, the attribute "exquisite refinement" had a somewhat negative connotation in Eddy's terminology, suggesting that he had certain reservations about Klee's idiosyncrasy. Significantly, he reproduced Klee's pen-and-brush wash drawing *Das Haus an der Brücke [The House by the Bridge]* (1911.58, fig. 5) in the chapter "What Is Cubism," which was devoted to Pablo Picasso, and not where it rightly belonged, in "The New Art in Munich."[24] Apparently Klee's delicate "Post-Impressionist" drawing did not fit into Eddy's concept of the new art in Munich, which he described, using the example of Kandinsky, as "*spiritual … based on the inner [world]*" and future-oriented ("before him an unlimited view").[25] This was in contrast to the Cubism of Picasso, which he characterized as "*physical*" and "based on the *outer* world"—further describing Picasso's work as at an "impasse," with the explanation that "further progress is impossible, further scientific subdivision is unattainable, his art in that direction is finished."[26]

Eddy represented the type of middle-class collector that was typical of America but new to Europe, collectors who had amassed a considerable fortune as entrepreneurs, merchants, or attorneys. In the eyes of established European collectors, who came from the nobility and the upper class, these Americans were parvenus lacking in family tradition. But it was precisely this supposed lack that proved to be these collectors' strength. They viewed the artists they supported as kindred spirits who, like themselves, had shrugged off inherited values and traditions to seek new ways of self-realization as individualists capable of taking risks. In his foreword to *Cubists and Post-Impressionism*, Eddy explicitly referred to this spiritual affinity between the rising class of business and professional people in America and contemporary artists: "The young painter looks at the great painters of yesterday and exclaims, 'What is the use? I cannot excel them in their way; I must do something in my own way.' It is the same in business; the young merchant studies the methods of the successful men in his line and says, 'It is idle form to copy their methods. I will do something in my own way,' and he displays his goods differently, advertises differently, conducts his business differently, and if successful is hailed as a genius, if a failure he is regarded as a visionary or an eccentric—the result making all the difference in the world in the verdict of the public."[27]

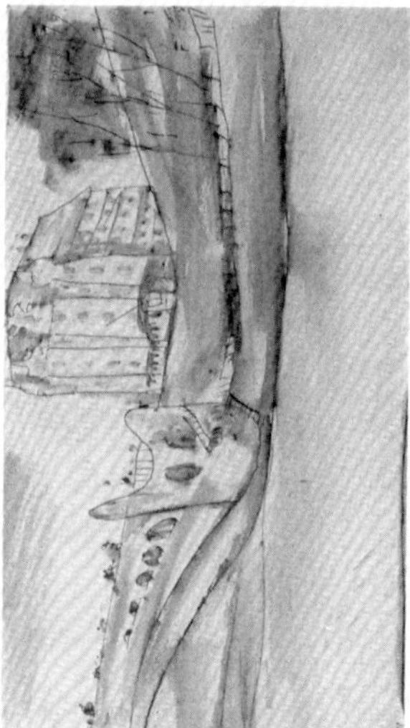

symbol. Without the double delight — the combination of these two quite distinct delights, there can be no art.

To the writer of prose there may come a beautiful fancy; he delights in it and hastens to record his thought. He may write the most flowing, the most perfect prose, but as he writes he is still occupied with his thought; his sole object is to find words which will but express it. The same fancy comes to the poet; he, too, delights in it, and seeks to record it; but when the poet touches pen to paper he is seized with a new and an entirely distinct delight, a delight *in his method of expressing* his thought; he may even permit his delight in his symbol, the flow, rhythm and ring of rhyme, to sweep him onward in forgetfulness of his first fancy — literature is filled with such examples.

Now and then a writer of prose expresses himself so finely, writes so well, that we feel instinctively and immediately not only the delight in the thought, but also a certain amount of delight in the manner of expressing the thought, in the style, . . . and to the extent of the *double* delight such prose is art, for art, as we shall see, is by no means confined to the five so-called fine arts.

No hard and fast line can be drawn between that which is art and that which is not art, the one fades imperceptibly into the other.

And farther on in the same little volume:*

The current notions of art are such and the current notions of labor are such that it may seem to most of you as though any attempt to discuss the two together could result only in a waste of words; yet time was when art and labor were so intimately united in the great domain of human effort that the one almost invariably implied more or less of the other; and the time will yet be when there will be no labor without at least some art, even as there is now and ever has been no art without at least some labor.

Art lies not in the employment, but in the *manner* of the employment of the powers of nature for an end; not in the task, but in the *attitude* of the worker towards his task.

 ◇ ◇ ◇

Whether a Cubist painting is or is not art does not depend upon the opinion of either critic or multitude; if it did it would be art to one man and not to another, art to one generation and not to another — an illogical conclusion.

* "Delight; the Soul of Art," lecture V, " Delight in Labor."

KLEE
House by the Brook

Fig. 5
Paul Klee, *Das Haus an der Brücke [The House by the Bridge]*, 1911.58. Pen and brush wash on paper mounted on cardboard, dimensions unknown. Location unknown. Reproduced in Arthur Jerome Eddy, *Cubists and Post-Impressionism* (Chicago: A. C. McClurg, 1914), 87–88.

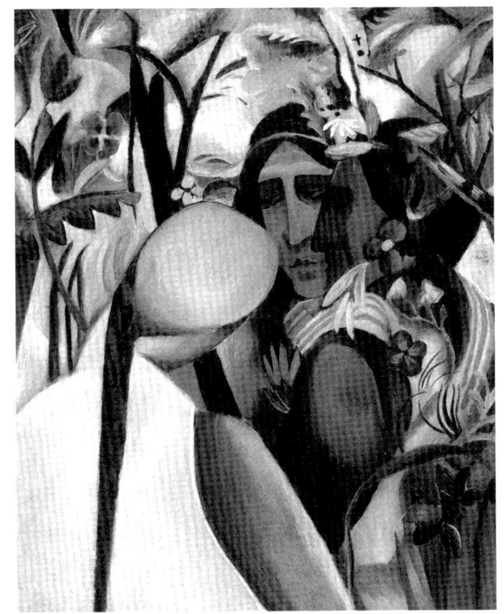

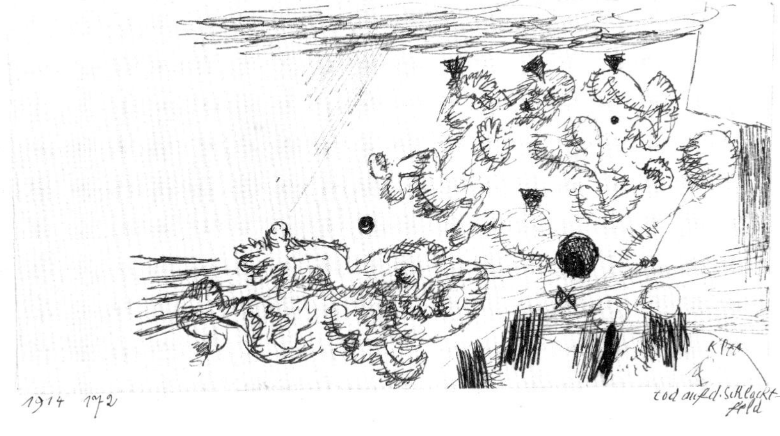

Klee and America

But what was Klee's relationship to American culture? His intellectual and artistic consciousness was informed by the classic Western intellectual and educational canon—even though, in the manner of Friedrich Nietzsche, he was wholly critical and confrontational in his approach to it. Yet his engagement was largely with European artists and thinkers. In his creative work, in his writings—some several thousand pages of them—and in his personal library, there are only marginal traces of any reaction to America before 1920. He mentioned Whistler (who was American by birth, to be sure, but was considered an English painter)[28] and made passing reference to Loie Fuller, the American dance icon of the Belle Epoque whom Klee had seen in Rome in 1902.[29]

This relative indifference to American culture was in contrast to his friends Münter and August Macke. Münter, who had visited her relatives in Texas with her sister Emmy in 1898, encountered important stimuli during her stay, while Macke, Klee's friend and traveling companion in Tunisia in 1914, adored the writings of Walt Whitman and the world of the American Indian, both of which left their mark on his art (fig. 6). Klee's attitude was also quite unlike that of such fellow painters as George Grosz, Otto Dix, or Rudolf Schlichter, who were fascinated by the myth of the "Wild West" and who saw America as a source of artistic inspiration, a screen on which to project one's ideal of a free, self-directed life.[30]

The Coming of the First World War

Artistic exchange between Germany and the United States came to an abrupt end with the outbreak of World War I. Relations between artists and collectors from the two countries were almost completely severed in 1917 as the two nations became enemies battling each other with propaganda. Under the circumstances, Herwarth Walden was taking a risk when he gave Feininger his first one-person show in the Galerie Der Sturm in Berlin in September 1917, succeeding only because in Germany Feininger was not perceived as American. Once the United States entered the war, however, the artist himself came under police surveillance as an enemy alien.

As a reservist, Klee was drafted into the German army on March 11, 1916. A week before, the artist Marc, who had welcomed the war as an act of major renewal, had been killed at the front near Verdun. In contrast to his friend, Klee saw the war as a senseless human catastrophe instigated by the great powers, and he portrayed it in that light in his work (fig. 7). At the same time—in a wholly different way—Marsden Hartley, one of the few American abstractionists at the Armory Show in 1913, was also dealing with the militarization of Germany, where in 1912 he had become fascinated with Kandinsky's artistic concepts. On a return trip in 1914–15, he noted the military splendor of Berlin at the beginning of the war, and he would later transform the display of such military insignia as medals, banners, and flags into emblematic, brightly colored paintings that absorb the abyss of war into their pattern of ornamental decor (fig. 8).[31]

Fig. 6
August Macke, *Indianer [Indians]*, 1911. Oil on canvas, 34¼ x 27¼ inches (88 x 70 cm). Private collection.

Fig. 7
Paul Klee, *Tod auf dem Schlachtfeld [Death on the Battlefield]*, 1914.172. Pen on paper on cardboard, 3½ x 6⅞ inches (9 x 17.6 cm). Zentrum Paul Klee, Livia Klee Donation, Bern, Switzerland.

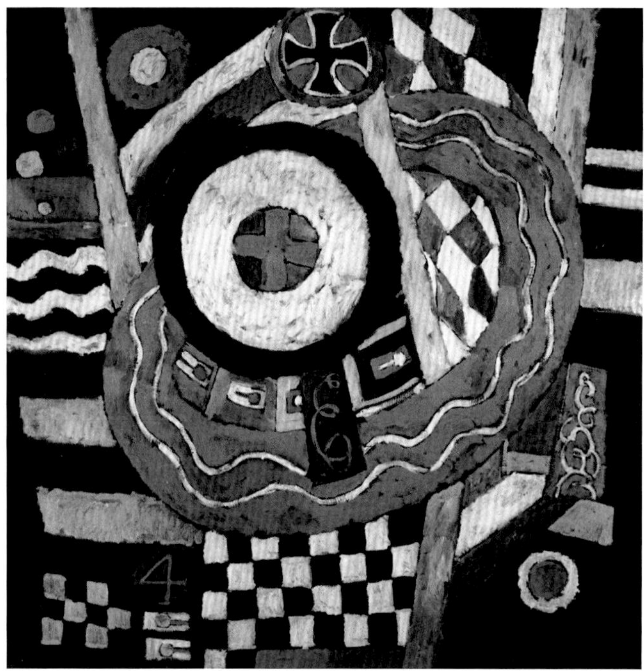

Klee's relationship with America during the war years and up until 1920 was limited to his encounters with the American painter Albert Bloch, who lived in Munich between 1909 and 1921. Bloch was the son of a St. Louis wholesale grocer of Bohemian Jewish ancestry.[32] He had moved to Munich with the financial support of his patron William Marion Reedy, editor-in-chief of the weekly *Mirror*. Bloch had worked for the *Mirror* as a caricaturist and illustrator from 1905 to 1909 after studying for a short time at St. Louis's School of Fine Arts.[33] Until 1912 he served as a reviewer for the journal, writing essays on the art scene in Germany.

In 1911 Bloch became acquainted with Kandinsky and Marc. They saw Bloch's anti-academic, almost raw and "primitive"—in the positive sense—way of painting as an important instance of the new "spiritual" art they meant to show in their programmatic "First Exhibition by the Blaue Reiter Publishers."[34] That legendary show was held in Munich's Galerie Thannhauser from December 1911 to January 1912 and included six Bloch paintings—an astonishingly high number. Eight more were shown in the second Blaue Reiter exhibition held in Hans Goltz's gallery from February to April 1912.[35] By contrast, Klee was not represented at all in the first show, although he had seventeen works in the second one.

Bloch later discounted this association with Munich and the Blaue Reiter.[36] He did, however, value his friendship with Marc. In his reminiscences of his Munich years, Bloch wrote: "Only of Franz Marc may I say that our acquaintance deepened to something like true friendship."[37] After Marc's death in Verdun, Bloch drew somewhat closer to the deceased artist's best friends, Heinrich Campendonk and Klee. "With Klee, who joined the circle later, I exchanged pictures and visits, and found him an altogether delightful acquaintance,"[38] he wrote, and went on to describe Klee's art as follows: "Perhaps Paul Klee is the strangest figure in all that group of painters, who were my friends and comrades in Munich. Whimsical, winsome, wayward, his little sheets of drawing and watercolor, with an occasional small picture painted in oil, look at first sight like the daubs and scrawls of a willful, destructive child—of a child never grown up, living alone, walled off from the world in some undreamt garden of wonderland, or in some forgotten corner of hell.… Upon me the work of Paul Klee has from the beginning

Fig. 8
Marsden Hartley, *The Iron Cross,* 1915. Oil on canvas, 47¼ x 47¼ inches (120 x 120 cm). Washington University Gallery of Art, St. Louis, University Purchase, Bixby Fund, 1952.

exerted a strange fascination, as great a fascination as the man himself, with his rare, impish humor."[39] Bloch's retrospective judgment of Klee as a wondrous mystic who created his works as
though in a dream was influenced by the portrayal of the artist in
the first monographs on him, which appeared just after the First
World War, a portrayal encouraged by Klee himself.[40]

Early in their friendship, Klee and Bloch shared the two-
person show "Paul Klee and Albert Bloch," mounted in March
1916 by Walden in Berlin's Galerie Der Sturm.[41] The exhibition
featured sixteen paintings by Bloch and forty-five watercolors,
drawings, and paintings by Klee. The Berlin press responded
favorably to Bloch's work, but harshly criticized Klee's.[42] Out of
solidarity with Klee, Bloch wrote a letter of protest to Walden:
"It is unbearable to me to be praised this way in contrast to Paul
Klee.... I would like to protest publicly.... The only things that
prevent me are my dread of coming forward in such a personal matter and my fear of giving the impression that Paul Klee in any way
requires the assistance of others."[43] Walden promptly published
the letter in the April issue of his journal *Der Sturm*.[44]

As the relationship between the two artists intensified during
the war years of 1917–18,[45] Bloch's pictorial vocabulary began to
approach more closely that of Klee. Bloch's paintings from these
years—with their stylized plants or cipherlike trees blending with
architectural elements, small houses, and churches in fantastic,
often nocturnal landscapes—greatly resemble Klee's painting of
the time both in form and subject matter (figs. 9 and 10; see also
Schulhaus [Schoolhouse] [1920.23, pl. 4]). This affinity culminated in an untitled work from 1918 that Bloch considered an
"homage" to Klee, which he gave to him (fig. 12). He also presented
Klee with the watercolor and pen drawing *Zum Klownbild VI [For
the Clown Picture VI]* (1914), while it is probable that Klee left
Bloch three works as gifts.[46] Bloch's "homage" to Klee shows two
men, two houses, and a cow in a mountain landscape. Annegret
Hoberg interprets the figure on the left, wearing a hat, as a self-portrait of Bloch, and she suggests that he is wishing he could hold
back the Paul Klee figure, with the characteristic dark beard, who
has turned his back and is walking away from him. The ciphers
for trees and the whitish, transparent silhouettes of the houses look
as if they could have been taken from a picture by Klee. A photograph of Klee's atelier in Schlösschen Suresnes in Munich from

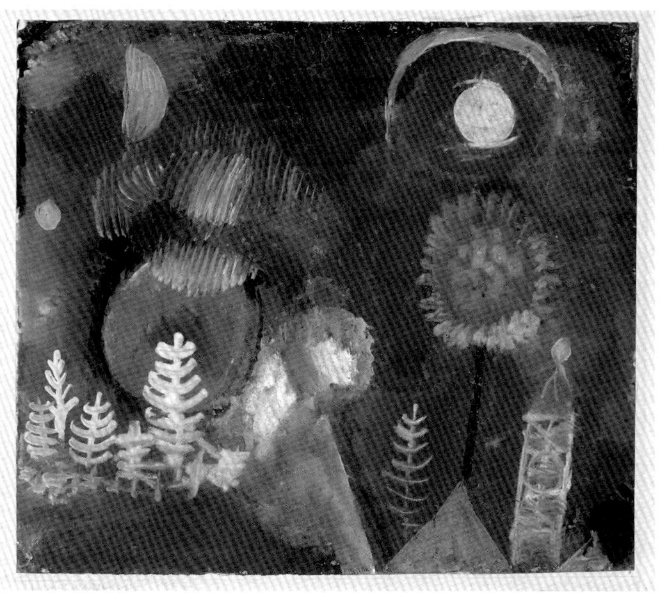

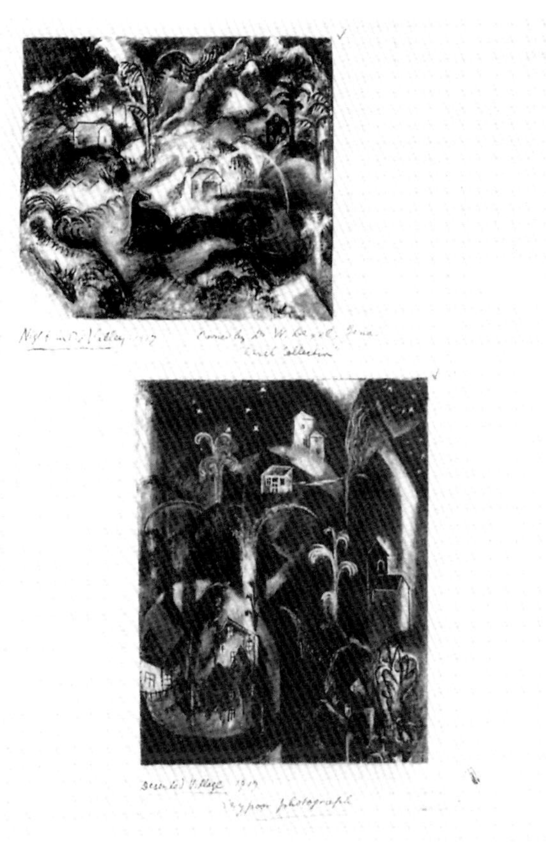

Fig. 9
Paul Klee, *Landschaft der Vergangenheit [Landscape of the Past]*,
1918.44. Watercolor and gouache on paper on cardboard, 8⅞ x 10⅜
inches (22.6 x 26.3 cm). Private collection.

Fig. 10
Photograph from Albert Bloch's record book, vol. 2; top: *Night in the
Valley*, 1917; bottom: *Deserted Village*, 1917.

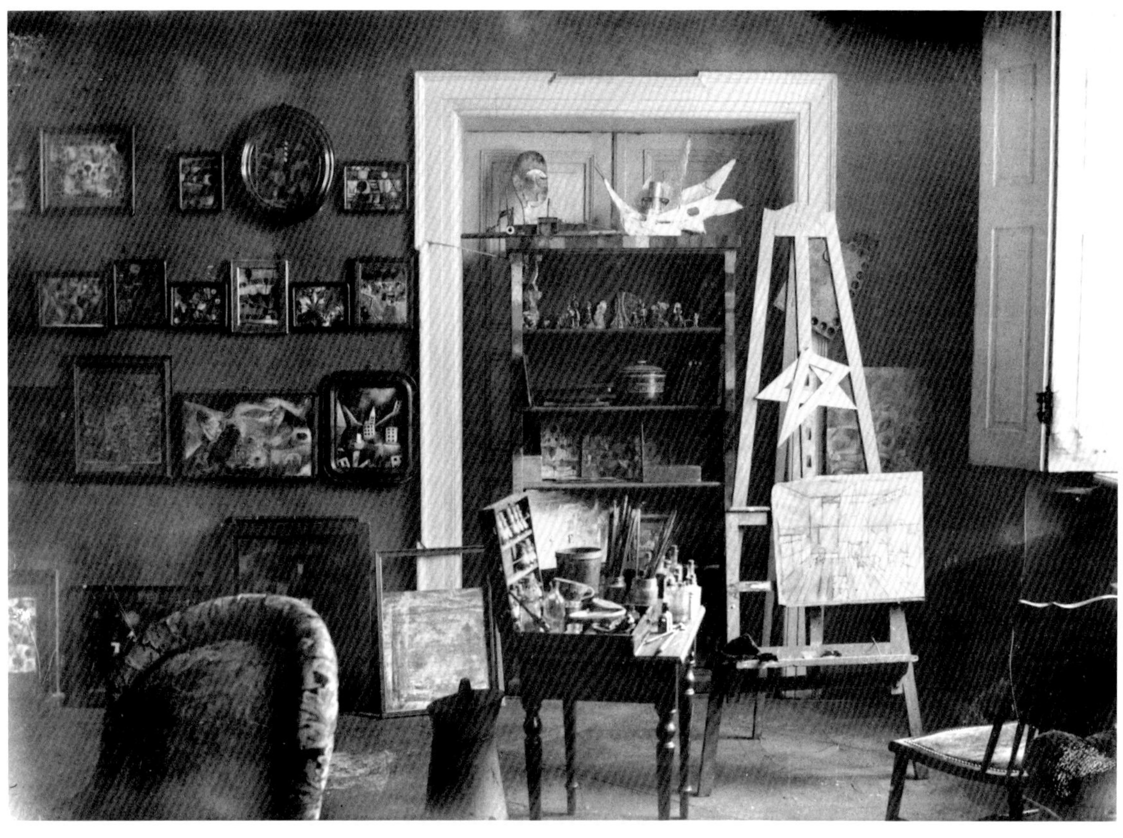

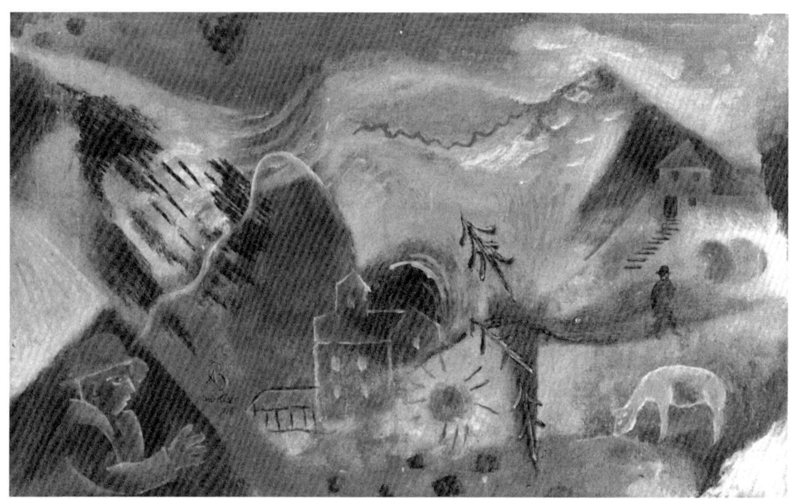

Paul Klee's atelier in Schlösschen Suresnes in Munich, 1920; to the left of the door frame in the bottom row: Paul Klee, *Zerstörtes Dorf [Destroyed Village]*, 1920.130; to the left of that: Albert Bloch, Untitled *(Landscape with Two Men, Two Houses, and a Cow)*, 1918.

Albert Bloch, Untitled *(Landscape with Two Men, Two Houses, and a Cow)*, 1918. Oil on canvas, 11¼ x 18¾ inches (29 x 48 cm). Kunstmuseum Bern, Gift of Livia Klee.

1920 (fig. 11) shows how much Klee valued Bloch's present, for he hung it next to his own oil painting *Zerstörtes Dorf [Destroyed Village]* (1920.130). That Klee should have placed precisely this work next to Bloch's landscape may have had to do with the fact that Bloch usually gave titles to his pictures that reflected the horrors of the war, like *Deserted Village*, *Deserted Villa*, and *Night in the Valley* (see fig. 10).[47]

Conclusion

The Klee works that once belonged to Eddy are now lost.[48] Records of those works, along with the memory of the friendship between Klee and Bloch, provide the few, nearly vanished traces of Klee's first weak contact with America. Yet they also serve as a prelude, as it were, to the lively appreciation that Klee's work would meet with in America in the 1920s.

For Eddy, the European avant-garde served as a stimulus to American artists: "The net result is that American art has received another impulse forward; it will do bigger and finer and saner things. It will not copy the eccentricities, the exaggerations, the morbid enthusiasms of [Europe], because America as yet is not given to eccentricities and morbidness—though it may be to a youthful habit of exaggeration. America is essentially sane and healthful—say quite practical—in its outlook, hence it will absorb all that is good in the extreme modern movement and reject what is bad."[49]

That willingness to absorb the "good" in the European avant-garde led both to Bloch's modernist-influenced paintings during his German sojourn, and to the early and tentative appreciation for the works of Klee on the part of collectors like Eddy. Indeed it was in part his unshakable optimism and faith in progress that enabled Eddy to risk embracing the unconventional in art, and that would make a subsequent understanding of Klee in America possible.

NOTES

1. Eddy wrote to the German artist Gabriele Münter, Vasily Kandinsky's lifetime companion and a friend of Paul and Lily Klee's: "I have just received notice from the American Express Co. that Paul Klee has shipped 25 watercolors. I am surprised he sent so many because I suggested his sending only two or three for my inspection." Arthur Jerome Eddy to Gabriele Münter, January 17, 1914, Gabriele Münter- und Johannes Eichner-Stiftung, Städtische Galerie im Lenbachhaus, Munich.

2. Hans Bloesch, "Ein moderner Graphiker," *Die Alpen* 6, no. 5 (January 1912): 264–65.

3. Impressed by what he saw of their work at the World Columbian Exposition in Chicago in 1893, Eddy came to admire Edouard Manet and Claude Monet in addition to Whistler and Rodin, and would soon buy works from them in Paris. Around the turn of the century, Eddy withdrew somewhat, devoting more of his time to his own professional advancement. It was after an encounter with the work of Arthur Dove, the first American abstractionist, and that of the Dutchman Otto van Rees that he turned his attention to modernism and artists like Kandinsky.

4. Paul Klee, "München," *Die Alpen* 6, no. 3 (November 1911): 184.

5. Most of the young painters who descended on Düsseldorf then were of German ancestry. They followed in the footsteps of such illustrious countrymen as Emanuel Leutze and Albert Bierstadt, acquiring an introduction to narrative and landscape painting. The best known of them were Karl Friedrich Lessing, Carl Ferdinand Sohn, and Eduard Julius. See Katharina Bott, *Vice Versa: Deutsche Maler in Amerika/Amerikanische Maler in Deutschland 1813–1913*, exh. cat. (Munich: Deutsches Historisches Museum, 1996), 11–16.

6. "The Düsseldorf school commanded the market, and I think of its exhibition as firmly seated, going on from year to year—New York, judging now [in 1910] to such another tune, must have been a brave patron of that manufacture; … though of what particular sacrifices to the pure plastic or undraped shocks to bourgeois prejudice the comfortable German genius of that period may have been capable history has kept no record." Henry James, *A Small Boy and Others* (New York: Charles Scribner's Sons, 1913), 266.

7. From 1820 to 1920, in what has been called the "century of immigration," 5.5 million Germans emigrated to America. The first surge came in the period after the revolutionary upheaval of 1848, followed by another in the years between 1880 and 1890, when roughly 1.5 million German immigrants entered the country. Recent research has determined that 1,336 artists emigrated from Germany to America between 1813 and 1913. See Bott, 11.

8. In addition to Duveneck and Currier, a number of other famous American artists belonged to the Munich "American Artists' Club" in the closing years of the nineteenth century, including John White Alexander, Otto Henry Bacher, William Merritt Chase, Joseph DeCamp, Julius Roishoven, Joseph H. Sharp, Walter Shirlaw, John H.

Twachtman, Theodore Wendel, and Theodore Wores. Most of them returned to the United States in the 1880s or 1890s, bringing back with them a free approach to painting that sparked violent controversy even before the appearance of the Impressionists. Currier, Duveneck, and Chase, as typical representatives of the Munich avant-garde, were the target of bitter attacks by the New York press. The resulting furor led American art dealers and collectors to shift their attention away from Düsseldorf to the Munich scene; the important art dealer Samuel P. Avery began to regularly visit the Bavarian metropolis on his trips to Europe. Close ties between American painters and Munich's art scene also stimulated the market for the works of their models and teachers. Chase, for example, bought works by Karl von Piloty, Wilhelm von Kaulbach, Ludwig Knaus, and Eduard Grützner for his patron Samuel A. Coale Jr., as well as two Wilhelm Leibl works for himself. America's appreciation for German art in the late nineteenth century paralleled its respect for German universities.

9. See Paul Klee, *Tagebücher 1898–1918*, ed. Wolfgang Kersten (Stuttgart/Teufen, Germany: Paul Klee-Stiftung, Kunstmuseum Bern, 1988), entries 70, 79, and 409. Few documents track Karfunkle's artistic activity in New York. In the 1910s his name turned up in the catalogues of Martin Birnbaum's exhibitions at the Berlin Photographic Company. Some of his works later found their way into the Museum of the City of New York. His best-known work is the fresco *Labor*, painted for the Harlem Court in New York around 1938.

10. For example, at the St. Louis World's Fair (Louisiana Purchase Exhibition) in 1904, the only moderately progressive German artist admitted was Adolf Hölzel. The Berlin and Munich Secessions were first shown in New York in 1909, in the Metropolitan Museum of Art exhibition "Contemporary German Art." Financed by the German-American businessman and collector Hugo Reisinger, the show featured the works of Wilhelm Leibl, Max Liebermann, Fritz von Uhde, Arnold Böcklin, Max Klinger, and Franz von Stuck. See Penny Joy Bealle, "Obstacles and Advocates: Factors Influencing the Introduction of Modern Art from Germany to New York City, 1912–33: Major Promoters and Exhibitions" (Ph.D. diss., Cornell University, Ithaca, New York, 1990), 40–49.

11. The exhibition traveled in 1913 to Buffalo, New York, and Chicago.

12. Martin Birnbaum, *Catalogue of an Exhibition of Contemporary German Graphic Art*, exh. cat. (New York: Berlin Photographic Company, 1913), 3.

13. Martin Birnbaum, *The Last Romantic: The Story of More than a Half-Century in the World of Art* (New York: Twayne, 1960), 52.

14. Stieglitz's parents were from Hessen. Stieglitz graduated from high school in the United States and then went to Germany to study mechanical engineering, but soon switched to photography. He had first been mainly interested in the French avant-garde. On his regular trips to Europe, he was one of the first to appreciate the pathbreaking artistic departure of Kandinsky. In 1912 he translated a passage from Kandinsky's *Concerning the Spiritual in Art* (1911) for his quarterly *Camera Work*, having presumably bought the book in Germany the previous winter. *Camera Work* 19 (July 1912): 34.

15. Paul Kruty, "Arthur Jerome Eddy and His Collection: Prelude and Postscript to the Armory Show," *Arts Magazine* 61 (February 1987): 40–47. At the Armory Show, of which he was a fervent advocate, Eddy bought works by Marcel Duchamp, Emilie Charmy, Maurice Denis, André Derain, Albert Gleizes, Leon Kroll, E. M. Manigault, Francis Picabia, Segonaz, Amadeo de Sousa-Cardoza, W. L. Taylor, Jacques Villon, Maurice de Vlaminck, and Edouard Vuillard. Kruty, 43.

16. According to Carter Harrison, "Eddy swept the [Kandinsky] studio clean." Carter Harrison, *Growing Up With Chicago* (Chicago: Ralph Fletcher Seymour, 1944), 216.

However, Vivian Barnett maintains that at that point Kandinsky was not even in Munich. Vivian Barnett, *Kandinsky: Watercolors and Drawings* (Munich: Prestel, 1992), 45.

17. "Second Group Exhibition," Galerie Neue Kunst Hans Goltz, Munich, April 8–10, 1913.

18. Arthur Jerome Eddy to Paul Klee, February 17, 1914, Archive of the Zentrum Paul Klee, Bern, Switzerland.

19. Eddy first selected eleven works from the two shipments and offered Klee 400 marks for the lot, which was the amount he had forwarded to the artist as an advance payment in February. From the entry in his handwritten oeuvre catalogue, it is clear that Klee did not agree to the lump sum offer and insisted on the prices he had set for the various genres. For his part, Eddy was unwilling to pay more than 400 marks total, and after receiving Klee's price list, he limited himself to six works, sending back the rest. Arthur Jerome Eddy to Paul Klee, February 17, 1914, and April 20, 1914, Archive of the Zentrum Paul Klee. The six works were: *Der Künstler (Dichtermaler) [The Artist (Poet-Painter)]* (1908.72); *Steinhauer II (getont) [Stonecutters II (tinted)]* (1910.74); *Das Haus an der Brücke [The House by the Bridge]* (1911.58); *Parkeingang (Seiteneingang) [Entrance to the Park (Side Entrance)]* (1913.74); *Bei Bern [Near Bern (Wittigkofen)]* (1913.96); and *Fensterausblick (München) [View from a Window (Munich)]* (1913.125).

20. Eddy wrote: "I have tried to make the selection in such a way that the individual phases in your work are represented." Arthur Jerome Eddy to Paul Klee, April 29, 1914, Archive of the Zentrum Paul Klee.

21. Arthur Jerome Eddy, *Cubists and Post-Impressionism* (Chicago: A. C. McClurg, 1914), 88 and 114.

22. See also Susan J. Nurse, "Arthur Jerome Eddy: Patron of Modern Art" (master's thesis, State University of New York at Buffalo, 1994), 37–58.

23. Eddy, *Cubists and Post-Impressionism*, 114.

24. Reproduced in Eddy, *Cubists and Post-Impressionism*, 88.

25. Eddy, *Cubists and Post-Impressionism*, 123.

26. Eddy, *Cubists and Post-Impressionism*, 123.

27. Eddy, *Cubists and Post-Impressionism*, 2.

28. Klee, *Tagebücher* (no. 644), 493 and 512.

29. Klee, *Tagebücher* (no. 403).

30. See *Envisioning America: Prints, Drawings and Photographs by George Grosz and His Contemporaries 1915–1933*, exh. cat. (Cambridge, Mass.: Busch-Reisinger Museum, Harvard University Art Museums, 1990).

31. See also Patricia McDonnell, *Painting Berlin Stories: Marsden Hartley, Oscar Bluemner, and the First American Avant-Garde in Expressionist Berlin* (New York: P. Lang, 2003).

32. See Annegret Hoberg and Henry Adams, eds., *Albert Bloch: Ein amerikanischer Blauer Reiter*, exh. cat. (Munich: Städtische Galerie im Lenbachhaus, 1997), 54, note 5. A smaller exhibition, "Albert Bloch: The American Blue Rider," traveled to the Nelson Atkins Museum of Art, Kansas City, Missouri, January 26 to March 16, 1994. See Frank Baron, Helmut Arntzen, and David Cateforis, eds., *Albert Bloch: Artistic and Literary Perspectives,* exh. cat. (Lawrence, Kan: Max Kade Center for German-American Studies, University of Kansas; and Munich: Prestel, 1997).

33. Bloch's portraits for the *Mirror* attest to his strong interest in the caricatures in Munich's satirical magazine *Simplicissimus*, most apparent in his appropriations from the styles of Olaf Gulbransson and Thomas Theodor Heine.

34. In Munich Bloch first adopted the highly simplified, almost posterlike style of painters like Alexander Kanoldt and Adolf Erbslöh.

35. Along with Marsden Hartley, who spent the first years of the war in Berlin, Bloch was one of the most important American modernists working in Germany.

36. In 1955 he described Marc and Kandinsky's invitation to take part in the Blaue Reiter exhibitions as a misunderstanding: "The point of Marc's and Kandinsky's misconception about me was simply that they believed in all good faith that I was a 'modern,' that it was my ambition to paint 'modernist' pictures, whereas I desired to do no such thing. I was not a modern in any real sense of the word…. I was in actual fact … a traditionalist to the core." Albert Bloch to Edward Maser, June 20, 1955; reproduced in Hoberg and Adams, 204.

37. Albert Bloch, quoted in Hoberg and Adams, 206.

38. Bloch, quoted in Hoberg and Adams, 207.

39. Bloch, quoted in Hoberg and Adams, 204.

40. See Hermann von Wedderkop, *Paul Klee,* Junge Kunst 13 (Leipzig, Germany: Klinkhardt & Biermann, 1920); and Leopold Zahn, *Paul Klee: Leben, Werk, Geist* (Potsdam, Germany: Gustav Kiepenheuer, 1920).

41. "Paul Klee und Albert Bloch. 39. Ausstellung" was held at Galerie Der Sturm, Berlin, in March 1916.

42. See Oscar Bie, "Bildende Kunst: Von Spitzweg bis in den Futurismus. Kunstausstellungen," *Berliner Börsen-Courier* 48 (March 5, 1916): 1st insert, 7f.

43. Albert Bloch to Herwarth Walden, March 29, 116; quoted in Hoberg and Adams, 69–70.

44. *Der Sturm* 7, no. 1 (April 1916): 11.

45. A passage from a letter from Lily Klee to Marianne von Werefkin shows that she, too, participated in the friendship with Bloch: "Bloch asks me to send you greetings—he had a retrospective show in Munich, at the Reich. He is striving and struggling very hard—has worked a lot. I see him now and then." Lily Klee to Marianne von Werefkin, August 22, 1918, Lietuvos Nacionaliné Martyno biblioteka, Vilnius; quoted in Annekathrin Merges-Knoth, "Marianne Werefkins russische Wurzeln—Neuansätze zur Interpretation ihres künstlerischen Werkes" (inaugural diss., University of Trier, 1996). I am grateful to Osamu Okuda for this reference.

46. They were: *Pferderennen I [Horse Race I]* (1911.47), *Landschaft mit Bergen [Landscape with Mountains]* (1917.139), and *Ein Knabe in jungem Wald [A Boy in Young Forest]* (1920.16).

47. Bloch destroyed many of the works he produced in 1917–18, but he documented the majority of them in photographs in his "record books." Klee could be critical of Bloch's painting, as is indicated by his comments on Bloch's one-person show in the Kunsthaus Reich in Munich from March to April 1918. In a letter to his wife, Lily, Klee wrote: "The exhibition in the 'Reich' for example, turned out better than I expected. Only Bloch once again hung in the left corner opposite the entrance some colored foolishness of the kind that only a person who understands little about color can produce. Who can make an exhibition? That is one of the most difficult things of all. Kandinsky could do it." Paul Klee to Lily Klee, May 1, 1918, Archive of the Zentrum Paul Klee; reprinted in Paul Klee, *Briefe an die Familie 1893–1940*, ed. Felix Klee, vol. 2 (Cologne: DuMont, 1979), 918.

48. Eddy died of acute appendicitis in 1920. Part of his collection went to the Art Institute of Chicago. The six works by Klee were still in the possession of the family until the early 1930s, but since then there is no trace of them. See *The Arthur Jerome Eddy Collection of Modern Paintings and Sculpture*, exh. cat. (Chicago: Art Institute of Chicago, 1931); and *Exhibition of Paintings from the Collection of the Late Arthur Jerome Eddy*, exh. cat. (Chicago: Art Institute of Chicago, 1922).

49. Eddy, *Cubists and Post-Impressionism*, 3.

From Both Sides of the Atlantic to the Pacific:
Klee and America in the Twenties

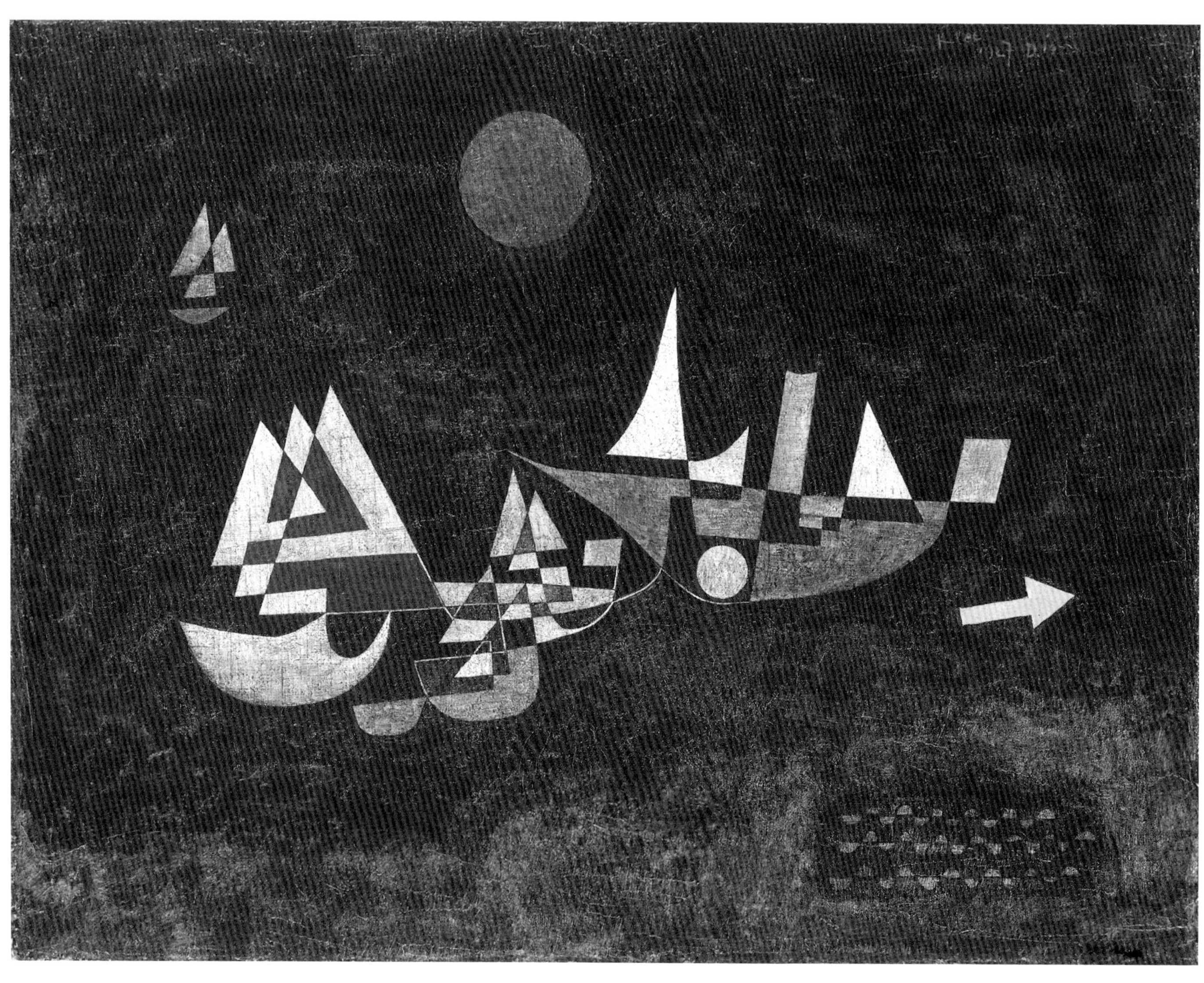

VIVIAN ENDICOTT BARNETT

Paul Klee's art first became known in America during the 1920s through artists, collectors, and dealers with close contacts in Germany. He was already well-known in Germany by 1920: his art was shown in numerous galleries and widely discussed in reviews and books. Although Klee had signed an exclusive contract with the Galerie Neue Kunst (Hans Goltz) in Munich in October 1919, his work continued to be on exhibit and for sale in Berlin in the early 1920s at the Galerie Der Sturm (Herwarth Walden), Galerie Fritz Gurlitt, Galerie Paul Cassirer, Graphisches Kabinett I. B. Neumann, and other galleries. By 1921 Hans von Wedderkop, Leopold Zahn, and Wilhelm Hausenstein had published monographs on the artist. That same year Klee began to teach at the Bauhaus, first in Weimar and then in Dessau.

Emmy E. (later known as "Galka") Scheyer was a young German artist, exhibition organizer, and enthusiastic promoter of the artist Alexei Jawlensky. When she traveled to Munich in October 1919, he gave her a letter of introduction to Klee. At the time she was planning a Jawlensky exhibition, which would open at the Galerie Fritz Gurlitt in June 1920 and would also be shown at Goltz's gallery. While it is unclear whether Scheyer met Klee in late 1919 or early 1920, it is certain that she knew the Klees by February 1920; she saw them in Munich in August and visited them in Possenhofen, Germany, in September. That year Scheyer received *Blüten und Ähren [Blossoms and Grains]* (1920.89) as the first of many gifts from Klee.[1] For Christmas 1921 he gave her *Die Heilige [The Saint]* (1921.107, pl. 12) with a dedication "to Emmy Scheyer in friendship." Two years later, in 1923, she received *Schauspieler als Frau [Actor as a Woman]* (1923.49, pl. 19) from the artist in exchange for an easel.[2]

During the same period of time, Katherine S. Dreier began to acquire works by Klee. Dreier was an American artist, collector, and educator of German ancestry who spoke German and traveled annually to Germany to visit relatives. In New York in January 1920, together with Marcel Duchamp and Man Ray, she founded the Société Anonyme, Inc., subtitled Museum of Modern Art, "for the study and research in the recent movements of Modern Art."[3] That same year, she purchased four Klee watercolors and two ink drawings from the Galerie Der Sturm, where they were exhibited in "89. Ausstellung Reinhard Goering—Paul Klee" held in September. The watercolors were *Mit dem roten X [With the Red X]* (1914.136, fig. 14), Ohne Titel [Untitled] (1914.147), *Teppich [Carpet]* (1917.70), and *Sonnenfinsternis [Solar Eclipse]* (1918.157). All six works were shown at the galleries of the Société Anonyme on East 47 Street in New York from March 15 to April 12, 1921— apparently the first public presentation of Klee's art in America. Years later Dreier recalled buying in 1922 *rot/grüne Stufung [Red-Green Gradation]* (1921.103) from Goltz in Munich and *Architectur rot/grün [Architecture Red-Green]* (1922.19) from the Galerie Der Sturm in Berlin. However, she met Klee only in October 1922, when she visited him and Vasily Kandinsky at the Bauhaus in Weimar.

Gradually Klee's work began to make an appearance in the American press. Early in 1923 two American magazine articles were illustrated with works by Klee. In February *Broom* interspersed three

Paul Klee, *Abfahrt der Schiffe [Departure of the Ships]*, 1927.140.2. Oil on canvas, 20 x 25¾ (51 x 65.5 cm). Nationalgalerie, Staatliche Museen zu Berlin, NG 22/67.

German Art," which opened in October 1923 at the Anderson Galleries in New York. Its organizer, William R. Valentiner, had visited Klee in March 1922 and purchased four works, including *Als Gott sich mit der Erschaffung der Pflanzen trug [When God Considered the Creation of the Plants]* (1913.176, pl. 1) and *Notturno für Horn [Nocturne for Horn]* (1921.91, pl. 8).[7] Valentiner, who was born in Germany and had been a curator at the Metropolitan Museum of Art in New York from 1908 to 1914, was at that time advisor to the Detroit Institute of Arts. The Berlin art dealer Ferdinand Möller assisted Valentiner in obtaining loans from Europe for the exhibition: his name appears on a document listing ten works by Klee that the artist signed on October 31, 1922.[8] According to the catalogue, nine of these were exhibited in "Modern German Art," among them *Kleine Komoedie auf der Wiese [Little Comedy in the Meadow]* (1922.107), *Schreck eines Mädchens [Fright of a Girl]* (1922.131, pl. 14), and *Blumenfamilie V. [Flower Family V.]* (1922.134, fig. 16). Dreier purchased the last from the show for $62.50.[9] In its review of the exhibition, the *New York Times* mentioned Lyonel Feininger, Erich Heckel, Emil Nolde, and Max Pechstein, but not Klee.[10] *Art News* stated that the show "gives New York its first comprehensive view of what German artists have been doing since the war,"[11] and a later issue reported that purchases by museums and private collectors from the show totaled more than $4,000.[12]

Because of the disastrous economic conditions in Germany, several art dealers came to New York, including J. B. Neumann, Paul Cassirer, and Möller, all of whom arrived in October 1923.[13]

drawings—*Selbstmörder auf der Brücke [Suicide on the Bridge]* (1913.100, page 17), *Der Mord [The Murder]* (1913.134), and *Akrobaten [Acrobats]* (1914.113)—between two unrelated essays, providing English titles for the drawings and noting that they had been included in the *Bilderbuch* published by Der Sturm in 1918.[4] An article by Tristan Tzara about the Weimar Bauhaus, which appeared in the April issue of *Vanity Fair*,[5] was illustrated with *Apparat für magnetische Behandlung der Pflanzen [Apparatus for Magnetic Treatment of Plants]* (1921.133, fig. 15) and *Gespenst eines Genies [Spectre of a Genius]* (1922.10). This almost forgotten article identified Klee as "one of the most celebrated of the German expressionist artists," and the caption under *Apparat* read: "the illustration of a subconscious poetry with a strong flavor of burlesque." In his discussion of the artists at the Bauhaus, Tzara wrote that "the painter who is the most remarkable personality of this school at Weimar is Paul Klee.... His exquisite water-colors might be likened to a child's drawing were they not so etherealized. But it is by the freshness of its imagination and its grotesque and ironic spirit that his talent charms us."[6]

Klee's work was included in the influential exhibition "Modern

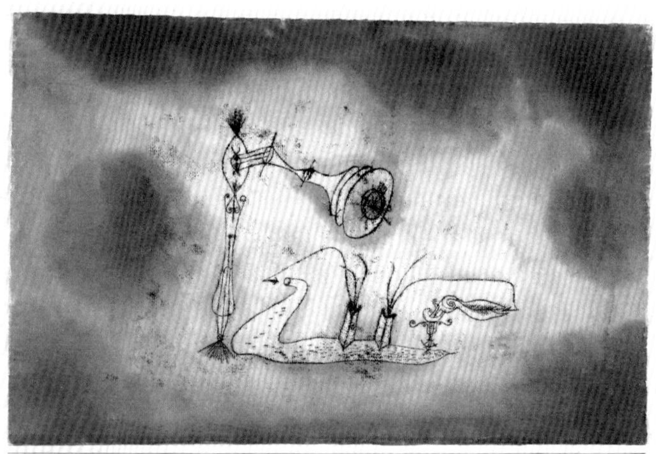

Fig. 15
Paul Klee, *Apparat für magnetische Behandlung der Pflanzen [Apparatus for Magnetic Treatment of Plants]*, 1921.133. Oil and watercolor on paper, mounted on cardboard, 12¼ x 18⅞ inches (31.1 x 47.9 cm). Busch-Reisinger Museum, Harvard University Art Museums, Cambridge, Massachusetts, BR34.80.

Möller came with the intention of opening a gallery, possibly collaborating with Erhard Weyhe, who had a bookshop and gallery in the city, but he did not stay. Neumann, however, moved permanently to New York and opened a gallery, where he would play a significant role in introducing curators and collectors to German art. Neumann had organized a Klee exhibition of thirty-four works at his Berlin gallery in March–April 1921 and had shown Klee's art again during the summers of 1921 and 1922. It remains unclear which works by Klee he might have brought with him to New York. In any case, Neumann did not present a Klee exhibition in New York in the twenties because, in his words, "the United States was then virgin territory for Klee."[14]

Through the Société Anonyme, Dreier organized Klee's first one-person show in America. The exhibition took place at the society's new galleries at 44 West 57th Street in New York from January 7 until February 9, 1924.[15] Dreier's book *Western Art and the New Era: An Introduction to Modern Art*, published the year before in 1923, curiously did not mention Klee, although she devoted several pages to Kandinsky. Her exhibition featured twenty-seven works by Klee along with several Kandinsky paintings that had appeared at the Société Anonyme the previous year.[16]

The review in the *New York Times* began: "The Société Anonyme are giving us another opportunity to struggle with a painting by Kandinsky." It referred to his book, *The Art of Spiritual Harmony* (1914), and continued: "Kandinsky's four or five paintings say nothing for themselves, are still in the laboratory state of research, and experimentation, unsolved problems. Paul Klee also builds with abstract form but understandably and musically. His scale is nearer the closer toned one of the East than ours of seven intervals, the forms are as easily related to music as his color. He directs the small colored forms, orders and arranges and without the aid of a book of explanation, forgetting books, one is drawn out of one's self by the joyousness of the designs."[17] The influential critic Henry McBride wrote in the *New York Herald* about Klee that "his color is always good and in a strange way he makes his mood felt without condescending to the details of description," citing the colors in *Sanft bewegter Garten [Gently Moving Garden]* (1920.217).[18] Elsewhere, McBride referred to "a most entrancing exhibition of that strange meteor from Switzerland—Paul Klee—an isolated figure in art.... The charm of his color and the delicacy of his lines

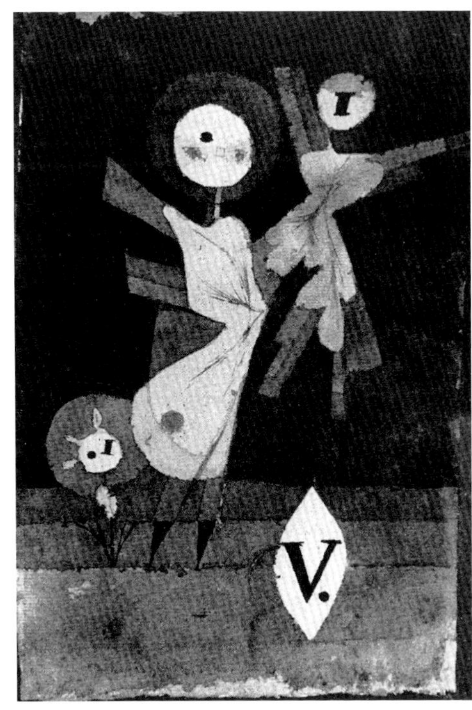

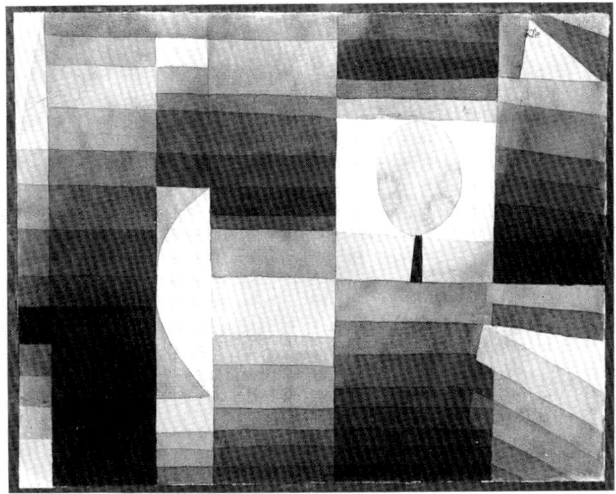

Fig. 16
Paul Klee, *Blumenfamilie V. [Flower Family V.]*, 1922.134. Watercolor and pen on paper, mounted on cardboard, 9 ½ x 6 ½ inches (24.2 x 16.5 cm). Location unknown.

Fig. 17
Paul Klee, *Der Bote des Herbstes (grün/violette Stufung mit orange Aczent) [Harbinger of Autumn (green/violet gradation with orange accent)]*, 1922.69. Watercolor and pencil on laid Ingres paper, 9⅝ x 12¼ inches (24.3 x 31.4 cm). Yale University Art Gallery, New Haven, Connecticut, Gift of Collection Société Anonyme, 1941.537.

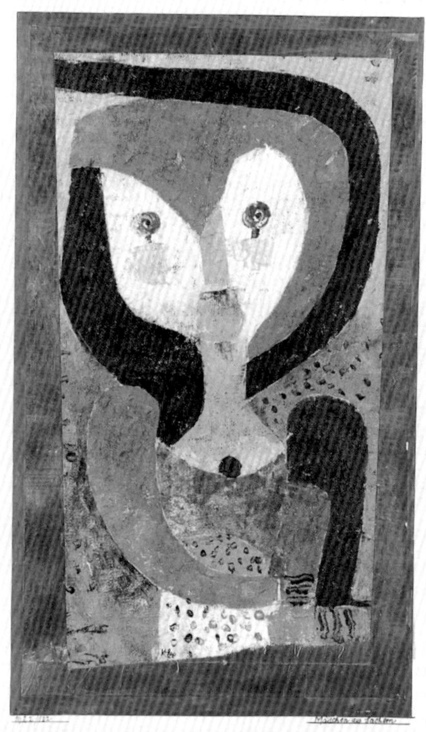

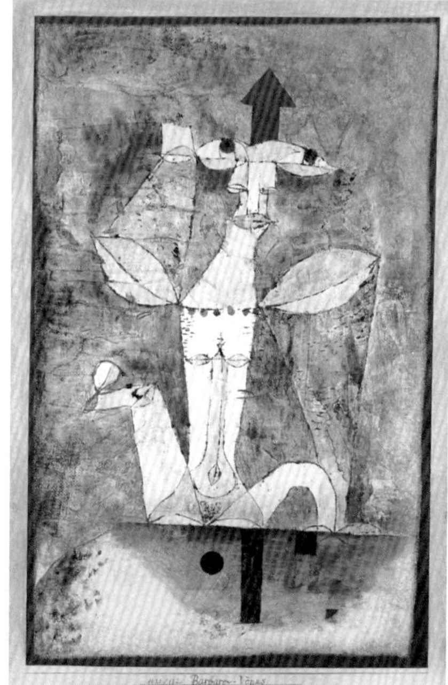

Paul Klee, *Mädchen aus Sachsen [Maid of Saxony]*, 1922.132. Oil on oil-primed muslin, mounted on gold foil, mounted on painted board, 14¼ x 8⅝ inches (36.2 x 21.9 cm). Norton Simon Museum, Pasadena, California, The Blue Four Galka Scheyer Collection, 1953.63.

Paul Klee, *Barbaren-Venus [Barbarian Venus]*, 1921.132. Oil, oil-transfer, and opaque watercolor on plaster-coated gauze on painted board, 16⅛ x 10½ inches (41 x 26.7 cm). Norton Simon Museum, Pasadena, California, The Blue Four Galka Scheyer Collection, 1953.62.

attract many to him."[19] Since no installation photographs of the gallery exist,[20] it is not known how the Klee and Kandinsky works were installed.

Dreier's logbook provides information about the eight oils and nineteen watercolors exhibited,[21] which included *Narr in Christo [Fool in Christ]* (1922.92, pl. 13), *Kleines Regattabild [Small Picture of a Regatta]* (1922.108, pl. 17), *Herbst Blume [Autumn Flower]* (1922.33), *Grundfeste [Foundations]* (1922.48), *Aquarell Skizze zu "MA" [Watercolor Sketch for "MA"]* (1922.51), *Der Bote des Herbstes [Harbinger of Autumn]* (1922.69, fig. 17), *Blumen im Wind [Flowers in the Wind]* (1922.106), *Kunstvoller Sternbehälter [Ingenious Star Container]* (1922.130), *Der König alles Ungeziefers [The King of All Vermin]* (1922.136), and *Guter Fischplatz [Good Place for Fish]* (1922.138). With one exception, the works dated from the early 1920s; the overwhelming majority of them were done in 1922. Although many works were emphatically figurative, others had strong architectural or structural elements. Dreier selected numerous pictures depicting flowers or plants. Moreover, she appreciated the humorous works and their titles. On the flyer for the exhibition, she wrote the since often quoted statement: "What is it that Klee wants to say in his quaint way? Is it only something whimsical, or beneath the whimsicality, is it something profound?" Yet in retrospect Dreier's selection seems more Constructivist than cute or whimsical.

Dreier had begun to make plans for the Klee exhibition at least a year earlier. When Klee wrote to her in June 1923, he also mentioned Scheyer: "I hear from Kandinsky that you plan to exhibit my collection in the best of months, January 1924, and I am agreeable to that. My main reason for writing is my desire to call your attention to the truly outstanding painter Alex[ei] von Jawlensky. . . . If you would like to have a [Jawlensky] show, you could get in touch with Frau Emmy Scheyer in Braunschweig, who handles his affairs. She is not a dealer, but rather a good friend to all of us. . . ."[22]

Their dear friend "Galka" Scheyer founded the Blue Four on March 31, 1924, in Weimar with the intention of disseminating the artistic ideas of Jawlensky, Kandinsky, Klee, and Feininger abroad, particularly through lectures and exhibitions. Scheyer took numerous works by Klee and the other members of the Blue Four with her when she left for the United States in May 1924. Soon after her arrival, she contacted Dreier and invited her to come to

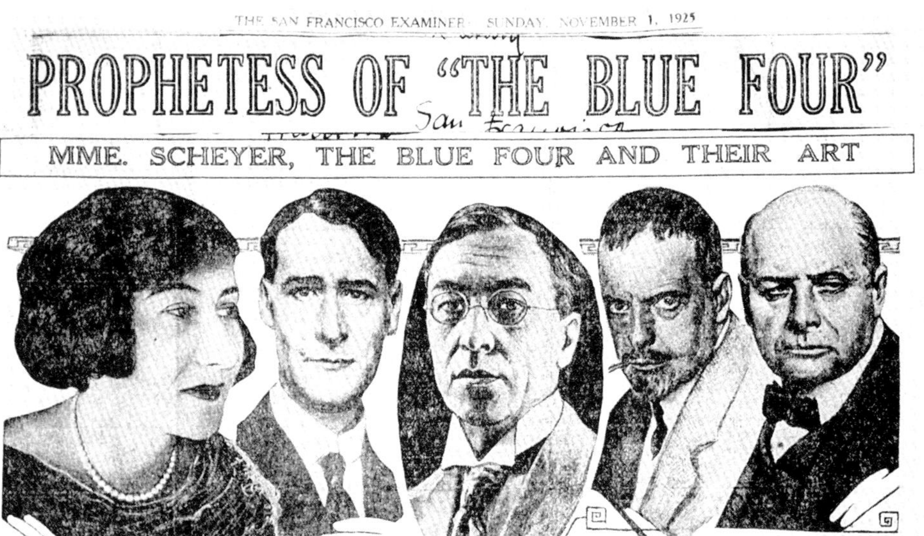

Ossining, New York, where she was staying. Dreier visited Scheyer briefly on June 20, saw some of the works by the Blue Four artists, and discussed the possibility of organizing an exhibition. However, the two women never worked closely together and tended to regard each other as competitors rather than friends.[23] The fact that Scheyer worked briefly at Neumann's Print Room on East 57th Street later that autumn further disconcerted Dreier, who had apparently invited Neumann to be director of the Société Anonyme galleries.[24]

Scheyer organized the first Blue Four show, which took place at the Daniel Gallery in New York from February 20 until March 10, 1925. *Die Heilige, Mädchen mit Puppen Wagen [Girl with Doll's Pram]* (1923.50, pl. 20), *Weisse Blüte im Garten [White Blossom in the Garden]* (1920.196), *Mädchen aus Sachsen [Maid of Saxony]* (1922.132, fig. 18), and *Barbaren-Venus [Barbarian Venus]* (1921.132, fig. 19) were among the seventeen works by Klee exhibited. Scheyer installed Klee's watercolors *Ausritt auf dem Oger [Ride on the Ogre]* (1923.157) and *Vogel Begegnung [Birds' Meeting]* (1918.202) on either side of the entrance so that visitors were immediately greeted with Klee's art. She had selected most of the works with the artist in Weimar and would later purchase several for her own collection. Of the four artists, McBride wrote that "Paul Klee is the best known in the United States and after this exhibition doubtless will remain so…. [Klee] is an Ariel. He is light, dancing, fantastic, but always the charmer. No matter what the motif, he plays with it with aston-

ishing agility and usually induces a mood. One of his pictures is called 'Mathematic Vision,' and a curiously illuminated pathway upon a strange world is ornamented with hieroglyphics that, as far as I am concerned, might easily pass for scientific notations. The artist evidently is mocking at the supermen of a too scientific age, but he achieves also a highly decorative page that ought to speak to the fancy of a playful mind."[25] A sarcastic review in *Time* magazine also mentioned *Mathematische Vision [Mathematic Vision]* (1923.76).[26] Although the exhibition at the Daniel Gallery received positive reviews in the *New York Times* and *Art News*, none of the works sold.[27]

Nevertheless, Scheyer succeeded in selling a Klee watercolor, *Scizze im Charakter eines Teppichs [Sketch in the Manner of a Carpet]* (1923.142, pl. 21), through the Walden School in New York, where she gave lectures and showed works of art.[28] In late May she left New York for California, bringing with her works on consignment from Klee and acquiring a group of his watercolors from Stadtsyndicus a. D. Kauth in Berlin—among them *Das Tor zum Hades [The Gateway to Hades]* (1921.29, pl. 9). In the San Francisco Bay Area, she found an enthusiasm for modern art and began to organize exhibitions, give lectures (fig. 20), and even sell a few prints. Although no list exists of the works she had on consignment from Klee, it is possible to reconstruct the selection from the exhibition catalogue checklists. Scheyer favored Klee's strikingly geometrical

Fig. 20
Photo illustration of Galka Scheyer, Lyonel Feininger, Vasily Kandinsky, Paul Klee, and Alexei Jawlensky, from the *San Francisco Examiner*, November 1, 1925, California.

works and bold figures as well as the more gentle and linear water-colors. She preferred art with enigmatic images, such as *Barbaren-Venus* and *Die Heilige*, appreciating the spiritual meaning of the latter.

A floor plan that Scheyer made of the Blue Four exhibition at Stanford University in October 1925 identifies the Klee water-colors on display. These included some works shown earlier at the Daniel Gallery in New York—*Vogel Begegnung, Architektur, transparent-structural [Architecture, transparent-structural]* (1921.120), *Choral und Landschaft [Chorale and Landscape]* (1921.125), *Die Schlange [The Snake]* (1923.87), *Perspective mit offener Türe [Perspective with Open Door]* (1923.143), and *Ausritt auf dem Oger*—as well as *Dünenflora [Flora of the Dunes]* (1923.184). At Stanford, however, the Klee works were presented in a separate room, rather than juxtaposed with those of Kandinsky and the others as they had been at the Daniel Gallery.

Scheyer's role in California was essentially that of a private dealer since she did not have a gallery. Instead she showed works of art to friends and prospective clients in her hotel room in San Francisco. She established contacts with several universities, museums, and women's clubs, where she gave lectures, and she mounted small group shows, such as the exhibition of prints that took place at the Paul Elder Gallery. She also taught art at the Anna Head School in Berkeley, both because she loved children and in order to earn money. Though Scheyer had little success as an art dealer during the 1920s, she nonetheless built up a remarkable network of friends and colleagues.

Scheyer's efforts to promote the Blue Four met with greater success in California than they had on the East Coast. When she informed the four artists on January 31, 1926, that an exhibition of their work would open at the Oakland Art Gallery in the spring, she exulted: "I can now say that I have found a footing in America, and more quickly than I had hoped. The best part is to have arrived without another German, as I did in New York, that is more of a hindrance than one might think, for everyone weighs you down with his own fate. Alone is the best of all." [29] Later she was appointed European representative of the Oakland Art Gallery, and its director, William H. Clapp, helped to arrange for the Blue Four exhibition to travel to museums in Los Angeles, San Francisco, San Diego, Portland, Oregon, Spokane, Washington, and Seattle under the auspices of the Western Association of Museum Directors. [30]

For the Oakland exhibition in May, Scheyer needed more works by Klee, and she turned to Dreier, who made five works available: Ohne Titel [Untitled] (1915.253), *Mit der sinkenden Sonne [With the Sinking Sun]* (1919.247), *Rosenbaum [Rose Tree]* (1920.219), *Keramisch/Erotisch/Religiös [Ceramic/Erotic/Religious]* (1921.97), and *Narr in Christo*. Dreier had a number of Klees on commission from the artist, but she could not lend Scheyer more than these five because she needed the rest for her own exhibitions later that year in Philadelphia and Brooklyn.

The installation of the Oakland show is known only from Scheyer's floor plan. The twenty-one works by Klee were shown in a separate rectangular gallery adjacent to the first room, where thirteen Kandinskys were hung, with the works by Feininger and Jawlensky installed on opposite sides of a large gallery beyond. In the Klee room, *Narr in Christo, Ausritt auf dem Oger, Choral und Landschaft, Flora in der toten Stadt [Flora of the Dead City]* (1922.92), and *Barbaren-Venus* (see fig. 19) filled the long wall, while *Matematische Vision* occupied the left corner and *Die Heilige* was placed in the right corner. Clapp's foreword in the small catalogue emphasized the abstract nature of the art exhibited and expressed the hope that "the Blue Four will lead the public to a fuller enjoyment of 'modern' art as well as to a greater appreciation and understanding of the types of art to which they are more accustomed." His remarks were undoubtedly directed more to the art of Kandinsky and Jawlensky than to that of Klee and Feininger. Six of the Klees listed in the catalogue belonged to Scheyer's private collection, but her annotated copy provided prices for the others, which ranged from $60 for *Mädchen aus Sachsen* (see fig. 18) to $750 for "Mummer," as Scheyer called *Schauspieler [Actor]* (1923.27). [31]

A typed list of works to be shipped from Oakland to Los Angeles, which is dated October 1926, records a total of thirty-three works by Klee, although the catalogue for the Los Angeles Museum show included only twenty-three. [32] The source of some of the works on that list remains unknown: *Stilleben mit Plastiken* [listed as *Still Life with Sculpture*] (1923.119), *Scene unter Mädchen* [listed as *Scenes with Girls*] (1923.148), and *Physiognomische Kristallisation* [listed as *Physiognomical Crystallization*] (1924.15). Other works on the list are not mentioned in the Los Angeles catalogue: *Architecture and Tree Rhythm, Scheidung Abends* [listed as *Separation in the Evening*] (1922.79), *Ablaufendes Meer* [listed as *Receding Sea*] (1923.183), and *Häuser in der Landschaft* [listed as *Houses in Landscape*] (1924.39). Scheyer noted on the list that *Architecture and Tree Rhythm* of 1920 (probably *Baum und Architectur=Rhythmen [Tree and Architecture Rhythms]* [1920.202]) had been sold to Dr. Karl Lilienfeld.[33] The sale stands out because Scheyer until then had been unable to sell Klee's pictures in California. Lilienfeld was, however, not a private collector but an art dealer who managed the Galerie Van Diemen-Lilienfeld in New York.

Reviews of the exhibition at the Los Angeles Museum in October provided biographical information about the four "ultra-modern artists" and characterized Klee as an Expressionist. Writing in the periodical *California Graphic*, Sonia Wolfson described Klee as "an artist of utter paradox. He gives us color patterns of amazing beauty in such whimsically-titled and conceived designs as 'House Tree.' In 'Physiognomical Crystallization,' he has decomposed the facial planes and recomposed them all slightly awry so that both the physical and psychological expression is attenuated. Then with apparently juvenile naivette [sic], he scratches such linear harmonies as 'Meeting of the Birds' and 'Departure of the Ogre.' Like a child's rough sketches, yet pictures palpitant [sic] with subtlety and satire." She characterized him as "an Expressionist who has exhibited frequently under the banner of the Dadaists," but emphasizing his association with Kandinsky at the Bauhaus, concluded that he is "one of the chief figures in German Expressionism today. . . . In America he is known chiefly through his first

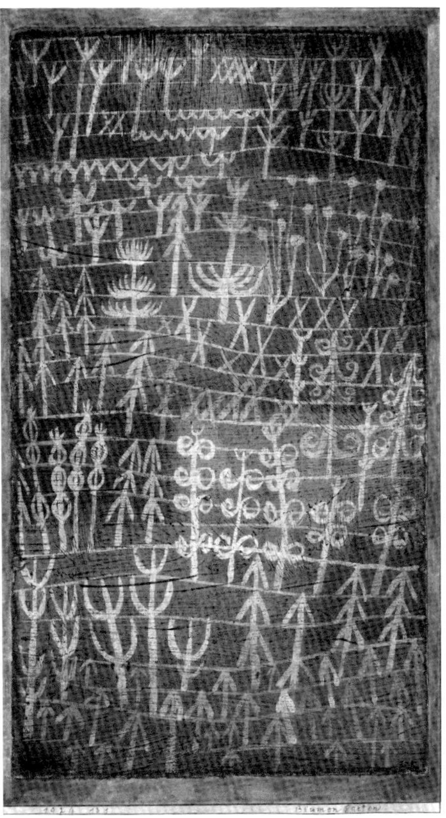

one-man exhibit, held in New York in 1924, under the auspices of the Society Anonyme."[34]

Back on the east coast, Klee's art was seen by a wider audience in 1926 than in previous years thanks to the efforts of Dreier (fig. 21). Dreier, who lived in New York City and West Redding, Connecticut, had traveled extensively in Europe to select works for her "International Exhibition of Modern Art" that would open that fall. Although Klee was not in Dessau to see Dreier in May, he later sent her seven watercolors for the exhibition. In a letter written to Dreier on June 17, Klee explained that he could send her the watercolors but that he did not have any framed paintings available since they were all in an exhibition in Europe. He also provided prices ranging from $100 for *Segelschiffhafen [Harbor for Sailing Ships]* (1925.45, pl. 37) to $175 for *Blumengarten [Flower Garden]* (1924.131, fig. 22), and he specified which works were on consignment and thus available for purchase while in exhibitions. Unlike Scheyer, Valentiner, and Neumann, Dreier herself did not sell works of art or function as a private dealer.

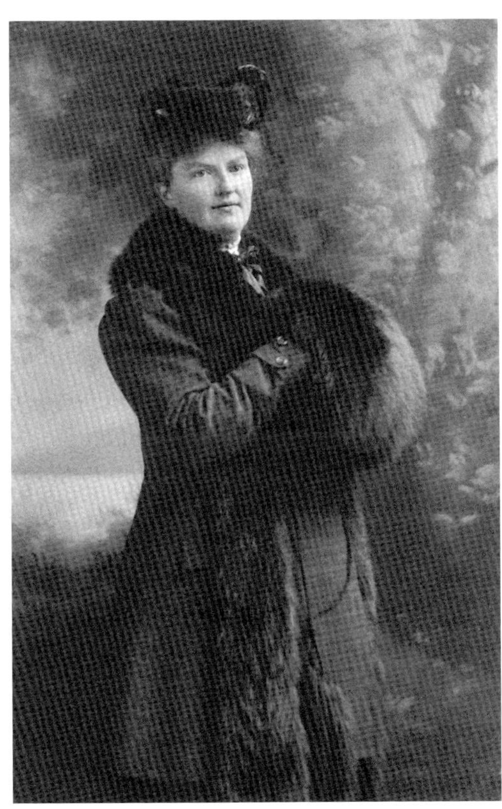

Fig. 21
Katherine Dreier, Munich, c. 1910.

Fig. 22
Paul Klee, *Blumengarten [Flower Garden]*, 1924.131. Black paste ground, gouache, and incising on paper mounted on board, 17 ½ x 12 ¾ inches (44.5 x 32.4 cm). The Museum of Modern Art, New York, Katherine S. Dreier Bequest, 166.1953.

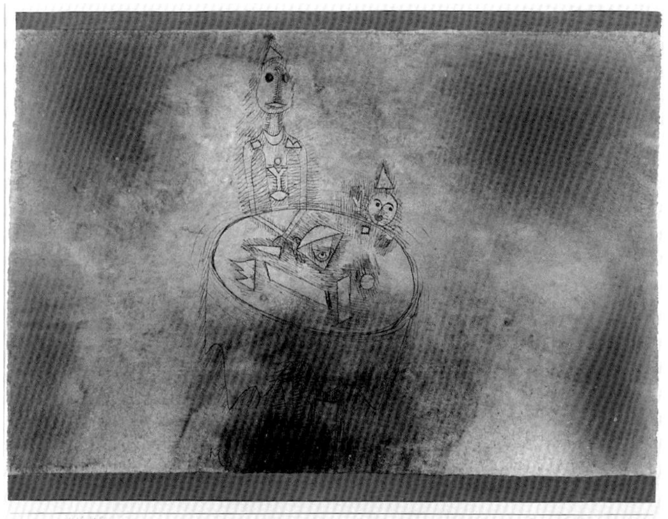

Dreier lent the twelve works by Klee to the German section that she organized for the "Sesquicentennial International Exposition" held in Philadelphia from June 1 until December 1, 1926. However, she focused most of her attention on preparing the ambitious and large "International Exhibition of Modern Art," which opened at the Brooklyn Museum on November 19, 1926, and traveled to other American venues as well as to Toronto. Among the works from twenty-three countries on display were four by Klee, whom she categorized as Swiss: *Blumengarten* (see fig. 22), *Reiher [Heron]* (1924.156), *Alte Stadt Architektur [Old Town Architecture]* (1924.158), and *Vast (Rosenhafen) [Vast (Harbor of Roses)]* (1925.8). Three others listed in the catalogue—*Madonna* (1923.2), *Schlussbild einer Tragikömodie [Final Scene of a Tragicomedy]* (1923.144), and *Segelschiffhafen* of 1925—were not hung.[35]

In 1926 Dreier also acquired several works from Klee that she had exhibited at the Société Anonyme two years earlier: she purchased *Herbst Blume* for $200, as well as *Grundfeste, Aquarell Skizze zu "MA,"* and *Der Bote des Herbstes* for $120 each. She also bought *Blumen im Wind, Kleines Regattabild, Maschinenanlage [Machine Plant]* (1922.110), *Kunstvoller Sternbehälter*, and *Der König alles Ungeziefers* for her own collection. Significantly, Dreier did not acquire any works by Klee dated later than 1925: she definitely preferred his work from the early 1920s.

Early in the summer of 1926, the young art historian Alfred H. Barr Jr. met Neumann at his New York gallery. Barr went there while he was preparing to teach a course on modern art at Wellesley College. Barr later recalled having seen Klee's art illustrated in *Vanity Fair* in 1922 when he was a senior at Princeton University,[36] and he may have visited the Blue Four exhibition in New York.[37] Neumann became a mentor to Barr, giving him advice not only about the bibliography for his course, but also about where to travel in Europe. He suggested which artists and art dealers to visit, emphasizing the importance of the Bauhaus. Later Neumann would play an important role in organizing the Klee exhibition that took place at The Museum of Modern Art, New York, early in 1930. The same year Barr bought *Abstraktes Terzett [Abstract Trio]* (1923.88, pl. 22) from Neumann for his own collection.

In 1927 Barr traveled to England, France, Germany, and Russia, accompanied by Jere Abbott, whom he had met at Princeton in 1924. They were disappointed that Neumann would not be able

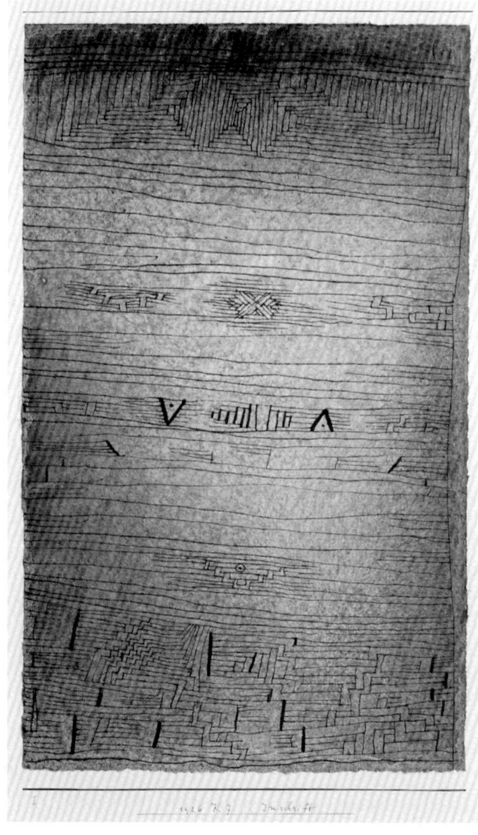

Fig. 23
Paul Klee, *Vater und Sohn [Father and Son]*, 1927.290. Pen and watercolor partially sprayed on paper, with paperstrips with gouache and pencil above and below, mounted on cardboard, 13⅛ x 18⅛ inches (33.5 x 46 cm). Private Collection. Courtesy Marlborough International Fine Art.

Fig. 24
Paul Klee, *Inschrift [Inscription]*, 1926.17. Watercolor and India ink on paper, mounted on cardboard, 9¼ x 5¾ inches (23.5 x 14.6 cm). The Solomon R. Guggenheim Museum, New York, Gift of Solomon R. Guggenheim, 41.343.

to travel with them. The two art historians spent four days at the Bauhaus in Dessau in early December, where Feininger introduced them to Klee.[38] It was probably on this trip that Abbott purchased a watercolor, *Bock [Billy-Goat]* (1925.198, pl. 48), from Klee.[39] Barr recalled that Klee was "the opposite of eccentric, in spite of his amazing art…. While one looks over his drawings in his studio one can hear his wife playing a Mozart sonata in the room below. Only in one corner are there curiosities, a table littered with such ornaments as shells, a skate's egg, bits of dried moss, a pine cone, a piece of coral, fragments of textiles, a couple of drawings by the children of his neighbor, Feininger."[40]

In May 1928 Scheyer went back to Europe for the first time since she had come to the United States four years earlier. She traveled with Evelyn S. Mayer, a professor at San Francisco State Teachers College. After attending the Sixth International Congress for Art Education in Prague, they went to the Bauhaus in Dessau, where they visited Klee and Kandinsky in June 1928. Scheyer returned works that she had on consignment and obtained new ones from the Blue Four artists. From Klee she received twenty-eight works, ranging in date from 1919 to 1928. They included *Pal* (1924.180, pl. 36), *Dorf-Carnaval [Village Carnival]* (1926.135, pl. 35), *Figurinensammlung [Collection of Figurines]* (1926.248, pl. 49), *Pflanzen Samen [Plant Seeds]* (1927.288, pl. 46), and *Vater und Sohn [Father and Son]* (1927.290, fig. 23). (Mayer would purchase the last in 1930 for a reduced price.)[41] Many of the works were recent ones from 1926–28: some featured a linear design with sprayed watercolor, whereas others displayed a more geometrical style. Klee designated two earlier works as belonging to a special "Sonder Classe" ("Separate Class"): a figurative work titled *Kopf [Head]* (1919.5) and the decorative *Tempel Wandmalerei II [Temple Mural Painting II]* (1920.114). Apparently they were not for sale, but Scheyer recorded prices for the others in marks as well as dollars—ranging from $110 to $360. She seems not to have exhibited these new works until 1930, selling most of them in 1930–31.

Back in California, Scheyer reached an agreement with the Los Angeles art dealer Harry Braxton in May 1929 to organize a series of four one-person shows (rather than a group show) of the Blue Four artists. She also decided to move to Los Angeles from San Francisco, although she did not settle there immediately, pre-ferring to spend time on the coast in Carmel while continuing to teach at the girls' school in Berkeley. Scheyer had hopes for the exhibitions at the Braxton Gallery, to be held the following year, and on June 7, 1929, she wrote to Klee: "With the hope of making a little money in Hollywood, I herewith inform you that I am BUYING the two pictures from the first shipment that I reserved for myself here and, therefore, as you will recall, did not bring back to Germany with me, namely *Das Mädchen von Sachsen* and the *Barbaren-Venus*. I am not making a partial payment to you, as I know that you prefer a lump sum."[42] Scheyer purchased both works (see figs. 18 and 19) for her own collection the following year. The Klee exhibition at the Braxton Gallery in May 1930 resulted in numerous sales.

Not only Scheyer and Dreier but also Hilla Rebay, a young German artist and the advisor to Solomon R. Guggenheim, became aware of Klee's art in Germany during the 1920s. Rebay first expressed her interest in acquiring his work in a letter written on March 27, 1929, to Rudolf Bauer, the Berlin dealer and artist: "I would so love to have a Kandinsky watercolor, they are so beautiful. What do you suppose they cost? And a Klee too, so that I can show different things."[43] It was not until July 1930 that she and Guggenheim went to the Bauhaus, where she purchased *Inschrift [Inscription]* (1926.17, fig. 24) for 500 marks from the artist.[44] During the thirties they acquired *Baum Kultur [Tree Culture]* (1924.245, pl. 32) and *Eulenkomoedie [Owl Comedy]* (1926.48, pl. 44), among other works, for the Solomon R. Guggenheim Foundation.

In May 1929 Dreier and Duchamp visited the Bauhaus again. Dreier did not acquire additional works by Klee for her own collection and her contact with the artist seems to have ended in 1930.[45] The Société Anonyme had been forced to close its galleries in April 1924 due to financial problems and lack of interest in modern art. Dreier, however, continued to fund concerts and lectures and, like Scheyer, arranged exhibitions in museums and galleries. In all, Dreier had more than forty Klees; of these, she acquired twenty-eight for her collection and that of the Société Anonyme during the 1920s.[46] Clearly she was the first person to present Klee's art in the United States. By the end of the twenties, the rising interest in modern art on the part of many people tended to eclipse her essential role.

The American artist and collector Albert E. Gallatin founded

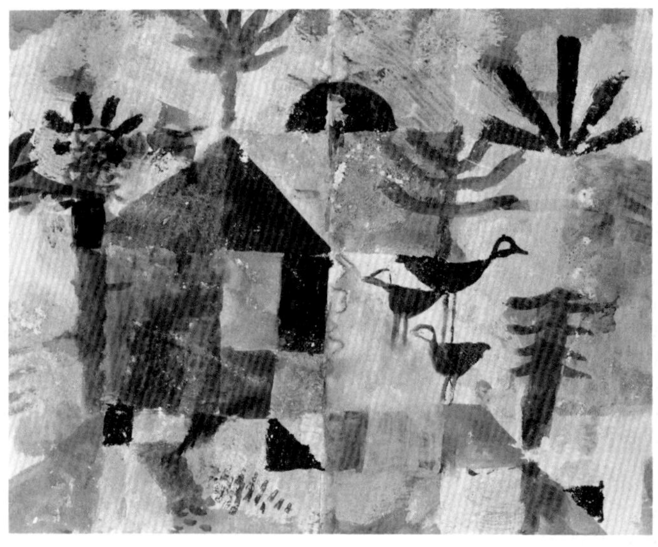

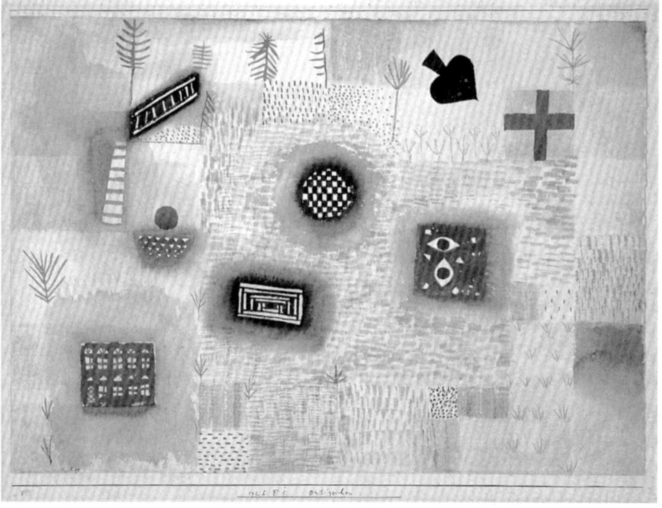

the Gallery of Living Art at New York University in 1927 "in order that the public might have an opportunity of studying at least some of the many phases of … progressive twentieth century painting, not only in private possession and at dealers, but in a public museum."[47] His statement brings to mind the intention of the Société Anonyme, stated a decade earlier, "to provide a public non-commercial center for the study and promotion of modern art." Gallatin purchased Klee's *Landschaft mit 3 blauen Vögeln [Landscape with 3 Blue Birds]* (1919.189, fig. 25) in Munich in 1929,[48] and by the following year, he had acquired *Weihnachtsbild 1B [Christmas Picture 1B]* (1923.178). Both works were exhibited at the Gallery of Living Art in New York in 1930.

Since Klee's work was not exhibited in the late 1920s, there was little or no mention of his art in reviews and no substantial articles were published. The periodical *Transition* reproduced two of Klee's drawings—*Mann Fisch Mann Esser [Man Fish Man Eater]* (1920.99) and *Kleiner Narr in Trance 3 [Small Fool in Trance 3]* (1927.171)—in November 1929.[49] Books such as *A Primer of Modern Art* by Sheldon Cheney, which appeared in 1924, responded negatively to Klee's art and struggled to categorize it. No monographs appeared about the artist in English, although the art historian Will Grohmann's book on Klee published in French in 1929 would have been available to a limited audience.[50] The absence of publicity about Klee in America during the late 1920s contrasts sharply with that in the following years.

Nevertheless, Klee's works were quietly being acquired in Europe by several American collectors. The Philadelphia businessman Albert C. Barnes, famous for his collection of Impressionism, Post-Impressionism, and French modernism, purchased *Sicilische Landschaft [Sicilian Landscape]* (1924.236) from the Galerie Alfred Flechtheim in 1930; he already owned another Klee work, *Ort-Zeichen [Place-Signs]* (1926.151, fig. 26). He had established the Barnes Foundation in 1922 outside Philadelphia as an edu-

Fig. 25
Paul Klee, *Landschaft mit 3 blauen Vögeln [Landscape with 3 Blue Birds]*, 1919.189. Watercolor on chalk-primed paper paper mounted on cardboard, 8 ½ x 11 ⅛ inches (21.5 x 28.2 cm). Philadelphia Museum of Art, A. E. Gallatin Collection, 1952.61.49.

Fig. 26
Paul Klee, *Ort-Zeichen [Place-Signs]*, 1926.151. Watercolor on handmade wove paper, artist-mounted to paperboard, 10⅞ x 14¾ inches (27.6 x 37.5 cm). Barnes Foundation, Merion, Pennsylvania, BF 1004.

cational institution and a place to show his extensive collection.

In Cambridge, Massachusetts, three undergraduates, Edward M. M. Warburg, Lincoln Kirstein, and John Walker III, founded the Harvard Society of Contemporary Art in February 1929. Warburg had admired Klee's work at the Galerie Alfred Flechtheim in Berlin and went to visit Klee at the Dessau Bauhaus. He recalled waiting to knock on the door until the artist finished playing a Bach sonata on the violin. Warburg eventually acquired *Abfahrt der Schiffe [Departure of the Ships]* (1927.140.2, fig. 13) and later *Romantischer Park [Romantic Park]* (1930.280).[51] The Harvard Society of Contemporary Art benefited from the attention of art professionals like Barr, who maintained close ties with its organizers and assisted with their exhibitions, as did Neumann and Valentiner.

Another Harvard student, Philip Johnson, bought a work by Klee, *Heilige Inseln [Sacred Islands]* (1926.6, pl. 40), in the autumn of 1929, probably at the Anhaltische Kunstverein in Dessau.[52] Johnson, who had met Barr earlier that year, was greatly impressed by the Bauhaus and modern architecture. He became a close friend of Barr's and would go on to work on exhibitions and architectural projects for The Museum of Modern Art, New York, for several decades.

In 1929 Barr was appointed founding director of The Museum of Modern Art, which opened that autumn. He presented the first large exhibition of Klee's work in March 1930. The catalogue listed four loans from private collections: *Mit der rotierenden schwarzen Sonne und dem Pfeil* [listed as *Escapement*] (1919.63) from Weyhe, *Landschaft mit 3 blauen Vögeln* (see fig. 25) from Gallatin, *Bock* from Abbott, and *Heilige Inseln* from Johnson. René Crevel's book *Paul Klee*, published the same year in Paris, included reproductions of *Landschaft mit 3 blauen Vögeln*, Ernest Hemingway's *Monument in Arbeit [Monument under Construction]* (1929.88, pl. 55), and *Der Fisch-Dampfer W [The Steam-Trawler W]* (1929.45) from the collection of N. St. Wolff, New York, and mentioned that Klee's work was also in the collection of the Detroit Institute of Arts.

Thanks to Valentiner, who had become the director, the Detroit Institute of Arts was the first American museum to purchase a work by Klee, *Lesende II [Woman Reading II]* (1925.147), in 1930.

Nevertheless, few American private collectors owned Klee's art at the end of the twenties—with the outstanding exceptions of Dreier and Scheyer. Scheyer had already informed Kandinsky in 1926: "Since there is not a single 'modern' collector here in America, and people simply do not buy pictures the way they do over there, you surely understand that the prospect of monetary success is virtually nil."[53] By the autumn of 1929, the crash of the New York stock market further quashed Scheyer's hopes for selling works of art; she told Jawlensky that "America is just now experiencing a dreadful stock market crisis…there has never been anything like it in American history."[54] Although obviously not all collectors—such as Guggenheim and the Rockefellers—were affected, the disastrous economic conditions hurt artists, collectors, and dealers. Scheyer, who had difficulty selling throughout the twenties, reported small sales. On December 5 she sent Klee $13.50 for two prints—*Garten der Leidenschaft [Garden of Passion]* (1913.155) and *Hoffmanneske Märchenscene [Hoffmannesque Fairy-Tale Scene]* (1921.123)—that she had sold. She had already sent the artist $12.50 for two lithographs bought by Jules Furthman in Los Angeles.[55] However, Klee's paintings and watercolors remained unsold.

The establishment during the twenties in America of institutions devoted to modern art—beginning with the Société Anonyme in 1920 and culminating with the founding of The Museum of Modern Art, New York, in 1929—set the stage for an increasing enthusiasm for Klee's art in the thirties. Although his work became known through group exhibitions organized by Dreier and Scheyer during the twenties, Klee would come into the spotlight only with the one-person exhibitions devoted to him in the following decade. It was then that private collectors across the country, not just on the East Coast or in California, would purchase his pictures.

NOTES

1. Vivian Endicott Barnett, *The Blue Four Collection at the Norton Simon Museum* (New Haven, Conn., and London: Yale University Press in association with the Norton Simon Art Foundation, 2002), 12 and 278.

2. Barnett, *The Blue Four Collection*, 292 and 308.

3. The flyers for the first exhibitions of the Société Anonyme are preserved with the Société Anonyme Papers, Beinecke Library, Yale University, New Haven, Connecticut.

4. *Broom* 4, no. 3 (February 1923): 171, 179, and 181.

5. Tristan Tzara, "Germany—A Serial Film: Some Consideration, without Malice or Enthusiasm, upon What Is Going On in Germany between the Acts," *Vanity Fair* 22, no. 2 (April 1923): 59 (illus.).

6. Tzara, 104.

7. Valentiner Papers, Roll 2142, Frame 646, Archives of American Art, Smithsonian Institution, Washington, D.C. Probably the other works were *Häuser u. reife Felder [Houses and Ripe Fields]* (1914.130), Ohne Titel [Untitled] (1914.148), or *Fische in der Tiefe [Fishes in the Deep]* (1921.87). Later he purchased *Mondspiel [Moonplay]* (1923.153) for $100 when he visited Klee again, probably in 1924.

8. Penny Joy Bealle, "Obstacles and Advocates: Factors Influencing the Introduction of Modern Art from Germany to New York City, 1912–1933: Major Promoters and Exhibitions" (Ph.D. diss., Cornell University, Ithaca, New York, 1990), 104–106 and 112a (illus.).

9. Katherine Dreier's annotated copy of the catalogue is preserved with the Société Anonyme Papers, Box 65, Folder 1709. However, according to *Art News* 22, no. 3 (October 27, 1923): 4, she purchased it for $75.

10. See "Modern German Art," *New York Times,* October 7, 1923, sec. 7, 12, and October 14, 1923, sec. 8, 7.

11. "Modern Germany Speaks by Its Art," *Art News* 22, no. 1 (October 13, 1923): 1.

12. "American Buyers Like German Art: Modernist Works at Anderson Galleries Bring More than $4,000," *Art News* 22, no.3 (October 27, 1923): 4.

13. Bealle, 143–44. Artists such as Alexander Archipenko and Georg Muche also went to New York in October 1923.

14. J. B. Neumann, unpublished manuscript,1958, files of The Museum of Modern Art, New York; cited in "Klee in America," in Carolyn Lanchner, ed., *Paul Klee,* exh. cat. (New York: The Museum of Modern Art, 1987), 94.

15. Robert L. Herbert, Eleanor S. Apter, and Elise K. Kenney, *The Société Anonyme and the Dreier Bequest at Yale University: A Catalogue Raisonné* (New Haven, Conn., and London: Yale University Press, 1984), 376, 754, and 777. Dreier's scrapbook contains the flyer and reviews (Société Anonyme Papers, Box 128, Folder 2872).

16. The exhibition listings in *Art News* (nos. 15–20, January 19–February 23, 1924) refer to a Klee and Kandinsky show. The Kandinsky paintings were probably *Entwurf I zu Bild mit weissem Rand [Sketch I for Painting with White Border]* (1913), *Bunter Kreis [Multicolored Circle]* (1921), *Kreise auf Schwarz [Circles on Black]* (1921), and *Blauer Kreis [Blue Circle]* (1922).

17. "Art Exhibitions of the Week." *New York Times,* January 20, 1924, sec. 7, 9.

18. Henry McBride, review, *New York Herald,* January 20, 1924, sec. 7, 15.

19. Henry McBride, "Notes and Activities in the World of Art," *New York Herald,* January 13, 1924. The clipping is one of seven preserved in Katherine Dreier's scrapbook, Société Anonyme Papers, Box 128, Folder 2872.

20. I am grateful to Kristin Henry, Yale University Art Gallery, New Haven, Connecticut, for providing me with this information and for bringing to my attention the original scrapbooks and logbook. The new gallery closed soon afterwards on May 1, 1924 (see Herbert, Apter, and Kenney, 754).

21. Société Anonyme Papers, Box 90, Folder 2330. The other works are: Ohne Titel [Untitled] (1915.253), *Mit der sinkenden Sonne [With the Sinking Sun]* (1919.247), *Tropische Blüte [Tropical Blossom]* (1920.203), *Sanft bewegter Garten [Gently Moving Garden]* (1920.217), *Rosenbaum [Rose Tree]* (1920.219), *Reifendes Wachstum [Ripening Growth]* (1921.71), *Keramisch/Erotisch/Religiös [Ceramic/Erotic/Religious]* (1921.97), *rot/grüne Stufung [Red-Green Gradation]* (1921.103), *Architectur rot/grün [Architecture Red-Green]* (1922.19), *Das Haus zum Fliegerpfeil [The Dart House]* (1922.56), *Ausschnitt aus einem Ballett zur Aeolsharfe [Fragment from a Ballet to Aeolian Harp]* (1922.87), *Maschinenanlage [Machine Plant]* (1922.110), *Urnensammlung [Urn Collection]* (1922.129), *Blumenfamilie V. [Flower Family V.]* (1922.134), *Schicksal-Stunde des Kaisers [The Emperor's Fateful Hour]* (1922.135), *Der Hügel [The Hill]* (1922.141), and *Der Heldentenor als Konzertsänger [The Heroic Tenor as Concert Singer]* (1922.144).

22. "Durch Kandinsky hörte ich dass Sie meine Kollection im besten Monat Januar 1924 ausstellen wollen und bin damit einverstanden. Der Anlass dieser Zeilen ist hauptsächlich mein Wunsch Sie auf den ganz ausgezeichneten Maler Alex. v. Jawlensky aufmerksam zu machen…. Wenn Sie Lust haben zu einer [Jawlensky] Ausstellung so können Sie sich an Frau Emmy Scheyer in Braunschweig wenden, die seine Geschäfte leitet. Sie ist kein Händler, sondern eine gute Freundin von uns allen…." Russell Stockman's translation. Paul Klee to Katherine Dreier, June 1923, Société Anonyme Papers, Box 20, Folder 582.

23. Vivian Endicott Barnett, "The Founding of the Blue Four and Their Presentation in New York in 1924–1925," in *The Blue Four: Feininger, Jawlensky, Kandinsky and Klee in the New World,* exh. cat. (Cologne: DuMont, 1997), 20–21 and 23.

24. Barnett, "The Founding of the Blue Four," 21–23. Scheyer, in a letter dated November 26, 1924, reported this information about Neumann to Kandinsky.

25. Henry McBride, review, *The Sun,* February 21, 1925, 12. McBride appears not to have written about Klee for *The Dial.*

26. *Time* 5 (March 9, 1925): 14.

27. See Barnett, "The Founding of the Blue Four," 26.

28. Scheyer wrote to Klee that she sold it for $50. Galka Scheyer to Paul Klee (carbon copy of letter), February 1, 1925, Blue Four Galka Scheyer Archives, Norton Simon Museum, Pasadena, California.

29. "Ich kann jetzt sagen, ich habe in Amerika Fuss gefasst und schneller wie ich hoffte. Das Beste ist mit keinem Deutschen zusammen zukommen, wie ich in New York tat, das hindert mehr wie man denkt, denn jeder belastet einen mit seinem Schicksal. Allein ist das Allerbeste." Isabel Wünsche's translation. Galka Scheyer to Blue Four group (carbon copy of letter), January 31, 1926, Blue Four Galka Scheyer Archives. The reference is to Neumann with whom she worked briefly in October–November 1924.

30. Galka Scheyer to Blue Four group (carbon copy of letter), March 10, 1926, Blue Four Galka Scheyer Archives.

31. "The Blue Four: Feininger, Jawlensky, Kandinsky, Paul Klee," The Oakland Art Gallery, Oakland, California, May 2–31 (extended to June 15), 1926. *Mit den schwarzen Tupfen [With the Black Spots]* (1915.251), *Der Häuserbaum [The Tree of Houses]* (1918.83), *Neue Häuser [New Houses]* (1919.246), *Flora in der toten Stadt*, and *Blüten und Ähren* belonged to Scheyer. The annotated copy of the exhibition catalogue is in the Blue Four Galka Scheyer Archives.

32. The list is in the Blue Four Galka Scheyer Archives.

33. A letter dated November 10, 1927, from Galka Scheyer to Lily Klee refers to $40 she had sent to Klee for a work sold in San Francisco to Dr. Lilienfeld. Carbon copy in Blue Four Galka Scheyer Archives. However, the catalogue raisonné does not cite either Lilienfeld or Scheyer in the provenance. Likewise, there is no mention of Scheyer for the above-mentioned works on the list dated October 1926.

34. Sonia Wolfson, review, *California Graphic* (October 1926). This review and clippings from the *Los Angeles Times* are preserved in the scrapbook for June–December 1926, Archives, Los Angeles County Museum of Natural History, Los Angeles.

35. Ruth L. Bohan, *The Société Anonyme's Brooklyn Exhibition: Katherine Dreier and Modernism in America* (Ann Arbor, Mich.: UMI Research Press, 1982), 146.

36. Alice Goldfarb Marquis, *Alfred H. Barr, Jr.: Missionary for the Modern* (Chicago: Contemporary Books, 1989), 29, and Sybil Gordon Kantor, *Alfred H. Barr, Jr. and the Intellectual Origins of the Museum of Modern Art* (Cambridge, Mass.: MIT Press, 2002), 158. Both books mention Barr's recollection without indicating the particular article. Undoubtedly the article by Tzara, published in April 1923, is intended.

37. Kantor, 159. The author does not provide a source. In addition, Feininger wrote to his wife, Julia, on December 6, 1927, that Barr had seen his work at the Blue Four show in California. Since Barr had not been to California, the reference must be to the Daniel Gallery show in New York. See Kantor, 160, and June L. Ness, ed., *Lyonel Feininger* (New York: Praeger, 1974), 160.

38. Ness, 161. Lyonel Feininger to Julia Feininger, December 6, 1927, Feininger Papers, Ms Ger 146, Houghton Library, Harvard University, Cambridge, Massachusetts.

39. Jere Abbott to Curt Valentin, September 30, 1940, files of Smith College Museum of Art, Northampton, Massachusetts. Abbott wrote that he acquired the work from the artist in 1926, although his visit took place in 1927.

40. Alfred H. Barr Jr., *Paul Klee,* exh. cat. (New York: The Museum of Modern Art, 1930), 8.

41. "Die Dame, die mit mir in Dessau war, Evelyn Mayer, kaufte No.I. [1927.10]. Vater und Sohn. anstatt für 700 Mk. 33 ein Drittel % weniger Mk. 467.00 oder 112.00 $ von Ihnen Direct." ("The woman who was with me in Dessau, Evelyn Mayer, bought no. 1 [1927.10], *Vater und Sohn,* from you directly for 33 1/3% less: 467 marks, or $112, instead of 700 marks.") Russell Stockman's translation. Galka Scheyer to Paul Klee (carbon copy of letter), June 1, 1930, Blue Four Galka Scheyer Archives.

42. "Mit der Aussicht in Hollywood etwas Geld zu verdienen, künde ich Ihnen hiermit an, dass ich die beiden Bilder von der ersten Sendung, die ich mir hier reservierte und deshalb, wie Sie sich erinnern werden, nicht mit nach Deutschland brachte, KAUFE. Nämlich 'das Mädchen von Sachsen' und die 'Barbaren-Venus'. Ich mache Ihnen keine Anzahlung, da ich weiss, dass Sie die Summe im ganzen vorziehen." Russell Stockman's translation. Galka Sheyer to Paul Klee (carbon copy of letter), June 7, 1929, Blue Four Galka Scheyer Archives.

43. "Ich hätte so gerne ein Aquarell von Kandinsky, sie sind doch zu schön, was kosten die wohl? U. einen Klee auch, damit ich verschiedene Sachen zeigen könnte." Russell Stockman's translation. Hilla Rebay to Rudolf Bauer, March 27, 1929, The Hilla von Rebay Foundation Archives, on deposit at The Solomon R. Guggenheim Museum, New York.

44. Louise Averill Svendsen, "Notes on Klee," in *Paul Klee in the Collection of the Solomon R. Guggenheim Museum,* exh. cat. (New York: Solomon R. Guggenheim Museum, 1977), 6.

45. In October 1930 Klee sent Dreier four works (see Société Anonyme Papers, Box 20, Folder 582) on consignment for an exhibition she organized at the Albright Art Gallery (later Albright-Knox Art Gallery) in Buffalo, New York, but they were soon returned to him. Their last letters date from 1926.

46. In contrast, Scheyer obtained more than two hundred works by Klee—most on consignment—over twenty-five years.

47. A. E. Gallatin, *Gallery of Living Art, New York University*, exh. cat. (New York: The Gallery, 1930), 1.

48. A. E. Gallatin Papers, Box 4, Folder 7, New York Historical Society, New York, contains a file card written by Gallatin stating "bought in Munich 1929."

49. *Transition,* no. 18 (1929): opposite 64 and 65.

50. See Sheldon Cheney, *A Primer of Modern Art* (New York: Boni and Liveright, 1924 and 1927) and Will Grohmann, *Paul Klee* (Paris: Editions Cahiers d'Art, 1929).

51. Nicholas Fox Weber, *Patron Saints: Five Rebels Who Opened America to a New Art 1928–1943* (New York: Knopf, 1992), 124–26. The exact date he acquired the works is unclear.

52. Johnson was enamored of Klee's work, having purchased a "charming one" at an exhibition in Dessau. Kantor, 280. In fact, the Anhaltische Kunstverein presented ninety-eight watercolors belonging to Klee that autumn. See *Der Cicerone* 21, no. 21 (1929): 622.

53. "Da es hier in Amerika gar keinen einzigen 'modernen' Sammler gibt, man überhaupt nicht in dem Sinne wie drüben Bilder kauft, so werden Sie begreifen, dass die Aussicht auf pekunaren Erfolg gleich 0 ist." Russell Stockman's translation. Galka Scheyer to Vasily Kandinsky, January 8, 1926, Bibliothèque Kandinsky, Musée National d'Art Moderne, Centre Georges Pompidou, Paris.

54. "Amerika hat im Moment eine fürchterliche Krise auf dem Stockmarkt … so was war noch nie in der Geschichte Amerikas." Russell Stockman's translation. Galka Scheyer to Alexei Jawlensky (carbon copy of letter), November 23, 1929, Blue Four Galka Scheyer Archives.

55. Galka Scheyer to Paul Klee (carbon copy of letter), December 5, 1929, with annotated typed list of prints "left over from first lot," Blue Four Galka Scheyer Archives.

Plates

1913–1929
with Selected Catalogue Entries

Around 1912–13 Klee began developing his new Cubist style. As this work shows, he soon adopted an abstract, densely articulated, graphic pictorial idiom that at first glance recalls the pictures of so-called Synthetic Cubism. Compared to those French precedents, however, Klee's Cubist compositions are far less centralized and hierarchical. The advantages and disadvantages of Cubism, which Klee first described as "a special branch of Expressionism," were the subject of intense debate among German avant-garde artists of the day. In his essay "On the Question of Form," published in May 1912 in the almanac *Der Blaue Reiter*, Vasily Kandinsky criticized Cubist practice, especially that of Pablo Picasso: "Such 'mathematical' construction is a form that often leads necessarily to the absolute destruction of the material coherency of the object's parts."[1] In his August 1912 review of the Swiss "Moderne Bund" exhibition in Zurich, published in *Die Alpen*, Klee was also critical, deploring the application of Cubism's formal disintegration to living creatures: "The animal and the human being, which are supposed to be alive, lose a measure of viability with each transposition. Especially if they are forced to integrate themselves into some heterogeneous pictorial organism, or—as in Picasso—are placed there, cut into separate motifs, for the sake of the pictorial idea. Destruction for the sake of construction?"[2]

Unlike Kandinsky, however, Klee tried to see how he might exploit Cubism in his own work. He had surely read Roger Allard's 1912 essay in *Der Blaue Reiter* and pondered the definition of Cubism it presented. "The first postulate of Cubism," according to Allard, "is the arrangement of things, not realistic things, to be sure, but abstract shapes. [The arranged shapes] fill a space viewed as a configuration of lines, spaces, quadratic and cubic equations, and weight relationships. The task of the artist is to introduce an artistic order into this mathematical chaos. His desire is to awaken the latent rhythm of this chaos."[3] Klee saw this process of creating order out of chaos as analogous to the working of nature, even the biblical story of Creation.

In the present work, various organic forms reminiscent of sprouts or leaves appear to be growing out of the small, inorganic rectangular shapes. Klee's minimally hierarchical network was ideally suited to suggesting this genesis of organic forms. His simple palette helps to fix the emergent scene, in which the primeval vegetation is apparently still surrounded by a blue haze. Double crosses become small stars. Light filters in from the orange corner in the upper left. In this twilight the fragments of vegetation gradually take on more recognizable shapes. This work embodies a different concept of Cubism than the one espoused later by Klee's biographer Wilhelm Hausenstein: "The Cubist approach effects the radical destruction of nature. And that is good. For nature is the enemy of art."[4] In 1913 Klee's artist friend Franz Marc proposed publishing a Bible with illustrations by such avant-garde artists as Kandinsky, Klee, Oskar Kokoschka, Alfred Kubin, and others. Klee elected to undertake the Psalms, and Marc himself was to illustrate Genesis. Owing to the outbreak of World War I, the project was never realized. In *Als Gott sich mit der Erschaffung der Pflanzen trug*, whose subject more properly belonged to Marc's part in the publishing project, Klee probed even deeper into the process of creation than did his friend with his romantic Cubist depictions of animals.

Osamu Okuda

1. Vasily Kandinsky, "Über die Formfrage," *Der Blaue Reiter* (May 1912), reprinted in Vasily Kandinsky and Franz Marc, eds., *Der Blaue Reiter* (Munich: Piper, 1965), 173.

2. Paul Klee, *Schriften: Rezensionen und Aufsätze*, ed. Christian Geelhaar (Cologne: DuMont Buchverlag, 1976), 107f.

3. Roger Allard, "Kennzeichen der Erneuerung in der Malerei," in Kandinsky and Marc, 79.

4. Wilhelm Hausenstein, "Vom Kubismus," *Der Sturm* 4, nos. 170 and 171 (July 1913): 68.

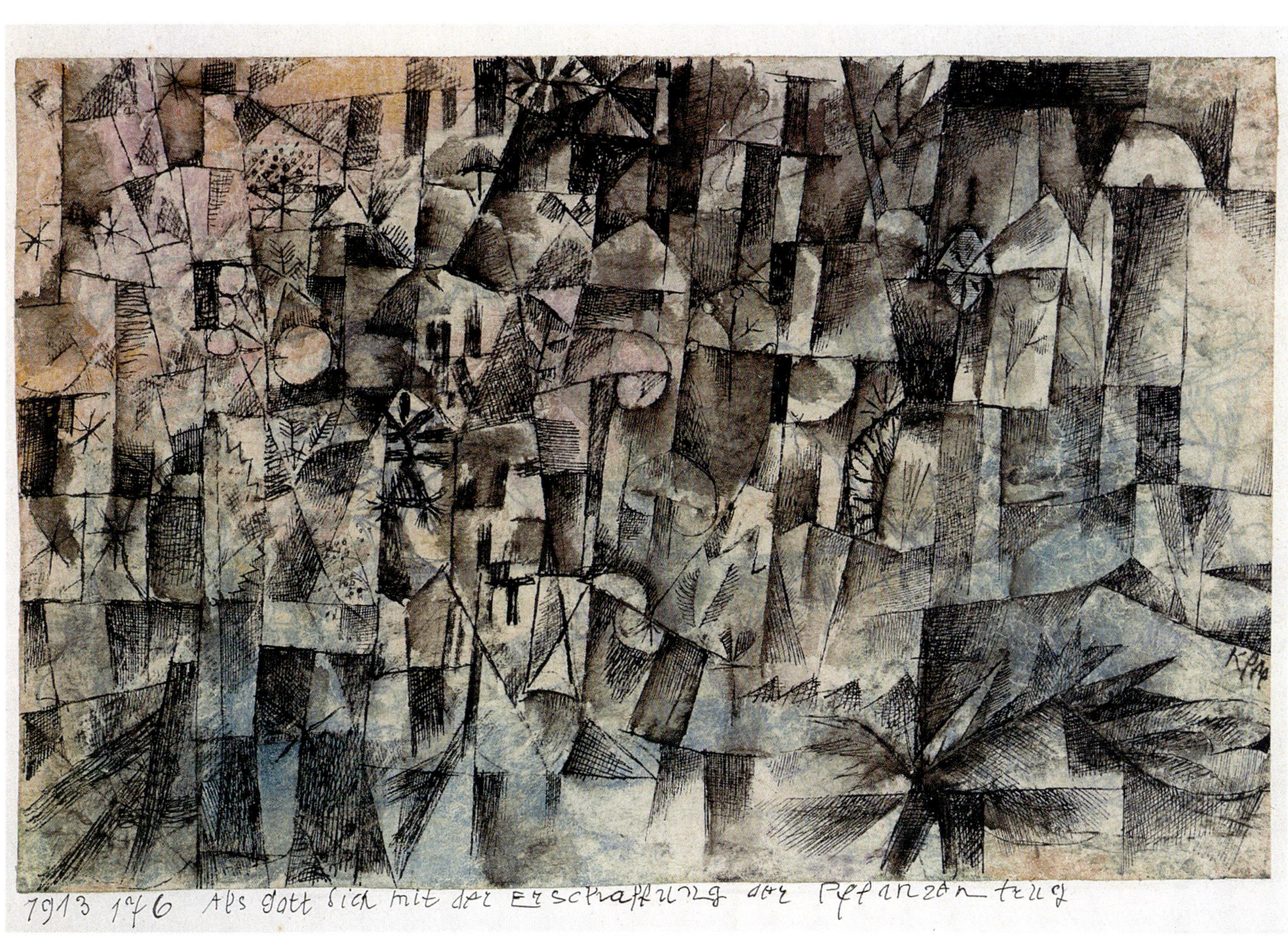

1 **ALS GOTT SICH MIT DER ERSCHAFFUNG DER PFLANZEN TRUG**, 1913.176
   [When God Considered the Creation of the Plants]

Pen, brush, wet in wet, and watercolor on paper, mounted on cardboard
6 x 8½ inches (15 x 21.5 cm)
Worthington Collection, Chicago

Around 1913–14, especially after his trip to Tunisia with August Macke and Louis Moilliet in April 1914, Klee devoted intense study to Robert and Sonia Delaunay's introduction of color into Cubist compositions. When Klee exhibited these works in Germany after the outbreak of World War I, they aroused considerable controversy. His Cubist abstractions were sharply criticized as "enemy art" or mere tapestry designs. But despite this criticism, Klee clung to his avant-garde style, as the example of *Gelbes Haus* shows. In it Klee reworked the subject of a watercolor he had painted during his 1914 trip to St. German (today Ez Zahra) near Tunis, consolidating the essences of the compositional vocabulary he had developed in the following year. The "X" shape, the central sign of abstract art in Klee's œuvre, appears prominently as an autonomous symbol.

Recent Klee scholarship has called attention to the special meaning of the "yellow house," a motif that the artist employed repeatedly in his works after 1912. One suggestion is that Klee was alluding to the yellow "artists' house" in Arles where Vincent van Gogh housed Paul Gauguin in 1888. Annette Baumann wrote: "Van Gogh seems to have figured as a spiritual father for the notion of an art collective, for the yellow house became a common motif in the Blaue Reiter circle and also turned up repeatedly in the work of Klee. His watercolor *Gelbes Haus [Yellow House]* (1914.26), painted immediately before his trip to Tunisia, was later owned by

[Alexei] Jawlensky. Klee's last two works from 1940, the year of his death, also carry this title, as if they were his last comments on the artist colony fallen victim to political conditions."[1] Indeed the 1915 picture, until now only rarely discussed, must be understood in the context of the subsequent evolution of the "yellow house" motif in Klee's work. It is significant that, as mentioned above, the artist reverted to this motif in his difficult wartime isolation. In this historical context, the yellow house can be seen as symbolizing an ideal bastion of the avant-garde that would survive the war in Klee's art. When Klee was serving in the army during World War I, working as a clerk in the finance office of the flying school in Gersthofen, Germany, he returned to the motif of his 1915 painting. In the watercolor *Himmelsblüten über dem gelben Haus (das auserwählte Haus) [Sky Blooms above the Yellow House (the Chosen House)]* (1917.74), the strange plants on the gable of the little yellow house are reaching up toward the sky, presenting the yellow house as a metaphor for artistic fertility in the midst of war. A similar cosmic, organic growth in his own commercial success began in 1917 as he turned away from the war.

Osamu Okuda

1. Annette Baumann, "Paul Klee als Sammler," in *Die Kunst zu Sammeln: Schweizer Kunstsammlungen seit 1948* (Zurich: Schweizerisches Institut für Kunstgeschichte, 1998), 299.

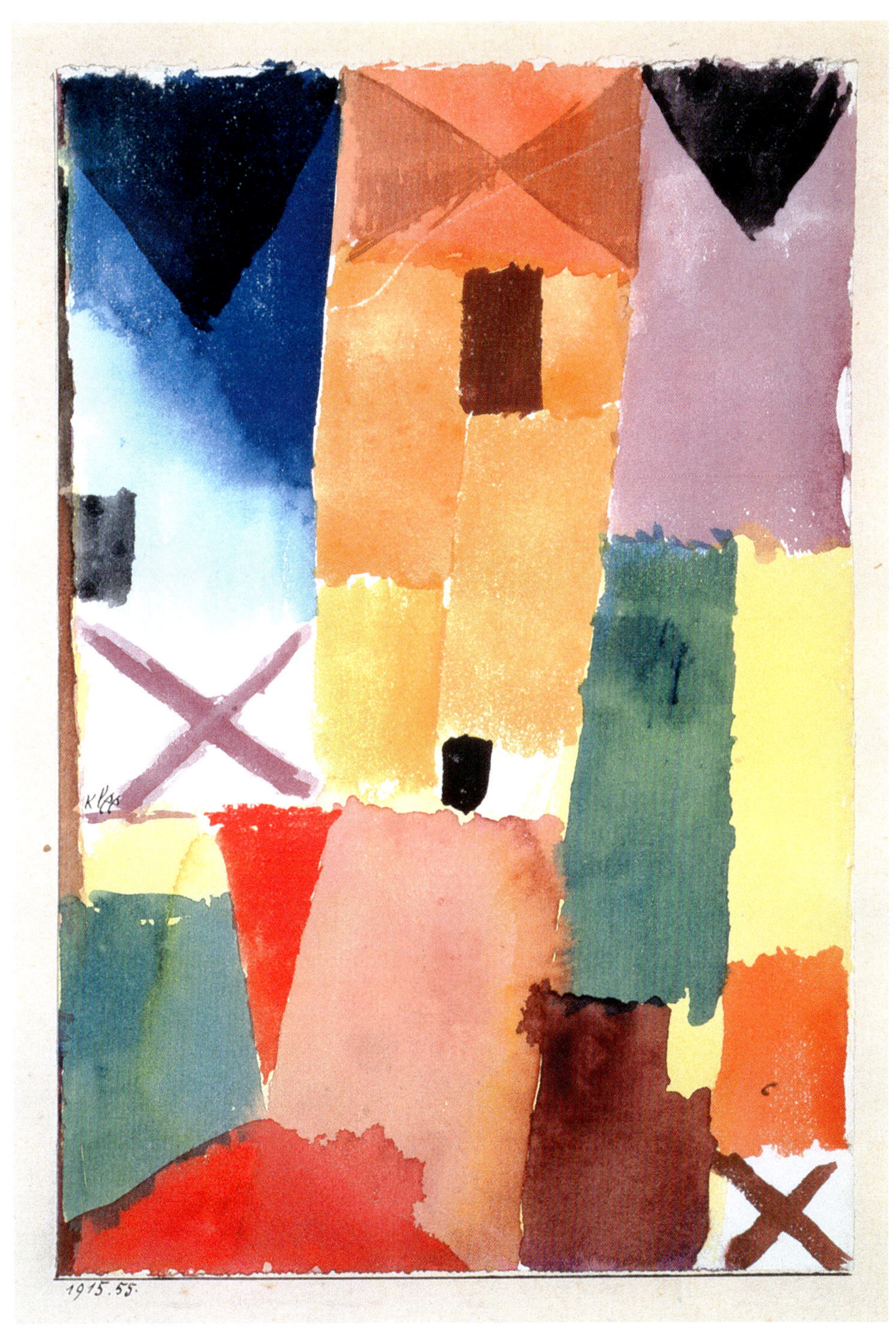

2   **GELBES HAUS**, 1915.55
[Yellow House]

Watercolor on paper, mounted on cardboard
8 x 5⅜ inches (20.3 x 13.8 cm)
Private Collection

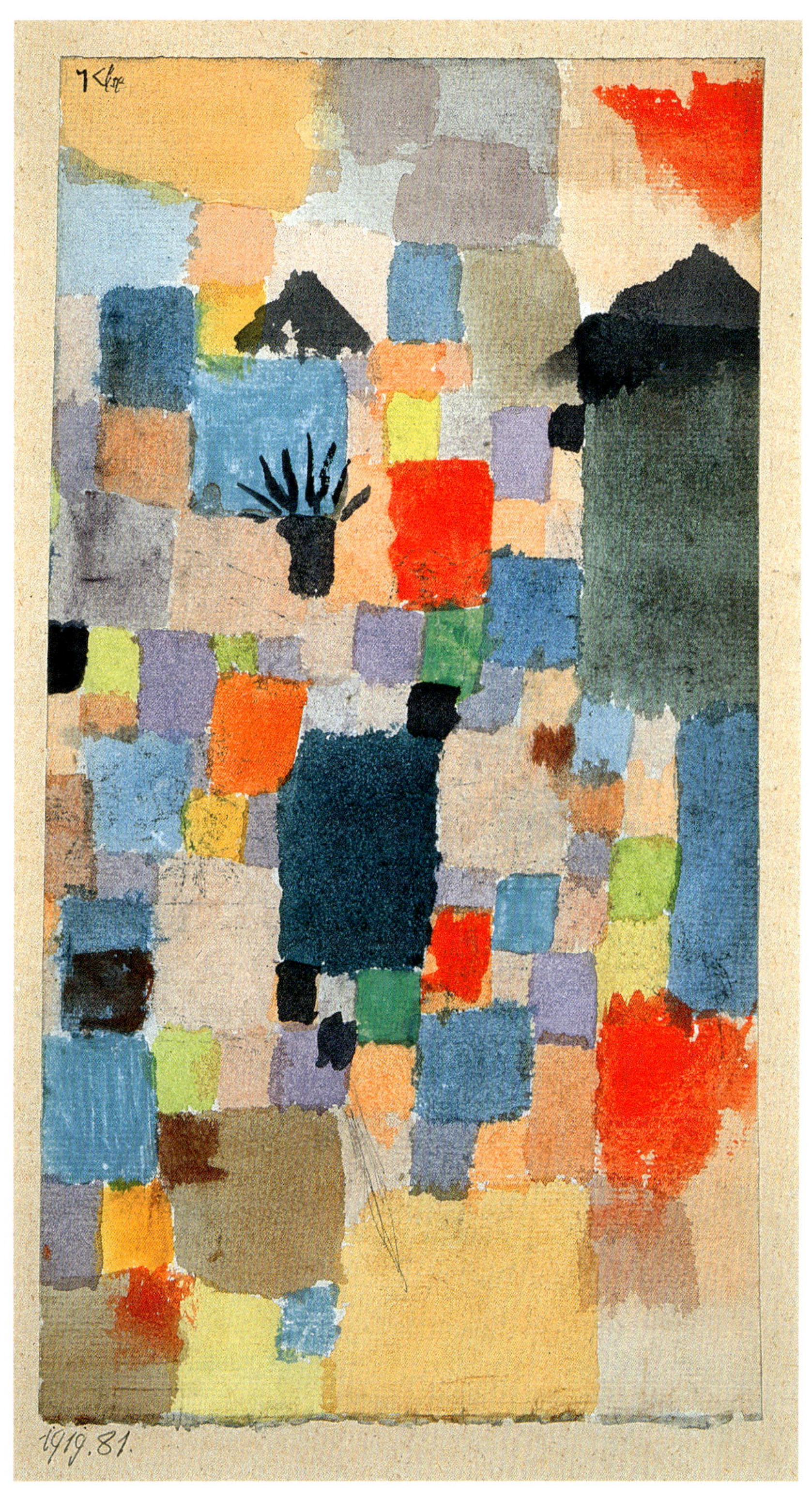

3   **TUNESISCHE GÄRTEN**, 1919.81
[Tunisian Gardens]

Watercolor and pen on paper, mounted on cardboard
9⅜ x 5⅛ inches (23.8 x 13 cm)
Private Collection

On a kind of stage set with a painted mountain backdrop, a flower, two houses, and a doll-like child emerge out of a deep, dark ground as though in a dream. The motifs are illuminated by white and colored—red, green, and violet—spotlights. A half moon shining through a flag in the upper corner is at the same time the eye of a laughing profile. The relative sizes of the various objects are incongruous: compared to the schoolhouse with its little bell tower, the child is a virtual Gulliver. The flower (a daisy?) could be even larger, especially as it stands back on a hill in the distance. Yet the structure of the landscape, with a foreground, middle distance, and background, is relatively conventional. The schoolhouse, which also stands on a rise, is largely rendered in perspective, whereas the second structure, on a hill in the right-hand middle distance, only presents its front façade parallel to the picture plane. Between the two buildings lies an illusionistic distance, and in this dark intervening space in the center of the picture, one is startled to discover a mouth, then a whole face, the upper part hidden behind the flower.

Klee played a similar game of hide-and-seek in several of his earlier works from 1918–19—for example, *Mit dem Adler [With the Eagle]* (1918.85) and *Kosmische Composition [Cosmic Composition]* (1919.165). Such picture puzzles were the result of his practice of overpainting, in which he formally or contextually combined earlier layers with newer ones painted on top. Thus it is possible that the fairy-tale landscape of *Schulhaus* took shape in the overpainting of a portrait. The discovery of the hidden face stimulates the imagination; it seems as if someone is watching us through the picture. Magical effects such as this are frequently linked to numinous childhood memories, or could the fantastic landscape be the dream of this ghostlike person in the picture? If the latter, this could be a kind of self-portrait of the artist, who, according to Leopold Zahn, after participating on the sidelines of the failed German revolution of 1918–19, continued his career as a painter of a "mystical fairy-tale" world. Klee first exhibited the picture in 1920 in his major retrospective at the gallery belonging to Hans Goltz in Munich. It is reproduced both in the catalogue of that show and in the Klee monograph that Zahn published at almost the same time. "What mainly distinguishes Klee from the other abstractionists," Zahn wrote in that book, "is the power of his imagination," adding, "Childlike imagination spins lovely, unheard-of fairy tales in an abstract language."[1] In support of this argument, he then quoted a long passage from Johannes Müller's esoteric "On Imaginary Visions of Faces."

Osamu Okuda

1. Leopold Zahn, *Paul Klee: Leben—Werk—Geist* (Potsdam, Germany: G. Kiepenheuer, 1920), 24.

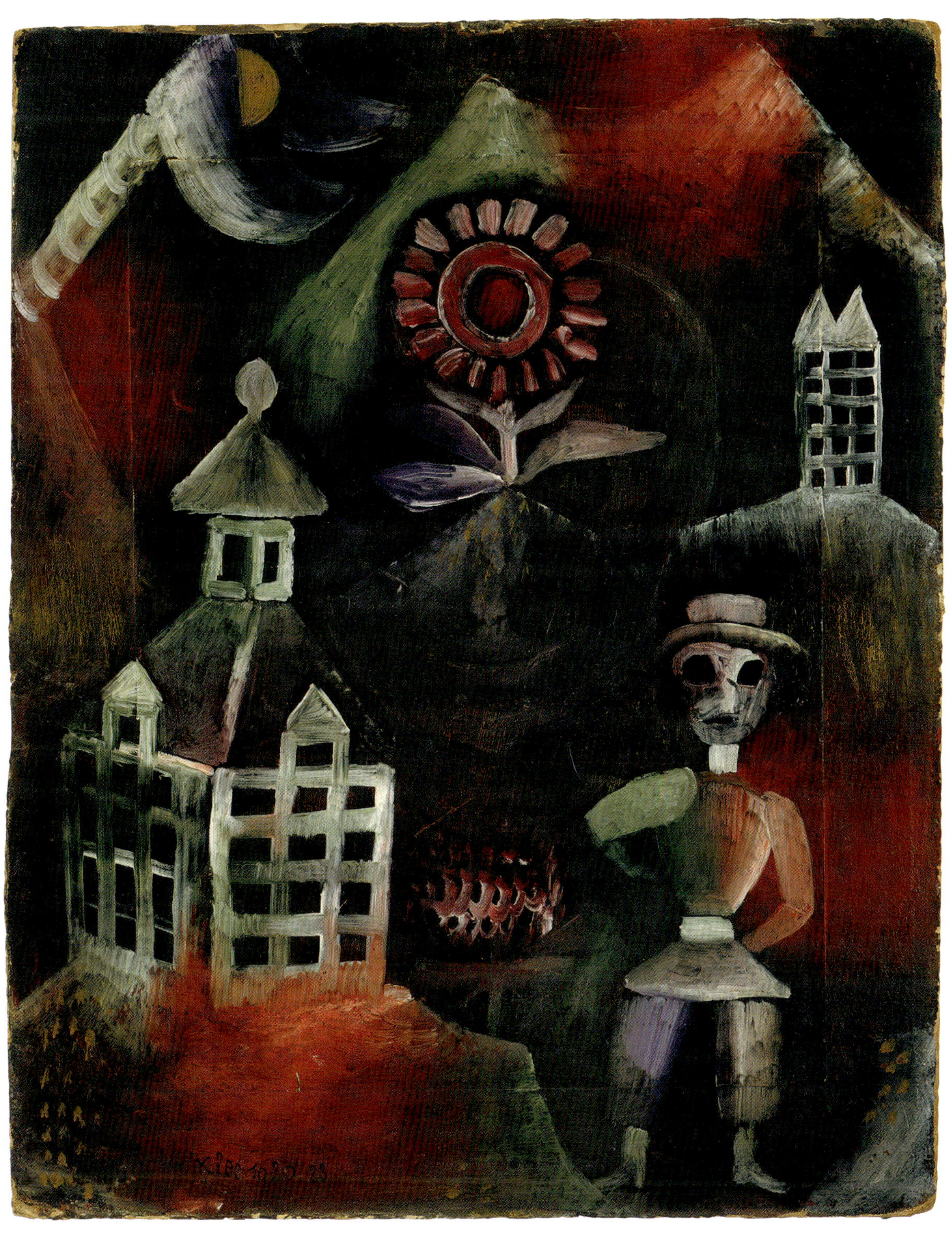

4 **SCHULHAUS**, 1920.23
[Schoolhouse]

Oil on paper, mounted on cardboard and mounted on stretcher
14½ x 11⅜ inches (37 x 29 cm)
The Art Institute of Chicago
Gift of Mr. and Mrs. Leigh B. Block, 1969.811

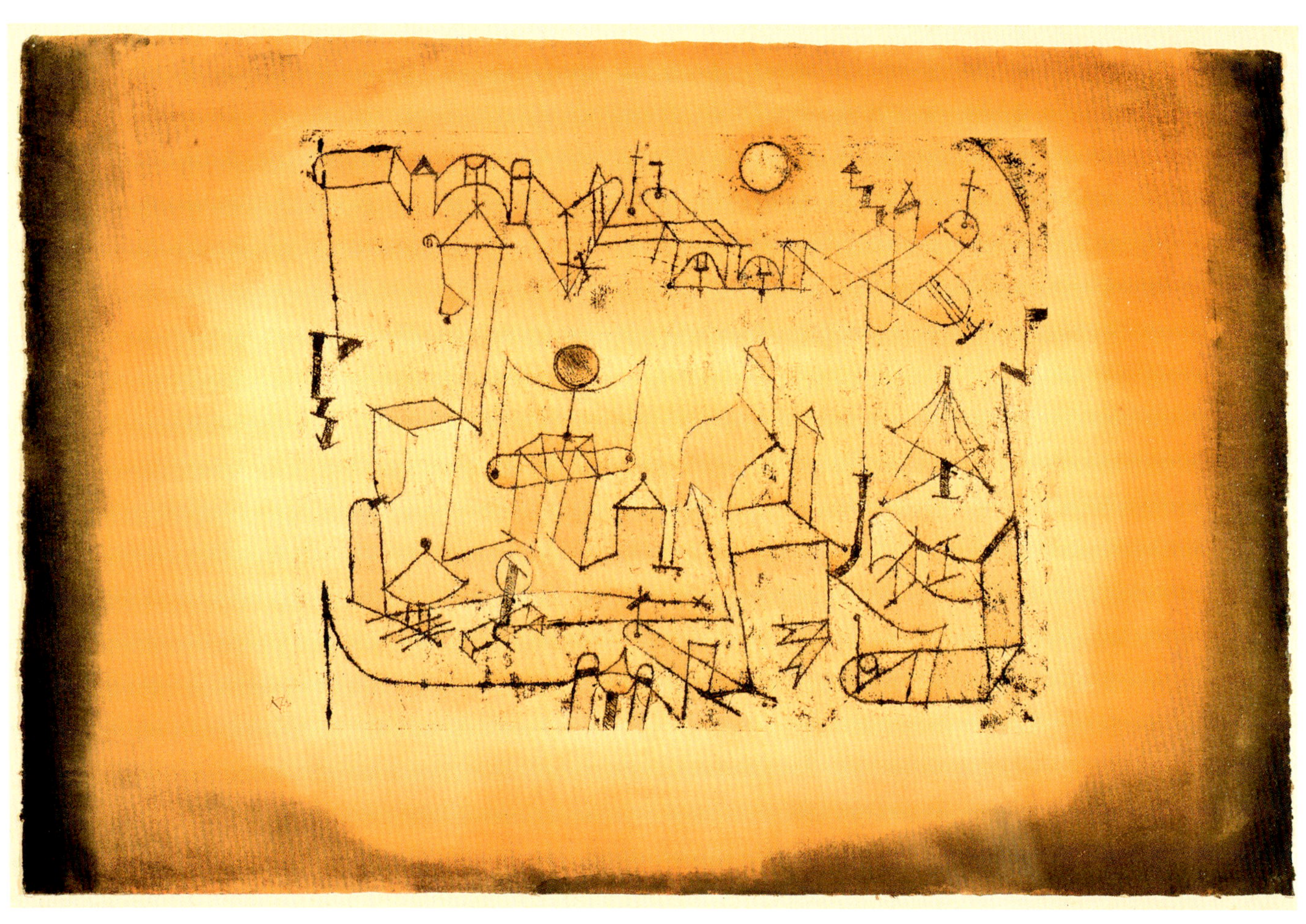

5 **STADT IM ZWISCHENREICH**, 1921.25
[City in the Intermediate Realm]

Oil transfer and watercolor on paper, mounted with glue spots on cardboard
12⅜ x 18⅞ inches (31.3 x 48 cm)
Columbus Museum of Art, Columbus, Ohio, Sirak Collection

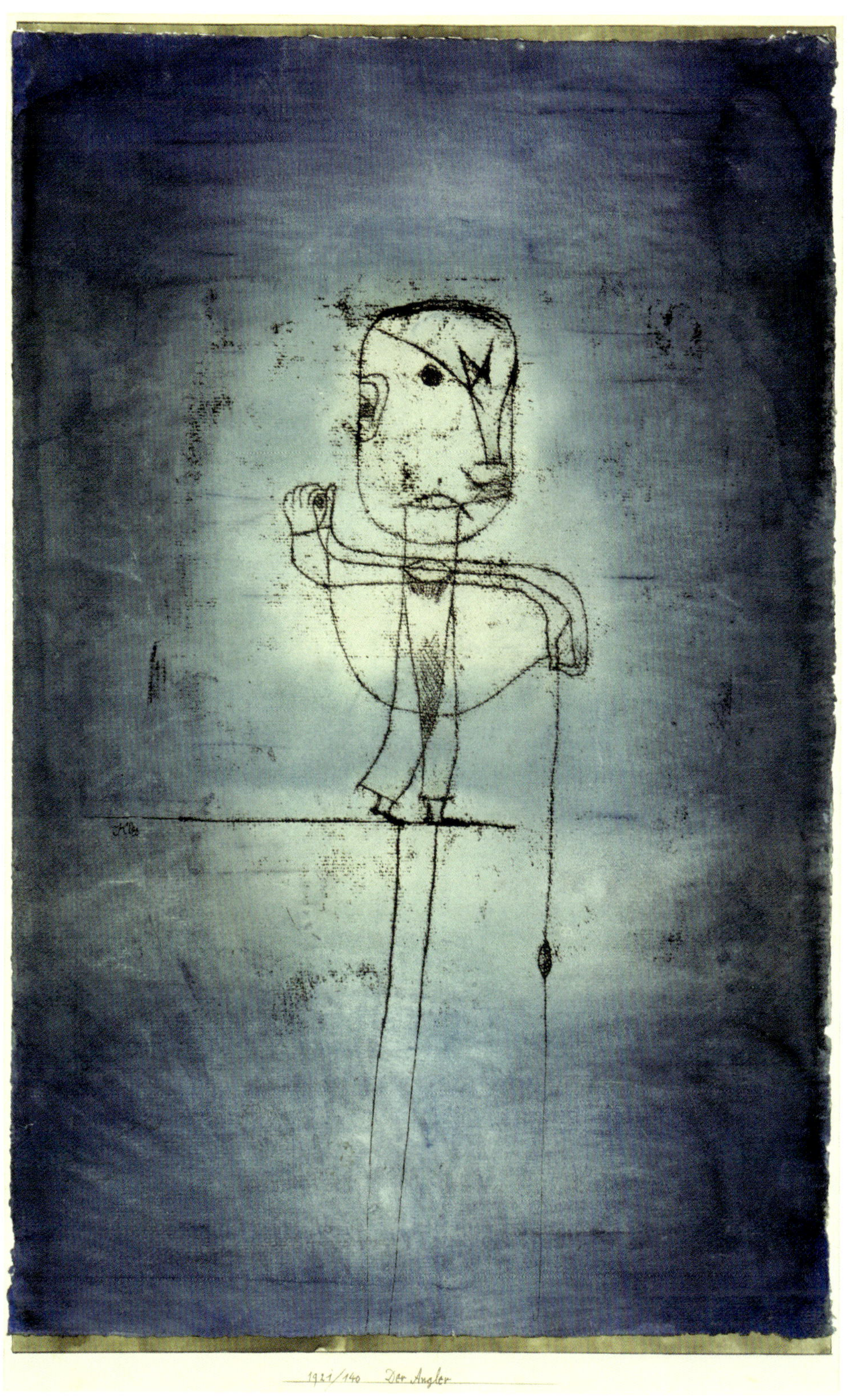

6   **DER ANGLER**, 1921.140
[The Angler]

Oil transfer and watercolor on paper, with watercolor and pen margin
above and below, mounted on cardboard
18¾ x 12¼ inches (47.6 x 31.2 cm)
The Museum of Modern Art, New York, John S. Newberry Collection, 64.61

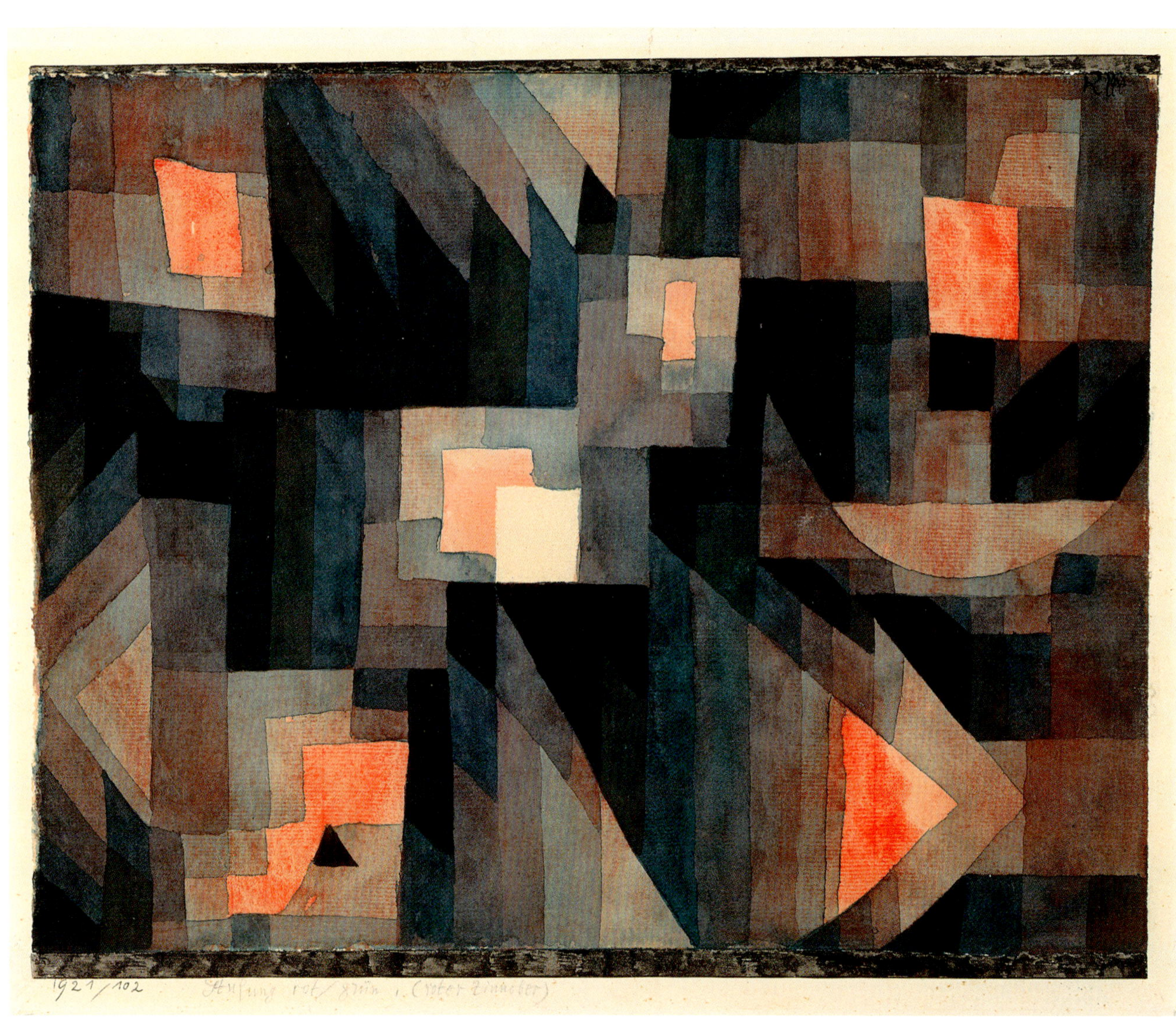

7 **STUFUNG ROT/GRÜN (ROTER ZINNOBER)**, 1921.102
[Gradation, Red–Green (Vermilion)]

Watercolor on paper, with watercolor and pen margin above
and below, mounted on cardboard
9½ x 12¼ inches (24.4 x 31.1 cm)
Pierpont Morgan Library, New York, Thaw Collection

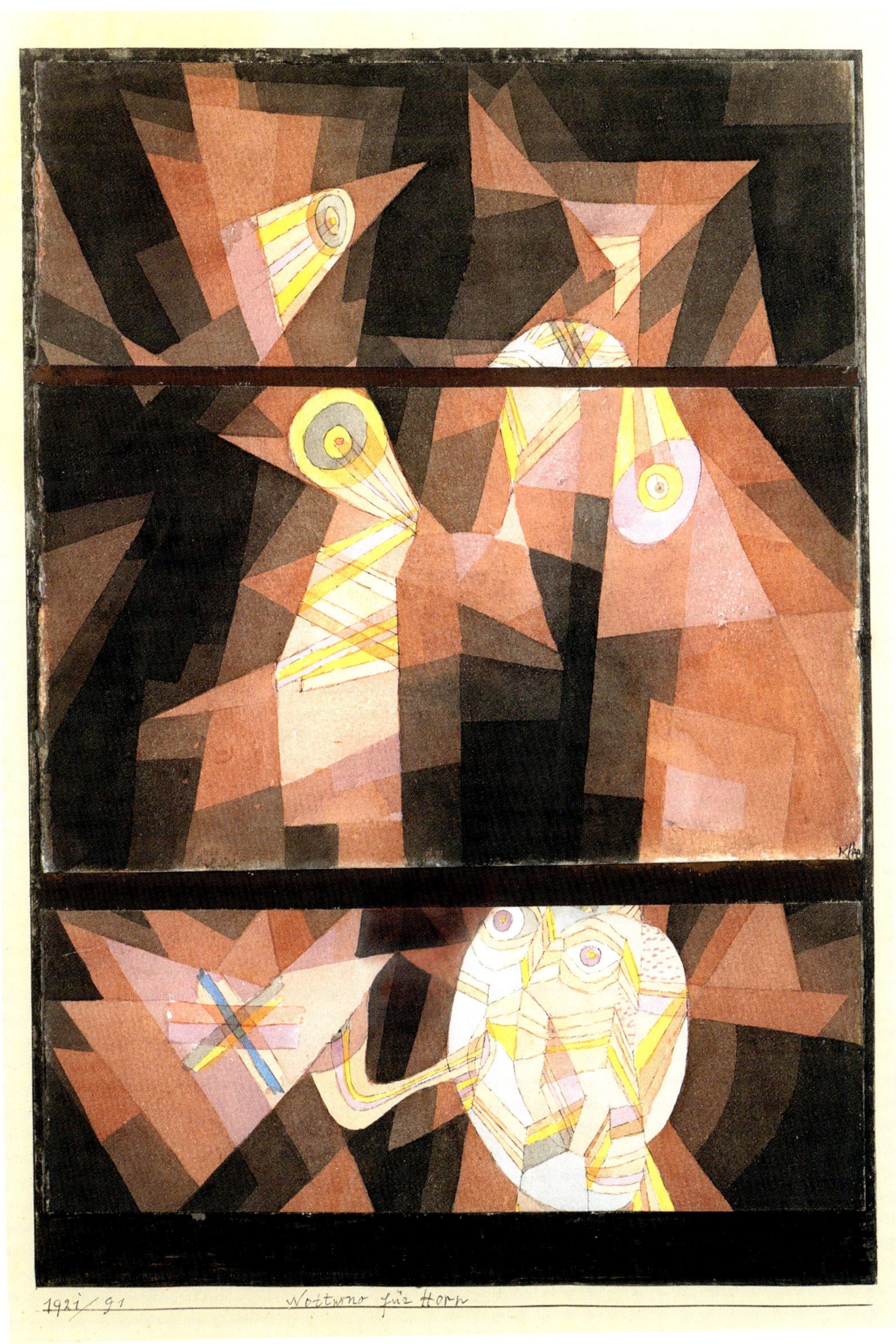

8 **NOTTURNO FÜR HORN**, 1921.91
[Nocturne for Horn]

Watercolor and pen on paper, cut and recombined, bordered
with gouache and pen, and mounted on cardboard
12¾ x 9½ inches (32.3 x 24 cm)
Private Collection

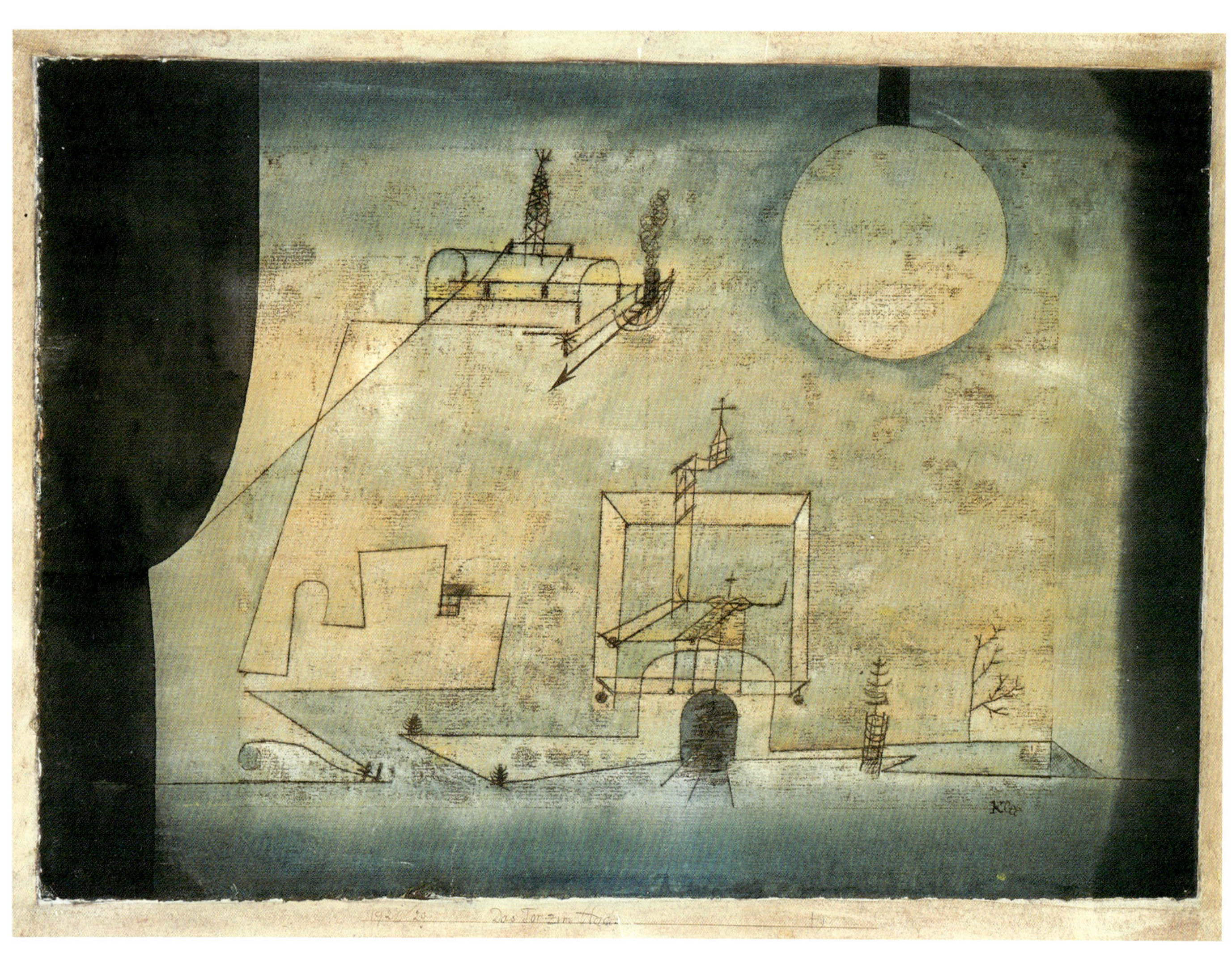

9 **DAS TOR ZUM HADES**, 1921.29
[The Gateway to Hades]

Oil transfer and watercolor on paper, mounted on cardboard
10¾ x 14⅜ inches (27.3 x 39.2 cm)
Norton Simon Museum, Pasadena, California
The Blue Four Galka Scheyer Collection

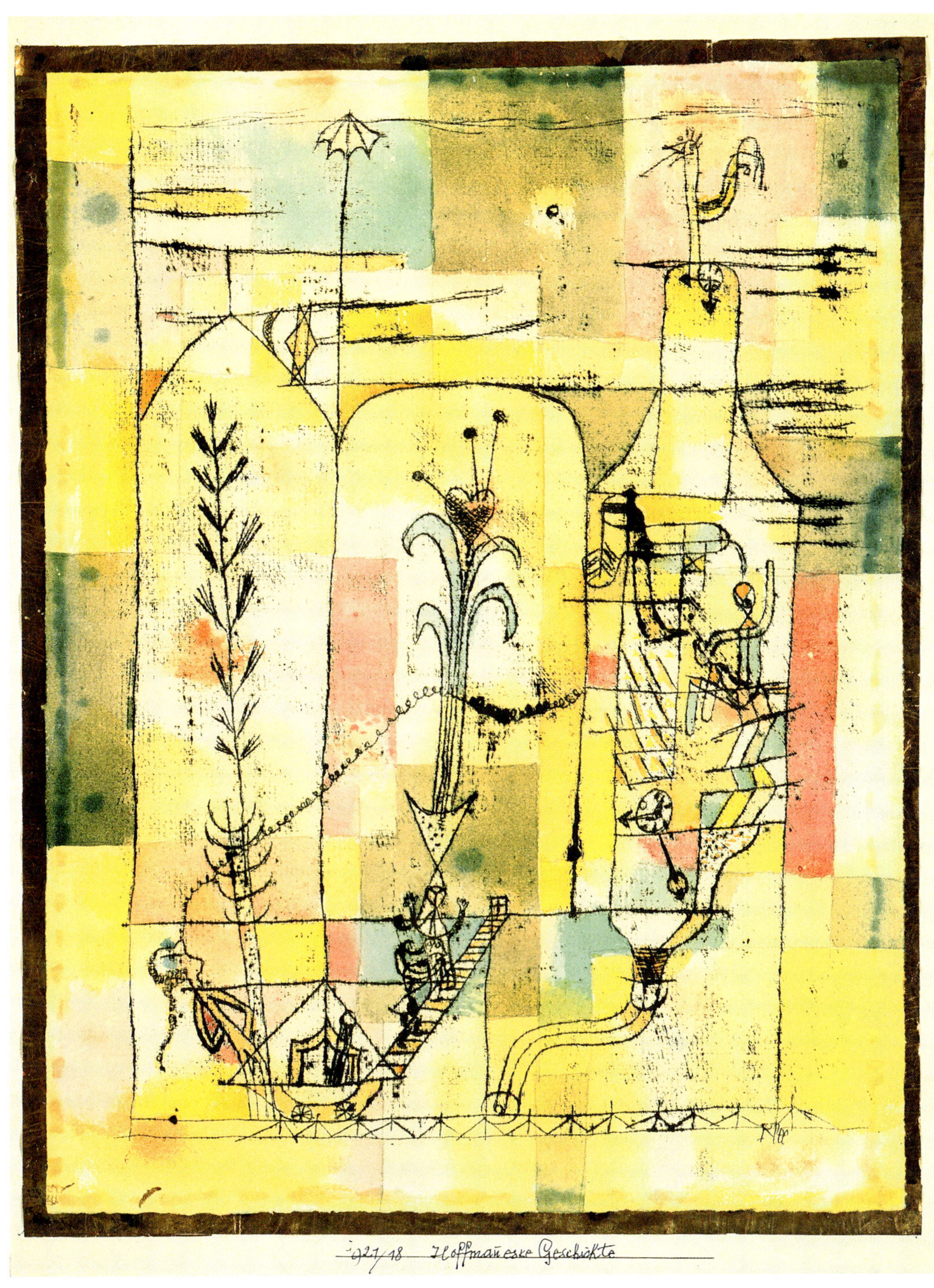

10   **HOFFMANNESKE GESCHICHTE**, 1921.18
[Hoffmannesque Tale]

Oil transfer and watercolor on paper, with watercolor
margin, mounted on cardboard
12¼ x 9½ inches (31.1 x 24.1 cm)
Metropolitan Museum of Art, New York
The Berggruen Klee Collection, 1984.315.26

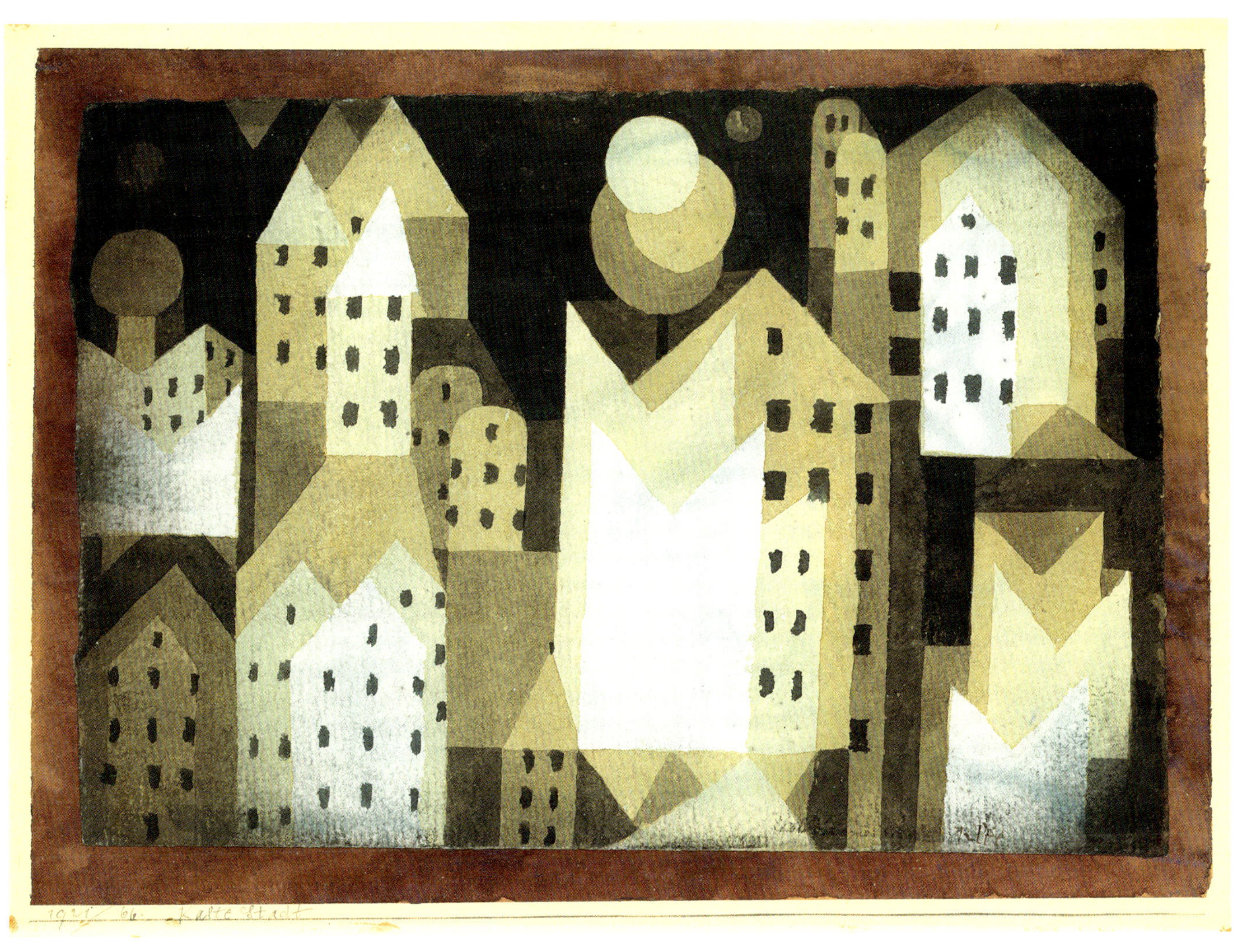

11 **KALTE STADT**, 1921.66
[Cold City]

Watercolor on paper, mounted on maroon paper and mounted on cardboard
8¼ x 11⅝ inches (21 x 29.5 cm)
Metropolitan Museum of Art, New York
The Berggruen Klee Collection, 1987.455.8

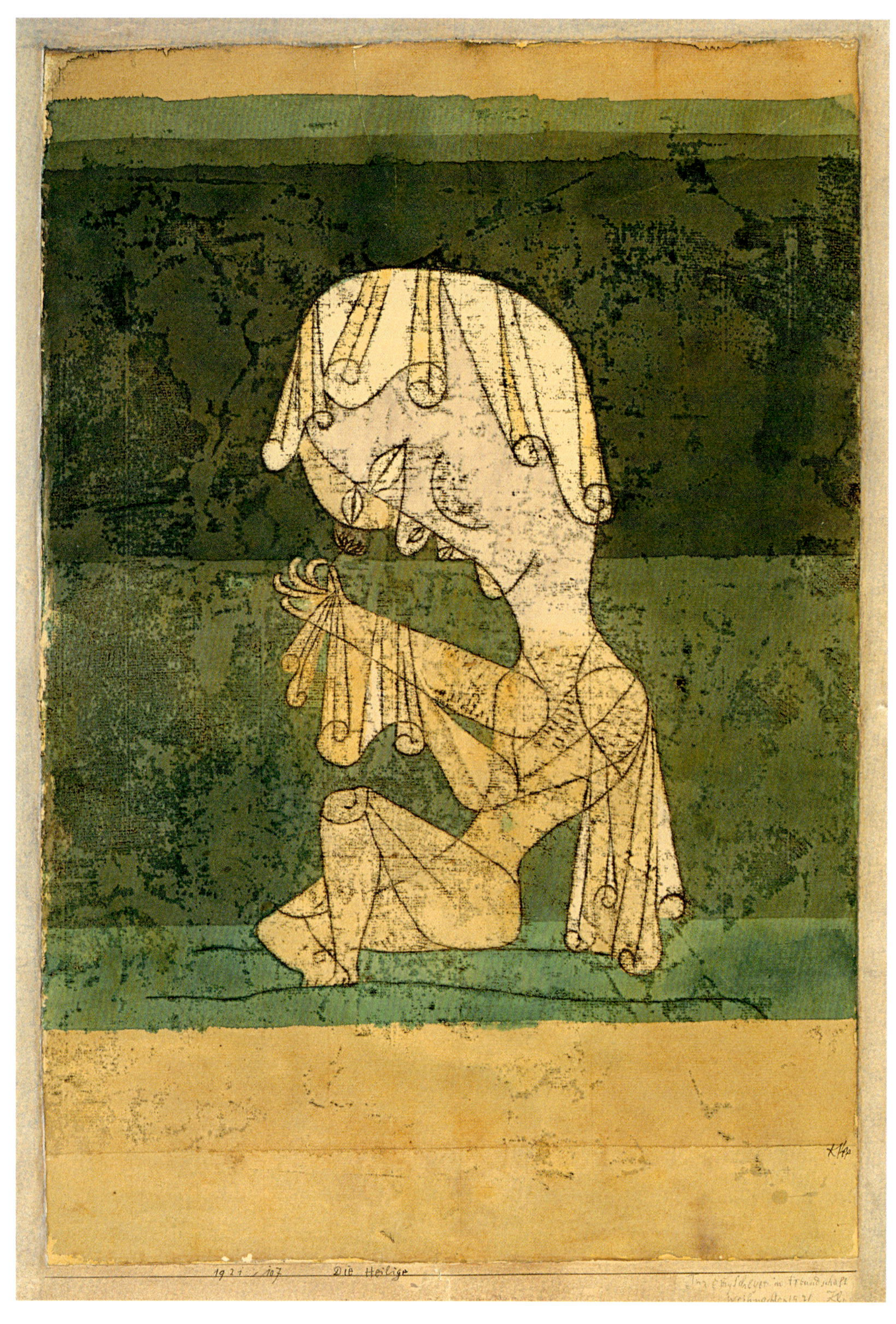

12   **DIE HEILIGE**, 1921.107
   [The Saint]

Watercolor and oil transfer on laid paper, mounted on thin cardboard
17 ¾ x 12 ¼ inches (45.2 x 31.1 cm)
Norton Simon Museum, Pasadena, California
The Blue Four Galka Scheyer Collection

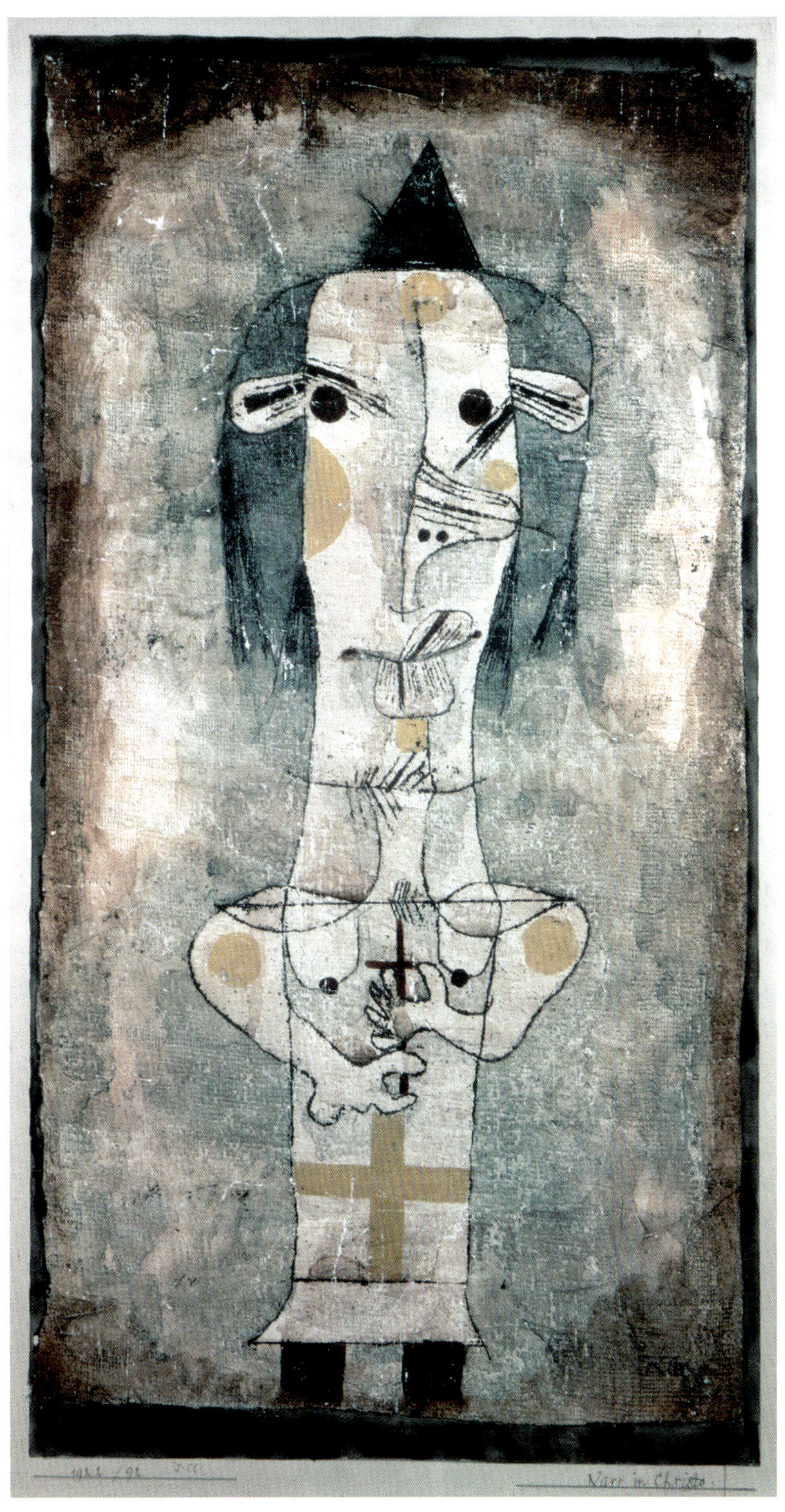

13 **NARR IN CHRISTO**, 1922.92
[Fool in Christ]

Oil transfer and watercolor on gypsum-primed gauze, bordered
with watercolor and pencil, and mounted on cardboard
17¾ x 9½ inches (45.1 x 24.1 cm)
Private Collection

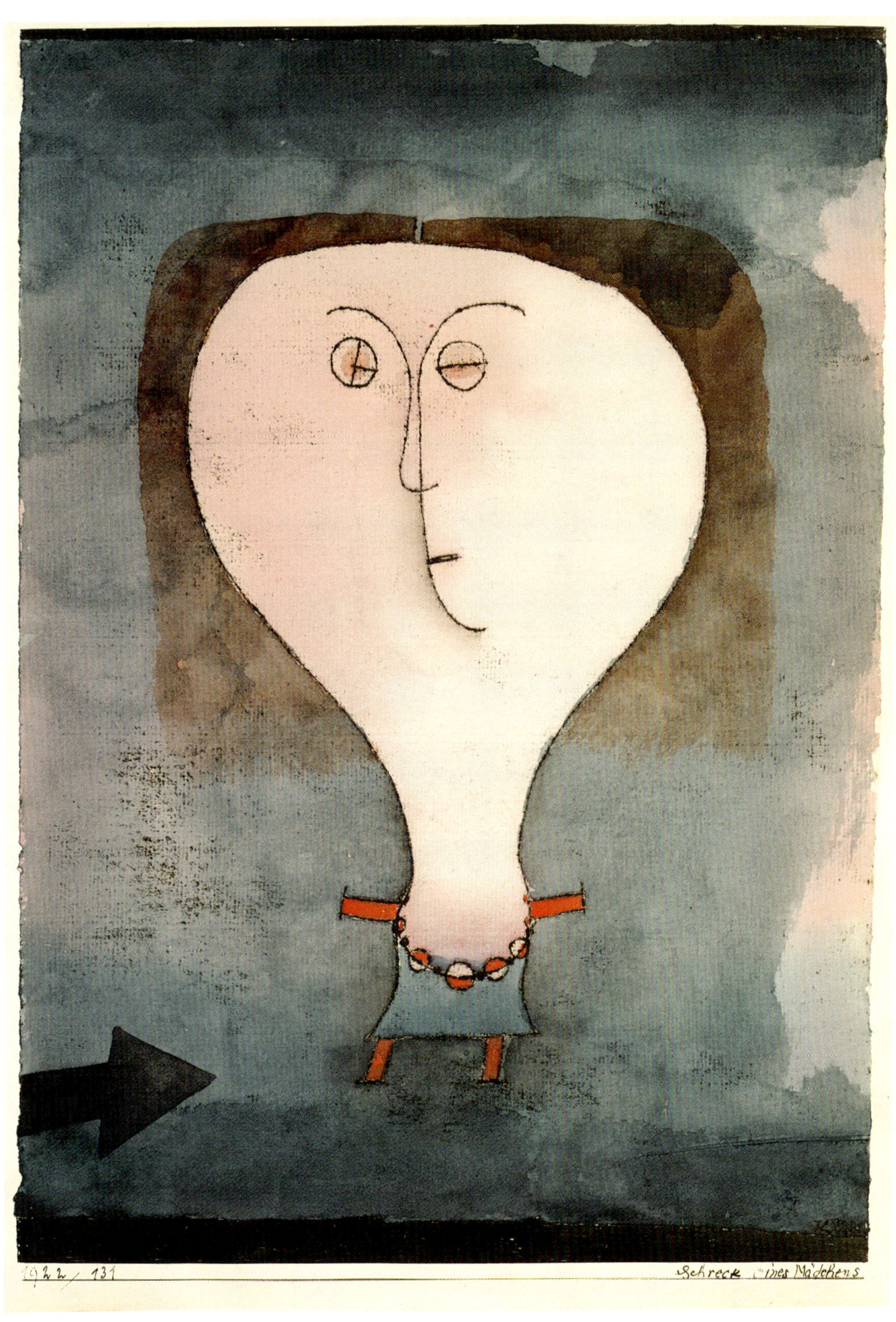

14 **SCHRECK EINES MÄDCHENS**, 1922.131
[Fright of a Girl]

Oil transfer and watercolor on paper, bordered with India ink
on paper and mounted on cardboard
11¾ x 8⅝ inches (29.7 x 22 cm)
Solomon R. Guggenheim Museum, New York. 48.1172x220

To create this painting, Klee copied his pencil drawing *Concert auf dem Zweig [Concert on the Branch]* (1921.188), using the oil transfer technique, onto a larger sheet with only slight modifications. Using pen and ink, he then added the machine parts, the crank, the handle, and the base. An entertaining little sketch of a quartet of birds thus became a kind of mechanical toy or musical instrument.

Klee had already depicted a hybrid between a bird and an airplane during World War I, when he used his preoccupation with the subject of the nightingale to distance himself from the real world of wartime. In those works, geometrical, mechanically constructed "bird planes," projected onto the wartime sky, do battle with each other and plummet down to earth. After the war, probably influenced by Dadaists like Max Ernst and Francis Picabia, Klee created more pictures of mechanisms. At that time the Constructivists associated with the Weimar Bauhaus—Theo van Doesburg, for example— were championing a new architectural and machine aesthetic, one that changed the direction of the school where Klee was teaching. In this context Klee's transformations of his bird-machine theme in the early 1920s, as exemplified in *Die Zwitscher-Maschine*, was altogether appropriate to the time, as was Klee's description of the organism in his Bauhaus lecture on February 13, 1922, as a "movement machine." Klee's Bauhaus colleague Oskar Schlemmer wrote: "Painting…is now attempting to be architecture or machine."[1]

Current avant-garde music and theater were also exploring the notion of a "twittering machine." In 1920 in Paris, Sergei Diaghilev's troupe premiered the ballet *Le chant du rossignol [Song of the Nightingale]* to the symphonic poem Igor Stravinsky had written based on his 1914 opera *Le Rossignol.* Henri Matisse created the sets and costumes. The Hans Christian Andersen fairy tale on which Stravinsky's opera and Diaghilev's ballet were based weighs the difference between nature and artifice. These works' contrast of a living nightingale with a mechanical one must surely have interested Klee, who enjoyed ballet: in 1913, as he excitedly noted in his diary, he had attended the Munich performance of the Ballets Russes with Vaslav Nijinsky and Tamara Karasavina. Geometric interpretations of the human body were also central to Schlemmer's *Triadic Ballet*, on which he was working in 1922.

Also at this time, Erwin Schulhoff, the young avant-garde composer from Prague who participated in the congress of Constructivists and Dadaists in Weimar in September 1922, along with van Doesburg, Jean Arp, Kurt Schwitters, and others, was working with birdsong as he composed his three pieces for contrabassoon titled *The Bass Nightingale.* The second of these, "Perpetuum mobile," is a repetitive scherzo that ironically recalls the utopian vision of the machine. It is also no coincidence that in 1924 Schwitters included a kind of cock-a-doodle-do-machine rooster-man dance (to the accompaniment of a violin) in his richly illustrated book *Die Märchen vom Paradies [The Tales of Paradise]*, written with Käte Steinitz. Klee, sensitive to the popularization of the motif, ceased producing pictures of mechanisms in 1923. He only employed the machine concept once more, in the drawing *Maschinenteile Serie elf [Machine Parts Series Eleven]* (1924.289), before returning to it for the last time, probably shortly before the outbreak of World War II, in his title for the *Kriegerische Maschine [Belligerent Machine]* (1939.607).

Osamu Okuda

1. Oskar Schlemmer to Otto Meyer-Amden, late March 1922, quoted in Oskar Schlemmer, *Idealist der Form: Briefe, Tagebücher, Schriften 1912–1943*, ed. Andreas Hüneke (Leipzig: Reclam, 1990), 84.

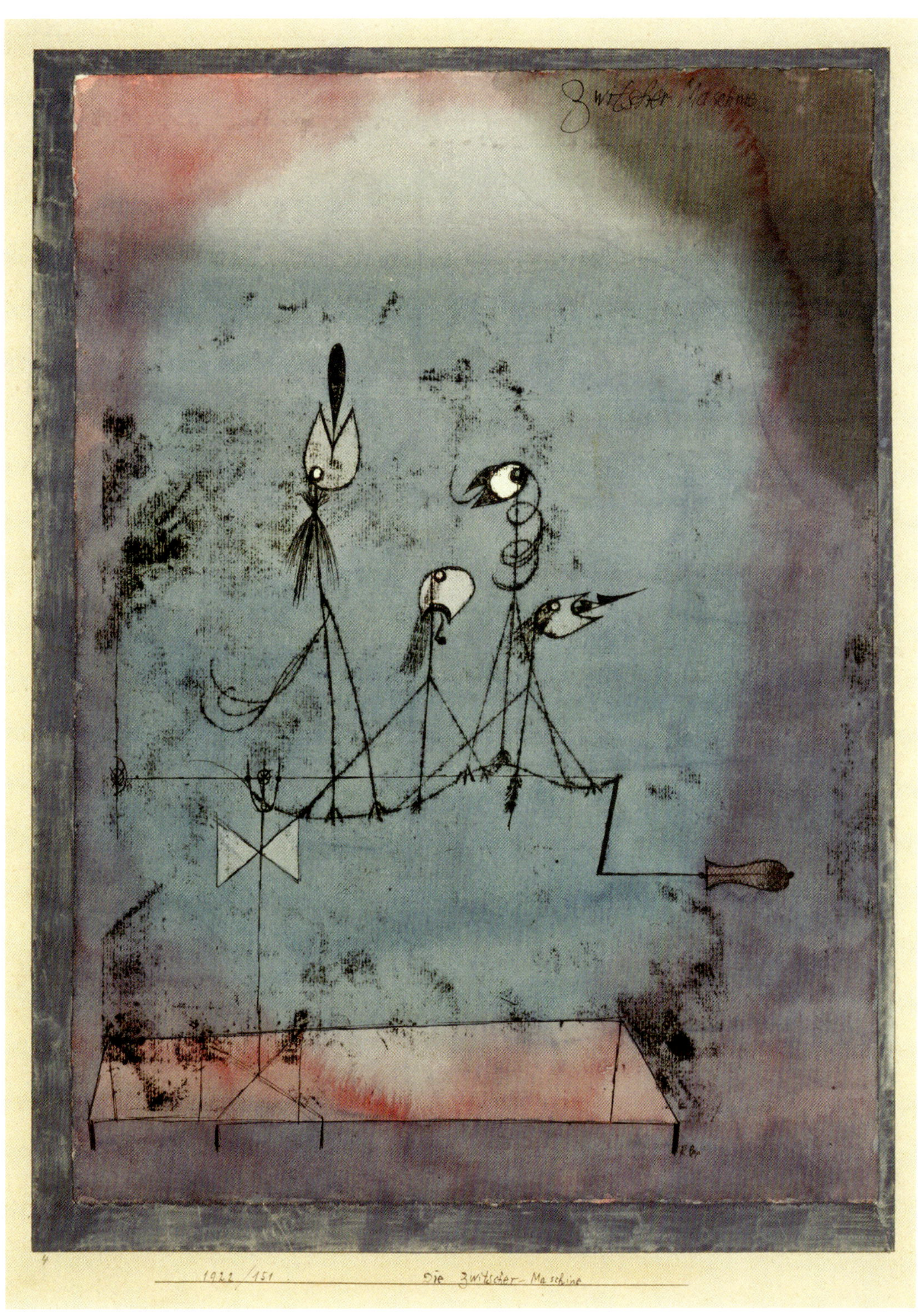

15 **DIE ZWITSCHER-MASCHINE**, 1922.151
[The Twittering Machine]

Oil transfer and watercolor on paper, bordered with
watercolor and pen, and mounted on cardboard
16¼ x 12 inches (41.3 x 30.5 cm)
The Museum of Modern Art, New York
Mrs. John D. Rockefeller Jr. Purchase Fund, 564.39

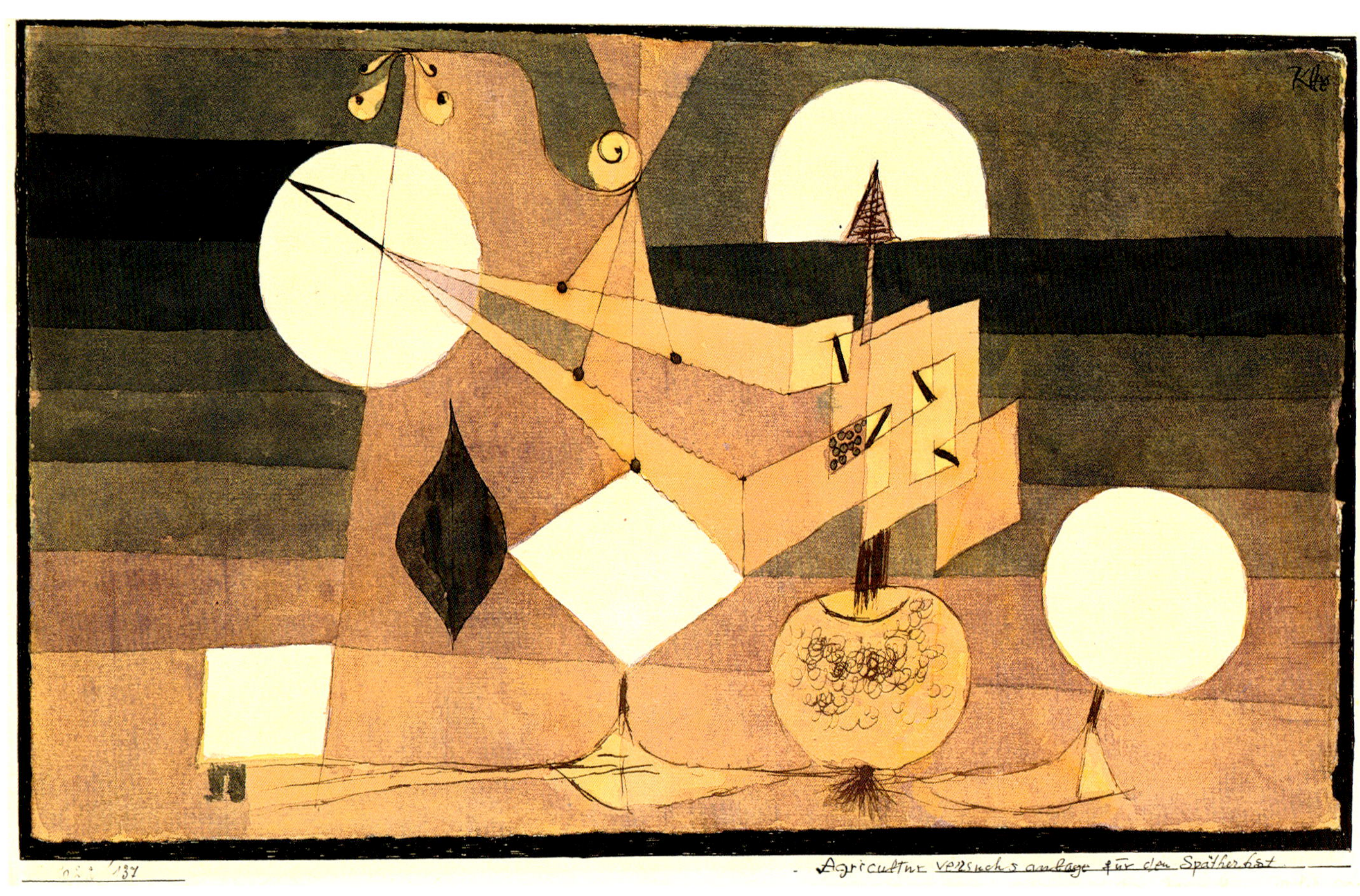

16   **AGRICULTUR VERSUCHS ANLAGE FÜR DEN SPÄTHERBST**, 1922.137
[Agricultural Research Station for Late Autumn]

Pen and watercolor on paper, lined with pen on cardboard
7 ⅜ x 11 ⅞ inches (18.6 x 30.1 cm)
Colby College Museum of Art, Waterville, Maine, Gift of Jere Abbott

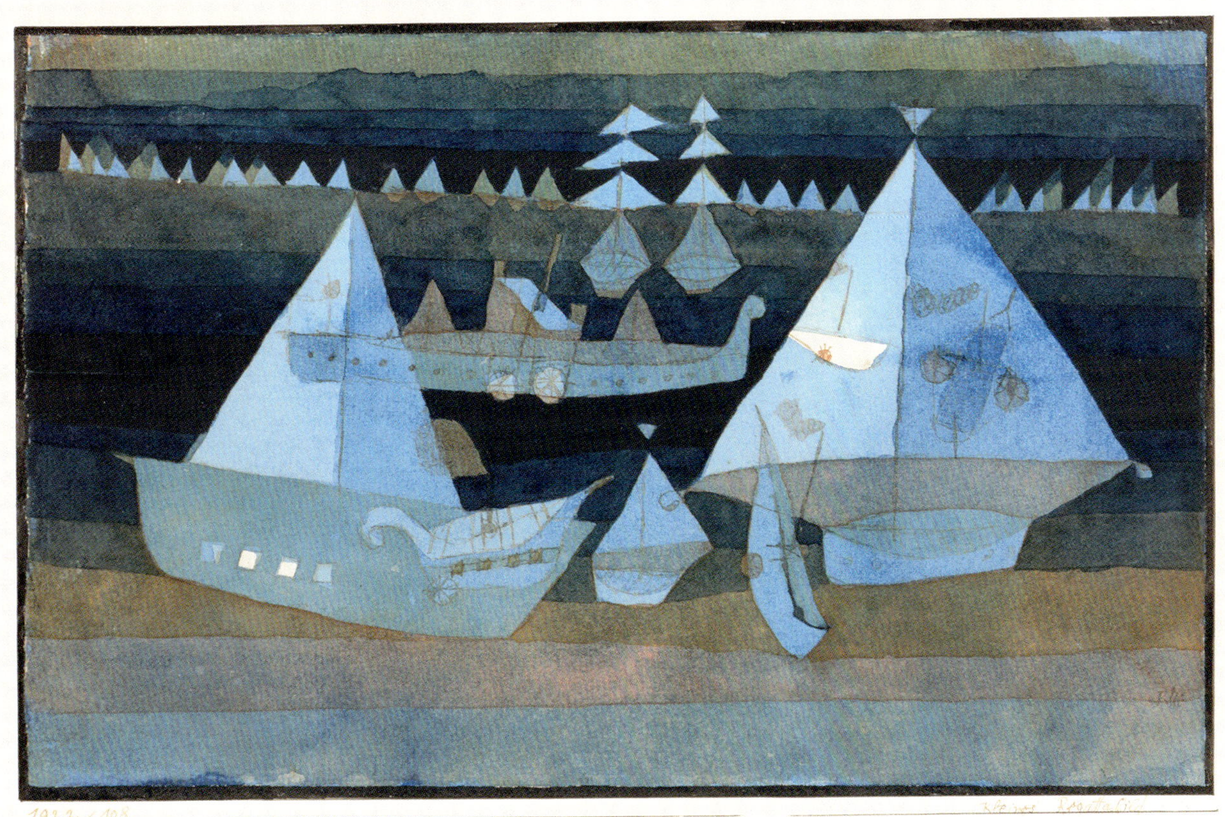

17 **KLEINES REGATTABILD**, 1922.108
[Small Picture of a Regatta]

Pen and watercolor on paper, bordered with
watercolor and mounted on cardboard
5 ¾ x 9 inches (14.6 x 22.8 cm)
The Phillips Collection, Washington, D.C.
Gift from the estate of Katherine S. Dreier, 0998

Originally this picture, along with *Kleines Tannenbild [Small Fir Picture]* (1922.176), was part of a larger, wide-format composition painted in oils on chalk-primed muslin (see below). In that geometric composition, a wide, dark green, trapezoidal elevation appeared in the bottom part of the picture. On the left edge of this rise stood a vertical pole with five staggered rectangles of decreasing size, each in a different color. (Klee employed a similar scheme to illustrate his Bauhaus lecture on the eye's receptive movement on February 27, 1922.) An identical construction, but with the rectangles projecting in the opposite direction, appeared on the right. On the rise, between these two vertical elements, stood a building with an entrance gate and a cupola. Directly to the left of the cupola stood a tree, which Klee probably drew in only provisionally. Between the building and the structure on the right, the sky opened up, revealing a red balloon hovering in the distance. Klee drew the lines in the composition with a ruler and painted flat reds, yellows, greens, and blues in the closed geometrical shapes that the lines created. The other elements were depicted as more or less atmospheric, with a translucence that allowed the texture of the support to show through. Klee was intent here on representing the contrast between nature (tree) and technology (balloon) in a Constructivist setting, as well as the contrast between stasis (the tree rooted in earth) and dynamism (the freely hovering balloon).

It is possible that Klee later found the careful disposition of the two vertical constructions too deliberately schematic, and the architecture complex in the center too dominant compared to the balloon and tree, through which he intended to convey the meaning of the work. For whatever reason, he decided to cut the composition in half vertically. In the taller left-hand portion, Klee added a fir tree on a raised area that earlier had been a part of the building, creating a contrast with the geometric construction to the left. The right-hand section is nearly square, so the remaining half of the building on the left and the vertical construction on the right more or less balance each other. The balloon, now lying on the central axis of the composition, is the main element in the picture. As Andrew Kagan aptly put it: "Here Klee conjures the most delicate color sensibility in floating areas of rectangle composition; the effect is to defeat the sense of pictorial gravity, to create a pictorial antigravity, which lifts the balloon from aloft and causes its gondola to swing gently."[1]

Osamu Okuda

1. Andrew Kagan, "Klee's Development," in *Paul Klee at the Guggenheim Museum,* exh. cat. (New York: Solomon R. Guggenheim Museum, 1993), 38.

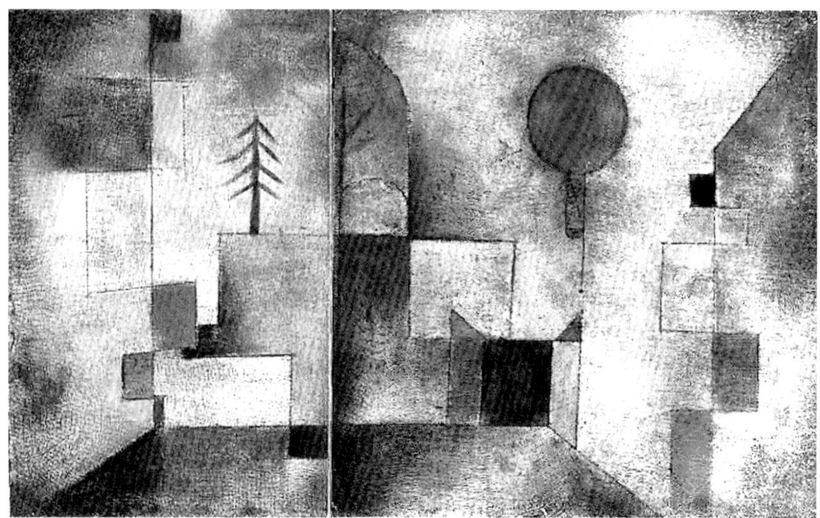

Reconstruction of original work combining:

Kleines Tannenbild, [Small Picture of Fir Trees], 1922.176 (left)
Oil on chalk-primed muslin mounted on cardboard
12½ x 8 inches (31.6 x 20.4 cm)
Öffentliche Kunstsammlung, Kunstmuseum Basel
Bequest of Richard Doetsch-Benzinger, G1960.24.

and
Roter Ballon [Red Balloon], 1922.179 (right)
Oil on chalk-primed muslin mounted on cardboard
12½ x 12¼ inches (31.7 x 31.1 cm)
Solomon R. Guggenheim Museum, New York, 48.1172x524

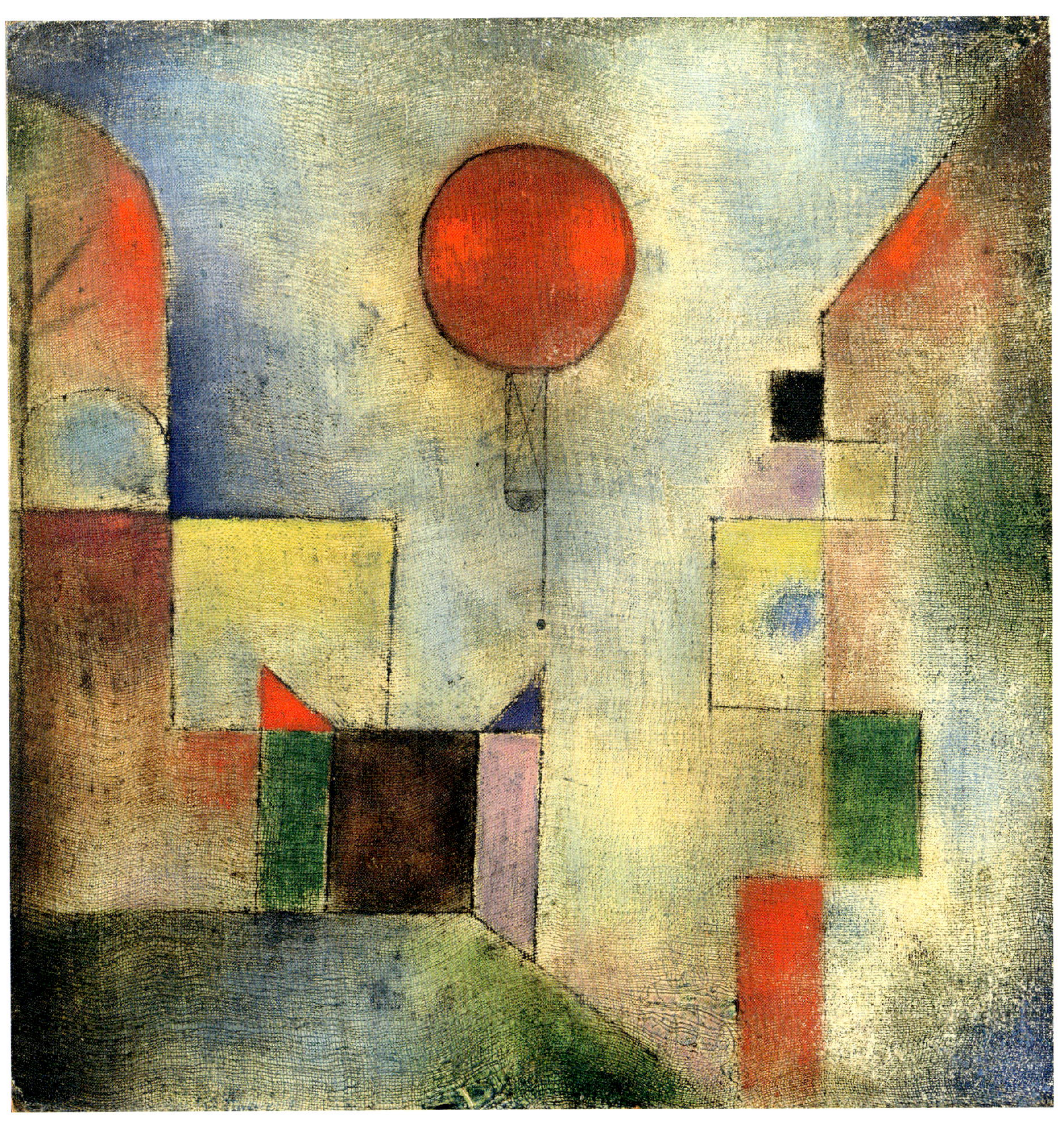

18 **ROTER BALLON**, 1922.179
[Red Balloon]

Oil on chalk-primed muslin, mounted on cardboard
12½ x 12¼ inches (31.7 x 31.1 cm)
Solomon R. Guggenheim Museum, New York, 48.1172x524

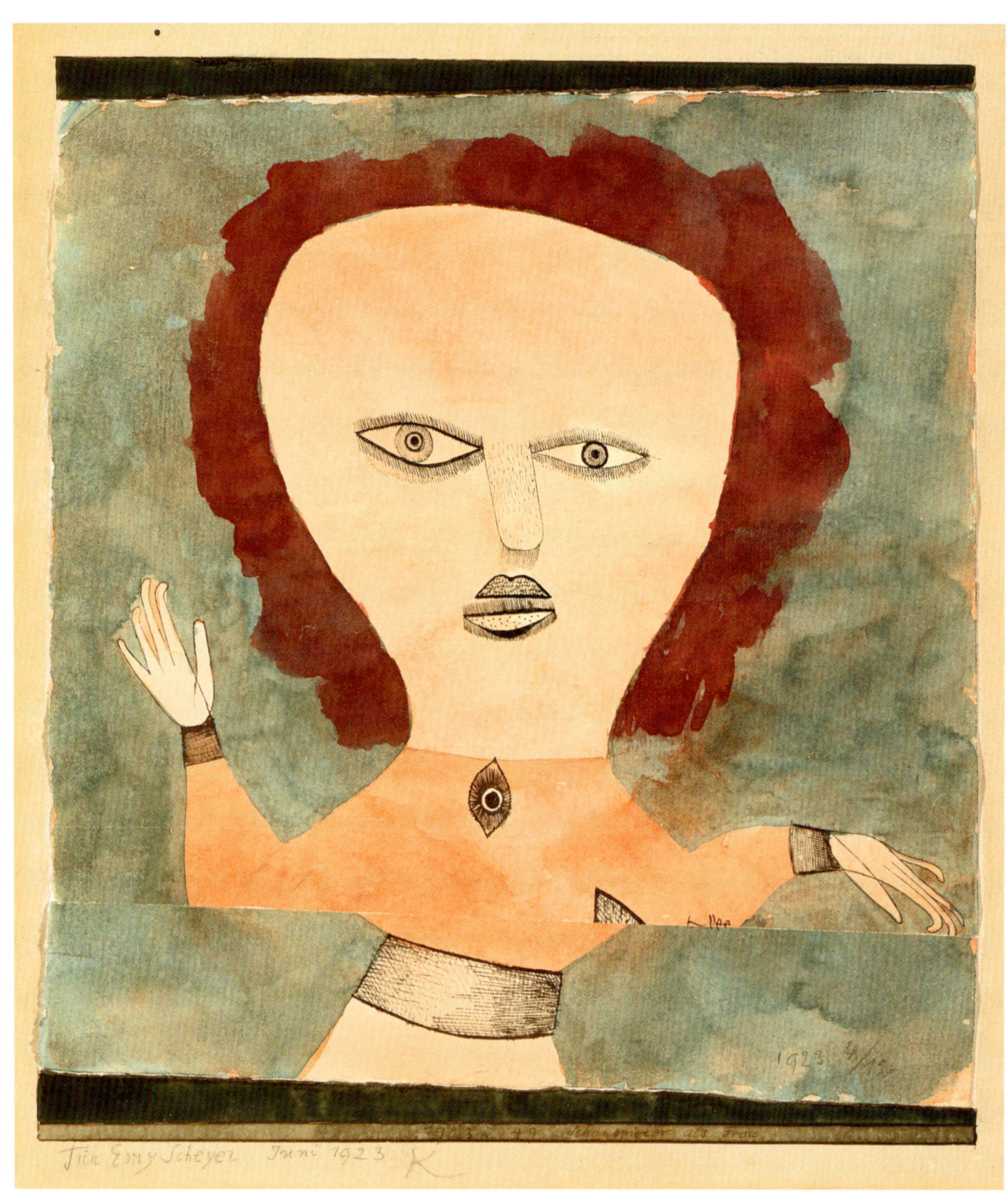

19 **SCHAUSPIELER ALS FRAU**, 1923.49
[Actor as a Woman]

Watercolor, ink, and pencil on paper, cut and recombined, with one
watercolor and pen margin above and two below, and mounted on cardboard
9 x 9 inches (22.9 x 23 cm)
Norton Simon Museum, Pasadena, California
The Blue Four Galka Scheyer Collection

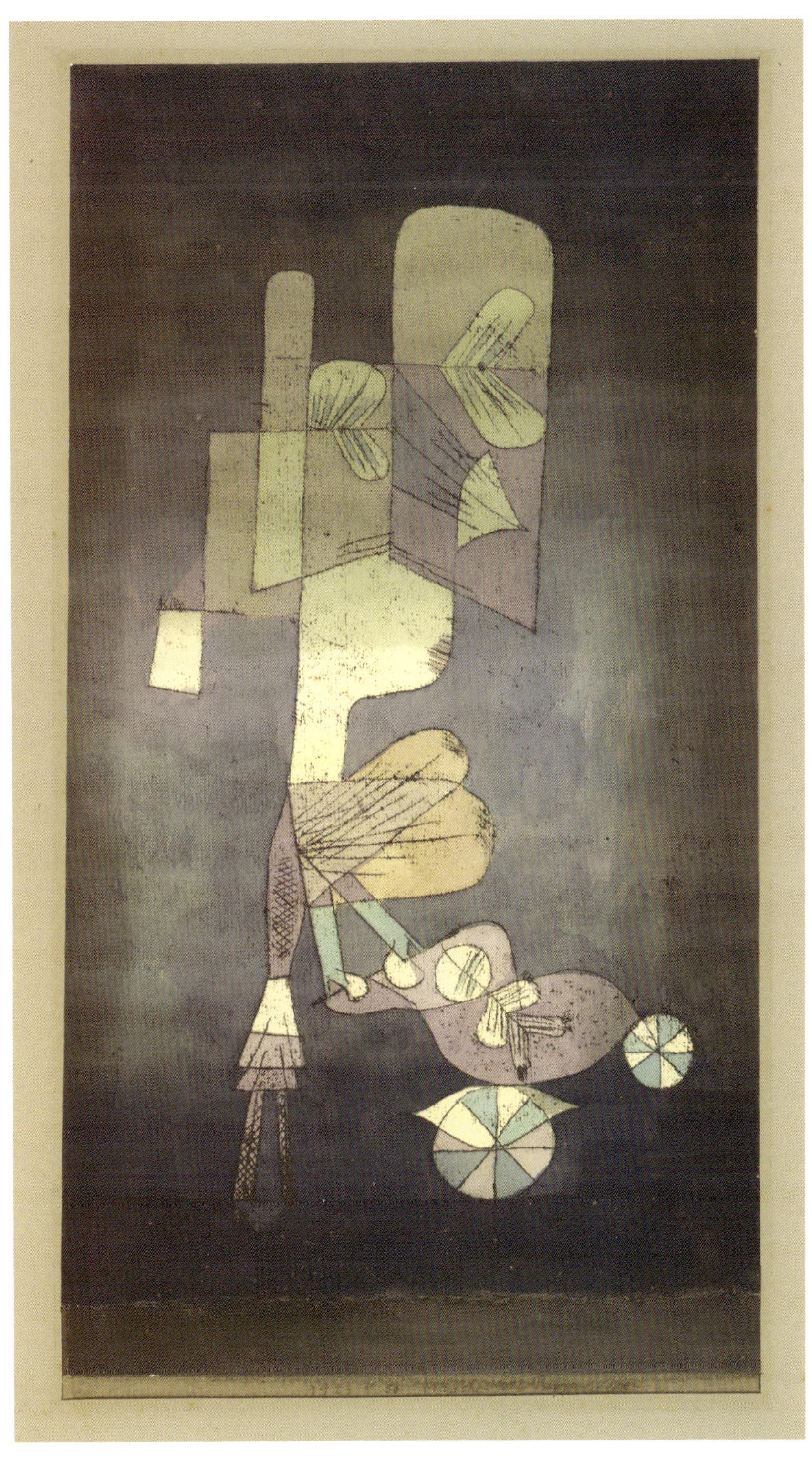

20 **MÄDCHEN MIT PUPPEN WAGEN**, 1923.50
[Girl with Doll's Pram]

Oil transfer and watercolor on paper, with added paper strip in watercolor
and watercolor and pen margin below, mounted on cardboard
15⅜ x 8⅜ inches (39 x 21.3 cm)
The Museum of Modern Art, New York, 13.51

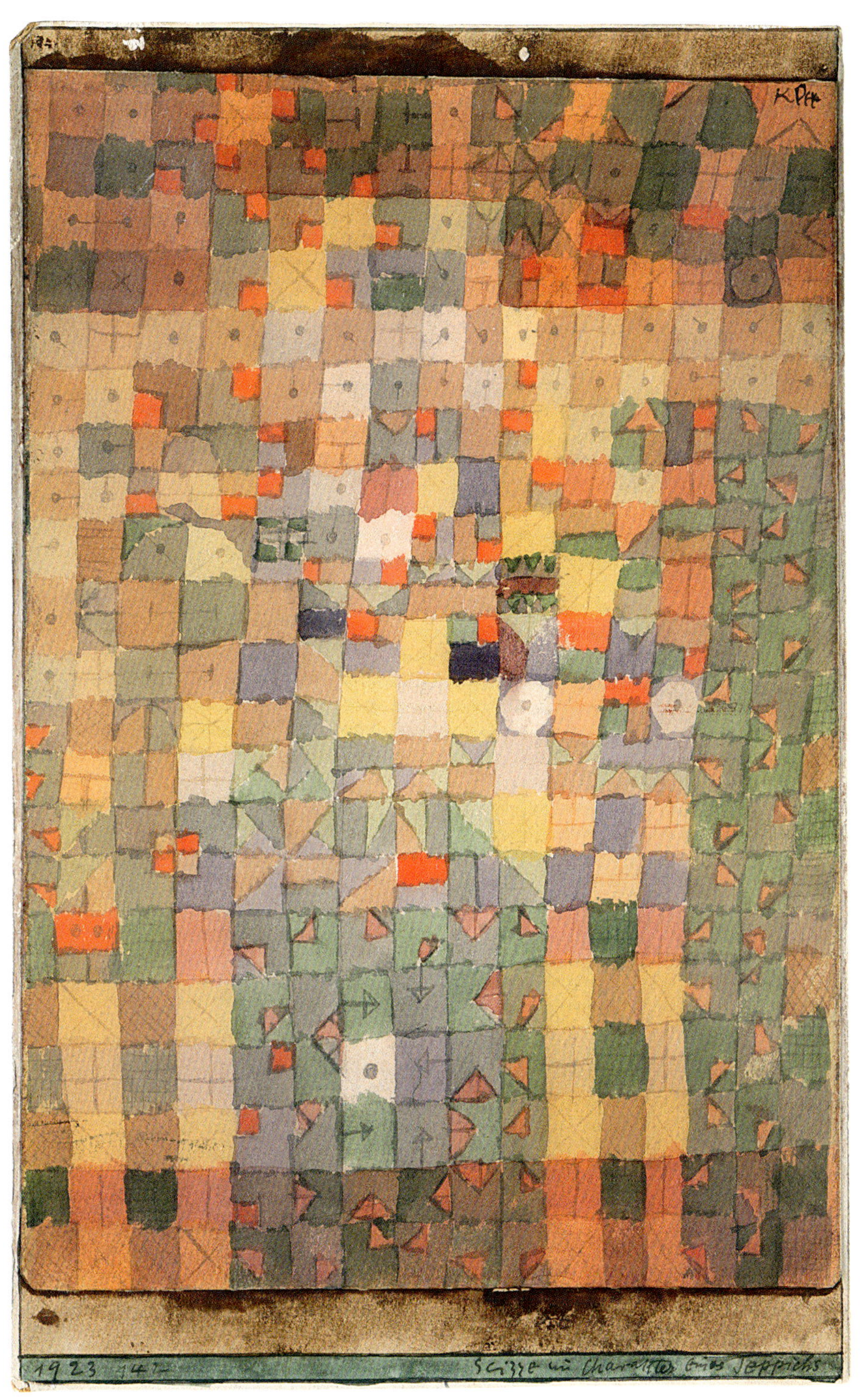

21 **SCIZZE IM CHARAKTER EINES TEPPICHS**, 1923.142
   [Sketch in the Manner of a Carpet]

Pen and watercolor on paper, with watercolor and pen margin
above and below, mounted on cardboard
8⅝ x 5¾ inches (22 x 14.7 cm)
Denver Art Museum, Gift of Katherine C. Detre

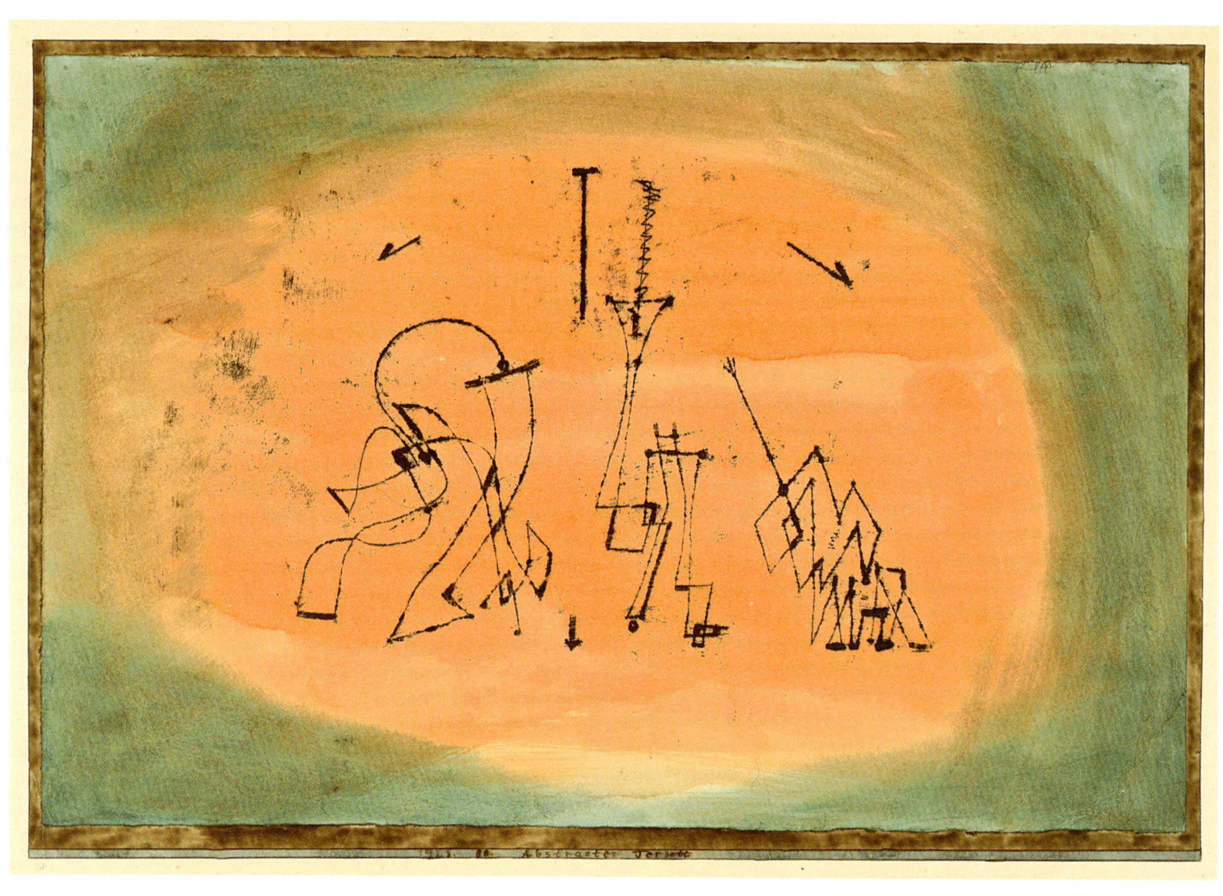

22 **ABSTRAKTES TERZETT**, 1923.88
[Abstract Trio]

Oil transfer (drawing), watercolor, and oil on paper, with
watercolor and pen margin below, mounted on cardboard
12⅝ x 19¾ inches (32.1 x 50.2 cm)
Metropolitan Museum of Art, New York
The Berggruen Klee Collection, 1984.315.36

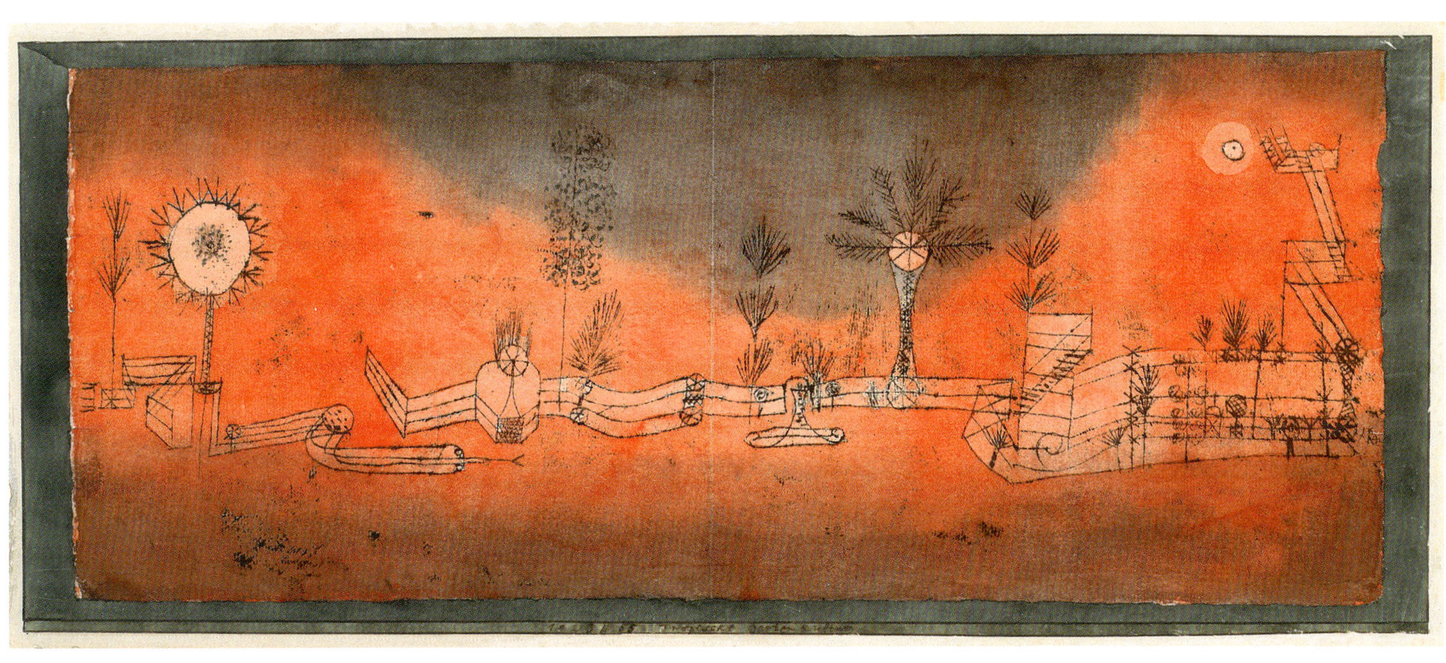

23 **TROPISCHE GARTEN KULTUR**, 1923.55
[Tropical Garden Plantation]

Oil transfer and watercolor on paper, with watercolor
and pen margin below, mounted on cardboard
7⅜ x 19¼ inches (18.7 x 48.9 cm)
Solomon R. Guggenheim Museum, New York
Gift of Solomon R. Guggenheim, 37.509

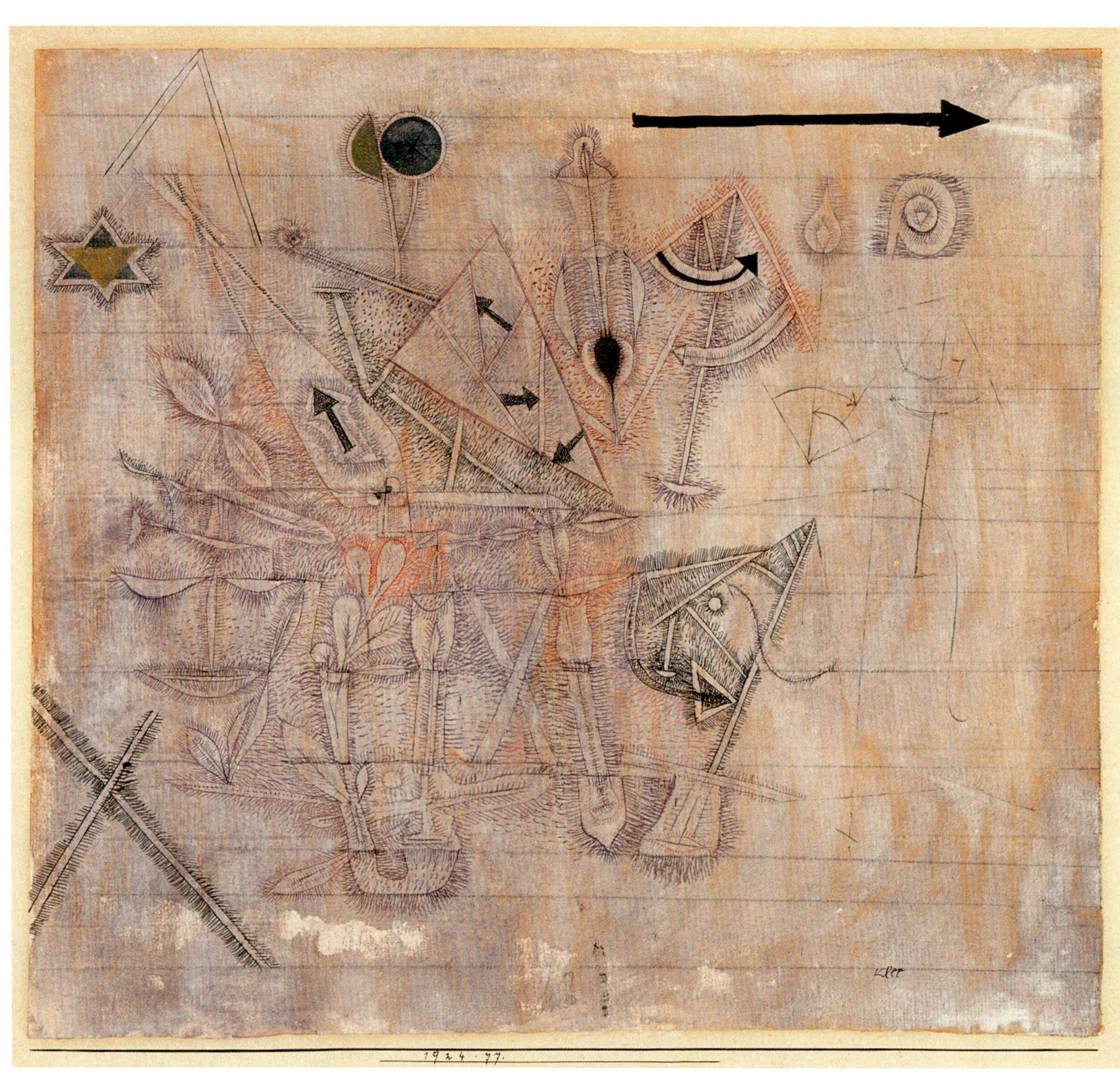

24   **UNTITLED**, 1924.77

Watercolor, pen, and pencil on paper, mounted on cardboard
11⅛ x 12⅜ inches (28.3 x 31.3 cm)
Marion Koogler McNay Art Museum, San Antonio
Mary and Sylvan Lang Collection, 1975.38

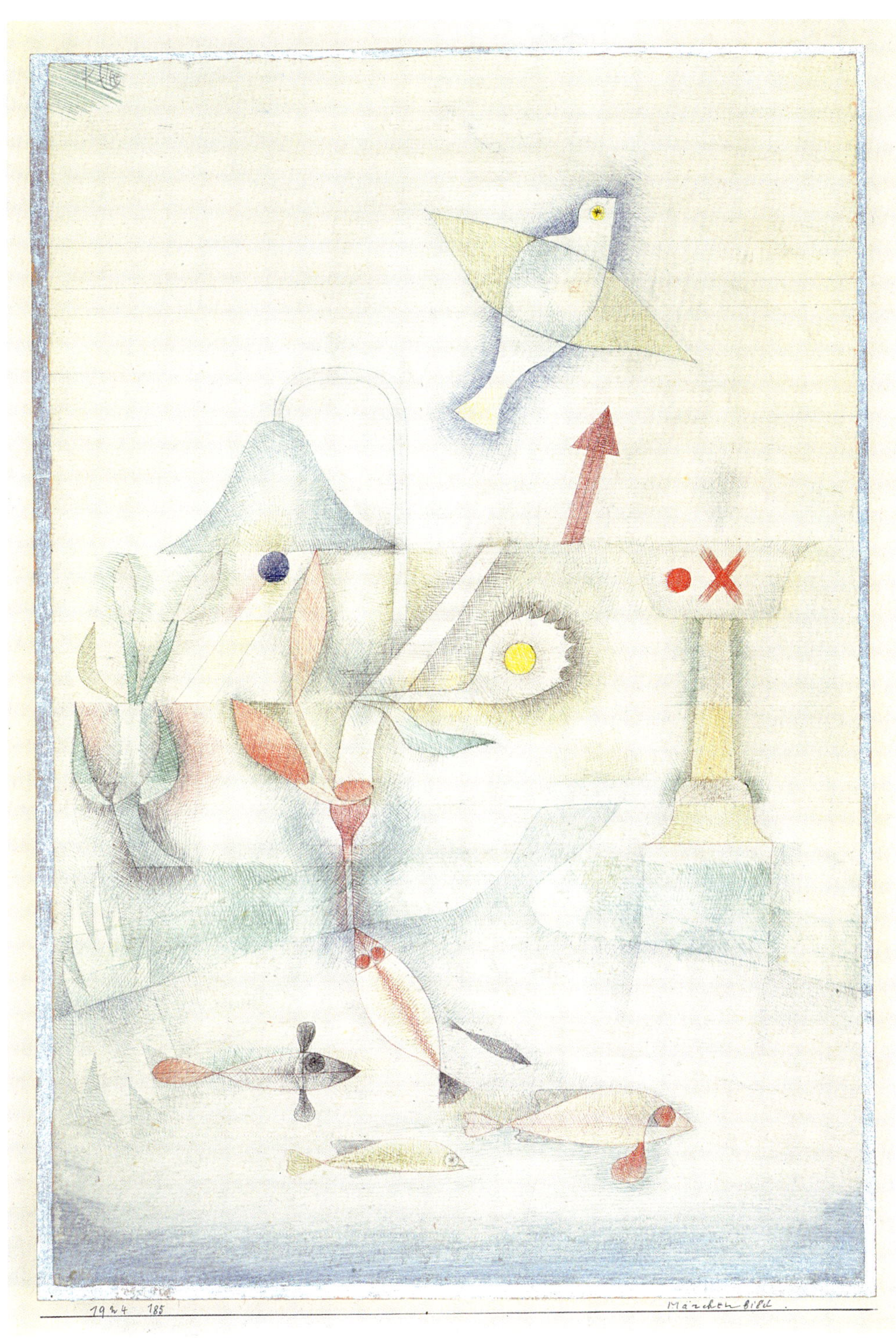

25 **MÄRCHENBILD**, 1924.185
[Fairy Tale Picture]

Watercolor on paper, mounted on silver
paper and mounted on cardboard
15 x 10¾ inches (38.1 x 27.3 cm)
Private Collection

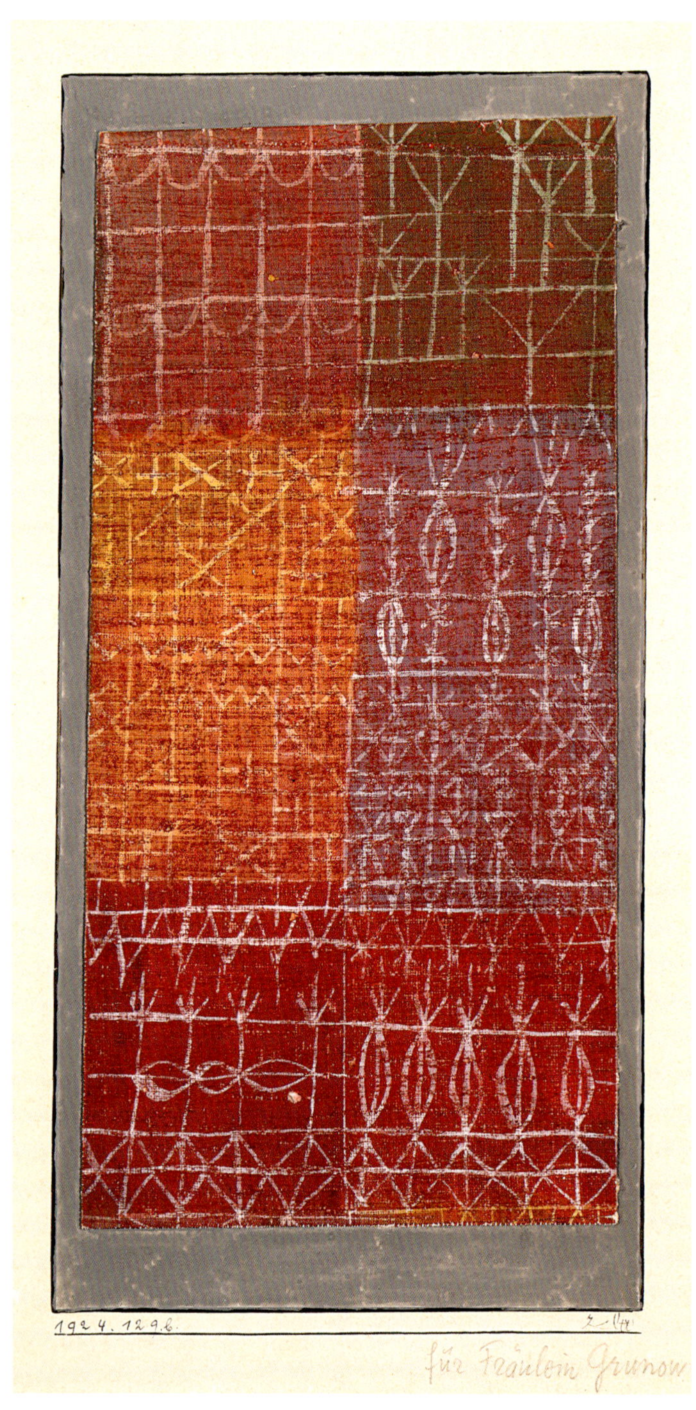

26 **VORHANG**, 1924.129b
[Curtain]

Watercolor and tempera on red paste-primed muslin, bordered
with gouache and pen, and mounted on cardboard
7⅛ x 3⅝ inches (18.1 x 9.2 cm)
Solomon R. Guggenheim Museum, New York
Hilla Rebay Collection, 71.1936 R115

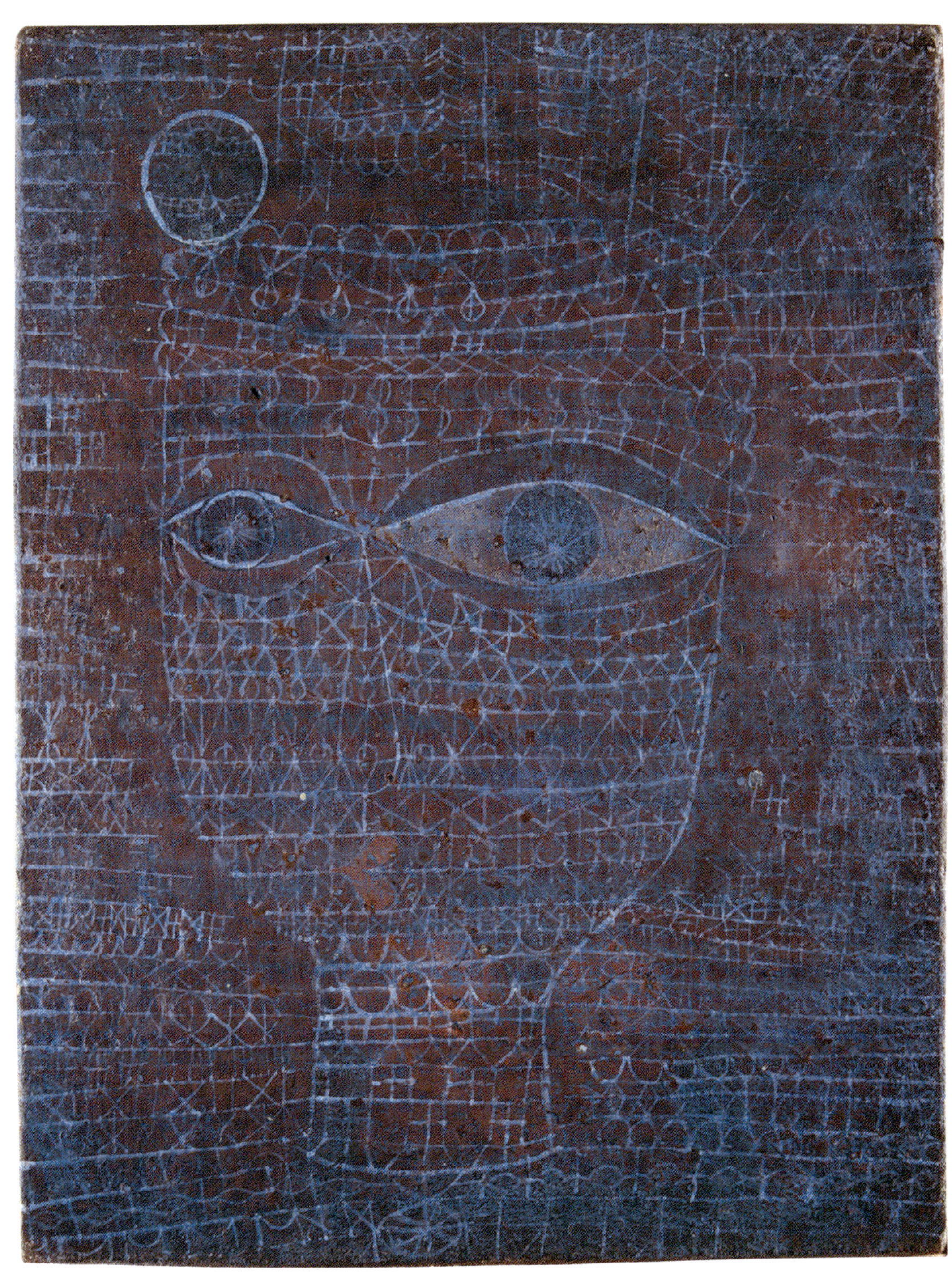

27 **PRINZESSIN VON ARABIEN**, 1924.136
[Princess of Arabia]

Watercolor and oil glazes on brown paste priming on cardboard
10 x 7¾ inches (25.5 x 19.7 cm)
The Baltimore Museum of Art
Gift of Blanche Adler, 1930.36.1

Ever since the appearance of Robert Goldwater's *Primitivism in Modern Painting* (New York: Harper, 1938), Klee scholars have repeatedly questioned whether Congolese masks or Japanese woodcuts may have served Klee as models for this picture. Jean Laude argued against the notion in 1984: "From this arises the delicate question of the limits of any comparative study."[1] But if one looks more closely at cultural currents in the air at the time, it is indeed possible to show connections between Klee and the art of the so-called "primitives." Of the suggestions made so far, Margaret Plant's that a Hokusai woodcut served as the direct inspiration for Klee's work is the most convincing.

The print she discussed, from the Japanese master's *100 Tales*, is reproduced in Wilhelm Michel's book *Das Teuflische und Groteske in der Kunst*. Klee owned the 1917 edition of that work, which also included a reproduction of his own watercolor *Maske [Mask]* (1912.58). Michel's caption for Hokusai's print reads: "a burning lantern … takes on the features of Oishi-san [Oiwa-san], tortured to death by her husband, above whose grave [it hangs]."[2] Plant described Klee's adaptation of the Japanese original: "The turned face of the Hokusai Klee rendered frontally; the eyes of the mask are closed in the inward-turning manner of his self-portrait of 1919, *Lost in Thought*. The spectre's spikey hair becomes a sharp childish haircut, surmounted by a peaked hat, and the cracks of the Hokusai face weave across the eyes and the mouth of the Klee face, creasing it into antiquity. Hokusai's graphic design is recast by Klee in complementaries of green and rusty red, against a background raised like armour with nails of paint."[3] One might add that Hokusai's lantern is hollow and that in the tale of Oiwa-san it embodies the soul of the deceased woman. The surface of the paper lantern,

with the parallel horizontals of its supporting frame, thus presents at the same time the magical vision of a ghostly face.

It is true that Klee had hit upon the scheme of using parallel horizontal lines beginning in 1917. But it was only in 1924 in the *Jugendlicher Schauspieler=Maske* that he clearly employed it in depicting a head. Regarding his early engraving *Komiker [Comedian]* (1904.14), Klee noted in his diary: "Of *Komiker* one could also say that the mask stands for art, and that the person hides behind it. The lines of the mask are ways of analyzing the work of art."[4] One suspects that in 1924 Klee, having seen masks on the stage at the Bauhaus, took up this earlier idea and with the help of parallel lines—borrowing from Hokusai—produced the facial features here that are reminiscent of the self-portrait Plant mentioned. He could have derived the strong green-red color contrast from the burning lantern and the grass in the background of Hokusai's picture. In Klee's depiction, art (the mask) and the young man blend together on the surface. That the introverted, inner-directed face is not bared, but becomes a mask, points to the surface of the picture as a setting for magical visions.

Osamu Okuda

1. Jean Laude, "Paul Klee," in *Primitivism in 20th Century Art*, exh. cat. (New York: Museum of Modern Art, 1984), 487.

2. Wilhelm Michel, *Das Teuflische und Groteske in der Kunst* (Munich: R. Piper, 1917), 85.

3. Margaret Plant, *Paul Klee: Figures and Faces* (London: Thames and Hudson, 1978), 38.

4. Paul Klee, *Tagebücher, 1898–1918*, ed. Wolfgang Kersten (Stuttgart: G. Hatje, 1988), 209 (no. 618, April 1905).

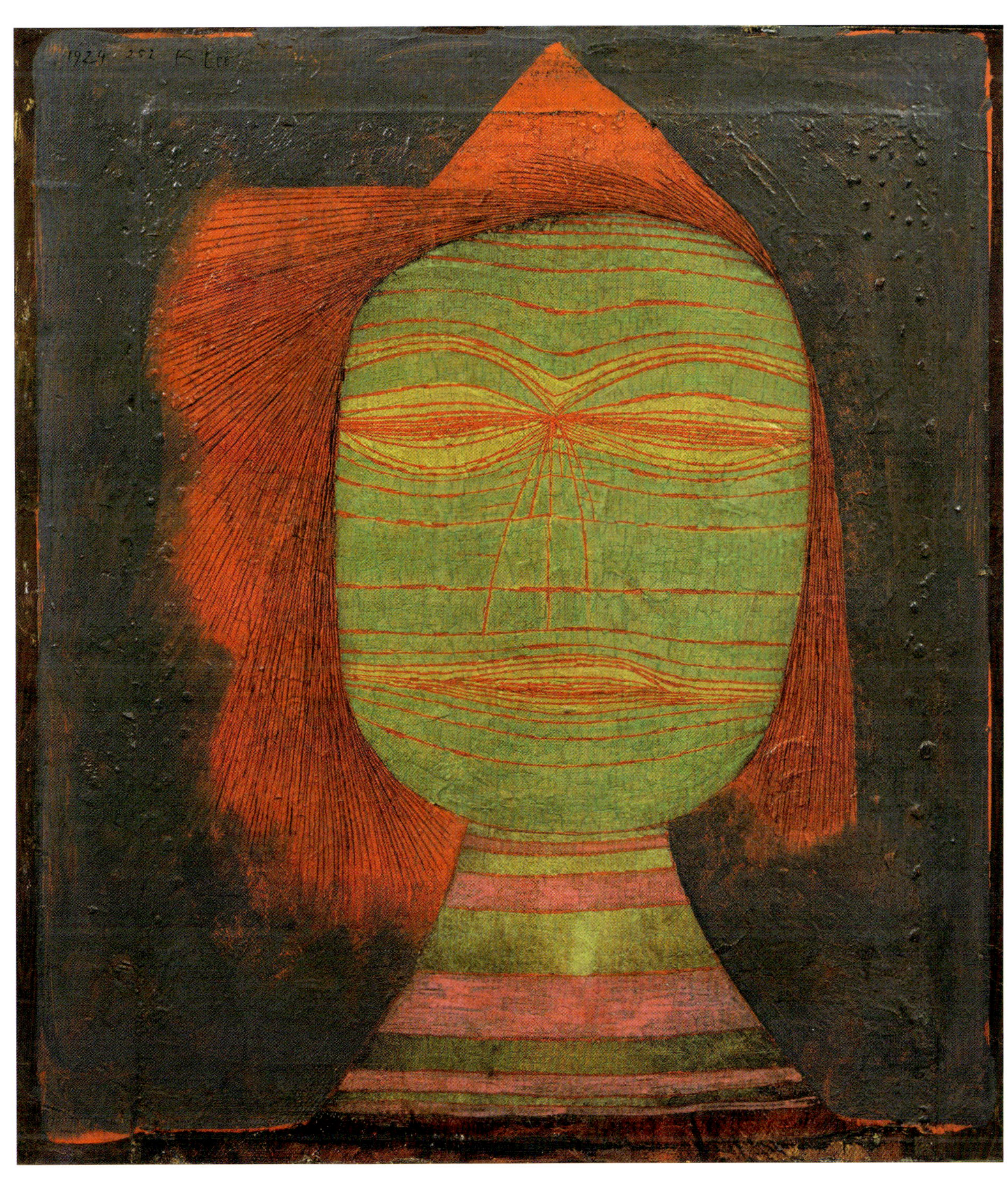

28 ~~JUGENDLICHER~~ SCHAUSPIELER=MASKE, 1924.252
[~~Youth~~ Actor's Mask]

Oil on canvas, mounted on cardboard and nailed on wooden panel
14 ½ x 13 ¼ inches (36.7 x 33.8 cm)
The Museum of Modern Art, New York
The Sidney and Harriet Janis Collection, 616.67

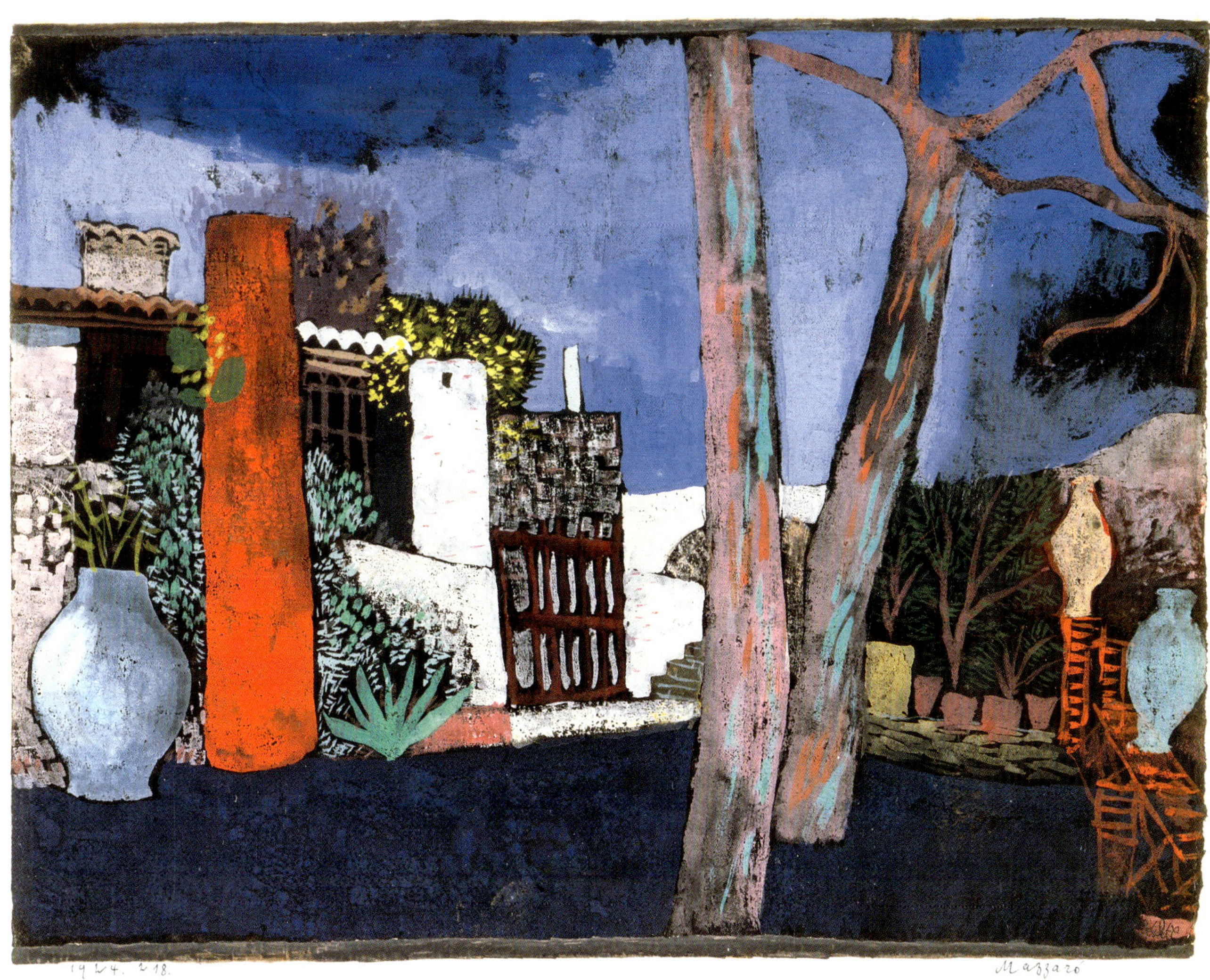

29   **MAZZARÓ**, 1924.218

Watercolor on black glue priming on paper, with watercolor
margins above and below, mounted on cardboard
9⅛ x 12 inches (23.3 x 30.5 cm)
Extended loan and promised gift of the Carl Djerassi Trust I
to the San Francisco Museum of Modern Art

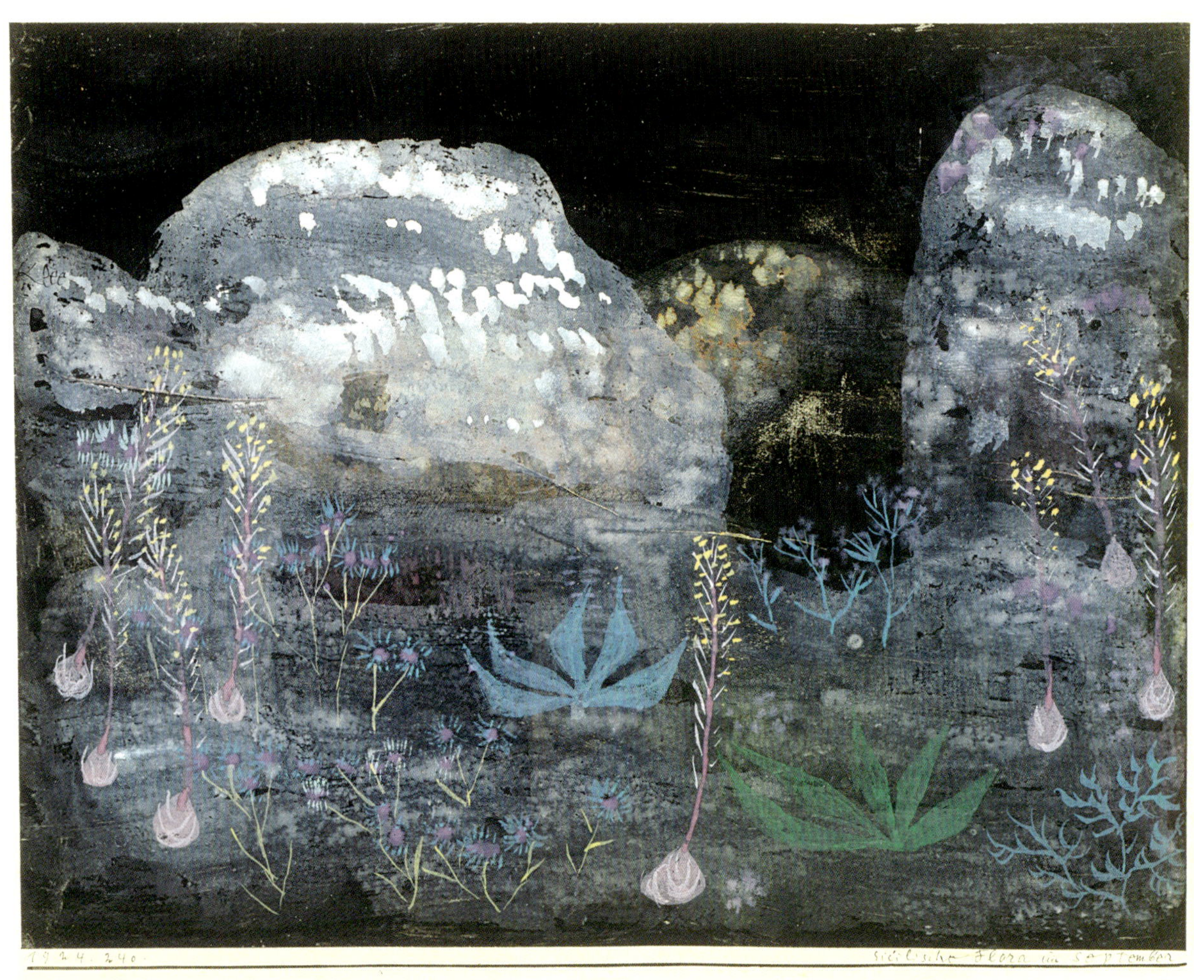

30 **SICILISCHE FLORA IM SEPTEMBER**, 1924.240
[Sicilian Flora in September]

Watercolor and pencil on black-primed paper, mounted on cardboard
8¾ x 11⅜ inches (22.2 x 28.8 cm)
Collection of The Arts Club of Chicago
Bequest of Arthur Heun, 1947

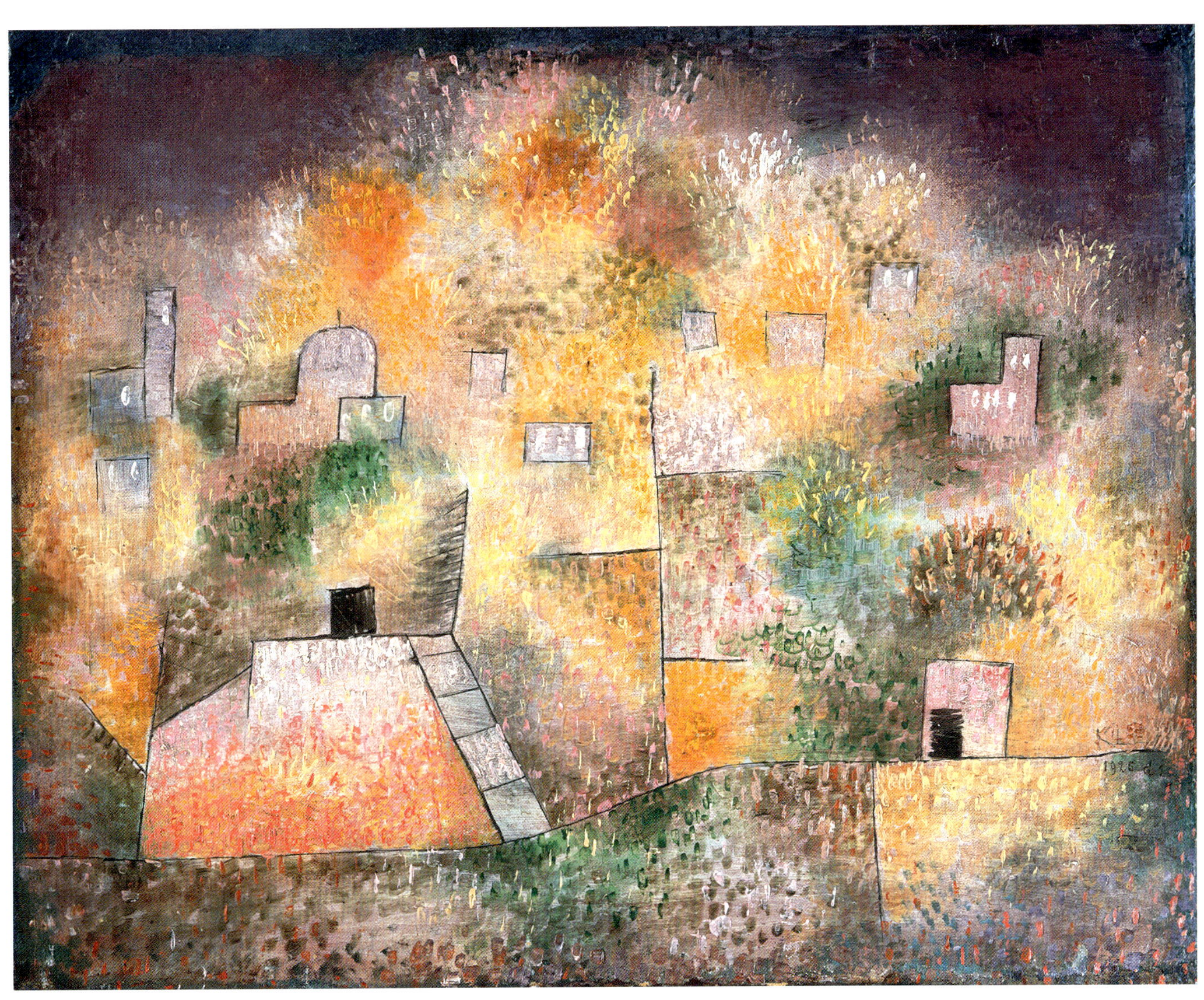

31 **ORIENTALISCHER LUSTGARTEN**, 1925.131
[Oriental Pleasure Garden]

Oil on cardboard
15¾ x 20½ inches (40 x 52 cm)
Metropolitan Museum of Art, New York
The Berggruen Klee Collection, 1984.315.41

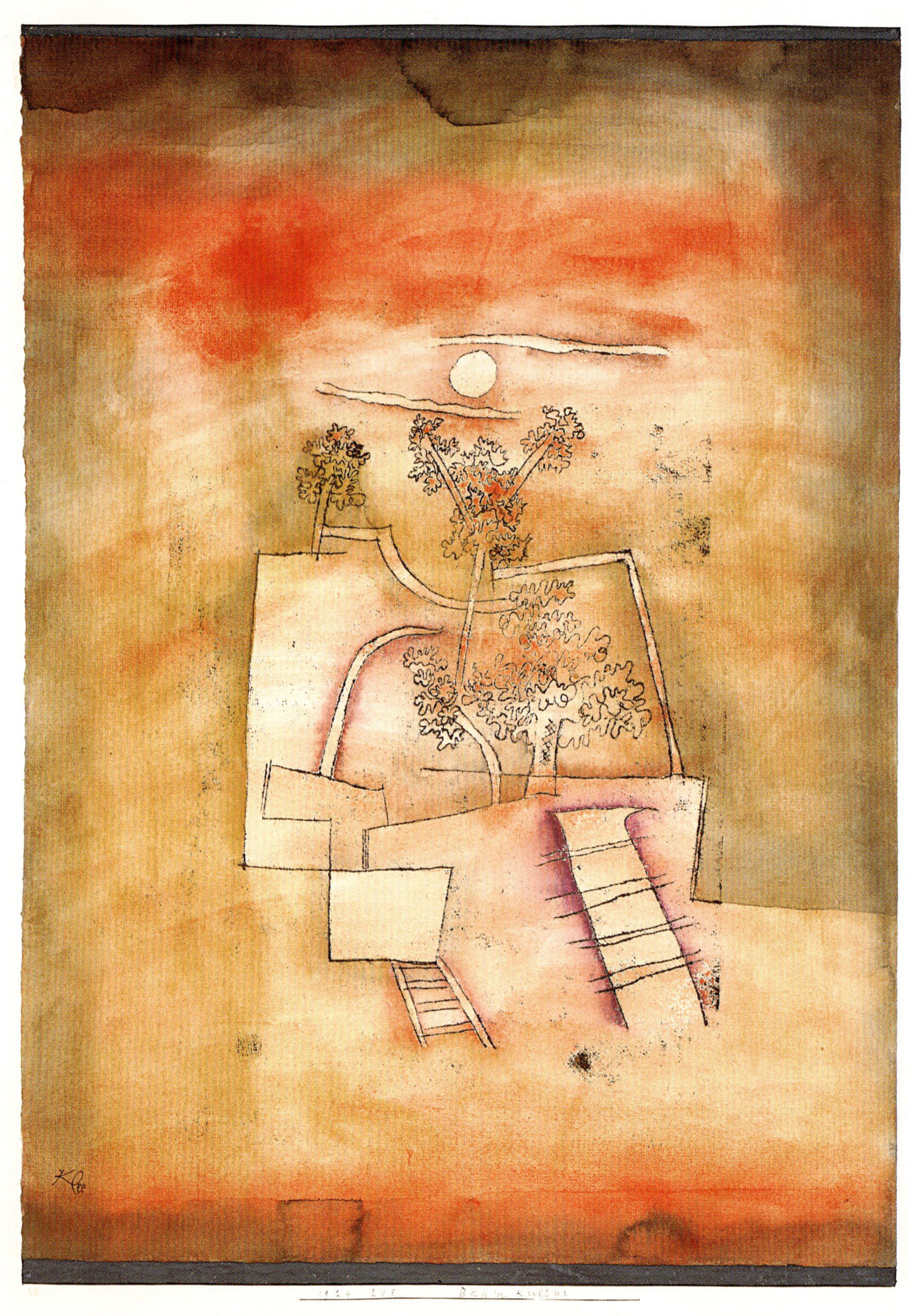

32 **BAUM KULTUR**, 1924.245
[Tree Culture]

Oil transfer (drawing) and watercolor on paper, with watercolor
and pen margin above and below, mounted on cardboard
19⅛ x 13¾ inches (48.7 x 34.9 cm)
Solomon R. Guggenheim Museum, New York, 38.511

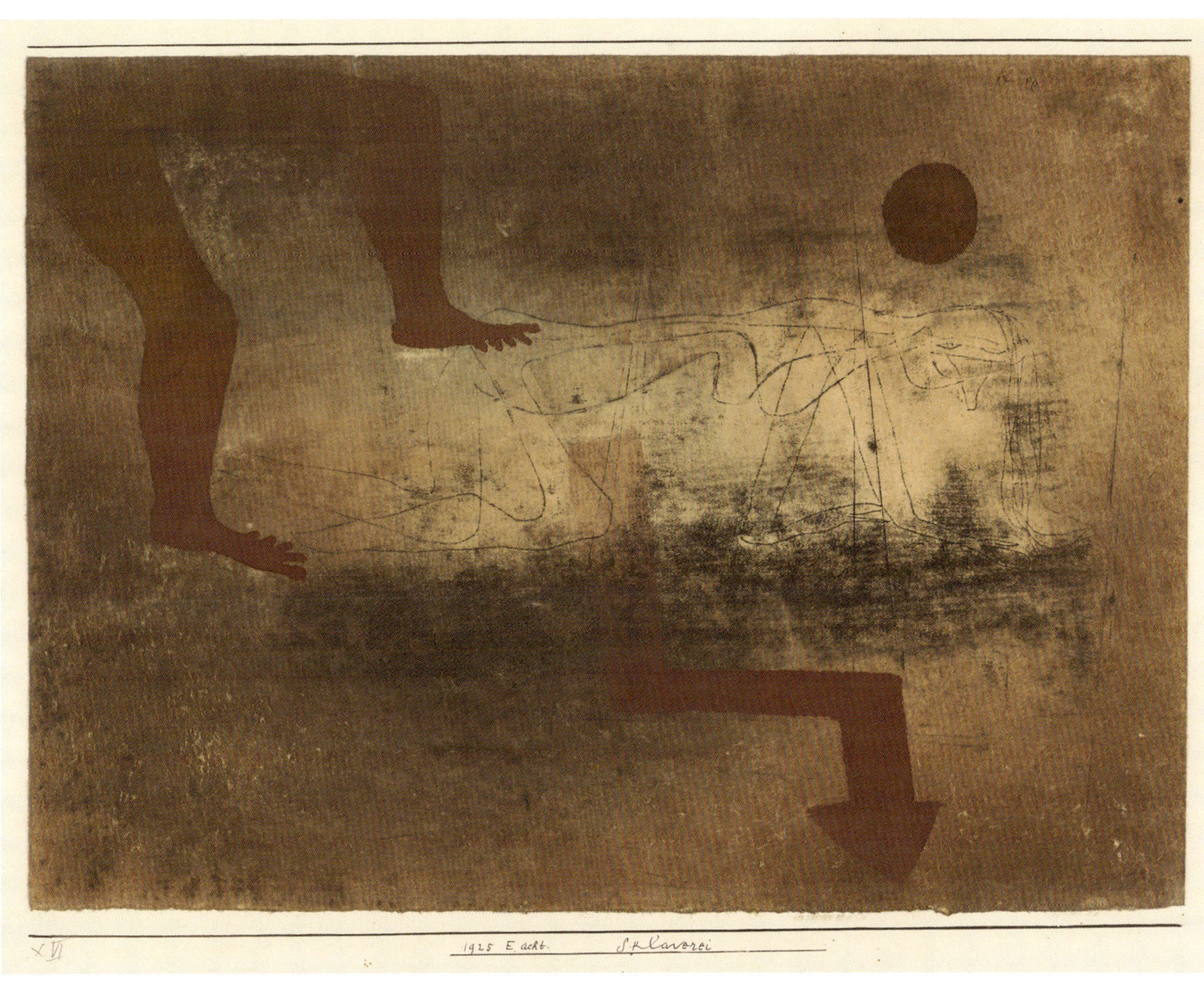

33 **SKLAVEREI**, 1925.148
    [Slavery]

Oil transfer drawing and watercolor on paper, mounted on cardboard
10 x 14 inches (25.4 x 35.6 cm)
The Museum of Modern Art, New York
Gift of Abby Aldrich Rockefeller, 96.35

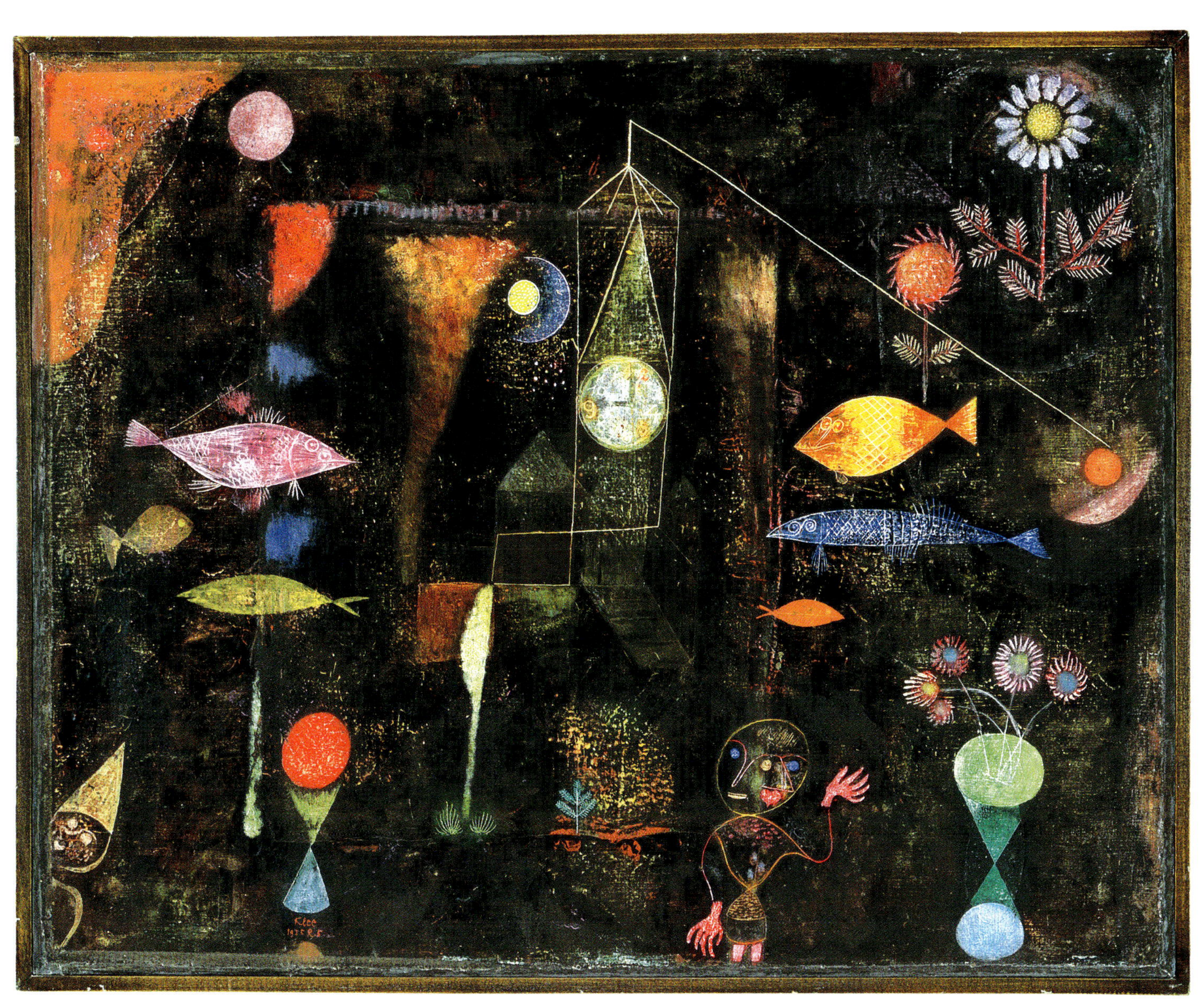

34 **FISCH ZAUBER**, 1925.85
[Fish Magic]

Oil and watercolor on muslin, mounted on cardboard
and mounted on stretcher
30¼ x 38¾ inches (77 x 98.3 cm)
Philadelphia Museum of Art
The Louise and Walter Arensberg Collection, 1950

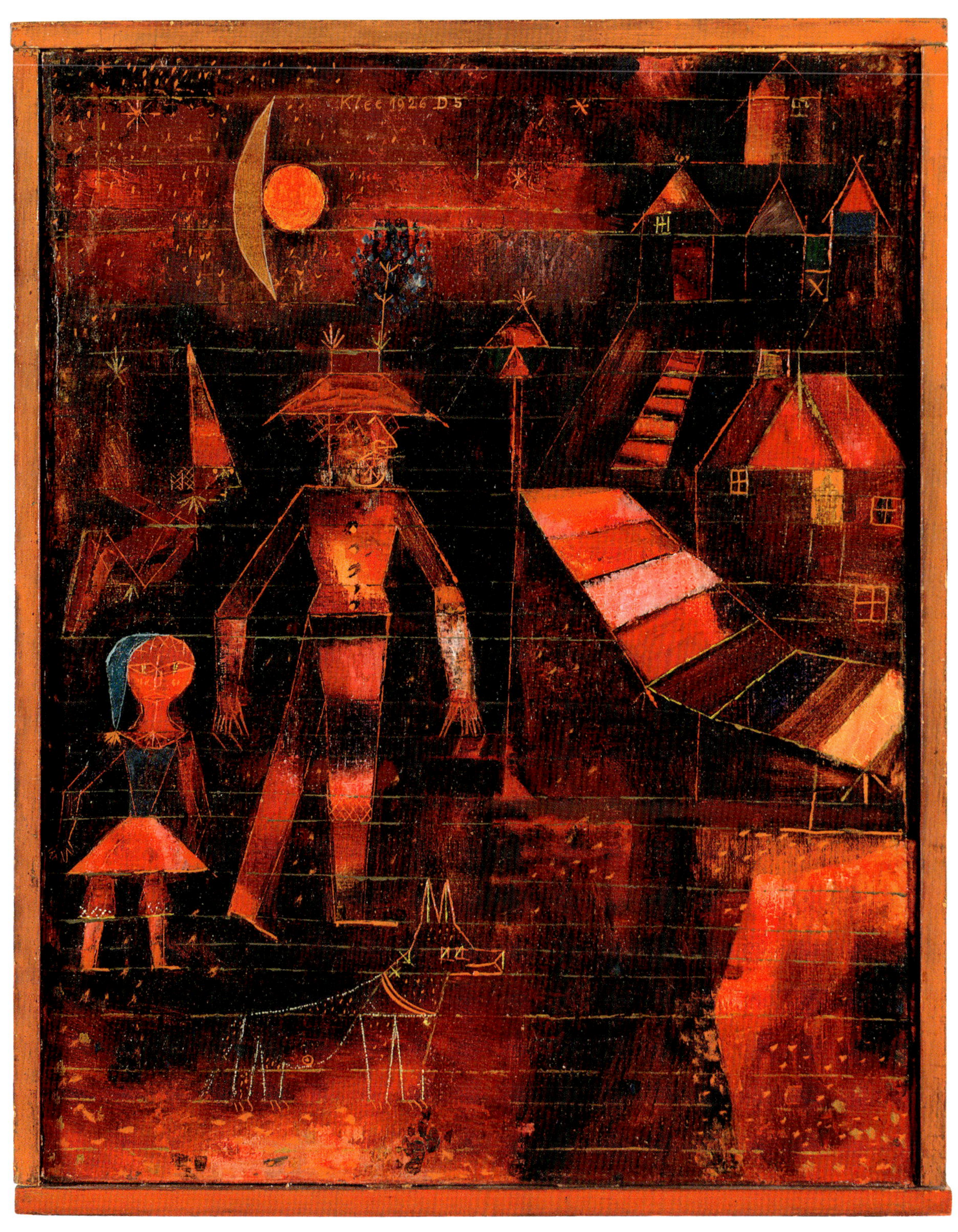

35 **DORF-CARNAVAL**, 1926.135
[Village Carnival]

Oil on muslin, mounted on cardboard,
with original painted strip frame
21½ x 17¼ inches (54.6 x 43.8 cm)
Philadelphia Museum of Art
The Louise and Walter Arensberg Collection, 1950

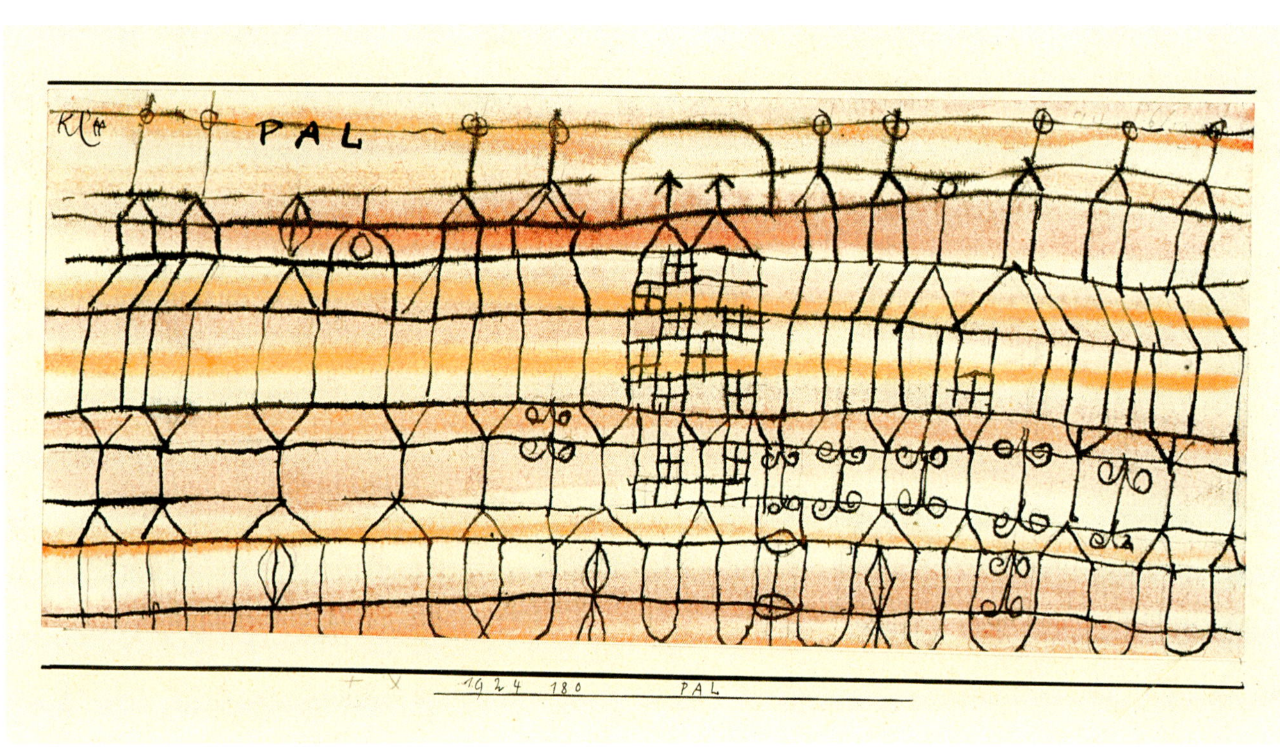

36 **PAL**, 1924.180

Pen and watercolor, wet in wet, and pencil
on paper, mounted on cardboard
3⅞ x 8⅞ inches (10 x 22.6 cm)
Private Collection

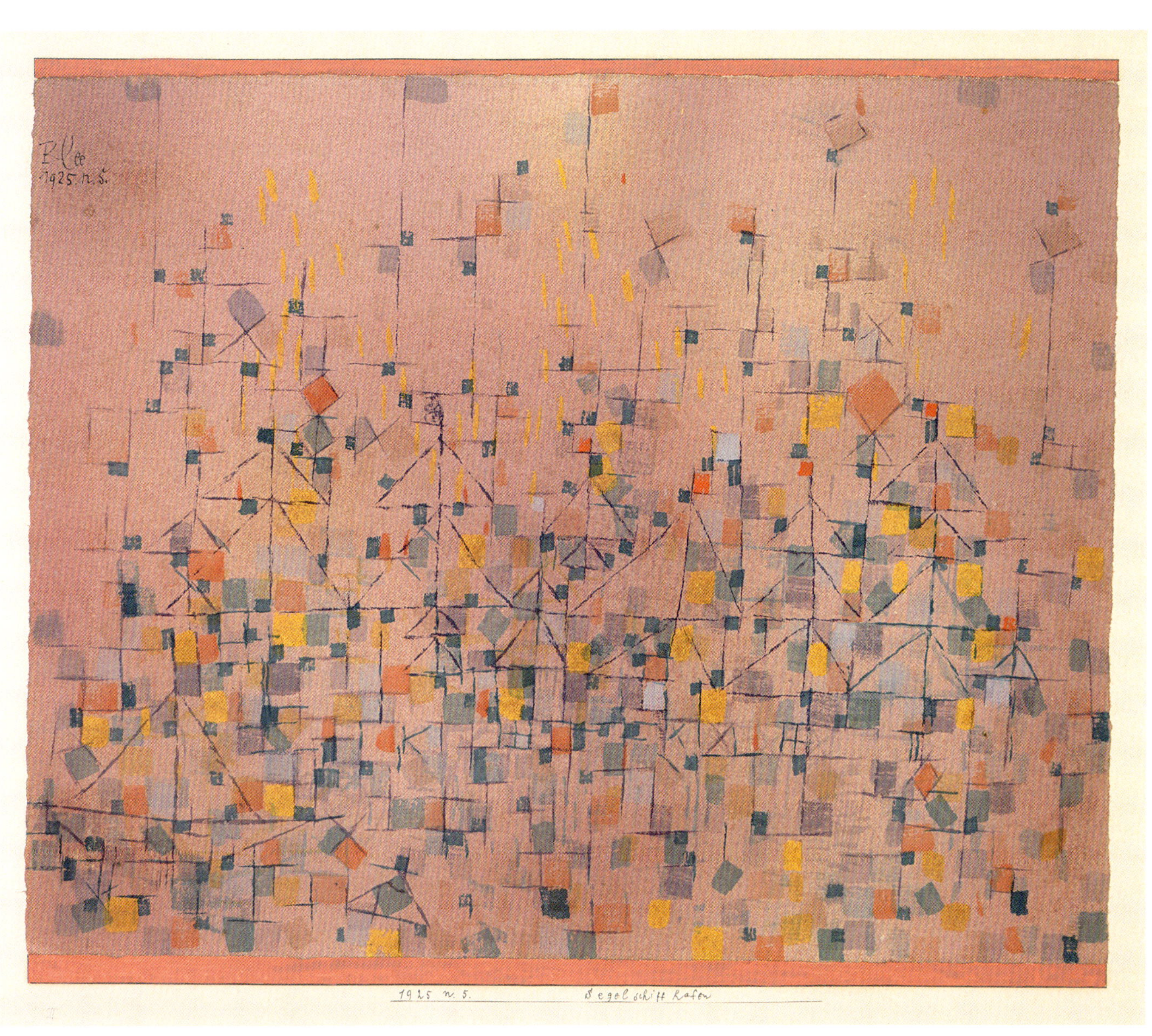

37 **SEGELSCHIFFHAFEN**, 1925.45
[Harbour for Sailing Ships]

Watercolor brushed and sprayed on paper
12⅝ x 17⅝ inches (32.1 x 44.7 cm)
Courtesy Calder Foundation, New York

Klee produced this work after his watercolor *Zimmerperspective mit der dunklen Tür [Perspective of a Room with the Dark Door]* (1921.23). Although no preliminary drawing for the work has as yet been discovered, one sees an almost identical perspective and interior in the original composition (see below) of the two, now separated, watercolors *Zimmerperspective rot/grün [Room Perspective Red/ Green]* (1921.46) and *Architektur in rot u. grün [Architecture in Red and Green]* (1921.47).[1] Klee possibly cut up that picture and made an oil transfer as described below, but certain steps cannot yet be verified.

Klee apparently first drew a single composition with two points of view, producing one perspective in the upper section and a different one in the lower one. He then applied watercolor to this drawing in the complementary colors of red and green, and afterward redrew the network of lines in the lower part with the help of a ruler. (He did not redraw the perspective of the upper section.) While redrawing the lines, Klee made a simultaneous tracing, which gave him a copy. Klee then cut the original composition in two. The upper picture is now simply a small architectural composition, dominated by its color gradations rather than perspective, since the more sharply focused lower section is missing.[2] Klee subsequently produced the watercolor *Zimmerperspective mit der dunklen Tür* on the copy he had made of the lower section. The spot where the upper arcades had been is now empty, and the large door acts like a kind of vortex. The space, with its various transparent furnishings, seems about to be sucked into the door's yawning opening. With the earlier elements cut away, the perspective picture seems all the more mysterious. Presumably, Klee then produced the "new version" of the work seen here, once again using the oil transfer method and working from the first or second copy.

In *Geisterzimmer mit der Hohen Türe (neue Fassung),* the lines have become clearer, and though there are various objects in it, the space seems even emptier. Klee heightened the effect of dematerialization with airbrushing, a technique that had become fashionable at the Bauhaus. The picture space seems even more closed and isolated because of the framing in black ink, which helps to draw the

Reconstruction of original work combining:

Architektur in rot u grün [Architecture in Red and Green], 1921.47 (top)
Watercolor and pen on paper, strips of paper at top and bottom, mounted on cardboard
6½ x 10¼ inches (16.5 x 26 cm)
Location unknown

and
Zimmer Perspective rot/grün [Room Perspective Red/Green], 1921.46 (bottom)
Watercolor and pen on paper, strips of paper at top and bottom, mounted on cardboard
7⅞ x 10⅜ inches (20 x 26.4 cm)
Norton Simon Museum, Pasadena, The Blue Four Galka Scheyer Collection, 53.55

viewer under its spell. Klee exhibited this adapted version in 1924 in Bern, Switzerland, and in 1926 in Prague and Dresden, Germany, and he included it in the large show "Art and Technology" in 1928 at the Museum Folkwang in Essen, Germany, organized to coincide with the convention of the Society of German Engineers. Interestingly, in 1925 Klee produced yet another variant of the perspective picture from 1921: *Das andere Geisterzimmer (neue Fassung) [The Other Ghost Chamber (New Version)]* (1925.109) is a new version of the watercolor *Zimmerperspective mit Einwohnern [Room Perspective with Inhabitants]* (1921.24). Klee exhibited this second version twice in Paris in 1925 under the title *Chambre spirite,* first in the Galerie Vavain-Raspail, then in the exhibition "La Peinture Surréaliste" at the Galerie Pierre.

These two new versions exemplify how in his recycling of early works, Klee deliberately performed a balancing act between Constructivist and Surrealist trends, strategically positioning his work within the range of contemporary art.

Osamu Okuda

1. See Wolfgang Kersten and Osamu Okuda, *Paul Klee: Im Zeichen der Teilung* (Stuttgart, Germany: Hatje, 1995), 344; and Vivian Endicott Barnett, *The Blue Four Collection at the Norton Simon Museum* (New Haven, Conn., and London: Yale University Press, 2002), 286–288.

2. Significantly, Klee presented the upper portion to his artist friend Alexei Jawlensky, probably in 1922. See Josef Helfenstein, "The Most Precious and Most Personal of Gifts: Pictures Exchanged Between Feininger, Jawlensky, Kandinsky, and Klee," in *Die Blaue Vier: Feininger, Jawlensky, Kandinsky, Klee in der Neuen Welt,* exh. cat. (Bern, Switzerland: Kunstmuseum Bern, 1997), 95.

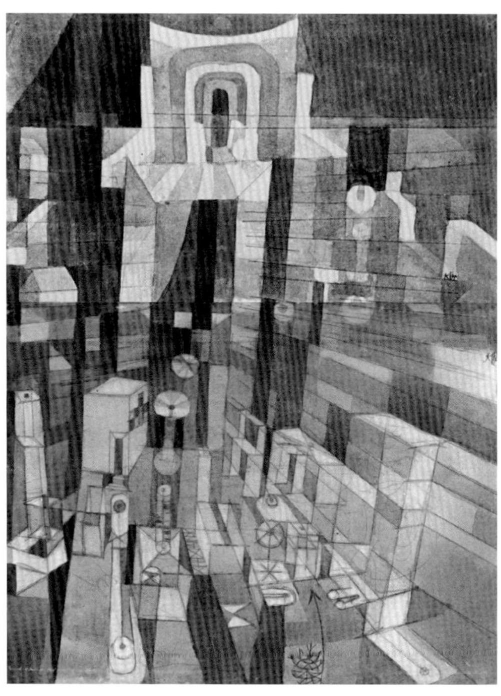

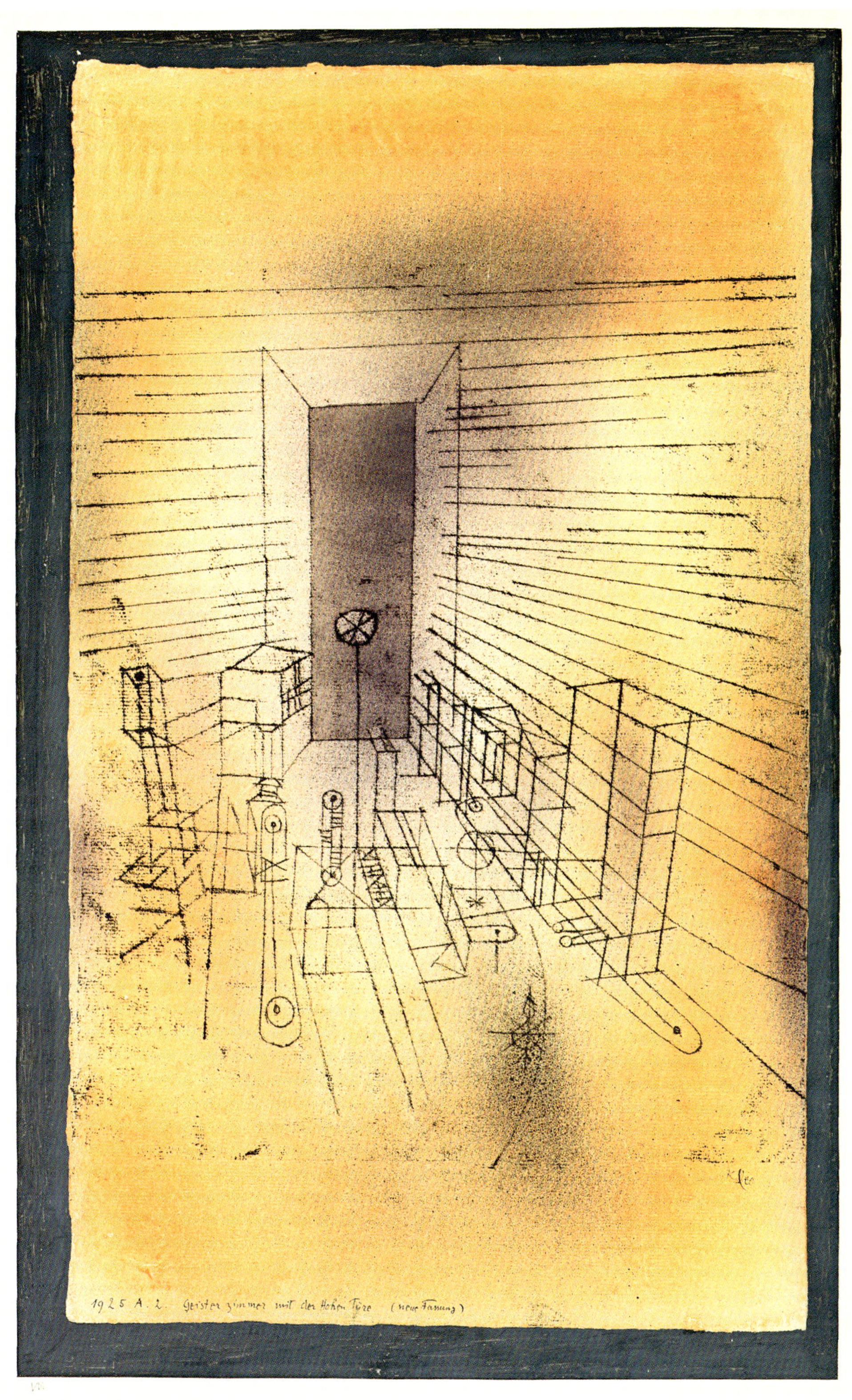

38 **GEISTERZIMMER MIT DER HOHEN TÜRE (NEUE FASSUNG)**, 1925.102
[Ghost Chamber with the High Door (New Version)]

Oil transfer (drawing) and partly sprayed watercolor on paper,
bordered with gouache and pen, and mounted on cardboard
19⅛ x 11⅝ inches (48.7 x 29.4 cm)
Metropolitan Museum of Art, New York, The Berggruen Klee Collection, 1987.455.16

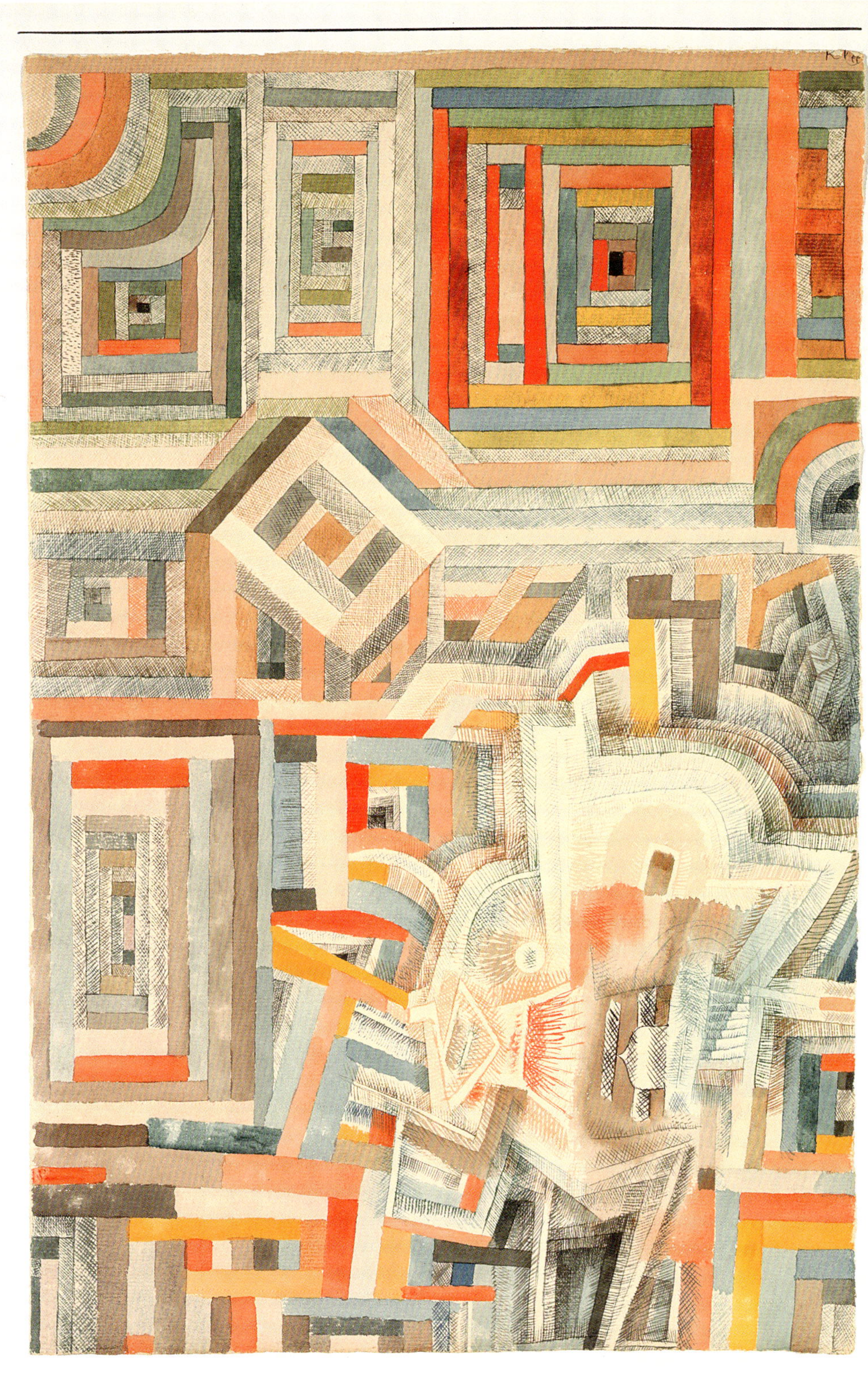

39 **PALAST, TEILWEISE ZERSTÖRT**, 1926.119
[Palace, Partly Destroyed]

Watercolor on paper, mounted on cardboard
20 x 13 inches (51 x 33 cm)
The Denver Art Museum
The Charles Francis Hendrie Memorial Collection

In the watercolored pen drawing *Heilige Inseln,* the form-giving energies crystallize in delicate structures of parallel lines, either lined up side by side or intertwining. Following the suggestion of the title, we can make out a landscape: a group of islands with grottoes and temples. On the right in the middle distance, the radiant sun is visible through a large pointed arch, with cross shapes below. These are apparently cult sites in the middle of an archipelago. This is one of the numerous compositions Klee produced between 1925 and 1927 using the graphic idiom of so-called "parallel configurations." Christian Geelhaar has emphasized the connection between these landscapes, with their varied sacred and mythological motifs, and German Romanticism. However, Christa Lichtenstern has pointed out that Klee also borrowed here and there from early Christian Byzantine culture.

In my opinion, the method of "parallel configurations" goes clear back to the very beginnings of art, as traced by Gottfried Semper. For one of his Bauhaus lectures, Klee drew on a sheet of paper various design possibilities based on the scheme of two overlapping triangles.[1] His last variant, with its interwoven narrow ribbons, is the prototype, so to speak, for his subsequent "parallel configurations." One sees similar forms in braided mats. In his book *Der Stil*, Semper pointed out that the ancient Egyptians and Assyrians employed this design as a pattern for brick walls. He added that "following age-old tradition … [it was] used to excess in the orientalizing style of Byzantine building and in the various branches of Arab architecture."[2] It was Semper's conviction that art developed out of the various techniques employed in working with textiles: knotting, knitting, and braiding. For his part, Klee devoted his Bauhaus lecture on October 23, 1923, to "the idea of braiding." Semper wrote: "The sole advantage of plaited ceilings over woven ones is that the strands of which they are composed do not have to cross each other at right angles, as weaving requires, but diagonals and threads running in all directions can be woven into the texture."[3] Klee made use of precisely this advantage in his "parallel configurations," then expanded this method in his drawing. Inasmuch as Klee's "decorative" style of painting and drawing was often criticized as mere "tapestry design," it is interesting that here Klee was presumably attempting to develop a commonality between drawing and textile making.[4] On this basis he built up his sacred, mythological landscapes of "parallel configurations." In *Heilige Inseln*, for example, he developed the spiritual dimension of "ornament" as derived from ancient cultures.

Osamu Okuda

1. Paul Klee, "Pädagogischer Nachlass," lecture notes, PN 12 M11/160, Zentrum Paul Klee, Bern, Switzerland.

2. Gottfried Semper, *Der Stil in den technischen und tektonischen Künsten oder Praktische Ästhetik*, vol. 1 (Munich: Bruckmann, 1860), 118f.

3. Semper, 118f.

4. On this subject, see Jenny Anger, *Paul Klee and the Decorative in Modern Art* (Cambridge, England, and New York: Cambridge University Press, 2003).

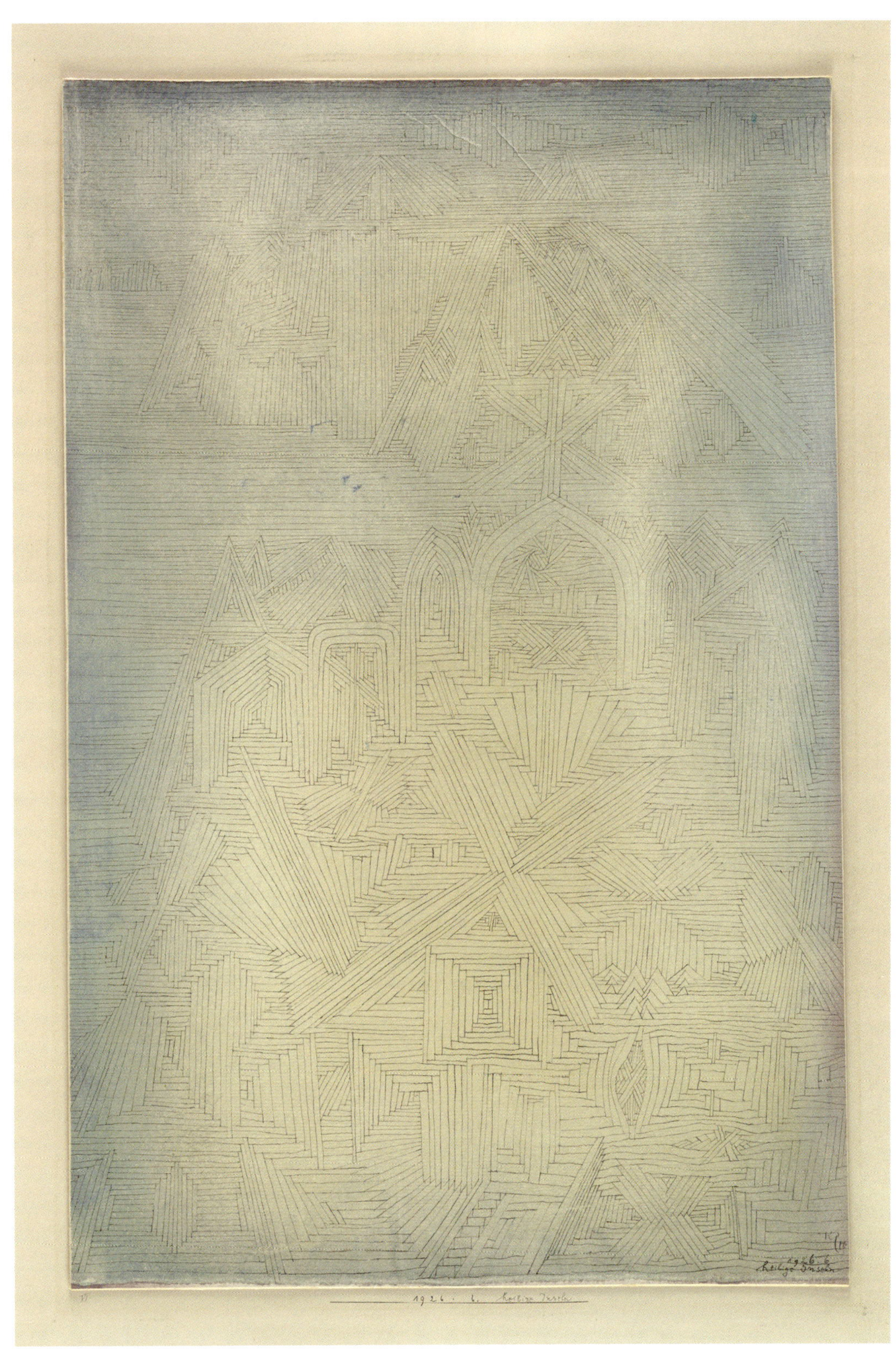

40 **HEILIGE INSELN**, 1926.6
[Sacred Islands]

Watercolor and pen on paper, mounted on cardboard
18½ x 12⅜ inches (47 x 31.5 cm)
The Museum of Modern Art, New York
Gift of Philip Johnson, 457

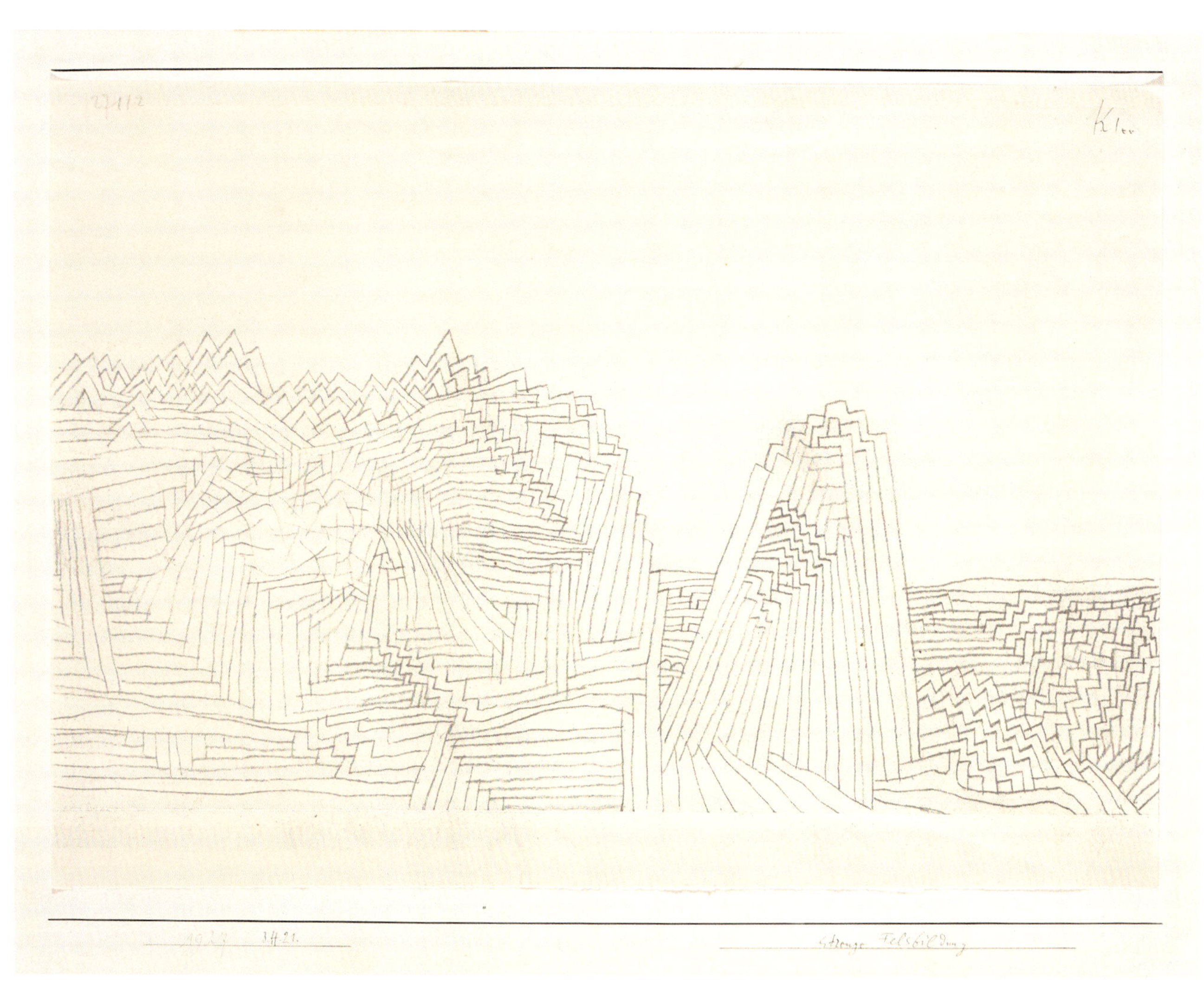

41 **STRENGE FELSBILDUNG**, 1927.321
[Austere Rock Formation]

Pencil on paper, mounted with glue spots on cardboard
8¾ x 13 inches (22.2 x 33 cm)
The Menil Collection, Houston

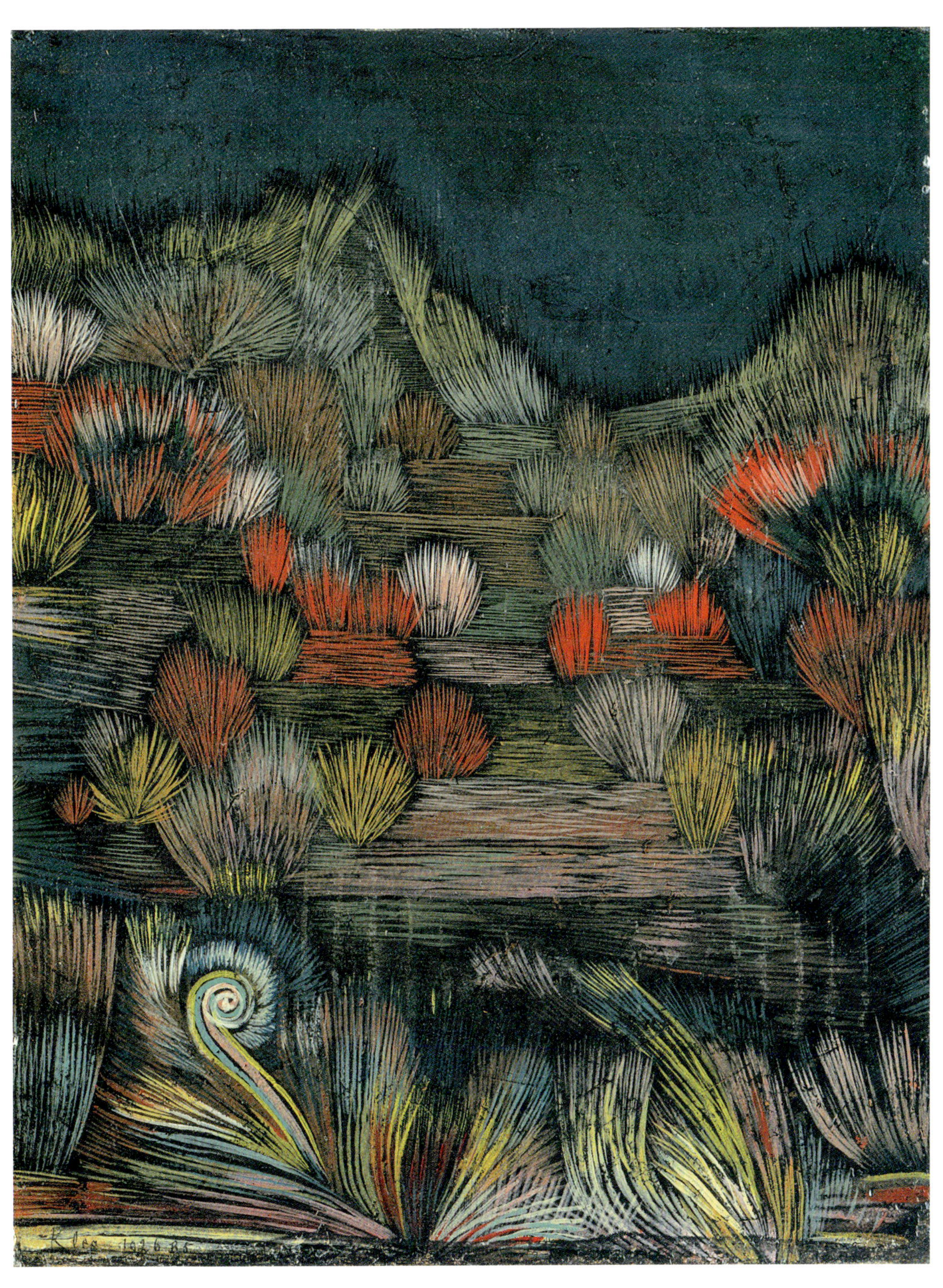

42 **KL. DÜNENBILD**, 1926.115
[Small Dune Picture]

Oil on black casein ground, mounted on cardboard
12¾ x 9⅛ inches (32.4 x 23.2 cm)
The Menil Collection, Houston

This work establishes a tense relationship between natural organic forms and strictly geometrical ones. In the center is a small rectangle whose lines extend outward until they nearly reach the edges of the sheet, so that they seem like pinwheeling arms or legs. The rectangle's tilted position heightens the dynamism of this schematic geometrical figure, which dominates the entire composition, threatening the animals in the upper right and lower left. The parallel lines depicting the two animals have a free calligraphic flow, in contrast to the precise straight lines of the rectangular construction, which Klee drew with a ruler. He further emphasized the power and menace of the central figure with sprayed red watercolor pigment. Careful observation reveals a small figure beneath the red surface, to the left of the animal on the upper right, which has apparently already fallen victim to the dominant red of the center construction. The situation of the two animals still visible is dire: they are trapped in the spaces formed by the limbs of the central figure and the edges of the sheet, an imprisonment that is further emphasized by the double molding of the cardboard mounting. What would happen if the central figure, obeying its immanent dynamism, were to suddenly turn?

The image can be understood as Klee's response to dogmatic Constructivism, of which he was highly critical. Klee hoped to create instead a "new naturalism" analogous with the Creation. The work possibly reflects Klee's precarious position at the Bauhaus, which shifted even more in the direction of Constructivism after its move to Dessau in 1926, pushing its teachers of painting more and more to the sidelines. Walter Gropius, the school's director, had said of his two painting professors as early as September 1925:

"…sadly, I see [Kandinsky] and Klee using the Bauhaus more and more only as a sinecure."[1]

One can assume that the picture's title refers to the central figure's arrogant attitude toward the animals. But in his handwritten œuvre catalogue, Klee registered the work under the title *Anmassung (der Missgeburten) [Arrogance (of the Monstrosities)]*. This additional information forces us to see the deformed animals as somewhat ambiguous and to recognize that Klee might have been engaging in a bit of self-mockery. Beginning in 1928, Klee's position at the Bauhaus under the direction of Hannes Meyer became even more problematic as Meyer steered the school in the direction of Functionalism. In a typical rant in 1930, after he had been dismissed, Meyer likened the Bauhaus artists to "exotic beasts." In an open letter to Dessau's mayor, Meyer continued his harangue: "Herr Oberbürgermeister! Zoos, museums, and racetracks are expressions of the desire for municipal stature. Along with Wörlitz and Junker, Dessau has now got itself a Bauhaus. Instead of exotic beasts, it shelters those strange people whom the world venerates as great artists. The young Bauhaus artists are but fields of clover cultivated by the most wondrous of painter-individualists, fields that will now lie fallow in our epoch of extreme social upheaval and collective adversity."[2]

In retrospect, then, Klee's *Anmassung* can be seen to be prophetic.

Osamu Okuda

1 Walter Gropius to Ise Gropius, September 1925; quoted in Reginald R. Isaacs, *Walter Gropius: Der Mensch und sein Werk*, vol. 1 (Berlin: Mann, 1983–84), 368.

2 Hannes Meyer, "Mein Hinauswurf aus dem Bauhaus," *Das Tagebuch* 11, no. 33 (August 16, 1930): 1311.

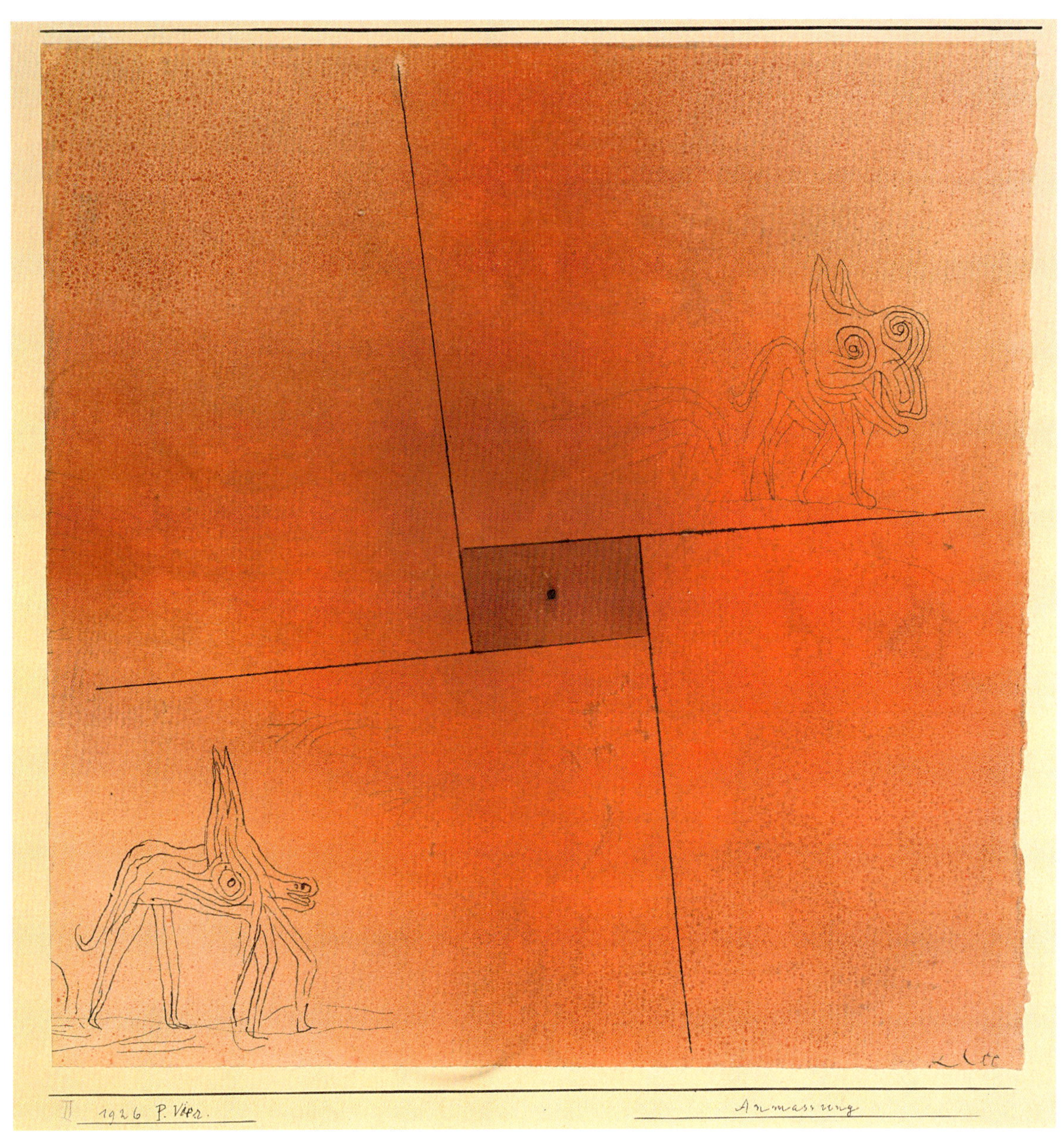

43 **ANMASSUNG**, 1926.64
[Arrogance]

Ink and partly sprayed watercolor on paper, mounted on cardboard
8¼ x 8¼ inches (21.1 x 21.1 cm)
Galerie Jan Krugier, Ditesheim & Cie, Geneva

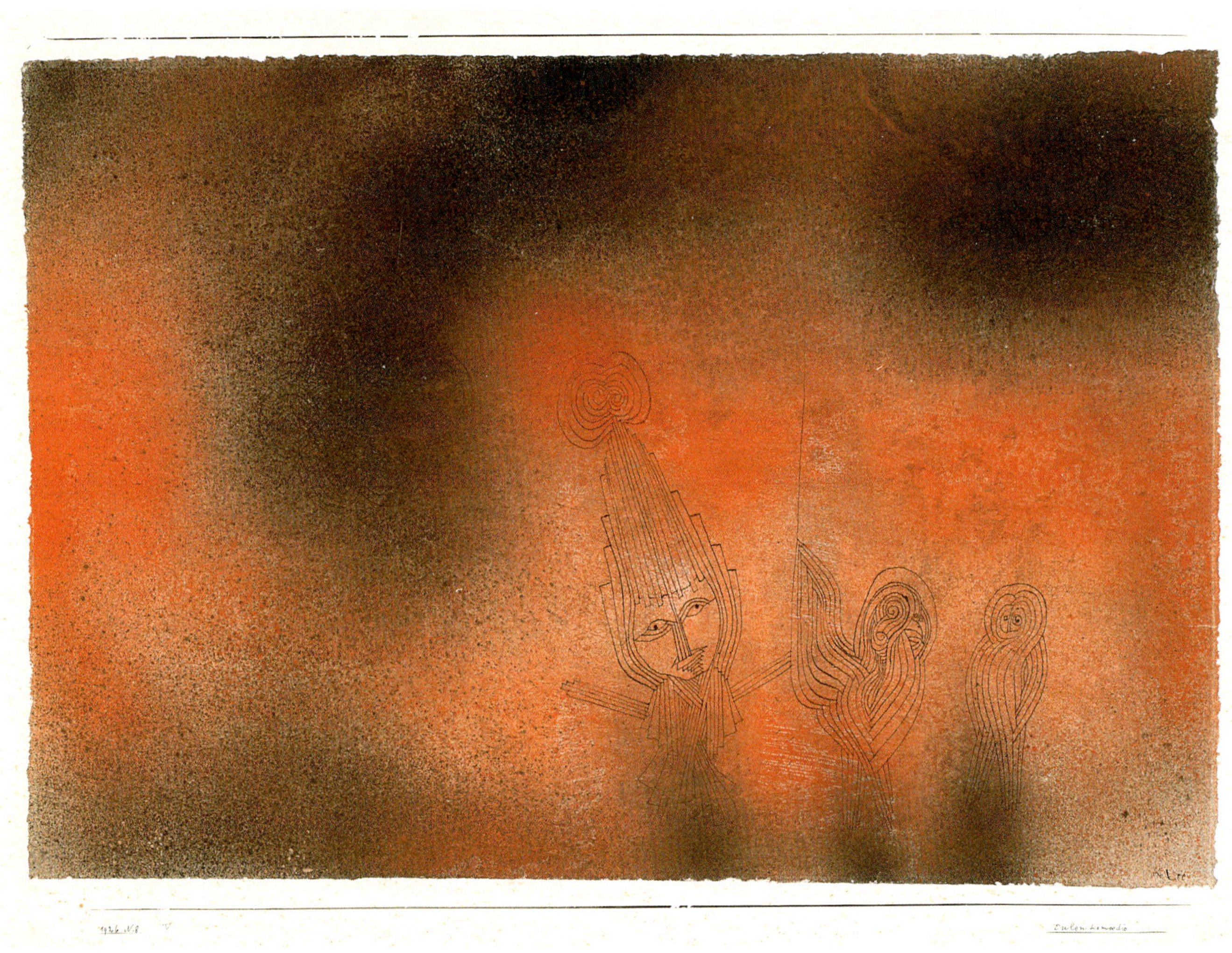

44 **EULENKOMOEDIE**, 1926.48
[Owl Comedy]

Partly sprayed watercolor and pen on paper, mounted on cardboard
12½ x 18½ inches (31.7 x 46.9 cm)
Solomon R. Guggenheim Museum, New York, 39.512

45 **ELEFANT UND LOEWE**, 1926.56
[Elephant and Lion]

Pen and sprayed watercolor on paper mounted on cardboard
12 x 18¼ inches (30.5 x 46.3 cm)
Museum of Art, Rhode Island School of Design, Providence
Gift of Bayard and Harriet K. Ewing Collection, 1993.105.15

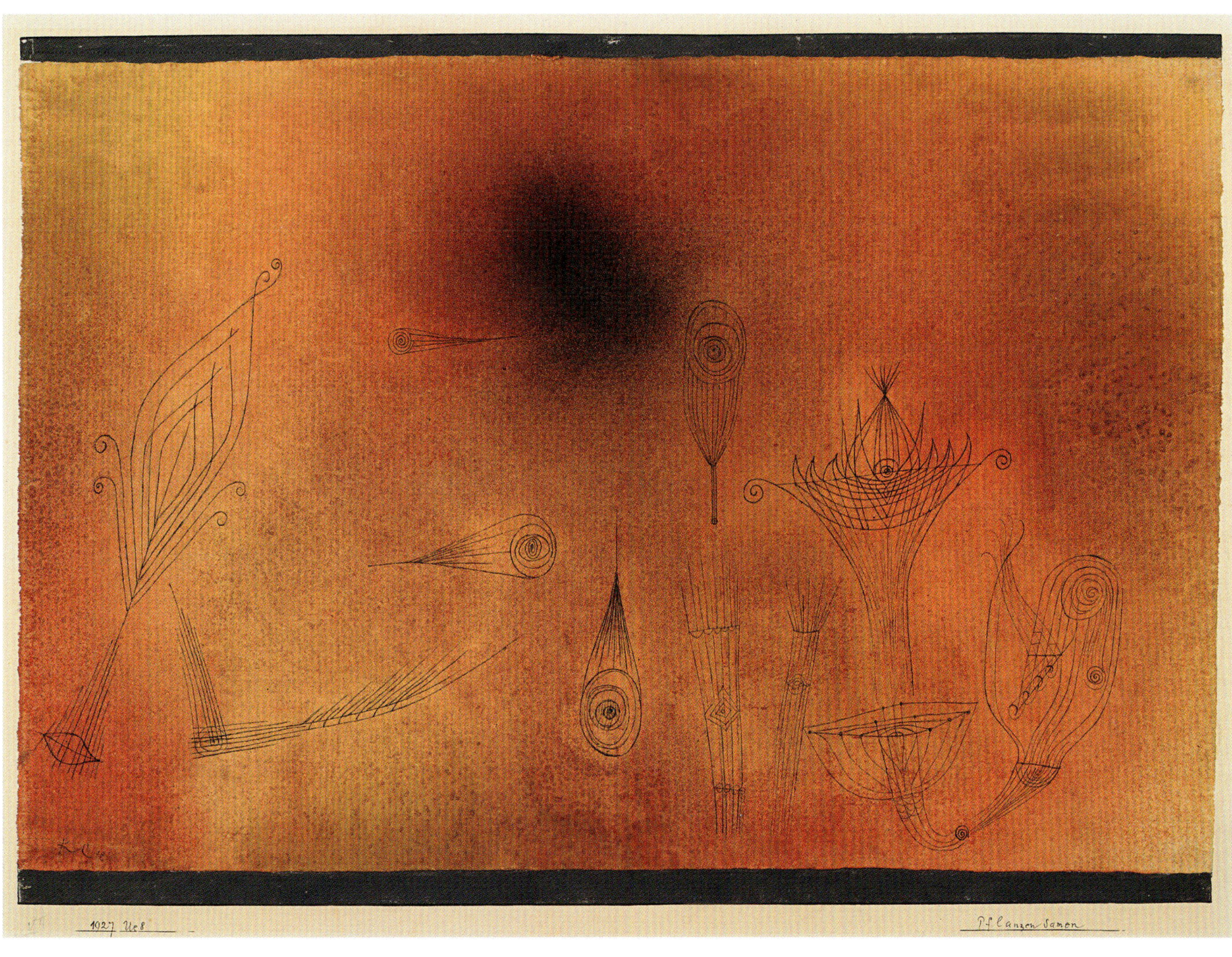

46 **PFLANZEN SAMEN**, 1927.288
[Plant Seeds]

Partly sprayed watercolor and pen on paper, with gouache
and pen margins above and below, mounted on cardboard
12⅛ x 18⅜ inches (30.8 x 46.7 cm)
Norton Simon Museum, Pasadena, California
The Blue Four Galka Scheyer Collection

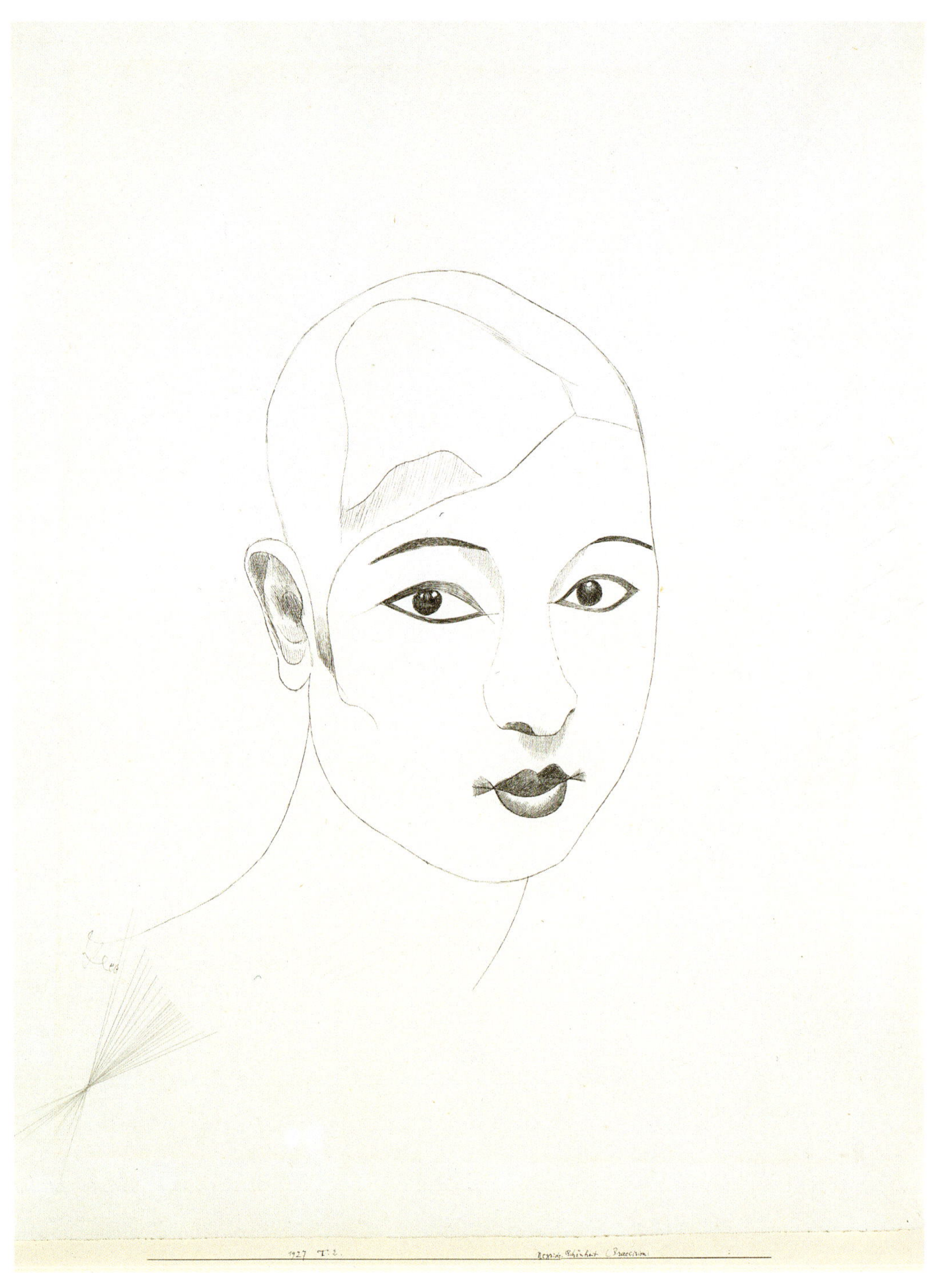

47   **NEGRIDE SCHÖNHEIT (PRAECISION)**, 1927.192
[Negroid Beauty (Precision)]

Pen on paper, mounted on cardboard
17⅜ x 13 inches (44 x 33 cm)
Extended loan of the Carl Djerassi Trust II
to the San Francisco Museum of Modern Art

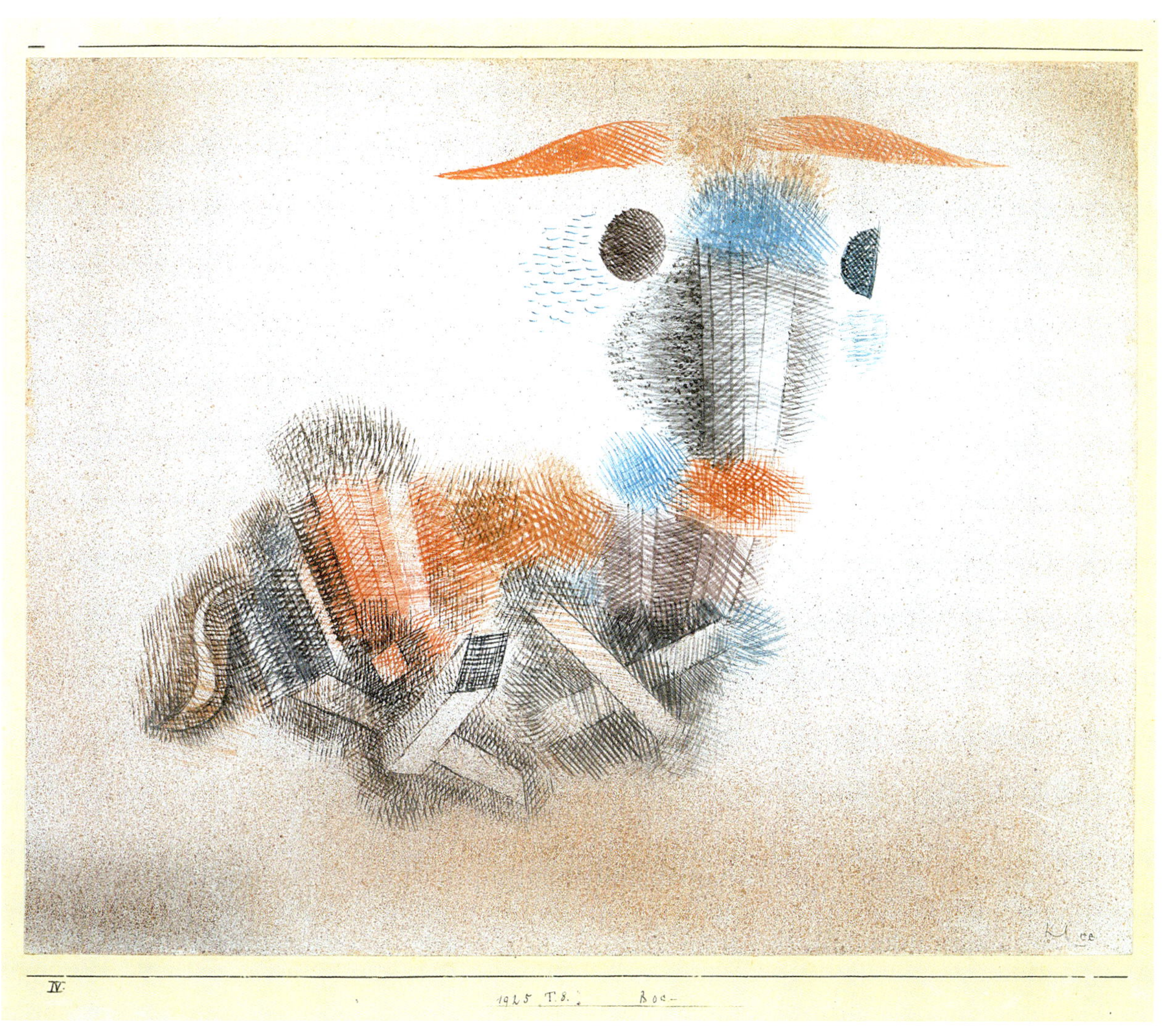

48 **BOCK**, 1925.198
[Billy-Goat]

Pen and sprayed watercolor on white chalk and
tempera-primed paper, mounted on cardboard
8⅝ x 11 inches (21.8 x 28.1 cm)
Smith College Museum of Art, Northampton, Massachusetts
Gift of Jere Abbott, 1976:23

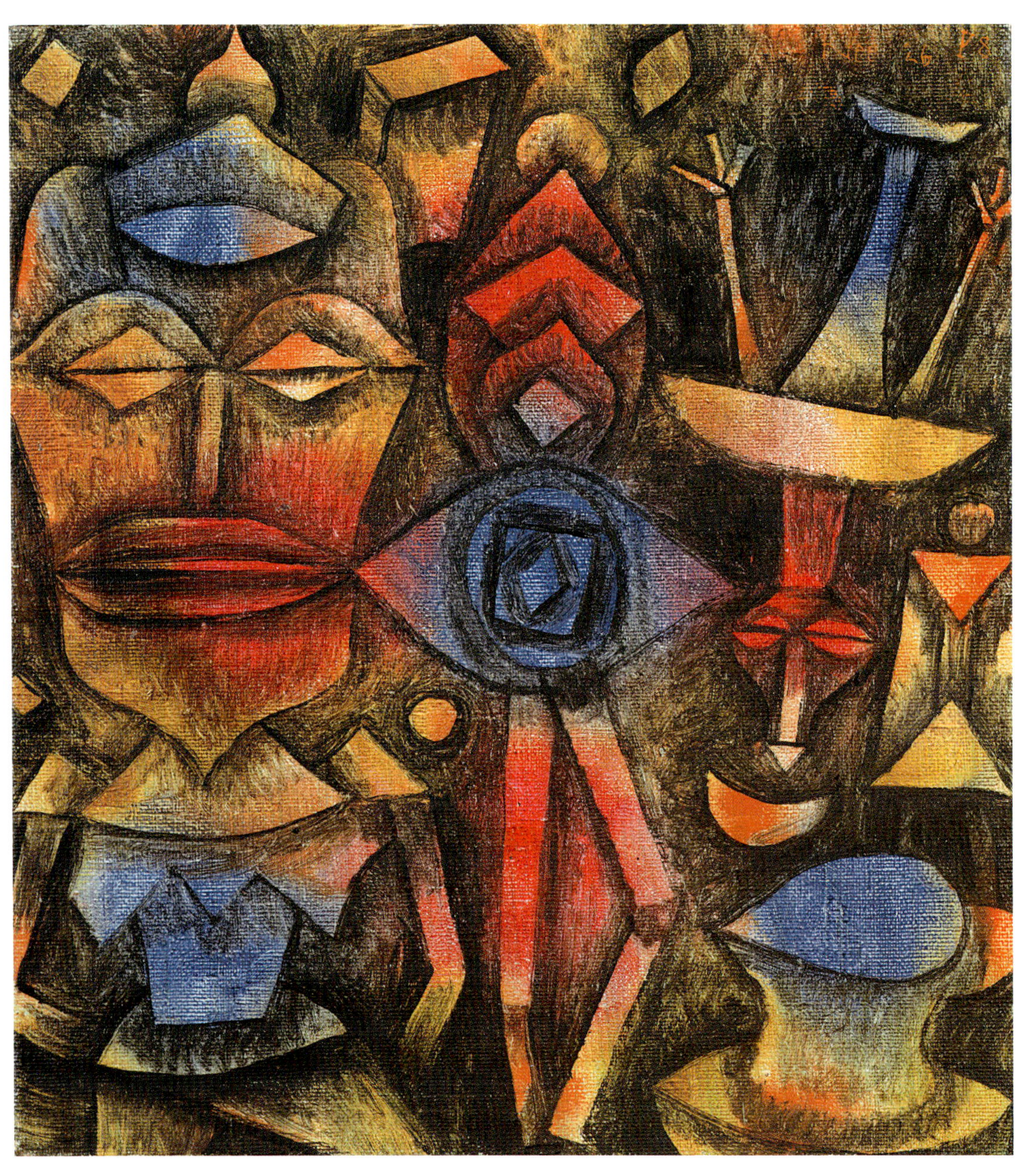

49 **FIGURINENSAMMLUNG**, 1926.248
[Collection of Figurines]

Oil on canvas, mounted on cardboard
10⅜ x 9⅝ inches (26.4 x 24.4 cm)
Metropolitan Museum of Art, New York
The Berggruen Klee Collection, 1984.315.47

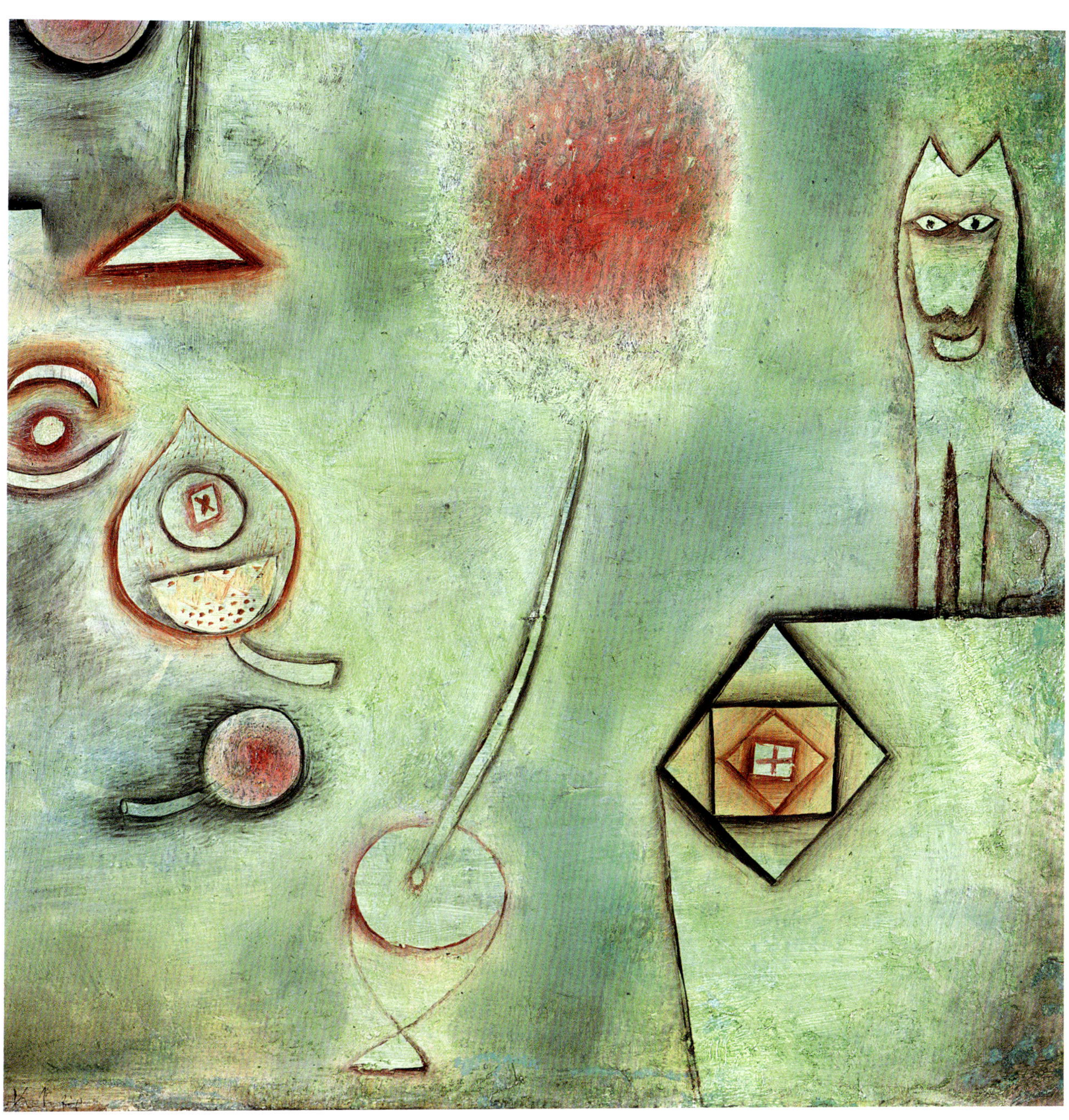

50 **STILLEBEN MIT TIERSTATUETTE**, 1928.158
[Still Life with Animal Statuette]

Oil and watercolor on white-primed canvas, bordered
with watercolor and pen, and mounted on cardboard
12⅜ x 12⅝ inches (31.5 x 32 cm)
Private Collection

STILL LIFE (POTS, FRUIT, EASTER EGG, CURTAINS, ETC.), 1927.18

COLORFUL MEAL, 1928.29

Black plays a special role in Klee's art, from his early pictures painted behind glass up to the so-called last still-lifes, those in front of which the artist had himself photographed for his sixtieth birthday in 1939. Since 1919 Klee had again and again used black as the base tone for his color compositions, whether abstract pictures of rectangles or fairy-tale fantasy scenes.

In the later 1920s, Klee painted a number of pictures on a black or very dark ground, borrowing from the traditional genre of the seventeenth-century Netherlandish still-life. In the present work, the allusion is unmistakable. In the seventeenth century, the playing cards and dice that Klee has arranged here, as if in a Netherlandish still-life, were "among the trifles treated with particular revulsion by popular moral tracts."[1] But Klee's depiction, as Christian Geelhaar has rightly observed, is no *nature morte* in the traditional sense. According to Geelhaar, "the small seeds on the outer left side and the orange-red fruit are thematically related: they symbolize the cycle of nature. Growth also promises the *ovum*, the concept of beginning and becoming."[2] In the background, much as in the painting *Schulhaus [Schoolhouse]* (1920.23), we can see two hidden figures who are apparently playing cards at a dining table. Narrative features such as this were not uncommon even in the early tradition of the still life, but to Klee this apparently meant that human activities are part of the "cycle of nature."

In the composition *Bunte Mahlzeit [Colorful Meal]*, produced a year later, Klee moved farther away from the traditional notion of the still life. Now the various objects simply hover in the dark mysterious space of the picture. The main protagonist, set in the center of the picture, is a cat that is reminiscent of a pre-Columbian ceramic figure. Despite its unpromising anatomy (large head, small legs), it seems to balance effortlessly atop a geometric construction. This construction is based on the pictorial idea of "tension," which Klee had taken from Russian and Hungarian Constructivists like El Lissitzky and László Moholy-Nagy around 1925–26 and integrated into his own theory. The cat wears a small red heart on its breast, recalling the drawing *Nicht ohne Herz [Not Without Heart]* (1928.33), produced at almost the same time. Klee exhibited the picture, shortly after he completed it, in a one-person show held from March 18 to Easter 1928 at the Galerie Alfred Flechtheim in Berlin. It had a featured place in the catalogue, and in his introductory text, Alfred Flechtheim proclaimed Klee's superiority to the Paris Surrealists, declaring on the facing page to *Bunte Mahlzeit*: "However, Surrealism's true creator is Paul Klee."[3] Hans Heilmaier also reproduced the work in his essay "Surrealism," which appeared in the fourth issue of the *Kunstblatt* in 1928. There he praised Klee as "one of the purest manifestations of 'surreal' art."[4] Thus, having noted and responded to the new Surrealist trend, Klee once again managed to ensure his success in the contemporary art market.

Osamu Okuda

1. Christian Klemm, "'Mors ultima linea rerum': Vorgeschichte und Grundlegung der Totenkopf-Vanitas," in Pieter Claesz, *Stilleben*, exh. cat. (Haarlem, Netherlands: Frans Hals Museum, 2004), 84.

2. Christian Geelhaar, *Paul Klee and the Bauhaus* (Greenwich, Conn.: New York Graphic Society, 1973), 107.

3. Alfred Flechtheim, "Paul Klee," in *Paul Klee*, exh. cat. (Berlin: Galerie Alfred Flechtheim, 1928), 4.

4. Hans Heilmaier, "Surrealismus," *Das Kunstblatt* 12, no. 4 (1928): 111.

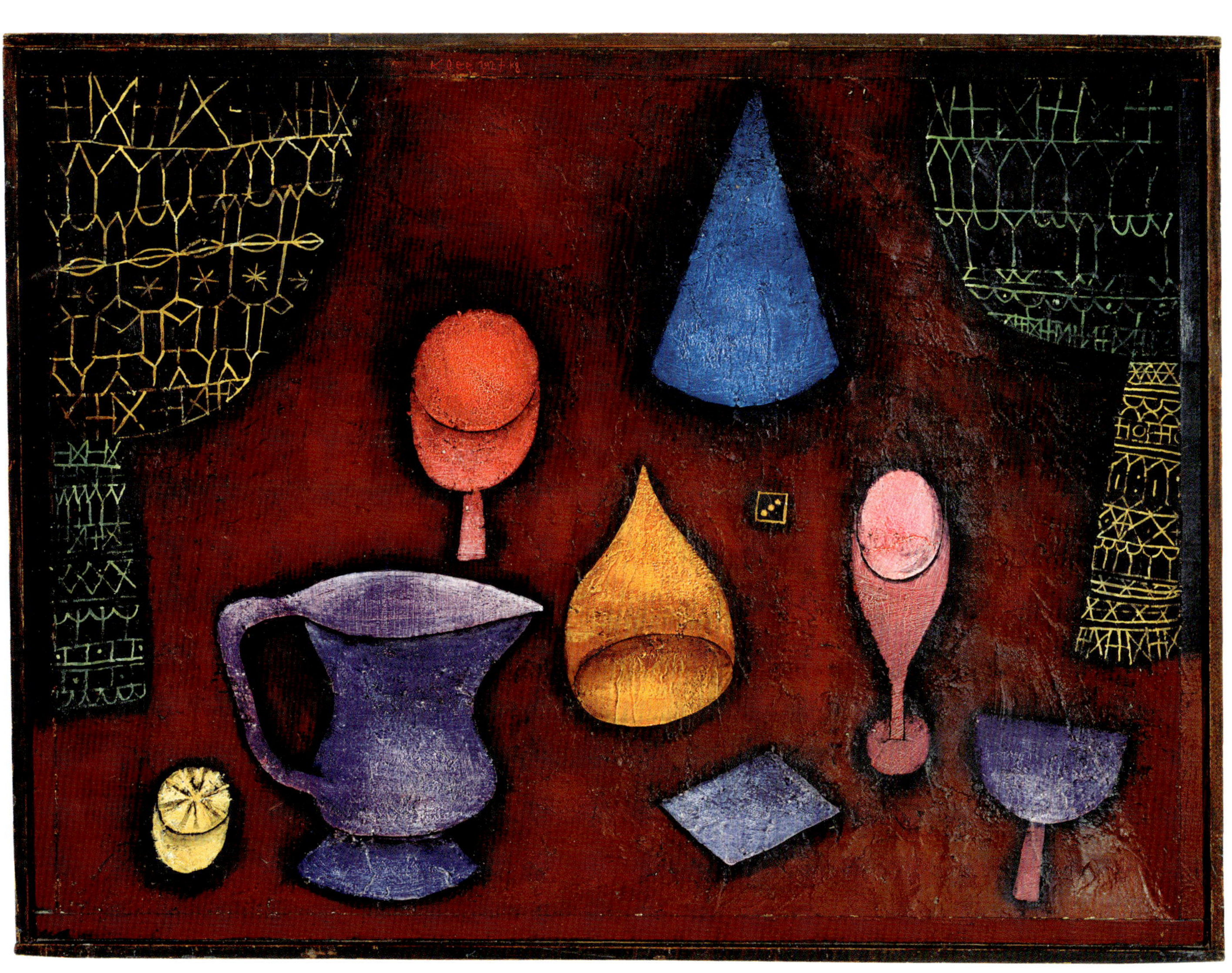

51 **STILLEBEN (TÖPFE, FRUCHT, OSTEREI, GARDINEN, ETC.)**, 1927.18
[Still Life (Pots, Fruit, Easter Egg, Curtains, Etc.)]

Oil on gypsum, with original strip frame
18⅞ x 25¼ inches (47.9 x 64.1 cm)
Metropolitan Museum of Art, New York
The Berggruen Klee Collection, 1984.315.49

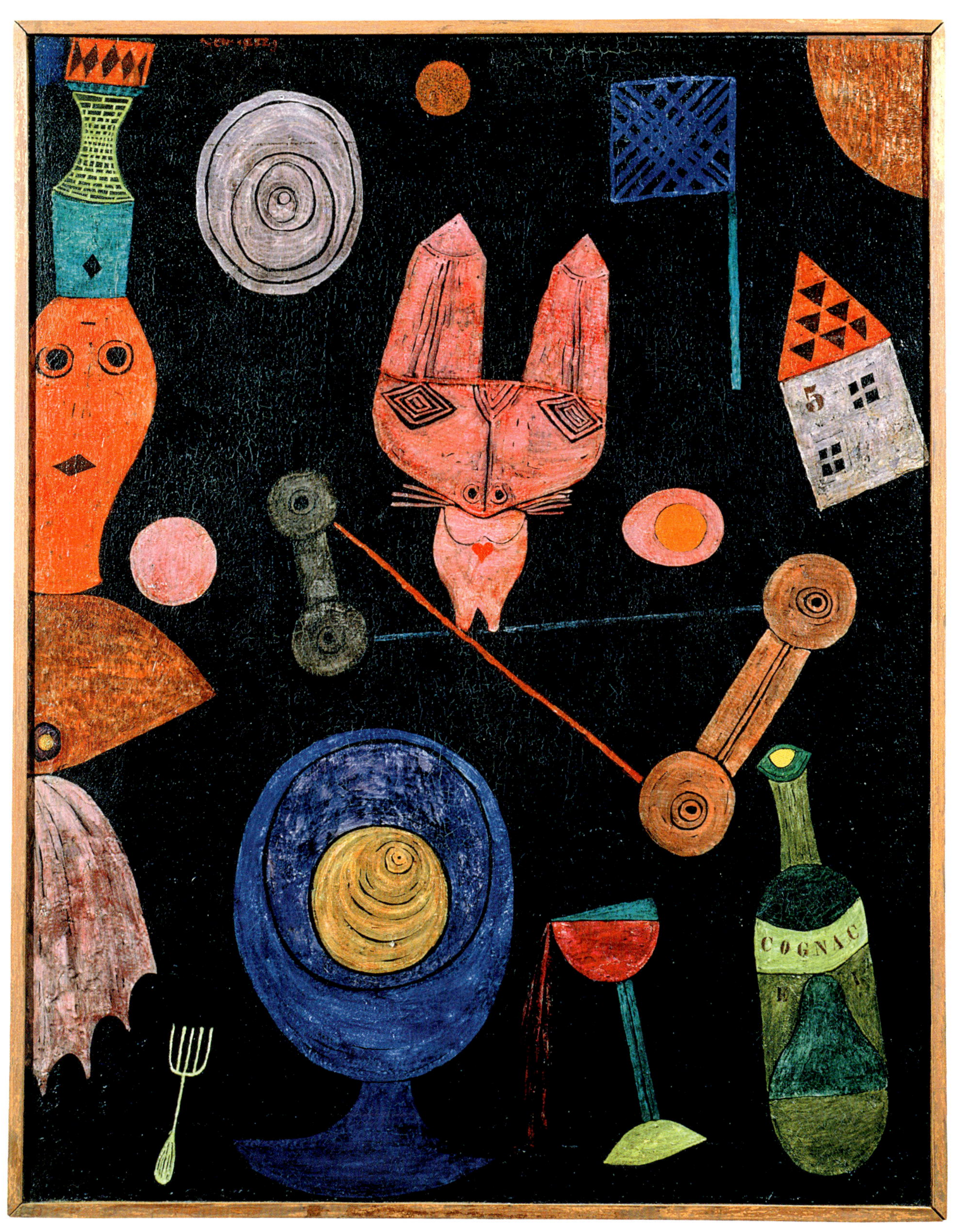

52 **BUNTE MAHLZEIT**, 1928.29
[Colorful Meal]

Oil and watercolor on canvas
31⅞ x 26⅜ inches (81 x 67 cm)
Private Collection, courtesy Neue Galerie New York

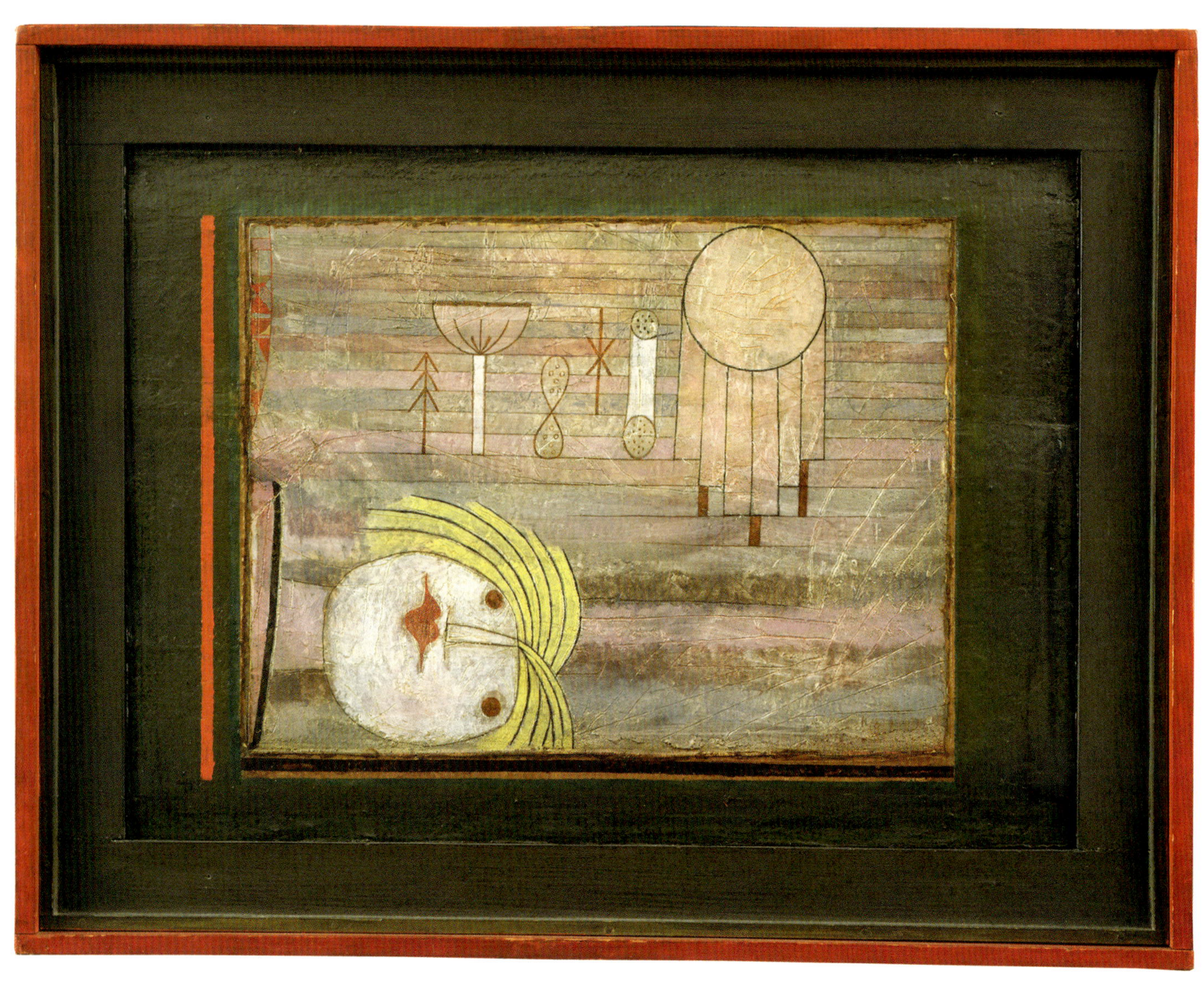

53 **GABEN FÜR "J."**, 1928.212
[Gifts for "J."]

Oil on chalk-primed canvas, mounted on wood
15¾ x 22 inches (40 x 55.9 cm)
The Museum of Modern Art New York
Gift of James Thrall Soby, 1092.69

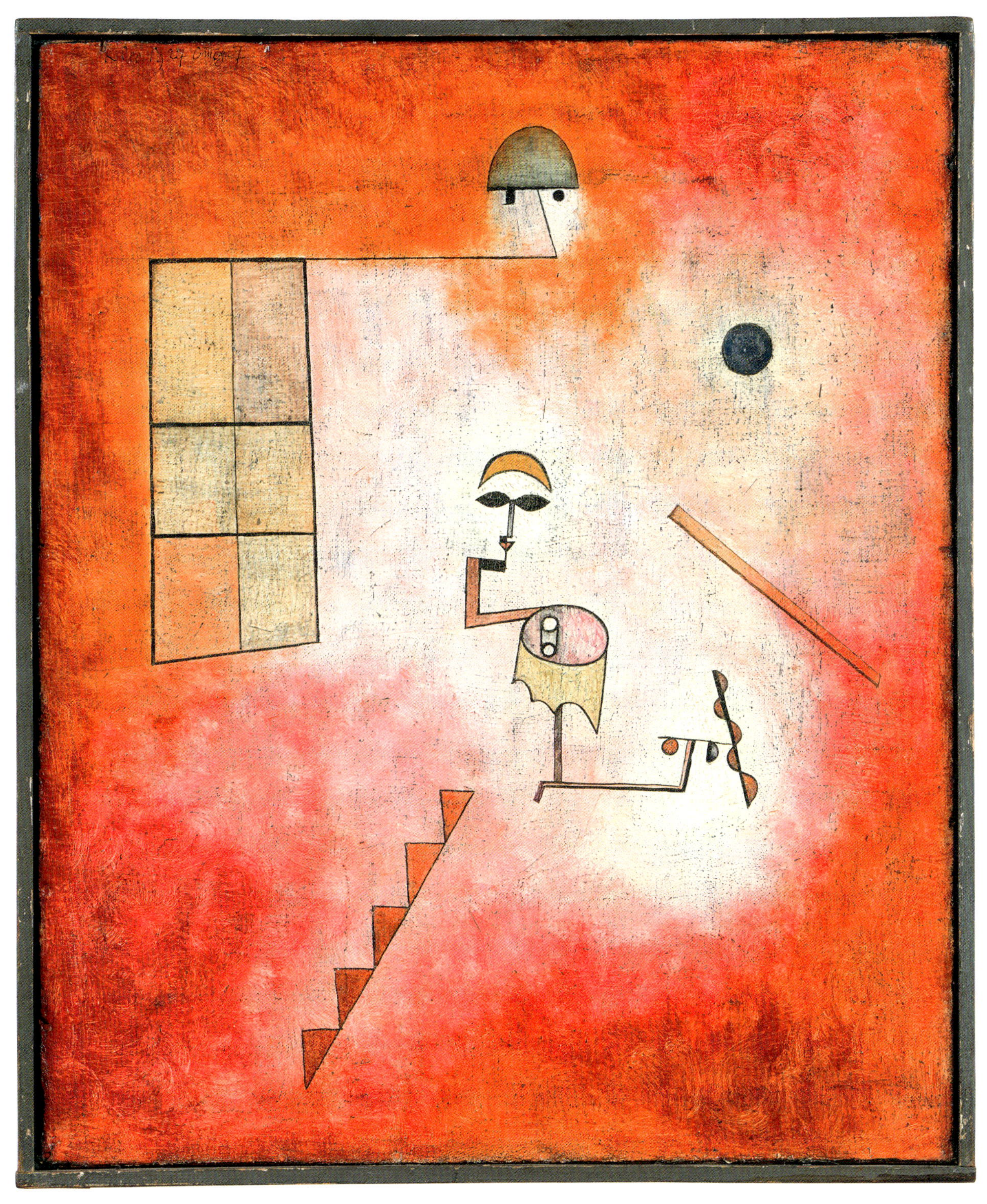

54 **ZAUBER KUNST STÜCK**, 1927.297
[Conjuring Trick]

Oil and watercolor on cardboard, with original painted strip frame
19⅝ x 16½ inches (49.8 x 41.8 cm)
Philadelphia Museum of Art
The Louise and Walter Arensberg Collection, 1950

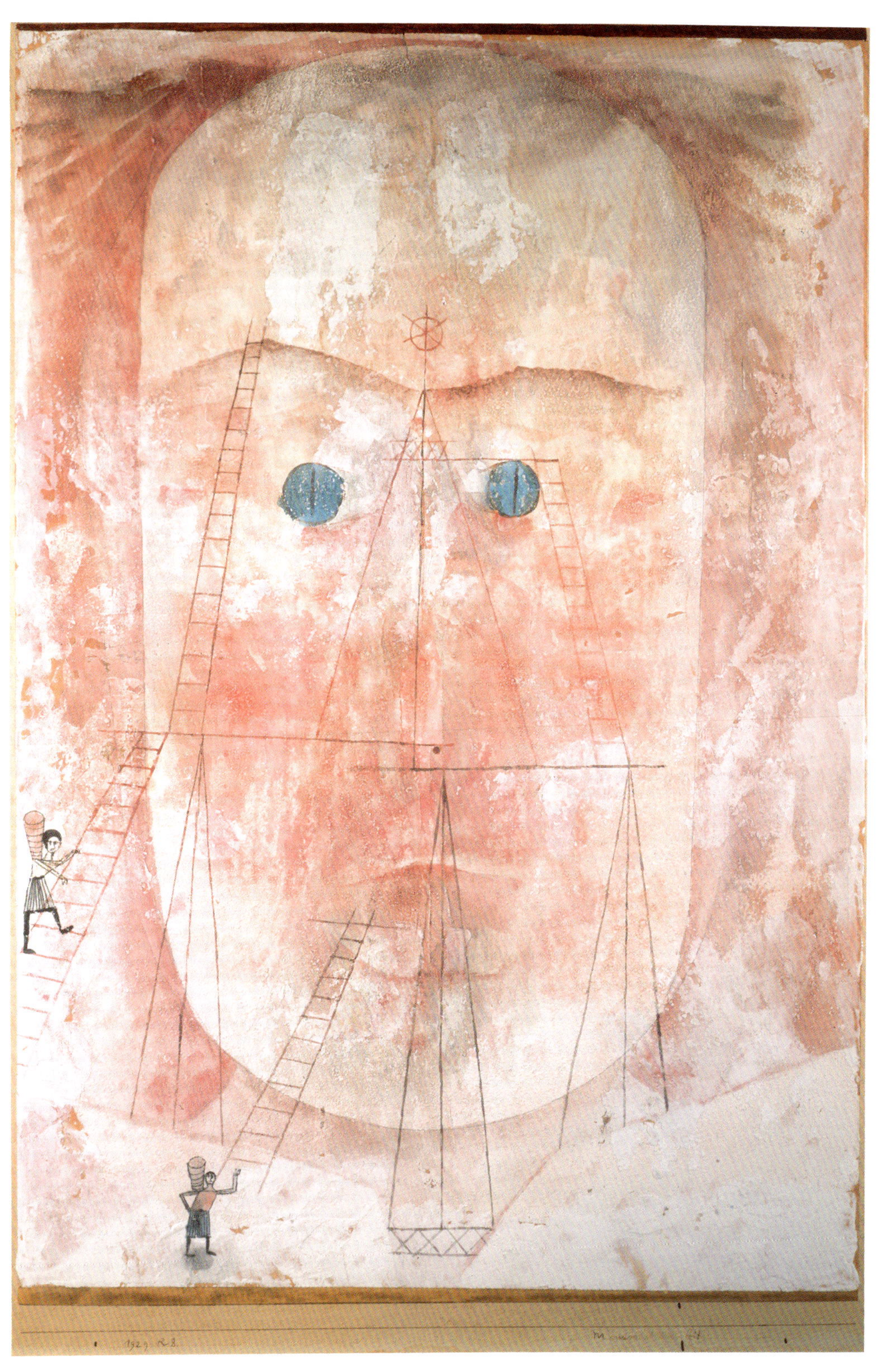

55 **MONUMENT IN ARBEIT**, 1929.88
[Monument Under Construction]

Watercolor on plaster-primed paper, with watercolor and
pen margins above and below, mounted on cardboard
22⅛ x 15¼ inches (56.3 x 38.6 cm)
Collection of Michael and Judy Steinhardt, New York

Around 1927–28 Klee based a number of works, which incorporated pure abstraction, landscape forms, and whimsical depictions of figures, on the design principle of progressions. In a lecture at the Bauhaus, Klee called this formal principle "the graduated accentuation of line." He then distinguished various types of such accentuation, including "linear nerve emphasis or incarnation of line" and "constructive broadening of line with strict integration into the construction thread." In the former, the "body" of the line expands: "in incarnation: the center line as skeleton."[1]

Klee employed this design method while working on the pen drawing *Nicht ohne Herz*. In this work he placed a loose arrangement of varied motifs on the sheet—three tables, a chair, a pendulum clock, a dog, a birdcage atop a column, a heart, and what might be a heavenly body. The objects for the most part are depicted three-dimensionally, but they do not share a common perspective focus. Despite their "incarnation," they seem weightless and transparent, aligned in casual groupings from left to right, never touching each other. The result of this unusual arrangement of spooky objects is the creation of a slightly bewildering, fascinating space.

In another drawing, *Möbelsammlung [Furniture Collection]* (1928.43), which he also composed using the principle of "incarnation of line," we find various chairs, a divan, stools, and tables that seem to be obvious parodies or caricatures of Bauhaus furniture. Beginning in 1925–26, Marcel Breuer had developed a number of epoch-making furniture designs using tubular steel, and he gave Klee, probably in 1926, a precursor of the tubular-steel B5 chair, which is still among his effects. By 1927 the new tubular pieces were found throughout the Bauhaus, as we see from historic interior photographs. As Mathias Remmele wrote, "tubular steel became *the* modernist material in furniture design. It perfectly conformed to the machine aesthetic being proclaimed as a guiding principle. It represented technology, industry, serial production, standardization, functionality, and hygiene—all of them central concepts and values of the international modern movement."[2]

In this context, one senses in Klee's work a gentle spoof on the new Bauhaus furniture. The furnishings in this drawing, by contrast, are the result of organic growth, of "incarnation." With the double negative of the title *Nicht ohne Herz [Not Without Heart]*, Klee even further emphasized the need for a measure of human warmth in the creation of such objects. In Klee's contribution to a celebration of the artist Emil Nolde on his sixtieth birthday, published in 1927, he concluded: "Every region shapes and colors its secrets, and the hands that produce them differ greatly, depending on the sphere of thought they have mastered. But the heart of creation, beating for all, supplies all regions."[3]

Osamu Okuda

1. Paul Klee, "Pädagogischer Nachlass," lecture notes, M11/79, Zentrum Paul Klee, Bern, Switzerland.

2. Mathias Remmele, "Marcel Breuer, Design und Architektur—Eine Einführung," in *Marcel Breuer, Design und Architektur*, exh. cat. (Weil am Rhein, Germany: Vitra Design Museum, 2003), 19.

3. Paul Klee, *Schriften: Rezensionen und Aufsätze*, ed. Christian Geelhaar (Cologne: DuMont, 1976), 129.

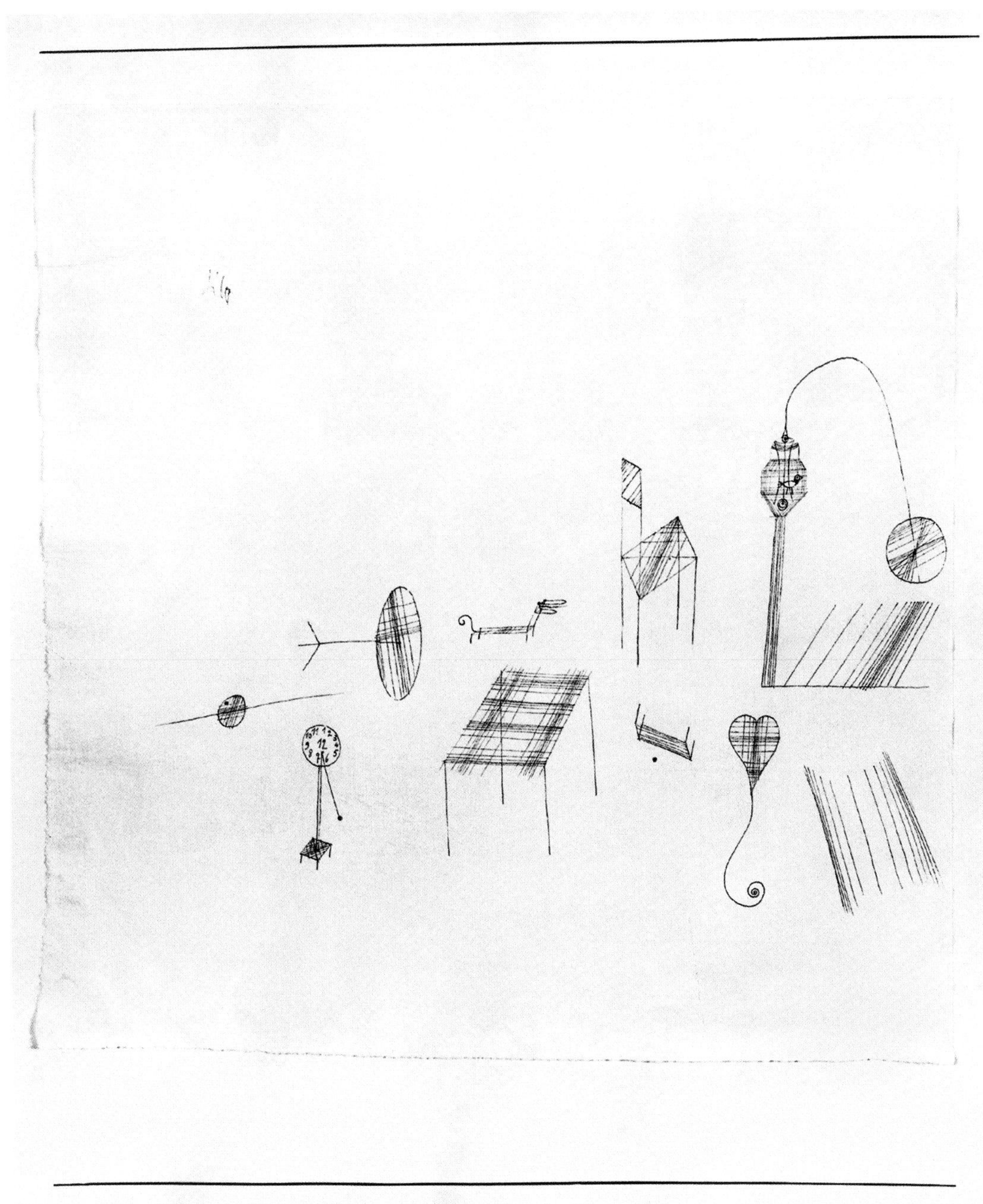

56 **NICHT OHNE HERZ**, 1928.33
[Not without Heart]

Pen on paper, mounted with glue spots on cardboard
12 x 11½ inches (30.5 x 29.2 cm)
Private Collection

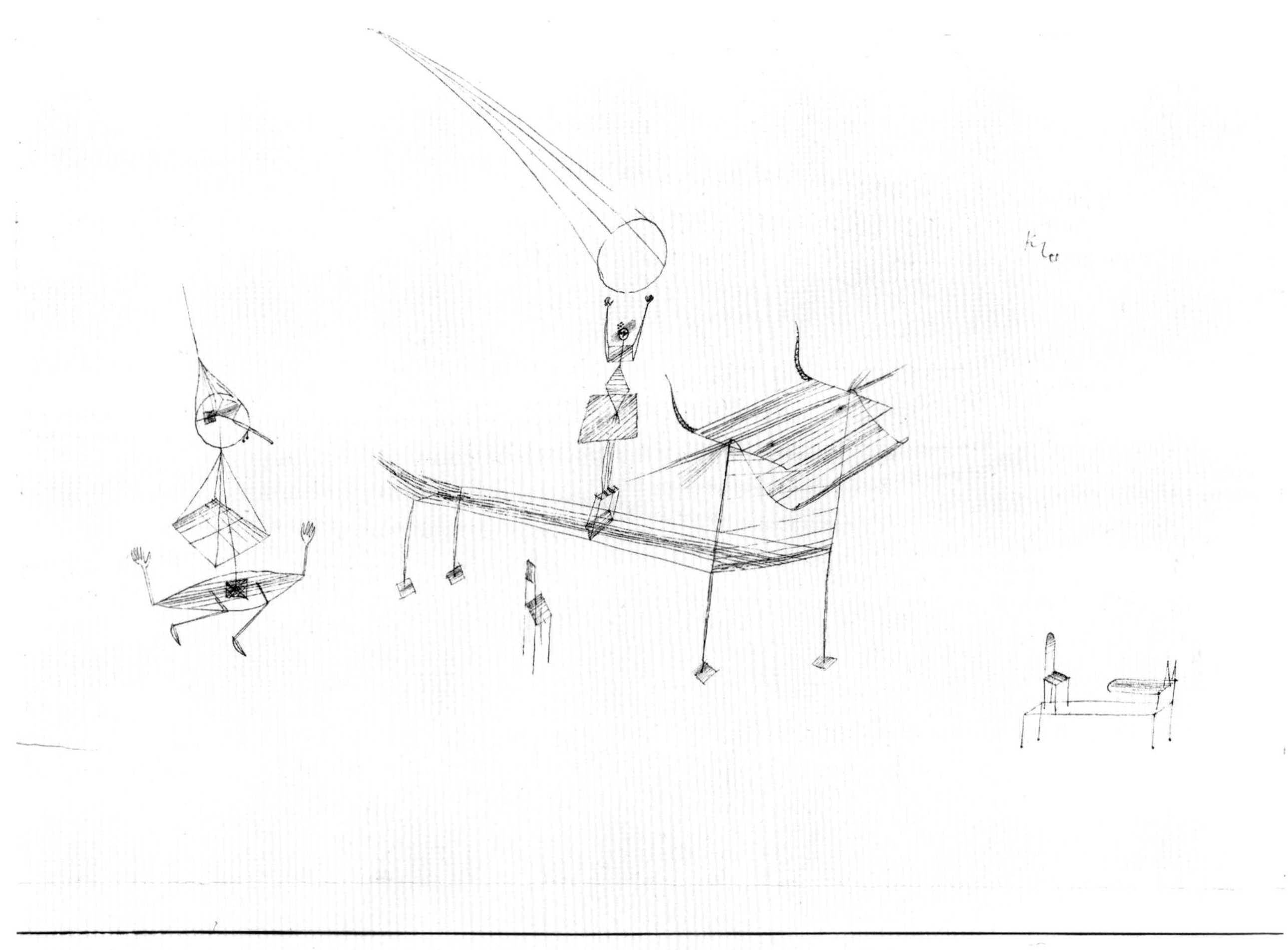

57 **SPUKENDE GAUKLER**, 1928.42
[Haunting Entertainers]

Pen on paper, mounted with glue spots on cardboard
11¾ x 18 inches (29.9 x 45.8 cm)
Courtesy Calder Foundation, New York

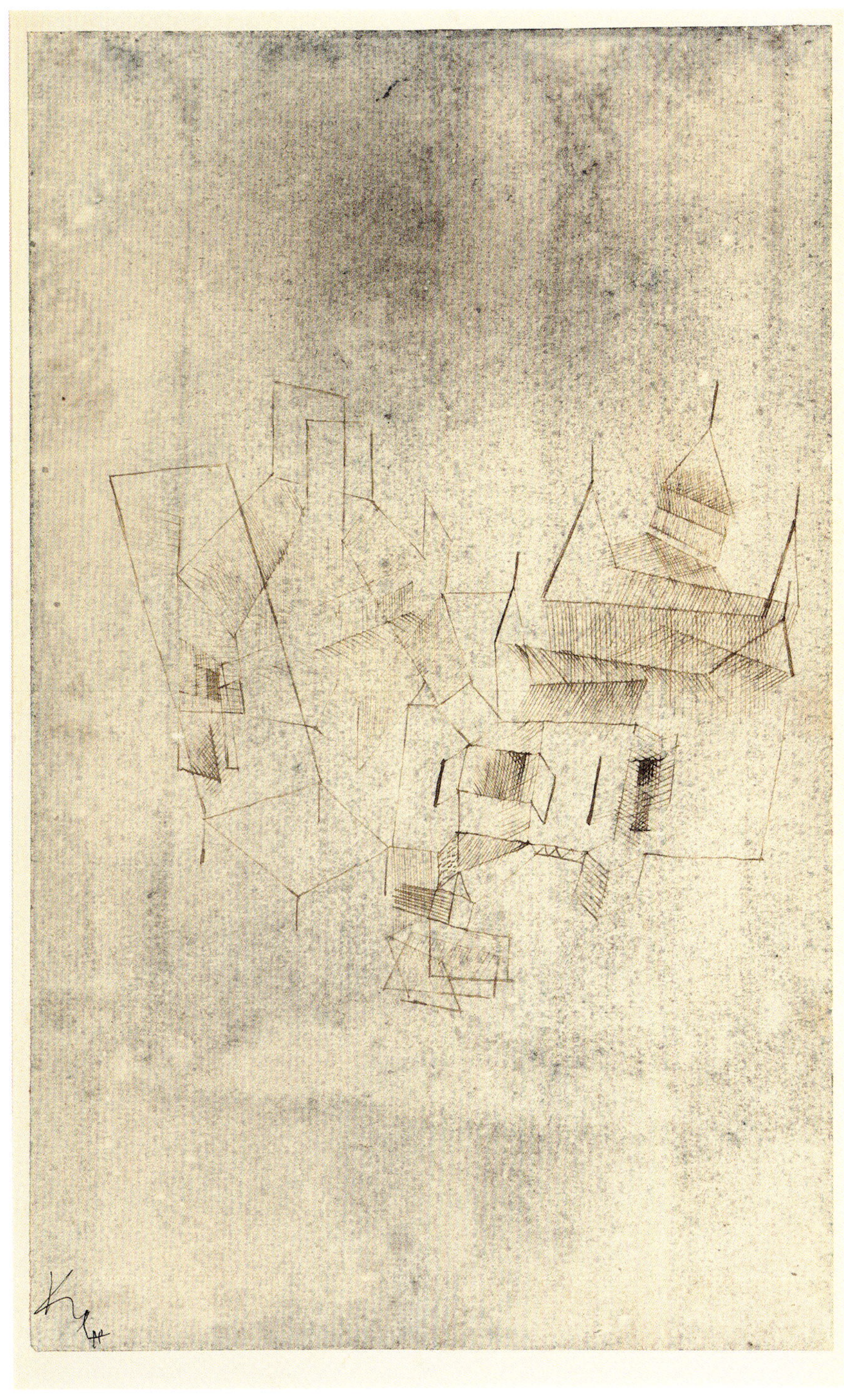

58   **BEBEN**, 1929.290
     [Quake]

Pen and sprayed watercolor on paper, mounted on cardboard
13 x 8 inches (33 x 20.5 cm)
Collection of the Tobin Foundation for Theatre Arts, long-term loan
to the Marion Koogler McNay Art Museum, San Antonio, R69.17

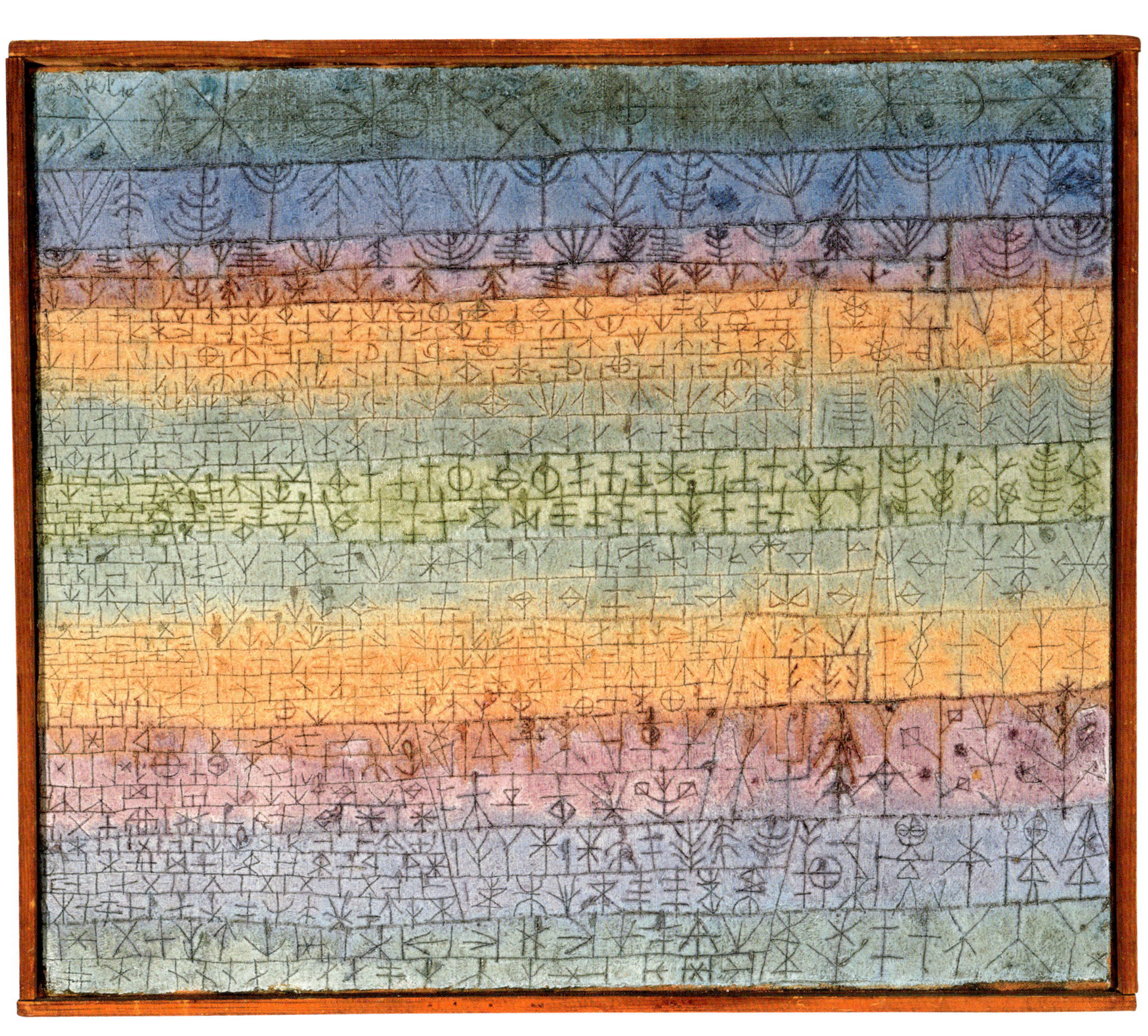

59 **JUNGE PFLANZUNG**, 1929.98
[Young Plantation]

Oil on primed canvas, with original strip frame
17 ¼ x 20 ⅝ inches (43.9 x 52.4 cm)
The Phillips Collection, Washington, D.C., 1000

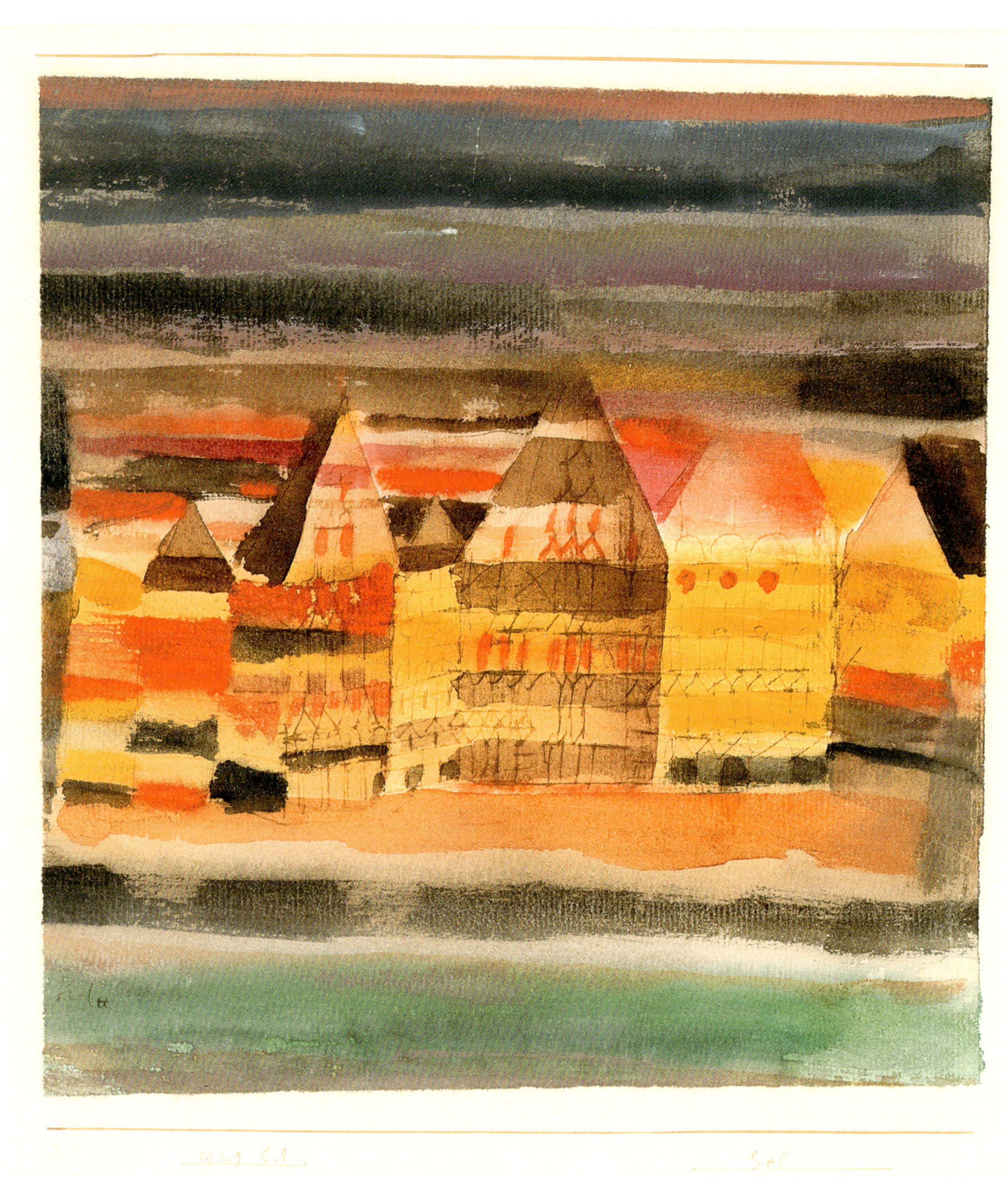

60 **SEL**, 1929.128

Watercolor and pen on paper, mounted on cardboard
9¼ x 8⅞ inches (23.5 x 22.5 cm)
The Museum of Fine Arts, Houston, Gift of Miss Ima Hogg, 39.110

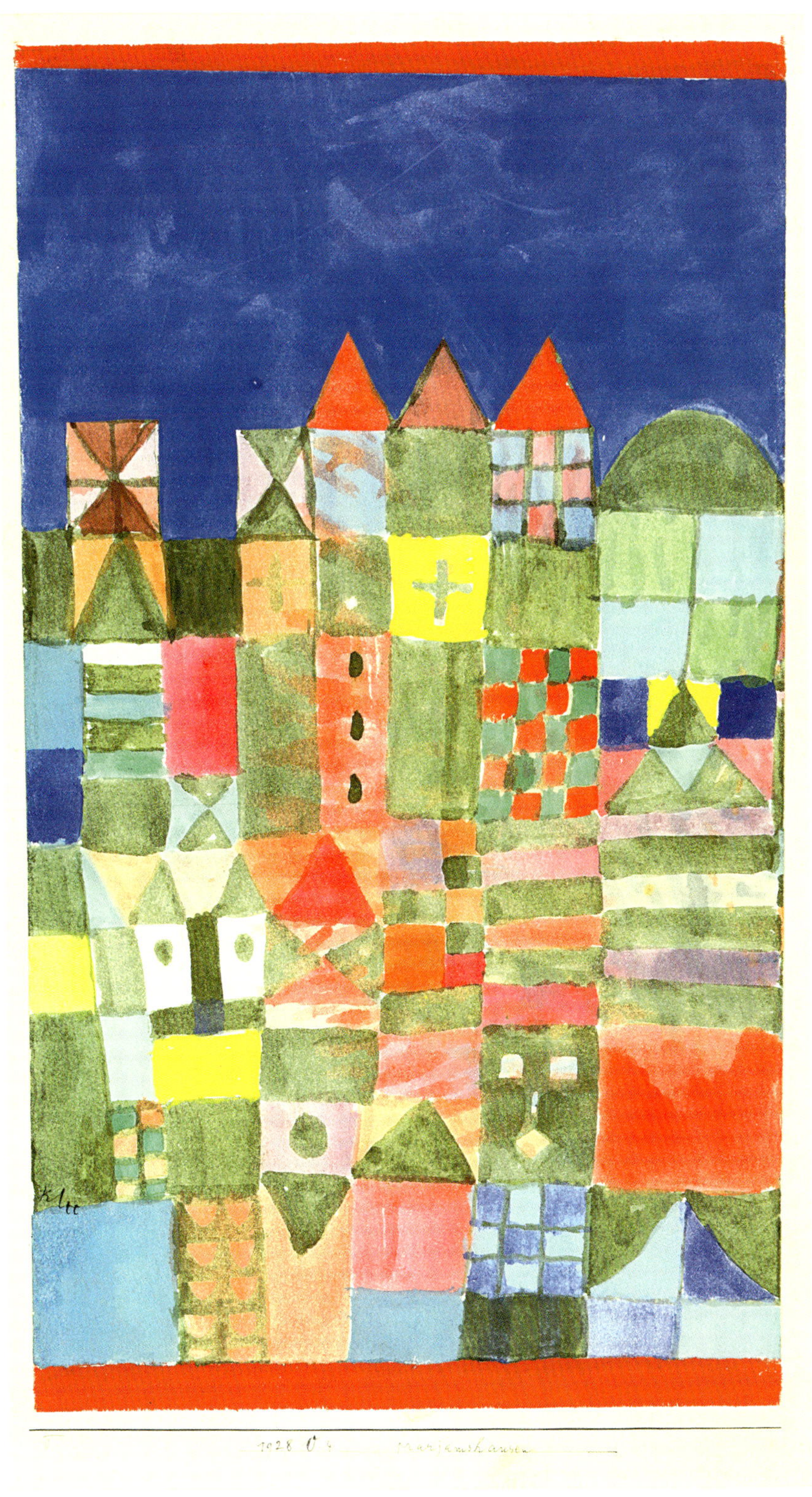

61 **MARJAMHAUSEN**, 1928.54

Watercolor on paper, with watercolor and pen margin above and
below, mounted on cardboard
14⅛ x 8 inches (36 x 20.5 cm)
The Museum of Fine Arts, Houston, Gift of Miss Ima Hogg, 39.111

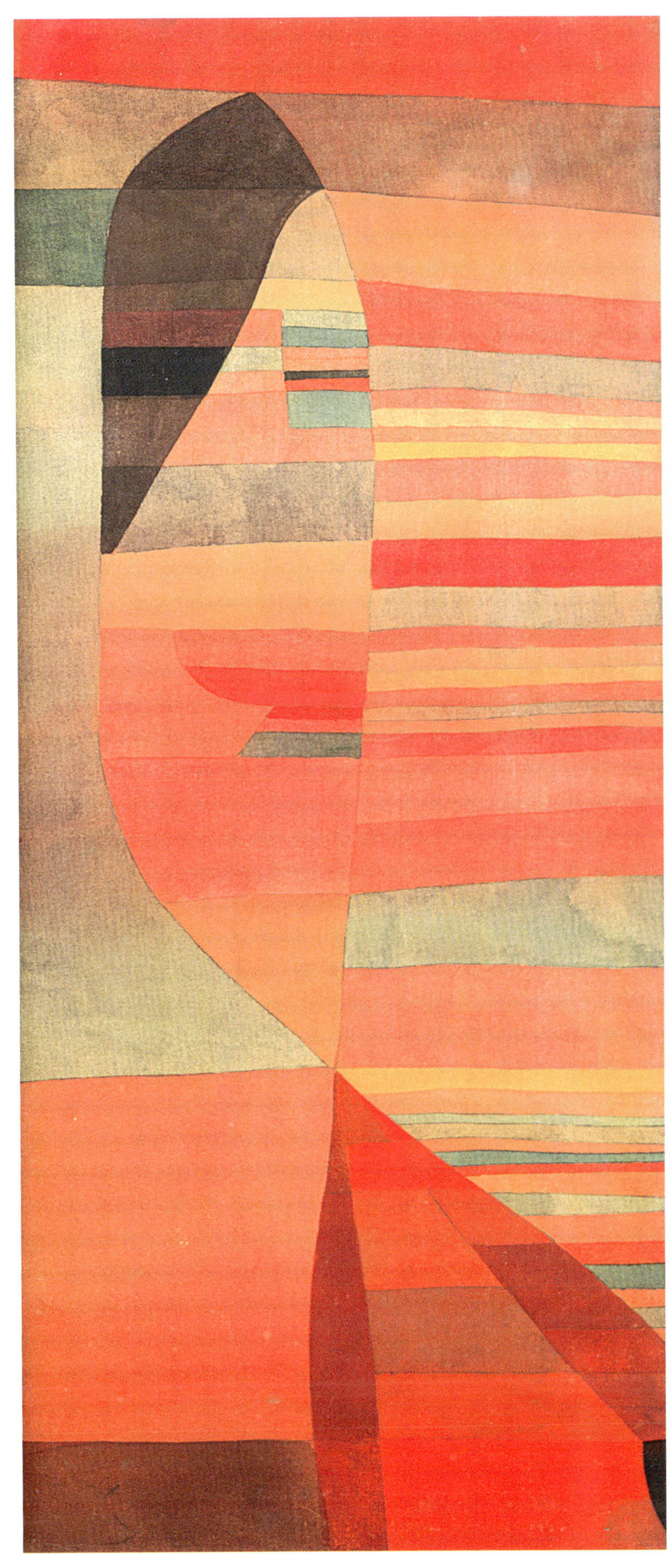

62 **ORPHEUS**, 1929.257

Watercolor on cotton, mounted on plywood
19¾ x 9½ inches (50.2 x 24.2 cm)
Private Collection

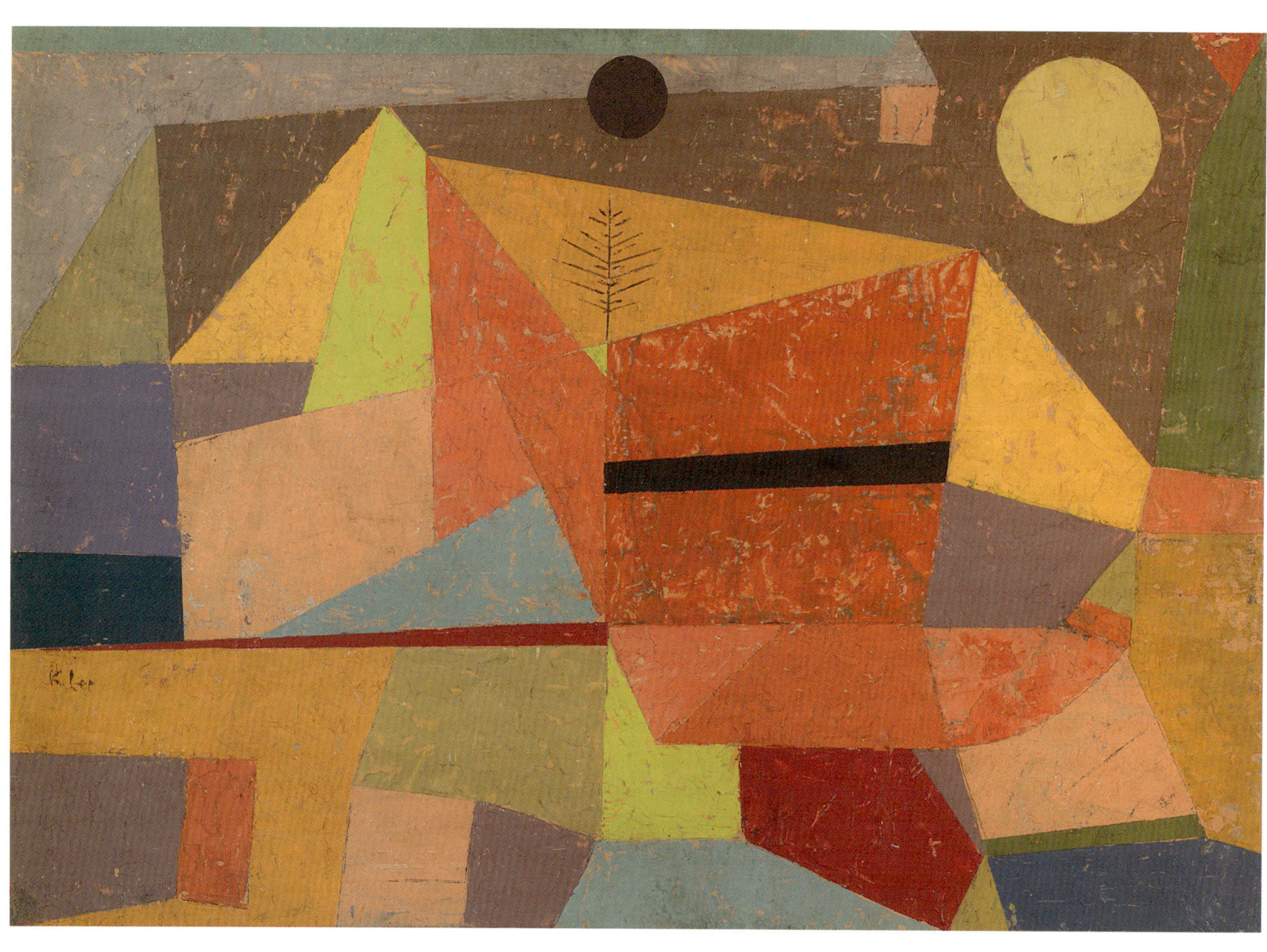

63 **HEITERE GEBIRGSLANDSCHAFT**, 1929.134
[Bright Mountain Landscape]

Oil on plywood
17¼ x 24⅞ inches (43.9 x 63.1 cm)
Yale University Art Gallery, New Haven, Connecticut
Katharine Ordway Collection, 1980.12.22

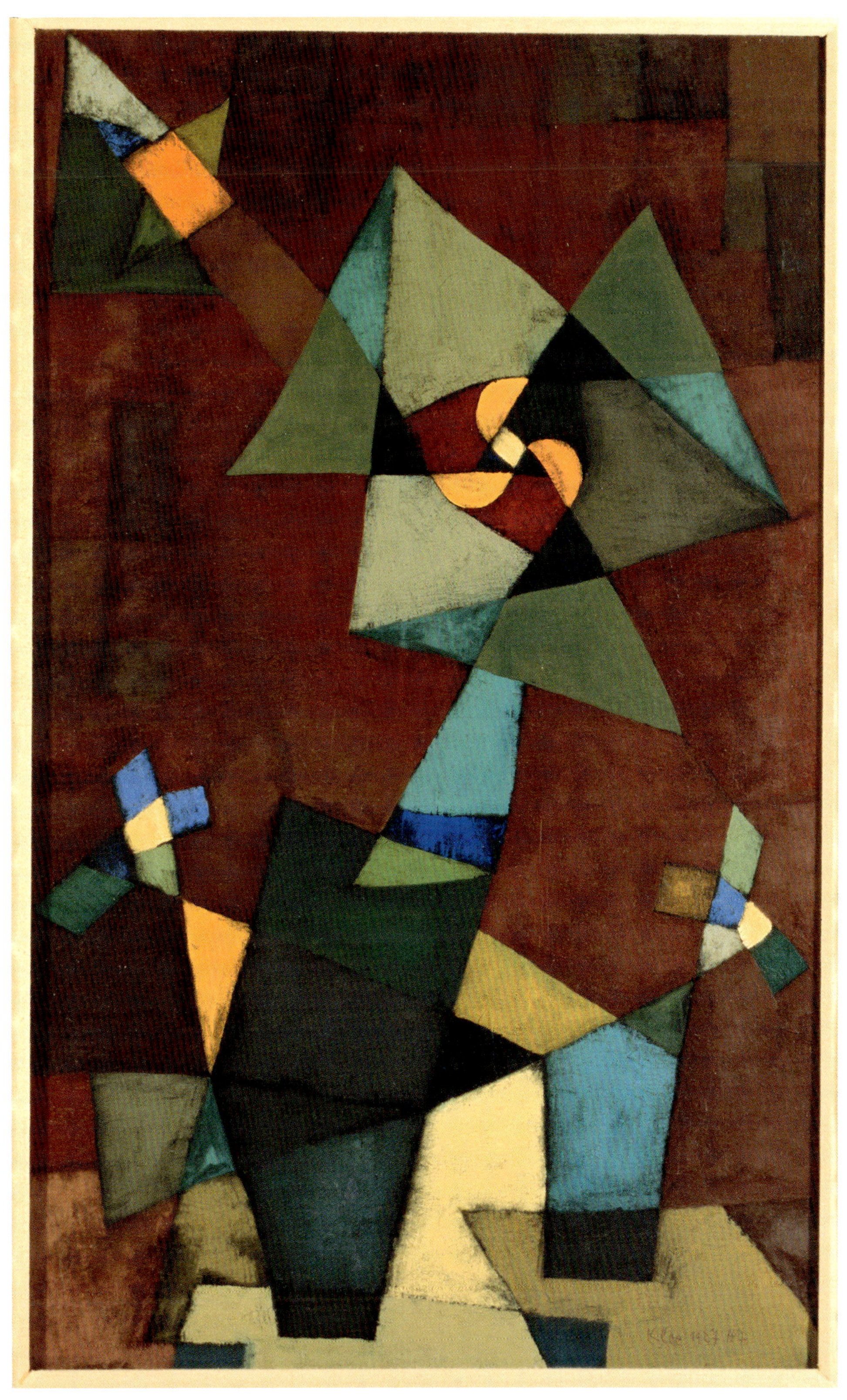

64   **MEGÁNTHEMUM**, 1927.177

Oil on wood, with original strip frame
28⅞ x 18 inches (73.3 x 45.7 cm)
Frelinghuysen Morris Foundation, Lenox, Massachusetts

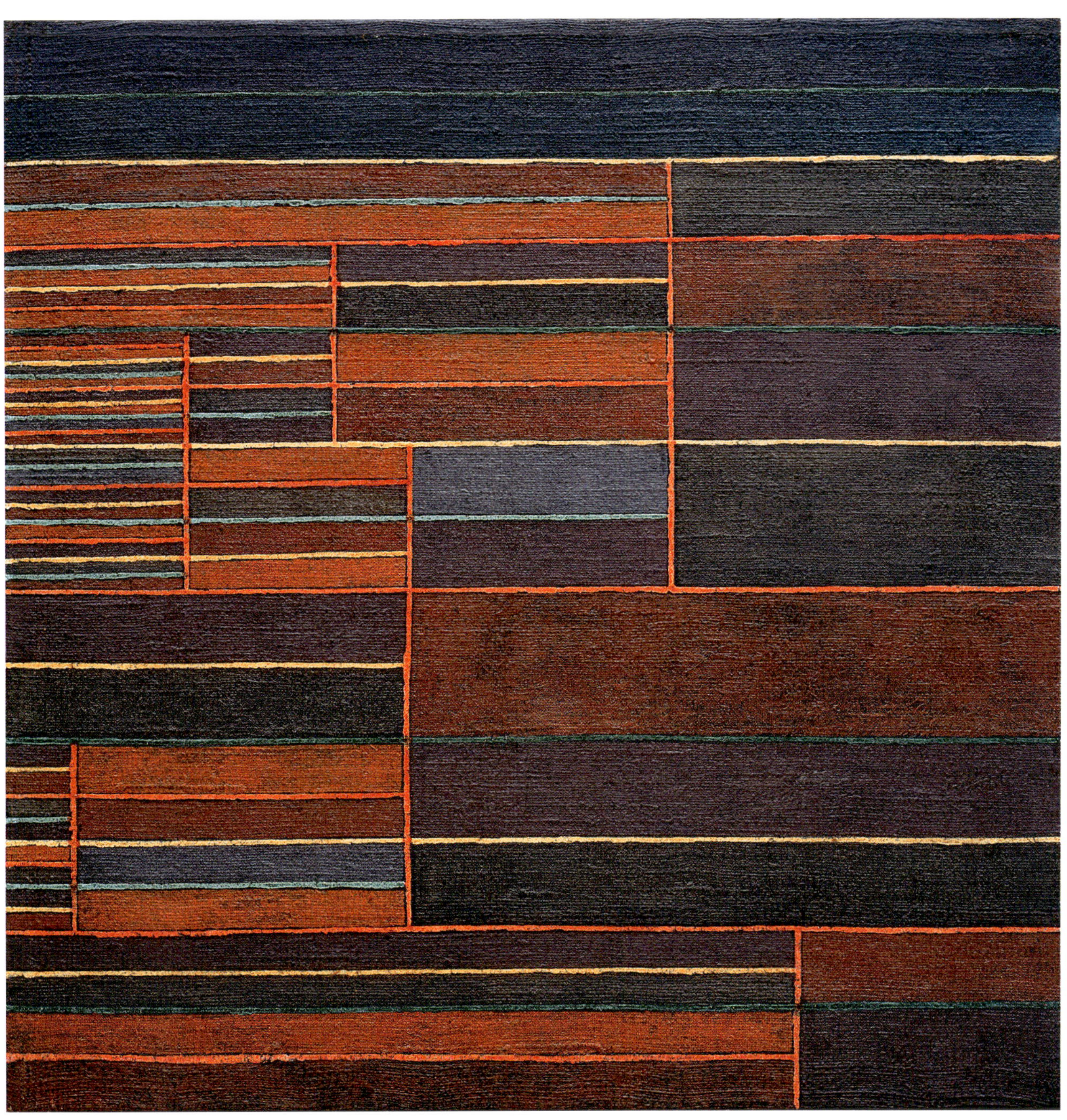

65 IN DER STRÖMUNG SECHS SCHWELLEN, 1929.92
[In the Current Six Weirs]

Oil and tempera on canvas
16⅝ x 16⅝ inches (42.2 x 42.2 cm)
Solomon R. Guggenheim Museum, New York, 67.1842

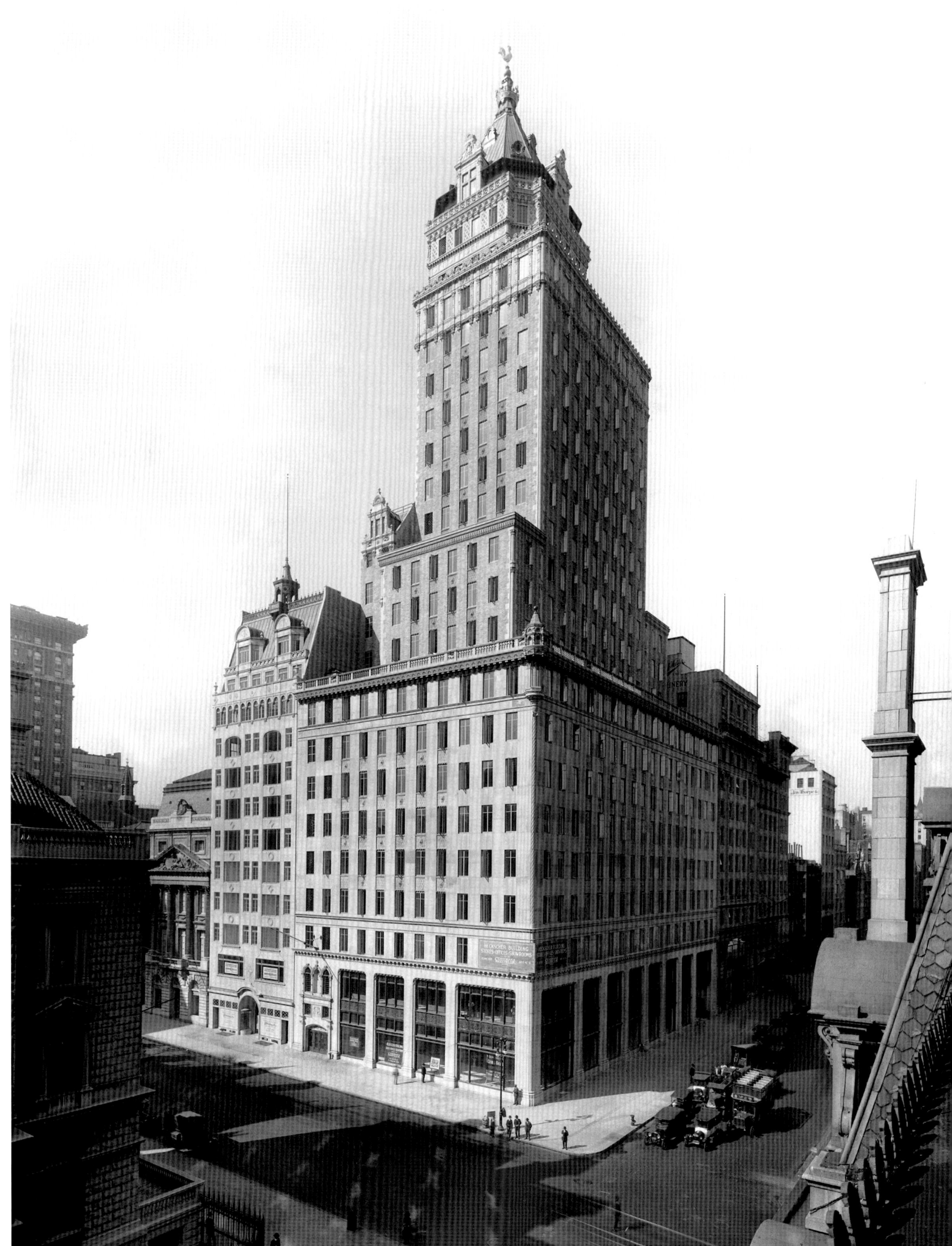

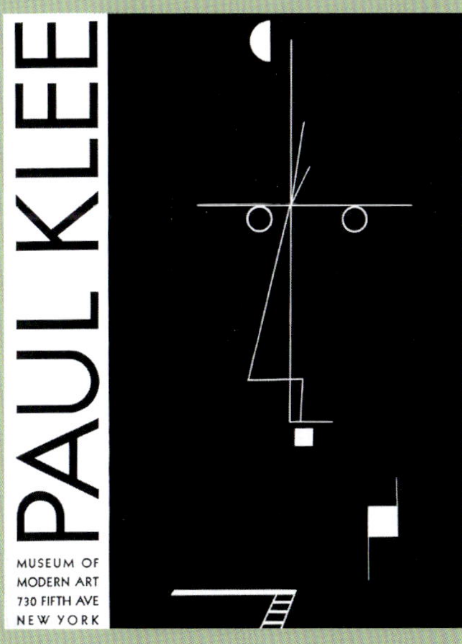
PAUL KLEE
MUSEUM OF
MODERN ART
730 FIFTH AVE
NEW YORK

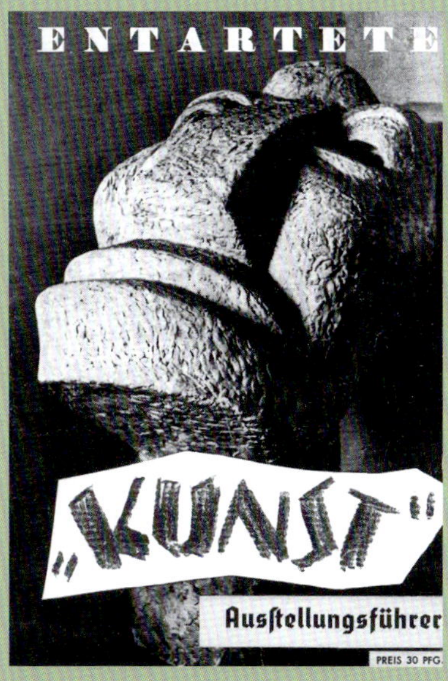
ENTARTETE
„KUNST"
Ausstellungsführer
PREIS 30 PFG.

Anticipating a Great Market:
Klee and America 1930–1933

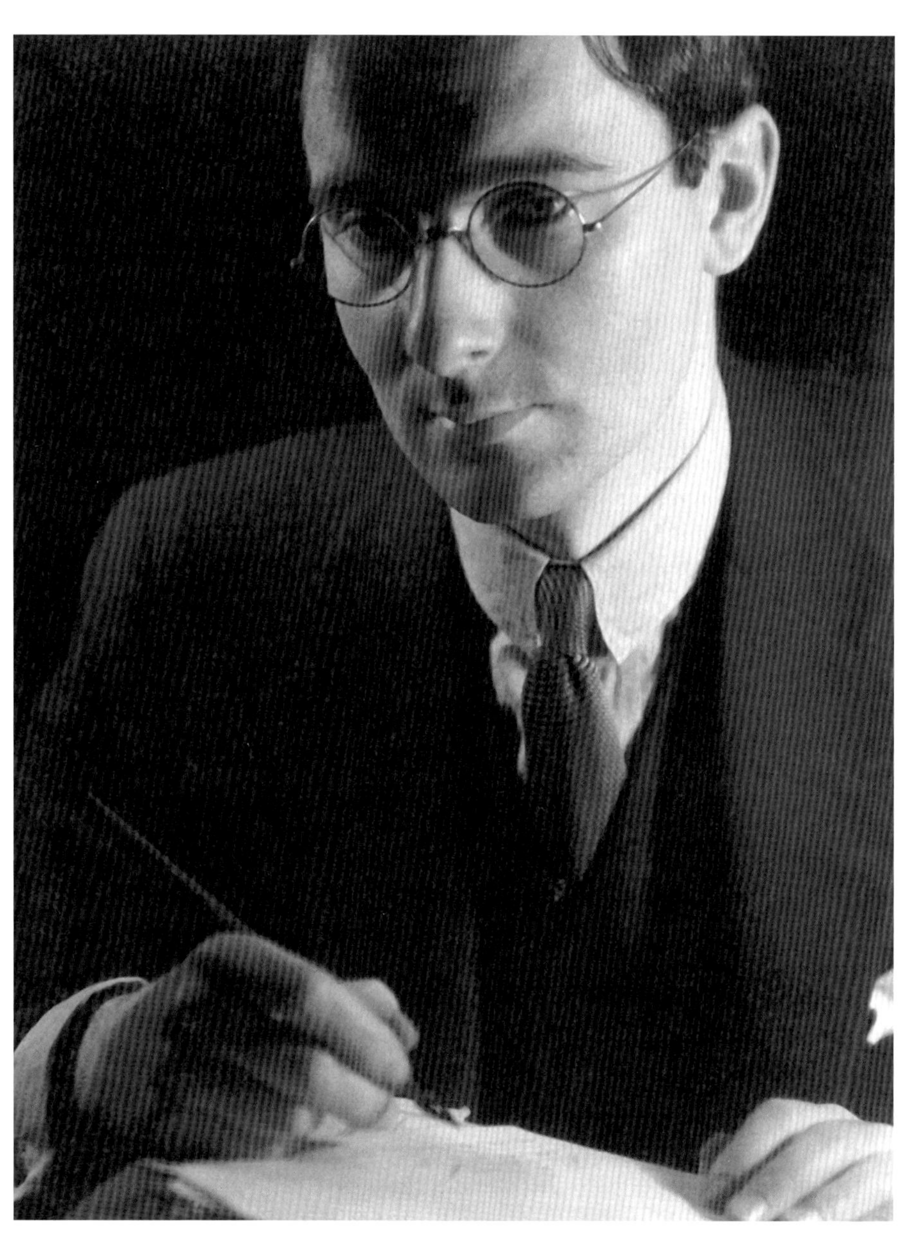

I prophesy a great market for you in America.
    —Galka Scheyer to Paul Klee, June 1, 1930

The years 1929 and 1930 marked a turning point in Paul Klee's career as an artist, both in Europe and in America. On December 18, 1929, Klee turned fifty years old, and to commemorate this occasion, large exhibitions of his work were held in Germany, first at the Galerie Alfred Flechtheim in Berlin (October 20–November 15) and a few months later at the Galerie Neue Kunst Fides in Dresden (February 1–beginning of March). Soon thereafter, the Nationalgalerie in Berlin presented Klee's work in two different exhibitions: in April the museum included Klee among a group of living artists in an exhibition of new acquisitions, and it simultaneously opened a monographic exhibition with fifty-six watercolors and drawings by Klee, all lent by the private collector Otto Ralfs from Braunschweig, Germany. This was the second one-person show the Nationalgalerie had offered Klee, the first one having occurred in 1923. The institution had collected works by Klee since 1923,[1] several of which would eventually play an unexpectedly important role in Klee's reception in America.

Toward the end of the 1920s, Klee's art was starting to receive wider recognition abroad, especially in France and Belgium. In 1929 Christian Zervos had published the first French monograph on Klee in his *Cahiers d'Art*, and in 1930 the French poet René Crevel, who was a member of the Surrealist group, published a small book on Klee in which he celebrated the artist's work as the quintessential expression of what he and his colleagues were aiming for. Crevel's monograph was part of the popular series Les peintres nouveaux [The New Painters], making Klee the first German artist to be included in that series. Klee's success in France and Belgium, and his popularity with key figures and movements in Paris and Brussels, including Marcel Duchamp, would eventually have a strong impact on his reception in the United States. Klee's breakthrough on the international art scene became a fact in 1930 when Alfred H. Barr Jr., the director of The Museum of Modern Art, New York (fig. 27), decided to present a Klee exhibition. Thus Klee became the first living European artist (followed two years later by Henri Matisse) to have a one-person show at the Modern.

At the same time, paradoxically, signs of unsettling developments in Germany were calling into question Klee's success, the world in which he had established himself, and the basis of his growing reputation. By 1929 the situation at the Staatliches Bauhaus in Dessau had been overshadowed by ideological controversies, and Klee was growing increasingly frustrated with his role as a teacher. He started looking for another job, and on April 1, 1931, he resigned from the Bauhaus and took up a position teaching at the more conservative Staatliche Kunstakademie in Düsseldorf. Klee decided, however, to keep his main residence in Dessau, where he and his wife, Lily, lived in one of the "Meisterhäuser" with Vasily and Nina Kandinsky as neighbors, and to commute to Düsseldorf, where he taught for two weeks each month. Klee's reluctance to permanently relocate to Düsseldorf drew suspicion from both the authorities in the Ministry of Culture and some of his new colleagues. This geographical ambivalence, working and living in two different places, seemed to mirror his vacillating status

---

Fig. 27
Alfred H. Barr Jr., director of the The Museum of Modern Art, New York, c. 1930.

Page 136
Heckscher Building, 730 Fifth Avenue at 57th Street, New York, 1921, site of the first American exhibition of Paul Klee works at the Société Anonyme (1924) and of "Paul Klee" (1930), his first one-person exhibition at The Museum of Modern Art.

Page 137
Cover of *Paul Klee*, exhibition catalogue, The Museum of Modern Art (New York: 1930).

Cover of the *Entartete Kunst* exhibition brochure, Verlag für Kultur- und Wirtschaftswerbung (Berlin: 1937).

and newly uncertain future as an artist. And indeed, as is now well known, political developments in Germany before long would undermine the security of his new position in Düsseldorf.

In January 1930 the National Socialist politician Wilhelm Frick became Minister of Internal Affairs and Education in Thuringia, the state where the Bauhaus had been founded in 1919 and where it remained until its move to Dessau in 1925. Soon the first signs of the democratic Weimar Republic's dramatic decline appeared: in March 1930 Chancellor Hermann Müller's coalition government resigned after failing to reach a compromise to address Germany's unemployment, social unrest, and economic crisis. During the run-up to the national elections in September 1930, Adolf Hitler offered a nationalistic, anti-Semitic, anti-reparations, anti-Versailles Treaty program, and as a result, the National Socialist party increased its seats in the German parliament (the Reichstag) from twelve to 107; the Social Democrats held 143 seats and the Communists had seventy-seven. After the elections, Nazi and Communist clashes, which had broken out in Berlin and other cities once the coalition government failed, continued. At the end of 1930, the evacuation from the Saar of the last Allied troops in Germany contributed to the country's increasing vacuum of power.

The worsening political climate translated immediately and directly into attacks on Klee and his like-minded colleagues. The Nazis launched their organized offensive against modern art in 1930, which included the "clearing" of the Schlossmuseum in Weimar, purging it of works by Klee, Kandinsky, and other contemporary artists. In hateful campaigns promulgated in local newspapers, Klee was charged with "mangelndes Deutschtum" ("lack of German patriotism") and "Kunstbolschewismus" ("art bolshevism").[2] Although not only Klee but many other artists and their supporters as well underestimated the power of these attacks, the situation was particularly delicate in his case because Klee's reputation was at least partly based on his success abroad, especially in France.

Klee's career between 1930 and 1933 must be seen in this dramatically conflictive context: just as he was receiving his most significant international recognition to date, political and socioeconomic developments in Germany were emerging that would steadily undermine and eventually destroy his standing as an artist. However, even as Klee's critical foundation crumbled in Europe, his reputation began spreading quickly in America.

ALFRED H. BARR JR. AND THE KLEE EXHIBITION AT THE MUSEUM OF MODERN ART IN 1930

In 1929 Barr was appointed founding director of The Museum of Modern Art, an institution that would play a critical role in introducing American audiences to European avant-garde art. Barr had met Klee for the first time in 1927 at the Bauhaus in Dessau, and his positioning of Klee's work within the modernist agenda of the museum would be crucial for Klee's reception in America.

Barr's early interest in the international aspects of the European avant-garde, particularly as expressed in the most recent movements in Germany and Russia, made him unique among American art historians of his generation. His friendship with the German art dealer J. B. Neumann, whom Barr first met in 1926, had fueled his interest in German art. Barr developed a close relationship with

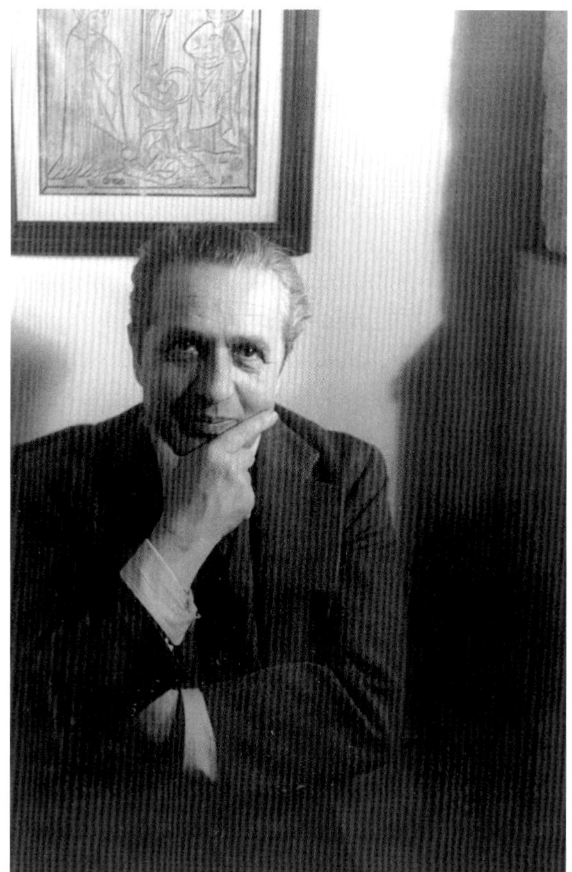

Fig. 28
J. B. Neumann, c. 1948–52.

Neumann, an unusual personality in New York's art world at the time, whose idealism and passion for contemporary art far exceeded his mercurial talents[3] (fig. 28).

By the end of the 1920s, encouraged by his partner in Berlin, Alfred Flechtheim, and by Klee's success in Europe, Neumann decided to "launch the first major Klee exhibition in America" at his New York gallery, The New Art Circle. Both German and American newspapers announced that the large Klee retrospective then at Flechtheim's gallery in Berlin would be on view in Neumann's gallery in early 1930. Ultimately, however, Neumann sought a broader audience for the exhibition and proposed it to Barr for The Museum of Modern Art, who seems to have accepted immediately.[4] The content of the show in New York, however, differed considerably from the earlier plan: in the end fewer than thirty works from Flechtheim's large retrospective in Berlin appeared in the exhibition at the Modern.[5]

The Exhibition and Barr's Writing

The presentation of Klee's work was The Museum of Modern Art's fourth exhibition in a lineup that included shows for two sculptors and another painter: Wilhelm Lehmbruck, Aristide Maillol, and Max Weber. Astonishingly, Klee thus became the first living European artist to receive a one-person exhibition at what was at the time the most highly regarded institution of modern art in the United States.

The catalogue for the exhibition listed sixty-three works—most, but not all, sent from Germany. Assembled by Neumann and Barr, the exhibition strongly focused on Klee's years at the Bauhaus in Weimar (1920–1925) and Dessau (since 1926), with only two works dating from before 1920—Barr borrowed both of these early works from private collections in New York.[6] The owners of two additional works in the show, Jere Abbott (fig. 29) and Philip Johnson, were close friends of Barr's who had only recently purchased Klee's work, largely motivated by Barr's interest in the artist. Barr's role in developing early support for Klee in America is evident in his influence on both collectors, who played significant roles in the early years of the museum.

Johnson had entered Barr's inner circle in the late 1920s, and Barr helped shape Johnson's knowledge of, and taste in, modern art and architecture, as well as his early interests as a collector. Johnson acquired his first Klee in 1929, most likely the watercolor

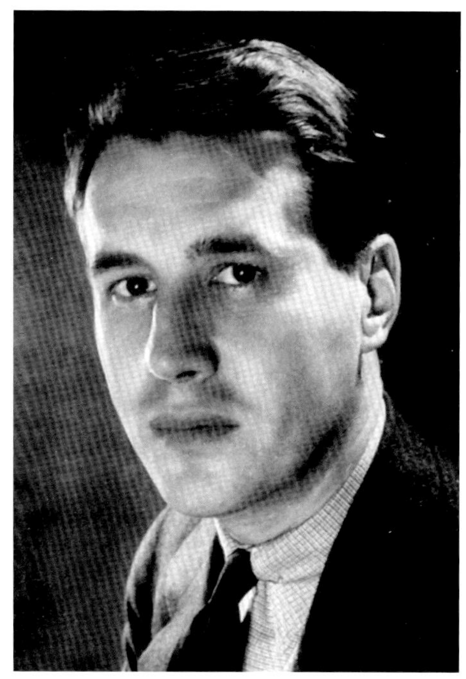

Heilige Inseln [Sacred Islands] (1926.6, pl. 40), which he later donated to The Museum of Modern Art's collection. This was the first work of art Johnson ever purchased for himself.[7] In the succeeding years, Johnson would acquire at least four more of Klee's works.[8]

Abbott had studied both at Princeton and with Barr's teacher Paul J. Sachs at Harvard, where he and Barr were roommates. He joined Barr on his trip to Europe in 1927–28, which featured long stays in Germany and Russia, and became Barr's associate director when The Museum of Modern Art opened in 1929. Abbott seems to have shared Barr's interest in Klee early on. He had spent considerable time in Europe in the 1920s and eventually purchased two Klees during his travels in Germany—*Bock [Billy-Goat]* (1925.198, pl. 48), which he anonymously lent for the 1930 show at the Modern,[9] and *Agricultur Versuchs anlage für den Spätherbst [Agricultural Research Station for Late Autumn]* (1922.137, pl. 16), which he acquired at a later date.[10]

Barr wrote the introduction to the exhibition catalogue. This text, though only four pages long, would shape the perception and interpretation of Klee's work in America for at least the next ten years. His straightforward essay followed the chronological structure of

Fig. 29
Jere Abbott, n.d.

Klee's biography, but Barr seemed especially keen to discuss the work in the broader context of key European avant-garde movements as well. According to Barr, an indefinable and idiosyncratic stylistic and thematic variety characterized Klee's work from early on. Despite the artist's solitary status, Barr made a point of stressing Klee's interest in, and connection with, movements and artists in Paris before and after the First World War.[11] He also emphasized Klee's seminal role for the Surrealist group, which allowed him to position Klee within the newest artistic movement: "His work is, however, perhaps the finest realization of their ideals of an art which appears to be purely of the imagination, untrammeled by reason or the outer world of empirical experience."[12]

Barr followed this with a description of Klee's personality based on their encounter in Dessau in 1927. The artist's quiet, inconspicuous demeanor, Barr observed, was in striking contrast to "his amazing art." The only evidence of eccentricity in the artist himself were the bizarre objects from nature that Klee kept in his studio and his interest in children's drawings. Barr assumed they enabled Klee, working at the school, "to break the logical severity of the [Walter] Gropius interior and Bauhaus furniture—and perhaps also serve as catalytics to Klee's creative activity."[13] Barr's focus on Klee's personality began a trend that would become commonplace in the critical reception of Klee's work in America.

Because The Museum of Modern Art in 1930 was still in the initial stages of defining its profile, it seemed consistent with that effort that Barr seized the opportunity to discuss Klee's work in the larger context of modernism. Barr's exhibition program at the museum articulated, especially in the first fifteen years, a decidedly international and multicultural vision of modernism, one formed in the intellectual and artistic circles in France, Germany, Holland, Belgium, Russia, and other European countries. Several trips to Europe in the 1920s had exerted a strong influence on Barr's intellectual formation and interests, enriching his definition of modernism. Barr was convinced that modernism as an international movement was an evolving, "open-ended phenomenon," capable of including both aesthetically and ideologically opposed tendencies (Constructivism and Surrealism, to name just two) as well as a broad range of non-Western cultures, which he referred to as "sources" of modernism.[14] Pointing to those sources, he positioned Klee's work within the context of children's drawings and drawings of the insane, then compared it with a wide range of prehistoric and non-Western art, including hieroglyphs, "paleolithic bone carvings, Eskimo drawings and Bushmen paintings, the pictographs of the American Indian," and "masks in theatrical and ethnographic museums."[15]

Barr's pluralistic view of modernism as open-ended and multifaceted, rather than as a strictly linear movement, was reflected both in The Museum of Modern Art's exhibition program as well as in his writings. It seems therefore consistent that Barr underscored Klee's artistic and intellectual independence—both his idiosyncratic art and his singular status within the modernist movement—which made it impossible to categorize him as an artist: "Indeed few living painters have been the object of so much speculation."[16] Barr saw Klee as an artist who "defies purism" and, like Giorgio de Chirico and Pablo Picasso, insists on his artistic freedom—an idea that was central to his own thinking. What Barr observed in Klee's work—its extraordinary artistic freedom, derived from the variety of Klee's inventions—was something that Barr had reflected about and cultivated for a number of years. Moreover, he seems to have advocated freedom for the artist at this historical moment for a very specific reason—namely, to counter "the growing isolationism and provincial conservatism in the United States."[17]

After a few brief observations on a number of pictures in the show, Barr concluded his essay by stressing the lack of precedent for Klee's "pure inventions": "Here are forms which live and breathe with convincing actuality, though their like has never been seen."[18] When Barr celebrated "Klee's infinitive variety" above all, he once again was advocating artistic and intellectual freedom. In this he seemed in agreement not only with the Surrealists, who celebrated Klee's art, but also with Duchamp, one of Klee's first admirers[19] and undoubtedly one of the most influential tastemakers in the history of modernism in the United States.[20] In 1936, when The Museum of Modern Art's profile had become much clearer, Barr acknowledged again Klee's impact on his vision of modernism by giving the artist a significant presence in his two most important and influential exhibitions to date, "Cubism and Abstract Art" and "Fantastic Art, Dada, Surrealism"[21] (fig. 30).

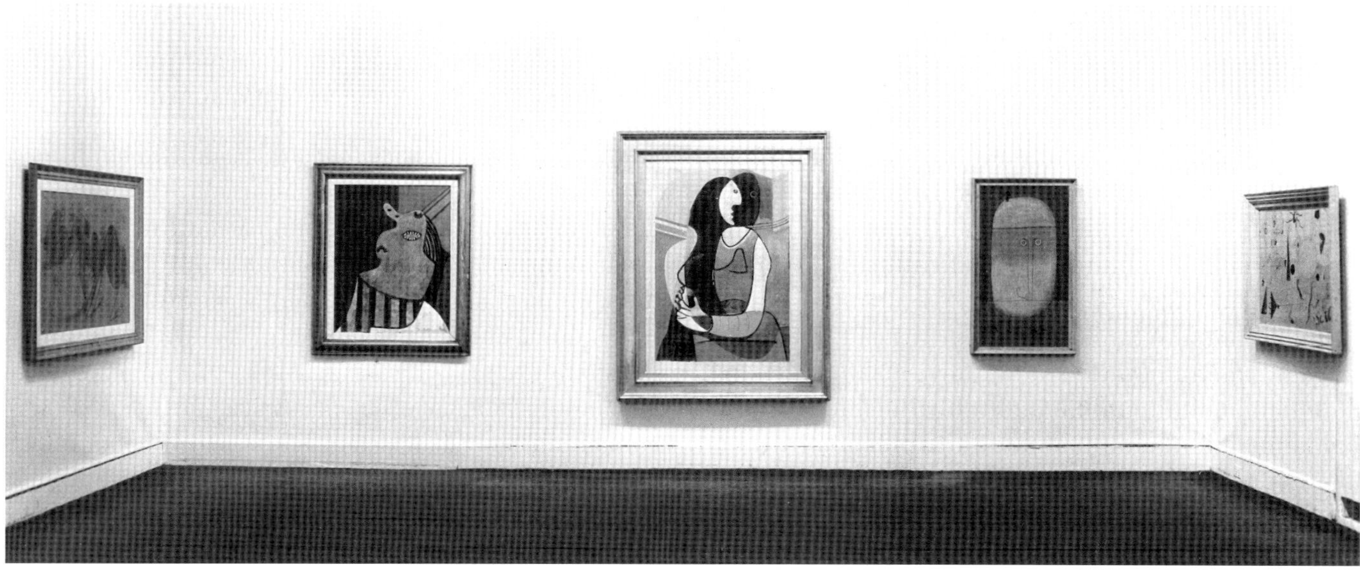

Reactions

From the beginning, the exhibitions at The Museum of Modern Art had been well attended; therefore Klee's work in the 1930 show reached a wide American audience for the first time. Reactions in the press were numerous and differed widely, though in general the critics struggled with the subject matter and small format of Klee's art, with skeptical reactions outnumbering cautiously positive reviews.[22] Barr, always aware of the impact that negative criticism could have on the young institution (and especially on his trustees), usually succeeded by dint of considerable personal engagement to navigate the situation and to defend his program at the museum. One year after the show, however, when Klee's work again appeared at The Museum of Modern Art in the exhibition "German Painting and Sculpture" (March 31–April 26, 1931), a controversy developed. One visitor's objections to Klee's work, and to modernism in general, was published in the *New York Times*,[23] and when Barr saw his 1930 catalogue text on Klee misrepresented, he felt obliged to respond.

The irritated visitor was Robert Macbeth, described in the paper as the owner of an art gallery, and he had seized the opportunity of this exhibition to question modern art in general, using Klee and Picasso as typical and especially problematic examples. His criticism may have differed in tone, but it was substantially the same as denunciations that Klee had earlier encountered in Germany.[24]

When Macbeth proceeded to distort Barr's argument showing an affinity between Klee's art and the art of young children and the insane by using it to dismiss Klee's work altogether, Barr rushed to defend the artist. He clarified the misused text, with regrets "that I cannot send Mr. Macbeth a copy of the Klee catalog —it happens to be the only one of the museum's fourteen catalogs out of print." Barr then found himself compelled to defend Klee's mental health, adding "that Paul Klee is a gentleman, intelligent, modest and charming, with no apparent traces of eccentricity, much less of insanity." Emphasizing how well respected Klee's work was in both Europe and America, Barr concluded his response with an impressive enumeration of private collectors in the United States: "It must seem strange to Mr. Macbeth that Duncan Phillips, A. Conger Goodyear, Dr. Albert Barnes, Dr. W. R. Valentiner (an authority on Rembrandt), Mrs. John D. Rockefeller and some dozen more American collectors own examples of Klee's 'degenerate' art, and that in the present exhibition of German painting and sculpture at the Museum of Modern Art, Klee's two paintings lent by the Berlin National Gallery are among the most enthusiastically admired."[25]

Around this same time, Barr was offered the opportunity to address the subject of Klee's art before a purportedly friendlier audience, the collectors and supporters of modern art in Germany. Barr had met a number of German museum colleagues on his European trip in 1927–28 and was eager to establish an international dialogue

Fig. 30
Installation view, "Fantastic Art, Dada, Surrealism," The Museum of Modern Art, New York, December 7, 1936–January 17, 1937.

between his institution and Europe. As a sign of his rising stature abroad, Barr was invited to share his experience with the 1930 Klee show and the exhibition of contemporary German art that followed in the newly founded German magazine *Museum der Gegenwart*. He used this platform to point out that even though Klee's art remained controversial in the United States, The Museum of Modern Art show had made "a deep impression on artists and collectors."[26] The exhibition moreover seemed to have had a delayed effect on the public, as visitors who initially rejected Klee's work eventually came to admire it. Barr also reported, as he had already pointed out in his defense of Klee's work in the *New York Times*, that the two Klee watercolors lent by the Nationalgalerie in Berlin (fig. 31), *Der Angler [The Angler]* (1921.140, pl. 6) and *Die Zwitscher-Maschine [The Twittering Machine]* (1922.151, pl. 15), had been "public favorites" in the exhibition of contemporary German art, which had been, even by the Modern's standards, very well attended.[27] Neither Barr nor his German readers could have suspected that both watercolors, lent by one of the most respected and progressive museums in Europe, one whose director Barr greatly admired, would eventually become part of the permanent collection of The Museum of Modern Art.[28]

Although the reactions to the presentation of Klee's art at The Museum of Modern Art in the early 1930s were mixed, and sales were sparse, the long-term effect of the 1930 monographic exhibition was considerable. A significant number of the works in the show would become part of American private collections, most of them eventually moving to prominent American museums. The leading beneficiary in that list would be The Museum of Modern Art: eight works figuring in the 1930 exhibition, among them icons like *Jugendlicher Schauspieler=Maske [Youth Actor's Mask]* (1924.252, pl. 28), *Artistenbildnis [Portrait of an Artist]* (1927.13), *Pastorale (Rhythmen) [Pastorale (Rhythms)]* (1927.20, fig. 48), and *Katze und Vogel [Cat and Bird]* (1928.73), would eventually, mostly through bequests, become part of its collection.[29] Barr himself, who had started collecting modern art in the 1920s, acquired *Abstraktes Terzett [Abstract Trio]* (1923.88, pl. 22) from his Klee show at the museum. He therefore joined a small but distinguished group of collectors who had been nurtured by his own program, among them one of the museum's wealthiest and most powerful trustees, Abby Aldrich Rockefeller, with whom Barr had developed a close personal relationship.[30] Rockefeller acquired the watercolor *Sklaverei [Slavery]* (1925.148, pl. 33), and this work with its ambivalent title and subject matter became the first unique work by Klee to enter The Museum of Modern Art's permanent collection in 1935.[31]

Through the individual efforts of Neumann and Barr, and the agency of The Museum of Modern Art, the most powerful institutional platform for promoting modern art in America, Klee saw a significant increase in his exposure on the East Coast of the United States. In 1930 alone, his work appeared in twelve exhibitions in the United States, seven of them in New York.[32] This was a sharp increase over his American presence in the 1920s. Although exhibition activity declined in 1932 and 1933 due to the Great Depression, it regained momentum, and Klee's work continued to be displayed at an even higher level after 1935. Even so, Klee remained skeptical of this success. Though pleased with the attention from "over there," he unquestionably thought of himself as a European artist, one whose recognition would eventually depend on Europe, rather than the New World.

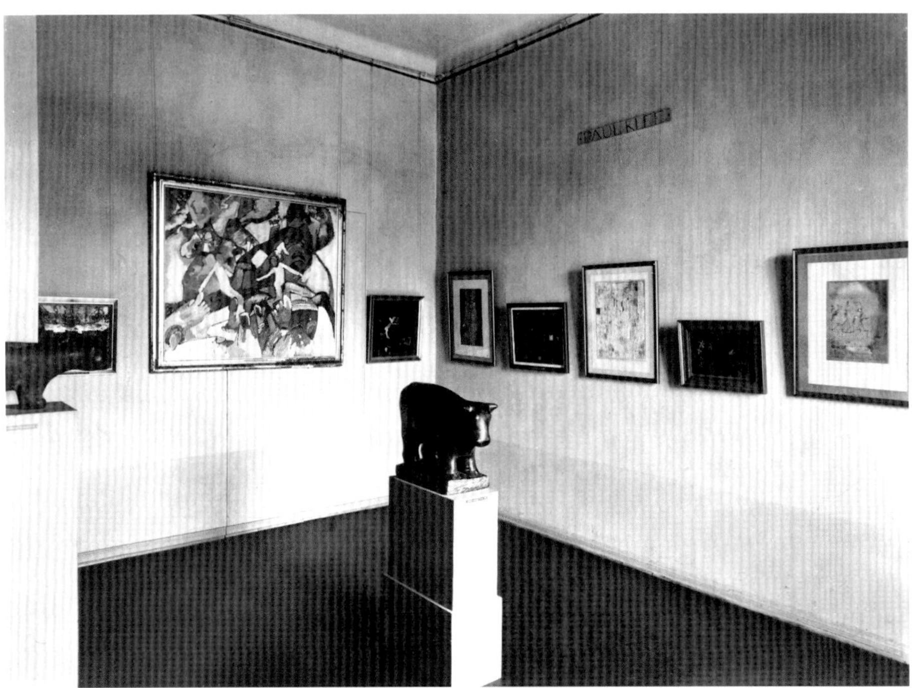

Fig. 31
Installation view, "Modern Section," Nationalgalerie in the former Kronprinzenpalais, Berlin, 1930; with works by Paul Klee: *Der Angler [The Angler]*, 1921.140; *Das Vokaltuch der Kammersängerin Rosa Silber [Vocal Fabric of the Singer Rosa Silber]* (1922.126); and *Die Zwitscher-Maschine [The Twittering Machine]*, 1922.151 (right wall: left, center, and right); and other works by Klee, Vasily Kandinsky, and Heinrich Campendonk, with animal sculptures by Ewald Matare.

Barr's show at The Museum of Modern Art in 1930 was the cul-
mination of an initial wave of efforts on behalf of Klee and the German avant-garde carried out by a group of loosely related German
émigré dealers, as outlined in Vivian Endicott Barnett's essay in
this book (pages 30–43). By far the most passionate, although not
the most successful, promoter of art by Klee and his friends was
Galka Emmy Scheyer, who had left Germany after founding the
group called the Blue Four (Lyonel Feininger, Alexei Jawlensky,
Kandinsky, and Klee) in 1924. Even though she and Barr did not
communicate directly, the results of her mission came to fruition
on the West Coast of the United States at the very same time as
Barr's exhibition at the Modern. After a brief stay in New York,
where she became friends with Neumann, Scheyer had moved to
San Francisco in 1925. In 1929 she decided to move to Hollywood, after Harry Braxton, owner of the Braxton Gallery in Hollywood, invited her to arrange four successive exhibitions of the Blue
Four artists. Scheyer based her decision to leave the Bay Area,
where she had achieved mixed success with her artists, on her conviction that Los Angeles, a quickly growing center of movie stars,
studio magnates, and oil tycoons, was "the ideal location for the
promotion of the Blue Four."[33]

Scheyer's expectations for success in Hollywood at first
proved unrealistic. The crash of the stock market immediately after
her arrival in Los Angeles made her mission—as a promoter and
dealer of virtually unknown European art in a milieu driven by en-
tertainment rather than by interest in art—even more difficult.
However, her series of four exhibitions, each devoted to a single
member of the Blue Four, finally took place in the spring of 1930.
Klee's show was the last in the series, presented from May 1 to 15.[34]
The short introductory text in the catalogue that accompanied the
exhibition stressed the presence of Klee's work in the permanent
collection of the Kronprinzenpalais at the Nationalgalerie in Berlin
and his success in Paris where, as the text claimed, Klee was considered "the father of the new movement—Surrealism." All of the
three statements printed in the catalogue—excerpts from texts by
German critics Will Grohmann and Wilhelm Hausenstein and a
statement from Klee's dealer in Dresden, Rudolph Probst—underlined the "otherworldly," mystical qualities of Klee's art.[35]

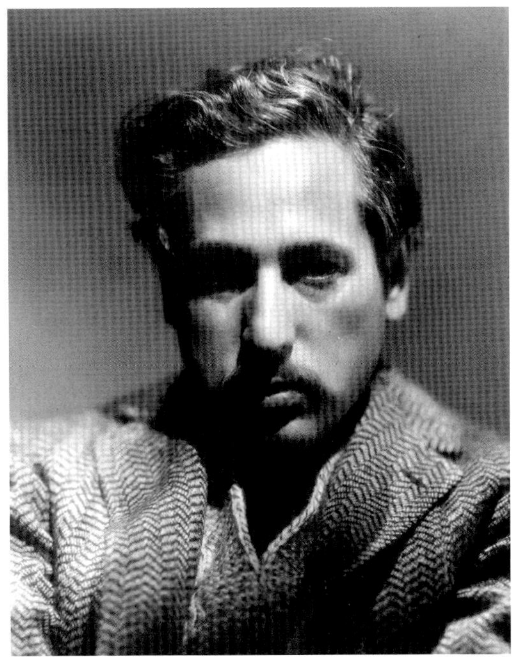

1930: First Success in Hollywood

As it soon turned out, the series of exhibitions at the Braxton
Gallery proved to be a success for Scheyer, a welcome surprise after
six years of disappointments and persistent financial setbacks.
Scheyer managed to get the film director Josef von Sternberg
(fig. 32) as a co-sponsor of the show, which generated public and
press attention. Most importantly, the most distinguished collectors of modern art in Los Angeles, Walter and Louise Arensberg,
showed an interest in the exhibition, especially in Klee's work. The
Arensbergs, following Duchamp's advice, had started to build their
collection of avant-garde European art in the 1910s in New York,
where their apartment became the center of the Dada movement.
In the 1920s they started to divide their time between New York
and Los Angeles, moving permanently to California in 1927 (fig. 33).
Their home in Hollywood became a meeting point for a circle of
friends that included artists, collectors, and intellectuals.[36]

The chance to build a relationship with a pair of serious collectors was a major breakthrough for Scheyer. Before 1930 her
missionary work on behalf of Klee and the Blue Four had mainly
resulted in the cultivation of a few female friends with mostly small
incomes, all of whom lived in the San Francisco Bay Area; none of

Fig. 32
Film director Josef von Sternberg, c. 1930.

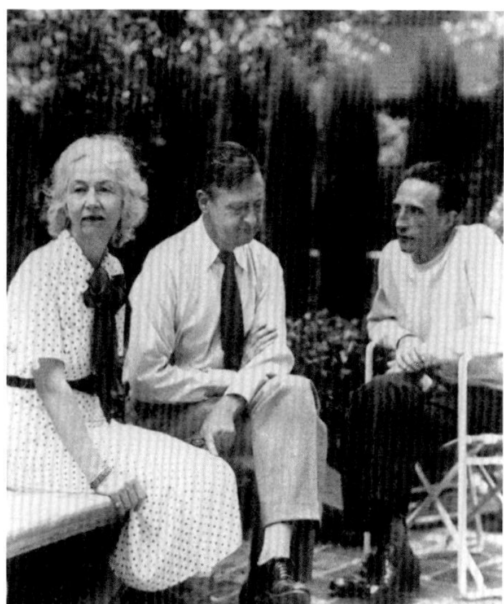

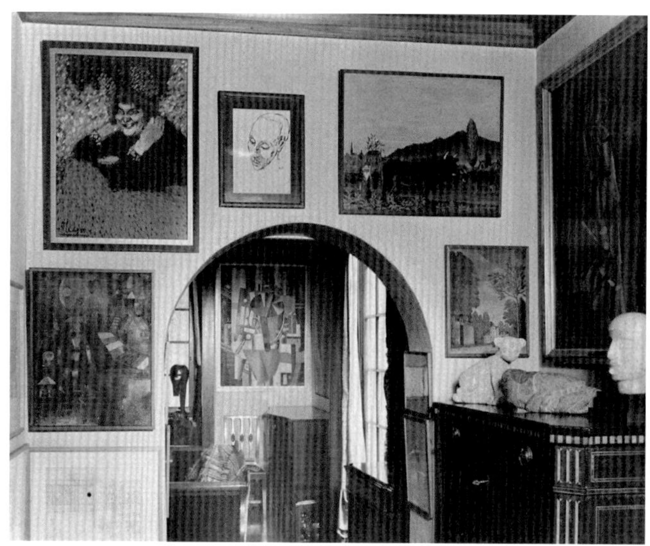

them had collected art before.[37] Scheyer's accounts showed meager sales, mainly of the Blue Four's graphic works. The success in Los Angeles was therefore a cause for excitement, which she quickly conveyed in her letters to Klee and the other artists of the Blue Four.

On April 22, 1930, before the Klee show had even opened, Scheyer wrote to the artist that the Arensbergs had purchased their first work, the painting *Dorf-Carnaval [Village Carnival]* (1926.135, pl. 35, see fig. 34). Scheyer pointed out that Walter Arensberg, a Shakespeare scholar who had stopped collecting ten years ago, had now decided to resume collecting "because the Blue Four made such a big impression on him. You are in the distinguished company of wonderful Cezannes, Rousseaus, Picassos, Brancusis, Renoirs, Gauguins."[38] Anxious to make the sale, Scheyer had asked Arensberg to propose a price, which she then telegraphed to Klee. After Klee had accepted the price, the Arensbergs embraced her and the transaction was reality. Scheyer seemed even more pleased that she had aroused in the Arensbergs a passion for Klee's art than about the sale itself: "We sat many nights for hours, drunk from looking at the pictures; to find that in America is a big relief and gave me huge comfort."[39] Klee reacted with typical understatement in a letter to his wife, Lily, noting that he was "no longer as disenchanted with 'over there' as I was before."[40]

A few weeks later, Scheyer had more good news. She informed Klee that the night before the opening of his show at Braxton Gallery on May 1, she had carried the pictures to the Arensbergs'

home, and they had picked out six watercolors for their collection. With one exception, all the works the Arensbergs had selected remained, after the closing of the show, in their collection.[41]

Scheyer's acquaintance with the Arensbergs brought her into contact with other collectors in Los Angeles, especially Ruth Maitland and Aline Barnsdall, and with the artist Beatrice Wood.[42] In addition to the Arensbergs, Scheyer sold works by Klee to several local collectors, among them Jules Furthman, a Hollywood scriptwriter who had been introduced to Scheyer by Von Sternberg; he purchased *Figurinensammlung [Collection of Figurines]* (1926.248, pl. 49). Von Sternberg himself and Maitland showed a strong interest in Klee and would eventually acquire works by the artist.[43] On June 5, 1930, Scheyer noted in a postscript to her long letter of June 1 (which she had not yet sent off to Klee) that her friend Marjorie Eaton from San Francisco had purchased the painting *Attrappen [Traps]* (1927.295), a work that had not been in the Braxton Gallery show. Soon thereafter, Eaton acquired *Zeichnung für Pflanzen, Erd- und Luftreich [Drawing for Plants, Realms of Earth and Air]* (1920.205) once Klee had reluctantly agreed to sell the drawing.

Klee's exhibition at The Museum of Modern Art around this time, which provided considerable exposure for his work, may have favorably influenced his outlook on the West Coast. Scheyer, at least, was convinced of the connection, as she noted in her letter to Klee on April 22, 1930: "Congratulations on your success in

Fig. 33
Louise and Walter Arensberg with Marcel Duchamp, Los Angeles, 1936.

Fig. 34
View of Louise and Walter Arensbergs' residence, Los Angeles, c. 1945; Paul Klee, *Dorf-Carnaval [Village Carnival]*, 1926.135 (left of the archway).

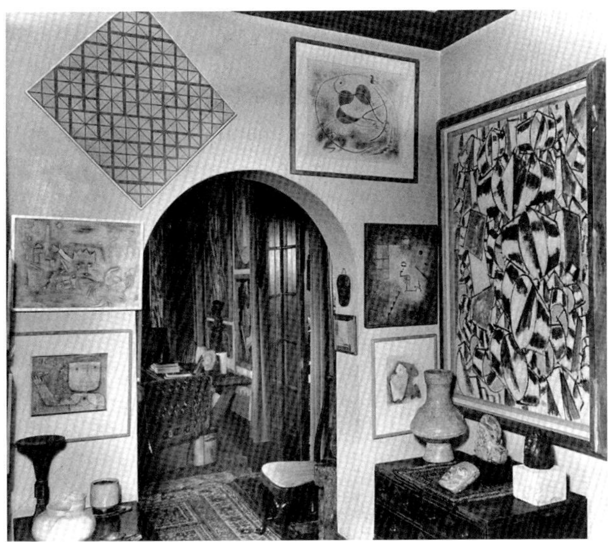

New York. I can feel the influence of it here. Your exhibition is to open here on May 1. Braxton had scheduled your show for last, because he didn't know what to make of your art. Now, after your success in New York, the tables are turned; he's a typical dealer, in the worst sense of the word."[44] Two weeks after the closing of the Braxton Gallery show, Scheyer had become even more optimistic about Klee's future in the United States and was ready to make a bold forecast: "I prophesy a great market for you in America!"[45]

The success of the Braxton Gallery exhibition may have prompted Scheyer to add more works by Klee to her own collection. By early 1930 Scheyer owned at least thirty drawings, watercolors, and prints by Klee; she had exchanged several works with the artist before her departure from Germany in 1924, and Klee had offered several works to her as gifts. In the same letter from April 1930 in which she announced Arensberg's new passion for his art, Scheyer signaled her decision to purchase two works that she had wanted to buy earlier. After Klee agreed and offered her special prices, she added *Barbaren-Venus [Barbarian Venus]* (1921.132, fig. 19) and *Mädchen aus Sachsen [Maid of Saxony]* (1922.132, fig. 18) to her personal collection. *Barbaren-Venus* had apparently been among the Arensbergs' favorites, and in September 1931 Scheyer agreed to lend it to them, together with the watercolor *Goldfischweib [Goldfish Woman]* (1921.93).[46] Scheyer would eventually bequeath *Goldfischweib* to Walter Arensberg as a token of her esteem for him.[47] In June 1930 Scheyer expressed interest in two additional watercolors, *Götzenbild für Hauskatzen [Idol for House Cats]* (1924.14) and *Pflanzen Samen [Plant Seeds]* (1927.288, pl. 46). The transaction was settled the following year when Klee agreed to sell *Götzenbild für Hauskatzen* for a reduced price and to offer *Pflanzen Samen* as a gift to Scheyer, "in grateful recognition of your activity over the last year."[48]

Initially compelled by Scheyer's enthusiasm, the Arensbergs would continue to purchase Klee works for their collection, among them *Zauber Kunst Stück [Conjuring Trick]* (1927.297) and the print *Seiltänzer [Tightrope Walker]* (1923.138) in 1932 (fig. 35). By then they owned the most significant collection of works by Klee on the American West Coast.[49]

1931: Diego Rivera Promotes the Blue Four

Scheyer in her promotion of Klee pursued various co-sponsors for her exhibitions, including the artists Diego Rivera and Frida Kahlo (fig. 36), who would become supporters of Klee in their own right. In January 1931, after traveling for six months through Bali, the Philippines, China, and Japan, Scheyer returned to California. She initially settled in San Francisco, where she met Rivera and Kahlo, over time developing a close friendship with the two, especially Kahlo. Rivera had come to San Francisco for his 1930 retrospective exhibition at the California Palace of the Legion of Honor and was currently working on two commissions: the mural *Riches of California* for the Stock Exchange Building and another mural for the California School of Fine Arts.[50] When Scheyer's Blue Four exhibition was due to open at the California Palace of the Legion of Honor on April 8, 1931, she invited Rivera to install the exhibition with her.

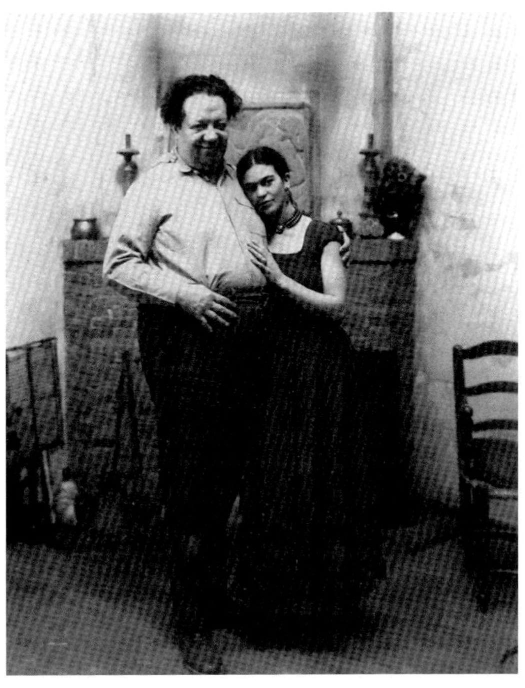

Fig. 35
View of Louise and Walter Arensbergs' residence, Los Angeles, c. 1945; works by Paul Klee: *Der Tierschreck [Animal Terror]*, 1926.204 (left of the archway, top) and *Jörg*, 1924.141 (bottom); *Zauber Kunst Stück [Conjuring Trick]*, 1927.297 (right of the archway, top; pl. 54).

Fig. 36
Diego Rivera and Frida Kahlo in the studio of Ralph Stackpole, San Francisco, 1931.

Just as her exhibition the year before in Hollywood had led to her fruitful encounter with the Arensbergs, the San Francisco exhibition would culminate in an important contact: the San Francisco philanthropist Charlotte Mack made her first purchases from Scheyer at this time. Mack's continued patronage of Klee's work through Scheyer would eventually result in her building the most important collection of the artist's work in San Francisco.[51]

Even more significant, however, was Rivera's agreement to co-sponsor the exhibition with Scheyer. It took place in two parts, with the work of Kandinsky and Feininger shown first (April 8–22, 1931), followed by the work of Jawlensky and Klee (April 23–May 8, 1931). The exhibition catalogue showed that a majority of the works on display were already part of American collections, thereby testifying to the growing success of Klee's work in the United States.[52] Rivera also agreed to help promote the show by writing a brief introduction for the catalogue, an abbreviated version of which was published in the *San Francisco Chronicle*.[53] In the catalogue essay, Rivera stressed the newness of the art presented in the exhibition and defended it against the accusations of "decadence" by describing the work as being "anticipated for a better organized world." Touching on a standard theme in the Klee literature—the combination in Klee's work of age-old tradition and revolutionary, child-like genius—Rivera described Klee and his friends as "pure creators whose work contains all the science of the great masters and all the freshness of the genius of children."[54]

Rivera also made a point of strongly underlining what he saw as the universal spirit of the work of all artists, unhindered by national borders or traditions. Alluding to the perception of America as the world's most forward-thinking country, he wrote that artists "are beings of the very first quality, who progress faster than phys-ical time, and who for this reason are already working in the future reality."[55] He stressed the present moment as a historical opportunity to discover the work of these four artists, linking the spirit of "newness" in their art with the vast potential in America for rapid cultural and economic development.[56] As Kandinsky reported to Scheyer, Rivera's short essay made a strong impression in Germany, especially on Grohmann, both Klee's and Kandinsky's leading critic.[57]

Rivera's interest in the Blue Four artists initially tended toward a partiality for Kandinsky, whereas Kahlo's preference from the beginning lay with Klee. Scheyer had agreed to lend the couple a group of Kandinsky's works for their rooms in San Francisco, and in the spring of 1931 she announced in a letter to the artist that Rivera was interested in acquiring his work. Rivera did subsequently acquire several works by Kandinsky. He seems to have been less familiar with Klee's work at the time, though Scheyer mentioned in her letter to Klee that the exhibition as a whole made a big impression on him. Shortly before the end of the exhibition's run in early May 1931, Scheyer sent a telegram to Klee requesting a price reduction for three watercolors Rivera wished to purchase: *Kinder und Hund [Children and Dog]* (1920.90), *Pal* (1924.180, pl. 36), and *Palast [Palace]* (1928.133). Klee immediately agreed, and on May 8, the final date of the exhibition, Rivera took ownership of the three Klee watercolors, which he then offered as a gift to Kahlo.[58]

Following the show in San Francisco, and almost a year of travels and work abroad, Scheyer returned to Hollywood, where she rented a room in Rudolph Schindler's famous house at Kings Road (fig. 37).[59] From there on June 14, 1931, she sent Klee an update on her recent transactions and mentioned that the Arensbergs were

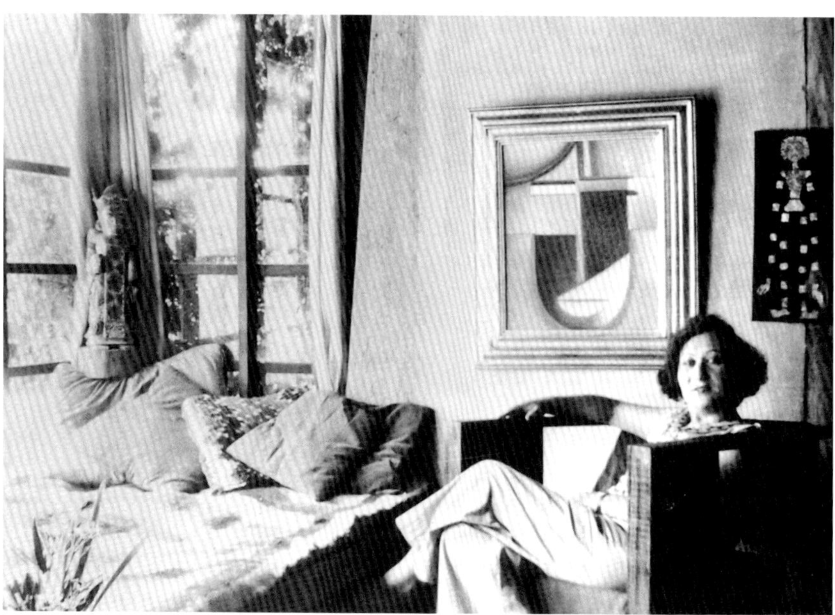

Fig. 37
Galka Scheyer at the home of architect R. M. Schindler, Los Angeles, early 1930s.

interested in purchasing yet another watercolor that she had lent to them, *Bewegung um ein Kind [Movement around a Child]* (1928.62).[60] Scheyer also mentioned how close she had become with her Mexican friends Rivera and Kahlo. She described Rivera's decision to purchase the three watercolors as a response to Kahlo's great affection for the works: "I have become quite friendly with Rivera, who has now gone back to Mexico. At first he was incredibly enthusiastic about Kandinsky's pictures, which were exhibited for the first two weeks along with Feininger's. Then when he saw yours, he was amazed at how infinitely more your work means to him than he earlier thought. His wife, Frida, loves your art most of all, so he presented her with the three Klees."[61]

End of 1931: The Exhibition of the Blue Four in Mexico City and Rivera's Essay on Klee

By the time the Blue Four exhibition closed in San Francisco, Scheyer and Rivera had already made plans to organize a similar exhibition in Mexico later that fall. As soon as Scheyer had established herself in Los Angeles, she began preparing for the project in Mexico. As their correspondence shows, Kahlo became Scheyer's most reliable source of information and support, advising her on all practical details—the venue (which was unclear), transportation issues, and how to deal with the local bureaucracy as well as with the Mexican Ministry of Foreign Affairs and Education in order to get both approval and financial support for the show.

Mounting the exhibition in Mexico promised to be an adventure from the outset, but the economic crisis, both in Mexico and internationally, made the organization of the show even more difficult than expected. Kahlo was very outspoken about the problems that continually surfaced: "The economic situation is terrible, you can't imagine, but in [the] first place, Goberment [sic] people are absolutely stupid and [it] is almost impossible to get something about art etc from them."[62] She also warned Scheyer that it would be "difficult to sell anything."[63]

In mid-September 1931, Scheyer traveled to Mexico City, where she stayed with Rivera and Kahlo.[64] They finally managed to secure the Biblioteca Nacional in Mexico City as the venue for the exhibition. Surprisingly for the effort involved, this first presentation of the four artists to the Spanish-speaking world lasted only one week, from November 24 to December 1, 1931. How-

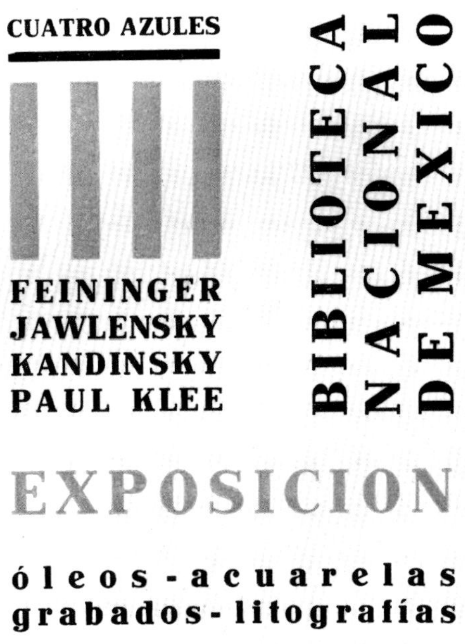

ever, Scheyer did succeed in publishing a catalogue for the show (fig. 38), with brief introductions for each artist. Rivera wrote short essays on Kandinsky and Klee, and his writing on Klee remains an interesting historical document of Klee's reception early on by one of the most prominent artists in the Americas.

Rivera was at this point an exceptionally successful artist both in Mexico and abroad, particularly popular in the United States and Europe. His promotion of the art of the Blue Four was therefore—as Kandinsky was well aware of, and eager to capitalize on—an important event with potentially far-reaching consequences.[65] Unlike in the catalogue for the San Francisco exhibition, where Rivera had written an introduction to the Blue Four with an unmistakable emphasis on Kandinsky, he now wrote statements on both Klee and Kandinsky, followed by an afterword on the Blue Four as a whole. In his writing on Klee, he focused more on the artist's personality than on his art. Without discussing specific works or addressing formal or technical aspects of Klee's art, he emphasized what he called Klee's outstanding sensibility and his capacity to transform the real world into visual poetry. The key

Fig. 38
Cover of the catalogue from the "Cuatro Azules" ("Blue Four") exhibition in Mexico, 1931.

metaphor for Klee's character as an artist seemed for Rivera to be the term "magician," which he applied to both Klee's unique use of materials and his ability to capture free-floating imaginings in a new form of pictorial language. Here, Rivera was clearly referring to the victory of imagination over reason, a crucial theme for the Surrealists who had celebrated Klee's work since the 1920s. As in his first description of the Blue Four, Rivera seemed enthralled by the concept of an artist's incorporating the experiences of both a pioneer of old age and a three-year-old boy, combining the wisdom of an advanced stage of life with the newness of a child genius. Rivera suggested that Klee's art transcended the present historical moment to represent a far greater extent of time, reaching far into the future.[66] Klee's reaction to Rivera's text is unknown.

Rivera and Kahlo had left Mexico for New York before the exhibition at the Biblioteca Nacional opened so Rivera could start work on the mural *Man at the Crossroads* in the Rockefeller Center. Kahlo wrote Scheyer from New York, worried about the difficulties the dealer had encountered in Mexico prior to the exhibition's opening,[67] and sent the names and addresses of friends to call upon for assistance if needed. On April 11, 1932, Kahlo mentioned her homesickness for Mexico, declaring she would "love to see my Klees again."[68]

In a letter to Kandinsky dated December 22, 1931, Scheyer reported in detail on her problems with the Mexican authorities, summarizing a frustrating experience with the comment: "Never again an exhibition in Mexico."[69] Nevertheless, despite the fact that the difficulties had far exceeded the show's material gains, Scheyer was convinced the exhibition had been successful. She was impressed with the attendance and the generally enthusiastic response from the Mexican people: "The exhibition in Mexico was a great success. People streamed in and looked and talked for hours. Selling to the collector there, who doesn't understand a thing about art, was most demoralizing, yet the non-buying but very enthusiastic public made up for it."[70] A few weeks later, on January 16, 1932, Scheyer sent Klee a summary of recent sales, including works sold from the exhibition in Mexico.[71] But even as Klee's success mounted in America, the intellectual and economic foundations in Germany were being pulled out from under his feet.

THE SHIFT FROM EUROPE TO AMERICA: THE TURNING POINT IN 1933

By the beginning of 1933, the political situation in Germany, marked by the steady disintegration of the democratic Weimar Republic, had worsened considerably. The collapse of the Austrian bank Kredit-Anstalt in the spring of 1931 triggered a financial crisis all over Central Europe, with many German banks going bankrupt. In the same year, the German millionaire and conservative politician Alfred Hugenberg decided to support the National Socialist party in an alliance that was soon joined by other powerful magnates.[72] Following elections in November 1931, the Nazis became the strongest party in the city council in Dessau, where Klee still had his main residence. In early 1932 the number of unemployed in Germany reached over six million. In June the government lifted the ban on Nazi storm troopers, causing riots in Berlin and other cities. In the Reichstag elections of July 1932, the Nazis became for the first time the dominant political party in Germany. Although they lost votes in the next national election in November, their influence grew and the street terror became more visible. In January 1933 the elderly Reichstagspräsident Paul von Hindenburg accepted Hitler's candidacy for chancellor. The transfer of power occurred on January 30, 1933. After the March election, in which the Nazis won 44 percent of the vote but failed to achieve a majority, Hitler assumed dictatorial power. He initiated drastic constitutional changes, ordering the liquidation of all opposition parties and the persecution of the Jews. By July 1933 the National Socialists had become Germany's only political party. Also by that time, 27,000 political prisoners had been detained in Germany in new prisons called "concentration camps." In the fall Hitler finally decided to withdraw Germany from the League of Nations and the Disarmament Conference.

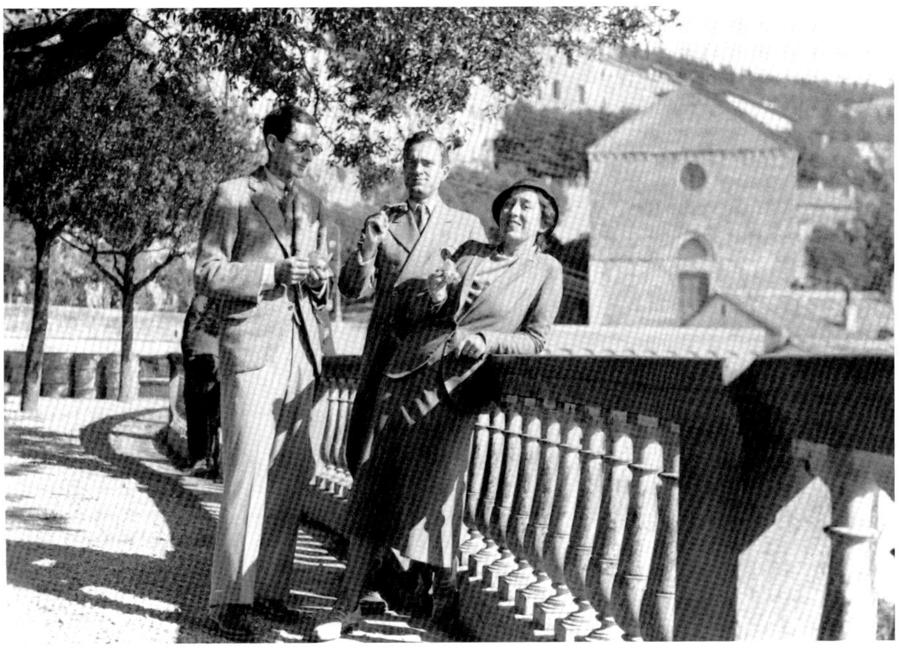

Barr's Stay in Europe in 1932–33

In the spring of 1932, the trustees of The Museum of Modern Art gave Barr, who was suffering from nervous exhaustion and severe insomnia, a leave of absence. In September 1932 Barr left New York for Europe, where he stayed until the summer of 1933.

Barr first traveled to Italy, where he joined his wife, Margaret Scolari Barr. The couple then traveled to Zurich to visit a large Picasso exhibition. In Switzerland they met Philip Johnson, with whom they drove on a long sightseeing tour through northern and central Italy to Rome (fig. 39). After Christmas 1932 Barr and his wife traveled to the ski resort of St. Anton in Austria, and from there in late January 1933, they went to Stuttgart, Germany, to undergo psychotherapy to cure his insomnia.[73]

Barr arrived in Stuttgart just days before Hitler was named chancellor of the Reich, making Germany the least suitable place for him to regain his mental and physical balance.[74] In the weeks that followed, Barr and his wife watched with astonishment and increasing indignation as the dictatorship of the National Socialists unfolded. Barr, from his days as a student at Princeton and Harvard, had always admired the progressive aspects of contemporary German culture. Now he saw firsthand the parades going on day and night, listened in the evenings to "the strained voices of Hitler and Goebbels shouting over a Berlin microphone," and witnessed the renaming of streets and the first boycotts of Jewish businesses. Like almost everyone else, Barr was surprised "at the thoroughness and rapidity with which the new order invaded every business and profession, every intellectual and cultural activity."[75] On April 9 he attended the first public meeting of the Kampfbund für Deutsche Kultur [The Battle Band for German Culture], organized by the National Socialist party, and saw with what fanatical dedication the new government sought to dominate "every phase of the cultural life in Germany."[76] He was increasingly alarmed by the systematic "cleansing" of German culture, removing all international or un-German elements, and by the Nazis' public humiliation of modern artists, scholars, and museum directors. Barr was still in Stuttgart undergoing psychotherapy when the Nazis in April closed the Bauhaus in Berlin and Klee was dismissed in Düsseldorf.

Barr had difficulty conveying to American audiences the severity of the political situation in Germany. In late May or early June 1933, following the advice of his psychiatrist in Stuttgart, Barr and his wife left Germany and spent several weeks in Ascona in southern Switzerland. Here, still struggling with his insomnia, Barr started to work feverishly on several articles describing the "cultural crisis" in the wake of the National Socialist dictatorship. He wrote four

Fig. 39
Alfred H. Barr Jr., Philip Johnson, and Margaret Scolari Barr
in Cortona, Italy, 1932.

articles and tried to publish them, but his attempt to raise the alarm in the United States about the political events in Germany proved unsuccessful. One essay was published in 1934, but most of his writing from his stay in Germany would not appear in print until the end of the Second World War.[77] In addition to reporting what he had seen, Barr became active on behalf of German scholars and artists, many of whom eventually were offered positions in the United States.[78]

Barr had admired the professionalism and high standards of German art museums and academies, especially their unparalleled institutional support for modern art, for many years, and he observed with increasing repulsion how the Nazis within weeks systematically destroyed a system that had been a model for Barr's own institution. When he left Germany in the late spring of 1933, he must have realized that Hitler's policy would drastically change the conditions under which contemporary German art was introduced to the United States. Yet despite his firsthand knowledge of the extreme situation, Barr could not have predicted that The Museum of Modern Art would within a few years acquire several works by Klee, deaccessioned under the new Nazi rule from the same institutions Barr had admired the most. After a short stay in Paris, Barr returned to the United States in July 1933.

Scheyer's Last Trip to Europe in the Fall of 1932

Like Barr, Scheyer also returned in the early thirties to a drastically changed environment in Germany. On October 15, 1932, Scheyer left for Europe to visit her family in Braunschweig as well as the artists—Feininger, Jawlensky, Kandinsky, and Klee—to whom she had dedicated all her efforts and most of her resources since moving to America in 1924. Her trip was partially funded by the Oakland Art Gallery, with which Scheyer had been affiliated for years. The professional purpose of the trip was to reconnect with the artists in Germany and to select pictures by the Blue Four for future exhibitions in the United States. Just a year earlier, Scheyer had become an American citizen.

Scheyer first spent four weeks in Paris, where she met Duchamp, among other artists, and acquired a painting by Picasso. When she arrived in Germany in late November 1932, she realized how dramatically the situation there had changed. Lily Klee had warned Scheyer in her letter in July ("In Germany bleak economic and political situation"),[79] but in the meantime things had grown worse.

In September the Nazis had closed down the Bauhaus in Dessau; it reopened two months later as a private institution in Berlin. On February 1, 1933, immediately after Hitler had been appointed chancellor, a National Socialist Party newspaper carried a hate article attacking the director of the Academy of Art in Düsseldorf, Walter Kaesbach, as well as Klee, whom the article denounced as a "typical Galician Jew."[80] Shortly thereafter, in February 1933, Scheyer spent a holiday with Lily Klee in the Harz region, followed in March and April with visits to Feininger in Dessau, Jawlensky in Wiesbaden, and Kandinsky in Berlin, but she did not meet with Klee. Dramatic events intruded: on March 17 Sturmabteilung, or Nazi storm troopers called SA men, searched Klee's house in Dessau when he and his wife were not there. Fearing arrest, Klee fled to Switzerland on March 19, remaining there until April 2. On April 3, when Klee returned to Düsseldorf, he met with the interim director of the Academy of Art, who counseled a "wait and see" approach.[81] Then on April 21 Klee received a telegram from the Academy of Art informing him that he had been suspended from his teaching post, "effective immediately."

Scheyer, distressed by the situation in Germany, decided to cut short her trip and started making last-minute travel arrangements on April 29, even as Klee was packing his studio in Düsseldorf. Lily Klee summarized the recent events in a letter to Scheyer, full of regret that she had not been able to meet Klee.[82] With an urgency never expressed before, she asked for Scheyer's help in creating opportunities for Klee to show his work in the United States.[83] She closed in a prophetic tone, forecasting the positive posthumous reception of Klee's work: "I know it is likely that the work in all its complexity will only be appreciated by posterity, and you, my dear Emmy, are one of the few people who give it its due."[84]

Ironically, on May 5, right after Klee's position at the Academy had been terminated, the Klees moved into their newly rented house in Düsseldorf, a home they had searched for over many months, now a place fraught with misfortune. Only one day later, on May 6, Scheyer left Germany from Hamburg on her trip back to America. She would never return to Europe. A few weeks later, Klee in a letter to Scheyer commented sarcastically on the bad luck of their missed encounter and the fateful last months: "The fact that we brushed-and-rushed past each other is almost fantastic, if only more had come out of it in these fantastic times."[85]

Conclusion

In the period of 1930 to 1933, only a handful of devoted individuals played a decisive role in promoting and presenting Klee's work in America. First was Neumann, who prepared the ground for Klee in New York and whose "contagious enthusiasm"[86] had a strong impact on prominent leaders of the New York art world, especially on its most influential figure, Barr. Next was Barr, whose exhibition at The Museum of Modern Art in 1930 was the breakthrough for Klee's reception in America. And finally Scheyer played a critical role for the visibility of Klee's work on the West Coast. By 1933 Klee's art was entering the visual culture in the United States, through exhibitions, publications, and a slowly increasing representation in public and private collections. Scheyer's instrumental role in that effort until now has not been sufficiently recognized: without Scheyer's lonely and often unsuccessful efforts, however, Klee's work would never have made its appearance on the West Coast as early as it did. Not only did her organization of dozens of shows across America add a remarkable geographic distribution to Klee's work in North America, but she was also responsible for the formation of the most significant private collection of Klee's work on the West Coast—that of the Arensbergs. This handful of dedicated individuals laid a remarkably sturdy foundation for the increased demand for Klee's work in the second half of the 1930s, when works deaccessioned in Germany began to find their way to the American market.

In 1933 Klee noted in his pocket calendar: "Is Europe limping or am I limping?"[87] His note seemed more than a rhetorical question, manifesting a deep insecurity about how intertwined his personal circumstances and, even more so, his career as an artist had become with the political situation in Europe. The story of Klee's reception in America between 1930 and 1933 is closely linked to the political and economic crisis in Germany, given that the collapse of the democratic structures and of the free art market in Germany were the preconditions for Klee's breakthrough in the United States in the second half of the 1930s.

Meanwhile, Klee's art in Germany disappeared almost entirely from public view. Just a few years earlier, in 1930, Klee had considered his future to be in Europe, primarily focused in Germany and France. His interest in America had been modest at best, reflecting his skepticism regarding the potential profit among collectors and exhibitions in the New World. By the end of 1933, however, that assessment had been brutally revised. Forced by the catastrophic turn of political events in Germany, Klee began to look for new markets for his work. In October 1933 he stayed briefly in Paris on his way back from a trip to the French Mediterranean coast, preoccupied with making arrangements for his future. While there, he met both with Flechtheim, his previous dealer who had been forced to flee Germany, and with Daniel-Henry Kahnweiler, signing a general contract with the latter. On December 23, 1933, Klee left Germany for good and emigrated to Switzerland. By then the prospects for his art had dramatically changed. Now America had become the most promising territory for its future.

NOTES

I am grateful to Sarah Eckhardt for her excellent research assistance and suggestions. My thanks go to Sarah, Kristina Van Dyke, and Kristin Schwartz-Lauster for their critical reading of this essay.

1. Christine Hopfengart, "Klee an den deutschen 'Museen der Gegenwart,' 1916–1933," in Oskar Bätschmann and Josef Helfenstein, eds., *Paul Klee: Kunst und Karriere, Beiträge des Internationalen Symposiums in Bern* (Bern, Switzerland: Stämpfli Verlag, 2000), 74–76 and 88.

2. Christine Hopfengart, *Klee Vom Sonderfall zum Publikumsliebling: Stationen seiner öffentlichen Resonanz in Deutschland 1905–1960* (Mainz, Germany: Philipp von Zabern, 1989), 90–92.

3. Penny Bealle, "J. B. Neumann and the Introduction of Modern German Art to New York, 1923–1933," *Archives of American Art Journal* 29, nos. 1/2 (1989): 2–15; Sybil Gordon Kantor, *Alfred H. Barr, Jr., and the Intellectual Origins of the Museum of Modern Art* (Cambridge, Mass.: MIT Press, 2002), 93–94.

4. Carolyn Lanchner, "Klee in America," in Carolyn Lanchner, ed., *Paul Klee,* exh. cat. (New York: Museum of Modern Art, 1987), 94.

5. Flechtheim, honoring Klee's fiftieth birthday, had organized a retrospective held October 29–November 15, 1929, with 150 works spanning Klee's entire career from 1910–1929, including loans from fifteen private and public collections. *Paul Klee*, exh. cat. (Berlin: Galerie Alfred Flechtheim, 1929).

6. The works were *Mit der rotierenden schwarzen Sonne und dem Pfeil [With the Rotating Black Sun and the Arrow]* (1919.63) (for the American audience, the unusually complicated title was modified to *Escapement*), Collection Erhard Weyhe, and *Landschaft mit 3 blauen Vögeln [Landscape with 3 Blue Birds]* (1919.189), Albert E. Gallatin's collection. See Alfred H. Barr Jr., *Paul Klee,* exh. cat. (New York: Museum of Modern Art, 1930), 13, no. 1 and no. 2, respectively. In December 1927 Gallatin had opened his private collection of modern art to the public in rooms provided by New York University at Washington Square.

7. Kirk Varnedoe, "Philip Johnson as Donor to the Museum Collections: An Overview," in *Philip Johnson at the Museum of Modern Art* (New York: Museum of Modern Art, 1998), 13.

8. *Schlussbild einer Tragikömodie [Final Scene of a Tragicomedy]* (1923.144) and *Nicht ohne Herz [Not Without Heart]* (1928.33, pl. 56), both of which Johnson traded with or sold to Andy Warhol in the 1950s, and *Ort der Seltenheiten [Place of Rarities]* (1929.303) and *Plan einer Burg [Plan of a Castle]* (1930.218, pl. 69). Johnson became a member of The Museum of Modern Art's advisory committee when it was founded in 1930, and when Barr created the curatorial department of architecture in 1932, Johnson became that department's first director.

9. Barr, *Paul Klee,* 13, no. 9.

10. Abbott left The Museum of Modern Art in March 1932 to become director of the Smith College Museum of Art, Northampton, Massachusetts. Margaret Scolari Barr, "'Our Campaigns': Alfred H. Barr, Jr., and the Museum of Modern Art, A Biographical Chronicle of the Years 1930–1944," *New Criterion* (Summer 1987): 28.

11. This was only partially accurate—Klee did visit Paris in 1912, but stayed only for two weeks, not "for over a year," as Barr stated. He also did not develop a friendship with Pablo Picasso (whom he met only twice, in 1933 and 1939) and Guillaume Apollinaire (whom he never met). Barr, *Paul Klee,* 8.

12. Barr, *Paul Klee,* 8.

13. Barr, *Paul Klee,* 8.

14. Kantor, 146–89. See also Josef Helfenstein, "From the Sidewalk to the Marketplace: Traylor, Edmondson, and the Modernist Impulse," in *Bill Traylor, William Edmondson, and the Modernist Impulse,* exh. cat. (Champaign, Ill.: Krannert Art Museum: and Houston: The Menil Collection, 2004), 45–67.

15. Barr, *Paul Klee,* 9–10.

16. Barr, *Paul Klee,* 8.

17. Kantor, 139–40.

18. Barr, *Paul Klee,* 10.

19. Lanchner, 86.

20. It is interesting to compare Duchamp's interpretation of Klee's work, although published at a later date, with Barr's essay. Duchamp wrote: "A deep conception of the use of watercolor, a personal method in oil painting applied to apparently decorative forms, have made Klee stand out in contemporary painting as unrelated to anyone else.… His extreme fecundity never shows signs of repetition as is generally the case." Marcel Duchamp, *The Writings of Marcel Duchamp,* eds. Michel Sanouillet and Elmer Peterson (New York: Oxford University Press, 1973), 151.

21. "Paul Klee … influenced both Dadaism and Surrealism by the inexhaustible variety of his ingenious fantasies." Alfred H. Barr Jr., *Cubism and Abstract Art,* exh. cat. (New York: The Museum of Modern Art, 1936), 174. See also Lanchner, 100–101.

22. "In the catalogue note on Klee it is stated that 'in Europe he is considered one of the most important artists working outside of Paris.' We wonder by whom he is so considered, and why? There is, as a matter of fact, nothing whatever about his productions here shown that is 'important.'" *The Art Digest* (March 1930): 8.

23. I am grateful to Sarah Eckhardt for bringing this document to my attention.

24. Described as the "president of the Macbeth Gallery," Macbeth had written: "I am against the acceptance as fine art of the products of degenerates when those products themselves are degenerate." *New York Times*, March 22, 1931.

25. Alfred H. Barr Jr., letter, *New York Times*, March 29, 1931.

26. Cary Ross, Barr's colleague on staff at The Museum of Modern Art, wrote: "In seiner vierten Ausstellung räumte das Museum eine seiner Abteilungen für eine Schau von dreiundsechzig Ölbildern, Aquarellen, Gouachen und Zeichnungen von Paul Klee und zeigte so die erste Sonderausstellung des Meisters in Amerika. Durch den Auftrieb, den diese Ausstellung im Museum gab, wurde Klee in eine Anzahl bedeutender Privatsammlungen New Yorks eingeführt." ("In its fourth exhibition, the museum cleared out one of its sections for a show of sixty-three oil paintings, watercolors, gouaches, and drawings by Paul Klee, and thus presented the master's first one-person show in America. Because of the boost provided by this museum exhibition, Klee was introduced into a number of New York's important private collections.") Cary Ross, "Deutsche Kunst in den Sammlungen New York," *Museum der Gegenwart* 2, no. 1 (1931): 7. Among the twenty-one private collections of contemporary German art listed by Ross, Klee was represented in twelve, among them the collections of Mrs. John D. Rockefeller and of the writer Ernest Hemingway (10–11). Barr, probably influenced by the recent controversy, reported in a more direct way: "Die Klee-Ausstellung rief lebhafte Gegnerschaft hervor, die noch nicht abgebrochen ist. Wieder neigten die Künstler eher

als die Kritiker dazu, das Neue und Fremde aufzunehmen." ("The Klee exhibition provoked lively opposition that has still not died down. Once again, it is the artists who are more inclined to accept the new and unfamiliar than the critics.") Alfred H. Barr Jr., "Deutsche Kunst in New York: Ein Rückblick," *Museum der Gegenwart* 2, no. 1 (1931): 4. See also Lanchner, 97.

27. Lanchner, 97. Barr wrote: "Hingegen hat sich Klee als ein sehr beachtenswerter Künstler nunmehr einen festen Ruf bei Künstlern und Sammlern erworben. Ganze Scharen von Besuchern, die voriges Jahr über die Klee-Ausstellung im Museum empört waren, fanden ihn diesmal hinreissend, zumal das Bild *Ma* der Sammlung Koehler und die beiden vorzüglichen Aquarelle, die die National-Galerie hergeliehen hatte." ("On the other hand, Klee has by now acquired a solid reputation among artists and collectors as a very noteworthy artist. This time hordes of visitors who had been enraged by the museum's Klee exhibition last year found him entrancing, especially the picture *Ma* from the Koehler Collection and the two excellent watercolors lent by the National Gallery.") Alfred H. Barr Jr., "Die Wirkung der deutschen Ausstellung in New York," *Museum der Gegenwart* 2, no. 2 (1931): 60.

28. Lanchner, 97. *Die Zwitscher-Maschine* was purchased in 1939, and *Der Angler* was bequeathed as a gift to The Museum of Modern Art in 1961.

29. The other works are *Sklaverei [Slavery]* (1925.148, pl. 33), *Sakrale Inseln [Sacred Islands]* (1926.6, pl. 40), *Gaben für "J." [Gifts for "J."]* (1928.212, pl. 53), and *Im Gras [In the Grass]* (1930.18). A list of institutions that would eventually acquire or be given works out of The Museum of Modern Art's Klee show in 1930 includes the Harvard University Art Museums, Denver Art Museum, Metropolitan Museum of Art (two works), The Art Institute of Chicago (three works), San Francisco Museum of Modern Art, Yale University Art Gallery, and The Phillips Collection.

30. Kantor, 193 and 213.

31. The first work by Klee to be acquired by The Museum of Modern Art was in fact the print *Seiltänzer [Tightrope Walker]* (1923.138) in 1931. I am grateful to Allyson Wolfe, Office of the Registrar, The Museum of Modern Art, for making this information available to me.

32. In New York Klee's work continued to be on view at The Museum of Modern Art in the "Summer Exhibition: Retrospective" (two works) and at Neumann's gallery, New Art Circle. Neumann presented a large selection of Klee's work in his gallery in June–August 1930. For detailed exhibition information, see the bibliography in Josef Helfenstein and Christian Rümelin, eds., *Paul Klee: Catalogue Raisonné,* 9 vols. (London and New York: Thames and Hudson, 1998–2004).

33. Christina Houstian, "Minister, Kindermädchen, Little Friend: Galka Scheyer and the Blue Four," in Vivian Endicott Barnett and Josef Helfenstein, eds., *The Blue Four: Feininger, Jawlensky, Kandinsky, Paul Klee in the New World,* exh. cat. (Cologne: DuMont; and New Haven, Conn.: Yale University Press, 1997), 43.

34. The dates for the individual artists in the 1930 exhibition "The Blue Four" at Braxton Gallery, Hollywood, were Kandinsky in March 1–15, Jawlensky in March 16–31, Feininger in April 15–30, and Klee in May 1–15.

35. Will Grohmann wrote: "Klee has the ability to make invisible things seen. His intuition reaches planes in which we are not yet at home when we see his pictures." Rudolph Probst wrote: "Paul Klee has overcome the gravity of the earth.… The dream of the romantic poet becomes reality." See *The Blue Four,* exh. cat. (Los Angeles: Braxton Gallery, 1930), 13.

36. Houstian, 44, and Naomi Sawelson-Gorse, "Narrow Circles and Uneasy Alliances: Galka Scheyer and American Collectors of the Blue Four," in Barnett and Helfenstein, 55–56.

37. Sawelson-Gorse, 54.

38. Galka Scheyer to Paul Klee, April 22, 1930, Zentrum Paul Klee Archives, Schenkung Familie Klee, Bern, Switzerland.

39. "Wir sassen Nachte [sic] lang wie betrunken mit Bilder anschauen. So etwas in Amerika zu finden ist ein Trost, ist ein doppelter Trost wenn der Kunsthandler [sic], lieber ein Strumpfnadler sein sollte." Scheyer to Klee, April 22, 1930, Zentrum Paul Klee Archives, Schenkung Familie Klee, Bern, Switzerland.

40. "Die Ausstellung in Hollywood wird noch einiges bringen. Es steht also nicht ganz schlimm mit Amerika, und wenn dann in New-York etwa I.B. Neumann noch ein Resultat zu Wege bringt, bin ich nicht mehr so unzufrieden mit 'drüben' wie bisher." ("The exhibition in Hollywood will bring in a bit more. So America is not altogether a loss, and if I. B. Neumann perhaps manages to produce results in New York, I am no longer as disenchanted with 'over there' as I was before.") Paul Klee to Lily Klee, May 27, 1930; reproduced in Paul Klee, *Briefe an die Familie*, vol. 2, 1907–1940 (Cologne: DuMont, 1979), 1125.

41. Galka Scheyer to Paul Klee, June 1, 1930, Zentrum Paul Klee Archives, Schenkung Familie Klee. The six works were *Jörg* (1924.141), *Blick einer Landschaft [Glance of a Landscape]* (1926.219), *Dämon als Pirat [Demon as Pirate]* (1926.221), *Kosmische und irdische Zeit [Cosmic and Earthly Time]* (1927.285), and *Kleine Gartenstadt-Häuser [Small Houses in the Garden City]* (1928.52); the Arensbergs only traded the painting *Vast (Rosenhafen) [Vast (Harbor of Roses)]* (1925.8) with the watercolor *Reise auf Korsika [Journey on Corsica]* (1927.239), "with great regret," as Scheyer noted, "since they could not live without Corsica."

42. Houstian, 44, and Sawelson-Gorse, 56–61.

43. Scheyer sold the print *Hoffmanneske Märchenscene [Hoffmannesque Fairy-Tale Scene]* (1921.123) to von Sternberg. Vivian Endicott Barnett, *The Blue Four Collection at the Norton Simon Museum* (New Haven, Conn., and London: Yale University Press in association with the Norton Simon Art Foundation, 2002), 295.

44. "Ich gratuliere Ihnen zu Ihrem Erfolg in New York. Ich spüre den Einfluss hier. Ihre Ausstellung wird am ersten Mai hier eröffnet. Braxton hat ihre Ausstellung an das Ende gestellt weil er keine Beziehung zu Ihrer Kunst hatte. Jetzt mit Ihrem Erfolg in New York hat sich das Blatt gewendet, er ist der typische Händler im schlimmsten Sinn des Wortes." Scheyer to Klee, April 22, 1930, Zentrum Paul Klee Archives, Schenkung Familie Klee, Bern, Switzerland.

45. "Ich prophezeihe Ihnen einen grossen Markt in Amerika." Scheyer to Klee, June 1, 1930, Zentrum Paul Klee Archives, Schenkung Familie Klee.

46. I am grateful to Vivian Endicott Barnett for sharing this information with me. See also Barnett, 300.

47. Winfried Haines Higgins, "Art Collecting in the Los Angeles Area, 1910–1960" (Ph.D. diss., University of California, Los Angeles, 1963), 178.

48. Klee's irony-dosed humor is typical in his correspondence with Scheyer: "Besagtes Werk das Euer Wohlgefallen in hohem Masse erregt hat, soll durch diese Urkunde ohne Entgelt in Ihren Besitz übergehen, als Anerkennung für die von Uns gnädig beurteilte Thätigkeit [sic] im letzten Jahre." ("The work in question, which delighted you so very

much, is hereby presented to you at no cost, in grateful recognition of your activity over the last year.") Paul Klee to Galka Scheyer, January 26, 1932, Blue Four Galka Scheyer Archives, Norton Simon Museum, Pasadena, California.

49.   Galka Scheyer to Lily Klee, May 6, 1932, Zentrum Paul Klee Archives, Schenkung Familie Klee.

50.   Sawelson-Gorse, 57.

51.   Sawelson-Gorse, 57–58.

52.   Sixteen out of thirty-one works by Klee were listed under private collections, among them the collections of Galka Scheyer, Evelyn S. Mayer, Walter and Louise Arensberg, and Marjorie Eaton.

53.   *San Francisco Chronicle*, April 19, 1931, 6.

54.   *The Blue Four—Feininger, Jawlensky, Kandinsky, Paul Klee*, introduction by Diego Rivera, exh. cat. (San Francisco: California Palace of the Legion of Honor, 1931), n.p.

55.   *The Blue Four—Feininger, Jawlensky, Kandinsky, Paul Klee.*

56.   An excerpt of Rivera's essay was published in several subsequent catalogues for Blue Four exhibitions, including shows at the Oakland Art Gallery held August–September 15, 1931 (in this catalogue the three Klee works eventually purchased by Rivera were listed as "Private Collection, Diego Rivera"); at Faulkner Memorial Art Gallery, Santa Barbara, California, held March 3–13, 1932; and at The Arts Club of Chicago held April 1–15, 1932.

57.   Vasily Kandinsky to Galka Scheyer, May 9, 1931. Kandinsky also wrote: "Den sehr schönen Katalogtext von Rivera habe ich auch englisch tatsächlich gut verstanden…. Dieser Text gefiel auch Grohmann sehr gut." ("Even in English I understood Rivera's very nice catalogue text perfectly well, in fact … Grohmann also liked this piece a lot.") Vasily Kandinsky to Galka Scheyer, May 28, 1931. And he later wrote: "Das Vorwort von Diego Rivera hat hier viele verständige Menschen direkt begeistert." ("The foreword by Diego Rivera has excited a number of knowledgeable people here.") Vasily Kandinsky to Galka Scheyer, June 17, 1931. For all correspondence, see Blue Four Galka Scheyer Archives.

58.   Galka Scheyer to Paul Klee, telegram, early May 1931, and Paul Klee to Galka Scheyer, May 8, 1931, Blue Four Galka Scheyer Archives.

59.   Scheyer had known both architects Schindler and Richard Neutra since 1927, when she briefly stayed at the Kings Road guest studio. Robert Sweeney, "Life at Kings Road: As It Was, 1920–1940," in Elizabeth A.T. Smith and Michael Darling, eds., *The Architecture of R.M. Schindler*, exh. cat. (New York: Abrams, 2001), 103. Schindler was also the architect in charge of remodeling Henry Braxton's gallery, where the series of Blue Four exhibitions took place in the spring of 1930. Smith and Darling, 45. For the first time, Scheyer had space to exhibit some of the works she had collected for more than ten years, hanging them in the compatible environs of one of the most remarkable modernist residences in Los Angeles. Scheyer now started to catalogue her personal collection of then over three hundred works, including works by Alexander Archipenko, Franz Marc, Emil Nolde, Oskar Schlemmer, and other artists.

60.   Although the Arensbergs eventually decided against the purchase, the work was consequently acquired by Charlotte Mack. Galka Scheyer to Paul Klee, June 19, 1931, Zentrum Paul Klee Archives, Schenkung Familie Klee.

61.   "Ich bin sehr befreundet geworden mit Rivera, der jetzt nach Mexico zurückgegangen ist. Er war erst schrecklich begeistert über Kandinsky's Bilder, die zusammen mit Feininger die ersten vierzehn Tage heraus-gestellt waren. Als er dann Ihre sah,

wunderte er sich selber darüber, wie unendlich viel mehr ihm Ihre Arbeit bedeutet als er glaubte. Seine Frau, Frieda, liebt Ihre Kunst am meisten, und so schenkte er ihr die drei Klees." Scheyer to Klee, June 19, 1931, Zentrum Paul Klee Archives, Schenkung Familie Klee, Bern, Switzerland.

62.   Frida Kahlo to Galka Scheyer, September 2, 1931, Blue Four Galka Scheyer Archives.

63.   Frida Kahlo to Galka Scheyer, July 28, 1931, Blue Four Galka Scheyer Archives.

64.   "Da lud mich Diego Rivera nach Mexico ein, und noch ehe meine Sammlung katalogisiert wurde, packte ich schon wieder die Bilder, lag 5 Tage und Nächte in der Eisenbahn, durch Wueste, wie eine totgedrückte Fliege landete ich 10 000 ft hoch, mit Schwierigkeiten der Behoerden, dass einem die Haare nicht nur zu Berge stehen konnten, sondern gleich ausfielen…. Zwei Monate hat es gedauert, bis die Bilder in Mexico reinkamen und einen [sic] Monat, bis ich sie wieder zurueck in Hollywood hatte. Dauernd ein Zittern, es koennte etwas den Bildern geschehen." ("Then Diego Rivera invited me to Mexico, and even before my collection was catalogued, I packed up the pictures again, rode on the train for five days and nights through deserts, got off like a squished fly at 10,000 feet up, had difficulties with the authorities that would make a person's hair not only stand on end but instantly fall out… It took two months before the pictures were allowed into Mexico and a month before I had them back in Hollywood. Constant worry that something could happen to the pictures.") Galka Scheyer to the Blue Four, May 6, 1932, Blue Four Galka Scheyer Archives.

65.   "Sagen Sie doch bitte Herrn Rivera meinen <u>herzlichsten</u> Dank für seine Zeilen im Katalog. Ich bedaure nur, dass sie nicht in meinem Buch der 'Cahiers d'art' aufgenommen werden konnten: sie würden die 'Hommages' noch klingender machen." ("Please pass along to Mr. Rivera my most heartfelt thanks for his lines in the catalogue. I only regret that they could not be included in my issue of the *Cahiers d'art*: they would make the 'Hommages' even more resonant.") Vasily Kandinsky to Galka Scheyer, May 9, 1931, Blue Four Galka Scheyer Archives.

66.   The translation of Rivera's text reads as follows:

"Paul Klee is the artist who, more than anyone else, deserves the designation 'magician,' high praise from the latest generation of art critics. He is undoubtedly one of the finest artists, or perhaps the artist with the finest sensibility, in the whole world. He has achieved the most complete miracle of current physiognomy, joining in one person a wise man of a thousand years with a three-year-old boy.

"Nobody but Klee is able to assert, using painting's own materials, how an artwork is a container for poetry manifested through plastic means. Klee's painting is sensitivity made real.

"Like no one else's, his paintings are something we can live on, receiving every day a new revelation of his infinite poetry.

"No work of art as much as one of Klee's can evoke emotion from both the most sophisticated and the most naïve viewer.

"No work of art like one of Klee's can be as distant from, and inaccessible to, the vulgar, the insensitive, and the trivial.

"Paul Klee is one of the wisest painters and one of the greatest child/poets of our world."

Diego Rivera, *Cuatro Azules: Feininger, Jawlensky, Kandinsky, Klee*, exh. cat. (Mexico City; Biblioteca Nacional de Mexico, 1931), n.p. I am grateful to Hector Olea and Clare Elliott for translating this text from the Spanish.

67. Frida Kahlo to Galka Scheyer, November 25, 1931, Blue Four Galka Scheyer Archives.

68. Frida Kahlo to Galka Scheyer, April 11, 1932, Blue Four Galka Scheyer Archives.

69. "Nie wieder eine Ausstellung in Mexico." Galka Scheyer to Vasily Kandinsky, December 22, 1931, Bibliothèque Kandinsky, Nina Kandinsky Bequest, Musée National d'Art Moderne, Centre Georges Pompidou, Paris.

70. "Die Ausstellung in Mexico war ein grosser Erfolg. Die Leute strömten hin und schauten und diskutierten stundenlang. Die Verkäufe an den Sammler dort, der nichts von Kunst versteht war sehr demoralisierend, das wurde aber wieder gut gemacht von dem nicht kaufenden, aber sehr begeisterten Publikum." Scheyer to Kandinsky, December 22, 1931, Zentrum Paul Klee Archives, Schenkung Familie Klee, Bern, Switzerland.

71. Galka Scheyer to Paul Klee, January 16, 1932, Zentrum Paul Klee Archives, Schenkung Familie Klee.

72. Hugenberg and Hitler established what they called the "Harzburger Front," a coalition of conservative industrialists and Nazi politicians determined to destroy the Weimar Republic. Hugenberg eventually became Minister for Economy and Alimentation in Hitler's cabinet (February–June 1933).

73. Scolari Barr, 28–31.

74. Alice Goldfarb Marquis, *Alfred H. Barr, Jr.: Missionary for the Modern* (Chicago: Contemporary Books, 1989), 105.

75. Alfred H. Barr Jr., *Defining Modern Art: Selected Writings of Alfred H. Barr, Jr.*, eds. Irving Sandler and Amy Newman (New York: Abrams, 1986), 163 and 164.

76. Barr, *Defining Modern Art,* 164.

77. Scolari Barr, 32.

78. Marquis, 109–110.

79. "In Deutschland trübe politische u. wirtschaftl. Situation." Lily Klee to Galka Scheyer, July 7, 1932, Blue Four Galka Scheyer Archives.

80. The same article was reprinted two months later in Düsseldorf. See Hopfengart, *Klee Vom Sonderfall zum Publikumsliebling*, 97–98.

81. Kaesbach had been dismissed a few days earlier and forced to leave the Academy of Art immediately. See Hopfengart, *Klee Vom Sonderfall zum Publikumsliebling*, 97. On April 3, 1933, Klee wrote to his wife: "Ich bin natürlich an der Reihe, beurlaubt zu werden; aber er [der Interim] hat noch einige Hoffnung, durch eine andere Eingliederung meiner Person in den Lehrbetrieb, ohne dass ich in meiner Lehrfreiheit beeinträchtigt werde. Ich bin ganz ruhig, nachdem ich Schlimmeres hinter mir habe, stelle mich auf das Negativste zum Vornherein ein und kann dann Alles abwarten." ("Naturally I am facing suspension, but he [the interim director] still has some hope of being able to integrate me at some other point in the teaching schedule without prejudicing my freedom of instruction. I am quite calm, having been through worse, but am still anticipating the most negative from the start, and so I can just wait and see how everything turns out.") Klee, *Briefe an die Familie*, vol. 2, 1233.

82. "Es ist ein wahres Verhängnis dass Sie Klee nicht gesehen haben diesmal. Dieser Aufenthalt stand unter keinem günstigen Stern. Wir hatten noch viel Schlimmes durchzumachen. . . . Kurz ein Jahr des Schicksals wie schon lange nicht." ("It is a true calamity that you did not see Klee this time. This stay was ill-starred. We still had to endure much unpleasantness. . . . In short, an unfortunate year, the like of which we have not had for a long time.") Lily Klee to Galka Scheyer, April 29, 1933, Blue Four Galka Scheyer Archives.

83. "Wie froh wären wir wenn für Kl. in USA Chancen wären seine Bilder betreffend." ("How delighted we would be if there were opportunities for Kl. in the U.S.A. regarding his pictures.") Lily Klee to Scheyer, April 29, 1933, Zentrum Paul Klee Archives, Schenkung Familie Klee, Bern, Switzerland.

84. "Ich weiss dass das Werk in seinem ganzen Umfang wohl [wol] erst der Nachwelt zugänglich sein wird und Sie, meine lb. Emmy, gehören zu den wenigen Menschen, die es würdigen." Lily Klee to Scheyer, April 29, 1933, Zentrum Paul Klee Archives, Schenkung Familie Klee, Bern, Switzerland.

85. "Dass wir aneinander vorbei-sausten- und- brausten, ist fast phantastisch, wenn nur mehr dabei herausgekommen wäre in diesem phantastischen Zeitalter." Paul Klee to Galka Scheyer, June 7, 1933, Blue Four Galka Scheyer Archives.

86. Bealle, 3.

87. Klee, *Briefe an die Familie*, 1242.

A "Degenerate" Abroad:
Klee's Reception in America, 1937–1940

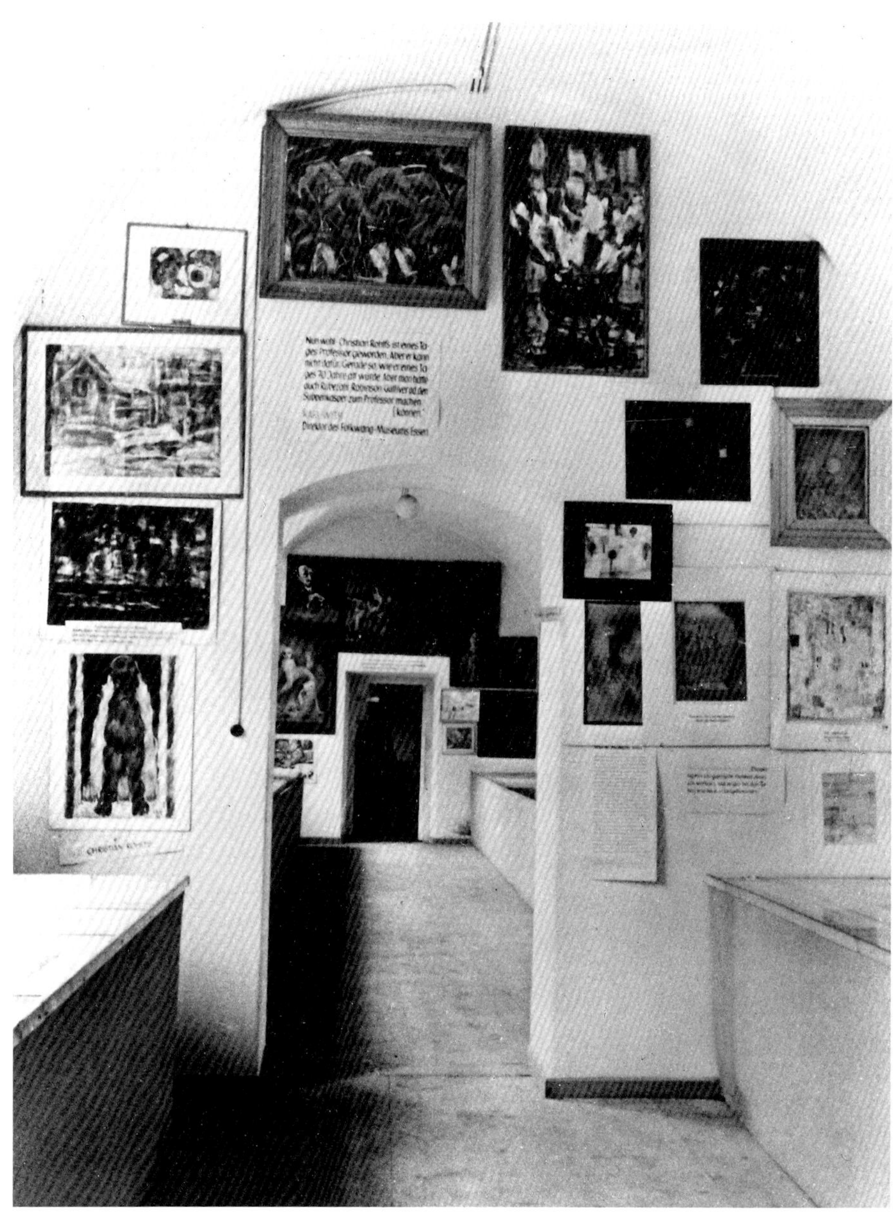

Prologue: Fate of a Watercolor

On November 14, 1937, as the Nazis' "Degenerate Art" exhibition neared the end of its four-and-a-half-month run in the galleries of the Archäologisches Institut in Munich's Hofgarten, an ambivalent, surprisingly thoughtful essay on the show, written by the art historian Carl Linfert, appeared in the *Frankfurter Zeitung:*

> This exhibition in Munich, which more than a million people saw during the summer … merits retrospective consideration. Reason enough is the polemical, condemnatory purpose of this enterprise, something without precedent throughout the long history of viewing art as a loftier, privileged domain of life. But also the *content*s of the exhibition, art rounded up from public museums, reflecting several decades that are also very much a part of the lives of today's visitors, these contents, too, deserve renewed scrutiny. For the artworks that have been brought together in this manner and presented as degenerate have undergone a curious transformation, even if their condition today appears no different than it was ten or so years ago. This transformation is due not merely to the nature of the retrospective view that the exhibition embodies. It is due above all to the "trend of the times," which always disavows a part—albeit this time a large part—of what has come before.[1]

Fifteen of the works that underwent this "curious transformation" were by Paul Klee.[2]

Among the "degenerate" Klees was the 1922 watercolor *Die Zwitscher-Maschine [The Twittering Machine]* (1922.151, pl. 15). Looking at this droll work today, probably the best known of the Klees in The Museum of Modern Art, New York, few viewers can imagine the vicissitudes it has endured in its odyssey through time and space, during which it has been an object both of delight and of vilification, inscribed with contradictory meanings both in Germany and in the United States. This trajectory is typical of many works of modern German art, and tracing it in some detail here should offer a trenchant illustration of Linfert's remark on how not only the changing historical context (the "trend of the times"), but also geographical relocation can alter the imputed meaning of an artwork.

Die Zwitscher-Maschine was first shown publicly in February 1923 at the Kronprinzenpalais on the boulevard Unter den Linden in Berlin, as part of a solo exhibition of 267 works. This was Klee's first large exhibition in Berlin, held in the city's most prestigious venue (following the abdication of the Hohenzollerns at the end of the war, the Kronprinzenpalais had been converted to display the Nationalgalerie's expanding holdings of twentieth-century art). In August 1923, after protracted negotiations with Klee, the museum's director Ludwig Justi purchased *Die Zwitscher-Maschine* and three other Klee works from the exhibition—*Der Angler [The Angler]* (1921.140, pl. 6), *Mond über der Stadt [Moon Over the Town]* (1922.18), and *Das Vokaltuch der Kammersängerin Rosa Silber [Vocal Fabric of the Singer Rosa Silber]* (1922.126, fig. 41)—for the price of 40 million grotesquely inflated and highly unstable Reichsmarks.[3] These four were among the first of Klee's works to be acquired by a major German museum.[4] Of the group, *Die Zwitscher-Maschine* would become by far the most cited and reproduced

Fig. 40
Installation view, room G2, "Degenerate Art," Archäologisches Institut, Munich, 1937.

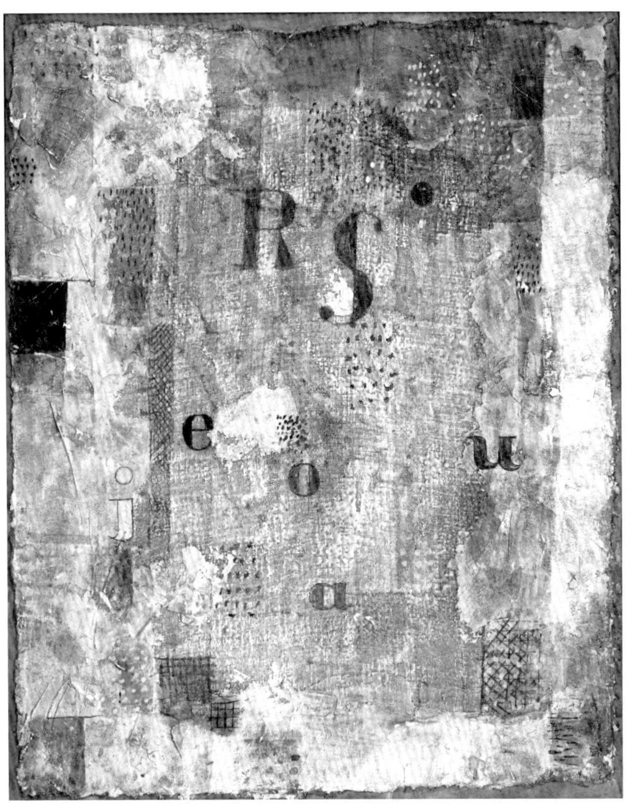

throughout the 1920s and early 1930s, appearing in texts in German, French, and English.[5] As Alfred H. Barr Jr. organized his landmark 1931 exhibition "German Painting and Sculpture" for The Museum of Modern Art, he borrowed *Die Zwitscher-Maschine* and *Der Angler* from the Nationalgalerie.[6] Thanks to these two splendid watercolors, Barr later wrote, Klee began to make inroads among artists and collectors who only a year before had been scandalized by his retrospective, also at the Modern.[7] By 1933 *Die Zwitscher-Maschine* had gained such fame that it was the one work that Richard Hamann chose to represent Klee in his nine-hundred-page history of art.[8]

Barr savored *Die Zwitscher-Maschine* for its "exquisite absurdity," which for him evoked the spirit of Lewis Carroll's "The Jabberwocky."[9] Yet Klee's bizarre contraption was not the product of pure fantasy, as Justi revealed in a handbook to the Kronprinzenpalais collections. It was inspired in fact by a music box made by Frenchman Blaise Bontemps around 1870, a highly naturalistic mechanical apparatus of a tree with animated birds, their lifelike song generated by bellows-driven cams, that was on view in Munich's museum of technology, the Deutsches Museum.[10] Justi wrote: "From the stimulus of this educational institution for technology, an astonishingly unreal machine has come into being: thin wires and birds that are nothing more than singing heads. On the right is a handle; if one turns it, there is twittering from all sides, and if one listens closely, one can hear the different pitches and little melodies." Playfully citing, without quotation marks, a line from Friedrich Schiller's "Ode to Joy," Justi concluded: "Whoever has failed in this, let him, weeping, steal away from our midst."[11]

Clearly many did fail, as not everyone in Germany admired Klee's wit or Justi's urbane joke. But those who failed did not "steal away." By the end of January 1933, they were in control, and the fortunes of *Die Zwitscher-Maschine*, Justi, and Klee changed drastically. On July 1, 1933, five months after Hitler took power, Justi was placed on "indefinite leave, effective immediately," by order of the Reichsminister for education, and the Kronprinzenpalais was ordered closed for reorganization.[12] On April 21 Klee was abruptly placed on leave from his teaching position at the Düsseldorf Academy; he was subsequently terminated in December. When the Kronprinzenpalais reopened that month under the directorship of Eberhard Hanfstaengel, *Die Zwitscher-Maschine* and four of the

Fig. 41
Paul Klee, *Das Vokaltuch der Kammersängerin Rosa Silber [The Vocal Fabric of Rosa Silber]*, 1922.126. Watercolor and plaster on muslin, mounted on cardboard, 24½ x 20½ inches (62.2 x 52 cm). The Museum of Modern Art, New York, Gift of Mr. and Mrs. Stanley B. Resor (13.1955).

other five Klee works in the collection had been removed from view.[13] Not until three years later, in November 1936, would *Die Zwitscher-Maschine* be exhibited once again, but under drastically different circumstances. It was seen not in Berlin but in Munich, at the very institution that housed the elaborate avian music box that had inspired Klee's watercolor—the Deutsches Museum. The occasion was the vast exhibition "Bolshevism—The Great Antibolshevist Exposition." Here *Die Zwitscher-Maschine* and its companion piece from the storage vaults of the Nationalgalerie, *Das Vokaltuch der Kammersängerin Rosa Silber*, were displayed not for their charm or aesthetic merits, but as scurrilous examples of the "cultural Bolshevism" allegedly rampant in the Weimar Republic.[14]

On July 7, 1937, the Nazi painters Adolf Ziegler, president of the Reichskammer of fine arts, and Wolfgang Willrich, author of the recently published *Säuberung des Kunsttempels [Cleansing of the Temple of Art]*,[15] arrived at the Berlin Kronprinzenpalais to select works to ship to Munich for display in the "Degenerate Art" exhibition, hastily conceived only a week earlier. *Die Zwitscher-Maschine* and four other Klees were among the 141 objects sent to Munich from the Kronprinzenpalais.[16] It hung, unframed, with eight of his other works beside a doorway in the ground floor galleries of the Archäologisches Institut (fig. 40).[17] Mounted directly beneath it, visible in the installation photograph, was a brief text by Klee: "I cannot be grasped in the here and now, for I dwell just as much with the dead as with the unborn."[18] This sentence, first published in 1920, had become a veritable mantra among Klee commentators in Germany during the Weimar Republic, shaping his image as an aloof, otherworldly, "cosmic" artist. Mounted alongside it at Munich was a longer wall text from a 1930 exhibition catalogue by Rudolf Probst that reinforced this image. Probst described Klee as one who worked "in dedicated seclusion," manifesting "Man's progressive loss of contact with his roots—which to those who remain earthbound is a sinister process, a vision of dread."[19] The context of the "Degenerate Art" exhibition crassly altered the implications of both texts: now they exemplified the estrangement of the modern artist from the *Volk*, a separation against which Adolf Hitler had railed in his speech dedicating the Haus der deutschen Kunst on July 18. It was, he declared, the task of German artists "to reach out from the very depths of the German heart to serve our people and its spirit.... They cannot hold themselves aloof from their people if their path is not to lead them into isolation."[20]

Shortly after the opening of the Munich "Degenerate Art" exhibition in July 1937, Hitler had authorized his propaganda minister, Joseph Goebbels, to order the confiscation of "all those products of the age of decadence ... still held by all the museums, galleries, and collections [under Nazi control], whether owned by the Reich, the individual regions, or the local communities."[21] Within three months German museums had been effectively purged of their modern art collections.[22] The following spring it was decided to exchange these confiscated "degenerate" works for desirable ones or to sell them abroad for hard currency: "We hope at least to make some money from this garbage," wrote Goebbels in his diary.[23] In autumn 1938 Goebbels established a Commission for the Utilization of Products of Degenerate Art (Kommission zur Verwertung der Produkte entarteter Kunst) to conduct the sales.

A major figure in these transactions was the Berlin book and art dealer Karl Buchholz. In the course of 1939, he acquired *Die Zwitscher-Maschine* and four of the other five Klees that had been in the Kronprinzenpalais collection. The authorities, however, confused the watercolor with Klee's easel painting *Die Pauken-Orgel [The Kettledrum-Organ]* (1930.212), mistakenly shipping the latter to the United States in place of *Die Zwitscher-Maschine,* for which Buchholz had paid $120 in February 1939. In response to Buchholz's follow-up query to the Propaganda Ministry on March 31, *Die Zwitscher-Maschine* was pulled from the touring "Degenerate Art" exhibition in Weimar in early April and finally shipped to America.[24] It was acquired by The Museum of Modern Art later that year and in November was seen for the first time since its return to America in the exhibition "Contemporary German Art" at the Institute of Modern Art in Boston.[25] It was one of twenty-three works that had once been the property of German museums (all were identified as such in the catalogue).

Ironically, the Boston catalogue note on Klee framed his work in essentially the same terms as had the "Degenerate Art" exhibition in Munich two years earlier: "His quest has led him to the very edge of our understanding; he has slipped just beyond the grasp of ordinary intelligence into a dream-world where only a few of the keenest minds can follow him." Yet the Boston curators, clearly counting themselves among this elite, lauded this hermeticism:

"Those who have been able to see what he sees…believe that Paul Klee is one of the great men of German art."[26] In October 1940, four months after Klee's death in Switzerland, *Die Zwitscher-Maschine* would be exhibited again, this time in the retrospective memorial exhibition that was a joint enterprise of the Buchholz Gallery and the Willard Gallery on East 57th Street in New York. This was the largest Klee exhibition yet held in North America and a manifestation of his triumph within the American culture of modern art.

The odyssey of *Die Zwitscher-Maschine* conforms to a now familiar American narrative that emerged as the first "degenerate art" began to be exhibited on these shores. It is a narrative of the rescue of artworks once collected by German museums that, only a few years before, Barr had held up to Americans as a model of a progressive and enlightened museum culture. Germany, he had written, was a place where "museum directors have the courage, foresight and knowledge to buy works by the most advanced artists long before public opinion forces them to do so."[27]

There is no question that the "cleansing of the temple of art" enriched American public and private collections. Yet that narrative, however eventful as in the case of *Die Zwitscher-Maschine*, played only a marginal role in Klee's reception among American critics, collectors, and curators. More crucial for Klee's growing fame in the United States was the presence in New York of two transplanted German dealers of modern art, Karl Nierendorf and Curt Valentin, each of whom opened galleries in 1937, two and a half years before the first confiscated Klees were exhibited in America. These dealers' relocation, too, was a consequence of the Nazi iconoclastic crusade against modern art.[28] Together with an earlier Berlin emigré, Israel Ber ("J. B.") Neumann, who had facilitated The Museum of Modern Art's Klee retrospective in 1930, they created a nucleus of galleries that made Klee's work more visible than ever before in the United States. Although some of the most important Klee collections in America were formed independently of these dealers, Klee's almost continuous exposure through their efforts and those of The Museum of Modern Art led between 1937 and 1941 to a dramatic growth in American Klee collections and the beginnings of an American critical discourse on the artist.

Klee's American Dealers and Collectors

The late 1930s marked a decisive geographical shift eastward in the exhibition of Klee's art in the United States. Until then Galka Scheyer, who had moved from Germany to America in 1924, settling in California, had been the primary promoter of Klee, whom she represented, along with Lyonel Feininger, Alexei Jawlensky, and Vasily Kandinsky, as a member of the so-called "Blue Four." She remained unchallenged in this role until 1935, and as a result, between 1925 and 1935 Klee's art was seen almost exclusively in the context of Blue Four exhibitions, primarily on the West Coast.[29]

The Museum of Modern Art did stage its groundbreaking Klee retrospective in 1930, but afterward the East Coast had to wait five years before encountering another comparably generous offering of Klee's art. In March 1935, Neumann mounted a solo exhibition of Klee's work in two sequential parts, showing first oils and then watercolors.[30] In the following year, he arranged a solo exhibition of fifty works at the Wadsworth Atheneum in Hartford, Connecticut.[31] Then in 1936 Klee was represented in the two most ambitious exhibitions that Barr had yet undertaken at The Museum of Modern Art: "Cubism and Abstract Art," from February to April, and "Fantastic Art, Dada, Surrealism," from December to January 1937 (both traveled to other major American cities).[32] But the real breakthrough began in 1937 when from January of that year through January 1941, Klee had twelve solo exhibitions in the United States—seven in New York, two in San Francisco, and one each in Hollywood, Chicago, and Cambridge, Massachusetts.

Nierendorf presented his first significant offering of Klee in the exhibition "Three Masters of the Bauhaus," which also included paintings by Kandinsky and Feininger. The show went on view around mid-December 1937 and was extended several times up to late February. The Klees outnumbered the works by his Bauhaus colleagues, and by early February Nierendorf had increased their share.[33] Less than a month later, on March 23, Valentin's Buchholz Gallery opened a Klee solo exhibition (fig. 42)—the first in the city since Neumann's shows of March 1935—with seventy-six works, thirteen more than in The Museum of Modern Art exhibition of 1930 and with a broader chronological range.[34] Beginning with two early etchings from 1903, which marked the beginning of Klee's mature production, the Buchholz show included eight more pictures from before 1920, twenty-seven works from the

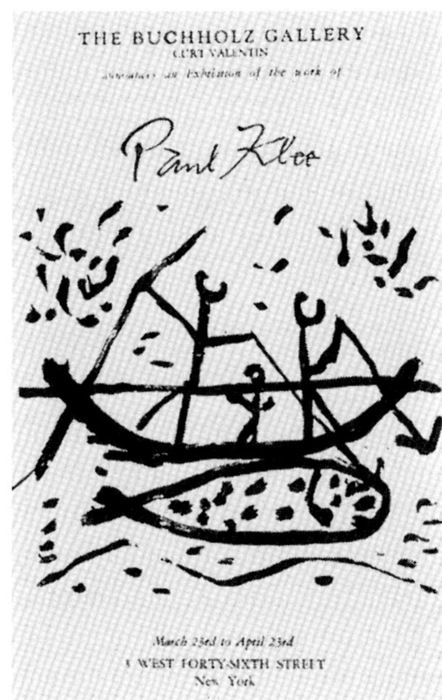

1920s, and thirty-nine from the 1930s. Prices ranged from $20 for the prints to up to $1,000 for the most expensive oil painting, *Gespenster-Abgang [Departure of the Ghost]* (1931.147), which belonged to Nierendorf and remained unsold.[35]

At this point Valentin's relations with Nierendorf were evidently still reasonably civil, though this would change in the fall of that year. The conflict between these two German dealers who were so crucial to Klee's success in America became acute after Nierendorf reached an agreement with Kahnweiler granting him the exclusive right to represent Klee in America.[36] Things came to a head in the fall of 1938, when Valentin made an advance announcement of his plan to mount a Klee exhibition "from a European private collection." He had acquired pictures from Klee himself and purchased others at auction in Switzerland or from other sources, but Nierendorf was adamant that Valentin had no authority to show Klee's work.[37] Valentin wrote to Lily Klee: "Nierendorf sent me a registered letter in which he informs me that he alone has the right to organize a Klee exhibition. It is my view that there is no such right; I know that I will not be able to organize a larger exhibition in the foreseeable future and that because of the Klee-Nierendorf contract, I cannot count on cooperation

from Klee or Kahnweiler. Still, no one can or will deprive me of the right to show to the public the small group of paintings and watercolors that I buy for myself."[38] Valentin claimed to feel "sorry for Mr. Nierendorf that I love Klee so much, over and above everything else." But he would not desist from exhibiting Klee, "even if I must go my own way."[39]

In the end there were two overlapping exhibitions, with a total of ninety-nine works spread between the two midtown galleries, a few blocks apart. It was the largest concentration of Klee's art yet seen in the United States. Nierendorf's show, with sixty-two paintings and watercolors, opened on October 24 and remained on view through November 15; Valentin's exhibition, with thirty-seven works, opened on November 1 and ran through November 26. Nierendorf printed a simple catalogue—a mimeograph of a typescript—with a three-page text by Perry Rathbone, who declared that "Klee is today second in importance only to Picasso as an exponent of the abstract wing in the modern tradition."[40] Only days after Valentin's exhibition closed, Klee gained further exposure when The Museum of Modern Art opened "Bauhaus 1919–1928," a huge exhibition in which he was prominently represented. It remained on view through January 1939.[41]

Although neither Valentin nor Nierendorf presented a solo Klee exhibition in 1939, each included works by Klee in group shows intermittently throughout the year. But Neumann, having just merged his gallery with that of Marian Willard, mounted a small Klee show of twenty-seven objects in May and June of that year in connection with the opening of the new building of The Museum of Modern Art, which was also celebrating its tenth anniversary.[42] To mark the occasion, Neumann donated *"oder der verspottete Spötter" ["Or the Mocked Mocker"]* (1930.246, pl. 67) to the museum.

It was around the time of the Neumann-Willard exhibition that the first "exiled" Klees acquired in Germany were seen in New York, although at first nothing was made of their provenance as "degenerate" art. In "Contemporary European Painters and Sculptors," Valentin showed four such Klees, including *Kalte Stadt [Cold City]* (1921.66, pl. 11), formerly of the Kunsthalle in Mannheim, Germany. At the same time, Valentin lent *Um den Fisch [Around the Fish]* (1926.124), formerly in the Dresden Gemäldegalerie, to The Museum of Modern Art for its tenth anniversary exhibition, "Art in Our Time." Buchholz had acquired it from the commission in

Fig. 42
Cover of the exhibition catalogue, *Paul Klee*,
Buchholz Gallery, New York, 1938.

January for $216.[43] Finally, on May 31 Solomon R. Guggenheim and Hilla Rebay opened "Art of Tomorrow," as the exhibition of their collection of "non-objective" painting was called, at temporary quarters on East 54th Street.[44] The catalogue included three Klees that had been confiscated from German museums.[45]

Yet it was not until mid-August, when The Museum of Modern Art acquired *Um den Fisch* and four other "degenerate" works—all on loan from Valentin to "Art in Our Time"—that the German provenance of these objects was publicized and the symbolic potential of their "exile" was exploited. The museum announced these new accessions, which besides the Klee included one painting each by Henri Matisse, Ernst Ludwig Kirchner, and André Derain, and a sculpture by Wilhelm Lehmbruck, with considerable fanfare: "By their exclusion from German museums these exiled works of art have joined the glorious company of paintings by van Gogh, Gauguin and other masters of modern art which have been banished from Germany to the enrichment of collections in other countries."[46] Barr, who had visited Nazi Germany in 1935, now related that even "the more cultivated elements in the Nazi party" were "embarrassed by the 'degenerate art' theories of Der Fuehrer. These men sincerely regret the loss of many works of art. They also regret the terrible damage done to Germany's reputation as a cultivated nation."[47] In a long article on the acquisitions, the critic Edward Alden Jewell declared their "sovereign significance." He recalled remarks President Franklin D. Roosevelt had made three months earlier in a radio address marking the dedication of the museum's new building: "The arts cannot thrive except where men are free to be themselves and be in charge of the discipline of their own energies and ardors. The conditions for democracy and for art are one and the same. What we call liberty in politics results in freedom in the arts."[48]

Under these circumstances, the acquisition activities of American collectors assumed for some the aura of a noble mission. After meeting Guggenheim in 1939, the exiled German artist and filmmaker Hans Richter was moved to write:

> To evacuate from endangered Europe works from all important periods, especially those of the last generation, that are so important for the future; to bring them to America and plant the 'Seed of culture' directly into America's soil.... That is a great thought.... This man is making *history*.[49]

Yet, rather than capitalizing on this notion of American rescue, Klee's growing popularity among American collectors during these years continued to depend chiefly on his enthusiastic promotion by his competing dealers Nierendorf and Valentin.

On December 18, 1939, Klee, by now seriously ill, marked his sixtieth birthday in Bern, Switzerland, and a little over a month later, on January 23, Nierendorf opened an exhibition of forty-four Klee pictures, with thirty-three dating after 1932, fourteen of which were from 1939.[50] He had also intended to bring out a substantive publication to mark the occasion: in his review of January 28, Howard Devree mentioned that "a book on Klee, including forty-eight plates, is to be published next week in connection with the exhibition."[51] This volume did not appear, however, until late 1941.[52] As a jubilee exhibition, Nierendorf's show was modest in size and scope—in lieu of the announced book, the gallery merely provided a checklist with the statement, "The entire collection has just been sent from the studio of the artist. Most of the works are being shown for the first time."[53]

Earlier, in January 1938, Nierendorf had written to his brother concerning his rival German *Galerist*: "For the moment V[alentin] has outdone me in every respect."[54] Where Klee exhibitions were concerned, that proved to be no less the case in 1940. Valentin, who had not mounted a Klee exhibition since the unpleasantness of the fall of 1938, now got his *revanche*—if not as the authorized dealer of Klee works, then at least as the artist's more enterprising promoter. Following Klee's death in June, Valentin joined forces with the Willard Gallery, now located in an adjacent space on the tenth floor at 32 East 57th Street, for a large memorial exhibition. With 101 works, the Buchholz and Willard exhibition of October–November 1940 was the largest showing of Klee ever held in the United States, and it would remain so until 1949.[55] The ambition of the exhibition was complemented by its catalogue—at thirty-four pages it was exceptional for a commercial gallery and longer than Barr's 1930 publication. It included a memoir from Lyonel and Julia Feininger, and a short appreciation by James Johnson Sweeney, who was then probably regarded as the most distinguished American commentator on modern art.[56]

With loans from over forty private and institutional lenders, the show demonstrated how a small elite of American collectors had gradually embraced Klee during the previous decade. Apparently to underline this point, appended to the catalogue was a three-page list of Klee collectors with, in some cases, an itemized list of their holdings. Together the catalogue and the supplemental list identified more than eighty collections and well over two hundred works.[57] Significantly, only twelve of the exhibited works had passed through Nierendorf's hands. Moreover, Valentin—through his partner Buchholz in Berlin—had obtained a small but significant number of Klees that had once been the property of German museums, some of which he had already sold to various American collectors and museums. Nineteen objects in the exhibition had this prestigious provenance, at least fifteen of which were purchased by Buchholz from the Nazi authorities for prices ranging from $50 to $300.[58] Two others were among the three Bauer had acquired in Germany and sold to Guggenheim in 1938.[59]

Nierendorf mounted a smaller Klee memorial show in the following January at the Art Students League, organized at the request of its newly formed student council. Echoing the language the dealer had used in the checklist of the sixtieth birthday exhibition a year earlier, the catalogue stated that this exhibition contained "pictures exclusively from the collection of the artist himself, who selected them to be shown in the United States," almost as if to suggest that somehow this more modest selection of forty-two works, with twenty-nine of them dating from the 1930s, offered a more privileged view of Klee's oeuvre than the works in Valentin's show, most of which had made their way to the United States by a more circuitous route, including those that had once been the property of German museums.

Devree, reviewing the Art Students League exhibition, commented on Klee's virtually continual exposure in New York's galleries: "Paul Klee we have with us almost every week."[60] Over the preceding three years, this had been almost literally true, and an exponential growth in the number of works by Klee in private and public collections was the net result. For all of Scheyer's years of tireless promotion, much of it during the Depression, the sole notable Klee collection that came into being as a result of her toil was that of Walter and Louise Arensberg.[61] The only other notable Klee collections in America before the late 1930s were those of W. R. Valentiner, the German emigré director of the Detroit Institute of Arts, and Katherine Dreier, who by the mid-1920s had already assembled significant holdings from European sources.[62] By 1931

Klee was represented in only perhaps a dozen collections in New York, led by that of Dreier.[63] By the fall of 1940, however, there were more than eighty Klee collectors in the United States, with more than thirty of them in New York City alone.[64] These included important new collections formed during the 1930s, most since 1937, although these remained few in number.

The Buchholz and Willard exhibition collectors list from 1940 provides a good overview of the state of Klee collecting in the United States in the year of the artist's death. The largest collections listed belonged to the architect Ludwig Mies van der Rohe (Chicago) with fifteen works and to the Solomon R. Guggenheim Foundation (New York) with fourteen. In third place was the Arensbergs' collection (Los Angeles) with twelve. Valentiner, who had formed his collection mostly in the 1920s, was listed with ten Klees, Duncan Phillips (Phillips Memorial Gallery, Washington, D.C.) with seven, Charlotte (Mrs. Adolph) Mack (San Francisco) and the Société Anonyme (New York) with six each, and Elmer Rice with five. Of these eight collections, only those of Mies, Phillips, and the Arensbergs consisted exclusively of works acquired in the United States: Mies had bought all fifteen of his Klees from Nierendorf, while Phillips had bought five from Nierendorf and one each from Neumann and Valentin. In contrast, Guggenheim had acquired all of his Klees but one from European sources, including the artist himself. Mack had acquired three in Europe and three from Scheyer. And all of the five Klees in Rice's collection he had bought in Europe.[65]

Once again, we see that the impact of the "Degenerate Art" purge on American Klee collections was a modest one. In his brief catalogue essay, Sweeney, himself an anonymous lender of two of the works, made only a brief mention of the critical world situation: "Today we are faced by another vast social crisis. We see a world torn between the two great forces, democracy and totalitarianism."[66] He did not mention that the very constitution of the exhibition reflected that crisis: twenty-five works had been in the possession of German dealers or collections after 1933, of which six had hung in the "Degenerate Art" exhibition. Indeed the exhibition included all but two of the Klees then in America that had once been the property of German museums. By the time the exhibition opened, some of these had already entered American collections, including The Museum of Modern Art.

"As far as American private collections were concerned, Klee proved one of the most popular European artists," wrote the *New York Times* in the artist's obituary.[67] The crucial factors in this phenomenon were the closing down of his major market in Europe, its displacement to America through the efforts of transplanted German dealers dedicated to promoting his art, and the activities of the young Museum of Modern Art. Taken together, they were more significant for establishing his reputation in America than the twenty-one paintings and watercolors that had been purged from German museums and subsequently found their way to these shores.

Incunabula of American Klee Criticism

Klee's virtually continuous exposure in New York solo and group exhibitions from 1938 through 1940 provided the conditions for the exponential growth of his reputation in the United States. Indeed, exhibitions were virtually the only way that anyone in America could become familiar with his art during these years. Not until Nierendorf's volume, with its sixty-five full-page plates and two essays, appeared in October 1941 would there be a book on Klee in the English language. Until 1937 Barr's four-page introduction to the 1930 exhibition catalogue remained the longest, most substantive text one could read on Klee's art—apart from an article by Jerome Klein published in a short-lived periodical of limited circulation.[68] Otherwise American writing on Klee was limited to the ephemera of exhibition reviews in newspapers and magazines and a few cursory mentions in general books on modern art, such as those by Sheldon Cheney and Sweeney.[69]

Two of the three substantive discussions of Klee's art that appeared during these years predated the flood of exhibitions of the late 1930s. These texts, by John Anthony Thwaites and Robert Goldwater, were probably based largely on a knowledge of Klee's art that they acquired through illustrations in German and French books and journals, since there was relatively little to be seen of his work in this country at the time they were writing—certainly the specific pictures they wrote about support this conclusion. In some instances, even as they crafted their commentaries around reproductions, the physical objects themselves were in Nazi hands, their fates uncertain.[70]

One of the more striking features of the Klee reception during the 1930s is how both Nazi and American commentators often agreed on what they saw as the dominant characteristics of his art—its childlike and primitive qualities, for example.[71] In the United States, such labels were used both to vilify Klee's art and to valorize it, just as they had been in Germany prior to 1933. The most striking instance of such convergence is in the comparison of Klee's art to that of schizophrenics. Klee himself had viewed the art of the insane with favor in a review he published in 1912, and according to his Bauhaus colleague Lothar Schreyer, had expressed admiration for Hans Prinzhorn's book *Bildnerei der Geisteskranken [Artistry of the Mentally Ill]* after it appeared in 1922.[72] By 1933 the valorization of the art of the mentally ill and its comparison with the art of the avant-garde had become an established trope. Barr had earlier pointed out this affinity with Klee's art in his 1930 catalogue, and he repeated it in 1936.[73] Yet as early as 1924, a right-wing German critic cited precisely this association in an attack on the Bauhaus as a symptom of "deepest spiritual decay," which compared the work of the Bauhaus masters with illustrations in Prinzhorn's book.[74] The "Degenerate Art Exhibition Guide" (page 137) devoted a sequence

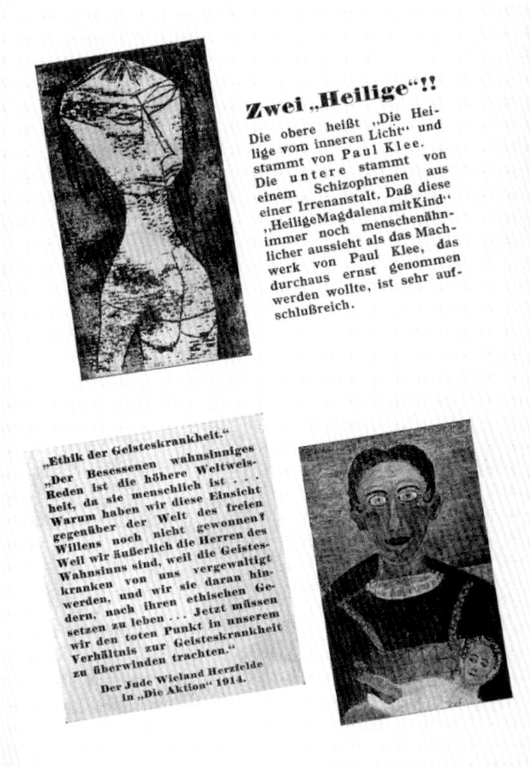

Fig. 43
Page 25 of *Entartete Kunst* exhibition brochure, Verlag für Kultur- und Wirtschaftswerbung (Berlin: 1937), captioned "Two Saints," reproducing Paul Klee, *Die Heilige vom innern Licht [The Saint of the Inner Light]* (1921.107) and *Mary Magdalene with Child* by a schizophrenic.

of four pages to such comparisons, the first of which juxtaposed Klee's lithograph *Die Heilige vom innern Licht [The Saint of the Inner Light]* (1921.122) with a painting from the well-known Prinzhorn collection (fig. 43). The caption reads:

> Two "Saints"!!
> The one above is called "The Saint of the Inner Light" and is by Paul Klee.
> The one below is by a schizophrenic from a lunatic asylum. That this "Saint Magdalene with Child" nevertheless looks more human than Paul Klee's botched effort, which was intended to be taken absolutely seriously, is highly revealing.[75]

Adjacent to the illustration by the schizophrenic is a quotation from "the Jew" Wieland Herzfelde in praise of the higher "worldly wisdom" of the speech of the insane.

In 1938, as the "Degenerate Art" exhibition was on tour throughout the Reich, the young American scholar Goldwater—in apparent innocence of the now politically charged implications of such comparisons in Nazi Germany—proposed that there were "clear analogies" between images in Prinzhorn's book and works by Klee. "Characteristic are the extension of the human features," he wrote, "especially the eyes and the mouth, into ornamental linear motives which are then, in neglect of the original intention, elaborated for their own decorative value.... In the *Dressed Doll* [sic] (1922) the eyes, ears, and elbows expand into symmetrical scrolls, while in the *Angelus Novus* (1920) hair, hands, and feet undergo a similar evolution."[76] Goldwater's comparison of Klee's *Kostümierte Puppen [Costumed Dolls]* (1922.85, fig. 44), as the drawing he cites is correctly titled, with one of the illustrations in Prinzhorn's book (fig. 45), like his other comparisons of this kind, hardly seems persuasive today.[77]

Goldwater's discussion appeared in the Paul Klee chapter of his groundbreaking book *Primitivism in Modern Painting* (1938), the first scholarly study in any language of this broader phenomenon. The focus of the chapter was not, however, the art of the insane, but the "Child Cult," an important aspect of early twentieth-century "primitivism," of which he considered Klee to be the primary exponent. Although Klee's art showed affinities with the art of the insane as well as with African and Oceanic art, he argued, the art of the child was the "predominant influence."[78] In taking up this issue, Goldwater honed in on the most pervasive theme of

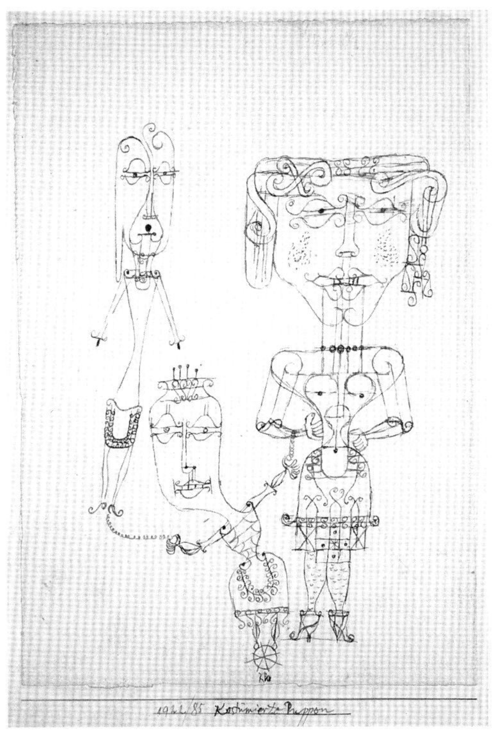

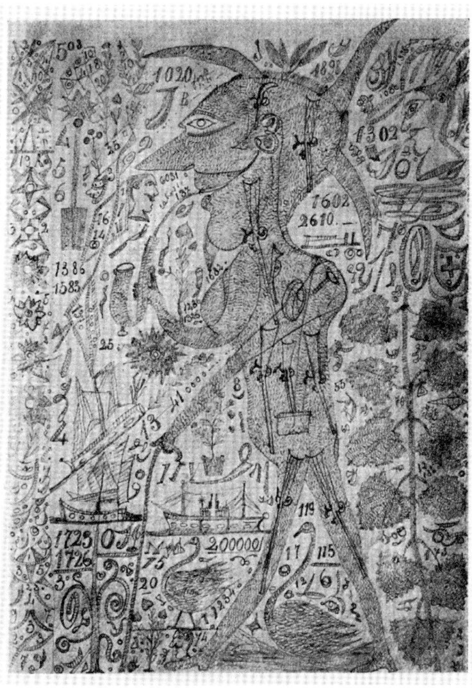

Fig. 44
Paul Klee, *Kostümierte Puppen [Costumed Dolls]*, 1922.85. Ink on paper, mounted on cardboard, 12 ½ x 9 ⅞ inches (31.8 x 25.1 cm). Solomon R. Guggenheim Museum, New York. (48.1172.481).

Fig. 45
"Figuren-Kritzelei," ill. 37, in Hans Prinzhorn, *Bildnerei der Geisteskranken* (Berlin: J. Springer, 1922).

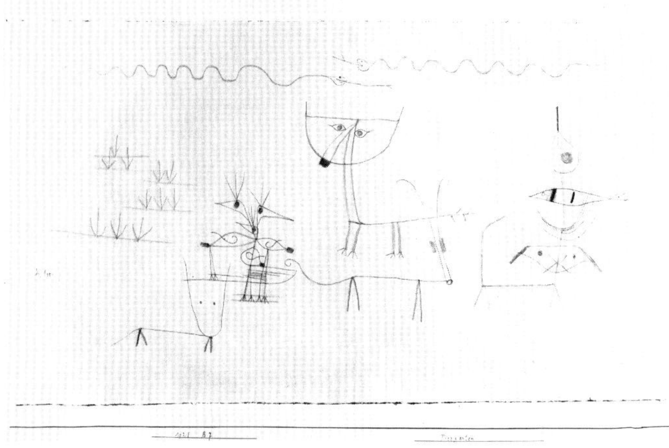

Klee commentary in the United States. One admiring critic saw in Klee's art the "aspect of a good and clever child," while a hostile one compared the artist to "a naughty child who draws pictures that he hadn't ought to in unseemly places," and a third dubbed him "the wistful little kindergartner."[79] Yet the majority of serious critics recognized the plastic sophistication that lay behind such ostensible naïveté. Reviewing the 1930 Museum of Modern Art exhibition, Jerome Klein wrote: "The knowing ones are already protesting that Klee draws like a child. Of course he does. So did the Egyptians. But he is one artist among a thousand moderns who has really recast his vision in the mold of the primitive.... It need hardly be said that primitive does not mean naïf, for Klee is one of the most sophisticated of contemporary artists."[80]

The professed admiration for children's art had since the early years of the century been a well-established feature of calls for a re-newal of art through various forms of "primitivism." Klee himself had espoused this position in several statements during his early prewar period, but by 1930 it had led to such misunderstandings that he felt obliged to distance himself from it.[81] If Goldwater was aware of the earlier controversy in Germany, he did not address it directly. Instead he identified a number of characteristics of chil-dren's art in Klee's work, grouping most of them under the rubric of "intellectual realism." By this term Goldwater meant the inclu-sion in a drawing or painting "of those features of an object which are considered important and which are *known* to be part of it, regardless of whether they could all be visually present at the same time."[82] The selective emphasis of certain features and the linear

drawing technique in *Tiergarten [Zoological Garden]* (1928.117, fig. 46) served as one example of Klee's childlike manner. Yet, Goldwater insisted, simply cataloguing Klee's various borrowings did not define his attitude toward children's drawings, "the uses he makes of them, or his reasons for both." Klee's childlike devices, he proposed, served a sophisticated strategy geared to a particu-larly refined pictorial poetics: "he is exercising a power of choice for certain controlled symbolic ends."[83]

In defining those "symbolic ends" and so offering a rationale for Klee's use of devices reminiscent of children's art, Goldwater broke new ground in identifying and explicating the artist's dis-tinctive visual poetics, a poetics that embraced and enhanced the beholder's share in creating content. This was why Klee, in con-trast to the child, "is careful to leave his figures indeterminate and his scenes unlocalized.... Through the reduction of the render-ing of the objects he makes their reference unspecifiable, and by floating them in a vague plane he then causes meanings which would otherwise be resented as purely private [i.e., known only to the artist] to have unlimited reference and importance." Klee's titles, in Goldwater's view, did not explain the work but increased its mysti-fication: "Thus the spectator is forced, rather than neglect the con-notations of these private symbols, to supply his own, and since the denotation furnished by Klee does not limit his fancy, he may extend without end the personal meanings suggested by *his own* associations." Klee used childlike forms, then, precisely "because they lend themselves to this, because, though they are common symbols which should be intelligible on a low level to everyone, they can, in the abstract manner in which Klee has employed them, have private and varying meanings attached to them. Since each observer will supply his own, they will necessarily seem important to him, and the painter is thus freed from the necessity of estab-lishing contact on direct and commonly meaningful ground." Such an art, with its deceptive "primitivizing through simplification," Goldwater concluded, "needs an acute, educated, and extremely subtle refinement of sensibility for its appreciation."[84]

Thwaites, like Goldwater, approached Klee by addressing a single issue. For him it was the status of the object in Klee's art—the relation between the abstract "visual symbol," the natural object it denotes and distills, and the response of the viewer. His article, published in the monthly journal of the College Art Association,

Fig. 46
Paul Klee, *Tiergarten [Zoological Garden]*, 1928.117.
Pencil on paper, 12⅞ x 23½ inches (32.7 x 59.8 cm).
National Gallery of Ireland, Dublin.

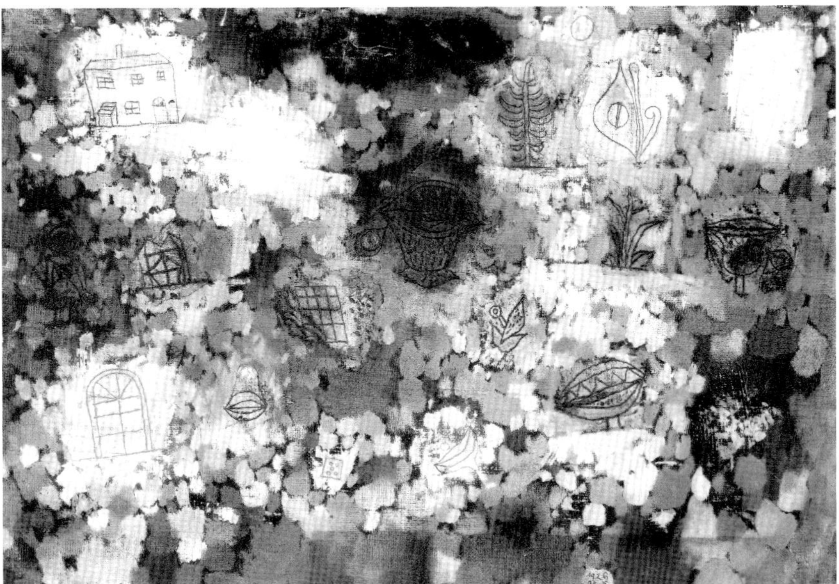

appeared in two parts in November and December 1937, and thus preceded Goldwater's discussion into print by several months.[85] Thwaites was British, not American, and he was at this time not even working in the art world, but was serving in the British diplomatic corps as vice consul in Chicago. He came to the United States in 1933 after having served two years in Hamburg where, one assumes, he had the opportunity to familiarize himself with Klee's work.[86] His article, the best thing published up to that time on Klee in English, must be in part the fruit of extended close looking during those years.

Thwaites argued that Klee's art, for all of its abstraction, was deeply grounded in the senses—and not just the sense of sight—and in an intimate knowledge of physical objects. He rejected the notion, espoused by Herbert Read, that Klee's was "an art of pure phantasy," one in which "the formal element is quite subordinate to the content," while the "content is subordinate to nothing: it is free fancy."[87] Instead of presenting the facts of visual phenomena, Thwaites countered, Klee "gives the symbol which frees your imagination to supply the whole." To the viewer this symbol becomes the object itself, but it is an object created and completed in the mind, one enriched by clusters of associations. Thwaites demonstrated his point with *Junger Park [Young Park]* (1926.206, fig. 47), an oil painting on gauze: "As sensual and emotional associations stir and supply their images there is the sense of flowers and leaves refracted through dusk and reflected from water. There are earth and plant textures here, and air spaces have the colors and smells of a wood. Nothing is representational. After you have looked for a while at the linear sketches they vibrate and glow with the same immediate reality. Not because they are fairy castles for Professor Read, but because they are conceptual and not only visual truth."[88]

The "childlike" aspect of Klee's art Thwaites touched upon merely in passing, as a feature that grew out of a mode of working in simplified pictorial symbols—in this assessment he anticipated Goldwater. Drawing on Klee's *Pedagogical Sketchbook* and his earlier text on graphic art,[89] Thwaites also stressed the centrality of the experience of movement as well as of temporality to Klee. Yet the artist was, he wrote, intelligent enough to know that one could not represent these things literally: "His forms are symbols which start things moving within ourselves." They are "packets of associations which explode like a firework and go off in different lines. So they make in us whole ways of perception, not only strong ways of seeing as Braque's forms do."[90]

Building on an observation made by Klee's German commentator Will Grohmann, Thwaites described how Klee used visual signs to evoke other, non-visual, sensations—of touch, of taste, of hearing. The 1921 watercolor *Kalte Stadt*, he wrote, "sets off associations

Fig. 47
Paul Klee, *Junger Park [Young Park]*, 1926.206. Oil on gauze,
13½ x 19¾ inches (34.3 x 50.2 cm). Location unknown.

in two ways at once, the formal way of its Cubism without volume and the human way of the moonlit town." These associations reinforced each other and were "brought together by the color which you can see into but not through like moonlight. So that at last the night and the cold are in you."[91]

Both Goldwater and Thwaites presented a view of Klee's visual poetics that was unlike any put forth by German critics. They saw his art not according to the Expressionist model of Kandinsky, where the artist communicates a specific emotion or experience to the viewer by means of the affective properties inherent in forms and colors, nor as a Surrealist revelation of the unconscious. As Thwaites commented, "Klee does not need to despise knowledge or to make his revolution in consciousness by a retreat from consciousness as they [the Surrealists] do. He can use knowledge in an intuitive way."[92] Rather Thwaites, like Goldwater, saw in the spare economies of Klee's abstract visual signs an enrichment, an augmentation of the beholder's share in completing the experience of the work of art. By contrast, Klee's most brilliant commentator in Germany, Carl Einstein, had understood the titles of his pictures as anchors, circumscribing the response of the viewer.[93] For both Thwaites and Goldwater, the brilliance of Klee's art was that it set no such limits—it embraced the possibility of endless interpretation and multiple layers of association, shaped by the memory and experience of the individual beholder.

A third major Klee commentator, Clement Greenberg, viewed the kind of aesthetic experience that was central to Goldwater's and Thwaites's analysis as a distraction at best and at worst as an aberration. While Greenberg conceded that we might be affected by "unconscious recognitions of 'literary' meanings and associations" when looking at Klee's pictures, he argued that in the end "we often overlook or forget the subjects." Ultimately it was the quality of the art "that may be responsible for our relative insensibility to anything except the abstract qualities of painting."[94]

The most distinctive feature of Greenberg's writing on Klee was that, for all of the artist's idiosyncrasies and "provincialism," Greenberg placed him at the very center of advanced painting. Earlier, in his now classic essays "Avant-Garde and Kitsch" (1939) and "Towards a Newer Laocoön" (1940), he included Klee in the circle of Pablo Picasso, Georges Braque, Henri Matisse, Joan Miró, Piet Mondrian, and a handful of others, as among the artists "who

derive their chief inspiration from the medium they work in" and as one who advanced the cause of abstract painting. With Valentin's memorial exhibition presumably acting as a catalyst, Greenberg was moved to write the first piece he would publish on a single artist. As he wrote to his friend Harold Lazarus, "I am trying to write a piece on Klee…. Klee, at least, and Picasso too, need a little deflating."[95] Greenberg labored on the short essay (six printed pages) for several months. Although it did not appear until almost a full year after Klee's death, its title, "On Paul Klee (1879–1940)," makes it clear that he intended it as a memorial assessment.

That Greenberg put Klee alongside Picasso as an artist in need of "a little deflating" is testimony itself to the stature Klee enjoyed in the American art world by this time. Greenberg did succeed in deflating him—a little. He did not think Klee's color measured up to his line, arguing that his pictures had "a tendency, when his inspiration flags …to close up on themselves and become too decorative," to be little more than "flat, tinted patterns." He also didn't care for the later work, describing it as "hard and flat, and at the same time heavy…. The color turns acid and rather garish."[96] Greenberg further asserted that "Klee's is perhaps the most literary pictorial art that has ever been attempted, since it tries to combine the ideographical and the representational, to be voluble through signs as well as through pictures of things."[97] From the author of "Towards a New Laocoön," in which he pronounced harsh judgment on "confusion of the arts," this might seem a damning assessment indeed.[98]

Yet for Greenberg, Klee's art manifested more clearly than any other the very problem of the "relations between 'literature' and the 'purely' plastic in pictorial art …because it embodies even better than Picasso's the transition from representational to abstract painting."[99] In contrast to Thwaites, who found the richness of Klee's art precisely in his reconstitution of the pictorial object, in which abstract symbols engendered layers of associations involving memory images of the natural world, for Greenberg it was their formal qualities that redeemed Klee's pictures from literariness: "We see an arrangement of color and line used not to reveal a human being, a house, an animal, a garden, but to take advantage of the themes they offer for the artist's revelation of his own nature. And resemblances are indicated only to have the reality to which they refer travestied and reduced in the interests of constructing an object largely independent of resemblances for its effect."[100] He suspected that the remnants of representation that Klee cultivated in his work were a response to the difficulties of purely abstract invention.[101]

One of the things Greenberg most admired about Klee was his "unconscious modesty, which accepted and accomplished the task of making an easel picture out of almost nothing." He worked "in the tradition of those who illuminated manuscripts and illustrated books and painted pictures for very private possession."[102] In an earlier review, Greenberg had expressed his belief that "as a rule the modern painter cannot cover large spaces successfully.... He is at his best when forced to compress and tighten.... The cases of Kandinsky and [Fernand] Léger demonstrate how easy it is for the abstract painter to degenerate into a decorator."[103] Greenberg suggested that because of Klee's intimate scale and his propensity for using his medium in novel and difficult ways that "help him to conceive freshly,"[104] he was successful in creating abstract pictures that flirted with decoration and yet resisted it. As an example he cited the 1927 painting *Pastorale (Rhythmen) [Pastorale (Rhythms)]* (1927.20, fig. 48). "In it Klee has isolated and concentrated the problem of decoration versus easel-painting, and he was able to solve the problem because he was very much aware of it."[105] It was precisely because of Klee's manipulations of his medium and his engagement with its resistance, so evident in *Pastorale (Rhythmen)* with its horizontal patterns somewhat crudely incised into the unevenly textured, shimmering paint surface, that he succeeded in avoiding decoration by asserting the physicality of the easel picture.

Despite their differences, one thing unites Goldwater, Thwaites, and Greenberg: each viewed Klee's art as one intended for private aesthetic experience—indeed Greenberg wrote that Klee was "complacent about the privateness of his art *qua* privateness and strove to accentuate rather than diminish it in his most characteristic productions."[106] A factor in the purge of Germany's museums was the belief, one that had been embraced by generations of German artists of various political persuasions, that art should be a collective expression and a collective possession. (It was not coincidental that the labels in the various "degenerate art" exhibitions from 1933 on usually included the price that had been paid, usually with tax revenues, for artworks that remained incomprehensible to a majority of the population.)[107] While American admirers of Klee

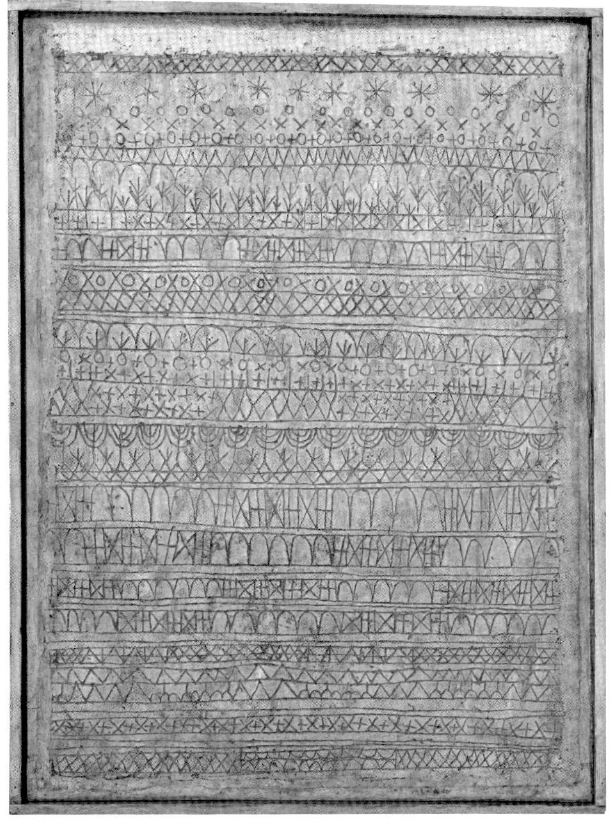

Fig. 48
Paul Klee, *Pastorale (Rhythmen) [Pastorale (Rhythms)]*, 1927.20.
Tempera on canvas, mounted on wood, 27 ¼ x 20⅝ inches (69.2 x 52.3 cm).
The Museum of Modern Art, New York, Abby Aldrich Rockefeller Fund
and exchange (157.1945).

accepted the isolation and seclusion of the contemporary artist, many in the Nazi rank and file instead dreamed of restoring a lost unity between *Kunst* and *Volk*—this same dream had just a few years before motivated segments of the German avant-garde, including the Bauhaus. But as Klee concluded in 1924, "uns trägt kein Volk" ("the people are not with us").[108] In Nazi Germany the supposed unity of art and the people resulted in a flowering of officially sanctioned *kitsch*. In truth, as Greenberg wrote in 1939, the avant-garde belonged not to the masses, who "have always remained more or less indifferent to culture in the process of development," but to "our ruling class … to which it has always been attached by an umbilical cord of gold."[109] In America, with its private collectors, its privately funded museums, and its tradition of art as an enhancement of bourgeois private life, Klee's art found a more agreeable haven.

Klee "has longed proved one of the most 'difficult' of the European moderns," Jewell wrote in 1935: while "appealing to a very limited group of enfranchised esthetes in this country, [his art] remained incomprehensible to the general public."[110] As we have seen, the "group of enfranchised esthetes" grew exponentially in the five years that followed, although it still remained almost infinitesimally small. Even in 1940 there were those who still dismissed Klee and did so in terms that echoed his vilification in Germany. Milton Brown, a professor of art history at New York University, declared, "Nowhere is there a better symbol of decadence, of a sophistication so cynical that it renounces itself, than in the work of Paul Klee."[111] In the popular press, negative criticism took more colorful forms. Reviewing the Buchholz and Willard memorial exhibition, *Time* magazine's critic probably represented the views of the majority of Americans who bothered to take notice at all: "In this world of screwball art," he wrote, "the most consistently screwy was Paul Klee's." He expressed his incredulity that "U.S. modern-art connoisseurs bought his ectoplasmic scratchings at $750 a canvas." Even Klee's death inspired no pretense of respectfulness:

> Last week Manhattan's Buchholz and Willard Galleries gathered together the largest Klee exhibition ever placed on view. The 100-odd drawings and canvases in the exhibition ranged from mad, wire-worky diagrams to basket-textured abstractions. Some, like the *Twittering Machine,* had an odd, disembodied relation to mechanical objects. Some looked like primitive drawings by U.S. Indians. Many were painted on coarse burlap, resembled intricate tattered rugs and tablecloths. All had a look of quiet, pastel-shaded insanity. The show was posthumous: short, sharp-faced Artist Klee had died at his Swiss home four months before. It was also posthumous in another sense. To the red-cheeked, goose-stepping Nazis who after 1933 scrubbed individualism from Germany's art galleries, Paul Klee had been the most degenerate of degenerate artists. Some day history will have to decide whether Hitler was right—about Artist Klee.[112]

During the next decade the growing acceptance and influence of Klee in the United States offered a decisive response to that question.

NOTES

I wish to thank Stefan Frey for his careful reading of the manuscript and his correction of several errors of fact.

1. Carl Linfert, "Rückblick auf 'Entartete Kunst,'" in Christoph Zuschlag, *"Entartete Kunst": Ausstellungsstrategien im Nazi-Deutschland*, Heidelberger kunstgeschichtliche Abhandlungen, neue Folge (Worms, Germany: Wernersche Verlagsgesellschaft, 1995), 197–99; first published in *Frankfurter Zeitung*, November 14, 1937, 4.

2. Of the seventeen works presented as works by Klee, two were actually by Vasily Kandinsky. For an illustrated reconstruction of the Munich exhibition, see Mario-Andreas von Lüttichau, "*Entartete Kunst*, Munich 1937: A Reconstruction," in Stephanie Barron, ed., *"Degenerate Art": The Fate of the Avant-Garde in Nazi Germany*, exh. cat. (Los Angeles: Los Angeles County Museum of Art, 1991), 45–81. A list of the Klee works can be found on pp. 283–84.

3. Christine Hopfengart, "Klee an den deutschen 'Museen der Gegenwart,' 1916–1933," in Josef Helfenstein and Oskar Bätschmann, eds., *Paul Klee: Kunst und Karriere: Beiträge des Internationalen Symposiums in Bern* (Bern: Stämpfli Verlag, 2000), 74–75, 88. See also Annegret Janda, "Paul Klee und die Nationalgalerie 1919–1937," in Verband bildender Künstler der DDR, ed., *Paul Klee: Vorträge der wissenschaftlichen Konferenz in Dresden* (Dresden, Germany: Staatliche Kunstsammlungen, 1984), 46–47. *Die Zwitscher-Maschine*, *Der Angler*, and *Das Vokaltuch der Kammersängerin Rosa Silber* are today in The Museum of Modern Art, New York; the present location of *Mond über der Stadt* is unknown.

4. For a detailed account of acquisitions of Klee's work by German museums during this period, see Hopfengart, "Klee an den deutschen 'Museen der Gegenwart,'" 68–92. Several museums in Germany had acquired works by Klee in 1922.

5. See Josef Helfenstein and Christian Rümelin, eds., *Paul Klee: Catalogue Raisonné*, vol. 3 (London and New York: Thames and Hudson, 1998–2004), 436 (cat. no. 2975).

6. Unaccountably, Janda writes that the Nationalgalerie denied Barr's request, agreeing to lend only *Der Angler*. Janda, "Paul Klee und die Nationalgalerie," 49. However, The Museum of Modern Art's file on the exhibition includes a letter of September 9, 1930, from Nationalgalerie deputy director Ludwig Thormaehlen agreeing to the loan. Registrar Exhibition Files, Exh. #11. The Museum of Modern Art Archives, New York (MoMA Archives).

7. Alfred H. Barr Jr., "Die Wirkung der deutschen Ausstellung in New York," *Museum der Gegenwart* 2, no. 2 (1931): 60.

8. Richard Hamann, *Geschichte der Kunst von der altchristlichen Zeit bis zur Gegenwart* (Berlin: Verlag von Th. Knaur Nachf., 1933), 878–80.

9. Alfred H. Barr Jr., *Modern German Painting and Sculpture*, exh. cat. (New York: Museum of Modern Art, 1931), 27. He quoted the line: "T'was brillig and the slithy toves did gyre and gimble in the wabe."

10. As described on the museum's website, which shows the object and a short video of it in operation: "Driven by four clockwork mechanisms, each of which pump up small bellows and steer several cams, birds sing, fly and peck, butterflies flutter by and a twisting glass rod produces a very passable imitation of a waterfall." See http://www.deutsches-museum.de/ausstell/dauer/musik/e_musik6.htm.

11. Ludwig Justi, *Von Corinth bis Klee* (Berlin: Julius Bard, 1931), 196–97.

12. Annegret Janda, "The Fight for Modern Art: The Berlin Nationalgalerie after 1933," in Barron, *"Degenerate Art,"* 107.

13. Janda, "The Fight for Modern Art," 110.

14. Zuschlag, 303–306. The exhibition was such a success that the ministry for Reich Propaganda decided to send it on a six-city tour. Since the final venue overlapped the opening of the "Degenerate Art" exhibition on July 19, 1937, Klee's artworks were presumably removed from the earlier show at some point.

15. Wolfgang Willrich, *Säuberung des Kunsttempels: Eine kunstpolitische Kampfschrift zur Gesundung deutscher Kunst im Geiste nordischer Art* (Munich and Berlin: J. F. Lehmans Verlag, 1937). Willrich's book, which appeared in the spring, was the primary stimulus for the "Degenerate Art" exhibition and shaped its concept. See Zuschlag, 172; and Lüttichau, 48.

16. Janda, "The Fight for Modern Art," 113.

17. Hanging works of art unframed seems to have been intended as yet another means of degradation. This was done in one of the earliest "degenerate art" exhibitions at the Kunsthalle Mannheim in 1933. See Zuschlag, 63.

18. Lüttichau, 80 (wall text d.); author's translation from the original German. This sentence, in a photomechanical reproduction of Klee's script, had appeared in a special issue of the journal *Der Ararat* on the occasion of the huge retrospective (371 works) that had been mounted in May and June 1920 by Klee's Munich dealer, Hans Goltz. It was reproduced again, later that same year, in Leopold Zahn's monograph on Klee. See *Der Ararat: Zweites Sonderheft: Paul Klee* (May/June 1920): 20; and Leopold Zahn, *Paul Klee: Leben—Werk—Geist* (Potsdam, Germany: G. Kiepenheuer, 1920), 5. Although both sources identify the passage as being from Klee's diaries, it does not exist in the surviving diary manuscript. See Thomas Kain, Mona Meister, and Franz-Joachim Verspohl, eds., *Paul Klee in Jena 1924: Der Vortrag*, Minerva, Jenaer Schriften zur Kunstgeschichte, Bd. 10 (Jena, Germany: Kunsthistorisches Seminar—Jenoptik AG; and Gera, Germany: Druckhaus Gera, 1999), 140.

19. The entire excerpt is reprinted, in English translation, in Lüttichau, 80 (wall text c.); Lüttichau's translation.

20. "Hitlers Rede zur Eröffnung der 'Großen deutschen Kunstausstellung' 1937," in Peter-Klaus Schuster, ed., *Nationalsozialismus und "Entartete Kunst": Die "Kunststadt" München 1937*, exh. cat. (Munich: Prestel, 1987), 252.

21. Andreas Hüneke, "On the Trail of Missing Masterpieces: Modern Art from German Galleries," in Barron, *"Degenerate Art,"* 124. See also Zuschlag, 205–21.

22. Goebbels's decree was issued on August 4. On this action see Hüneke, "On the Trail of Missing Masterpieces," 123–25; and Zuschlag, 205–21.

23. Joseph Goebbels, quoted in Hüneke, "On the Trail of Missing Masterpieces," 125.

24. Hüneke, "On the Trail of Missing Masterpieces," 130. For a more detailed account, see Andreas Hüneke, "'Weg mit Zwitschermaschine und Paukenorgel!' Paul Klee und die Aktion 'Entartete Kunst,'" in Verband bildender Künstler der DDR, *Paul Klee: Vorträge*, 65–70. On the trade between dealers and the commission involving works seized from German museums, see Andreas Hüneke, "'Dubiose Händler operieren im Dunst der Macht': Vom Handel mit 'entarteter Kunst,'" in Hans Albert Peters and Stephan von Wiese, eds., *Alfred Flechtheim: Sammler, Kunsthändler, Verleger* (Düsseldorf: Kunstmuseum, 1987), 101–105.

25. Although The Museum of Modern Art accessioned *Die Zwitscher-Maschine* on October 14, 1939, for some reason it was designated an anonymous loan in the catalogue of the Boston exhibition and, in October 1940, in that of the Klee exhibition

organized by the Buchholz and Willard galleries in New York. The museum did not announce its acquisition of the watercolor in a press release, but the Klee obituary published in the *New York Times* on July 3, 1940, included mention of *Die Zwitscher-Maschine* as one of six works by the artist in The Museum of Modern Art's collection. Christel Hollevoet-Force of the museum's Provenance Research Project suggested to me in an e-mail communication that the museum may have chosen not to identify its ownership of the work until it was shown in its own traveling Klee memorial exhibition, which opened at the Arts Club of Chicago on January 31, 1941, and was eventually presented at the Modern from June 30 to July 27 of that year. I wish to thank Ms. Hollevoet-Force for her assistance, including providing me with information on the exact accession date of the work.

26. James S. Plaut and Mary C. Udall, eds., *Contemporary German Art*, exh. cat. (Boston: Institute of Modern Art, 1939), 22.

27. Barr, *Modern German Painting and Sculpture*, 7–8. Barr's earlier remarks were cited in the catalogue of the 1939 Boston exhibition *Contemporary German Art*; see Plaut and Udall, 5.

28. The most extensive discussion of Klee's reception in the United States during these years is by Carolyn Lanchner, "Klee in America," in Carolyn Lanchner, ed., *Paul Klee*, exh. cat. (New York: The Museum of Modern Art, 1987), 83–101, particularly 100–104. See also Christine Hopfengart, *Klee: Vom Sonderfall zum Publikumsliebling: Stationen seiner öffentlichen Resonanz in Deutschland* (Mainz, Germany: Verlag Philipp von Zabern, 1989), 120–24; and Anja Walter-Ris, *Die Geschichte der Galerie Nierendorf: Kunstleidenschaft im Dienst der Moderne, Berlin/New York 1920–1995* (Zurich: Inter Publishers GmbH, 2003), 242–48. An indispensable examination of Klee's career, including his relations with his dealers, during these years can be found in Otto Karl Werckmeister, *Paul Klee in Exile, 1933–1940*, exh. cat. (Japan: Fuji Television Gallery, 1985), 27–43. For a more general account of the impact of the Third Reich and German exile culture in the United States, see Vivian Endicott Barnett, "Banned German Art: Reception and Institutional Support of Modern German Art in the United States, 1933–45," in Stephanie Barron, ed., *Exiles + Emigrés: The Flight of European Artists from Hitler*, exh. cat. (Los Angeles: Los Angeles County Museum of Art; and New York: Harry Abrams, 1997), 273–84.

29. For a list of Blue Four exhibitions, see Vivian Endicott Barnett and Josef Helfenstein, eds., *The Blue Four: Feininger, Jawlensky, Kandinsky, and Klee in the New World* (Cologne: DuMont; and New Haven, Conn.: Yale University Press, 1997), 356–59. Scheyer mounted only one solo exhibition for Klee, the 1935 show at the Hollywood Gallery of Modern Art, Los Angeles, and the Oakland Art Gallery, California.

30. In his memoirs Neumann relates that he wrote to Klee in 1934, "asking for the right to represent him." Klee politely referred him to his representative Daniel-Henry Kahnweiler of the Galerie Simon in Paris, through whom Neumann arranged the exhibition. J. B. Neumann, "Confessions of an Art Dealer," c. 1958, unpublished manuscript, K4-5, J. B. Neumann Papers, II.B.2. MoMA Archives. See also Walter-Ris, *Die Geschichte der Galerie Nierendorf*, 243, 273, and note 148.

31. Hartford, it seems, was not ready for Klee, as Neumann related in his unpublished memoirs: "One of my few untoward experiences occurred early in 1936, when I sent fifty oils and water colors to the Wadsworth Atheneum in Hartford, Connecticut, for a showing scheduled to run three weeks. At the end of the first week I went up to Hartford to have a look and found that all the pictures had been taken down because they had all caused so much antagonism." Neumann, "Confessions of an Art Dealer," K6-7.

32. Alfred H. Barr Jr., *Cubism and Abstract Art*, exh. cat. (New York: Museum of Modern Art, 1936), 212, cat. nos. 107–13; Alfred H. Barr Jr., *Fantastic Art, Dada, Surrealism*, exh. cat. (New York: Museum of Modern Art, 1936), 215–16, cat. nos. 229–48.

33. There is some confusion about what was on view in Nierendorf's gallery at this time. As related by Barnett, Nierendorf wrote to his brother Josef in Berlin on January 2, 1938, that he had just "installed a Klee exhibition that looks really wonderful and sumptuous." Vivian Endicott Barnett, "The Architect as Art Collector," in Phyllis Lambert, ed., *Mies in America* (New York: Harry Abrams, 2001), 96. Walter-Ris cites the same letter in *Die Geschichte der Galerie Nierendorf* (242) and uses it as a basis for including a Klee solo exhibition, opening January 2, 1938 (between separate shows of Klee, Kandinsky, and Feininger), in her list of Nierendorf exhibitions. Yet neither the weekly exhibition listings in *Art News* nor reviews of the show indicate a solo exhibition of Klee during this period, mentioning only the trio of Bauhaus painters. See, for example, "Works by 'Modernists,'" *New York Times*, January 9, 1938, 10. A month later (on February 13), the exhibition was reported as still on view and that "Carl Nierendorf has added to his current show of work by three masters of the Bauhaus—Klee, Kandinsky, and Feininger—a group of oils and water-colors by Paul Klee." Howard Devree, "A Reviewer's Notebook: Brief Comment on Some of the Recently Opened Exhibitions in the Galleries," *New York Times*, February 13, 1938, X162. In general, Nierendorf seems to have had a casual attitude about setting firm dates for his exhibitions. According to the *Art News* of December 11, 1937, the show of the month was "Vasily Kandinsky Paintings," on view until December 31. In the issue of the following week, however, the show had evolved into "Kandinsky; Klee; Feininger: Paintings till Dec. 31." This exhibition then remained on view until late February, with the closing date being revised several times, from December 31 to January 31, then to February 13, and finally, in the February 12 *Art News,* it was extended to March 1.

34. The exhibition is consistently reported in the literature as having seventy-five works, and indeed the highest catalogue number is 75, but this overlooks the fact that there was a number 26a, *Schwarze Schiffe [Black Ships]* (1927.22), an oil painting that was also the third most expensive item in the exhibition at $850. (See note 35.)

35. The Curt Valentin Papers (CV), I.4, MoMA Archives, include a copy of the printed checklist with the prices entered by hand.

36. Nierendorf signed the agreement with Kahnweiler on February 28, 1938. Nierendorf had known Klee since 1919 and claimed that it was the artist who had persuaded him to become an art dealer. See Walter-Ris, *Die Geschichte der Galerie Nierendorf*, 242–43. Walter-Ris also cites the terms of the contract and reproduces Nierendorf's letter of January 4, 1938, to Klee, in which he requested the right to be his American representative (244–45). Nierendorf had joined Neumann's gallery in Berlin in 1923, just before Neumann came to the United States. Neumann wrote that since Nierendorf "had a very close personal relationship with Klee and Mrs. Klee, I felt it proper that he should be given the representation of Klee in America…." Neumann, "Confessions of an Art Dealer," K8. On Nierendorf's campaign to gain the right to represent Klee, see also Barnett, "The Architect as Art Collector," 96–97.

37. In a letter to Lily Klee, Valentin described the planned exhibition as consisting of "works that I got from you, bought at auction from Gutekunst and Klipstein, or acquired elsewhere." Curt Valentin to Lily Klee, October 18, 1938, CV, III.A.16. MoMA Archives. Since the exhibition was assembled from various sources, initially announcing it as from a "European private collection" was misleading. Presumably Valentin was referring to fourteen works from the estate of Heinrich Stinnes, which are the ones he had acquired from the Gutekunst and Klipstein auction. See *Paul Klee*, exh. cat. (New York: Buchholz

Gallery Curt Valentin, 1938), n. p. (cat. nos. 2, 4, 5, 9–12, 14–16, 21, and 23-25). See also *Gutekunst and Klipstein, Moderne Graphik der Sammlung Heinrich Stinnes*, sale of June 20–22, Bern, 42–44.

38. Curt Valentin to Lily Klee, October 26, 1938, CV, III.A.16. MoMA Archives.

39. Curt Valentin to Lily Klee, October 18, 1938, CV, III.A.16. MoMA Archives. On the Valentin/Nierendorf rivalry see Walter-Ris, *Die Geschichte der Galerie Nierendorf*, 243 and 246.

40. Perry Rathbone, *Exhibition Paul Klee,* exh. cat. (New York: Nierendorf Gallery, 1938), 1.

41. Herbert Bayer, Walter Gropius, and Ise Gropius, *Bauhaus 1919–1928*, exh. cat. (New York: Museum of Modern Art, 1938). The exhibition opened on December 7.

42. Neumann, "Confessions of an Art Dealer," K8. As the *New York Times* reported, Neumann thought a Klee exhibition appropriate, since he had been instrumental in arranging The Museum of Modern Art's Klee exhibition in 1930, the first that the museum had given to a living European artist. Howard Devree, "A Reviewer's Notebook," *New York Times*, May 21, 1939, X8.

43. Andreas Hüneke, "'Weg mit Zwitschermaschine,'" 68.

44. A collection catalogue, lavishly produced for its time, was published on the occasion: Hilla Rebay, ed., *Art of Tomorrow: Fifth Catalogue of the Solomon R. Guggenheim Collection of Non-Objective Paintings* (New York: Solomon R. Guggenheim Foundation, 1939). See the anonymous notice on the opening in the *New York Times*, June 1, 1939.

45. The works were *Tanze Du Ungeheüer zu meinem sanften Lied [Dance, You Monster, To My Gentle Song]* (1922.54), cat. no. 508; *Baum Kultur [Tree Culture]* (1924.245), cat. no. 511; and *Vollmond über der Stadt Bejodte [Full Moon over the Town of Bejodte]* (1927.7), cat. no. 514. See Rebay, 174. All three works had been acquired from the Nazi commission by the Berlin dealer Ferdinand Möller, who sold them to Bauer. They are listed as cat. nos. 72, 73, and 75 among works that Möller acquired from "confiscated holdings" of the Nazis, in Eberhard Roters, *Galerie Ferdinand Möller: Die Geschichte einer Galerie für moderne Kunst in Deutschland 1917–1956* (Berlin: Gebr. Mann Verlag, 1984), 295. I am grateful to Stefan Frey for this reference.

46. Museum announcement, quoted in "Exiled Reich Art Put on View Here," *New York Times*, August 8, 1939, 15.

47. Alfred H. Barr Jr., quoted in Edward Alden Jewell, "The Creative Life vs. Dictatorship," *New York Times*, August 13, 1939, X7.

48. Jewell, "The Creative Life vs. Dictatorship," X7.

49. Hans Richter, quoted in Joan M. Lukach, *Hilla Rebay: In Search of the Spirit of Art* (New York: George Braziller, 1983), 122.

50. The concentration on the later work echoes the large sixtieth birthday exhibition (213 works) organized by the Kunsthaus Zurich in Switzerland. Klee had insisted that it focus on the work of the years 1933–39. Werckmeister recounts the conflict between Klee and the museum's director, Wilhelm Wartmann, on this point; see Werckmeister, *Paul Klee in Exile*, 38–39. To conclude, however, that Klee's decision to exhibit only late works from 1933–39 at this sixtieth birthday exhibition showed that he "was determined to stake his reputation on his most recent, most successful pictures" is not persuasive. In 1935 a large retrospective of Klee's career (273 works) had been shown in Switzerland at the Kunsthalle in Bern and had traveled later in the year (reduced to 191 works) to the Kunsthalle in Basel. To repeat such a show little more than four years later would have been redundant. Moreover, after a year (1936) in which illness had reduced his productivity to only twenty-five works, Klee had bounced back to have the most productive period of his career, and in 1939 he had produced the astonishing number of more than 1,250 works—constituting over one-eighth of his total output. It is only reasonable that he would want these works to be seen.

51. Howard Devree, "A Reviewer's Notebook: Brief Comment on Some of the Recently Opened Shows—A Klee Retrospective," *New York Times*, January 28, 1941, X10.

52. Karl Nierendorf, ed., *Paul Klee: Paintings, Watercolors, 1913 to 1939* (New York: Oxford University Press, 1941). It is mentioned as "just published" in late October. Howard Devree, "A Reviewer's Notebook: Brief Comment on Some of the Recently Opened Group and One-Man Shows," *New York Times*, October 26, 1941, X10.

53. Louise Averill Svendsen, *Paul Klee, 1879–1940, in the Collection of the Solomon R. Guggenheim Museum*, exh. cat. (New York: Solomon R. Guggenheim Museum, 1977), 7.

54. Karl Nierendorf to Josef Nierendorf, January 1938, unpublished letter, Archives of the Galerie Nierendorf, Berlin; quoted in Barnett, "The Architect as Art Collector," 96.

55. In the list of exhibitions appended to each volume of the Klee catalogue raisonné, the number of 100 works is given, and indeed the highest number assigned to the list of exhibited works *is* 100. Yet for some reason the first work in the exhibition, *Bildnis einer schwangeren Frau [Portrait of a Pregnant Woman]* (1907.25), was assigned the number "0." *Paul Klee: Exhibition*, exh. cat. (New York: Buchholz Gallery and Willard Gallery, 1940), n.p.

56. Sweeney had been praised for his book *Plastic Redirections in 20th Century Painting* (1934) by the recently transplanted Erwin Panofsky as one of the few authors anywhere who had approached "the problems of contemporary art history from the standpoint of scholarly art history." See Erwin Panofsky, review, *Bulletin of the Museum of Modern Art* 2, no. 1 (November 1934): 3.

57. The catalogue and the supplemental list account for 219 works, but in some instances the number of Klees in individual collections, such as Neumann's, is not given. In a note to the collectors' list, the Buchholz Gallery asked for further information on Klees in American collections that may have been overlooked. In July 1941 Valentin received a letter from Marjorie Woodruff of The Museum of Modern Art with what was intended as a comprehensive list of all the Klees then in American collections, both public and private. It lists an additional ten collectors by name, including Valentin and Marian Willard, who had organized the show. CV, I.4. MoMA Archives.

58. For an account of these transactions, see Hüneke, "'Weg mit Zwitschermaschine,'" 67–69. In the catalogue of the Buchholz and Willard exhibition, seventeen works were marked with an asterisk, signifying that they were "Formerly in the collections of museums in Germany."

59. See note 45.

60. Howard Devree, "A Reviewer's Notebook," *New York Times*, January 26, 1941, X10.

61. By 1932 the Arensbergs had acquired eight Klees, all of them from Scheyer. On Scheyer and the Arensbergs' Klee collection, see Naomi Sawelson-Gorse, "Narrow Circles and Uneasy Alliances: Galka Scheyer and American Collectors of the *Blue Four*," in

Barnett and Helfenstein, 56. Scheyer's limited marketing success and the growing discontent of her artists led to the unraveling of the group. See Vivian Endicott Barnett, "The Last Years of the *Blue Four, 1933–1945*," in Barnett and Helfenstein, 263–71. As Lyonel Feininger wrote Scheyer on January 2, 1936, "the 'Blue Four' do not exist any more, there are merely 'Blue Ones,' and I am herewith formally dissolving my connection with the group" (265).

62. Robert L. Herbert, Eleanor S. Apter, and Elise K. Kenney, eds., *The Société Anonyme and the Dreier Bequest at Yale University: A catalogue raisonné* (New Haven, Conn.: Yale University Press, 1984), 375–87, 772. On Valentiner, see Margaret Heiden, "Neue deutsche Kunst im Detroit Institute of Arts," *Museum der Gegenwart* 2, no. 1 (1931): 12–22.

63. Carry [sic] Ross, "Deutsche Kunst in den Sammlungen New Yorks," *Museum der Gegenwart* 2, no. 1 (1931): 7, 10–11. This does not include a lender who appeared in an annotated checklist intended as a gallery handout for "German Painting and Sculpture." It noted that a work entitled *The Reader*, lent by Mr. and Mrs. Eugene Klein of New York, was substituted for no. 46, *The Herdsman*, which, the handwritten annotation tells us, was "not shown." Registrar Exhibition Files, Exh. #11. MoMA Archives. The Klee catalogue raisonné does not list Eugene Klein in its provenance index.

64. I base these statistics on the 1940 Buchholz and Willard exhibition catalogue and the supplemental three-page list of Klee collectors appended to it. See *Paul Klee: Exhibition*, n.p.

65. The above is based on information gleaned from the provenance of the individual works in Helfenstein and Rümelin.

66. James Johnson Sweeney, "Paul Klee," in *Paul Klee: Exhibition*, n.p.

67. "Paul Klee: Artist Banned by the Nazis," *New York Times*, July 3, 1940, 17.

68. Jerome Klein, "The Line of Introversion," *New Freeman* 1, no. 4 (1930): 88–89.

69. Sheldon Cheney, *A Primer of Modern Art*, 7th rev. ed (New York: Liveright, 1932), 82, 141, 172, and 201; Sheldon Cheney, *Expressionism in Art* (New York: Liveright, 1934), 306–308; and James Johnson Sweeney, *Plastic Redirections in 20th Century Painting* (Chicago: University of Chicago Press, 1934), 30, 77, and 90.

70. *Grieche und Barbaren [Greek and Barbarians]* (1920.12), discussed by Goldwater (see below) and acquired by the Neues Museum in Wiesbaden, Germany, in 1932, was used by Willrich in a photomontage of "degenerate" works that he published in his book. See Willrich, *Säuberung Des Kunsttempels*, 7. See also Robert Goldwater, *Primitivism in Modern Painting* (New York and London: Harper, 1938), 43. Thwaites (see note 85) was writing about *Die Zwitscher-Maschine* even as it was on view in the "Degenerate Art" exhibition in Munich.

71. On the Nazi characterizations, see Hüneke, "'Weg mit Zwitschermaschine,'" 64.

72. Hans Prinzhorn, *Bildnerei der Geisteskranken: Ein Beitrag zur Psychologie und Psychopathologie der Gestaltung* (Berlin: Julius Springer, 1922). Klee's positive allusion to the art of the insane appeared in his review of the first Blaue Reiter exhibition, reprinted in Paul Klee, *Schriften: Rezension und Aufsätze*, ed. Christian Geelhaar (Cologne: DuMont, 1976), 97. He repeated the relevant passage from the review, with slight variations, in his diary; see Paul Klee, *Tagebücher, 1898–1918*, ed. Wolfgang Kersten (Stuttgart, Germany: G. Hatje, 1988), 322 (no. 905). See also Lothar Schreyer, *Erinnerungen an Sturm und Bauhaus* (Munich: Albert Langen Georg Müller Verlag, 1956), 168–69 and 170–71. For a rigorous and critical reassessment of the whole question, see Wolfgang Kersten, "Paul Klees kulturkritisches Ideal der 'Geisteskrankenkunst': Revision einer kunsthistorischen Bewertung," in *Vision und Revision einer Entdeckung* (Heidelberg: Sammlung Prinzhorn, 2001), 47–60.

73. Alfred H. Barr Jr., *Paul Klee*, exh. cat. (New York: Museum of Modern Art, 1930), 9; and Barr, *Cubism and Abstract Art*, 68.

74. Cited by Otto Karl Werckmeister in *Versuche über Paul Klee* (Frankfurt am Main: Syndikat, 1981), 156. See also Barron, *"Degenerate Art,"* 385, 387, and 389.

75. The entire brochure is reproduced with English translations in Barron, *"Degenerate Art,"* 358–90.

76. Goldwater, 155.

77. As Wolfgang Kersten has shown, critics continue to make such dubious comparisons up to the present. See Kersten, "Paul Klees kulturkritisches Ideal der 'Geisteskrankenkunst,'" 47–60, especially 59, n. 2.

78. Goldwater, 154.

79. Elisabeth Luther Cary, "Max Weber, Paul Klee, Aristide Maillol and Lehmbruck at Museum of Modern Art," *New York Times*, March 16, 1930, sec. 10, p. 18. Junius Cravens, review in the *San Francisco News*, quoted in "Junk?" *Art Digest* 8 (August 1934): 7. Edward Alden Jewell, "In the Realm of Art: From the Stone Age to Modernism: The Cave Man as Artist, Museum of Modern Art Shows Group of Facsimiles from the Frobenius Collection," *New York Times*, May 2, 1937, X9. Almost a year later, Jewell thought better of this characterization and offered a correction: "Paul Klee, I'm afraid, will never with preciseness be 'placed' (not that it matters). To dismiss him as a wistful and willful little kindergartner who never grew up won't quite do, for suddenly he will surprise us with a bit of sensitive drawing or color that betokens a highly developed intellectual and artistic coordination." Edward Alden Jewell, "Three Art Shows Are Opened Here," *New York Times*, March 22, 1938, 19.

80. Jerome Klein, "Weber, Once Held 'Lunatic,' Given Big Show," *Chicago Evening Post: Magazine of the Art World*, March 18, 1930, 6.

81. Hans-Friedrich Geist published an article in which young children gave their reactions to works by Klee. Hans-Friedrich Geist, "Kinder Über Paul Klee," *Das Kunstblatt* 14, no. 1 (1930): 21–26. The piece provoked a scornful attack on Klee and his admirers. Rudolf Arnheim, "Klee Für Kinder," *Die Weltbühne* 26, no. 5 (January 26, 1930): 170–73. This was in turn rebutted by Ernst Ludwig Kirchner, "Randglossen zum Artikel R. Arnheims," *Das Kunstblatt* 14, no. 3 (1930): 91–92. After the war Geist published another article, presumably based on notes from a studio visit with Klee in 1930, in which Klee insistently sought to differentiate his art from the work of children. For a thorough discussion of the issue, see Otto Karl Werckmeister, "The Issue of Childhood in the Art of Paul Klee," *Arts Magazine* 52, no. 1 (September 1977): 138–51, and Otto Karl Werckmeister, "Klees 'kindliche' Kunst," in *Versuche über Paul Klee,* 124–78.

82. Goldwater, 156.

83. Goldwater, 155–57.

84. Goldwater, 157–60. It is interesting to compare Goldwater's discussion with that of Carl Einstein from 1931, who saw in the childlike element in Klee's art the return of a mythic dimension, creating new forms in the world and ultimately contributing to a *collective* renewal. Carl Einstein, *Die Kunst des. 20. Jahrhunderts (1931)*, 3rd ed., Carl Einstein—Werke—Berliner Ausgabe, vol. 5 (Berlin: Fannei und Walz, 1996), 259–69.

85. John Anthony Thwaites, "Paul Klee and the Object," part 1, *Parnassus* 9, no. 6 (November 1937): 9–11; part 2, *Parnassus* 9, no. 7 (December 1937): 7–9, 33, and 34.

86. On the early career of Thwaites, see Beate Eickhoff, *John Anthony Thwaites und die Kunstkritik der 50er Jahre* (Weimar: Verlag und Datenbank für Geisteswissenschaften, 2004), 74.

87. Herbert Read, *Art Now: An Introduction to the Theory of Modern Painting and Sculpture* (New York: Harcourt, Brace, 1933), 140.

88. Thwaites, "Paul Klee and the Object," part 1, 9–10.

89. Paul Klee, *Pädagogisches Skizzenbuch.* (Munich: A. Langen, 1925); Paul Klee, *Pedagogical Sketchbook,* trans. Sybil Moholy-Nagy (New York: Praeger, 1953). The essay on graphic art was published in Kasimir Edschmid, ed., *Schöpferische Konfession,* vol. 13, Tribüne der Kunst und Zeit (Berlin: Erich Reiss, 1920); reprinted in English in Herschel B. Chipp, with Peter Selz and Joshua C. Taylor, eds., *Theories of Modern Art: A Source Book by Artists and Critics* (Berkeley, Calif.: University of California Press, 1969), 182–86.

90. Thwaites, "Paul Klee and the Object," part 1, 11.

91. Thwaites, "Paul Klee and the Object," part 1, 11. It is hard to know how much impact Thwaites's article had. To the best of my knowledge, it was never cited by other critics. Considering the scarcity of English-language writing on Klee, it is telling that it was omitted from the two-page bibliography in the catalogue of the 1940 memorial exhibition, with which Valentin took such obvious pains. Nierendorf listed it in his book of 1941, as did Barr in the Modern's catalogue of that year. In a note to his first article, Thwaites let it be known that his article "represent[ed] the first section of a proposed monograph" and invited "comment and criticism from students of Klee." He never wrote the monograph. Shortly after the publication of his article, he was transferred to the British consulate in Katowice, Poland. After a brief stint in Munich after the war, Thwaites left the diplomatic corps and became an art critic. See Eickhoff, *John Anthony Thwaites*, 74.

92. Thwaites, "Paul Klee and the Object," part 2, 9.

93. "Klee guides his beholder by means of clearly directive titles." Carl Einstein, *Die Kunst des 20. Jahrhunderts*, 2nd ed., Propyläen Kunstgeschichte, vol. 16 (Berlin: Propyläen-Verlag, 1928), 154.

94. Clement Greenberg, "On Paul Klee (1879–1940)," *Partisan Review* 8, no. 3 (May/June 1941): 228.

95. Clement Greenberg to Harold Lazarus, November 25, 1940, in Janice Van Horne, ed., *The Harold Letters, 1928–1943: The Making of an American Intellectual* (Washington, D.C.: Counterpoint, 2000), 229. He was, he reported to Lazarus, two-thirds finished in December, but it was mid-February 1941 by the time he was ready to type the final draft. It finally appeared in the May/June issue of *Partisan Review.* See Van Horne, 230 and 233.

96. Greenberg, "On Paul Klee," 227. Greenberg reaffirmed his judgment on the later Klee in his review of Nierendorf's book. "The only fault to be found is that over half of the pictures reproduced date after 1932, when Klee's best work was behind him, and his style had begun to harden and lose its precious lightness." Clement Greenberg, *Perceptions and Judgments, 1939–1944*, vol. 1 of *The Collected Essays and Criticism*, ed. John O'Brian (Chicago: University of Chicago Press, 1986), 95.

97. Greenberg, "On Paul Klee," 229. In this observation Greenberg seems to have been influenced by a remark by Grohmann, who wrote that "image and the signs of writing complement one another, letters stand for words, fragments for things, images of things for concepts." Will Grohmann, *Paul Klee: Handzeichnungen, 1921–30* (Potsdam and Berlin: Müller & Kiepenheuer, 1934), 5–6.

98. Greenberg, *Perceptions and Judgments*, 25.

99. Greenberg, "On Paul Klee," 228.

100. Greenberg, "On Paul Klee," 229.

101. In this he seems to have been influenced by Grohmann, 5.

102. Greenberg, "On Paul Klee," 225 and 227–28.

103. Clement Greenberg, "Review of Exhibitions of Joan Miró, Fernand Léger, and Wassily Kandinsky," *The Nation* (April 19, 1941); reprinted in Greenberg, *Perceptions and Judgments*, 65.

104. Greenberg, *Perceptions and Judgments,* 63.

105. Greenberg, "On Paul Klee," 226.

106. Greenberg, "On Paul Klee," 229.

107. On this point, usually ignored in the literature on the "degenerate art" phenomenon, Werckmeister has written: "The historical understanding of National Socialism is hampered by its continuing implicit or explicit invocation as a device of political combat rhetoric. . . . The decisive question is whether the commonplace inclusion of contemporary art in a government-organized and government-funded public culture is accountable to political constituencies, as are other policies of government institutions that claim democratic legitimacy." Otto Karl Werckmeister, review of *"Degenerate Art,"* by Stephanie Barron, and *"Entartete Kunst,"* by Christoph Zuschlag, *Art Bulletin* 79, no. 2 (June 1997): 338.

108. The phrase is from Klee's lecture in the Jena Kunstverein, 1924. It was not published until 1945. Paul Klee, *Über die Moderne Kunst* (Bern and Bümpliz, Switzerland: Benteli, 1945); and Paul Klee, *On Modern Art*, trans. Paul Findlay (London: Faber and Faber, 1958), 55.

109. Greenberg, "Avant-Garde and Kitsch," in *Perceptions and Judgments,* 10–11.

110. Edward Alden Jewell, "Oils by Klee Now on Exhibition," *New York Times*, March 11, 1935, 30.

111. Milton Brown, "Paul Klee Retrospective," *Parnassus* 12, no. 7 (November 1940): 37.

112. "Art: Fish of the Heart," *Time* 36, no. 17 (October 21, 1940): 57.

Plates

1930–1939
with Selected Catalogue Entries

In the late 1920s and early 1930s, Klee devoted much of his time to strictly geometrical constructions. At the same time, as a relief from such purely rational labor, he produced a series of dreamlike, calligraphic, and labyrinthine line compositions distinguished by their mysterious subjective features. At times these linear complexes take on figurative shapes, like *Narr in Trance [Fool in Trance]* (1929.46) or *"oder der verspottete Spötter"*; at other times they remain abstract compositions, like *Dynamisch-polyphone Gruppe [Dynamic-Polyphonic Group]* (1931.66).

Klee probably produced the painting *"oder der verspottete Spötter"* after the oil-pigment drawing *Der Mann mit dem Mundwerk*. At first glance *Der Mann mit dem Mundwerk* leaves the impression that Klee constructed this man from a single line. Only after careful study does it become apparent that Klee in fact combined four or five lines to create this image. Two large loops overlap in the area around the mouth where, between the pointed nose and the large chin, a small circular line was added. An unusual feature is the reversed signature, a result of the oil tracing, which means that the entire composition is a reverse copy of the preliminary drawing.

In the preliminary drawing, accordingly, "the man" would have faced to the right rather than the left. Presumably what we now see is actually the back of that preliminary drawing.

In the watercolor of the same name (see below), a nearly identical figure looks toward the right. It is interesting how the line composition's relationship to space has been altered by being reversed. In that watercolor (see below), Klee treated the complex of lines "polyphonically," applying different colors to its open spaces. By contrast, when working on the painting *"oder der verspottete Spötter,"* Klee chose to emphasize its purely linear quality. To that end he opted for a dark ground and drew the figure in lighter pigment with a peculiar sweep of the brush. In so doing, he playfully chose to create the impression of one line crossing on top of the other where the lines intersect, so that the viewer gets the impression that the work is a three-dimensional wire sculpture. The work's title also reflects somewhat the design principle of a line circling back on itself. Klee thus lent the tangle of lines a certain humanity with a dash of caricature.

Osamu Okuda

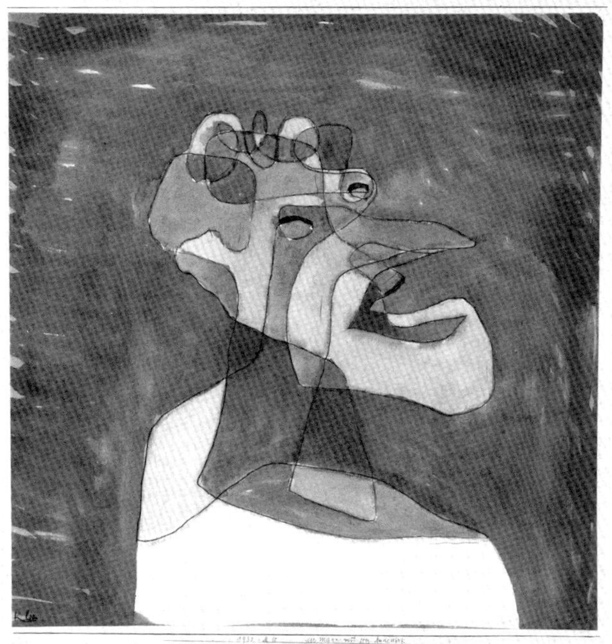

Der Mann mit dem Mundwerk [The Man with the Big Mouth], 1930.40
Pen, pencil, and watercolor on paper mounted on cardboard
17¼ x 17 inches (43.9 x 43 cm)
Zentrum Paul Klee, Bern, Gift of Livia Klee

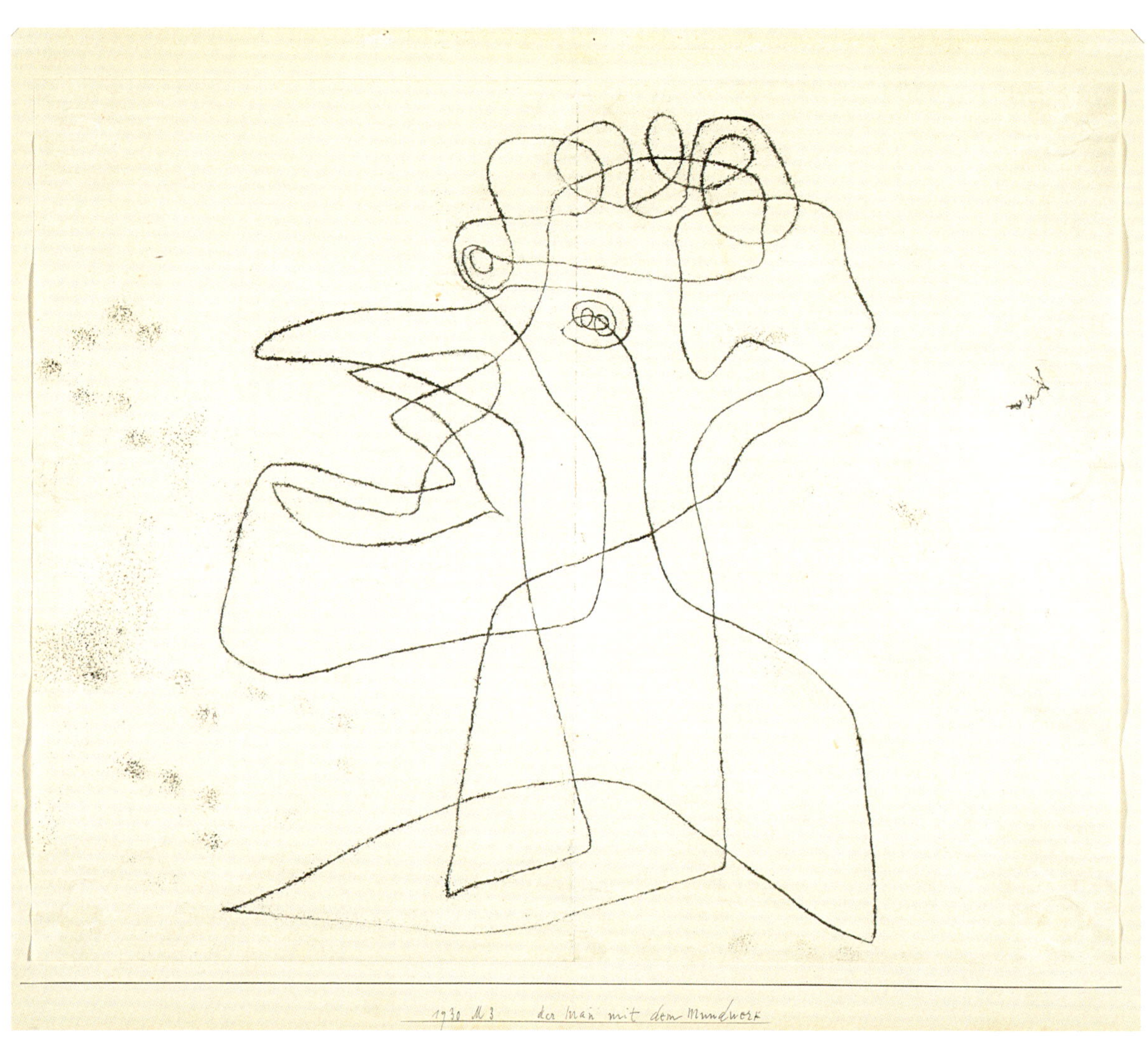

66 **DER MANN MIT DEM MUNDWERK**, 1930.33
[The Man with the Big Mouth]

Oil transfer (drawing) on paper, mounted with glue spots on cardboard
13 x 16½ inches (33 x 41.9 cm)
The Detroit Institute of Arts
Bequest of John S. Newberry, 65.187

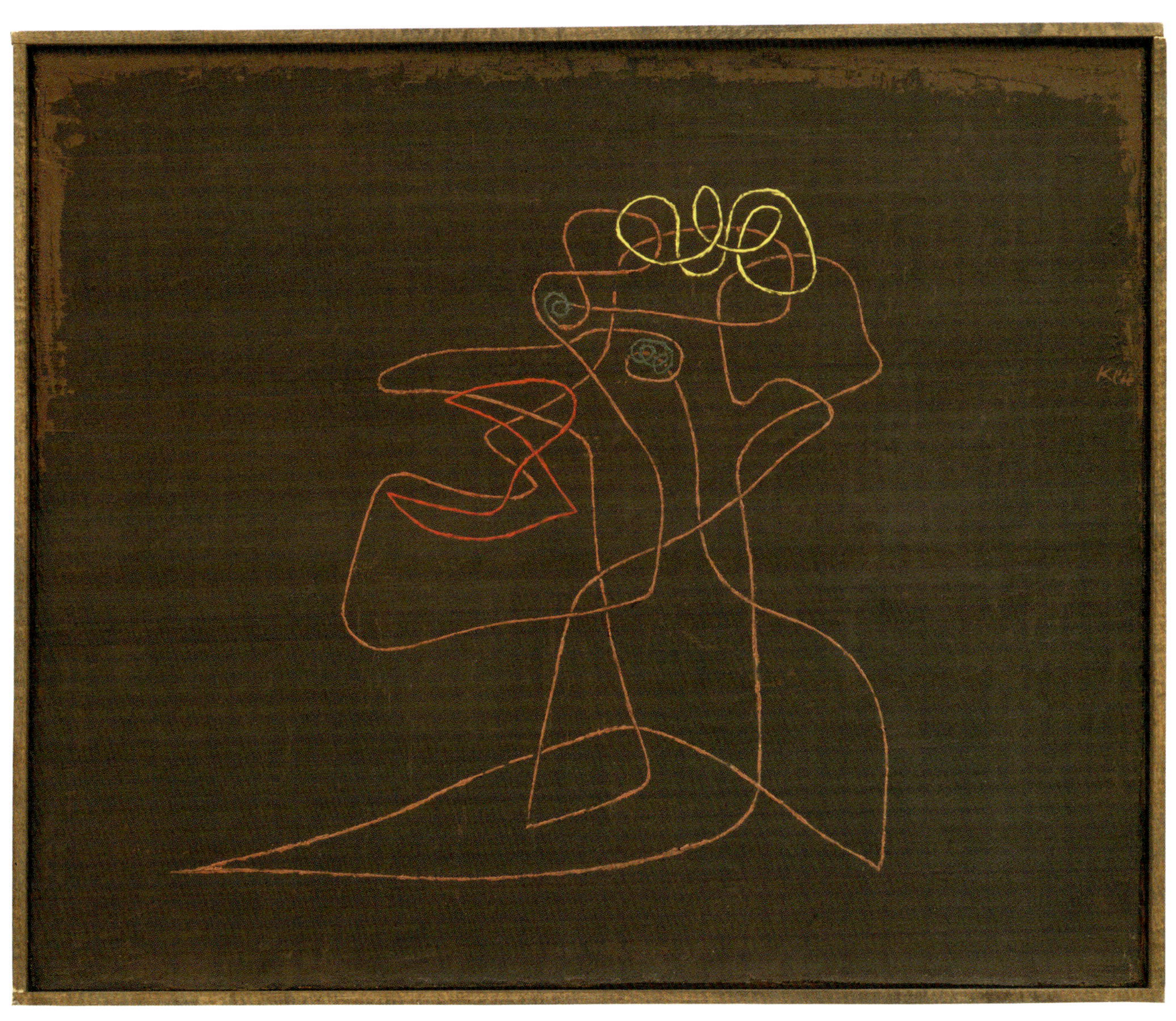

67   "ODER DER VERSPOTTETE SPÖTTER," 1930.246
["Or the Mocked Mocker"]

Oil on canvas
17 x 20½ inches (43 x 52 cm)
The Museum of Modern Art, New York
Gift of J. B. Neumann, 1939, 637.39

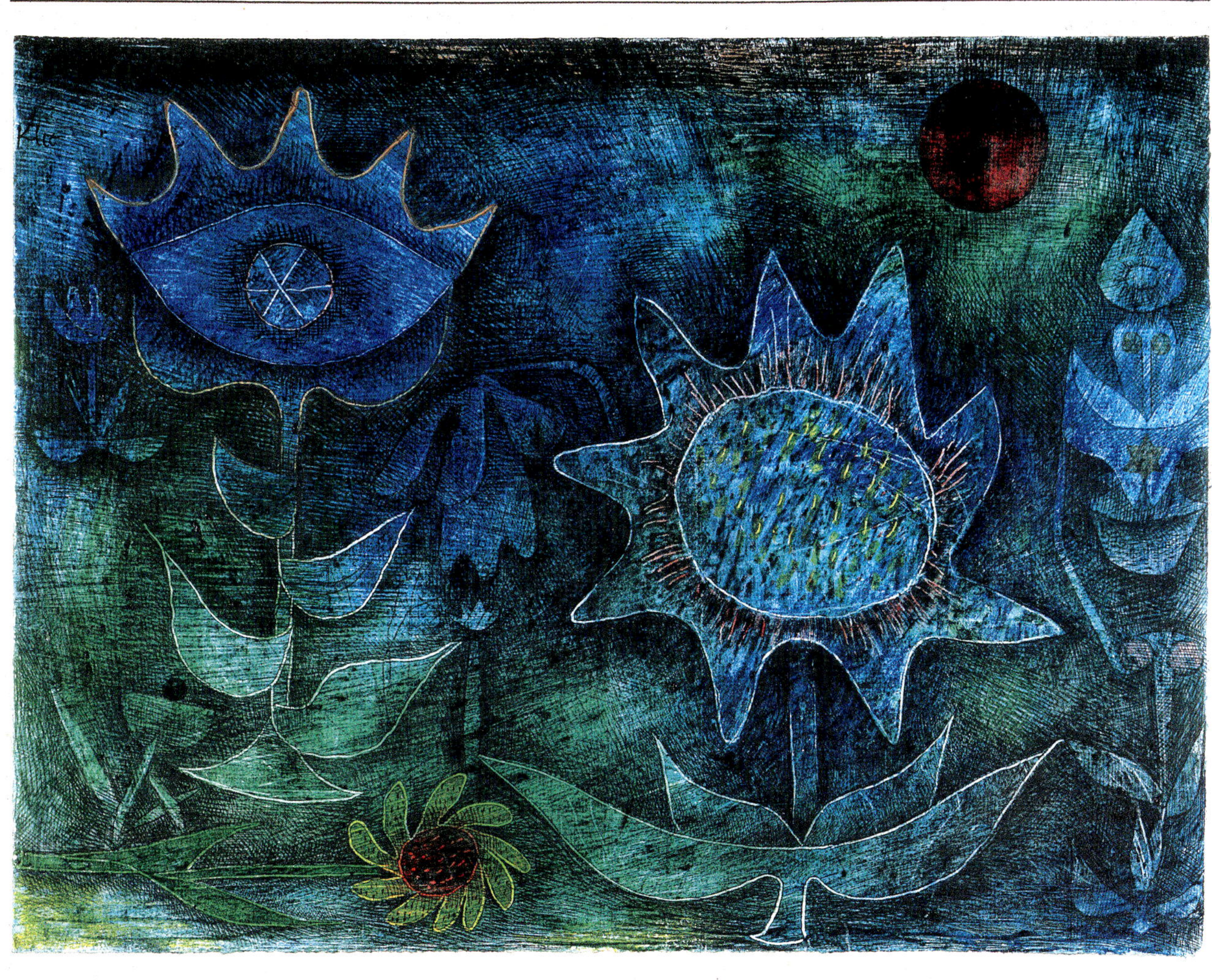

68 **BLÜTEN IN DER NACHT**, 1930.0207
   [Flowers in the Night]

Watercolor on paste-primed paper, mounted on cardboard
9¼ x 12¼ inches (23.5 x 31.2 cm)
San Francisco Museum of Modern Art, Gift of Charlotte Mack

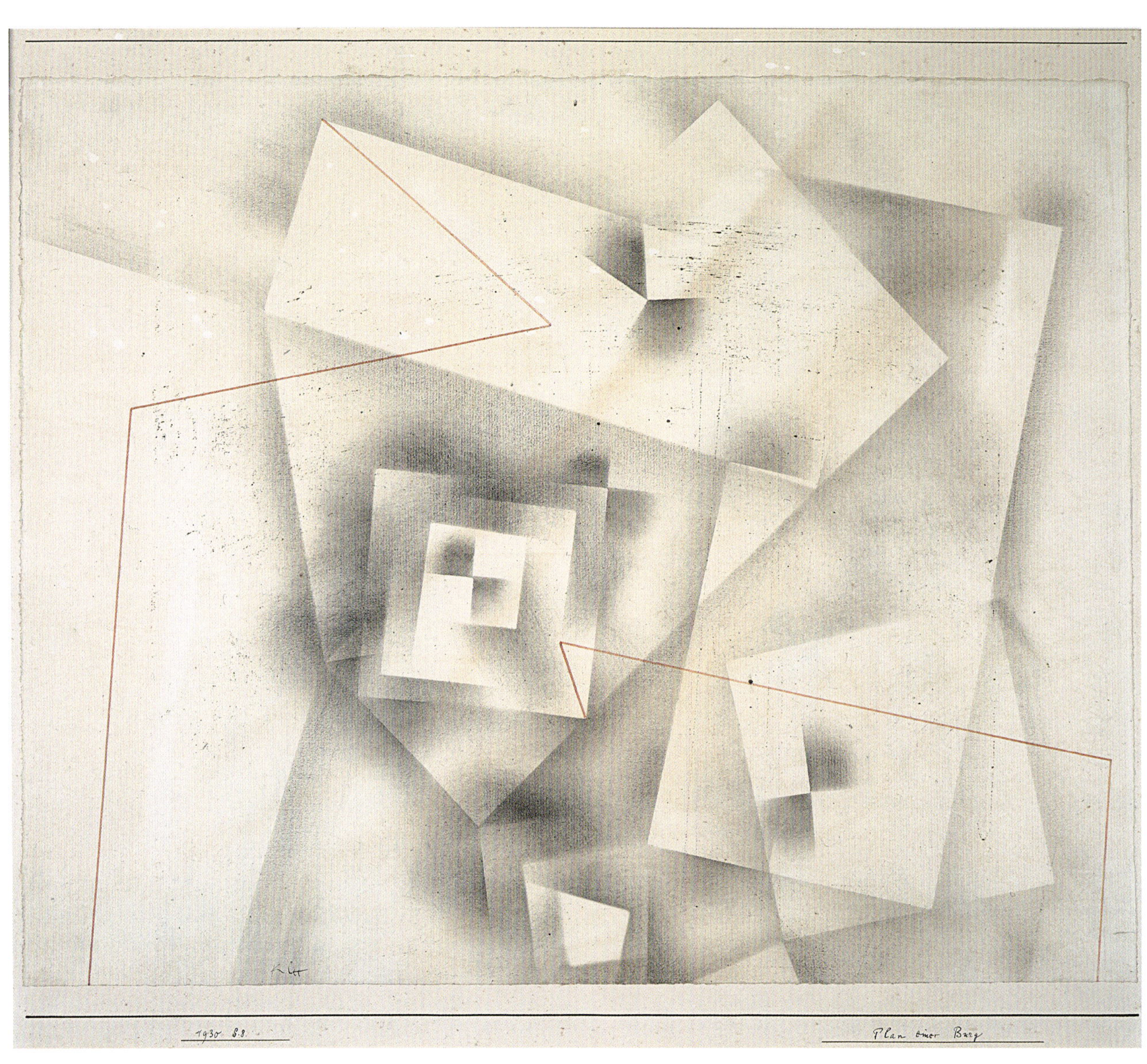

69 **PLAN EINER BURG**, 1930.218
[Plan of a Castle]

Watercolor and pen on paper, mounted on cardboard
15 x 19 inches (38.1 x 48.3 cm)
Collection of Hope Dempsey Hungerford

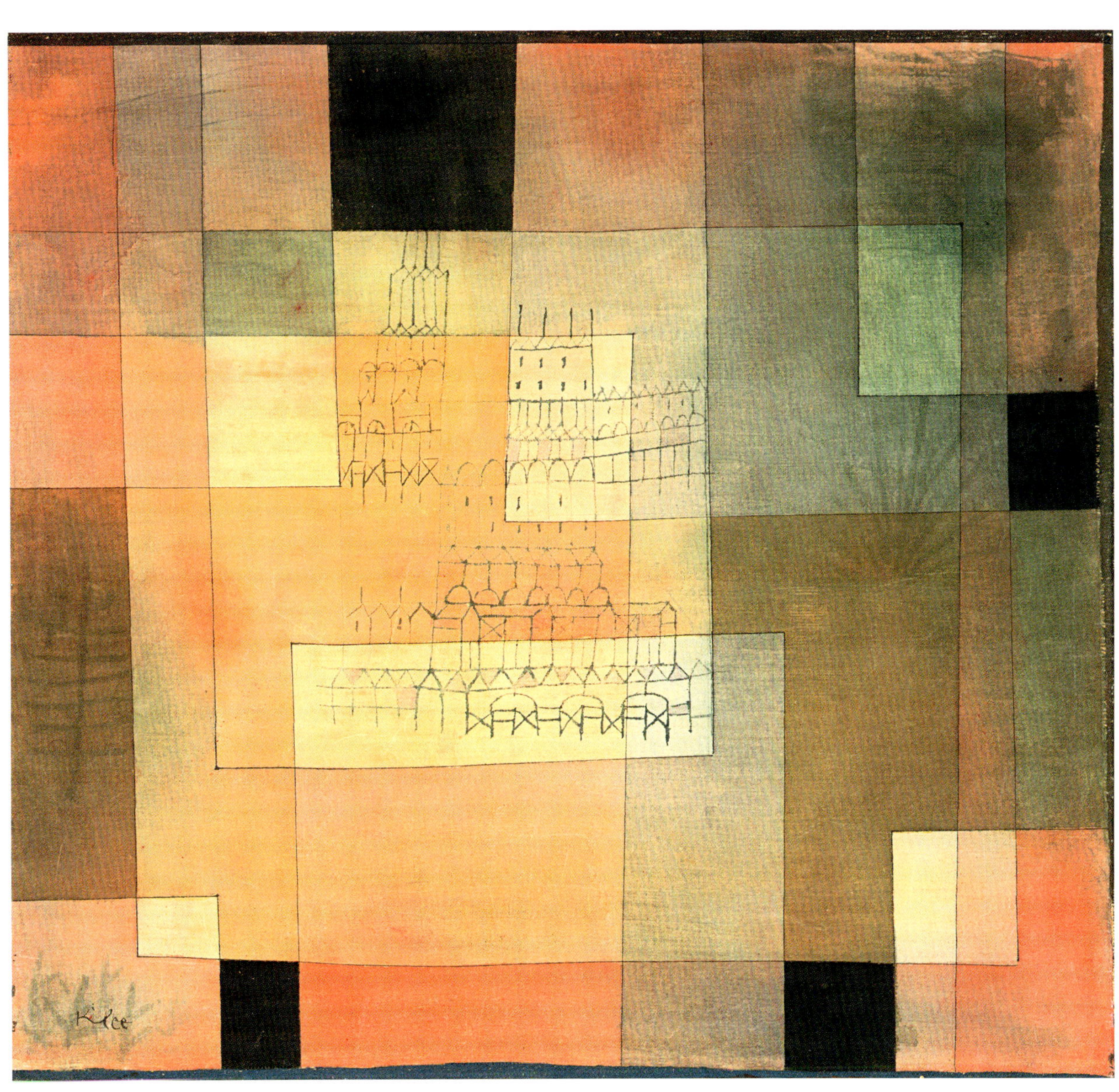

70 **POLYPHONE ARCHITEKTUR**, 1930.130
[Polyphonic Architecture]

Watercolor and pen on cotton on canvas
16½ x 18⅛ inches (42 x 46 cm)
The Saint Louis Art Museum, Purchase, 9:42

Much has been written about the "Pointillist" pictures Klee produced between 1930 and 1933.[1] Klee's own comments on these pictures appear in Rudolf Bach's "Gespräch mit Paul Klee [Conversation with Paul Klee]," but few writers have taken them into account. Bach visited Klee in his studio at the Dessau Bauhaus in the spring of 1931, just when the artist was working on his Pointillist works. After his visit on March 11, Bach noted: "They [the Pointillist pictures] delight him. One can conform everything to everything else, and it always fits, harmonizes. Just as everything in a landscape always harmonizes so wonderfully owing to the atmosphere, the narrow white interstices produce [harmony] in the paintings through the constant interruption (vibrato)."[2] Four days later Bach continued his conversation with the artist, and once again it revolved around the Pointillist works. Klee said: "But a pause is necessary in this kind of work. Your eyes get very tired, and the work is very tense and anxiety-producing internally, for more than anywhere else, [in making a Pointillist work,]one is unable to predict anything, to see the finished work in advance—the effect, the whole, only becomes apparent with the last dot. Until then it has been as though it were hidden and only now decides [what it will be]. But there is still much to do with the whole thing: weeks of work are required before it is resolved and takes shape. First on, some color different from the white ground, later on, a multicolored ground, lots of possible combinations."[3] A week later, on March 22, Klee was still working on the same picture, probably *Klippen am Meer [Cliffs by the Sea]* (1931.154), and Bach reported: "He has never succeeded in painting the sea with regular paint strokes, which troubles him. But in this way [painting the sea] has become possible for him. The white space in between, the air! The cliffs in the foreground were not intentional, but simply presented themselves, were accommodated."[4]

Klee's Pointillist technique culminated in a few delicately nuanced pictures that he created in the beginning of 1932. In the watercolor *Das Ganze dämmernd*, for example, the small flecks of color do not form clear contours. This sowing of pastel dots instead seems spherical, slowly moving. In the bottom half of the sheet, one glimpses vague architectural and landscape elements shining through; small fragmented shapes in the lower right look like abandoned ruins. In the upper section, where the rows of colored dots are arranged in horizontal rows, there is calm. The early English translation of the title, *All in Twilight*, came from Galka Scheyer. Using that English title, inspired by Klee's watercolor, the Japanese composer Toru Takemitsu in 1987 wrote four pieces for guitar on commission from the English guitarist Julien Bream. The heavenly "Takemitsu sound" is produced by combining stopped and open strings and overtones, creating unexpected sonorities. Like the painting, the music does not develop to a climax, but rather emerges from the silence and fades back into it again.

Osamu Okuda

1. See, for example, Josef Helfenstein, "Von der Synthese der Verschiedenheiten zur Negation der Malkultur: Zu den pointillistischen Bildern von Paul Klee 1930/33," in *Canto d'Amore: Klassizistische Moderne in Musik und bildender Kunst 1914–1935*, exh. cat. (Basel, Switzerland: Kunstmuseum Basel, 1996), 346–55.

2. Rudolf Bach, "Gespräch mit Paul Klee," transcribed by Thea Bach, unpublished typescript, 3, Klee family estate, Zentrum Paul Klee, Bern, Switzerland.

3. Bach, 3f.

4. Bach, 5.

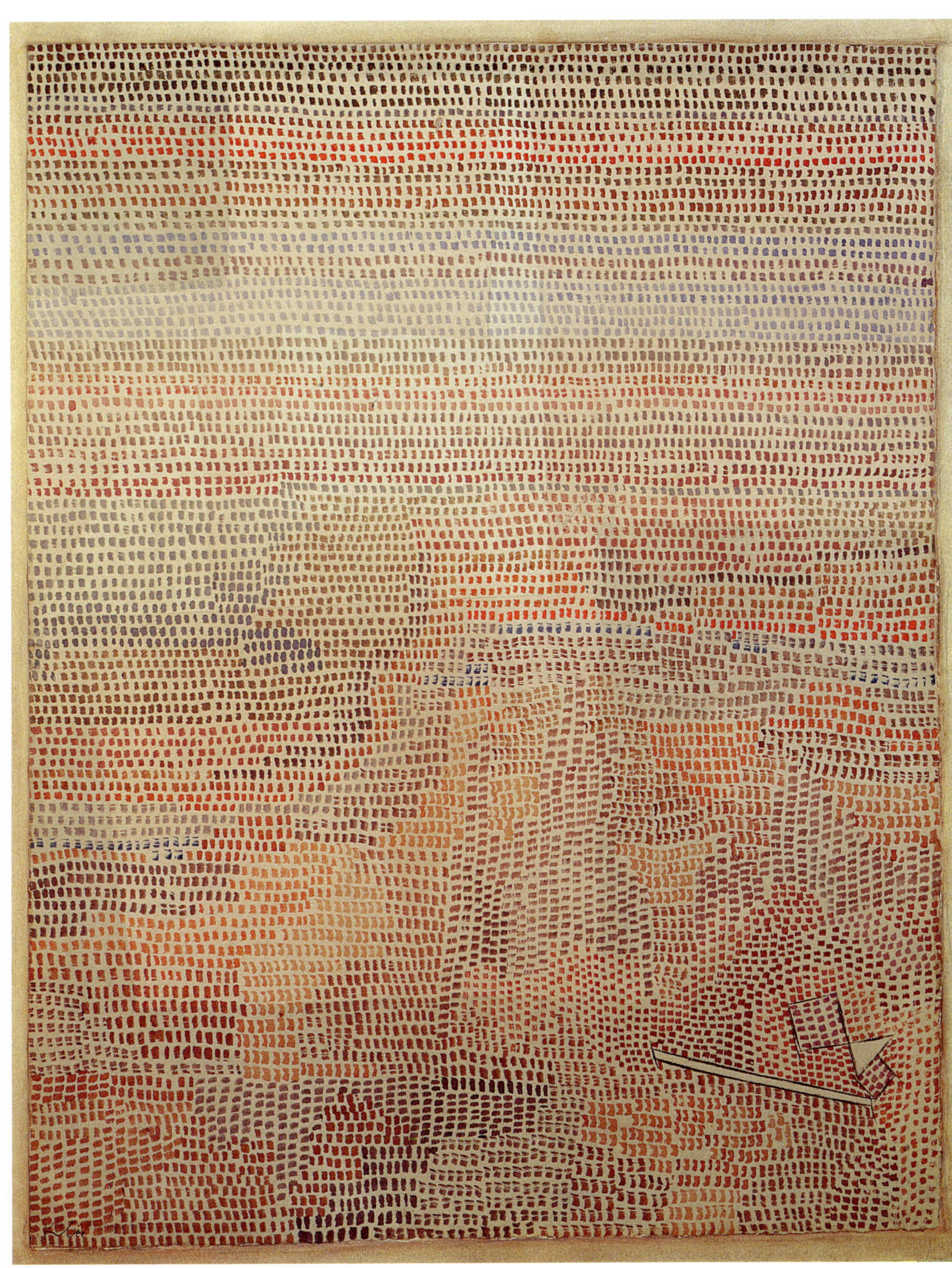

71 **DAS GANZE DÄMMERND**, 1932.4
[The Whole Is Dimming]

Watercolor on paper, mounted on cardboard
15¾ x 12⅜ inches (40 x 31.4 cm)
Private Collection

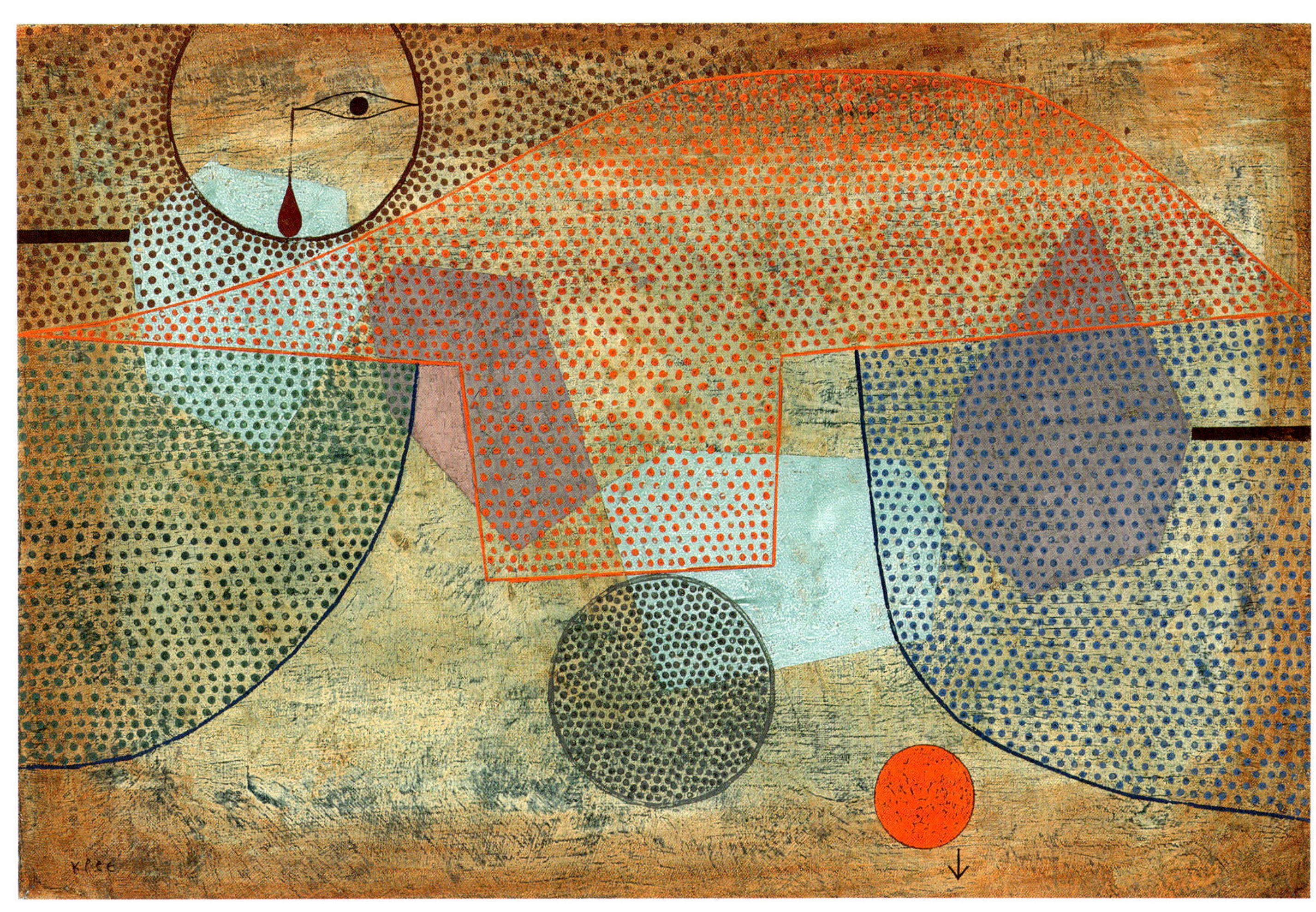

72 **SONNENUNTERGANG**, 1930.209
[Sunset]

Oil and pencil on primed canvas
18¼ x 27⅝ inches (46.2 x 70.2 cm)
The Art Institute of Chicago
Gift of Mr. and Mrs. Leigh B. Block, 1981.13

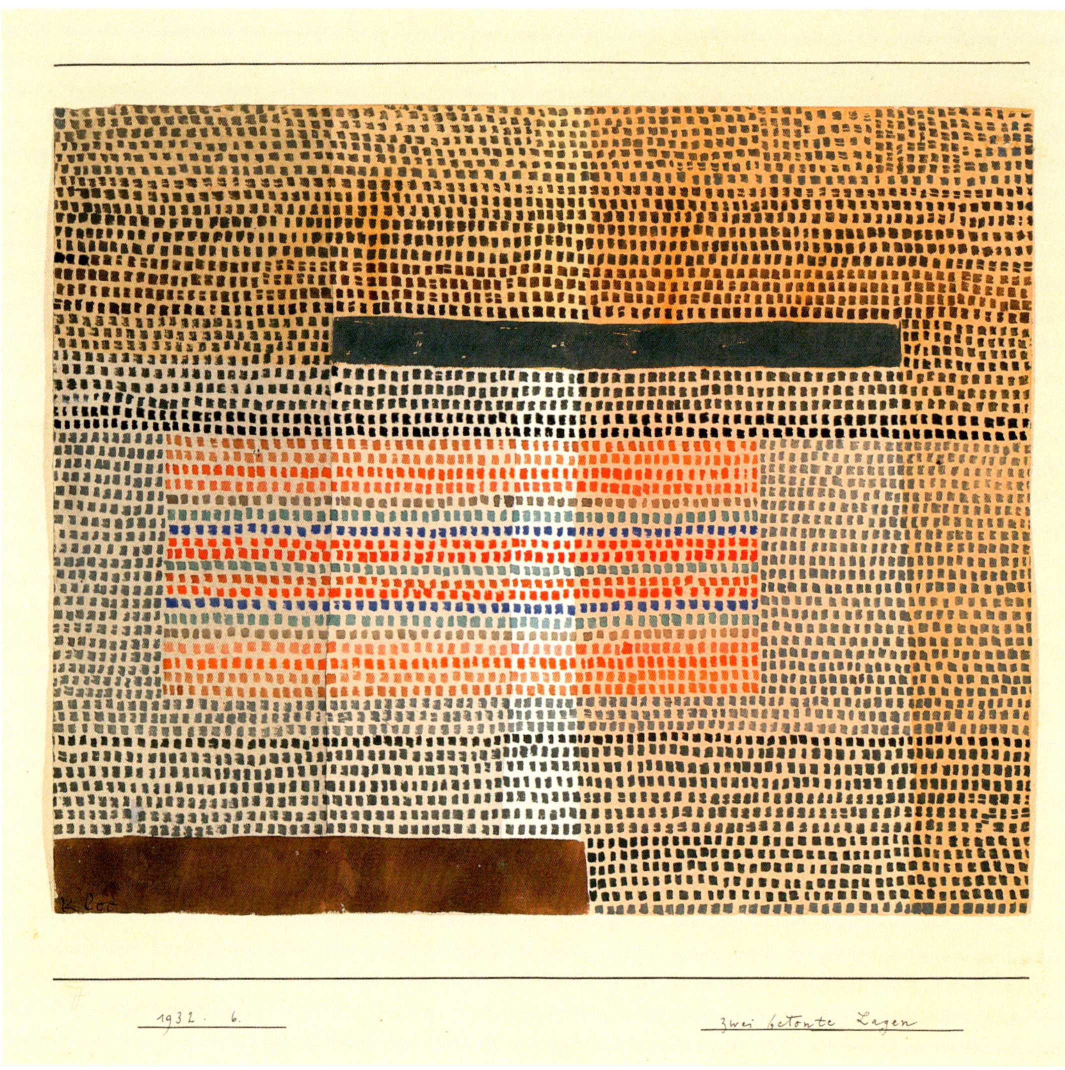

73 **ZWEI BETONTE LAGEN**, 1932.6
[Two Emphasized Layers]

Watercolor on paper mounted on cardboard
9½ x 12 inches (24.1 x 30.4 cm)
The Menil Collection, Houston

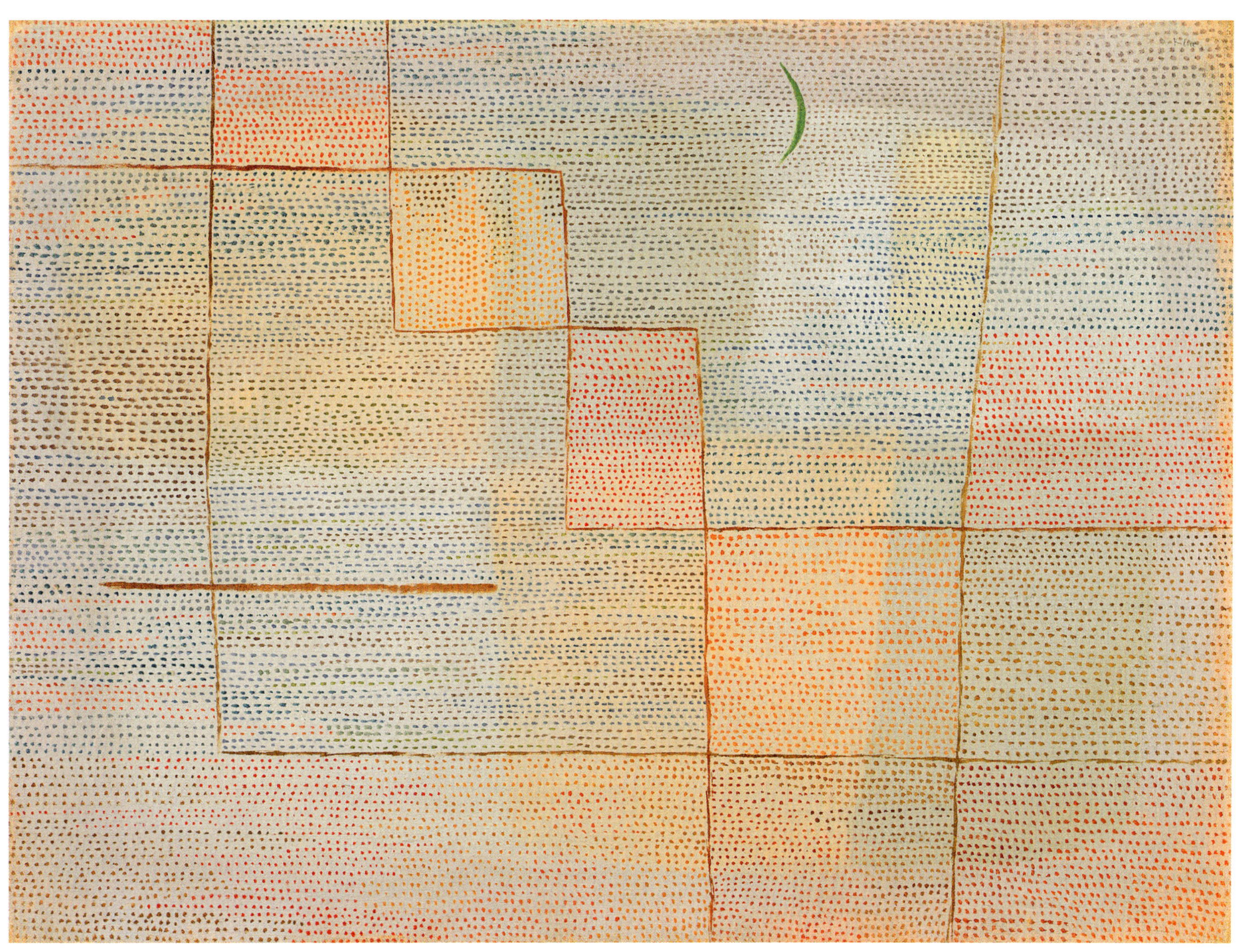

74 **KLAERUNG**, 1932.66
[Clarification]

Oil on canvas
27½ x 37¾ inches (70 x 96 cm)
Metropolitan Museum of Art, New York
The Berggruen Klee Collection, 1984.315.54

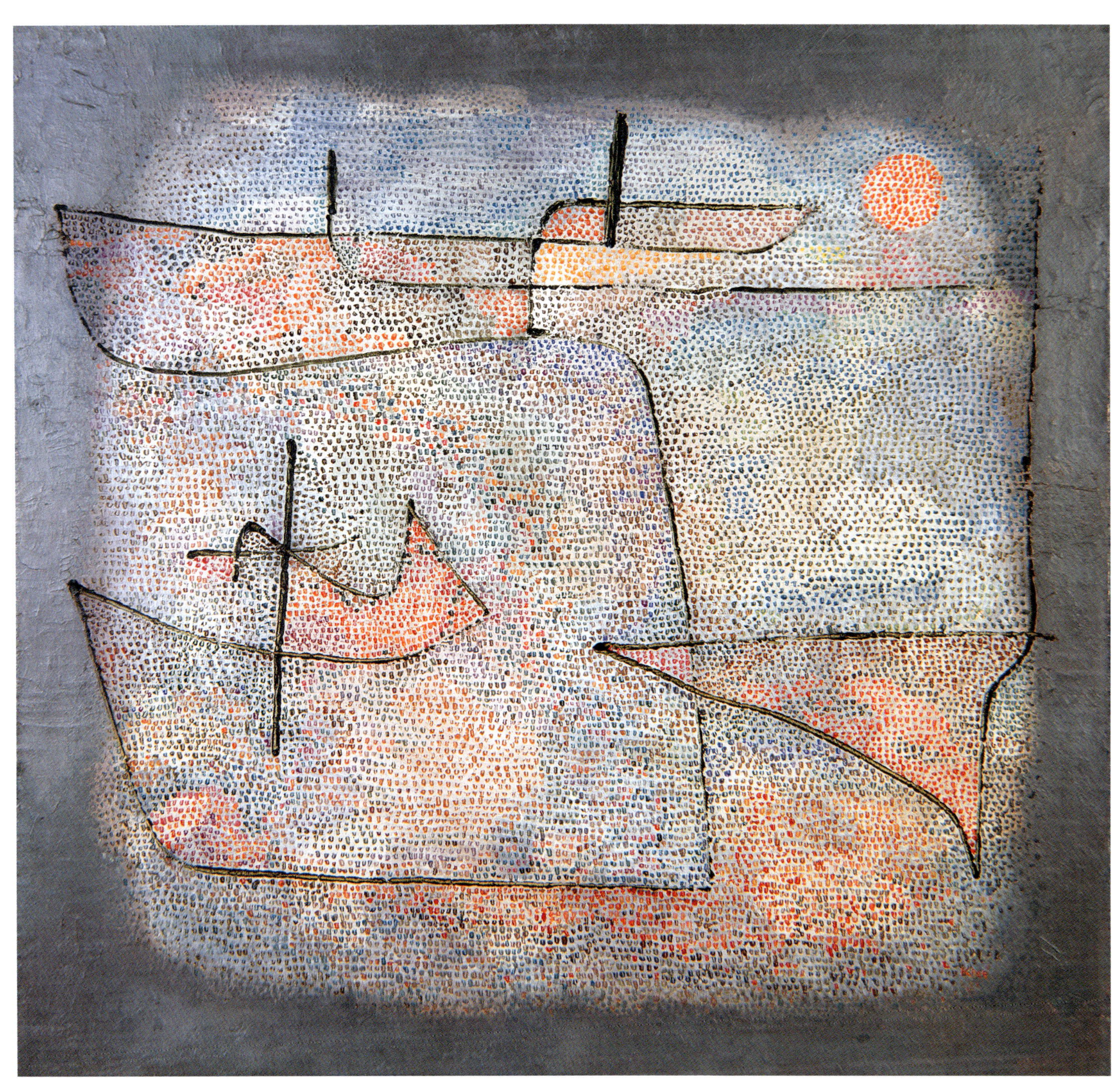

75 **VOR ANKER**, 1932.22
[At Anchor]

Oil on canvas
34¼ x 36⅝ inches (87 x 93 cm)
Private Collection

In 1932 Klee used coarse jute canvas for a number of his works. In the composition *Arabisches Lied,* he linked this material with the picture's subject. As Jenny Anger has noted: "This is a playful and loving homage to a mysterious figure wrapped in a chador; all we see of her, in fact, are her strangely hilly eyes above the drape. Indeed, her eyes are in one sense continuous with the drape; the gouache [sic] is so finely painted on burlap that the fabric insists on its presence, not simply as represented fabric (chador) but as real, material fabric support of the painting."[1] The painting is remarkable for its combination of the fabric's rough texture and the work's simple figurative motif. It is reminiscent of the pictorial textile works that became fashionable around 1930—for example, the tapestries by Johanna Schütz-Wolff. Schütz-Wolff's works had appeared in the traveling exhibition "Moderne Bildwirkereien [Modern Pictorial Weaving]," mounted in 1929–30 by Ludwig Grote and first shown in Dessau, for which Klee lent a tapestry by his student Ida Kerkovius. Apparently inspired by this novel concept of "pictorial weaving," Klee returned to the relationship between pictorial content and its support that he had explored earlier, around 1921–22, when he had completed his abstract composition *Teppich der Erinnerung [Tapestry of Memory]* (1914.196) by leaving the edges of the canvas unpainted in such a way as to give the impression of the frayed edges of an old "tapestry." But he did not repeat this tactic in 1932. This time Klee produced a variation on the newly fashionable "pictorial weaving" by applying thinned oil pigments directly onto the rough jute canvas.

Once again he chose an Eastern subject, one that presumably had autobiographical resonances. In 1919 Klee had delivered to Wilhelm Hausenstein, who was then planning a monograph on the artist, an autobiographical extract from his diaries in which he alluded to his mother's possible Eastern ancestry. Thanks to Hausenstein's book more than anything else, the myth arose in the 1920s that Klee's artistic roots were to be found in the Middle East: the book described Klee's journey to Tunisia in 1914 as a return to his homeland. As late as 1925, Hausenstein was characterizing Klee's "Arabesque" works as "the applied art of someone who is a blood relative of those orientals who still pray—and for whom each line of weaving is nothing less than a precise analogy for the incomprehensibility of a metaphysical idea."[2] And in 1931, in conversation with the writer Rudolf Bach, Klee ventured that the tapestries from the Bauhaus weaving shop, where he had taught from 1927 to 1930, could hardly be compared with authentic Eastern craftsmanship.

In *Arabisches Lied,* the fabric, which Klee subtly incorporated by painting onto it a depiction of a typical Muslim costume—the *niqab* (veil) and chador—becomes a metaphor for the inscrutable East. Somewhat ironically, the creator of the true art of rug making stands unmistakably before us. Despite her veils, the Arab woman's face does not appear introverted, like the face in ~~Jugendlicher Schauspieler~~=Maske [~~Youth~~ Actor's Mask] (1924.252). Both eyes gaze directly at the (presumably Western) viewer. They suggest what lies behind them and open up an imaginary, but—in view of what is depicted—quite "real" dimension of the picture. In October 2001, still feeling the impact of 9/11, Anger wrote: "Here in this late painting [Klee] honors the fabric that for many non-Muslims enfolds the mystery of Islam and he lets the imaginary Muslim woman peer out at him, at us, with an even, steady gaze. She is looking at us and we must try, to save us all, to look back with an equally open and friendly gaze."[3]

Osamu Okuda

1. Jenny Anger, "Paul Klee: 'Seeing the Other,'" in *Paul Klee and His Travels*, exh. cat. (Nagoya-shi: Chūnichi Shinbunsha, 2002), 276.

2. Wilhelm Hausenstein, "Paul Klee: Ausstellung bei Hans Goltz in München," *Frankfurter Zeitung*, May 26, 1925, first morning edition.

3. Anger, 277.

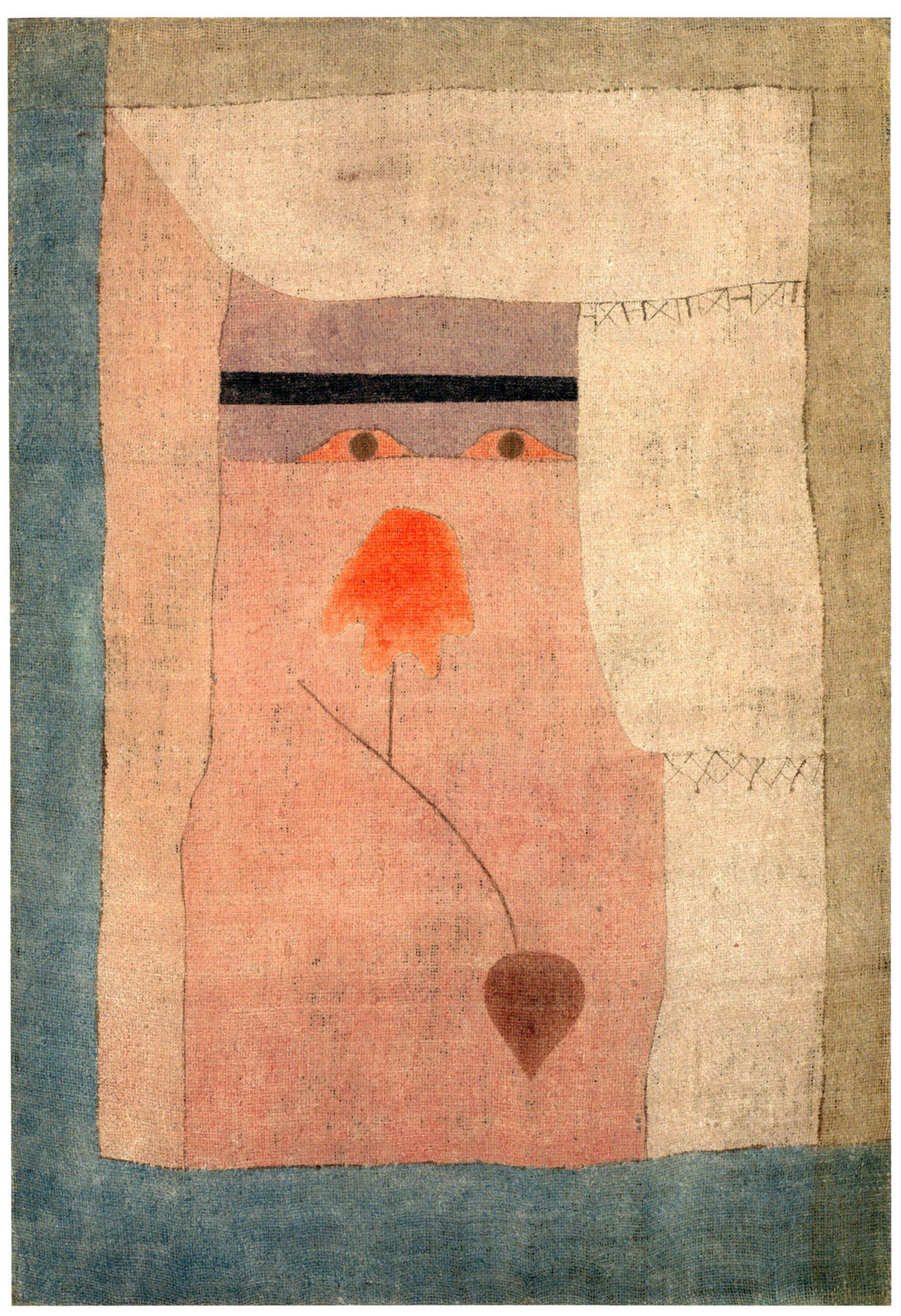

76 **ARABISCHES LIED**, 1932.283
[Arabian Song]

Oil on jute
35⅞ x 25½ inches (91.1 x 64.7 cm)
The Phillips Collection, Washington, D.C., 0990

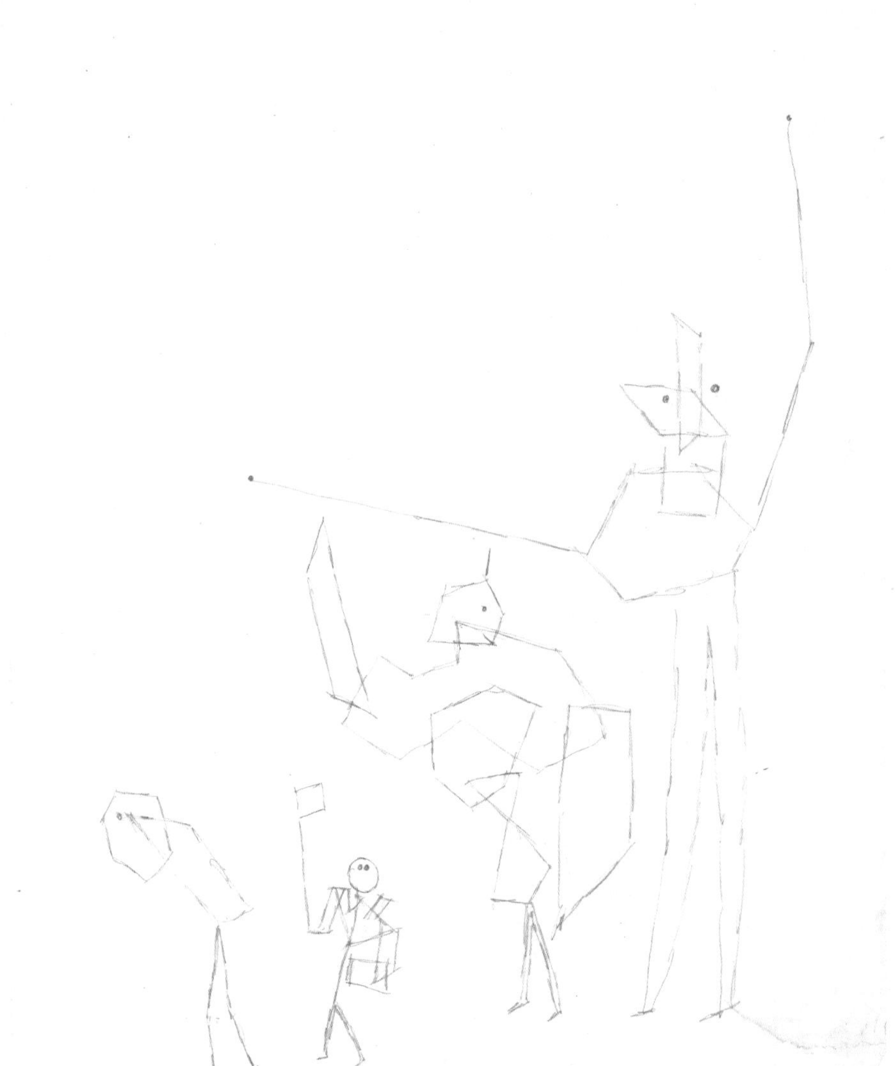

77 ERNEUERUNG DER MANNSZUCHT, 1933.71
[Revival of Manly Discipline]

Pencil on paper, mounted on cardboard
17 x 12¾ inches (43.2 x 32.4 cm)
Colgate University, The Picker Art Gallery, Hamilton, New York
Gift of Herbert Mayer, 1966.1.324

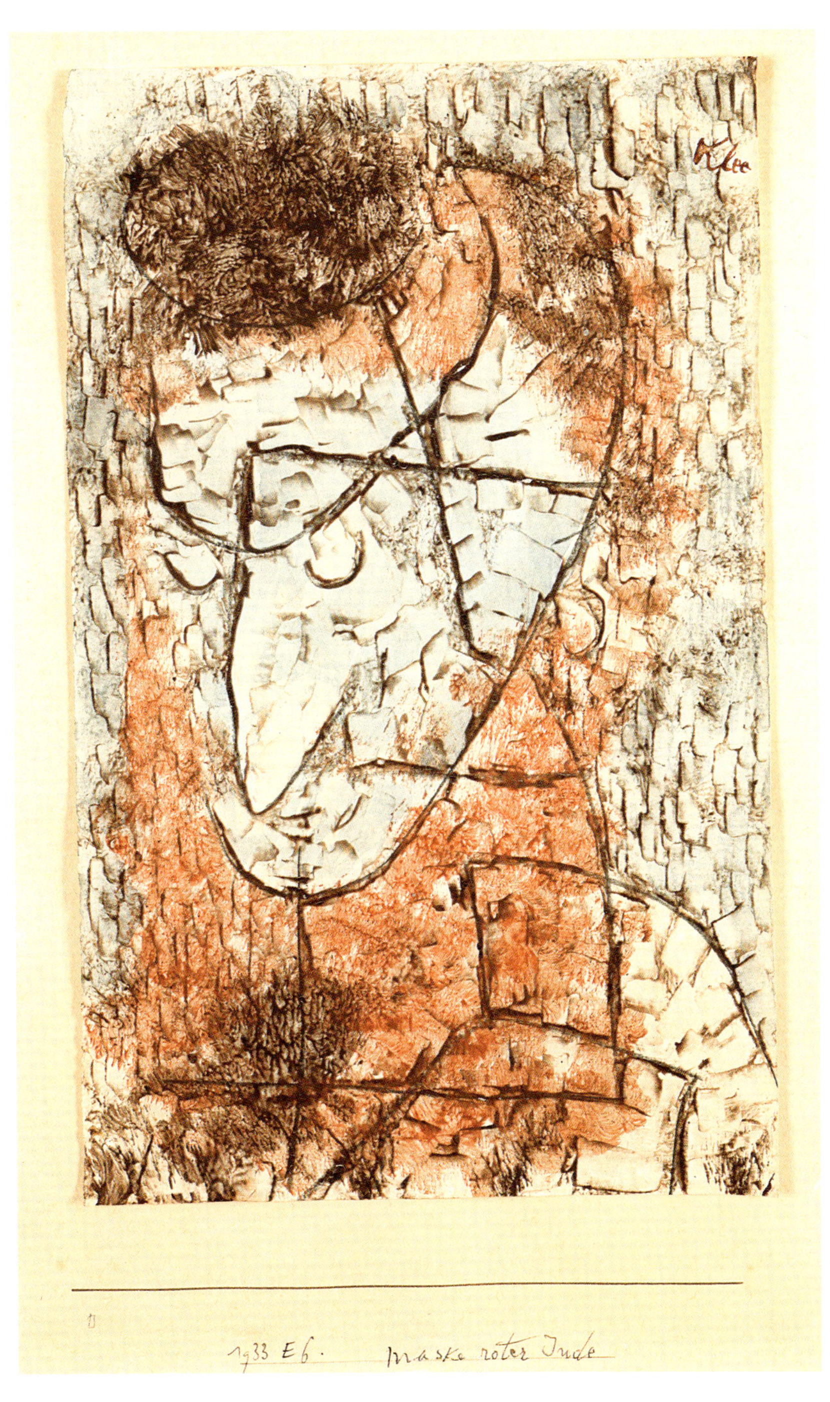

78 **MASKE ROTER JUDE**, 1933.386
[Mask: Red Jew]

Paste paint on paper, mounted on cardboard
12¾ x 8⅛ inches (32.5 x 20.6 cm)
Collection of Michael and Judy Steinhardt, New York

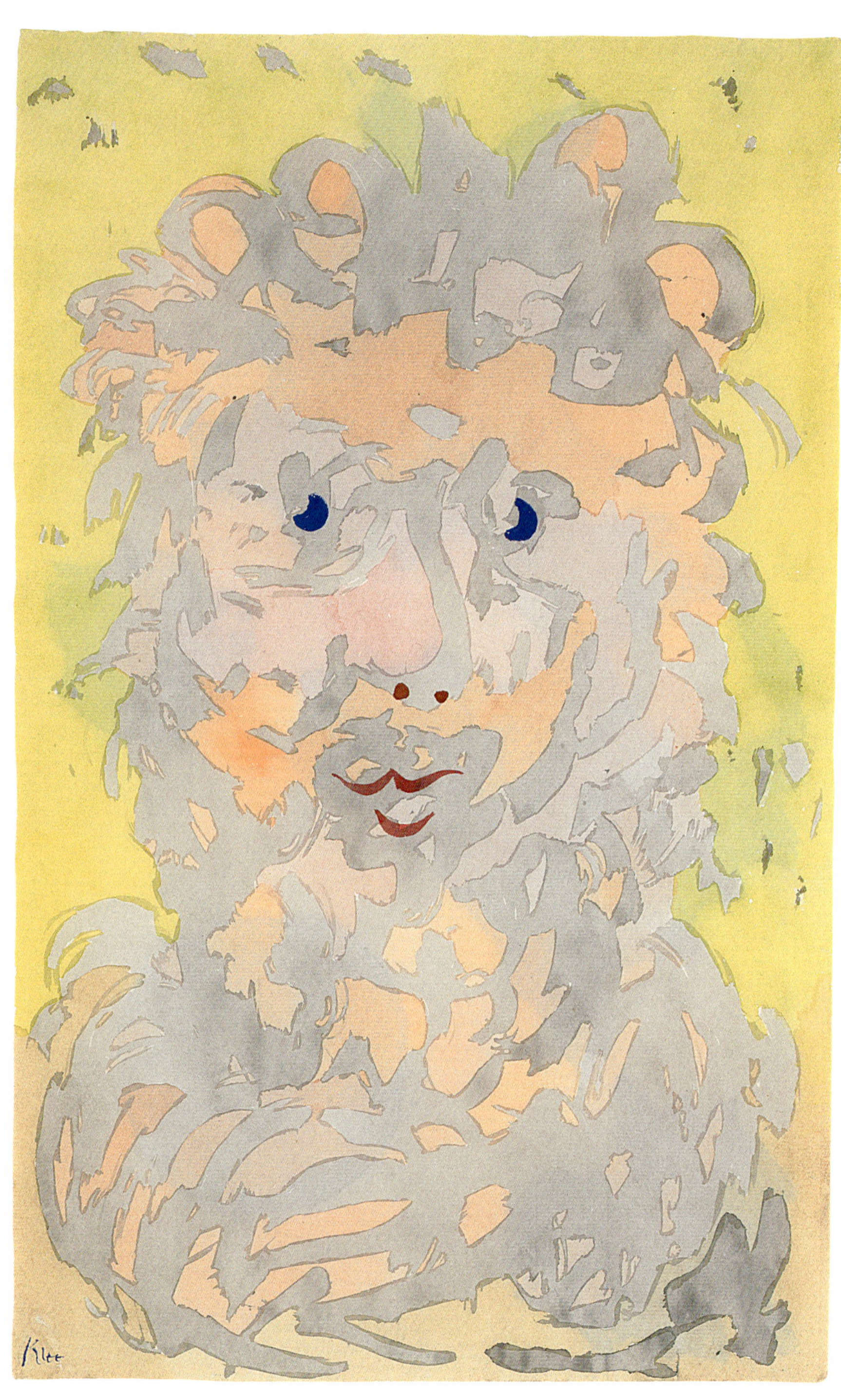

79 **LÖWENMENSCH**, 1934.2
[Lion Man]

Watercolor on paper
18¾ x 12 inches (47.6 x 30.6 cm)
Fractional and promised gift of the Djerassi Art Trust
to the San Francisco Museum of Modern Art

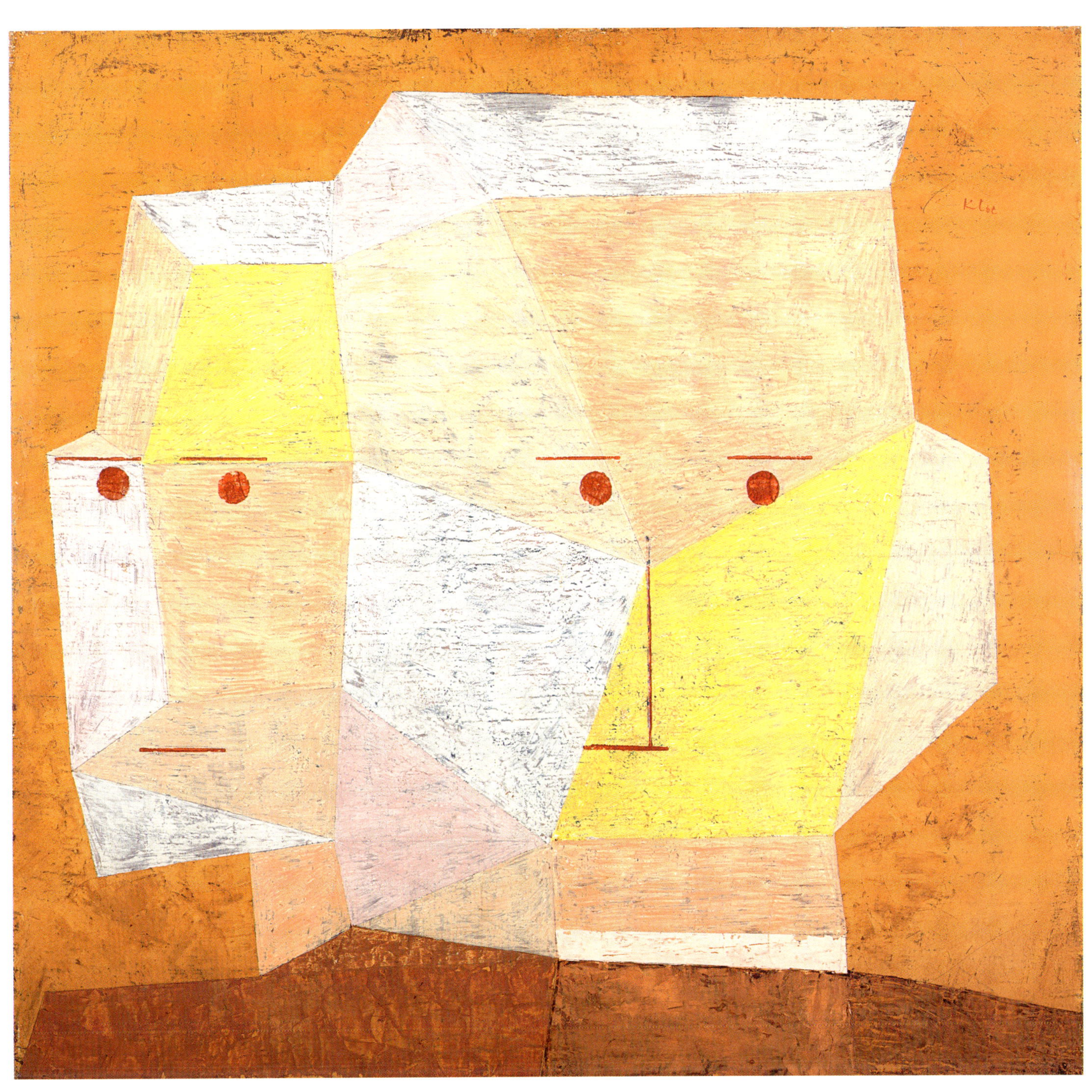

80 **ZWEI KÖPFE**, 1932.332
[Two Heads]

Oil and pencil on canvas
31¾ x 33⅜ inches (80.8 x 84.7 cm)
Norton Simon Museum, Pasadena, California
The Blue Four Galka Scheyer Collection

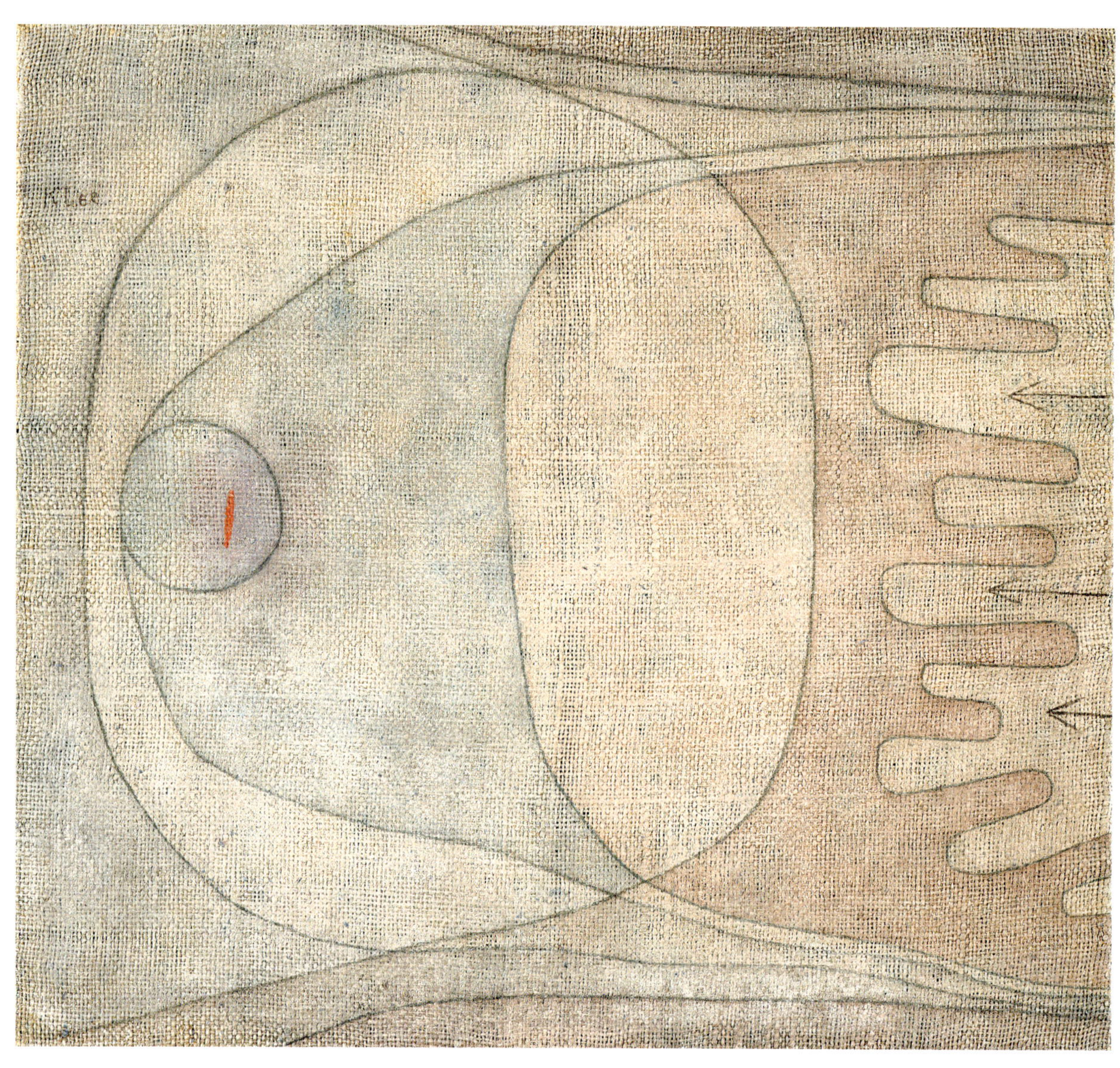

81 **ANGST**, 1934.202
[Fear]

Watercolor on chalk-primed jute
(verso: gouache and wax on jute)
19⅝ x 23⅝ inches (49.9 x 60 cm)
National Gallery of Canada, Ottawa, Purchased 1979

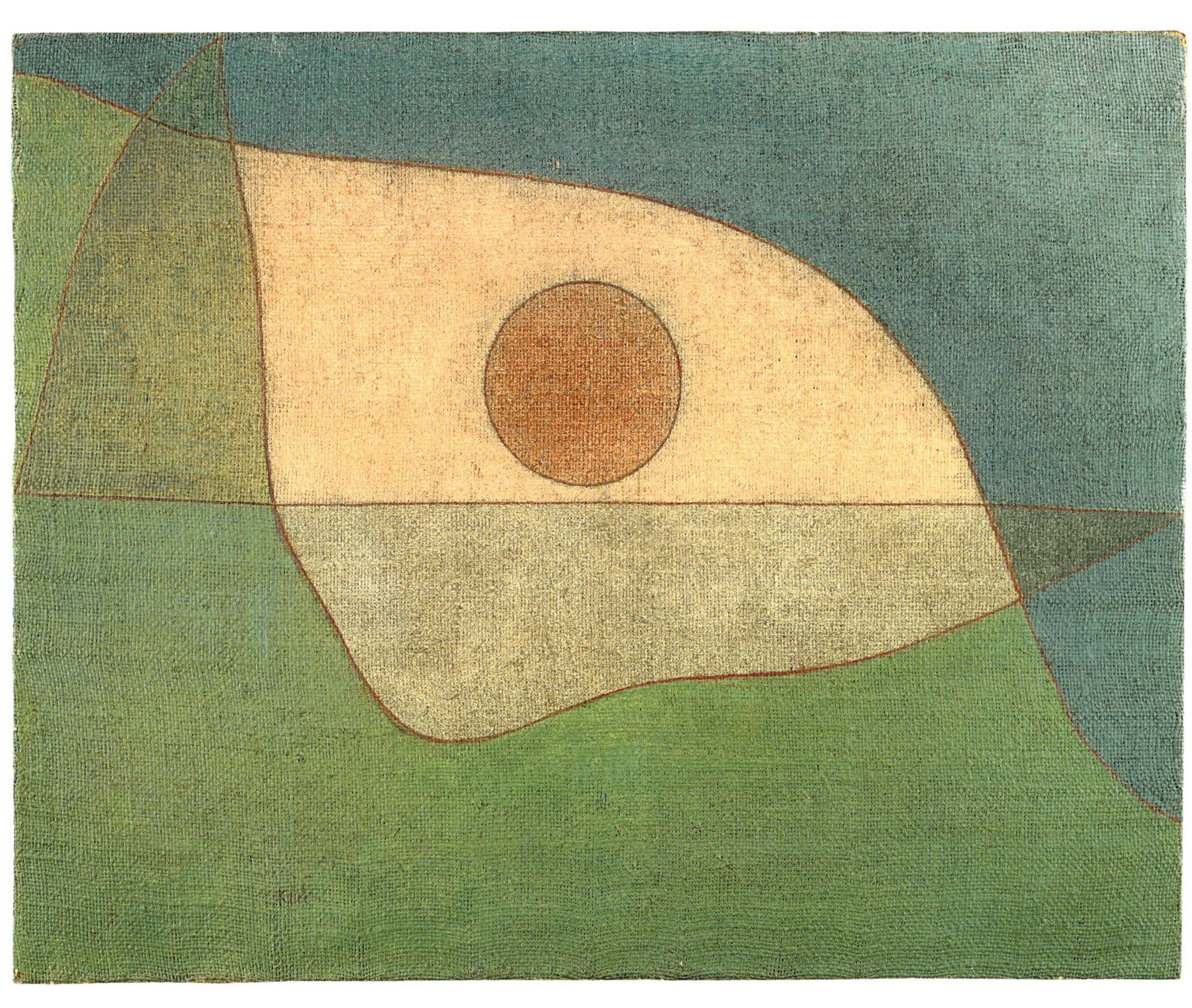

82 **BLICK DER STILLE**, 1932.285
[Gaze of Silence]

Oil on jute
21⅞ x 27¾ inches (55.6 x 70.5 cm)
The Menil Collection, Houston

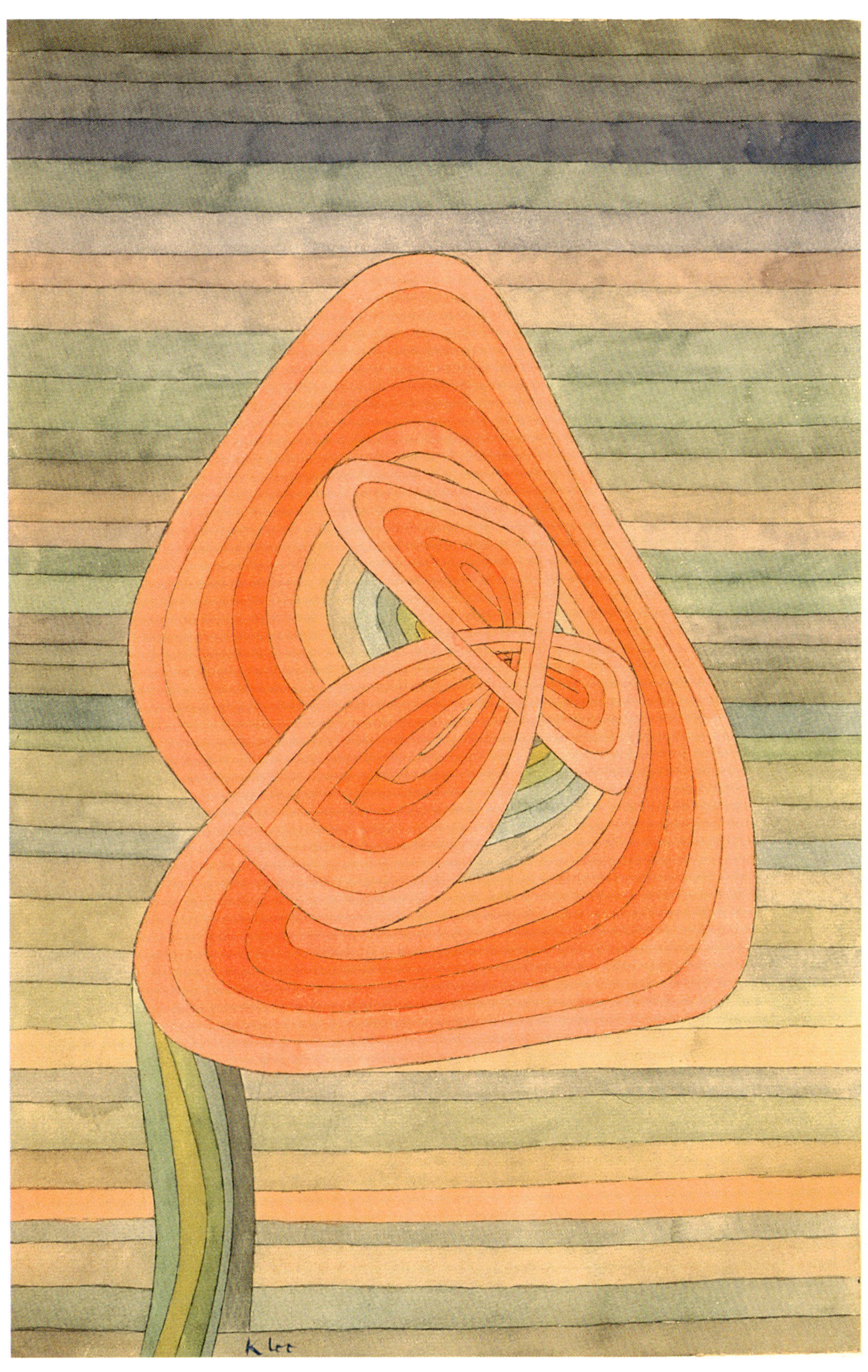

83 **EINSAME BLÜTE**, 1934.5
[Lonely Flower]

Watercolor, pen, and pencil on paper
18⅞ x 12⅜ inches (47.8 x 31.5 cm)
Columbus Museum of Art, Ohio
Sirak Collection, 1991.001.025

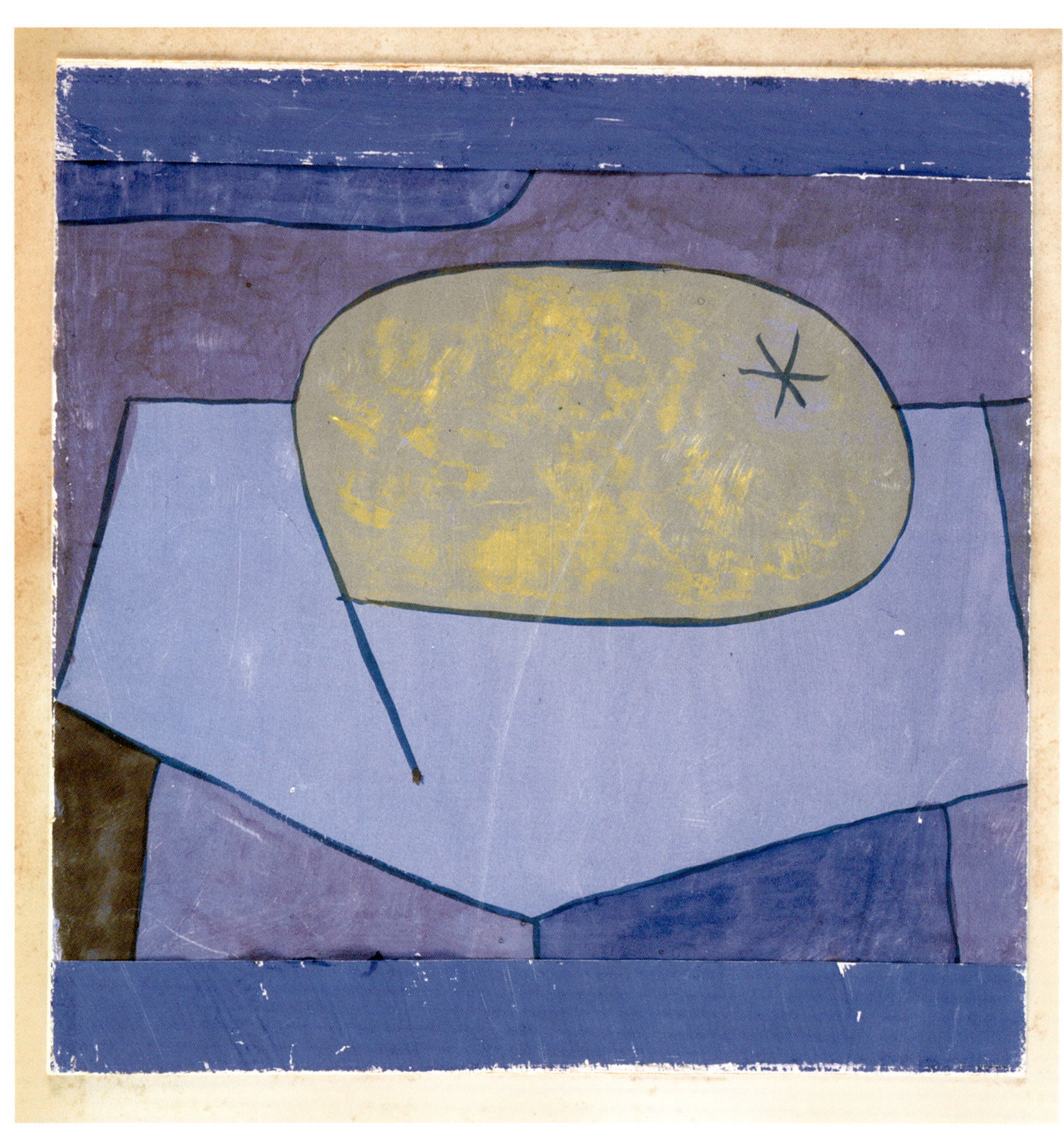

84   **BEULEN BIRNE**, 1934.164
[Bulgy Pear]

Watercolor and oil on primed paper, with colored paper
strips placed above and below, mounted on cardboard
8¼ x 8½ inches (21 x 21.6 cm)
Private Collection, New York

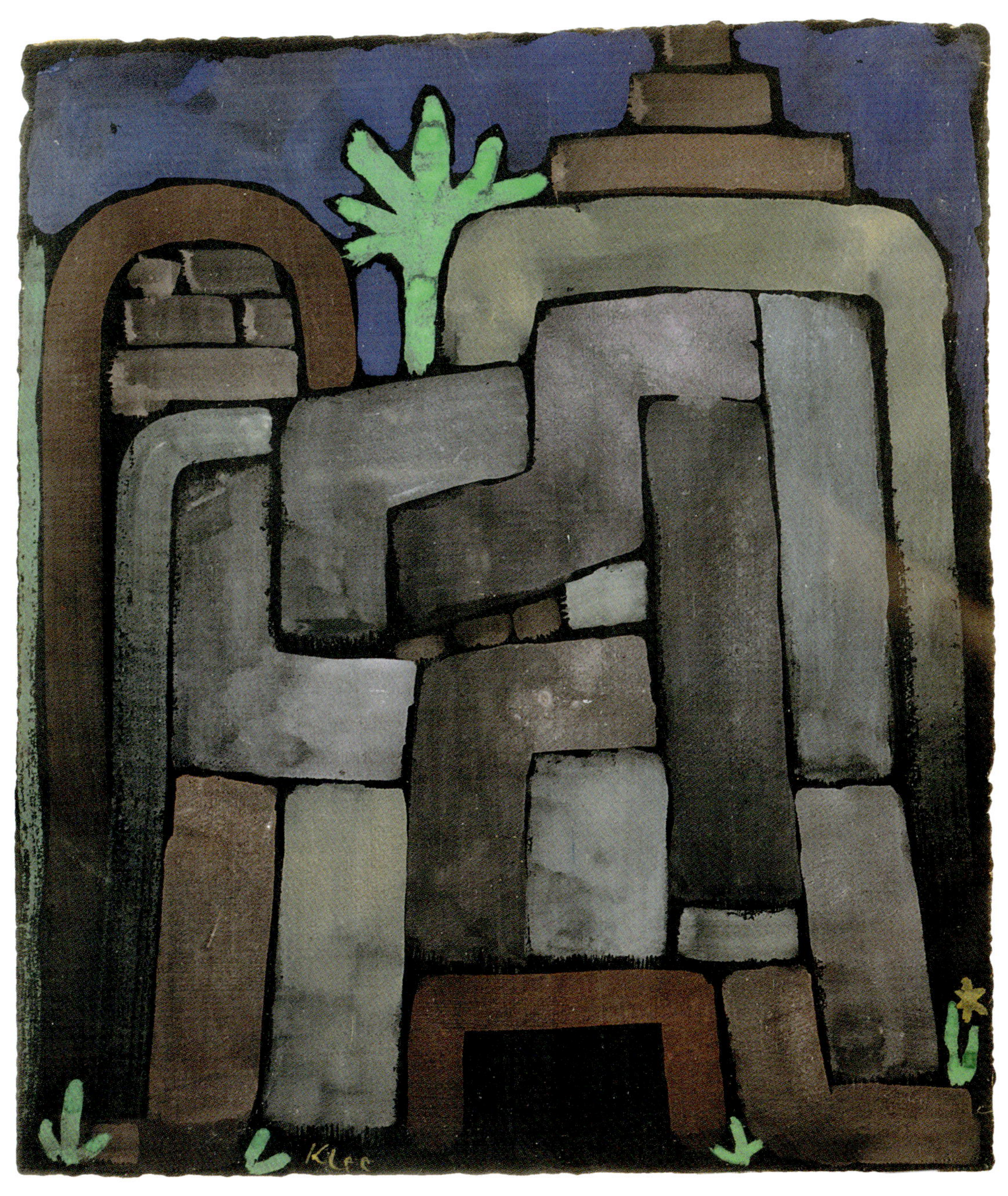

85 **ILFENBURG**, 1935.109

Watercolor on primed paper, mounted on
silver paper and mounted on cardboard
11⅞ x 10⅜ inches (30.3 x 26.2 cm)
Columbus Museum of Art, Ohio
Sirak Collection, 1991.001.028

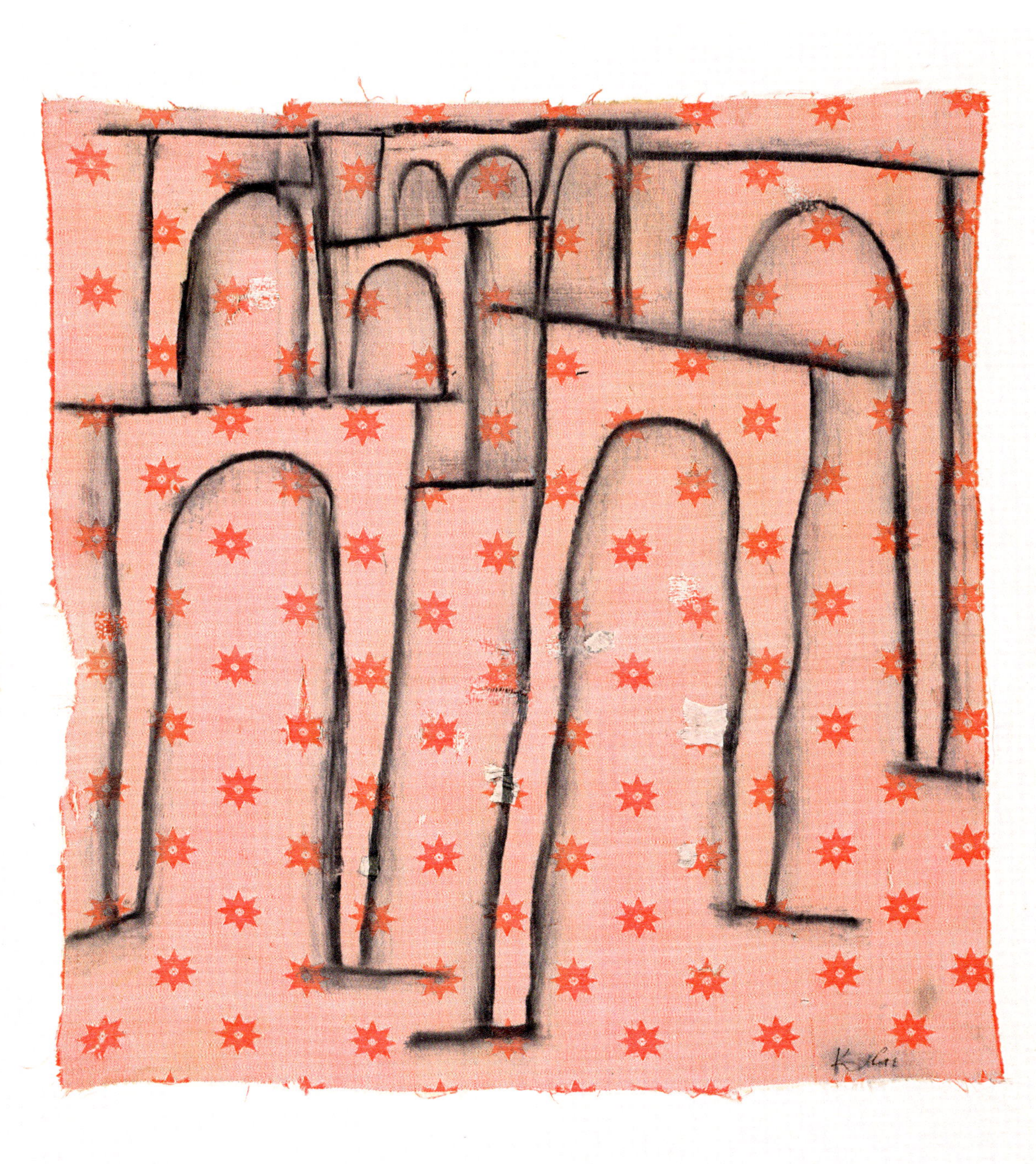

86 **BRÜCKENBOGEN TRETEN AUS DER REIHE**, 1937.111
[Arches of the Bridge Stepping Out of Line]

Charcoal and red chalk on linen, mounted on cardboard
16¾ x 16½ inches (42.6 cm x 42 cm)
Solomon R. Guggenheim Museum, New York, 48.1172x59

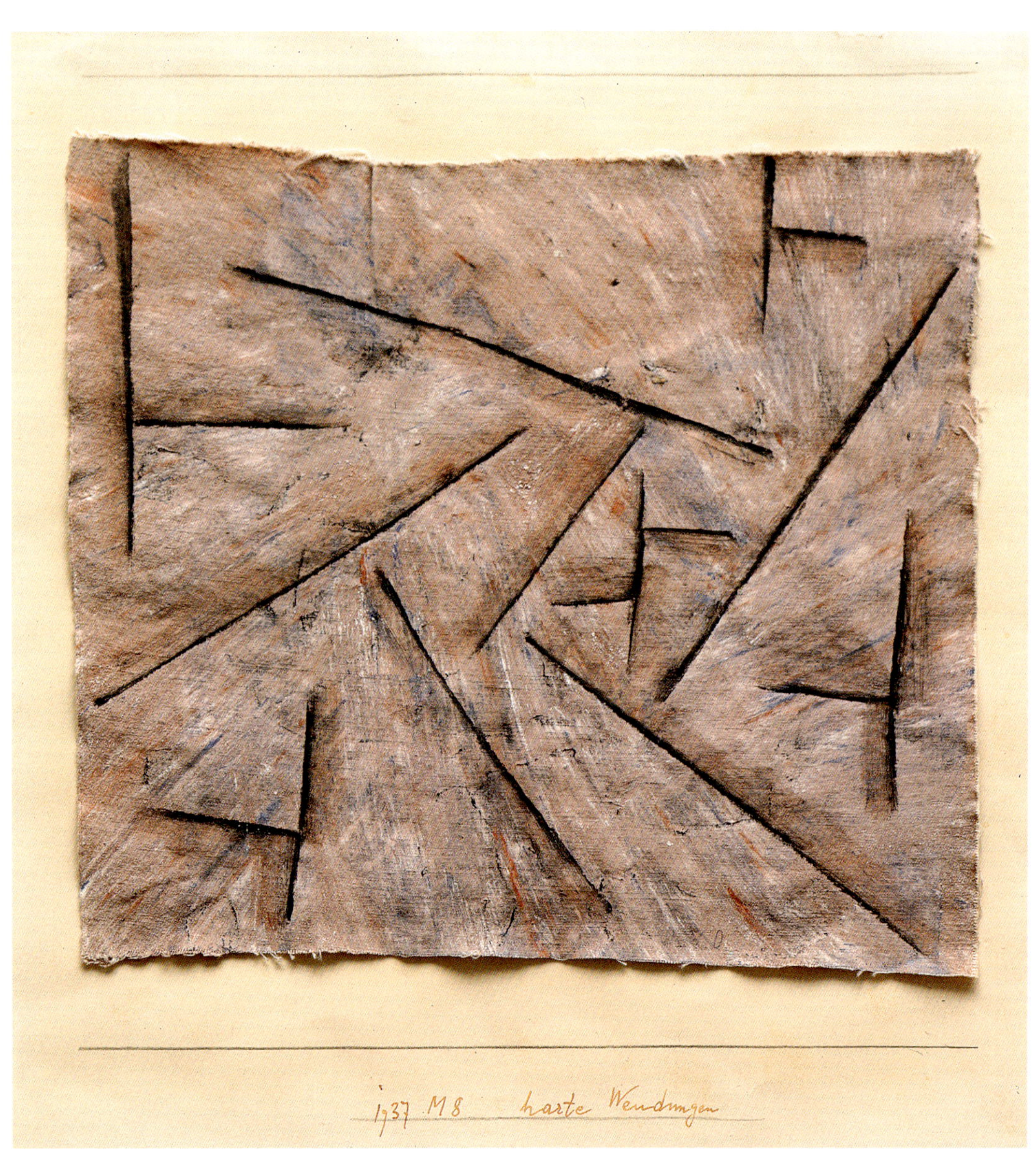

87 **HARTE WENDUNGEN**, 1937.68
[Sharp Turns]

Colored paste on cotton canvas, mounted on cardboard
8½ x 10 inches (21.6 x 25.4 cm)
The Menil Collection, Houston

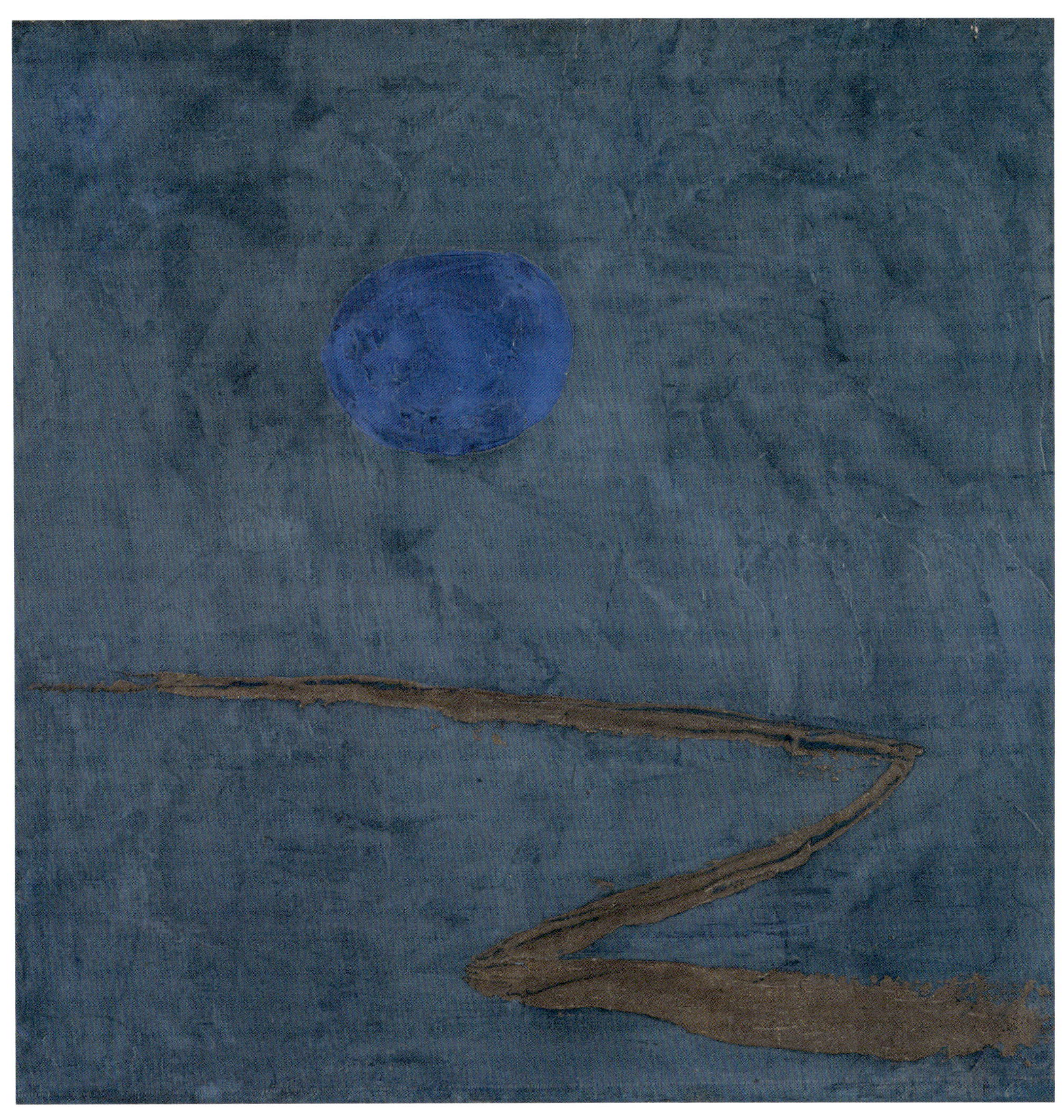

88 **DER WEG INS BLAUE**, 1934.203
[The Path into the Blue]

Oil on wood
16¼ x 16½ inches (41.3 x 41.9 cm)
The Old Jail Art Center, Albany, Texas
Gift of Bill Bomar, 1991, 91.002

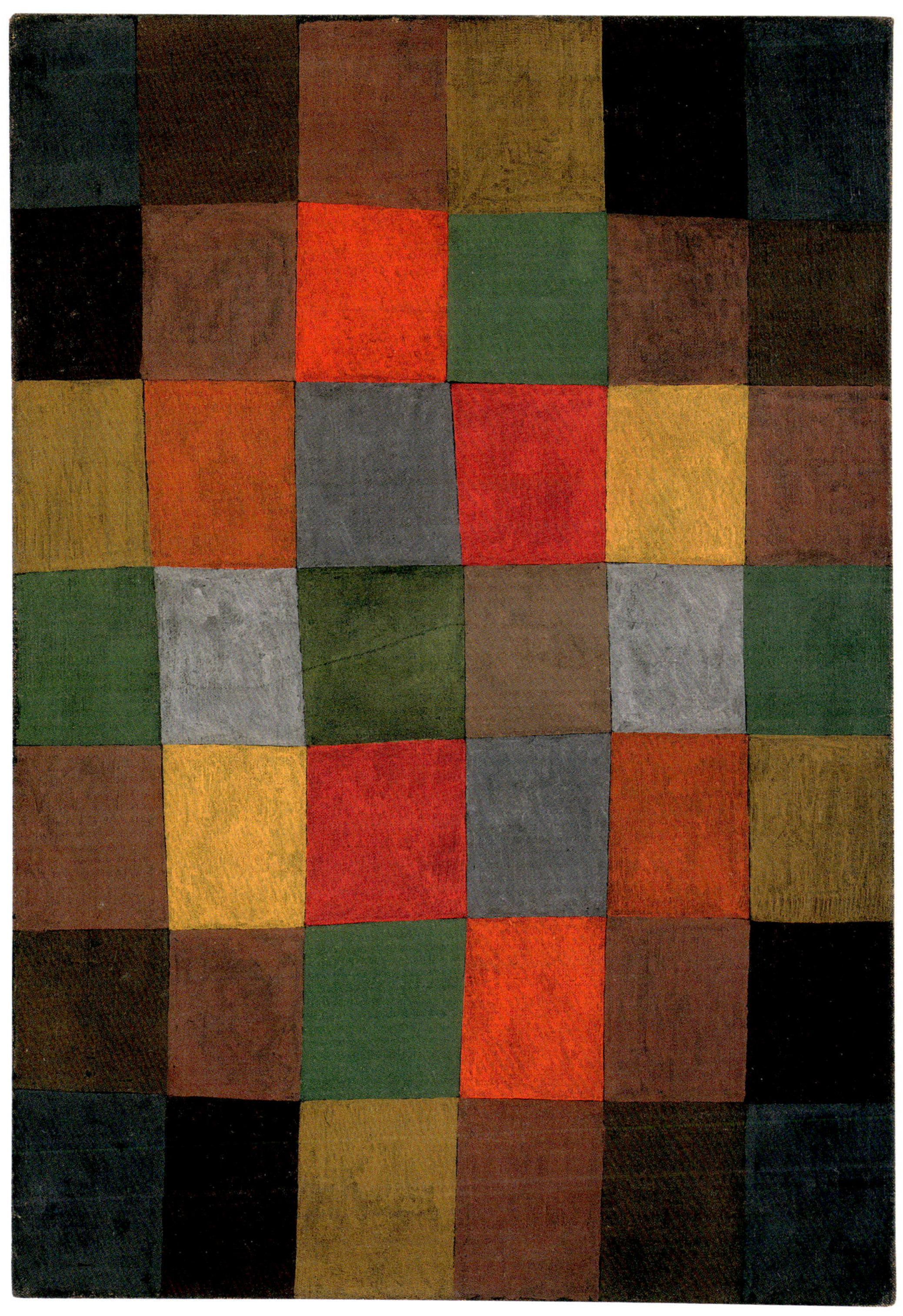

89 **NEUE HARMONIE**, 1936.24
[New Harmony]

Oil on canvas
36½ x 26⅛ inches (93 x 66 cm)
Solomon R. Guggenheim Museum, New York

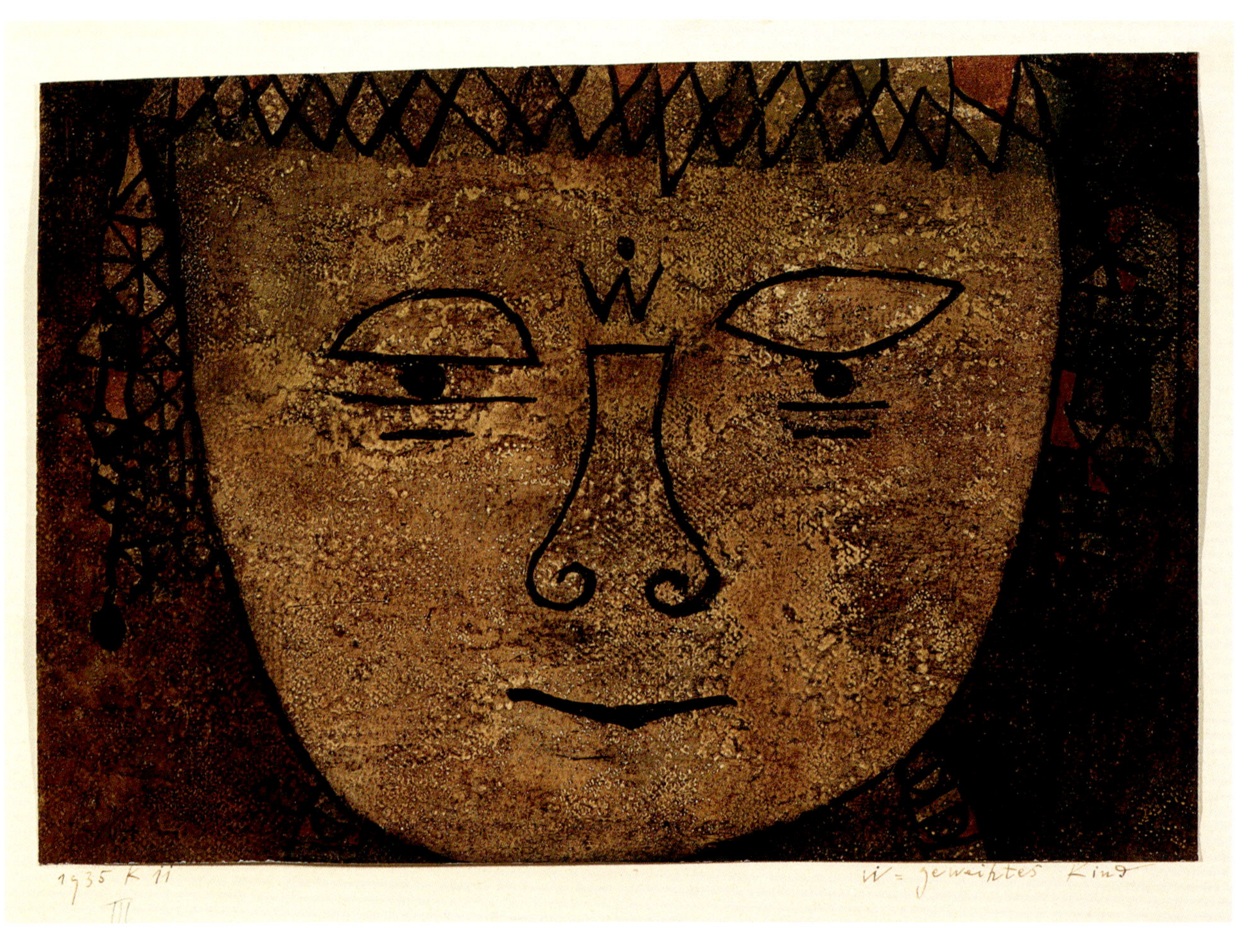

90   **W = GEWEIHTES KIND**, 1935.31
[W = Consecrated Child]

Oil and watercolor on primed paper, mounted on cardboard
6⅜ x 9⅜ inches (16 x 23.9 cm)
Albright-Knox Art Gallery, Buffalo, New York, RCA 1940:12

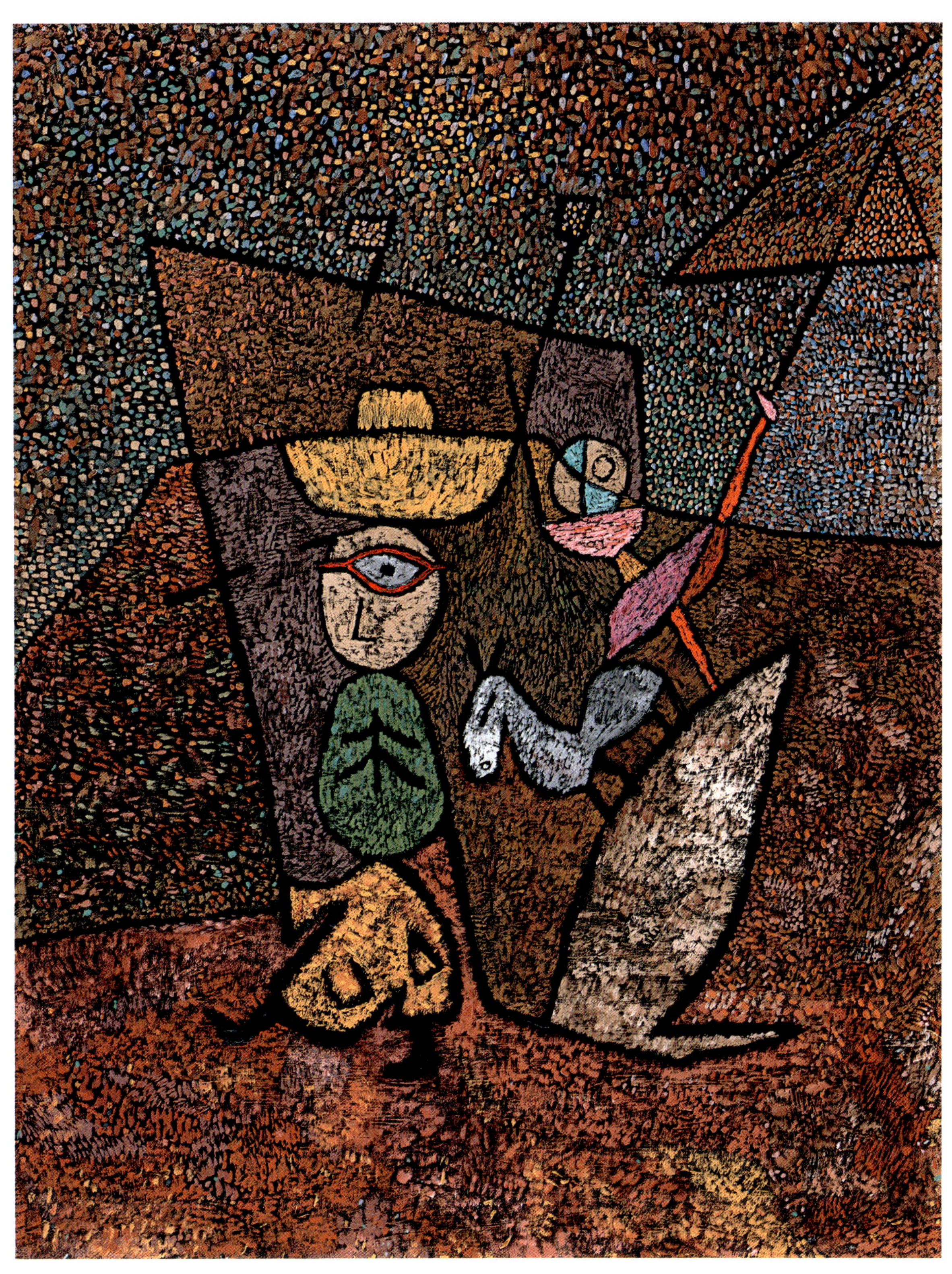

91 **WANDER-CIRCUS**, 1937.139
[Traveling Circus]

Oil on canvas
25⅝ x 19⅝ inches (65 x 50 cm)
The Baltimore Museum of Art
Bequest of Saidie A. May, 1951.317

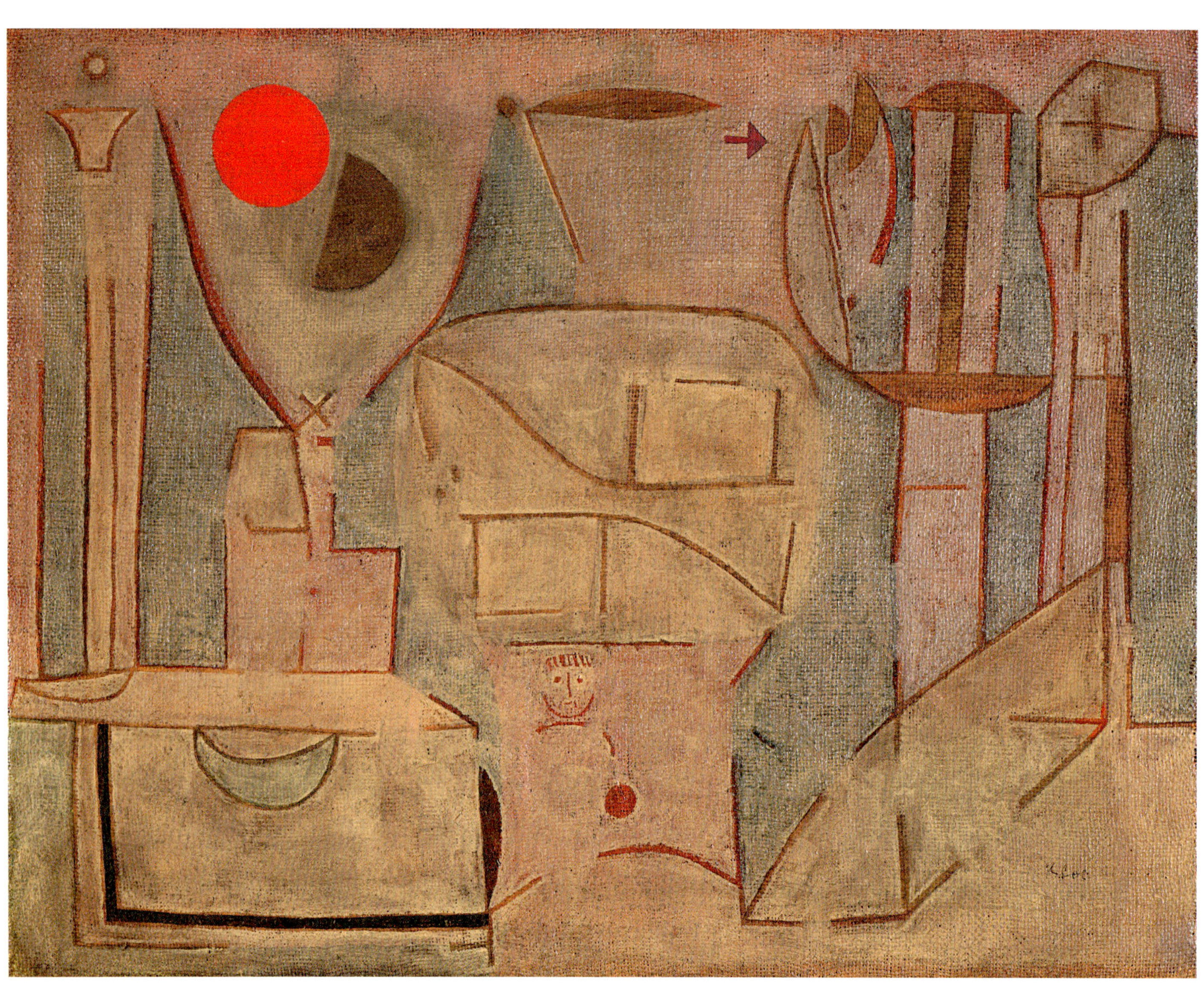

92 **FRAGMENTE**, 1937.132
[Fragments]

Oil on jute
21⅝ x 28 inches (55 x 71 cm)
San Francisco Museum of Modern Art
Gift of Wilbur D. May

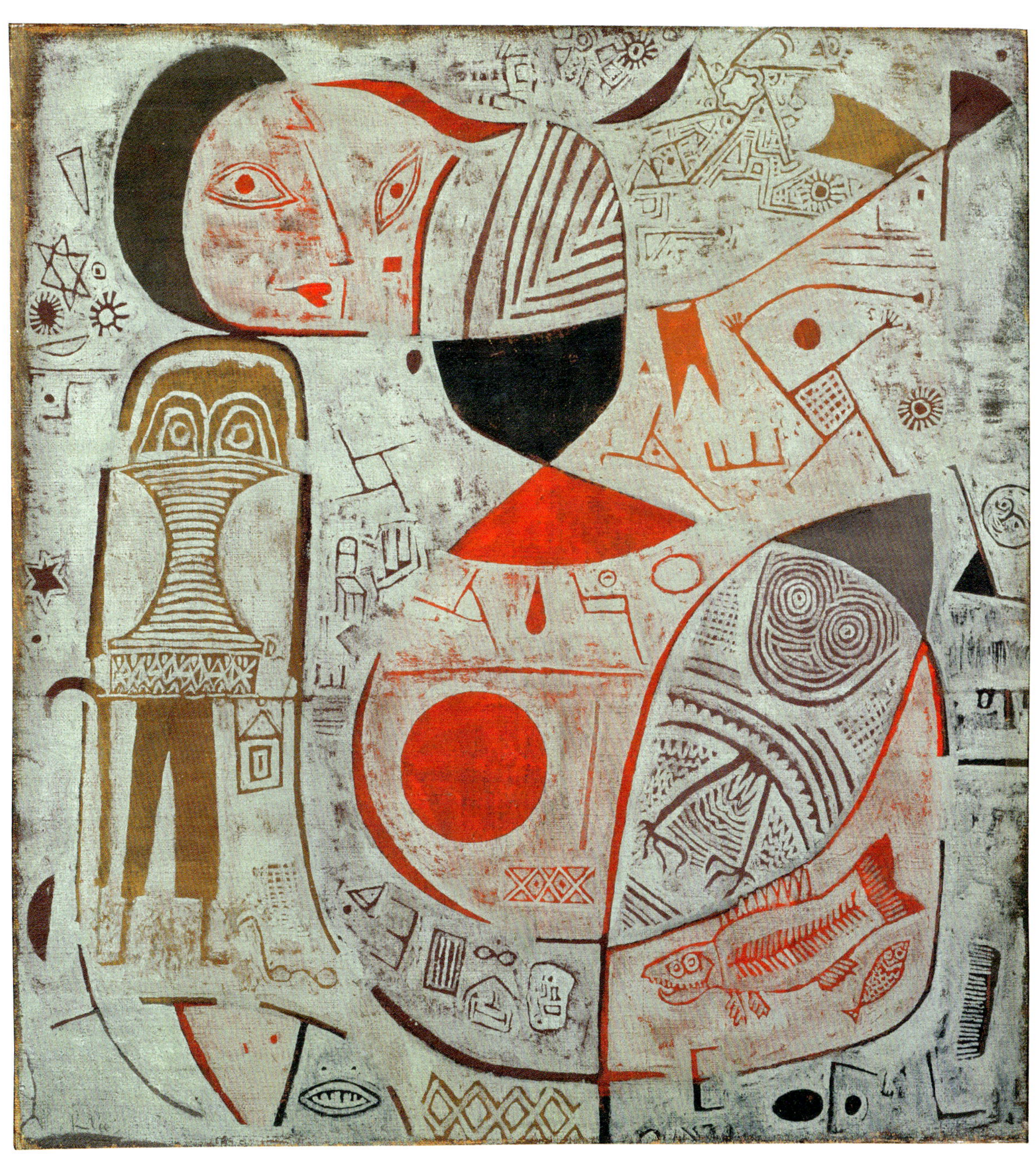

93   **BILDERBOGEN**, 1937.133
[Printed Sheet with Picture]

Oil on canvas
23¼ x 22 inches (59 x 56 cm)
The Phillips Collection, Washington, D.C., 0999

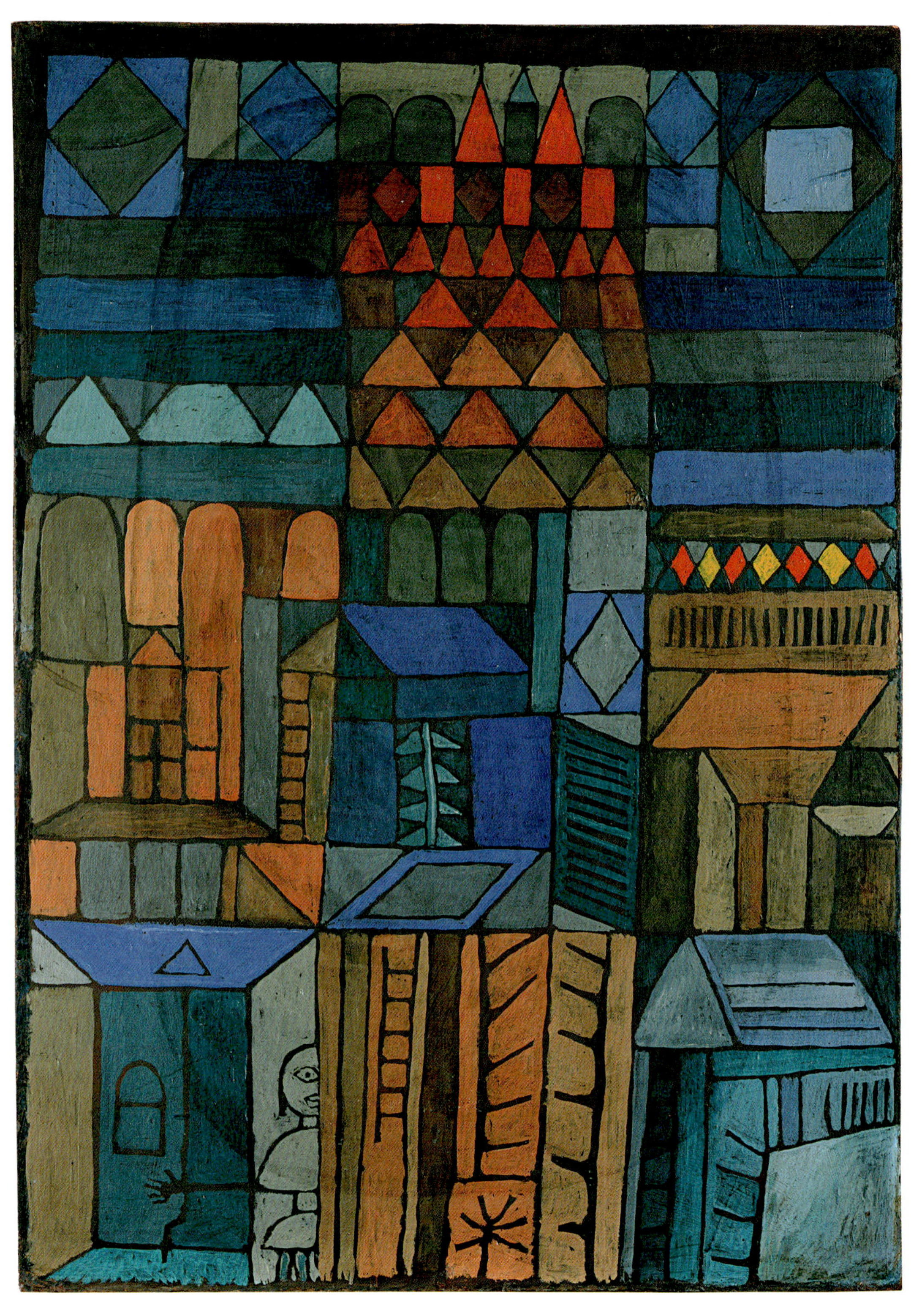

94 **BEGINNENDE KÜHLE**, 1937.136
[Incipient Coolness]

Oil on cardboard, nailed on stretcher
29½ x 20⅞ inches (75 x 53 cm)
Galerie Jan Krugier, Ditesheim & Cie, Geneva

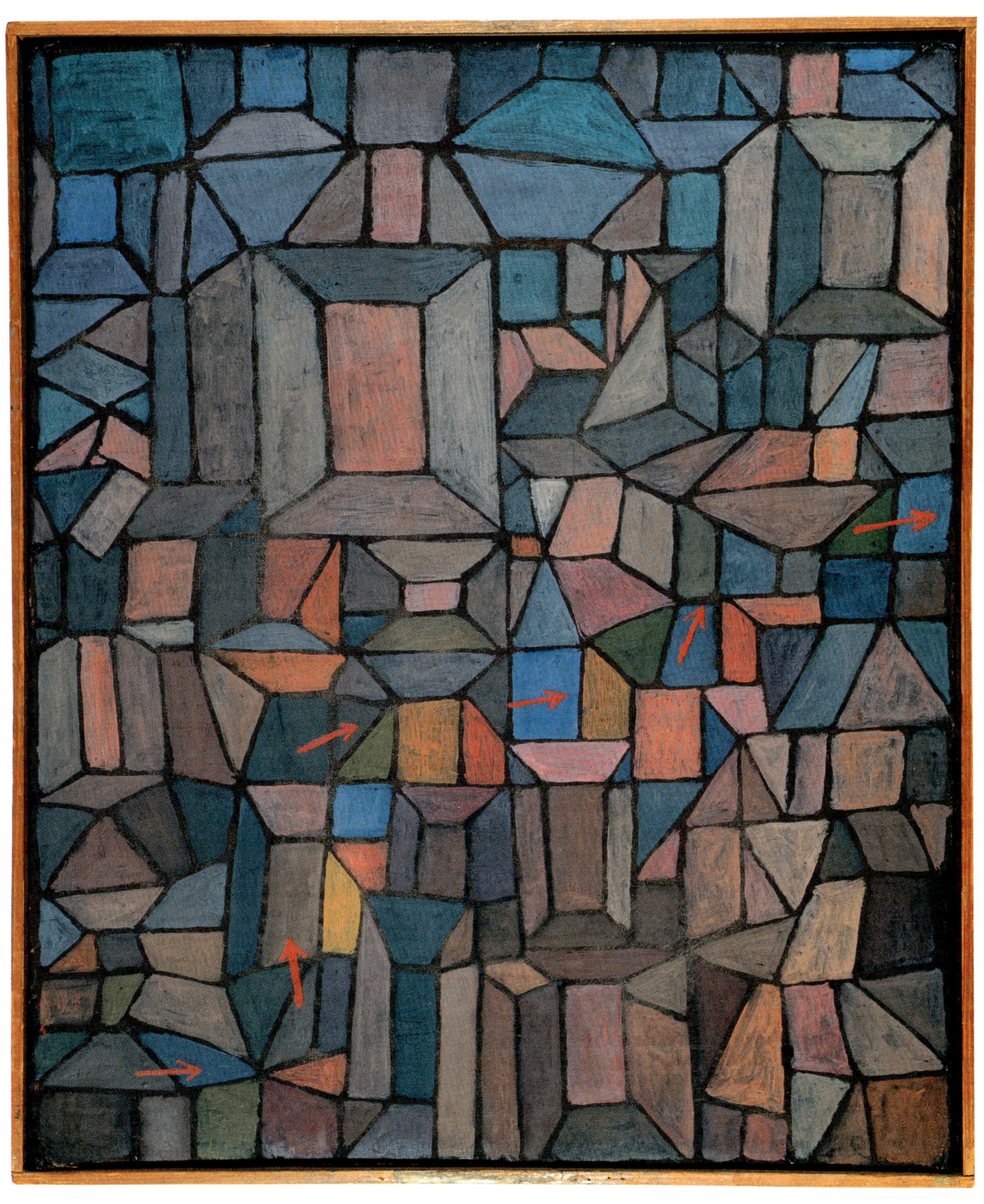

95 **DER WEG ZUR STADTBURG (STÄDTEBILD)**, 1937.137
[The Way to the Citadel (Picture of a City)]

Oil on canvas, mounted on cardboard and nailed on stretcher,
with original strip frame
26⅜ x 22½ inches (67 x 57 cm)
The Phillips Collection, Washington, D.C. , 1001

From the end of 1938 to roughly the spring of 1939, Klee worked with closed shapes that were isolated from each other, frequently representing human limbs. Jürgen Glaesemer has seen this fragmentation of the body as an extreme reflection of human suffering. According to Glaesemer, in this group of works, we see "figures disintegrating in agony. Hands, arms, legs, and indeterminate pieces of the body have broken apart into separate, self-contained forms and lie scattered over the paper like islands. The heads stand out from the other parts because of their inner details; but in them, too, the large eyes, noses, and open mouths have lost their stability and fall pell-mell."[1] One of the most arresting of these works, along with the watercolor *Angstausbruch III [Outbreak of Fear III]* (1939.124), is the panel *Der Mann der Verwechslung [The Man of Confusion].*

Klee's *membra disjecta* can also be understood, given the contemporary situation, as expressing the very antithesis of the Nazis' idealized, classically oriented cult of the body. They also relate to the theory of Jacques Lacan. In the summer of 1936, Lacan presented a lecture at the International Psychoanalytical Congress in Marienbad, Czech Republic, on the "mirror stage" (*le stade du miroir*), in which he spoke of the fear of the "I" when faced with the threat of the dismembered body. According to Lacan, the mirror stage is that impressionable period between six and eighteen months when the child, still in a condition of helplessness from a lack of coordinated motor ability, imagines taking hold and mastering the unity that is its body. This imaginary integration comes about through the child's identification with the image of a being, similar to itself, as a whole Gestalt, which comes from the child's concrete experience of seeing its own image in a mirror. It is this mirror stage that retrospectively leads to the fearful imagining or fantasy of the dismembered body: when the integrity of the "I" is lost, the fear of dismemberment appears, and vice versa.[2]

In the panel *Der Mann der Verwechslung,* this "fantasy of the dismembered body" is apparently the result of a psychic chaos that has flung the subject back into the archaic phase. (Furthermore, the "man's" necklace and hilly breast section provide a suggestion of sexual ambiguity.) Klee matter-of-factly titled the three preliminary drawings for the painting *Vertauschte Plätze [Transposed Places]* (1938.427; 1939.109; 1939.191). Apparently it was only when translating them into a color composition that he realized the motif's deeper significance. The broad orange shape lying beneath the "man" now appears to be a matrix out of which the body fragments emerge. Klee often depicted the dismembered body in the process of becoming whole, as in the picture *Wird es ein Mädchen? [Will It Be a Girl?]* (1939.384), where one can anticipate the emergence of a more or less integrated body out of the geometric fragments.

Julia Kristeva's theory of the "semiotic" (drives and their articulation) helps to provide a deeper understanding of Klee's destructive-constructive method. According to Kristeva, the "semiotic" refers to the mother-child relationship in the pre-Oedipal phase, the period that precedes the mirror stage. Kristeva called attention to "the relations (eventually representable as topological spaces) that connect the zones of the fragmented body to each other and also to 'external' 'objects' and 'subjects,' which are not yet constituted as such. This type of relation makes it possible to specify the semiotic as a psychosomatic modality of the signifying process...."[3] Klee's pictures of *membra disjecta* doubtless show this "signifying process" with its manifold associations and fantasies.

In the panel *Das kranke Herz,* the heart motif turns up once again in the midst of dismembered body parts or undefined fragments. The isolated heart with its wound recalls depictions of the Sacred Heart from the late Middle Ages, but there is no clear cross shape (one of the instruments of Christ's ordeal). The choice of motif must surely have roots in the artist's own experience. At the onset of Klee's illness in the fall of 1935, diagnosed in 1938 as "vasomotor neurosis" and posthumously as "scleroderma," his main symptoms were heart pains. But by April 1936, as his wife, Lily, reported,[4] his heart was once again in good shape. Klee was apparently remembering that critical period as he painted this picture with its sick heart. Ten years earlier he had written: "One learns that particular kind of progress from a critical penetration of the past, of what came before, on which what follows can build."[5]

Osamu Okuda

1. Jürgen Glaesemer, *Paul Klee: The Colored Works in the Kunstmuseum Bern*, trans. Renate Franciscono (Bern, Switzerland: Kornfeld, 1979), 322.

2. Klee could have learned of Lacan's theory from his friend the neurologist Fritz Lotmar. Lacan published his essay "Le complexe, facteur concret de la psychologie familiale," which described the mirror stage and the dismembered body, in 1938 in volume 8 of Larousse's *Encyclopédie française*, the same volume in which Lotmar is mentioned as involved in the newest direction in research on aphasia. In any case, Lacan was not an unknown quantity to Klee. In 1932–33 Klee was close to the Surrealists, especially Salvador Dalí and René Crevel (Crevel was a Klee enthusiast and in 1930 had published a Klee monograph in Paris). In 1933 Lacan published articles on paranoia in the first issue and the subsequent double issue (nos. 3–4) of the Surrealist journal *Le Minotaure.* Klee owned both issues and participated in the "Exposition Minotaure" held in Brussels in May and June of 1934.

3. Julia Kristeva, *Revolution in Poetic Language,* trans. Margaret Waller (New York: Columbia University Press, 1984), 28.

4. See Lily Klee to Nina Kandinsky, April 14, 1936, Fonds Kandinsky, Centre Georges Pompidou, Paris.

5. Paul Klee, "Exakte versuche im bereich der kunst," in Paul Klee, *Schriften: Rezensionen und Aufsätze*, ed. Christian Geelhaar (Cologne: DuMont, 1976), 130.

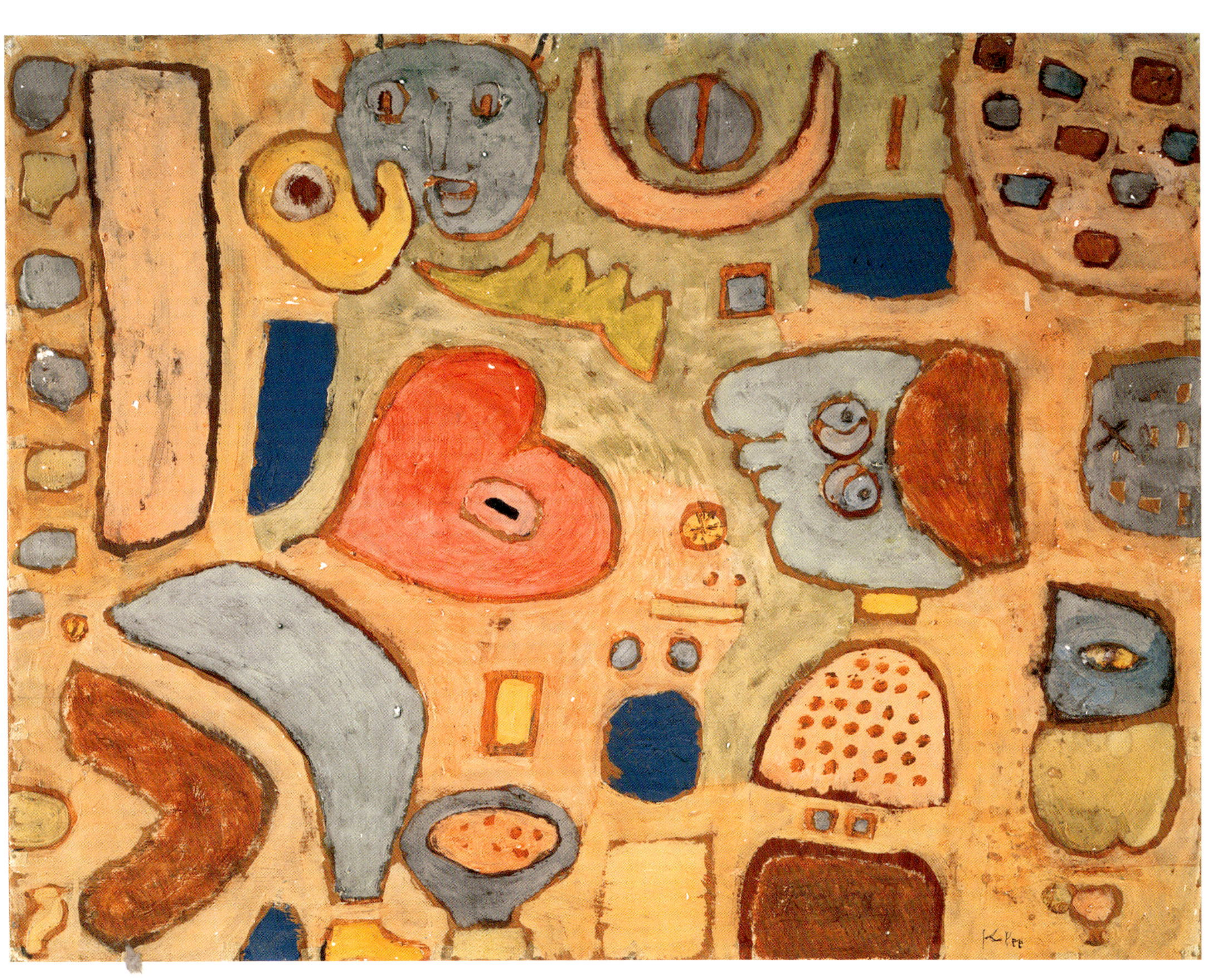

96 **DAS KRANKE HERZ**, 1939.382
[The Sick Heart]

Watercolor and paste paint on cardboard,
nailed on stretcher, with original strip frame
16 x 21¼ inches (40.7 x 54 cm)
Private Collection, New York

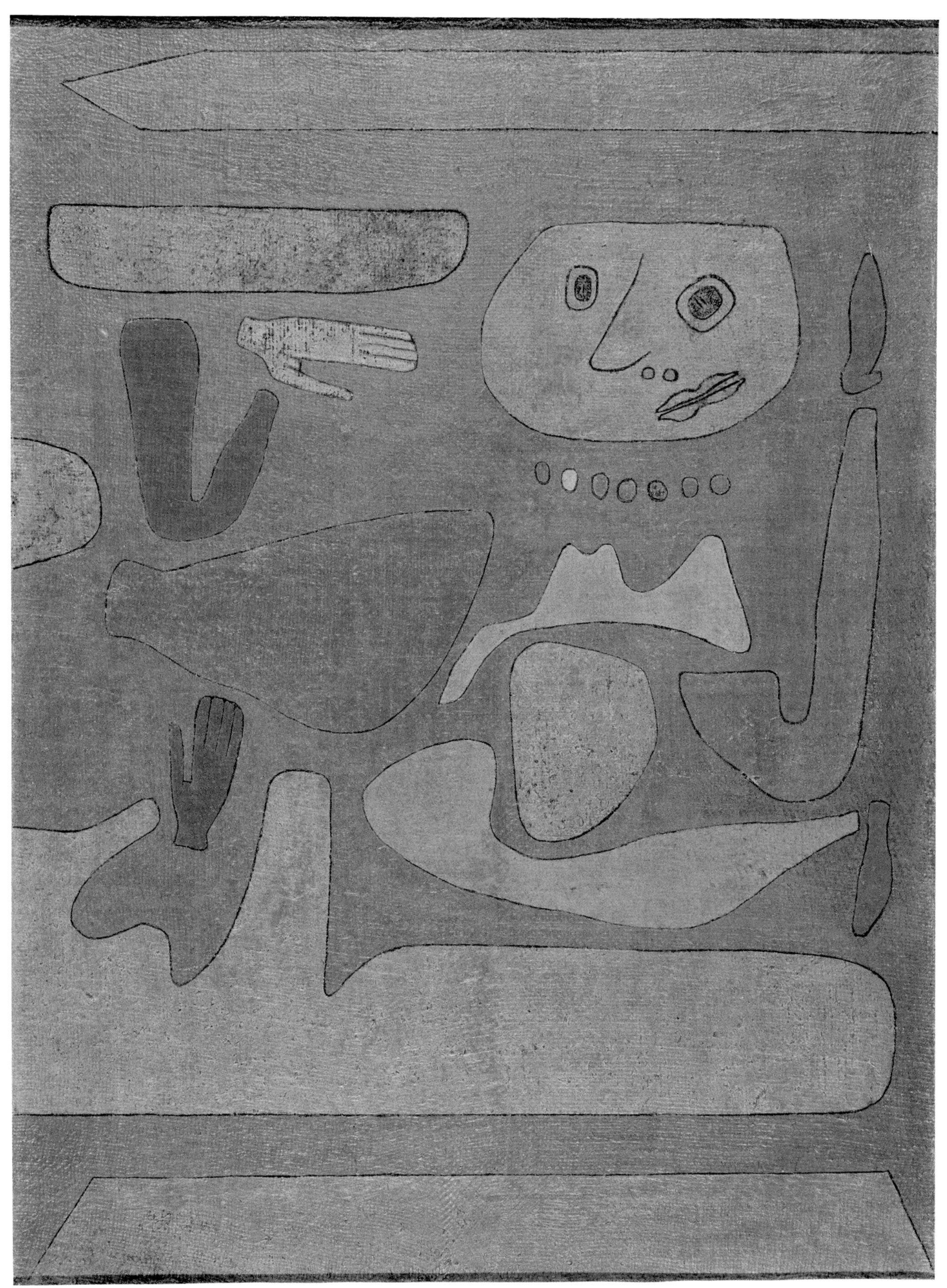

97 **DER MANN DER VERWECHSLUNG**, 1939.350
[The Man of Confusion]

Watercolor and oil on jute
26 x 19⅝ inches (66 x 50 cm)
The Saint Louis Art Museum
Gift of Mr. and Mrs. Joseph Pulitzer Jr., 410:1952

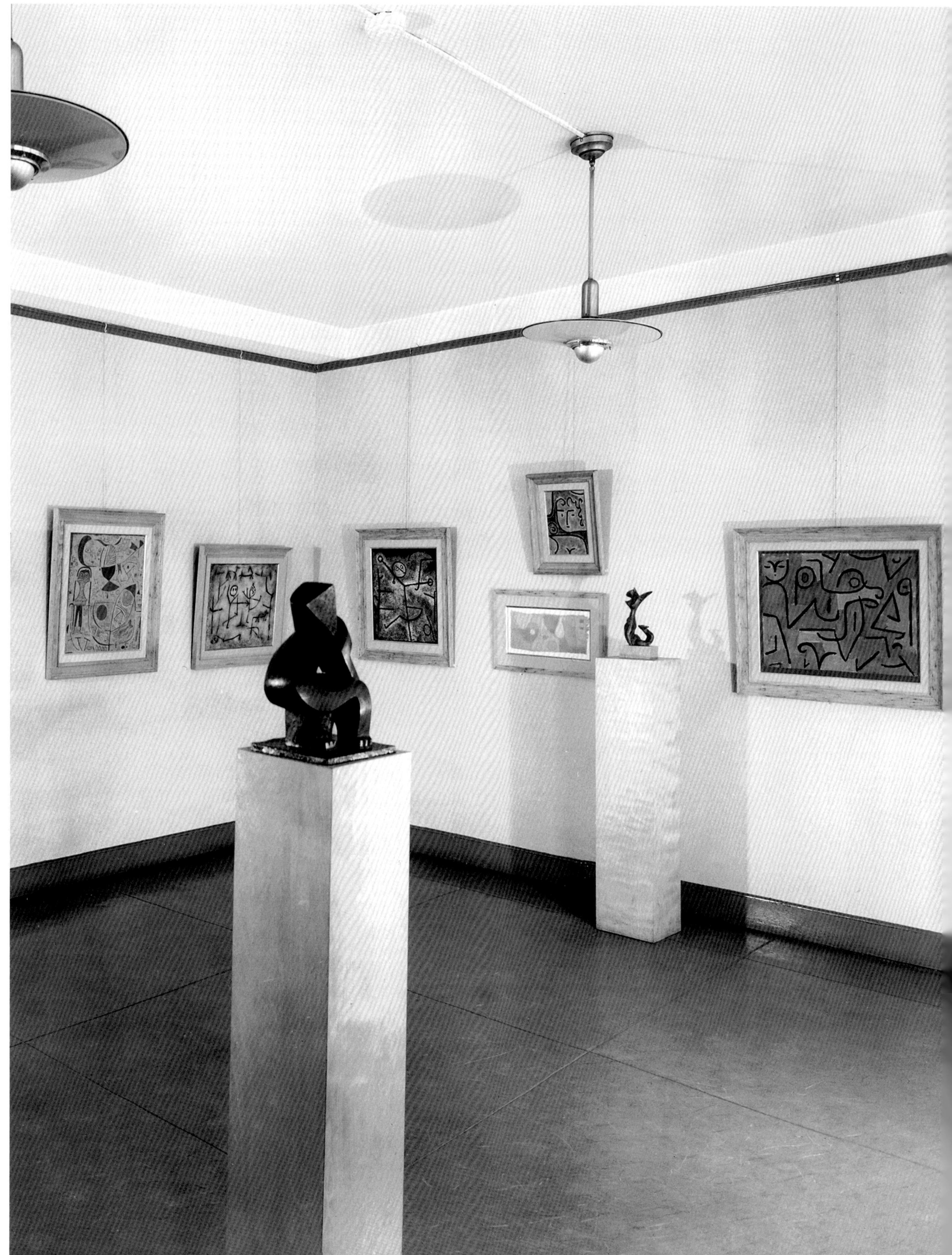

Impact and Legacy

1940s and 1950s

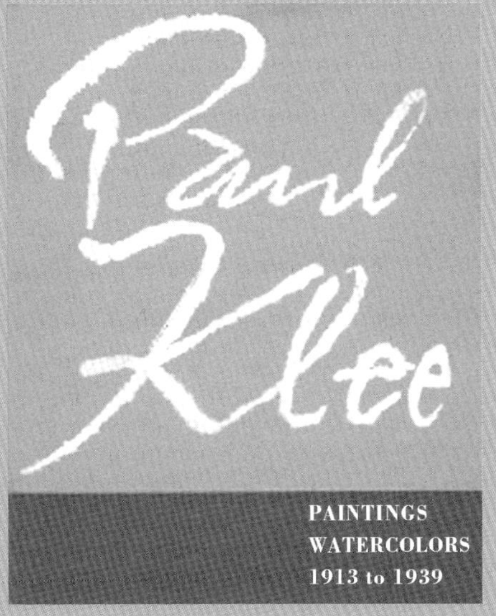

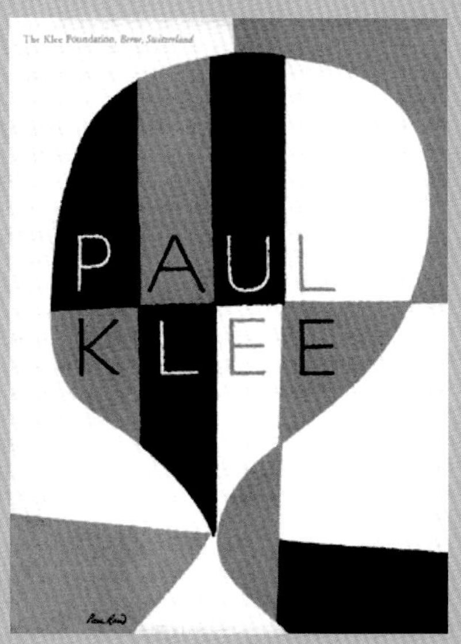

"Our Adopted Ancestor":
America's Postwar Embrace of Klee[1]

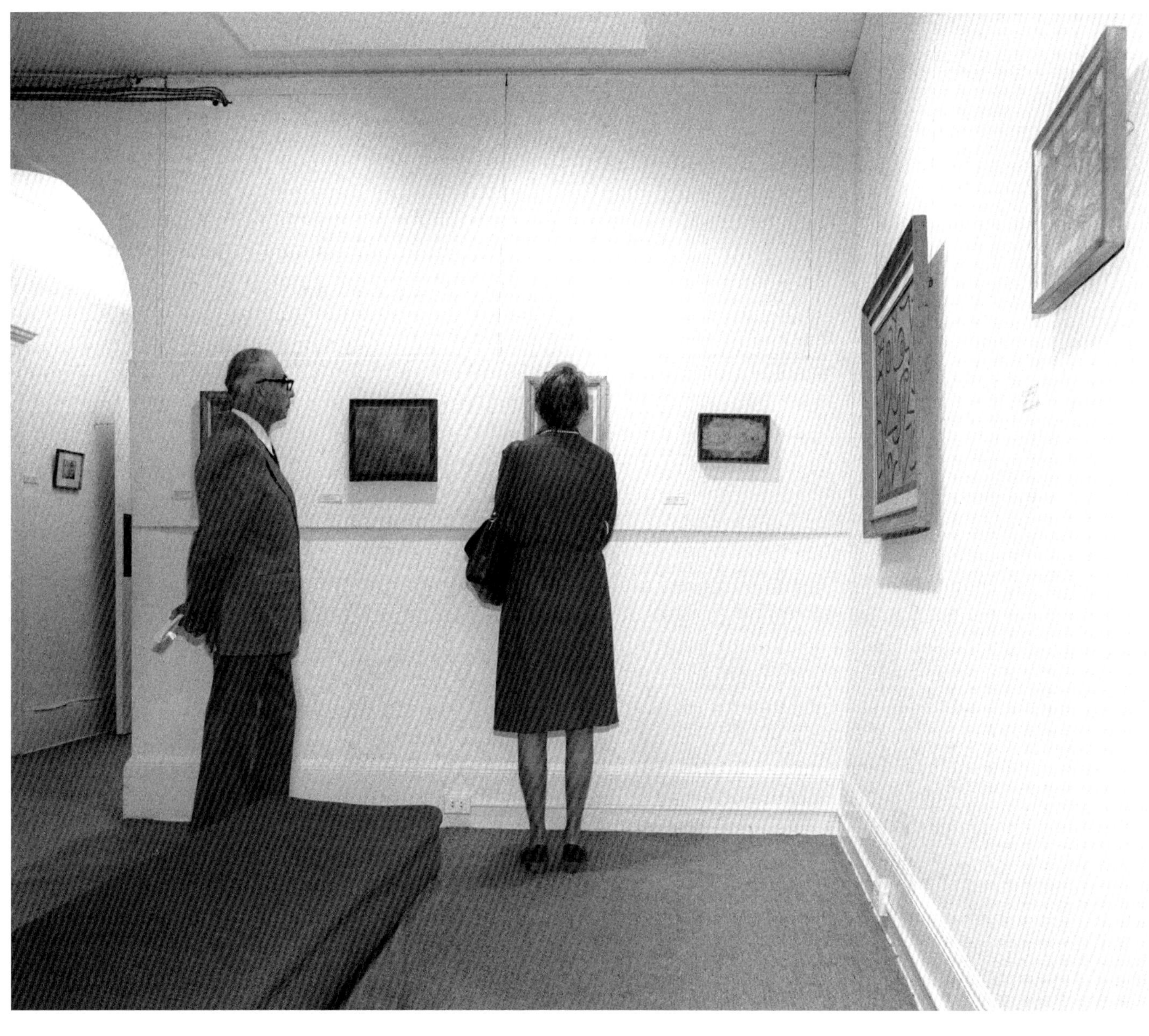

Klee had a way of leaping ahead of our understanding and trusting us to catch up with him. Posterity has proved that he had the right idea. His harbors are our harbors, his birds, our birds, his feasts our feasts.[2]   — John Russell, 1987

The Room

For over thirty years, from 1948 to 1982, in the brownstone at the corner of 21st and Q Streets N.W. that comprised Duncan Phillips's museum of modern art in Washington, D.C., visitors found, tucked by the landing on the second floor, an old sewing room hung with paintings by Paul Klee (fig. 49). It was seemingly the smallest space that could still make a room—just over 9 x 18 feet, according to the drawings of the original architects, Hornblower and Marshall. Size of course had nothing to do with the importance of the display—the room's scale and proportions were perfectly attuned to Klee's cabinet-sized pictures, and Phillips took great care to block the direct light coming through its sole window, completing the intimate enclosure. Phillips, who had begun collecting Klee in 1930, and redoubled his efforts in the late '30s and '40s, meant to represent in the sixteen paintings on display the range of Klee's research, including the late calligraphic works—not conventional choices among American collectors. To his way of thinking, the 1948 purchase of *Bilderbogen [Printed Sheet with Picture]* (1937.133, pl. 93) made it complete. Along the north wall, on the baffle covering the window, typically hung *Figur des Östlichen Theaters [Character of the Oriental Theater]* (1934.218) (fig. 50); on the opposite wall was a group of watercolors including *Botanisches Laboratorium [Botanical Laboratory]* (1928.131) and *Citronengegend [Region of Lemons]* (1929.335, fig. 51); and

occupying the walls on east and west, a procession of oils or oil mixtures ended with a face-off between *Arabisches Lied [Arabian Song]* (1932.283, pl. 76) and *Der Junge Moe [The Young Moe]* (1938.121). The quality and constancy of the display drew many pilgrims, most significantly artists Ken Noland, Morris Louis, Mark Tobey, and Mark Rothko. Legend has it that sometime in the late 1970s, when author Philip Rieff found the room, he was overheard to have exclaimed, "Oh, the bones of the martyrs!"[3] What of the sacred was enshrined along the perimeter of this tiny room? If not the bones of the sainted Klee, then at least the essence of a faith in the autonomy of the artist's vision. No doubt Phillips was a believer: Klee, by virtue of his humanity and humility, had showed him the way and the truth of abstraction. The abiding presence of Phillips's room sustained the collector's own belief—and in many ways bolstered the conviction of generations to come—that Klee's lifework pointed to a new era in modern art.

A Question of Influence

This is a story about the metaphysics of influence. The legacy of Klee as articulated in America in the 1940s, a time when his work appeared almost continually in exhibitions, was a story told at the right time in the right place to the right audience. Already known variously as a Cubist, a Surrealist, and a Bauhaus artist, Klee had stellar credentials in the international art world by the time of his

Fig. 49
Installation view, The Klee Room, The Phillips Collection, Washington, D.C., 1986.

Page 222
Installation view, "Paul Klee," Buchholz Gallery, New York, 1948. Also pictured are sculptures by unidentified artists.

Page 223
Cover of Karl Nierendorf's monograph *Paul Klee: Paintings, Watercolors, 1913–1939*, Oxford University Press (New York: 1941).

Cover of exhibition catalogue (designed by Paul Rand), *Paintings, Drawings, and Prints by Paul Klee*, The Museum of Modern Art (New York: 1941).

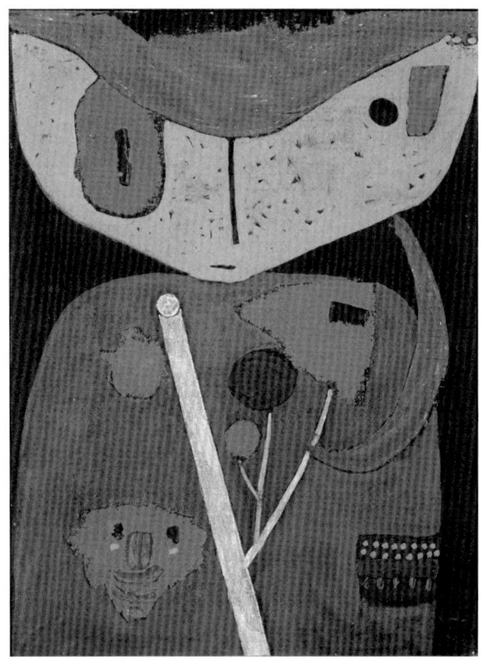

death in 1940, as well as a reputation untainted by art world politics. In an isolationist America just emerging from the Great Depression, critics saw a clear divide between abstraction and representation for which the lionized Klee supplied a much needed bridge. Thanks to two great memorial Klee retrospectives at The Museum of Modern Art, New York, which bracketed the decade—the first in 1941 drew from predominantly American collections, and the second in 1949 completed the picture with more of the drawings and late works from the artist's estate—Klee gained historical stature after his death.

The 1940s also saw the first complete translations of two of Klee's publications. Klee was the only founding father of modern art to publish a pedagogical discourse. Students used the combination of graphics and commentary in his *Pedagogical Sketchbook*[4] like an owner's manual, its precepts giving shape and direction to the work of a new generation of American abstract artists. Klee's interest in myth and archetype was timely; his pictorial solutions were even more so, as he translated his exploration of the unconscious mind into form and gesture. Looking back, critic Harold Rosenberg believed this was exactly what the next generation needed: "In sum, what the new American artist sought was not a richer or more contemporary fiction (like the Surrealists), but the formal sign language of the inner kingdom—equivalents in paint of a flash, no matter how transitory, of what had been known throughout the centuries as spiritual enlightenment."[5] Though he couched the matter in formalist terms, critic Clement Greenberg's assessment was much the same. He believed that the central issue for the artists of the emerging New York School was personal autonomy—more specifically, how to exercise autonomy within the seemingly restrictive grid of Cubist space. Greenberg thought in retrospect that Klee played a central role in determining the answer: "And almost everybody, whether conscious of it or not, was learning from Klee…."[6]

Awaiting Adoption

When Klee died on June 29, 1940, in Lugano, Switzerland, it was already a well-known fact that Germany's earlier loss of Klee had been somehow America's gain. On July 3, 1940, the headline of Klee's obituary in the *New York Times* read: "Paul Klee, Artist Banned by Nazis."[7] The obituary acknowledged the Swiss-born

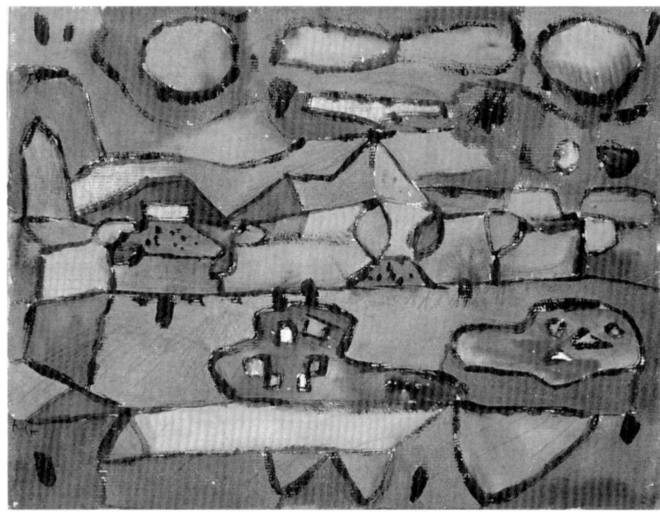

Fig. 50
Paul Klee, *Figur des Östlichen Theaters [Character of the Oriental Theater]*, 1934.218. Oil on canvas mounted on plywood, 20½ x 15½ inches (52 x 39.3 cm). The Phillips Collection, Washington, D.C.

Fig. 51
Paul Klee, *Citronengegend [Region of Lemons]*, 1929.335. Watercolor and pen on paper, mounted on cardboard, 9 x 12 inches (22.8 x 30.4 cm). The Phillips Collection, Washington, D.C.

artist's unique prominence in German modern art and repeated the oft made connection of his art with the "innocent eye" of childhood. Further, it duly noted that even if he had not been widely understood by general audiences, Klee had exhibited his work across America and been popular since the 1920s among collectors described as "a limited group of esthetes in this country." Finally, the *Times* credited American collectors and museums with the rescue of certain of Klee's works that had been deaccessioned from German museums in the 1930s: "Many examples of his art are in museums in this country, among others, in Detroit and in the Gallery of Living Art at the New York University Museum. The Museum of Modern Art, 11 West Fifty-third Street, has six of his canvases, among them 'Around the Fish,' formerly at the Dresden Gallery, and 'The Twittering Machine,' previously owned by the National Gallery of Berlin."[8] So even as American collectors took up Klee, Europe, convulsed by political events, was shunning him: disowned by Germany, his home for nearly thirty-five years, he had found even his native Switzerland, to which he returned in 1933, slow to embrace him. Klee's second application for Swiss citizenship was still pending and was said to have been approved only on the day he died. Meanwhile, thanks to his dealers J. B. Neumann, Curt Valentin, and Karl Nierendorf, Klee was practically on continuous view in New York—even at death, an artist open for adoption.

Memorials

In October 1940 Klee's memorial in America began with a joint exhibition by Buchholz Gallery and the Willard Gallery in New York. Selections from this show, together with key additions from the collections of Neumann and Nierendorf, in turn became the basis for a traveling exhibition organized by The Museum of Modern Art and launched in January 1941. That show, consisting of sixty-six works—all from American collections—opened in Northampton, Massachusetts, and circulated to Chicago; Portland, Oregon; San Francisco; and St. Louis before returning to New York six months later.[9] Its opening at the Modern on June 30 marked the first anniversary of Klee's death as well as the eleventh anniversary of Klee's first retrospective, organized by Neumann and Alfred H. Barr Jr. for The Museum of Modern Art in 1930.

There was very little overlap between the 1930 and the 1941 exhibition checklists: most notable were *Abstraktes Terzett [Abstract Trio]* (1923.88, pl. 22), ~~*Jugendlicher*~~ *Schauspieler=Maske [~~Youth~~ Actor's Mask]* (1924.252, pl. 28), and *Gemischtes Wetter [Unsettled Weather]* (1929.343). Important additions to the 1941 show included *Jungfrau (Träumend) [Virgin (Dreaming)]* (1903.2), *Kleinwelt [Little Cosmos]* (1914.120), *Die Zwitscher-Maschine [The Twittering Machine]* (1922.151, pl. 15), *Maske Furcht [Mask: Fear]* (1932.286), and *W=geweihtes Kind [W=Consecrated Child]* (1935.31, pl. 90).[10] The titles of Klee's later paintings brought attention to the brewing political turmoil in Germany. As critic Elizabeth McCausland observed, "Klee's work is a monument to the tortured sensibilities of a period." She wondered whether Klee's art represented his own personal solution to hardship or whether it constituted, as she said, "an ideal for the future,"[11] a question addressed in the 1941 catalogue.

The reprinting in the 1941 catalogue of Barr's landmark assessment of Klee from the 1930 exhibition served to codify Klee's claims upon the unconscious realm and primal sources. After all, as Barr said in 1930, Klee, together with Giorgio de Chirico and Pablo Picasso, was the one who initially had won "the right of the painters to excite the imagination and to consider dreams."[12] But in a newly drafted conclusion for the 1941 catalogue, Barr pressed his case further to position Klee more firmly within the modernist pantheon. Barr asserted, as he had in 1930, "Nothing is so astonishing to the student of Klee as his infinitive variety," then added the following rejoinder: "Not even Picasso approaches him in sheer inventiveness. In quality of imagination also he can hold his own with Picasso." Barr continued the comparison, observing that Picasso's paintings "roar" while Klee's "whisper," positioning the two artists like the yin/yang of modern painting, bound in balance and opposition. Thus Klee, or rather the spirit of Klee—the lyrical, the "incalculably sensitive" Klee that Barr described—was accorded new historical stature.[13]

It remained for the second catalogue essayist, the curator and poet James Johnson Sweeney, to articulate Klee's legacy. Departing from the conventions of art history that Barr had followed and taking a page from literary criticism, Sweeney began his tribute to Klee with a metaphor: "In an age that blasted privacy, Paul Klee built a small but exquisite shrine to intimacy."[14] Avoiding the pitfalls of stylistic labels, Sweeney thus brilliantly conveyed the essence of Klee by conjuring a verbal image. This type of fluid exchange between vision and perception is as universal as the idea of language itself. In fact, Sweeney proposed that the rhythms and repetitions explored in Klee's imagery—"a curious pictorial poetry" and "a mixed tongue of representation and technical phantasy"—could and "should be read and re-read."[15] Sweeney's emphasis upon reading (metaphorically speaking) provided a way of extricating Klee from the past so as to actively experience Klee's art in the present. (Certainly, this focus on the free-flowing interactivity of perception would have been a welcome concept to young painters at the time seeking to create their own language of abstraction and to communicate something about their world.) The agent in this approach to art that Sweeney proposed was line—in particular a moving graphic line that can be equated with a line of thought and a line of action as it collects feelings and forms from the unconscious and releases them upon the compositional field. Sweeney found such a fluidity in Klee's calligraphic expression, which he described as "sensitive to the most delicate suggestions of the nervous system, responsive to the most subtle unconscious associations." (Here Sweeney echoed Klee's stated goal: "I should like to create an order out of feeling and going still further, out of motion.")[16] Moreover, Sweeney maintained that such a seemingly automatic approach to painting exerted a powerful influence on other artists. As he said, "This was the Klee whom the Surrealists recognized as a precursor." And Sweeney predicted that Klee's "free sensibility and intelligence" would be needed again "to give life to a renewed art in a renewed world."[17]

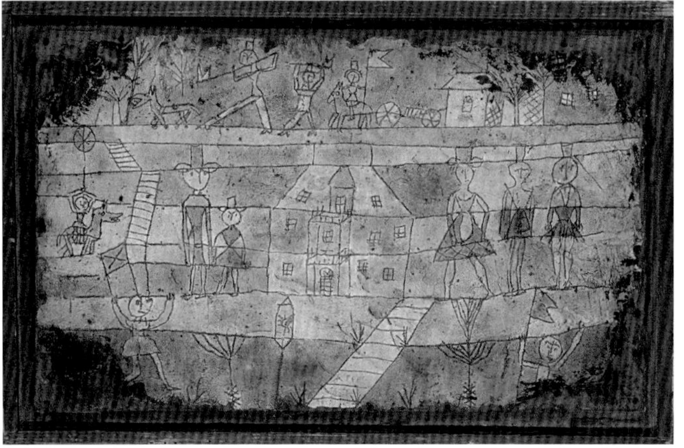

Miró

It was Joan Miró who provided the first clear demonstration of Klee's impact on younger artists. Painter and teacher Hans Hofmann often spoke of Klee's importance for Miró. In particular he cited Klee's fluency of expression in painting, which, like handwriting, "characterizes a complete personality."[18] It was this aspect of Klee that Miró cultivated when he began, as Hofmann put it, "relating and spacing these shapes to a sur-real expression."[19] By 1941 painter André Masson, Miró's former neighbor from the rue Blomet in Paris, had arrived in New York and could corroborate Hofmann's story with his own firsthand account (albeit in French) of the day in 1922 when he retrieved the German art historian Wilhelm Hausenstein's 1921 monograph on Klee from the bookstall on the quay and showed it to Miró.[20]

In November 1941 there were ample opportunities for comparison when The Museum of Modern Art opened a Miró retrospective exactly commensurate with a Klee retrospective at the Nierendorf Gallery.[21] (Sweeney curated both.) According to Sweeney, Miró had responded to his generation's need for "a recall of the imagination to painting."[22] However, his work from the twenties also introduced the question of influence. At times in his

Fig. 52
Paul Klee, *Ankunft der Gaukler[Arrival of the Jugglers]*, 1926.203. Oil on putty-primed cardboard, mounted on second cardboard, with original frame, 6⅞ x 10¾ inches (17.4 x 27.3 cm). The Phillips Collection, Washington, D.C.

Fig. 53
Joan Miró, *Peinture (Personnages: Les Frères Fratellini) [Painting (Personage: The Fratellini Brothers)]*, 1927. Oil on canvas, 51⅛ x 38⅜ inches (130 x 97.5 cm). Fondation Beyeler, Riehen, Switzerland.

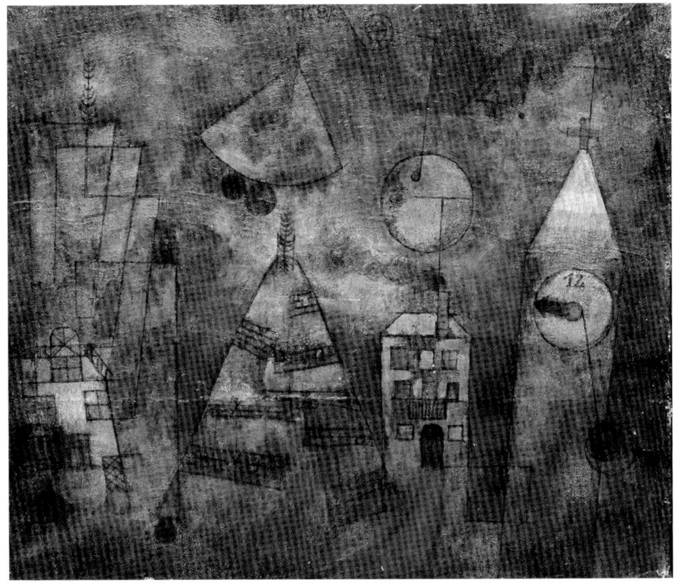

paintings, aspects of Miró's deeply felt and intensely described inventory of memories, such as those given expression in *The Farm* (1921), launch upward and become airborne fantasies, such as elements in *The Hunter* (1923). Suitable comparisons with Klee paintings, if not the exact source of Miró's inspiration, could be found in nearby Nierendorf Gallery, where Sweeney lauded Klee for his reflection of "the world of imagination."[23] Works such as *Orakel [Oracle]* (1919.98), *Ankunft der Gaukler [Arrival of the Jugglers]* (1926.203, fig. 52), *Urnensammlung [Urn Collection]* (1922.129), and *Schicksalstunde um Dreiviertel Zwölf [Fateful Hour at a Quarter to Twelve]* (1922.184) demonstrate a propensity to subvert Cubist structure along with a predilection for fantastic, self-effacing humor that was similar to Miró's. Had Klee led the way? Without question. Miró himself later would say simply: "My encounter with Klee's work was the most important event in my life."[24]

Seeing Miró in light of Klee in New York in 1942—seeing *Fratellini* (1927, fig. 53) in light of *Schicksalstunde um Dreiviertel Zwölf* (fig. 54), for example—was to witness how Miró had gained entry to an autonomous sphere of abstraction and the unconscious via Klee's seemingly boundless atmosphere of color and running lines. Soaring in pictorial space, Miró's painting abandoned the descriptive trappings of the outer world and expressed simply the action of his being. Klee understood this aesthetic response to the world, saying, "Thus am I abstract with memories."[25] Miró adopted from Klee, not a style, but a pictorial process of inquiry with infinite potential for future discoveries. This included new materials: Klee often combined the effects of paste and plaster variously on canvas, paper, or panel, as in *Ankunft der Gaukler* or *Vögel Versammeln Sich [Birds Flock Together]* (1937.195). Like Klee, Miró reignited his process in painting by experimenting with new materials. In *Women and Kite among the Constellations* (1939), Miró painted with oil on burlap, an unusual surface that unpredictably resisted or accepted the movements of his line. That sense of experimentation was key. As Klee said, "When intuition is joined to exact research, it speeds the progress of exact research.... Mathematics and physics furnished the means in the form of rules to be followed and to be broken."[26] As more of Klee's writings—particularly the *Pedagogical Sketchbook* and Klee's 1924 lecture *On Modern Art*—became translated, and his diagrams were reprinted, the empirical aspect of Klee's artistic process would become better known.

Calder

Alexander Calder may have learned about the importance of Klee from Miró—perhaps as early as January 1929 when he visited Miró's studio in Paris. Surely by April 1929, when Calder showed his work in Berlin at the Neumann-Nierendorf Gallery, he would have seen Klee's work. Klee's influence was clearly present in the work that Calder exhibited in a range of media, from sculpture and painting to textile designs, at the Fifty-sixth Street Galleries in New York in late 1929.[27] The exhibition included a wire fishbowl with a crank, essentially a simple machine whose action in many ways appears as a parody of Klee's *Die Zwitscher-Maschine*.[28] Looking

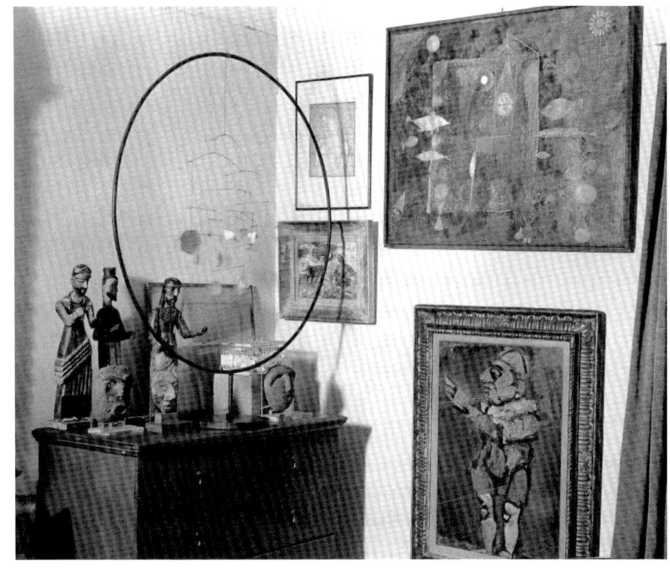

Fig. 54
Paul Klee, *Schicksalstunde um Dreiviertel Zwölf [Fateful Hour at a Quarter to Twelve]*, 1922.184. Oil on chalk-primed muslin mounted on wood, with original frame, 16⅛ x 18⅞ inches (41 x 48 cm). Private collection, Great Britain.

Fig. 55
Walter and Louise Arensberg residence, Los Angeles, showing Alexander Calder, *Mobile* (1934, left), along with Paul Klee, *Fisch Zauber [Fish Magic]* (1925.85, upper right, pl. 34) and Georges Rouault, *Polichinelle* (c. 1930, lower right), c. 1945.

back, Calder said he would have exhibited a bird that opened and closed its beak, but he found out that Klee had beaten him to it.[29] Following his own propensities toward what Klee would call science and intuition, Calder later announced his Klee-like intent in art: "Compose motions."[30] (see fig. 55)

In April 1942 the Cincinnati Modern Art Society mounted an exhibition of works by Calder and Klee—at that point a winning combination, given the popularity of both artists. With the Nierendorf Gallery drawing record crowds in New York and the Klee catalogue in its fourth printing, *Art News* reported Klee to be in the midst of a revival.[31] Calder's profile also was on the rise, given his growing international reputation, his name in the latest edition of *Who's Who,* his regular exposure at the Pierre Matisse Gallery in New York, and a retrospective planned by The Museum of Modern Art for 1943. Would seeing the larger-scale works by Calder somehow make Klee's animated, cabinet-sized paintings more visible? Perhaps.

The Cincinnati exhibition of the historical Klee (including forty-three drawings and paintings from 1907 to 1937) with the contemporary Calder (nine mobiles and four stabiles from around 1939 to 1942) brought to light a new dimension of the older artist. Few in America would have known, if the Cincinnati catalogue had not told them, that Klee, like Calder, had also made "arrangements with cloth, wood and metal which functioned by crank or by draft."[32] Seeing Calder's *Castle with Flags* (1939) (fig. 56) in light of Klee's *Beginnende Kühle [Incipient Coolness]* (1937.136, pl. 94),

for example, demanded that viewers give process—that is to say, the artist's way of seeing and constructing—primary significance. From cut and bolted steel and bent wire, Calder assembled an arched and stair-stepped composition, culminating in mobile wire extensions that delicately pivot and balance. Likewise, in *Beginnende Kühle*, within a composition of oil on cardboard not much longer than the extension of a forearm, Klee built a virtual city out of the movement of line—a structural rhythm dense with irregular patterns—and rectangles within rectangles that bring intonations of blue out of orange. Despite the artists' use of vastly different media and scale, a similar vibrancy emerges from their respective discipline in approaching their materials. As the catalogue stated, "Although their media differ, Klee and Calder are allied by a rhythmic lightness and balance, a gay vibrancy and, especially in Klee, by an unequalled sense of empathy."[33] The "keenly felt diagrams" of Klee's *Pedagogical Sketchbook* had already suggested as much.[34]

Perhaps Klee was akin to Calder in much the same way that Klee was akin to the physical movement expressed in his own diagram of the waterwheel and triphammer (fig. 57; this well-known image from Klee's *Pedagogical Sketchbook* was reproduced on the back of the 1941 Museum of Modern Art catalogue). The artist transformed his preoccupation with the physics of movement through his sense of play in the act of drawing his machine. Klee's stick-figure rendering of the water, wheels, transmission belt, lever, and hammer tells us very little about industrial mass or energy— ironically we fear more for the fate of the spindly table beneath the

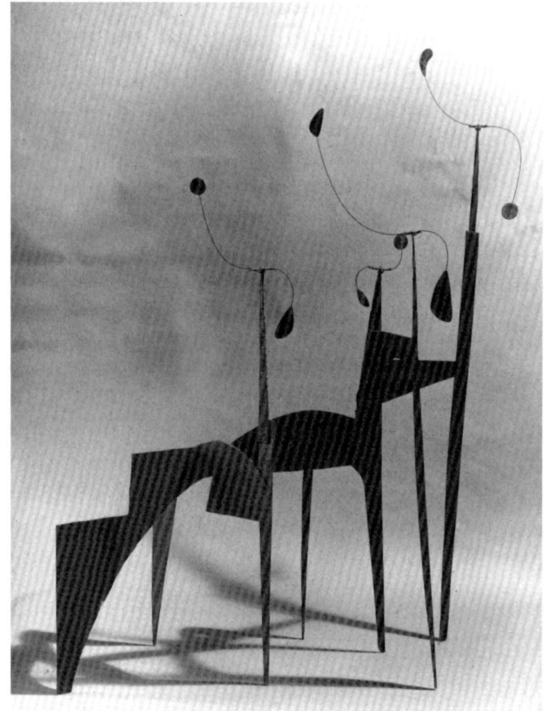

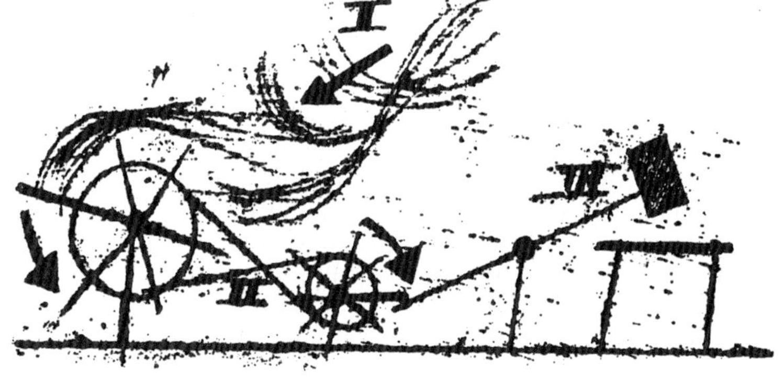

Fig. 56
Alexander Calder, *Castle with Flags*, 1939.
Sheet metal and paint, 28½ x 22½ x 12⅝ inches
(72.4 x 57.1 x 32 cm). Courtesy Calder
Foundation, New York.

Fig. 57
Paul Klee, "Figure 25," in *Pedagogical Sketchbook,* 5th ed. (1925; reprint, New York: Frederick A. Praeger, Inc., 1967).

heavy hammer.[35] In this latter aspect, Klee differed from Calder. Directing irony toward industrial machinery was not Calder's province—with the exception of a few motorized actions, Calder used only simple machines—but this aspect of Klee would be readily enlisted in 1942 for a Surrealist demonstration of his work at Peggy Guggenheim's new gallery in New York.

New Visionaries

In the fall of 1942, the installation of Klee's work at Guggenheim's Art of This Century gallery in New York provided one of the most engaging experiences of the inaugural exhibition. Positioned in a long darkened room called the Kinetic Gallery, a "Klee paternoster" operated behind a black panel to automatically display the artist's work. Activated by an electric eye that crossed the corridor, selections from Guggenheim's collection of Klee works, which at the time included *weibliche und männliche Pflanze [Female and Male Plant]* (1921.76), *Frau R. auf Reisen im Süden [Mrs. R. Traveling in the South]* (1924.248), *Ebene Landschaft [Flat Landscape]* (1924.134), *HM. Idyll* (1932.112), *Überkultiviertes Land [Over-cultivated Land]* (1935.81), *Kind vom Berg [Child of the Mountain]* (1935.50), *Eisenbahn im Gebirge [Railway in the Mountains]* (1936.20), and *Rotes Raubtier [Red Predator]* (1938.198), began rotating in and out of view, courtesy of a moving conveyor belt that would pause at approximately ten-second intervals.[36] Even though the viewer could push a button to stop the mechanism in order to look at an individual work for a longer time, the mechanical motion was mesmerizing. As one critic described it, "Each Klee appears and halts a short while before the next one rolls in with clangor and grind."[37] Another said, "You feel like a child with a new toy that does all sorts of unpredictable things."[38] Obviously a ten-second pause on the awkward conveyor belt was not enough time to appreciate the intricacies of each Klee painting—it is impossible to quickly assimilate his images—but the glimpse itself afforded the chance to experience, if only by way of parody, the temporal nature of Klee's approach to painting. Alternately, a shadowbox device in the Abstract Gallery featured a closed circular peephole that the viewer could open to reveal Klee's *Zaubergarten[Magic Garden]* (1926.141, fig. 58, 59; see fig. 105). At the time, designer Frederick Kiesler explained that his installation for Art of This Century would enable "the artist's work to stand forth as a vital entity in a

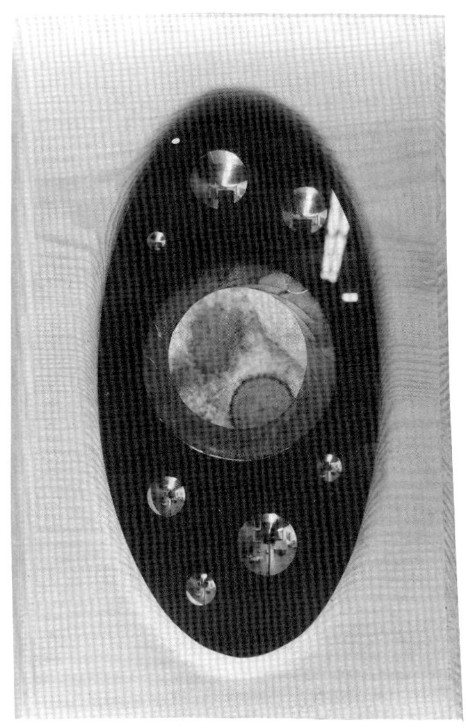

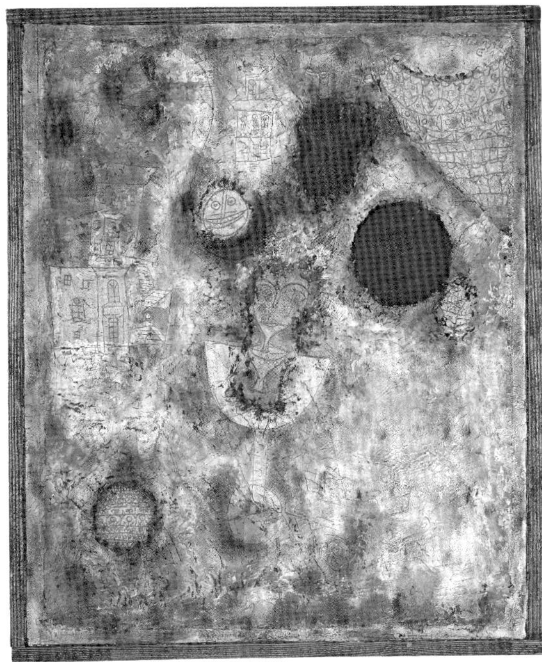

Fig. 58
Shadowbox viewing mechanism with shutter open to show detail of Paul Klee's *Zaubergarten [Magic Garden]* (1926), Kinetic Gallery, Art of This Century, New York, 1942.

Fig. 59
Paul Klee, *Zaubergarten [Magic Garden]* (1926.141). Oil on gypsum plaster-filled wire mesh with original wood frame, 20⅞ x 17¾ inches (52.9 x 44.9 cm). Solomon R. Guggenheim Foundation, Peggy Guggenheim Collection, Venice, 1976, 76.2553.90.

spatial world and art [to] stand forth as a vital link in the structure of a new myth."[39] Certainly the fact that Kiesler's "Klee paternoster" remained on continuous view as part of the permanent installation at Art of This Century made it available to visitors with a stake in that new myth—particularly to Robert Motherwell, Jackson Pollock, and Rothko, who themselves would later exhibit at the gallery. Looking back, Motherwell recalled how the planning for another exhibition (possibly Art of This Century's "Exhibition of Collage" in the spring of 1943) following the gallery's inaugural display of Surrealist and abstract art, became the pretext for a discussion with Pollock that focused on Klee's automatic way of beginning a picture.[40] Two years later, weary of Surrealist dogma, particularly its disregard for the formal values of painting, Motherwell may well have been thinking of the heroic example of the exiled and tragic Klee when, in a lecture at Mount Holyoke in 1944, he defined his ideal in painting as "the mind realizing itself in color and space. The greatest adventures, especially in the brutal and policed period, take place in the mind."[41]

Stanley William Hayter was among those at the forefront of new research in art. An English engraver befriended by the Surrealists in Paris, he had reestablished his printmaking Atelier 17 in New York in 1940 in space borrowed from the New School. Atelier 17 had no organized program of instruction but provided equipment and technical assistance for those interested in graphic methods. Learning came by doing. Painters like Rothko, Pollock, Motherwell, and Adolph Gottlieb were given carte blanche to explore ideas and to follow up on questions in a fresh medium—with no interference. True to the workshop setting, learning also came by example. Looking back, Hayter named Klee as the major influence on those working at Atelier 17.[42] By 1944, when a selection of Atelier 17 works was shown at The Museum of Modern Art, a number of works on paper by Rothko bore the hallmarks of Klee's floating, transparent, linear figures.[43] This was the same year that the *Pedagogical Sketchbook* was translated in its entirety, asserting Klee's faith that his art was communicable and subject to rational analysis; also available, published ten years after its suppression by the Nazis, was Will Grohmann's *The Drawings of Paul Klee* (New York: C. Valentin, 1944), including excerpts from Klee's notebooks.

In 1946 Hayter paid tribute to Klee by publishing the ideas derived from Klee's art and writing that he had shared with the artists who had come to work in his studio. Hayter began his article, entitled "Paul Klee: Apostle of Empathy," by asserting that Klee provided a prescient model for the attitudes of "artists today." Klee embraced, as he said, "everything within man as well as everything within the grasp of the senses of man." Moreover, Klee's empathy enabled him to identify the physical action of his marks with their metaphysical consequence. For example, the drawing of the turning spiral (fig. 57) from the *Pedagogical Sketchbook* posed both an artistic and a moral question: Klee asked whether it would indicate "the release from the center in freer and freer movements, or …an increasing dependence upon a finally destructive center. This question means life or death, and the decision rests with a small arrow." And how, he continued, did this aspect of Klee's philosophy, one concentrating on the physics of movement, reconcile with the artist's use of automatism? Hayter explained that although Klee was willing to risk the venture into the unknown and to rely upon the instinctive or unconscious gesture as a technique of research—"the least of his lines is charged with an extremely high voltage"—he was able to avoid danger (in the form of deadly repetitions) through his predetermined, rational understanding of his physical relationship to the surface upon which he was working. Reflecting his musical inclination, Hayter estimated Klee's physical range was most often the spread-fingered reach of two octaves, observing that Klee's "spirit came into focus on a small surface." But his imagination activated that space as a buoyant antigravitational field—what Klee described as "fish swimming in all directions." Hayter concluded that Klee had the power to lead others into unlimited fields of "unrestricted motion in a medium with no other resistance than that of time." Whether we undertake the journey is contingent upon our ability to "leave everyday baggage behind."[44] To follow Klee, according to Hayter, was to empathize with his quest—to acknowledge that the artist's search for truth is the real subject of art. Even though by 1947 Greenberg was describing works by Tobey and Morris Graves as belonging to "the School of Klee,"[45] Hayter, like Klee, understood that there could be no such thing.

In 1948, the same year that Klee's 1924 lecture *On Modern Art* was translated and published (London: Faber and Faber, 1948), William Baziotes, David Hare, Motherwell, and Rothko founded a small school, which they called Subjects of the Artist, located at

35 East Eighth Street in New York. Barnett Newman joined the faculty in January 1949. The school ran for three ten-week terms before closing in May 1949 and had in all about seventeen regular students. Subjects of the Artist advertised a new approach to learning art.[46] According to the one-page catalogue written by Motherwell, admission was not based upon previous experience or academic courses. As he said, "Those attending the classes will not be treated as 'students' in the conventional manner, but as collaborators with the artist in the investigation of the artistic process, its modern conditions, possibilities, and extreme nature, through discussions and practice."[47] On Friday nights they opened the school to the public, and other artists such as Willem de Kooning, Jean Arp, and John Cage were invited to speak on topics that interested them. In March 1949, in his lecture before the Seventh Annual Conference of the Committee on Art Education, Motherwell explained that learning in his "little school of art" began by providing a place "to hang around artists." As Motherwell said, "We talk to students as we do to one another, trying to break down ignorance and clichés, encouraging each individual to find his own expression of his inner life. This kind of teaching must be done by artists. No one else 'reads' plastic expression quickly or subtly enough. Still, in a basic sense art cannot be taught, and we do not try to. Yet paradoxically it can be learned—in the beginning from other artists, and then from oneself."[48] In so doing, students learn "what [their] subjects are, how they are arrived at, methods of inspiration and transformation, moral attitudes, possibilities for further explorations, what is being done now and what might be done and so on."[49] In this regard, Motherwell had adopted Klee.

Similarly, Klee's 1924 lecture saw the artist as kinsman to the student—"as a being like you." According to Klee, our artist guide, having already made sense of the stream of images and experience, takes us, as companions in the creative process, on his inward journey. Fittingly, Klee began with an analogy from the everyday: "May I use a simile, the simile of a tree?" he said. Like a tree, the artist channels and transforms what he has found from the roots to the glory of the crown. However daunting the effort to probe experience, the true artist must continue: "The deeper he looks, the more readily he can extend his view from the present to the past, the more deeply he is impressed by the one essential image of creation itself, as Genesis, rather than by the image of nature, the finished product." At the source of creation—what Klee called "the powerhouse of all time and space"—we will find a key that unlocks variously "dream, idea or phantasy." It is not enough simply to find it: one must retrieve it. As Klee said, the artist's uncovered dream lives on the surface of consciousness only if it unites with the proper form in an autonomous construction. Klee attached particular importance to color for providing variation of meaning: "Color as tone value: e.g., red in red, i.e., the entire range from a deficiency to an excess of red, either widely extended, or limited in range. Then the same in yellow (something quite different). The same in blue—what contrasts! Or colours diametrically opposed— i.e., changes from red to green, from yellow to purple, from blue to orange. Tremendous fragments of meaning."[50] Klee ended his lecture by revealing his own dream for the future: "Sometimes I dream of a work of really great breadth, ranging through the whole region of element, object, meaning and style. This, I fear, will remain a dream, but it is a good thing even now to bear the possibility occasionally

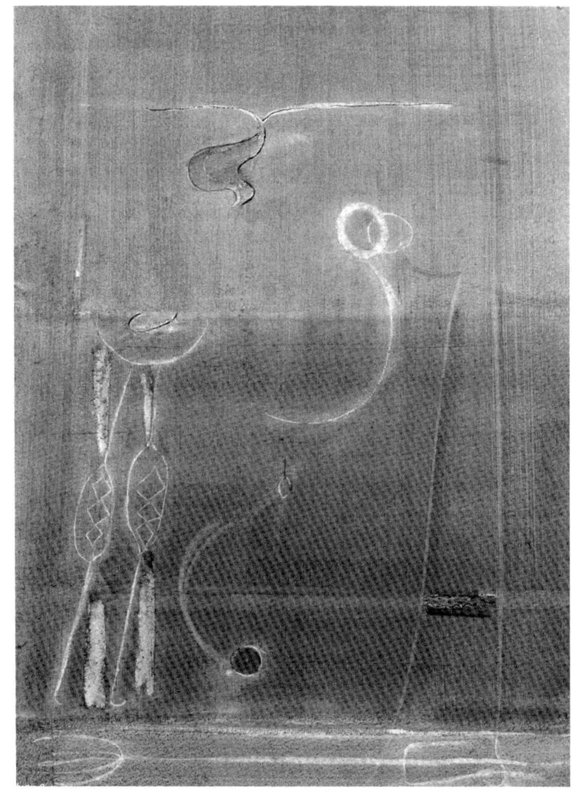

Fig. 60
Mark Rothko, *Aubade,* 1944. Gouache on paper, 25 ¼ x 19 inches (64.1 x 48.3 cm). The Phillips Collection, Washington, D.C., Gift of Rebecca B. and Julius W. Allen, 1994.

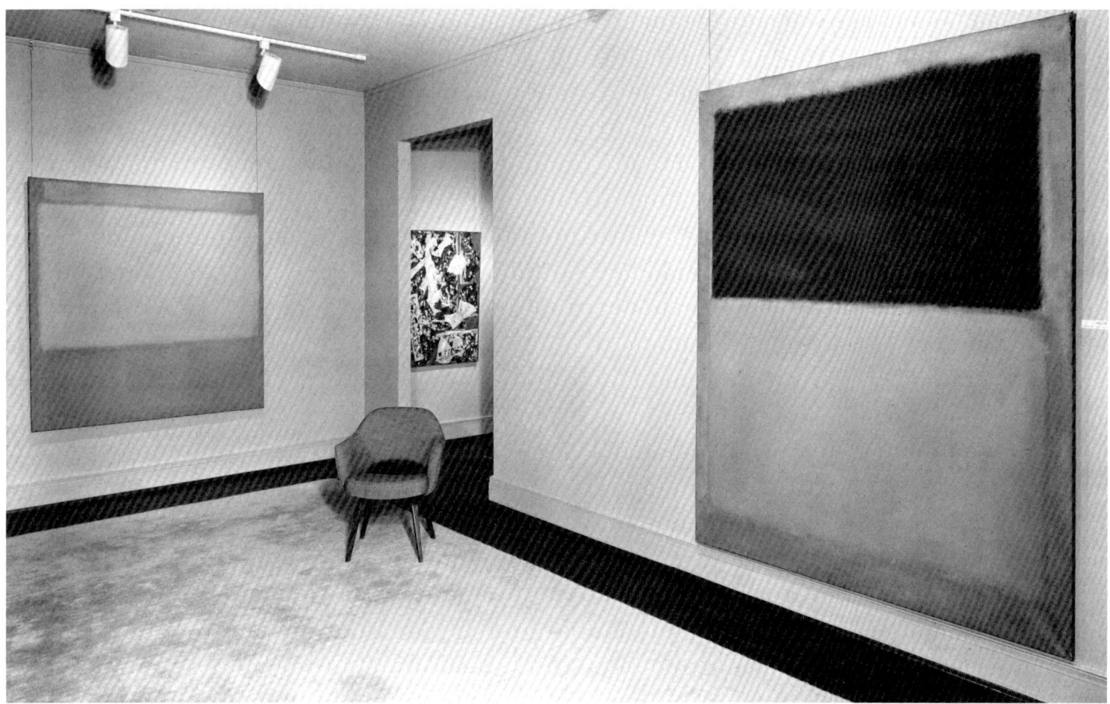

in mind…. We must go on seeking it! We have found part, but not the whole! We still lack the ultimate power, for: the people are not with us. But we seek a people…."[51] A generation after Klee's lecture, the congregants at Subjects of the Artist were well on their way to realizing, as Klee put it, "a work of really great breadth."

During his time on the faculty, Rothko characterized his own artistic quest as a desire for transcendence in his work. Through painting Rothko forged a physical connection with the metaphysical realm (fig. 60). He said, "I do not believe that there was ever a question of being abstract or representational. It is really a matter of ending this silence and solitude, of breathing and stretching one's arms again."[52] From 1944 through 1949, his work changed as he began abandoning Surrealist figuration in favor of loosely shaped patches of paint floating in an atmosphere of color. His echoing forms emanate their own light. They move as animate beings—as actors in a theatre of the artist's imagination—in an all-over space characterized by forms continuously fading in and out.

Rothko pursued this effect, first achieved in watercolor, in oils by methodically applying sheer screens of dilute paint upon carefully prepared surfaces.[53] Visiting Rothko's 1948 show at Betty Parsons Gallery in New York , critic Sam Hunter described it as "an art solely of transitions without beginning, middle or end."[54]

What Rothko wanted was nothing less than the ravishment of the sublime. He said that he was working "toward the elimination of all obstacles between the painter and the idea and between the idea and observer."[55] In 1949, at the same time that Rothko's artist's statement was being published in *Tiger's Eye,* The Museum of Modern Art mounted its great and final Klee memorial exhibition. In a manner that suggested a precedent (a spiritual ancestor, if you will) for Rothko, critic David Sylvester spoke of the sublime aspect of late Klee: "With a Klee, the relationship between the picture and yourself is reciprocal…. You are part of it as you are part of the sea when you go swimming; you plough your way through it and, in turn, are buffeted by the waves—lines continually chang-

Fig. 61
Installation view, The Rothko Room, The Phillips Collection, Washington, D.C., 1986: Mark Rothko, *Orange and Red on Red*, 1957 (left) and *Green and Tangerine on Red*, 1956 (right); and Jackson Pollock, *Collage and Oil*, c. 1951 (visible through doorway into adjoining gallery).

ing in plane and direction. For the picture is always changing, always becoming."[56] If sublime pictorial space exists to define and extend the experience of seeing, then it is not surprising that Rothko's paintings would increasingly lay claim to an all-enveloping space. As Rothko explained, "By saturating the room with the feeling of the work, the walls are defeated and the poignancy of each work . . . become[s] more visible."[57] Presumably, the people Klee sought in his 1924 lecture would provide a setting for such a communion with "a work of great breadth."

The Room

In 1960 Phillips created a room for Rothko.[58] The room (fig. 61) —precursor to the Rothko Chapel in Houston, completed in 1971—was, within the context of Phillips's modern museum, an heir to the room for Klee. In 1959, just over ten years after completing his room of Klee works, Phillips began planning a space for Rothko in a small ground floor room of the new annex being designed by Wyeth and King of New York. This room, measuring about 24 x 24 feet, was specifically proportioned to accommodate a single work on each wall. As realized in November 1960, the Rothko room installed *Green and Maroon* (1953, fig. 62), measuring 91⅛ x 54⅞ inches, on the north wall opposite *Green and Red on Tangerine* (1956), measuring 93⅝ x 69¼ inches, on the south wall; on the east wall hung *Orange and Red on Red* (1957), measuring 68⅞ x 66⅜ inches. (Originally the west wall was left empty.) The effect was one of immersion within the artist's palette. Being in the room brought Phillips into a state of reverie, or what he described as "some sense of well-being suddenly shadowed by a cloud—yellow ochres strangely suffused with a drift of gray, prevailing over an ambience of rose, or the fire diminishing into a glow of ember, or the light when the night descends."[59]

Indeed Phillips had been prepared for that moment by Klee. Before encountering Klee's work, abstract art—particularly geometric abstraction—seemed as an empty house to Phillips. After Klee, however, Phillips recognized abstraction's humanity—its generative life-giving force. As he said, "Love must come back to its vacant dwelling."[60] And that unity of abstraction with personal experience may well have been the ultimate legacy of Klee to America.

Fig. 62
Mark Rothko, *Green and Maroon*, 1953. Oil on canvas, 91⅛ x 54⅞ inches (231.5 x 139.4 cm). The Phillips Collection, Washington D.C.

NOTES

I would like to thank Merry A. Foresta, Mary Lord, and Evelyn Braithwaite for their thoughtful reading of my manuscript. Many thanks are also due Elsa Smithgall, Karen Schneider, Sophie Cikovsky, Allison Wood, Cecily Boles, Rebecca Seltzer, and Katie Pfieffer, for their research assistance. Last but not least, I would like to dedicate this essay to Marion Bolton Stroud, whose kind hospitality enabled me to finish it.

1. "Klee's influence . . . has been tremendous on contemporary America art. [The exhibition] . . . is not only a memorial to a modern master, but also to one of our adopted ancestors." Henry A. LaFarge, "Klee: The Old Magician in a New U.S. Look," *Art News* 48, no. 2 (April 1949): 42. Also cited in Carolyn Lanchner, "Klee and America," in Carolyn Lanchner, ed., *Paul Klee,* exh. cat. (New York: Museum of Modern Art, 1987), 83. In addition to Lanchner's writing, the landmark essay on Klee's importance to postwar American artists was by Andrew Kagan. See Andrew Kagan, "Paul Klee's Influence on America Painting: New York School," Part I, *Arts Magazine* 49, no. 10 (June 1975): 54–59, and Andrew Kagan, "Paul Klee's Influence on American Painting," Part II, *Arts Magazine* 50, no. 1 (September 1975): 84–90.

2. John Russell, "The Legacy of Klee Is Everywhere," *New York Times*, February 8, 1987, sec. 2, 1.

3. Klee Paintings Files, Hanging Records, Phillips Collection Archives, Washington, D.C. My thanks to chief registrar Joe Holbach for sharing the legend.

4. Paul Klee, *Pedagogical Sketchbook,* trans. Sibyl Peech (New York: Nierendorf, 1944).

5. Harold Rosenberg, quoted in Dore Ashton, *About Rothko* (Cambridge, Mass.: Da Capo Press, 2003), 107.

6. Clement Greenberg, "The Late Thirties in New York" (1957), in Clement Greenberg, *Art and Culture: Critical Essays* (Boston: Beacon Press, 1965), 232.

7. "Paul Klee, Artist Banned by Nazis," *New York Times*, July 3, 1940, 17.

8. "Paul Klee, Artist Banned by Nazis," 17.

9. There is a discrepancy in the number of paintings given in the 1941 exhibition catalogue and in the Klee catalogue raisonné listing for this show.

10. See *Paul Klee,* exh. cat. (New York: Museum of Modern Art, 1941).

11. Elizabeth McCausland, "Paul Klee's Paintings in Memorial Showing," *Springfield, Massachusetts, Sunday Union and Republican,* July 13, 1941, 6E.

12. Alfred H. Barr Jr., *Paul Klee,* exh. cat. (New York: Museum of Modern Art, 1930), 8–10.

13. See Barr, *Paul Klee* (1930), 8; revised and reprinted in *Paul Klee* (1941), 6. Also note Barr's comparison of Picasso and Klee—most specifically the comparison of Klee's *Mädchen aus Sachsen [Maid of Saxony]* (1922.132) with Picasso's *Seated Woman* (1927)—which dates back to his essay in Alfred H. Barr Jr., *German Painting and Sculpture,* exh. cat. (New York: Museum of Modern Art, 1931), 27; reprinted in Lanchner, 97. Picasso continued to be the means by which both artists and critics distinguished Klee. For further examples of his comparison with Picasso, see Jacob Kainen, "An Interview with Stanley W. Hayter," *Arts Magazine* 60, no. 5 (January 1986): 65; Clement Greenberg, "Essay 2," in Merle Armitage, et al., *5 Essays on Klee* (New York: Duell, Sloan & Pearce, c. 1950), 49–53; Howard Devree, "Essay 3," in Armitage, et al., 83; and Mark Tobey, quoted in Selden Rodman, *Conversations with Artists* (New York: Devin-Adair Co., 1957), 18.

14. James Johnson Sweeney, "Paul Klee," in *Paul Klee* (1941), 6. Sweeney's essay had appeared in the exhibition catalogue for the Buchholz Gallery and Willard Gallery show in November 1940. Sweeney's essay was also the basis for the introduction in Karl Nierendorf, ed., *Paul Klee: Paintings, Watercolors, 1913 to 1939* (New York: Oxford University Press, c. 1941), 13–17. The Museum of Modern Art later reprinted the entire 1941 Klee catalogue with expanded reproductions in Margaret Miller, ed., *Paul Klee* (New York: The Museum of Modern Art, 1945). Though his themes remained much the same, Sweeney continued to publish new commentary on Klee. See James Johnson Sweeney, "Essay 5," in Armitage, et al., 115–21.

15. Sweeney, "Paul Klee," 6. Clement Greenberg credits Will Grohmann with first connecting Klee with poetry: "As Grohmann, Klee's commentator, has pointed out, objects served him more or less as words. . . . He used the visible figuration of an object as one uses the sound of a word, and was controlled and impelled by appearances as one is in making poetry by the sounds of words." Clement Greenberg, "Art Chronicle: On Paul Klee (1879–1940)," *Partisan Review* 8, no. 3 (May/June 1941): 228. Sweeney most likely "read" Klee by reaching back to his own background—possibly to sources such as Ernest Fenollosa's posthumously published *Epochs of Chinese & Japanese Art,* 2 vols., ed. Mary Fenollosa (London: W. Heinemann, 1912; revised and reprinted, New York: Frederick A. Stotes, 1921), and to Ezra Pound, who collaborated with Mary Fenollosa on *Epochs* and was widely known among the generation of formalist poets and writers who came of age at the time of World War I. Sweeney would read Klee the way that Pound and Fenollosa read the ancient Chinese characters, which they considered to be the earliest form of visual metaphor: in the fluid action of the mind, eye, and hand, they discerned the essential rapport among things. On two occasions Sweeney quoted Fenollosa's timeworn adage that "relations [sic] are more real and more important than the things they relate." See James Johnson Sweeney, "Introduction," in Nierendorf, 13; and James Johnson Sweeney, essay in *Paul Klee: Paintings, Drawings, Prints,* exh. cat. (Philadelphia: The Philadelphia Art Alliance, 1944), 3. American writers shared a similar desire to articulate sensations moving between the conscious and the unconscious realms. Sweeney himself was a collector of works by Klee, as was Ernest Hemingway, who owned *Monument in Arbeit [Monument under Construction]* (1929.88, pl. 55). For the American writer-collector's perspective, see Nancy Wilson Ross, "Essay 4," in Armitage, et al., 97–113. It should be noted that even Greenberg was not averse to comparing Klee to American poets: "Let him be put next to Marianne Moore and Wallace Stevens, and we in America shall have a more correct idea of the place of his art and a truer estimation of its intense but circumscribed power." Clement Greenberg, "Essay 2," 29.

16. Paul Klee, diary entry, quoted in Lanchner, 85.

17. Sweeney, "Paul Klee," 7.

18. Hans Hofmann, quoted in "Artists' Session at Studio 35," in Clifford Ross, ed., *Abstract Expressionism: Creators and Critics: An Anthology* (New York: Abrams, 1950), 222.

19. Ben Wolf, "The Digest Interviews: Hans Hofmann," *Art Digest* 19, no. 13 (April 1, 1945): 52.

20. The story was first told in Jacques Dupin, *Miró,* trans. Norbert Guterman (New York: Abrams, 1962); it is cited in Lanchner, 88.

21. The following spring a Klee show at Nierendorf Gallery also coincided with a Miró show at Pierre Matisse Gallery.

22. James Johnson Sweeney, *Joan Miró,* exh. cat. (New York: The Museum of Modern Art, 1941), 13.

23. James Johnson Sweeney, "Introduction" in Nierendorf, 13.

24. Joan Miró, quoted in Brassaï, *The Artists of My Life,* trans. Richard Miller (New York: Viking, 1982), 143; also quoted in Lanchner, 88 and 109.

25. "My heart which was wont to beat for this world has been mortally wounded. . . . One leaves the realm of here and now and builds forward into the beyond which is still allowed to be an absolute 'Yes'. . . . To work my way up from my ruins I had to fly. And

I did fly. I live in the world of destruction merely in memory, in the way we sometimes recall the pasts …thus am I abstract with memories" (1915). Paul Klee, diary entries 950–952, quoted in Carola Giedion-Welcker, *Paul Klee*, trans. Alexander Gode (New York: Viking, 1952), 33.. Around 1939–40 Mark Rothko experienced a similar moment of reckoning as he abandoned his earlier Social Realist concerns and turned increasingly toward myth and abstraction. See Ashton, 40–41.

26. Paul Klee, "Excerpts from Notes," in Herbert Bayer, Walter Gropius, and Ise Gropius, eds., *Bauhaus: 1919–1928*, exh. cat. (New York: Museum of Modern Art, 1938), 172.

27. James Johnson Sweeney, *Alexander Calder*, exh. cat. (New York: Museum of Modern Art, 1943), 25–26. Calder had known Klee's work since the 1920s, though it is difficult to pinpoint the exact moment of initial contact. An engineer by training, he was still only a student at the Art Students League at the time of Galka Scheyer's lectures and Katherine S. Dreier's Klee show in 1924 in New York. In 1926, the year of Dreier's "International Exhibition of Modern Art," Calder was shuttling back and forth between Paris and New York. In April 1928 dealer and bookseller Erhard Weyhe, an early collector of Klee's work, gave Calder his first one-person show, including his wire sculptures, in New York. In November 1928 Jules Pascin, a former illustrator for *Jugend* and *Simplicissimus* who was known to Klee, wrote the introduction for Calder's first one-person show of wire sculptures in Paris.

28. Joan Marter, *Calder* (New York: Cambridge University Press, 1997), 85.

29. "Alexander Calder," in Katherine Kuh, *The Artist's Voice: Talks with Seventeen Artists* (New York: Harper & Row, 1962), 39. Klee's *Die Zwitscher-Maschine* was illustrated as "La Machine à gazouiller" in *Cahiers d'Art* 2, no. 7 (1928): 298. By the time of Calder's visit to Berlin in 1929, *Die Zwitscher-Maschine* had entered the collection of the Nationalgalerie Berlin.

30. Alexander Calder, artist's statement, in *Modern Painting and Sculpture,* exh. cat. (Pittsfield, Mass.: Berkshire Museum, 1933), n.p. Klee wrote in his diary, "I should like to create an order out of feeling and going still further, out of motion." Paul Klee, diary entry, quoted in Lanchner, 85.

31. Rosamund Frost, "Klee: Pigeons Come Home to Roost," *Art News* 41, no. 8 (June/July 1942): 24.

32. "Foreword," in *Paintings by Paul Klee and Mobiles and Stabiles by Alexander Calder,* exh. cat. (Cincinnati: Cincinnati Art Museum and Cincinnati Modern Art Society, 1942), n.p.

33. "Foreword," in *Paintings by Paul Klee and Mobiles and Stabiles by Alexander Calder*.

34. Klee's *Pedagogical Sketchbook* was organized into four chapters: "Line, Structure, Movement," "Dimensions," "Earth, Water, Air," and "Symbols of Movement." The book describes elements of composition and style in terms of mathematics, physics, and biology. For a contemporary review, see H. W. Janson, "Letters on the Education of Artists in Colleges," *College Art Journal* 4, no. 4 (May 1945): 232–35.

35. My reading of Klee's *Pedagogical Sketchbook* is indebted to Roger Lipsey. See Roger Lipsey, *An Art of Our Own: The Spiritual in Twentieth-Century Art* (Boston: Shambhala, 1988), 188.

36. See Peggy Guggenheim, ed., *Art of This Century: Objects, Drawings, Photographs, Paintings, Sculpture, Collages, 1910 to 1942* (New York: Arno Press, 1942).

37. Edgar Kaufmann Jr., "The Violent Art of Hanging Pictures," *Magazine of Art* 39, no. 3 (March 1946): 109.

38. Emily Genauer, "Surrealist Paintings Hung Surrealistically," *New York World Telegram,* October 24, 1942, 7.

39. Frederick Kiesler, quoted in Genauer, 7.

40. Lanchner, 104. For a thorough documentation of Kiesler's installation of Klee see: Don Quaintance, "Modern Art in a Modern Setting: Frederick Kiesler's Design of Art of This Century," *Peggy Guggenheim & Frederick Kiesler: The Story of Art of This Century,* Susan Davidson and Philip Rylands, eds. (Vienna: Austrian Frederick and Lillian Kiesler Private Foundation, 2004), 207–273. I am very grateful to Don Quaintance for his reading of this essay.

41. Robert Motherwell, quoted in Ashton, 97.

42. Jacob Kainen, "An Interview with Stanley William Hayter," *Arts Magazine* 60, no. 5 (January 1986): 66.

43. Compare Klee's *Abstractes Terzett* to Rothko's Untitled (1944), which is reproduced in Lanchner, 99.

44. Stanley W. Hayter, "Apostle of Empathy," *Magazine of Art* 39, no. 4 (April 1946): 127, 129, and 130.

45. Clement Greenberg, "The Present Prospects of American Painting and Sculpture," *Horizon* 16, nos. 93–94 (October 1947): 25.

46. Howard Singerman, *Art Subjects: Making Artists in the American University* (Berkeley: University of California Press, 1999), 131.

47. Singerman, 140.

48. Robert Motherwell, "A Personal Expression, 19 March 1949," in *The Collected Writings of Robert Motherwell,* ed. Stephanie Terenzio (New York: Oxford University Press, 1992), 62.

49. Robert Motherwell, quoted in Singerman, 141–42.

50. Paul Klee, *On Modern Art,* intro. Herbert Read, trans. Paul Findlay (London: Faber and Faber, 1948; reprint, Trowbridge, Wiltshire: Redwood Burn, 1989), 40–41. My reading of Klee's Jena Lecture is indebted to Roger Lipsey. See Lipsey, 179.

51. Klee, *On Modern Art*, 54–55.

52. Mark Rothko, "The Romantics Were Prompted," *Possibilities* 1 (Winter 1947–48): 84.

53. Lipsey, 310.

54. Sam Hunter, review, *New York Times*, March 14, 1948; cited in Ashton, 105.

55. Ashton, 103.

56. David Sylvester, "Auguries of Experience," in "The Ides of Art: Six Opinions on What Is Sublime in Art," *The Tiger's Eye* 1, no. 6 (December 15, 1948): 50.

57. Mark Rothko to Katherine Kuh, archives of the Art Institute of Chicago; quoted in Eliza E. Rathbone, "The Rothko Room at The Phillips Collection," in *Mark Rothko*, exh. cat. (Basel, Switzerland: Fondation Beyeler, 2001), 49.

58. For a complete history of the creation of the Rothko Room at The Phillips Collection, see Rathbone, 47–53.

59. Duncan Phillips, "Mark Rothko," undated manuscript, Phillips Collection Archives, Washington, D.C.

60. Duncan Phillips, "Paul Klee," undated manuscript, Phillips Collection Archives, Washington, D.C.

Paul Klee, Anni and Josef Albers, and Robert Rauschenberg:
Weaving and the Grid at Black Mountain College

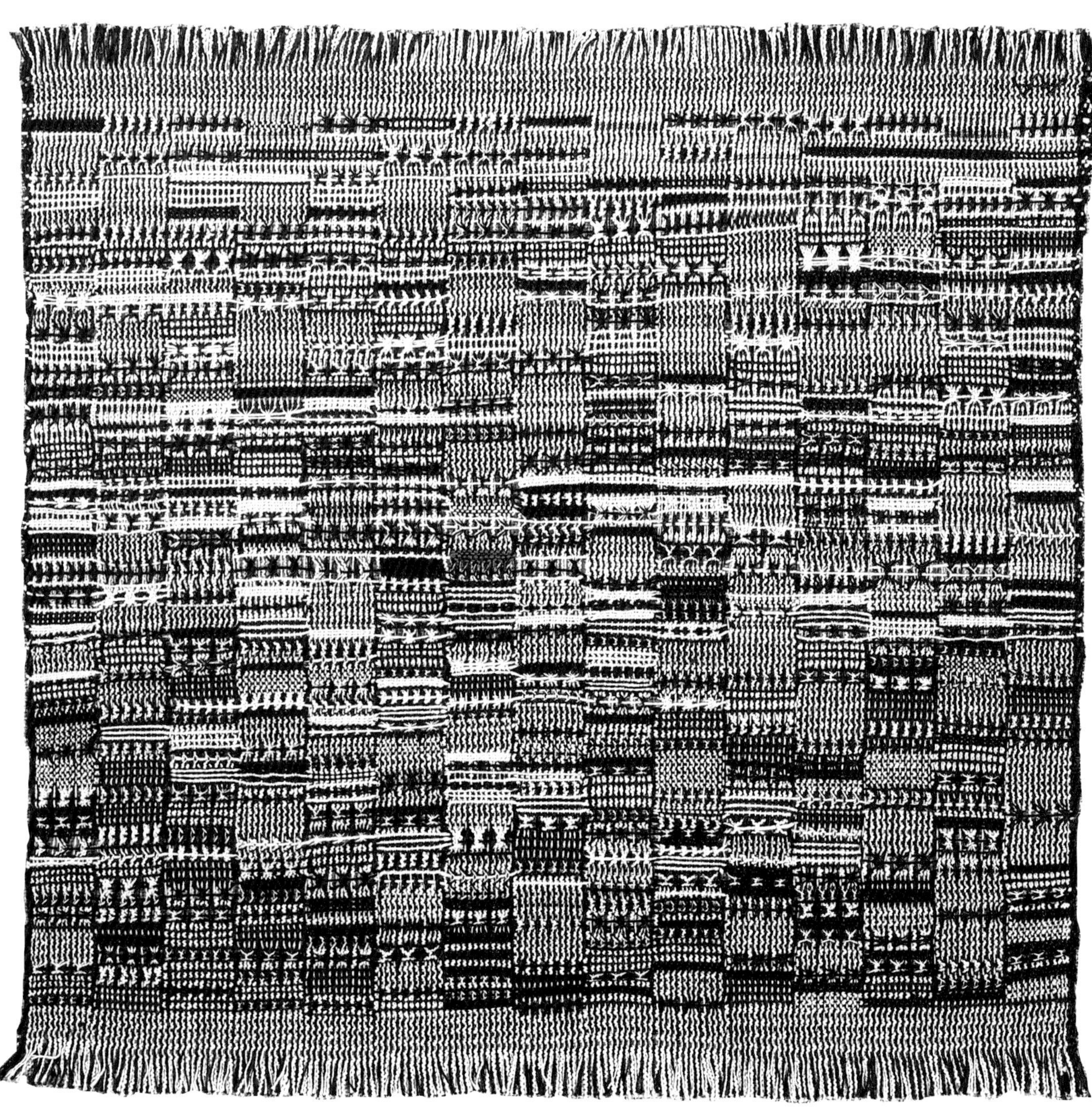

JENNY ANGER

We construct and construct.

In 1928 the magazine Bauhaus—*under new direction—*
    appeared with its largest issue yet (Volume 2, Issues 2–3).
In it, we, the remaining faculty members, wrote on the aims
    of our teaching.
Paul Klee wrote "Exact Experiments in the Realm of Art."
His article began with the statement:
"We construct and construct, and intuition is still a good thing."
We younger teachers—then—read this as addressed to us.
For a long time I have tried to find an answer to this statement.
Finally, after many years, on the other side of the Atlantic,
    a parallel formulation came to me:
"We construct and construct, because intuition is still
    a good thing."
I feel certain that if Klee were to read this, he would smile
    his calm and measured smile.

                                        —Josef Albers[1]

This epigraph represents a rare moment when Josef Albers openly claimed to have internalized and promulgated the teachings of Paul Klee. Much has been written about Bauhaus influences in the United States, with the architecture of Martin Gropius, Marcel Breuer, and Mies van der Rohe garnering the most attention, followed by the teaching and painting of Josef Albers, and then by the weaving of Anni Albers.[2] The case of Klee, who never came to the U.S., is more subtle, but perhaps as significant as any of these. Although the weavers at Black Mountain College, where the Alberses came to teach in 1933, produced some of the most "Klee-like" work there, just as they had at the Bauhaus,[3] the teaching principles of Klee—especially his commitment to construction *with* intuition—inflected all of the art instruction at Black Mountain, at least for the sixteen years (1933–49) in which the Alberses were art professors there.[4] We might call the emblem of that teaching the grid: *not* the grid that Rosalind Krauss famously characterized as a closed, static, modernist system, but rather the grid as an open weave that welcomes endless variation and that can expand infinitely.[5] It is this model for art that inspired Black Mountain students such as Robert Rauschenberg, who arguably initiated postmodernism in this country.

Tracing Klee's legacy requires, shall we say, intuition, because it has remained veiled for several reasons.[6] Anni was effusive in her admiration for Klee—he was "my god," she once wrote[7] –but as her students' notes reveal, she taught complicated weaving patterns and techniques, including multiweave, discontinuous warp

Fig. 63
Anni Albers, *Open Letter*, 1958. Weaving, 23 x 23½ inches
(58.4 x 59.7 cm). Collection of The Josef and Anni Albers
Foundation, Bethany, Connecticut.

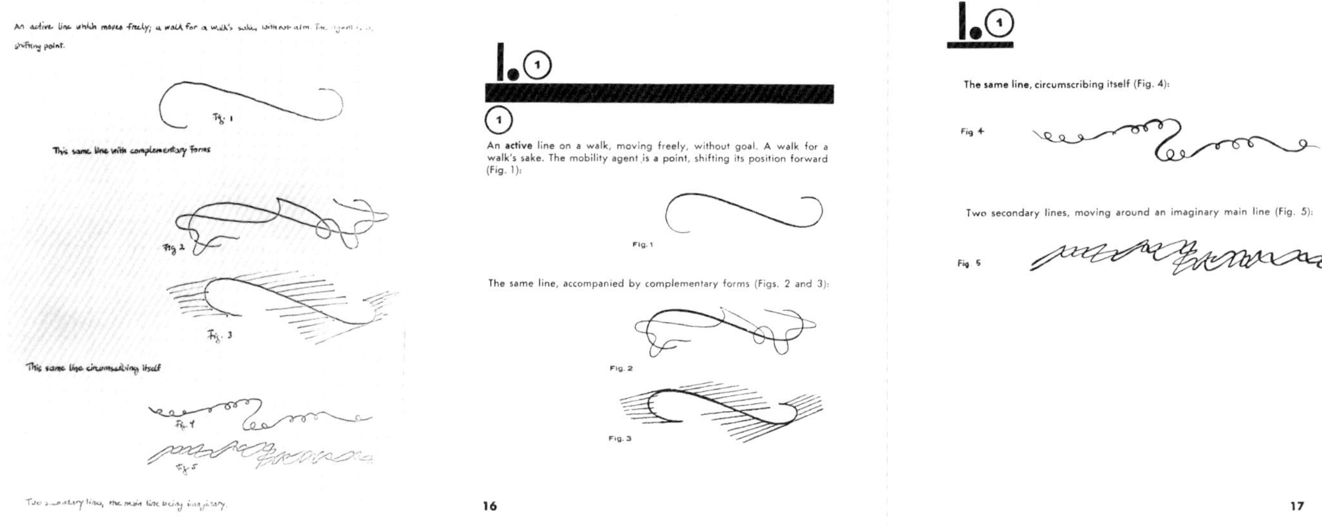

and weft, and floating weft, that were almost certainly beyond Klee's ken.[8] She once took the time and effort to translate Klee's famous lecture "On Modern Art" (1924), showing her devotion to his thought even though the intended purpose of the typescript remains obscure.[9] The awkward phrasing in English dates the translation to Anni's early years at Black Mountain, but her students' notes make no mention of it. Paul Findlay's translation appeared in 1948,[10] but as late as 1960 Anni expressed hope that hers might also circulate, writing that publication "would be an enormous pleasure for me and would give me a feeling of having said at last in some way THANK YOU to Klee."[11] Such hope remained unfulfilled.

If Anni's tributes to Klee were not always successfully transmitted, Josef often kept his deliberately under wraps. He developed approaches and a vocabulary in his design courses that are recognizably his, including his use of the term *matière* to describe an intensive study of materials and their combination.[12] He was especially proud of the teaching program that he developed, first at the Bauhaus (1920–33), then at Black Mountain (1933–49), and finally at Yale University (1950–58). He boasted years later that in 1928 Alfred H. Barr Jr., then director of The Museum of Modern Art, was so impressed by the design course materials Josef had shown him at the Bauhaus that he wanted to write his very "first book" on Josef's teaching, though the book never materialized.[13]

Josef's emphasis on his original teaching is complicated by evidence that suggests that he sought to emulate, perhaps even to outdo, Klee. In a sense, even Josef's statement, "we construct and construct, because intuition is still a good thing," is more emphatic than Klee's, given the causality of "because" that links construction and intuition all the more tightly together. Josef's library provides material evidence of a competitive spirit.[14] For example, in his copy of *Paul Klee: Leben und Werk in Dokumenten [Paul Klee: Life and Work in Documents]* (1960), Josef wrote across one of the opening pages: "According to Will Grohmann, in 40 years Paul Klee produced 9 thousand works."[15] After underlining the last figure, Josef—a prolific artist himself—signed his own initials, effectively declaring himself worthy of mention in this context. In the pages of his copy of Klee's diaries in the original German, Josef kept a clipping of Clement Greenberg's review of the book's English translation in which he underlined three things: (1) Greenberg's name, (2) "The diaries close with Klee's discharge from the army on Dec. 16, 1918," and (3) the last part of the last sentence, which reads in full: "I do not know what the effects of Klee's teaching were—perhaps they have not been important in any *direct* way—but on the evidence of these diaries he had the makings of a great art teacher."[16] By noting that Klee

Fig. 64
Page of anonymous student notes, c. 1945–48.
Black Mountain College Research Project.

Fig. 65
Paul Klee, "I.1, Active Line," in *Pedagogical Sketchbook*,
trans. Sybil Moholy-Nagy (New York: Praeger, 1953), 16–17.

had had the "makings of a great art teacher" by 1918, when Klee was thirty-nine, Josef may have been comparing his own record (he was thirty-five when he started teaching at the Bauhaus and forty-five when he began at Black Mountain). Perhaps he also wondered whether Klee's—or his own—teaching had had direct effects despite Greenberg's doubts. Josef's only handwriting within the book itself is underneath a photograph of Klee labeled "Dessau 1933." Josef crossed out "1933" and added, "photo by J.A. (retouched) / but 1928 Dessau / he left 1929 for Düsseldorf."[17] At the very least, all of these signs suggest that Josef was interested in his own legacy—as artist and teacher—as much as he was in that of Klee.

The reader and viewer sensitive to Klee, however, can find signs of the artist in both Josef's and Anni's teaching. Occasionally, as in the statement about intuition, their words and drawings —and those of their students—echo Klee's almost exactly. An excellent example is a page of notes from Josef's class at Black Mountain (fig. 64).[18] The unidentified student copied Klee's drawings exemplifying "active line" from the 1925 *Pädagogisches Skizzenbuch [Pedagogical Sketchbook]* (see pages from 1953 English edition, fig. 65), adding notes that are a loose translation of recognizably playful Klee-ian prose, including: "An active line which moves freely; a walk for a walk's sake, without aim." Whether or not Josef assigned Klee's book or provided the translation, the lineage is unmistakable.[19] Another example points more broadly to a shared philosophy. Klee opened his oft-quoted "Creative Credo" (1920) with the statement: "Art does not reproduce the visible, but renders visible."[20] In 1965 Josef said in a published lecture: "Art makes the invisible—visible."[21] Here he quoted Klee almost word for word, but then masked the reference by attributing the insight *not* to Klee, but to Geoffrey Chaucer—an unlikely source. Later in the same lecture, however, Josef inadvertently suggested another reason for his repression of Klee as the source: "Why did the masters become masters? And why are the great ones great? Because they tried to say something other than *their* masters had, not only different and new, but alive and ahead. Therefore they chose to follow themselves and search, not re-search; to move forward rather than backward."[22]

Thus Josef in particular faced a logical dilemma: how does one repeat the teacher's lesson not to repeat? Josef frequently tried to skirt the problem by claiming the philosophy as his own—or attributing it far afield—but Klee often hovers over such efforts. For example, in an interview in the 1970s, Josef reiterated the need to create anew immediately after declaring his own independence from Klee: "I do not come from Klee and Kandinsky because—you think [that I do] because I come from the Bauhaus[—]…in the end I come from Adam.… What we are suffering from so much today is not very helpful at all because it is reproductive. Retrospection means reproduction. But tradition in art is not to revive but to produce. To create: [that] is tradition in art."[23] Josef likened the problem of copying that he had observed at Yale to diseases: "One was called Picassobia, another Matisseitis, and, in addition, I discovered Kleeptomania."[24] Clearly, in warning students of the dangers of copying, especially of copying an artist like Klee, and in encouraging students to follow their own intuition, one would not wish to emphasize that one had learned this principle from someone else—namely, Klee.

Perhaps because weaving might seem unrelated to painting, Anni did not go to such lengths to repress her indebtedness to Klee. In 1965 she recounted in an interview that "I think I owe most of my insight into problems of form to Klee."[25] Anni could have learned about form from Klee either in his regular course or in one specifically for the weavers—Klee most likely taught the same principles of formal composition in both. The surviving student notes from these classes, including Anni's, record precise and logical elements of design, including methods of multiplying a pattern (simple repetition, mirroring, turning) and examples of overlapping patterns.[26] Klee called the latter "polyphony," exemplified in *Polyphone Architektur [Polyphonic Architecture]* (1930.130, pl. 70), in which he has combined fine overlapping tones with a delicate interlacing of line to signify architecture. Klee addressed the creative spark that led him to combine these forms by showing students his own paintings; he discussed them in class and occasionally hung some on the walls of the school. Anni is said to have "admired them tremendously."[27] In 1924, in fact, she bought one that must have had particular significance for her, *Zwei Kräfte [Two Forces]* (1922.23, fig. 66).[28] Albers historian Virginia Gardner Troy has noted that the two (almost) perpendicular arrows are "like the warp and weft of a weaving."[29] The entire composition is bound by the dark horizontals at top and

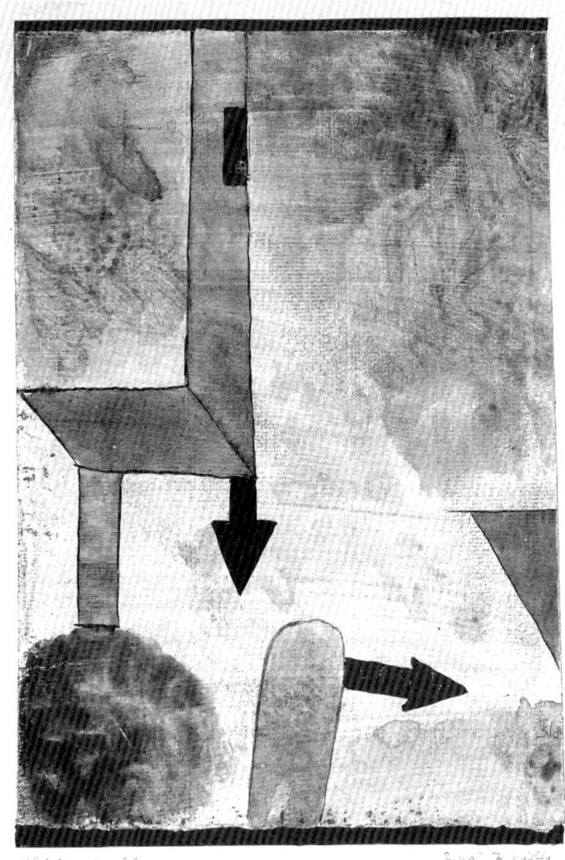

bottom, but equilibrium appears fragile or momentary at best: the slight lean of the lower central shape pushes the "horizontal" arrow down to the right, while the imminent fall of the vertical arrow would upset the lower central shape further. With the mysterious round blob on the bottom left and the fluid presence of the washes throughout the work, Klee has taken design essentials and jiggled them, rendering the work vibrant and slightly odd. Anni learned form in Klee's classes, but it was probably in seeing his works that she recognized "the proper creative means" that unite with "dream, idea or phantasy…to form a work of art," as Klee had put it in his lecture "On Modern Art."[30]

Anni articulated this principle in relation to her own medium in the following way: "The interlacing of the vertical and the horizontal threads is in thousands of variations possible, a constructive task that gives free play to phantasy and intellect."[31] In her weaving *Open Letter* (1958, fig. 63), we can recognize the regular horizontal and vertical threads, but following any one of them leads to surprising turns—a knot, a twist, a disappearance—followed by a sudden resurfacing in the next gridlike unit. There is a structure of perpendiculars, in other words, but Anni has not let it bind her imagination. On the contrary, the irregular regularity of the work recalls paintings by Klee, such as *Vorhang [Curtain]* (1924.129b, pl. 26) and *Junge Pflanzung [Young Plantation]* (1929.98, pl. 59), whose interlaced threadlike line evokes a wide range of subjects (curtains and gardens here, but also script, architecture, and music in other works). Anni's title, *Open Letter*, also invokes the weave as writing. Troy has written at length on Anni's use of "thread as text," arguing that Klee's pictographs, letters, and signs of all sorts are an important source for her (the other being Andean textiles).[32] Troy wrote that with *Open Letter* Anni created "a composition of individual pattern units that, when taken or 'read' as a whole, implies content and meaning through the arrangement of codified visual information, analogous to the way one reads a paragraph composed of letters, words, and sentences."[33] The allusions to writing, it seems, provided Anni with a way to free her line from the reign of the horizontal and vertical, allowing her to join form and fantasy. While many of Anni's weavings are strictly rectilinear, she always emphasized "a playful beginning, unresponsive to any demand of usefulness, an enjoyment of colors, forms, surface contrasts and harmonies—a tactile sensuousness."[34]

Fig. 66
Paul Klee, *Zwei Kräfte [Two Forces]*, 1922.23. Watercolor on chalk ground on paper mounted on cardboard, 9½ x 6¾ inches (24 x 17 cm). Nationalgalerie, Museum Berggruen, Staatliche Museen zu Berlin.

Indeed, Nicholas Fox Weber related that Anni always remembered that Klee had "suggested that one could 'take a line for a walk,'" just as we saw in the student's notes from Josef's class. In Weber's estimation, the grid did not bind Anni, who instead "decided to let thread do all it could do."[35]

Did Klee similarly influence Josef's work? Some have thought that Josef's paintings show lamentably little fantasy. Greenberg wrote in 1949, "One has to regret that Albers has so rarely allowed the warmth and true plastic feeling we see in his color to dissolve the ruled rectangles in which all these potential virtues are imprisoned."[36] And thirty years later, Josef's painting figured prominently in Krauss's well-known critique of the grid, which she called "emblematic of the modernist ambition…." She continued: "[T]he grid announces, among other things, modern art's will to silence, its hostility to literature, to narrative, to discourse." Further, the grid has "sustained itself so relentlessly while at the same time being so impervious to change…. [T]he grid is the means of crowding out the dimensions of the real and replacing them with the lateral spread of a single surface."[37] Krauss conceded that the grid is "simultaneously transparent and opaque," but rather than recognizing that multiplicity as potential openness, she wrote that "an artist would certainly not want to confuse the issue by seeming to imply both."[38] According to Krauss, such confusion is actually sickness: "we also know that this schizophrenia allows for many artists—from Mondrian, to Albers, to Kelly, to Lewitt—to think about the grid in both ways at once." In her estimation, this "schizophrenia" is not productive: she concluded by asserting that the late work of Piet Mondrian and Josef Albers shows a "lack of development" attributable to the stymieing effect of the grid.[39]

Thus Greenberg read the grid as Josef's prison, and Krauss read the grid as modernism's great sickness—worse, one presumes, than Kleeptomania—exemplified by Josef's painting. Yet, as we will see, Josef's earlier work, his photo-collages, and even the later paintings all point to a Klee-ian play with the grid that requires a much freer understanding of the grid than Krauss provides. A text that does not mention Josef is enormously helpful here. In *A Thousand Plateaus*, Gilles Deleuze and Félix Guattari compared the open sea with the "map, which intertwines meridians and parallels, longitudes and latitudes, plotting regions known and unknown onto a grid."[40] They thus formulated an opposition between what they called "smooth" space (e.g., the sea) and "striated" space (e.g., the grid of the map): "…the striated is that which intertwines fixed and variable elements, produces an order and succession of distinct forms, and organizes horizontal melodic lines and vertical harmonic planes. The smooth is the continuous variation, continuous development of form; it is the fusion of harmony and melody in favor of the production of properly rhythmic values, the pure act of the drawing of a diagonal across the vertical and the horizontal."[41]

Whereas Deleuze and Guattari addressed both the grid and what they perceived to be its opposite—free, open, continuously varied space—Krauss found opposition within the grid itself: at first it appears to shut out all time and space, but later it is seen as transparent and opaque, open and closed at the same time. Krauss disparaged this multiplicity as stultifyingly "schizophrenic," but a reading of Deleuze and Guattari's description of textiles makes one wonder if multiplicity might not point instead to the infinite possibility of the grid. Fabric, for Deleuze and Guattari, seems at first to fall on the side of striation: "It is constituted by two kinds of parallel elements; in the simplest case, there are vertical and horizontal elements, and the two intertwine, intersect perpendicularly."[42] Warp and weft, they maintained, order everything, and the writers contrasted that striation with felt, which "is in principle infinite, open, and unlimited in every direction; it has neither top nor bottom nor center…."[43] However (and this is crucial), "There are many interlacings, mixes between felt and fabric. Can we not displace the opposition…?" They then proceeded to do so, especially in their evocation of patchwork, which "may display equivalents to themes, symmetries, and resonance," but is nevertheless "[a]n amorphous collection of juxtaposed pieces that can be joined together in an infinite number of ways."[44] Deleuze and Guattari concluded that "we must remind ourselves that the two spaces [striated and smooth] in fact exist only in mixture: smooth space is constantly being translated, transversed into a striated space; striated space is constantly being reversed, returned to a smooth space."[45] For Deleuze and Guattari, this is not schizophrenia, but *reality*.[46]

Hence, it is possible to read the grid as limit *and* potential.[47] There is ample evidence that both Anni and Josef Albers did so.

Where Deleuze and Guattari characterized the "smooth" as the "pure act of the drawing of a diagonal across the vertical and the horizontal," Anni expanded the possibilities beyond the diagonal, saying, "The interlacing of the vertical and the horizontal threads is in thousands of variations possible, a constructive task that gives free play to phantasy and intellect."[48] She understood the restrictions of warp and weft, but she played between the lines (and welcomed writing, contra Krauss) to create intuitive constructions of great beauty.

Similar insights are possible by looking at Josef's *Gitterbild [Grid Mounted]* (1921, fig. 67), which art historian Michael Baumgartner rightfully compares with Klee's own grid pictures from the period.[49] Close examination of *Gitterbild* reveals that it has been pieced together in such a whimsical, unregimented fashion that the language of textiles seems absolutely appropriate for discussing it. Reproductions tend to flatten the work, but in fact the large grid structure was woven together, and the thin wires that make tic-tac-toe boards out of each pane of glass run vertically in front of the work and cross horizontally on its backside. Each wire wraps around the major structure whenever it crosses it,

thereby joining the major structural weave and holding the glass pieces in place. The glass patches seem to have been placed together intuitively, in a playful quilt of tone and value, while little cutouts of window screen behind selected pieces of glass reiterate the grid just as their unpredictable placement delights the eye and the inconsistent tightness or openness of their weave reminds the viewer that these are found objects, like the glass, fancifully ordered together.[50] Thus the open weave—not Krauss's grid—describes this work most closely.

The grid and Klee come together more overtly in Josef's photo-collages, including *Paul Klee, Dessau XI '29* (1929, fig. 68). With its productive mix of construction and intuition, photo-collage—while not literally woven—can be understood so figuratively. The large photograph of Klee on the left is beautifully balanced by seven contact strips in vertical columns on the right. The photo and the seven strips, forming two large rectangles, share a baseline rather high on the page, causing them to hover against the ground. The seven strips of the right-hand block form an almost regular grid, although slight irregularities reveal cutting and arrangement by hand. The penetrating image of Klee on the left is an enlargement of the image in the top left square of the grid. However, as Brenda Danilowitz notes in reference to another Klee photo-collage by Josef, we never see all of Klee in Josef's photo-collages, despite the enlargements and repetitions: Klee is always partially obscured, in some cases hidden in shadow or blowing a puff of smoke between himself and the camera.[51] In this series, from left to right, Klee seems cumulatively to turn toward the viewer, only to turn his head back toward the left in the last shot at the top right. In fact, in the twenty-one headshots plus the enlarged image of one, we never see the right side of Klee's face. The photo-collages seem to say that the spirit of the artist cannot be contained. One can piece together and order a lot of information, but threads always weave in and out of view.

Even Josef's later (more "imprisoned" or "stymied") work, which includes his long-running series titled Homage to the Square, shows signs of the open weave. While he did repeat inset squares with the same proportional relationships over and over in these paintings, his intuitive color combinations are frequently surprising and often very moving.[52] After all, as Josef once said, "color is a magic force."[53] We can experience this in the exhibition

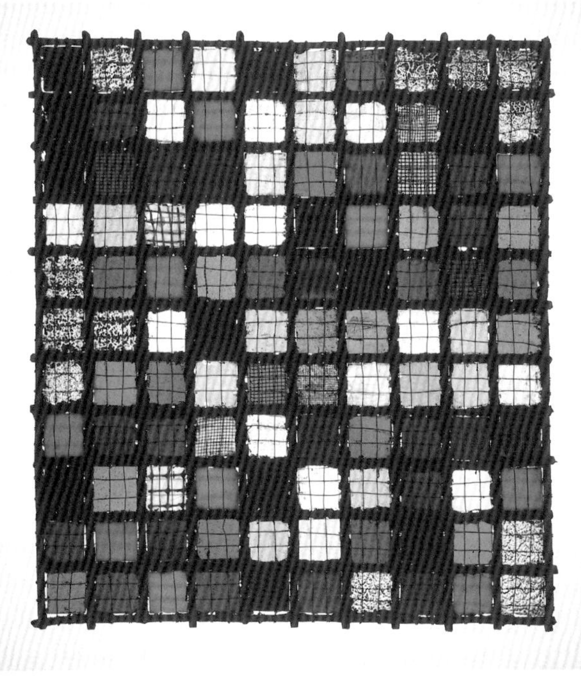

Josef Albers, *Gitterbild [Grid Mounted]*, 1921. Glass, metal, and wire, 12 ¾ x 11 ⅜ inches (32.4 x 28.9 cm). Collection of The Josef and Anni Albers Foundation, Bethany, Connecticut.

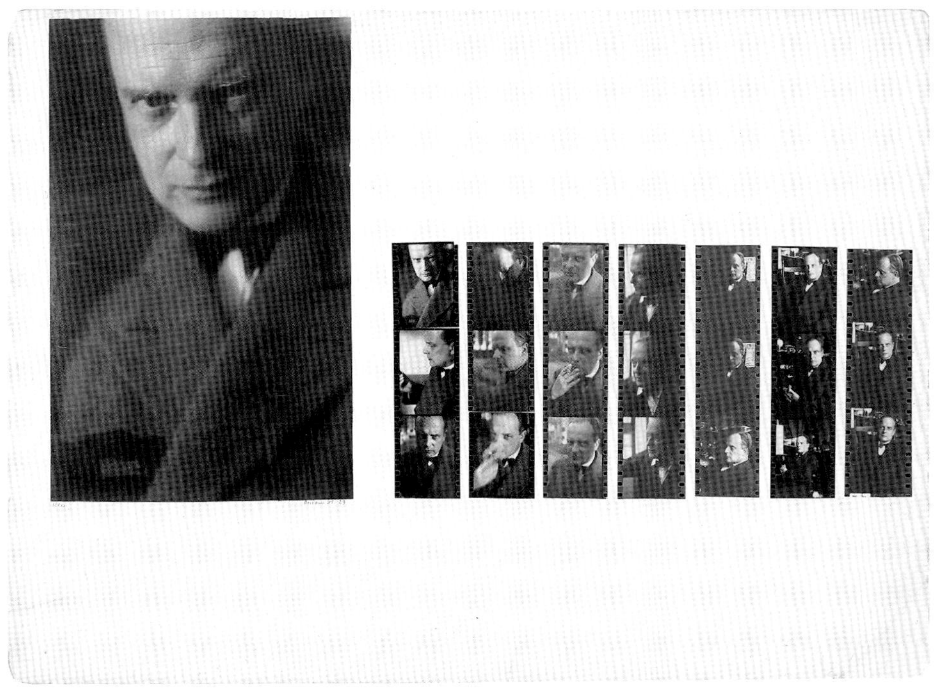

catalogue *Josef und Anni Albers: Europa und Amerika*, which shows Klee's *Individualisierte Höhenmessung der Lagen [Individualized Altimetry of Layers]* (1930.82) facing Josef's *Study for Homage to the Square "Inductive"* (1957).[54] The color harmonies of each are intoxicating on their own, but here the central bright orange squares also sing to each other across fields of purple and green.

We can follow this open weave, the legacy of their studies with Klee, through Josef and Anni to their students at Black Mountain and the Klee-inflected work they in turn produced. Indeed, if we conceive of the grid as limit and potential, then the humor and patchwork composition of various student paintings and the weaving students' lively abandonment of the grid, as well as a notable experiment in "weaving" together a geodesic dome, all foreshadow the art of Robert Rauschenberg, who perhaps carried Klee's ideas of construction and intuition the furthest. Among the painters, Sewell (Si) Sillman, according to former Black Mountain student Mary Lou Mitchell, "painted meticulous Paul Klees by the dozen."[55] Her choice of adjective points to a certain austerity in Sillman's painting, but his work is not without its own admittedly dry humor. *Untitled Painting* (c. 1948), for example, *is* geometric, but a circle seems to bounce gleefully

across the page.[56] The spareness and grace of the work is comparable to that found in Klees such as *Sonnenuntergang [Sunset]* (1930.209, pl. 72), and the minute size of Sillman's painting (7 x 14½ in.) also harks back to Klee. Another painter, Joseph Fiore, wrote that Klee "has been an inspiration to me for 60 years."[57] In his *Untitled Landscape* (c. 1947, fig. 69), a mountain landscape dotted with simplified Klee-ian trees emerges from a patchwork grid. It references paintings by Klee such as *Ilfenburg* (1935.109, pl. 85), as well as echoing the diminutive scale of so many Klees. Describing another Fiore work from this period, James Thompson wrote: "Klee again is the obvious influence in *Early Pictograph* [1948], a patchwork composition of bright colors and strong shapes, the most obviously identifiable of which are fish and vessels…. As with many fine quilts, the dialogue in this work between light and dark color and between horizontal and vertical shapes is an important feature of the work."[58] Ranging from tighter to looser, both Sillman's and Fiore's paintings reveal Klee's grid as their model.

The open weave metaphor resonates directly in the Black Mountain student work in textiles as a result of the joint tutelage of Anni and Trude Guermonprez, who replaced Anni in 1946–47

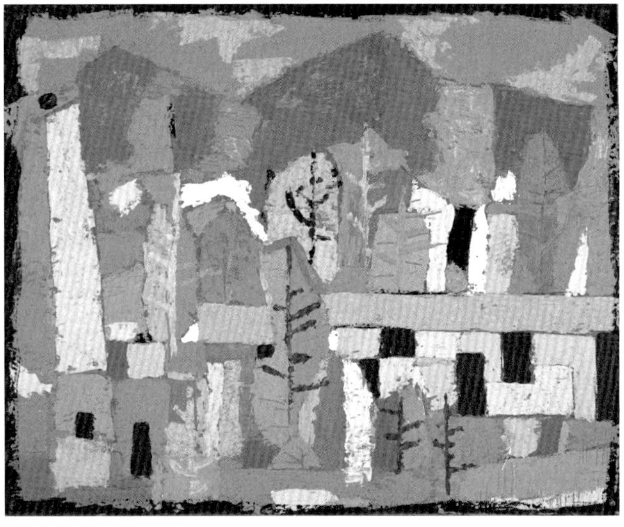

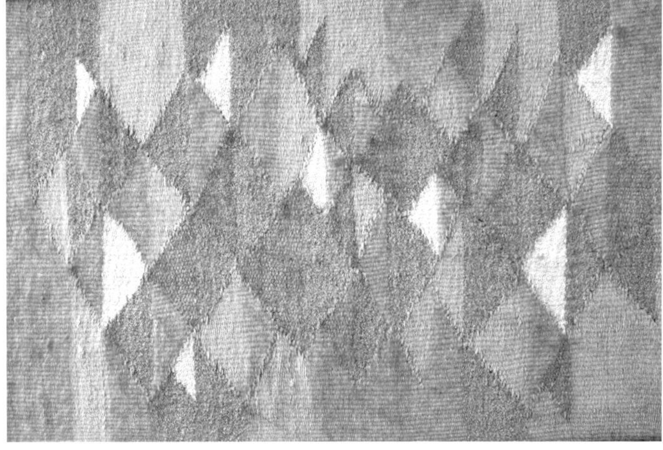

when she went on sabbatical and who continued to teach with her after her return. Guermonprez had not studied at the Bauhaus, but Benita Koch-Otte, her teacher at Burg Giebichenstein in Halle, Germany, *had* studied with Klee at the Bauhaus—one watercolor of hers, with its Tunisian-like domes set within the shadow of a grid, is remarkably Klee-like—and she purposefully brought Klee's lessons (on color, in particular) to the school in Halle.[59] Anni and Guermonprez extended this legacy to students like Eini Sihvonen, whose imaged triangles in the undated *Constellation Pleiades* (fig. 70) abandon the grid for the diagonal through lovely mid-tones that produce a polyphonic overlap. These triangular "stars" pointing like arrows in space provide movement and verve to the work. (Klee, we might note, had a particular fondness for stars, and he is known to have suggested the heavens in an equally small format.)[60] Lore Kadden Lindenfeld experimented with a wide range of fabrics—as did Klee.[61] And while Don Page made bold wall hangings more reminiscent specifically of Anni's rectilinear works with their horizontal bands, on occasion he added a frolicking deer in an abstracted and simplified landscape, whose playful tone is like some Klees.[62] Thus the evidence suggests that Anni and Guermonprez's students understood the Klee-ian open weave.

As Rauschenberg would famously demonstrate, other Black Mountain students moved from the home base of construction and intuition to altogether new territory. Ruth Asawa is one such case. She came to Black Mountain in the summer of 1946, hoping to take weaving, but "Anni told me that she couldn't teach [weaving] in 8 weeks," so Asawa started (and continued) to study with Josef, for whom she at one point typed out pages of quotations from Klee's "Creative Credo."[63] She wrote later, "I remember Josef Albers talking about 'Klee's line' when teaching us about figure/background."[64] Her drawing from his class, *Exercise in Figure-Background and Disposing Using the Triangle* (1946–48, fig. 71), shows something like Sihvonen's triangles freely meandering off of the grid, and some of her paintings reflect Klee's influence, too. Her mature work consists of hauntingly beautiful hanging wire sculpture that is woven or crocheted, confirming that the principle of the open weave extended beyond the weaving workshop.[65]

Indeed, a large project in the summer of 1948 palpably demonstrates the profound influence of the open weave on the

Fig. 69
Joseph Fiore, *Untitled Landscape*, c. 1947. Oil on board, 8¼ x 11½ inches (21 x 29.2cm). Collection of the artist.

Fig. 70
Eini Sihvonen, *Constellation Pleiades*, n.d. Weaving, 10½ x 16 inches (26.7 x 40.6 cm). Private collection.

creative lives of Black Mountain students and faculty alike. Some months before Rauschenberg's arrival, Buckminster Fuller reputedly mesmerized students with a three-hour lecture at the end of which, according to Elaine de Kooning, "he began making diagrams on a blackboard. He drew a square, connecting two corners with a diagonal line. 'Ah,' he said affectionately, 'here's our old friend, the hypotenuse.'"[66] Fuller then went on to activate the hypotenuse in three dimensions by attempting to build the first geodesic dome at Black Mountain College. The dome did not rise that summer—everyone referred to it as the "Supine Dome"—but the process of connecting Venetian-blind strips in a huge web that had the possibility of supporting itself excited a lot of people.[67] The process was something like life-size weaving. De Kooning wrote in 1952 that "the geodesic dome outstrips any other framework of comparable size. Its properties seem magical: constructed of a discontinuous three-way grid which stresses its members equally and acts almost as a membrane in absorbing and distributing loads…the dome can be built in several layers and then trussed together.…"[68] Guermonprez appears to have intuited the relationship with weaving as well. She photographed the construction of the first dome from near and far, and her many images of students carefully binding the Venetian-blind strips (fig. 72) read like figures weaving a gigantic web.[69] The fact that the "Supine Dome" remained flat adds to this textile impression: it was as if one had joined the threads and entered the loom. This interpretation does not seem at all far-fetched when one reads Fuller's own words describing the weaving of Anni Albers: "From aeronautical altitudes, the criss cross grids of earth's cities seem to be two-dimensional planar arrangements, as do woven fabric surfaces, seen from a distance. Seen from inside the city streets or within the loom, both cities and fabrics disclose multidimensional structuring of great complexity. Anni Albers, more than any other weaver, has succeeded in exciting mass realization of the complex structure of fabrics. She has brought the artist's intuitive sculpturing faculties and the age-long weaver's arts into historically successful marriage."[70] Here Fuller eloquently described that mixed state of smooth and striated space—some of which depends on perspective—that Deleuze and Guattari would articulate more than two decades later.

It was at this moment, in the fall of 1948, that Rauschenberg,

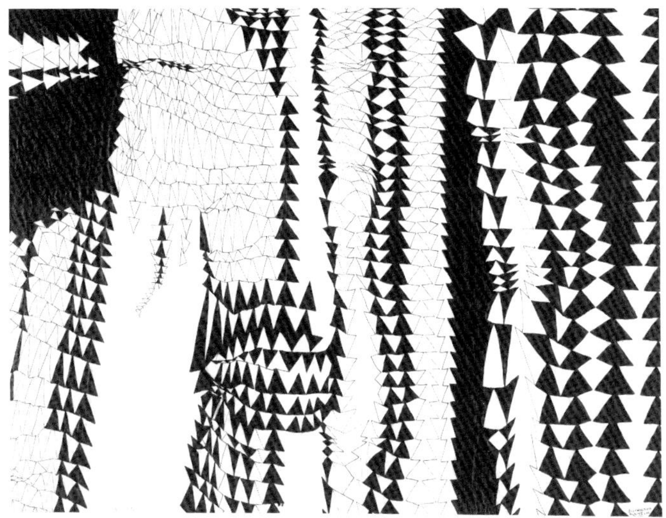

arguably Black Mountain's most famous alum, arrived at the school with his wife-to-be, Susan Weil, reportedly because he had heard about Josef's teaching. While he developed a less than congenial relationship with Josef, Rauschenberg eventually would say, "I consider [Josef] Albers the most important teacher I've ever had."[71] One can argue further that the open weave of the teaching legacy that winds back to Klee also provided the framework for Rauschenberg's art. Does he not to this day combine construction and intuition? Mary Emma Harris has summarized the story of Rauschenberg at Black Mountain:

> Robert Rauschenberg came to Black Mountain because he felt he needed more discipline and had read that [Josef] Albers was "the greatest disciplinarian in the United States." Albers shared his self-evaluation, noting at the end of his first semester that in painting he "could be better with more discipline" and that "with more effort and concentration, [he] could have achieved better results" in drawing. Apparently Rauschenberg found what he was seeking because four months later Albers applauded his progress: "finally discovered that intensive work and discipline are the means of development." In the end, Rauschenberg generously assessed Albers as a teacher: "Albers was a beautiful teacher and an impossible person.… He wasn't easy to talk to, and I found his criticism so excruciating and so devastating that I never asked for it. Years later, though, I'm still learning what he taught me, because what he taught had to do with the entire visual world.… I consider Albers the most important teacher I've ever had, and I'm sure he considered me one of his poorest students."[72]

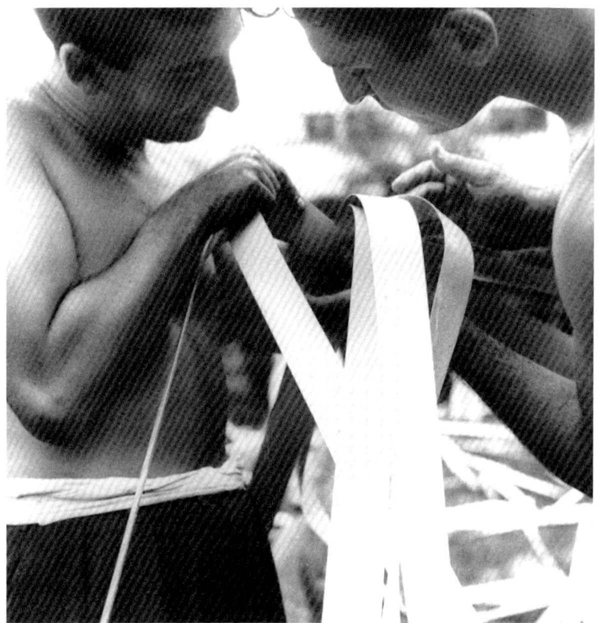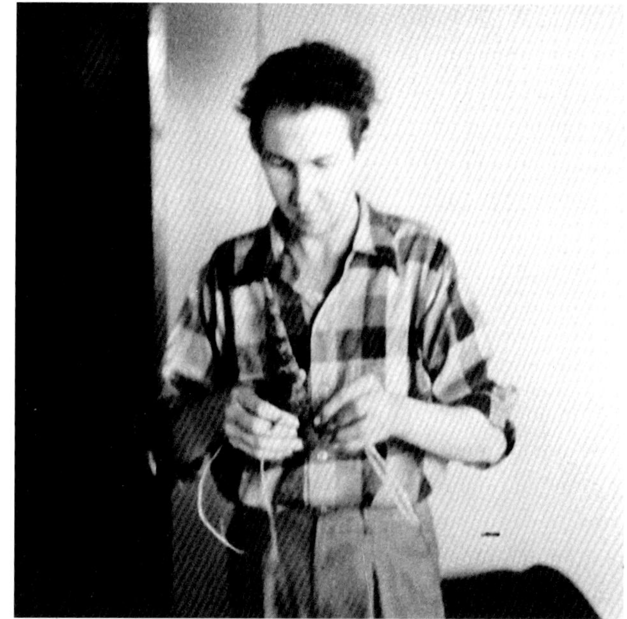

For his part, when Black Mountain historian Martin Duberman asked Josef around 1970 what he thought he might have taught Rauschenberg, the former teacher replied, "He was a little stubborn and doing his own [thing]—but what he is doing now is much more a part of my classes he participated in than he will ever recognize.... [W]e played a lot with combinations of materials, 'combination' was a great word in our [vocabulary]—and changing surface qualities.... And I think that is what lives on in his work now."[73] Rauschenberg's Red Paintings, which he initiated at Black Mountain, and the Combines soon to follow would support Josef's theory that the idea for a combination of materials —what he also called *matière*—came from his classes.

That hardly accounts, however, for the breadth of work that we associate with Rauschenberg. In truth, nothing can encapsulate Rauschenberg's work, but it nonetheless emerged from a certain place and time that we can map—with an open grid. Just as she photographed students weaving Fuller's first dome, Guermonprez also caught Rauschenberg on film engaged in the binding of some threads or strings (fig. 73).[74] Guermonprez maintains that she had Rauschenberg in her class, while Rauschenberg biographer Mary Lynn Kotz reports that he studied weaving with

Anni.[75] A comment by Guermonprez suggests, in fact, that the intuitive side of Rauschenberg was nurtured at Black Mountain in the realm of textiles: "I had given once as a task, as a challenge, to design garments where you would not cut the fabric, only retain it in its rectangular shape. And Bob [Rauschenberg]...came to the class period—you know, they were there to show me what they had thought of—and he made a whole fashion show. He had all white muslin, white monks cloth, and he made all kinds of versions of rectangular pieces. It was wonderful. Most imaginative."[76] So here was Rauschenberg creating fanciful fabric work while respecting the restriction of the square (or the rectangle, to be precise). It seems that he was finding a productive mix of construction and intuition of his own. Guermonprez, when asked about Josef's teaching style, agreed that he was strict, but with a caveat: "I think Albers was a great disciplinarian. You see, in spite of [it, in fact,] ...on the basis of the discipline freedom was possible."[77] Rauschenberg no doubt struggled with Josef's discipline, but his experience with weaving and fabric may have helped him eventually to see the grid as open weave.

Rauschenberg created *Bed* (1955, fig. 74), that landmark of twentieth-century art, some years after the Alberses and Guermonprez had left Black Mountain College. But in it we can see the potential of the grid. *Bed*'s unmistakably real quilt—which Rauschenberg acquired, incidentally, in Black Mountain[78]—not to mention the pillow and crumpled sheets, renders Krauss's understanding of the grid as "crowding out the dimensions of the real" unrecognizable. Much more fitting is Deleuze and Guattari's evocation of the mix of smooth and striated space, symbolized by patchwork. Let Rauschenberg play with that patchwork grid and a magical work of art is created.[79]

Leo Steinberg, in a landmark essay that provides one of the most compelling accounts of a shift from modernism to postmodernism, described the orientation of Rauschenberg's work as pivotal in that shift. Steinberg contended that painting for centuries had had a vertical orientation associated with human vision, but that Rauschenberg rotated the plane to a horizontal spread associated with culture, specifically the accumulation of information. Rauschenberg, according to Steinberg, effected that switch with works that appear to have been arranged horizontally on a "flatbed," but are then hung vertically on the wall.[80] *Bed* is an obvious example of such a work. However, there is nothing marvelous or revolutionary about arranging a quilt, pillow, and sheet horizontally. Textiles, especially carpets, are usually laid out flat, and as Joseph Masheck has argued, the carpet made to look flat while actually lying flat was a major inspiration for modernist abstraction in painting.[81] Thus a switch from verticality to horizontality-hung-vertically occurred long ago, and textiles inspired the change. As Masheck noted, Josef in his precise study *Interaction of Color* reported that the nineteenth-century German who discovered "optical mixture," Wilhelm von Bezold, did so "in practical connection with von Bezold's hobby, rug design."[82] Masheck also quoted Josef saying that his exercises with stripes "will readily remind us of textiles, and we may read and interpret them as fabrics of wool or cotton…."[83] Yet the artist who articulated the phenomenon of horizontality displayed vertically with the greatest clarity is Anni Albers. She wrote, "To let threads be articulate again and find a form for themselves to no other need than their own orchestration, not to be sat on, walked on, only to be looked at, is the *raison d'être* of my pictorial weavings."[84]

Anni wanted to take line for a walk, but then hang it on the wall for all to see. Rauschenberg may have combined all sorts of

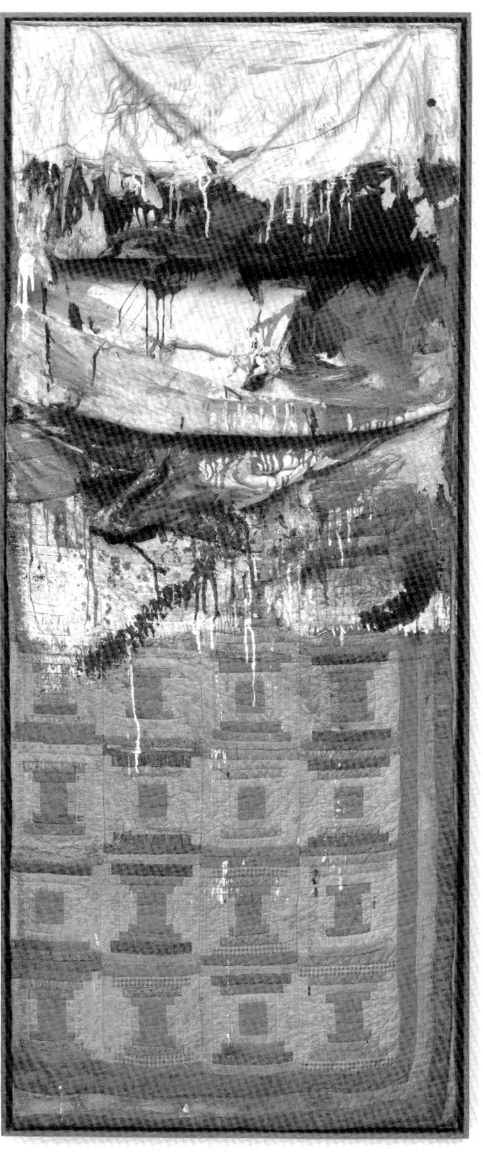

Fig. 74
Robert Rauschenberg, *Bed*, 1955. Combine painting: oil and pencil on pillow, quilt, and sheet, mounted on wood supports, 75 ¾ x 31 ½ x 8 inches (192.4 x 80 x 20.3cm). The Museum of Modern Art, New York, Gift of Leo Castelli in honor of Alfred H. Barr Jr. (79.1989).

materials on a "flatbed" later in his career, but in Guermonprez's photograph of him, we see that he learned to look *down* while intuitively weaving line at Black Mountain College.   That *Bed* came from the man who studied with the Alberses and Guermonprez should therefore be no surprise.   It is an open question whether Klee, who had already been dead for fifteen years by the time *Bed* appeared, would have recognized it as his legacy, let alone as art. But I feel certain that he would have recognized the following teacher-student exchange at Black Mountain College recounted by former student Martha Rittenhouse Treichler:

I took two art classes from Josef Albers, drawing and color.… He was a wonderful teacher, and I loved his classes.   There was never a dull moment, either. He had a friendly argument going with Bob Rauschenberg. Albers thought Bob was just too wild sometimes. One day Bob brought in a color study that had Albers raving with admiration. "Bob," he said, "how did you do it?" Bob said, "I held it as tight as I could, and then I wiggled it a little bit!"[85]

I feel certain that if Klee, the lover of construction with intuition, were to have heard this, he would have smiled his calm and measured smile.   Josef probably did, too.

NOTES

I am grateful to Brenda Danilowitz, Molly Wheeler, and Jessica Csoma of The Josef and Anni Albers Foundation, Bethany, Connecticut (JAAF), for their willing help and engaging discussion during my research for this essay. I thank the staff at Manuscripts and Archives, Yale University Library, New Haven, Connecticut (MAYU) and the North Carolina State Archives, Raleigh, North Carolina (NCSA), especially Ashley Yandle. Warm thanks also to Sarah Eckhardt and Polly Koch, who provided expert assistance at The Menil Collection.

1. Josef Albers, "We construct and construct," undated typescript, Josef Albers Papers (JAP), Box 22, Folder 193, MAYU. The document survives in two versions, a German one (with "Josef Albers" typed at the bottom) and an English one (with Albers's handwritten initials). In an attempt to make the English as clear as possible, I have amalgamated both versions. The voluminous Albers archives (at several sites) contain many typescripts presumably typed by Anni Albers.

2. Margret Kentgens-Craig, *The Bauhaus and America: First Contacts, 1919–1936* (Cambridge, Mass.: MIT Press, 1999) continues the architectural emphasis, in force at least since William H. Jordy, "The Aftermath of the Bauhaus in America: Gropius, Mies, and Breuer," in *Perspectives in American History*, vol. 2 (Cambridge, Mass.: Charles Warren Center for Studies in American History, Harvard University, 1968), 485ff. A major exhibition in Germany, however, broadened this view of the Bauhaus dramatically: see Georg-W. Költzsch and Margarita Tupitsyn, eds., *Bauhaus: Dessau, Chicago, New York*, exh. cat. (Essen: Museum Folkwang, 2000).

3. See Jenny Anger, "Klees Unterricht in der Webereiwerkstatt des Bauhauses," in Magdalena Droste and Manfred Ludewig, eds., *Das Bauhaus webt: Die Textilwerkstatt am Bauhaus*, exh. cat. (Berlin: Bauhaus-Archiv, 1998), 33–41; reprinted in an expanded and revised version as "Carpets of Memory," in Jenny Anger, *Paul Klee and the Decorative in Modern Art* (Cambridge, England: Cambridge University Press, 2004), 164–90.

4. Anni and Josef Albers took sabbaticals in 1940 and 1946–47. I rely here and elsewhere on Mary Emma Harris's exhaustive study *The Arts at Black Mountain College* (Cambridge, Mass.: MIT Press, 1987), 265.

5. Rosalind Krauss, "Grids," *October* 9 (summer 1979); reprinted in Rosalind Krauss, *The Originality of the Avant-Garde and Other Modernist Myths* (Cambridge, Mass.: MIT Press, 1988), 8–22. I return to Krauss below. Virginia Gardner Troy defines "open weave" as produced by "periodically leaving areas unwoven or twisting and pulling aside the taut warp threads so that open spaces are created and held apart by weft threads." Virginia Gardner Troy, *Anni Albers and Ancient American Textiles: From Bauhaus to Black Mountain* (Burlington, Vt.: Ashgate, 2002), 90. I use "open weave" to mean an open and infinite variety of weaving possibilities. As Black Mountain student Lore Kadden Lindenfeld wrote, "Painting can be started at any point of the canvas, [but] it is limited in size to the canvas itself. [In contrast t]he woven piece grows…." Lore Kadden Lindenfeld, "Tapestry Now," undated typescript, 6, copy at Black Mountain College Research Project (BMCR), Series 5: Donated Materials, Box 71, NCSA. I am grateful to my research assistant, Katherine Rochester, for helping me to locate this and many other pertinent sources.

6. Hereafter I refer to Anni and Josef Albers by their first names, so as to avoid confusion and needless repetition.

7. Anni Albers, quoted in Nicholas Fox Weber, "Anni Albers to Date," in *The Woven and Graphic Art of Anni Albers,* exh. cat. (Washington, D.C.: Smithsonian Institution Press, 1985), 19.

8. See, for example, Harris, 20–24, and Troy, *Anni Albers and Ancient American Textiles,* 70, 75–79, and 117.

9. Paul Klee, "On Modern Art," trans. Anni Albers, undated, unpublished ms., JAAF.

10. Paul Klee, *On Modern Art*, trans. Paul Findlay (London: Faber and Faber, 1948).

11. Anni Albers to Charlotte Weidler, August 19, 1960, JAAF; emphasis in original.

12. This was an expansion upon the practice Josef had emphasized at the Bauhaus. See Harris, 78–83.

13. Josef said, "We had big walls with shelves all covered with glass doors and there we had saved our results of my basic course in design. And that was so exciting to Mr. Barr that he said … [he] would write his first book on my teaching." Anni and Josef Albers, undated interview with Martin Duberman, 4, Duberman Personal Collection (DPC), Series 4: Interviews, 1678.13, NCSA. This and many other interviews were conducted for Martin B. Duberman, *Black Mountain: An Exploration in Community* (New York: Dutton, 1972). Josef appears to have been concerned more than Anni with establishing that his teachings were his own. He even wrote from Black Mountain to implore László Moholy-Nagy to retract published statements that Josef had "continued" Moholy-Nagy's teachings at the Bauhaus: "As you know, I was at the Bauhaus for thirteen years, of which ten years were spent in teaching my own courses which were independent from your teaching." Josef Albers to Moholy-Nagy, August 28, 1938, JAP, Box 2, Folder 20, MAYU.

14. Josef's library is maintained at the JAAF. According to Danilowitz, the following Klee books and catalogues there were Josef's: *Paul Klee: Exhibition of Paintings and Drawings,* exh. cat. (New York: Saidenberg Gallery, 1963); Will Grohmann, *Paul Klee: Handzeichnungen, 1921–1930,* limited edition 284/525 (1934); Felix Klee, ed., *Paul Klee: Leben und Werk in Dokumenten* (Zurich: Diogenes Verlag, 1960); Paul Klee, *Pädagogisches Skizzenbuch,* Bauhausbuch 2 (Munich: Langen, 1925); Paul Klee, *Pedagogical Sketchbook,* trans. Sybil Moholy-Nagy (New York: Praeger, 1953); Paul Klee, *Tagebücher* (Cologne: DuMont, 1957); James Thrall Soby, *The Prints of Paul Klee* (New York: Curt Valentin, 1945); and Voltaire, *Candide,* illus. Paul Klee, limited edition (New York: Pantheon and Nierendorf Galleries, n.d.).

15. Author's translation; emphasis in original. *Paul Klee: Leben und Werk in Dokumenten,* JAAF.

16. Clement Greenberg, "Portrait of the Artist," *New York Times*, Book Review, December 27, 1964, JAAF. Italics in original; underlining by Albers.

17. Josef wrote this in English in Klee, *Tagebücher*, 336, JAAF.

18. This page can be found amidst copies of Lore Kadden Lindenfeld's notes from Josef's class at BMCR. Citing a difference in script, however, Lindenfeld has attested that this page is not hers. Letter to the author, September 8, 2005. See Lore Kadden Lindenfeld, undated notes, 26c, BMCR, Series 5: Donated Materials, Box 68, Josef Albers's course, NCSA.

19. Josef's library at JAAF includes both the German and English editions. The former is signed "Albers" in bold red pencil across black endpaper.

20. "Kunst gibt nicht das Sichtbare wieder, sondern macht sichtbar." Author's translation. Paul Klee, "Schöpferische Konfession," in Kasimir Edschmid, ed., *Schöpferische Konfession*, Tribüne der Kunst und Zeit: eine Schriftensammlung 13 (Berlin: Reiß, 1920).

21. Josef Albers, *Search Versus Re-search* (Hartford, Conn.: Trinity College Press, 1969), 9. This volume collects Josef's three lectures at Trinity College in April 1965. Josef and Anni rehearsed their views over the years, so the late date should not be problematic.

22. Albers, *Search Versus Re-search,* 12; emphasis in original.

23. Josef Albers, interview with Duberman, 71–72.

24. Albers, *Search Versus Re-search*, 11.

25. Anni Albers, quoted in Neil Welliver, "A Conversation with Anni Albers," *Craft Horizons* (July–August 1965).

26. Anni's notes from Klee's class are kept at the Bauhaus-Archiv, Museum für Gestaltung, Berlin. Her notes on repetition, or what Klee called *Schieben* and *Verschieben*, are reproduced in Troy, *Anni Albers and Ancient American Textiles*, 87, fig. 4.16.

27. Weber, "Anni Albers to Date," 19.

28. Michael Baumgartner, "Josef Albers und Paul Klee: Zwei Lehrpersönlichkeiten am Bauhaus," in Josef Helfenstein and Henriette Mentha, eds., *Josef und Anni Albers: Europa und Amerika*, exh. cat. (Bern: DuMont, 1998), 185–86. Baumgartner traces the Alberses' Klee collection, which included nine works, and notes that *Zwei Kräfte* was actually the most abstract Klee that they owned.

29. Troy, *Anni Albers and Ancient American Textiles*, 120.

30. Klee, *On Modern Art* (1948), 51.

31. Anni Albers, "Weaving in a College," undated typescript, 1, Anni Albers Personal Collection (AAPC), 1197.1, NCSA. I suspect that it dates from Anni's early years at Black Mountain, because she penciled in some marginalia in German.

32. This is the premise of Troy's "Thread as Text: The Woven Work of Anni Albers," in Nicholas Fox Weber and Pandora Tabatabai Asbaghi, eds., *Anni Albers*, exh. cat. (New York: Guggenheim Museum, 1999), 28–39, which she elaborated in *Anni Albers and Ancient American Textiles*.

33. Troy, *Anni Albers and Ancient American Textiles*, 156.

34. Anni Albers, quoted in Harris, 24.

35. Weber, "Anni Albers to Date," 19.

36. Clement Greenberg, "Art," *The Nation*, February 19, 1949, 222. A copy of this review is in Josef's papers at Yale (JAP, Box 4, Folder 47, MAYU). Seven presumably angry exclamation points, in Josef's recognizable hand, grace the margins.

37. Krauss, 9.

38. Krauss, 16 and 19.

39. Krauss, 21–22.

40. Gilles Deleuze and Félix Guattari, *A Thousand Plateaus: Capitalism and Schizophrenia*, trans. Brian Massumi (Minneapolis: University of Minnesota Press, 1987), 479.

41. Deleuze and Guattari, 478.

42. Deleuze and Guattari, 475.

43. Deleuze and Guattari, 475–76.

44. Deleuze and Guattari, 476.

45. Deleuze and Guattari, 474.

46. Elsewhere, Deleuze and Guattari regarded the mixed and messy state of the world as "schizophrenic," although they read the symptoms more productively than Krauss did.

47. An art-historical model for my analysis is Rico Franses, "Postmonumentality: Frame, Grid, Space, Quilt," in Paul Duro, ed., *The Rhetoric of the Frame: Essays on the Boundary of the Artwork* (Cambridge, England: Cambridge University Press, 1996), 258–73.

48. Albers, "Weaving in a College."

49. Baumgartner, 167–80.

50. I am grateful to Danilowitz and Csoma for showing me the work in storage at JAAF. Deleuze and Guattari also invoked scraps when they described patchwork. Deleuze and Guattari, 477.

51. Brenda Danilowitz, "Portraitphotographien," in Marianne Stockebrand, ed., *Josef Albers: Photographien 1928–1955*, exh. cat. (Cologne: Kölnischer Kunstverein, 1992), 24–25. Danilowitz discusses this in terms of the limits of photographic objectivity as well as Josef's admiration for Klee.

52. We might remember, too, that Homage to the Square was a potentially infinite series, not a closed and finished system. Mondrian, Krauss's other target, also used the grid consistently, but his intuitive handling of color placement, and the width and length of each band resulted in remarkably powerful breadth. See the astonishing formal descriptions of the works in Kermit Swiler Champa, *Mondrian Studies* (Chicago: University of Chicago Press, 1985).

53. Josef Albers, typescript of comments made at Sidney Janis Gallery, New York, for the exhibition "New Work by Josef Albers," January 7–26, 1952, JAP, Box 22, Folder 202, MAYU.

54. Helfenstein and Mentha, 210–11.

55. Mary Lou Mitchell to Martin Duberman, c. 1967, DPC, Series 1: Correspondence, 1678.3, Mary Lou Mitchell, NCSA.

56. See Si Sillman, *Untitled Painting* (c. 1948), in Harris, 131.

57. Joseph Fiore, letter to the author, July 26, 2005.

58. James Thompson, *Joseph Fiore*, Black Mountain College Dossiers 1, exh. cat. (Black Mountain, N.C.: Black Mountain College Museum and Arts Center, 1995), 19.

59. See Anger, "Carpets of Memory," 182–85, and *Farblehre und Weberei: Benita Koch-Otte, Bauhaus Weimar und Dessau, Burg Giebichenstein*, exh. cat. (Berlin: Bauhaus-Archiv, 1976). Guermonprez and Anni also shared a Jewish German heritage and had both left Germany because of National Socialism.

60. See Anger, *Paul Klee and the Decorative in Modern Art*, 126.

61. See, for example, Lore Kadden Lindenfeld, *Japanese Diary #12* (1982), at http://www.ibiblio.org/blackmountaincollege/kaddenfolder/pages/k_diary.htm.

62. See Sigrid Wortmann Weltge, *Bauhaus-Textilien: Kunst und Künstlerinnen der Webwerkstatt* (London: Thames and Hudson, 1993), 129 and 87.

63. Ruth Asawa, interview with Aiko Cuneo, December 19, 2003, and typescript of excerpts from "Creative Credo," c. 1946–48, Asawa Papers, San Francisco. I am grateful to Asawa and Cuneo for sharing this material with me.

64. Ruth Asawa, letter to the author, July 24, 2005.

65. See http://www.ruthasawa.com.

66. Elaine de Kooning, quoted in Harris, 151.

67. Guermonprez's account is typical: "…it was thrilling. Buckminster Fuller, he built the first geodesic dome there with the students, and it collapsed. I'll never forget that." Lisa Jalowetz Aronson and Trude Guermonprez Elsesser, interview with Martin Duberman, 26, DPC, Series 4: Interviews, 1678.14, NCSA.

68. Elaine de Kooning, "Dymaxion Artist," *Art News* 51, no. 5 (September 1952): 16.

69. At least a half dozen of these photographs are preserved at BMCR, Series 8: Visual Resources, Box 87, Guermonprez photographs.

70. Buckminster Fuller, quoted in "Exhibition at Yale Gallery to Have Pictorial Weavings of a Leading Pioneer Artist," *New Haven Evening Register*, December 8, 1959. A clipping of this article can be found in AAPC, 1197.1, NCSA.

71. Robert Rauschenberg, quoted in Harris, 126.

72. Harris, 126. Harris reports that although Rauschenberg claimed to have read about Josef as a disciplinarian in *Time*, she was not able to locate such a source.

73. Josef Albers, interview with Duberman, 62–63.

74. The plaid shirt and pleated slacks look like the ones Rauschenberg was wearing as he prepared the finishing touches for a unicorn costume of raffia in 1949, so it is possible that what he is binding here is that raffia. See Guermonprez's photograph in Harris, 126.

75. Guermonprez, interview with Duberman, 27 and 29; Mary Lynn Kotz, *Rauschenberg: Art and Life*, 2nd ed. (New York: Abrams, 2004), 66.

76. Guermonprez, interview with Duberman, 27.

77. Guermonprez, interview with Duberman, 11.

78. Joan Young and Susan Davidson, "Chronology," in Walter Hopps and Susan Davidson, eds., *Robert Rauschenberg: A Retrospective,* exh. cat. (New York: Guggenheim Museum, 1997), 554.

79. I have not been able to verify her contention, but Guermonprez claims to have initiated a practice at Black Mountain that may also have had its influence on Rauschenberg. In another interview, she said, "I made a tapestry there where I used painting as well as tapestry weaving combined." Trude Guermonprez, interview with Mary Emma Harris, December 8, 1971, 6, BMCR, Series 4: Released Interviews, Box 31, Guermonprez, NCSA.

80. I cannot do justice to Steinberg's brilliant argument in this limited space. Leo Steinberg, "Other Criteria," in *Other Criteria: Confrontations with Twentieth-Century Art* (New York: Oxford University Press, 1972), 55–91.

81. Joseph Masheck, "The Carpet Paradigm: Critical Prolegomena to a Theory of Flatness," *Arts Magazine* 51, no. 1 (1976): 82–109.

82. Masheck, 82. See Josef Albers, *Interaction of Color*, 2nd ed. (New Haven, Conn.: Yale University Press, 1975), 33 and 81.

83. Albers, *Interaction of Color*, 50, quoted in Masheck, 82.

84. Anni Albers, quoted in *Anni Albers: Pictorial Weavings,* exh. cat. (Cambridge, Mass: MIT Press; Pittsburgh: Carnegie Institute of Technology; Baltimore: Baltimore Museum of Art; and New Haven, Conn.: Yale University Art Gallery, 1959). A copy of this catalog is in AAPC, 1197.1, NCSA.

85. http://www.bmcproject.org/MEMOIRS/RITTENHOUSEtreichlerMarthaMEMOIR.htm.

Paul Klee's Frames:
Documenting Choices and Changes[1]

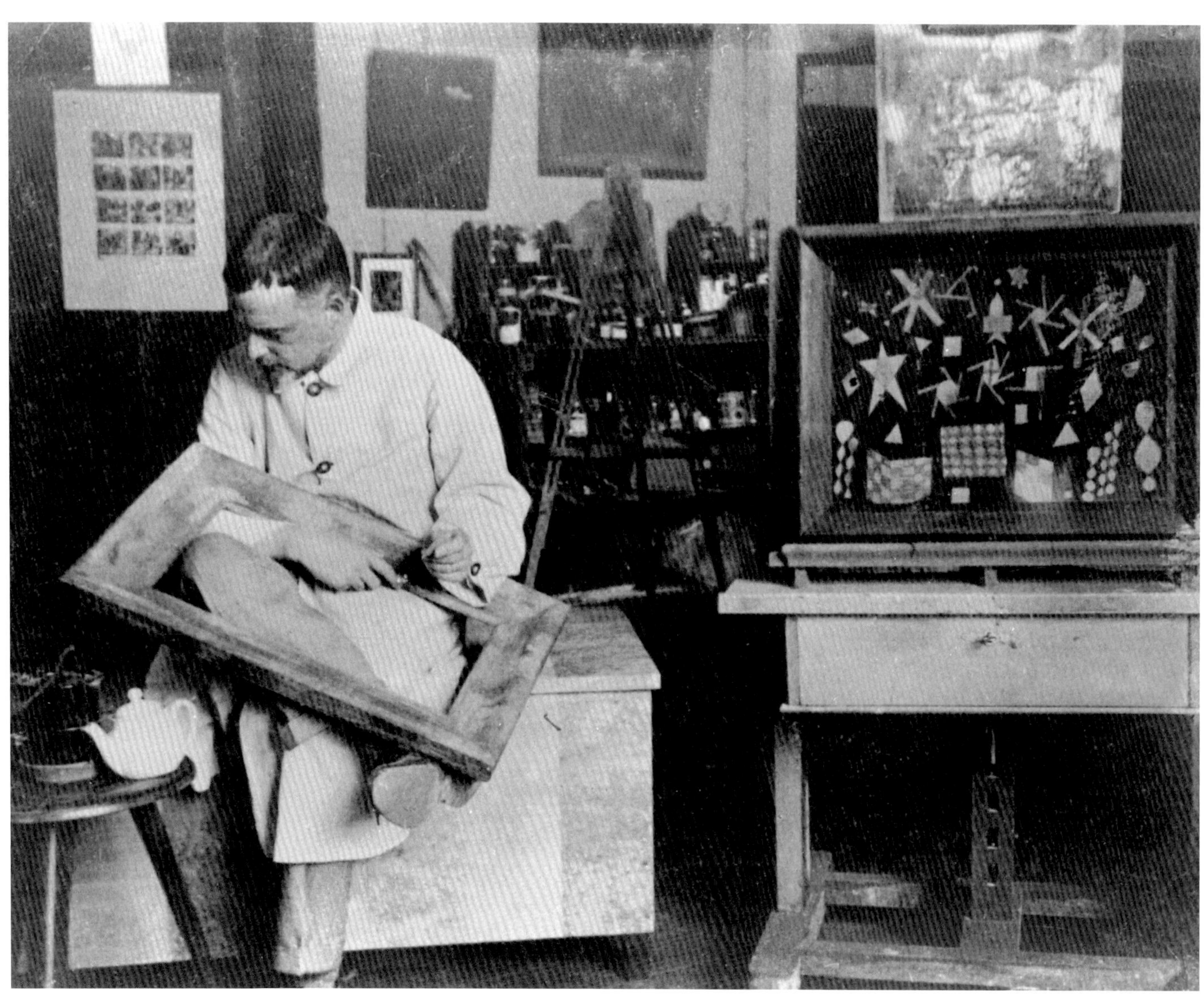

Paul Klee had very specific ideas about the presentation of his paintings. Unlike many artists who view mounting and framing as details to be handled by a dealer or eschewed altogether, Klee saw the presentation of a painting as a crucial step in its completion. In many cases where an original frame still exists, this emphasis is obvious: the painting and frame are intimately conjoined, conceptually and materially. For other works, however, the simplicity of Klee's style and method of framing led to the frame's replacement. Keeping in mind that all Klee works did not arrive in America with their original frames, in the current presentation of Klee's work in America, we can see framing solutions that illustrate the artist's aesthetic as well as those that reflect other individual personalities, institutional philosophies, and changes in ownership.

Klee's Original Frames

To determine the types of frames and mounting systems Klee originally used and to trace the modifications that occurred afterward, we used several resources. The primary one was archival photographic material documenting the artist's studios, his exhibitions in Europe from 1930 to 1941, and his exhibitions in the United States from 1936 to 1948. The studio photos show numerous empty frames, unassembled sections of frame molding, frames around completed paintings hung on the walls, and frames around paintings still in progress on an easel. In some cases Klee appears to have propped an unframed work within a frame for the sake of the photograph. Additionally, Klee's diaries, his correspondence, and his handwritten oeuvre catalogue, which he began in 1911 to systematically record his output, provided valuable information on original mounting and framing.

The frames Klee chose for his paintings can be grouped into several broad categories. The first group consists of wooden frames that Klee painted, stained, or gilded, or that he treated in a combination of these techniques. A photograph made by the artist in 1920 shows several works framed and hanging on the wall in his studio in the Schlösschen Suresnes, Munich (fig. 76). While the majority of these early works are in small dark-colored frames, Klee also utilized white painted versions of these simple frames. In a diary entry from 1918, Klee discussed framing a painting in this way immediately after its completion.[1] Additionally, *Bühnen-Gebirgs-Konstruction [Stage Mountain Construction]* (1920.28) can be seen in a painted white frame in another 1920 photograph (fig. 11). Four years later, larger and wider frames appeared. In a photograph from 1924, the artist can be seen preparing a frame of this type in his Weimar studio (fig. 75). Similar frames can also be seen on paintings in the studio in Weimar in 1925 (fig. 77). In addition to using painted frames, on several occasions Klee used a combination of paint and metal leaf, primarily silver, on his frames.[2] Sometimes he surrounded his works with antique lacquered or gilt frames. In a 1906 letter to his wife, Klee mentioned admiring a small Renaissance frame for its slight relief on the molding that made a "delightful contrast" with the

Fig. 75
Paul Klee preparing a frame in his studio in Weimar, Germany, 1924;
Assyrisches Spiel [Assyrian Game], 1923.79, sits on the easel framed
with a similar, though slightly more angular, frame.

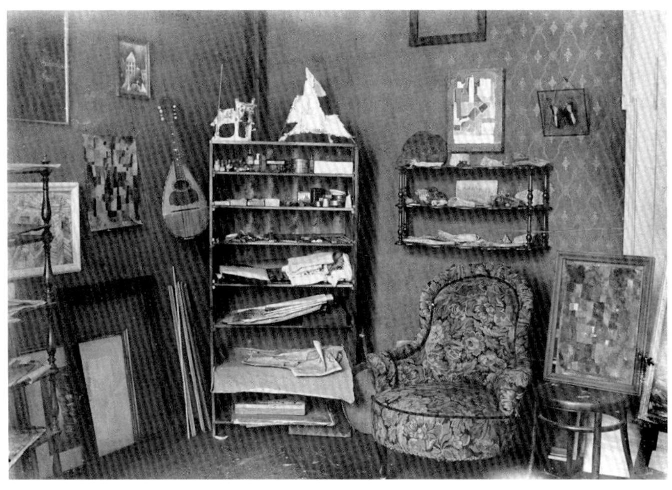

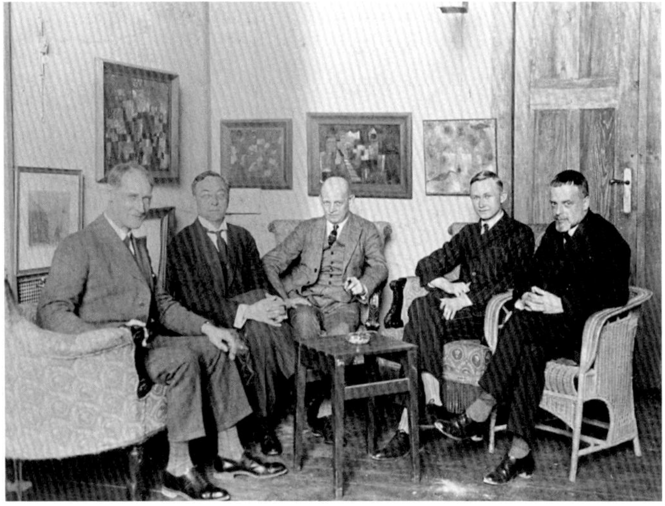

"flat style" of his works.[3] Several examples of antique frames chosen by the artist remain unaltered in the Paul Klee-Stiftung in Bern, Switzerland.[4] Due to Klee's use of standard simple moldings, along with the relative ease with which these frames could be removed, this group of frames is not well represented in American collections. Once the paintings began to change ownership, it is possible that these frames were misunderstood and discarded as an artifact of the previous owner's aesthetic, rather than a reflection of original artistic intent. While no longer extant, ~~Jugendlicher~~ *Schauspieler=Maske [~~Youth~~ Actor's Mask]* (1924.252, pl. 28) appears to have had a thick wood frame of this type in the 1940 exhibition at the Buchholz Gallery in New York.[5]

The second group of Klee's original frames consists of simple strip frames, typically noted in his oeuvre catalogue as "original strip frame, painted," as for *Um den Fisch [Around the Fish]* (1926.124), or simply "original strip frame," as noted for *Junger Garten (Rhythmen) [Young Garden (Rhythms)]* (1927.25). At different times opaquely painted, thinly washed with color, or left untreated, this was perhaps the frame that Klee used most frequently. The thickness of the frames' members varies from painting to painting; usually they were not mitered, but simply butt-joined in the corners.[6] *Dorf-Carnaval [Village Carnival]* (1926.135, pl. 35), *Artistenbildnis [Portrait of an Artist]* (1927.13), and *Junge Pflanzung [Young Plantation]* (1929.98, pl. 59) have frames typical of this group.

In this group we also find two variants of special interest. *Feuer Abends [Fire in the Evening]* (1929.95, fig. 78) has its original strip frame. However, the top and right strips are slightly shorter than the other strips. To compensate, small pieces of wood have been added in both top corners, oriented either vertically or horizontally as necessary. While at first glance these undisguised splices appear to derive from a need for thrift, the proportions and orientation of the added pieces reflect the overall intervals within the color bands in the painting.

Another interesting variant of the strip frame appears on several of his works on cardboard. Because these works were too thin to accommodate framing strips, Klee often mounted the cardboard works onto stretchers, usually with small tacks through the face of the painting, in order to create additional thickness. In many cases, such as with *Maibild [May Picture]* (1925.120c), Klee

Fig. 76
Paul Klee's studio in Munich, Schlösschen Suresnes, Werneck, 1920.

Fig. 77
Paul Klee's studio at the Bauhaus in Weimar, Germany, April 1925; left to right: Lyonel Feininger, Vasily Kandinsky, Oskar Schlemmer, Georg Muche, and Paul Klee.

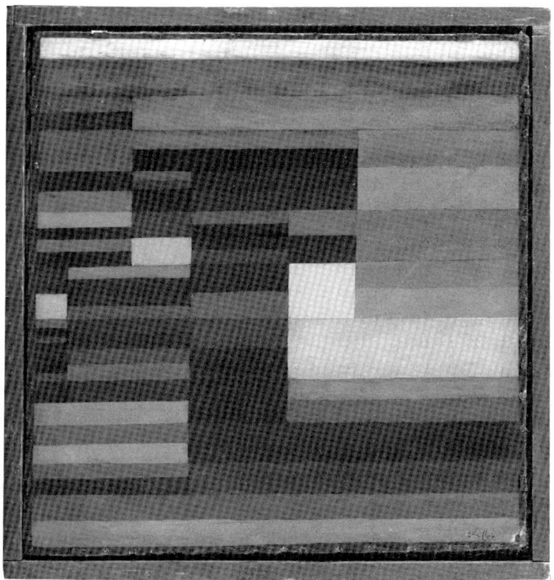

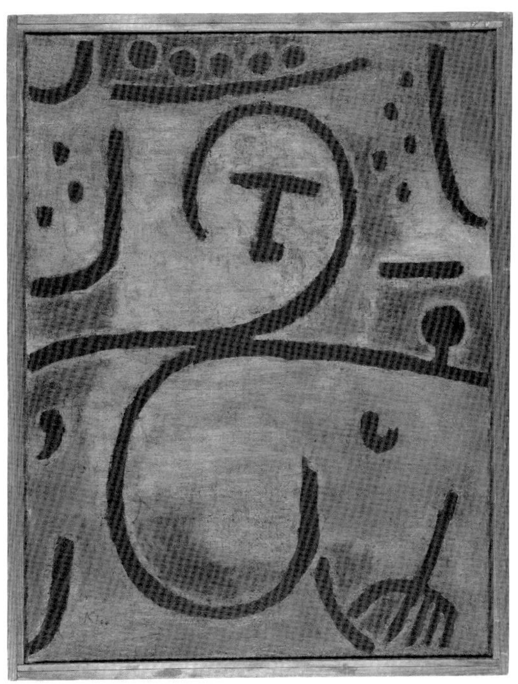

painted this supporting stretcher, which is just visible between the
image and frame, to integrate it with the work.[7] Around 1936 Klee
began to use a double strip frame, where a second strip surrounds
the original frame. *Blaue Nacht [Blue Night]* (1937.208) and
Pomona, Über-reif [Pomona, Overripe] (1938.134, fig. 79) have
frames typical of this variant. The stretcher, intermittently visible
around the perimeter of the cardboard paintings and thus acting
as an inner framing device, may have evolved into this double
strip frame that can be seen in later works. Unlike the previous
frame group, many of the paintings that arrived in America with
their original strip frames, such as those mentioned above, have
retained them.

The third group of Klee frames made its appearance around
1932.[8] These frames consist of two parts: a flat wooden liner
and a molding with a simple downward slant on the inside.
Though the structure stays the same, Klee introduced some variety in the finishes from painting to painting. Sections of the
frame may be completely or partially painted, and/or selectively
stained. *Hoch oder Tief? [High or Deep?]* (1934.20) has a partially
painted outer molding with its crown stained brown, while the
liner has a decorative pattern incised into the white paint (fig. 80).
While a group of at least seventeen paintings had this particular
frame, either still extant or documented photographically, no such

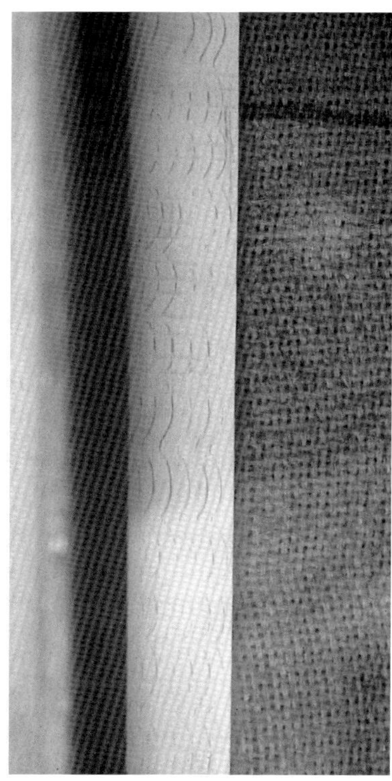

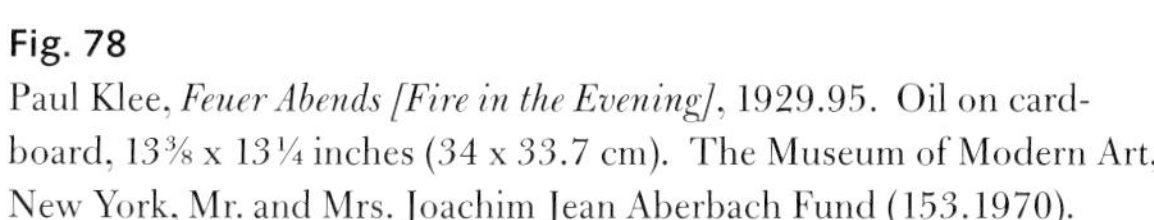

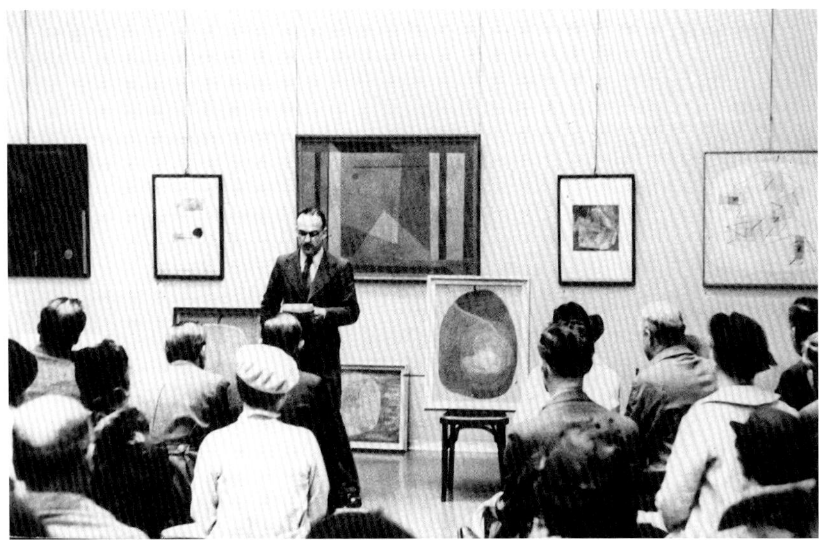

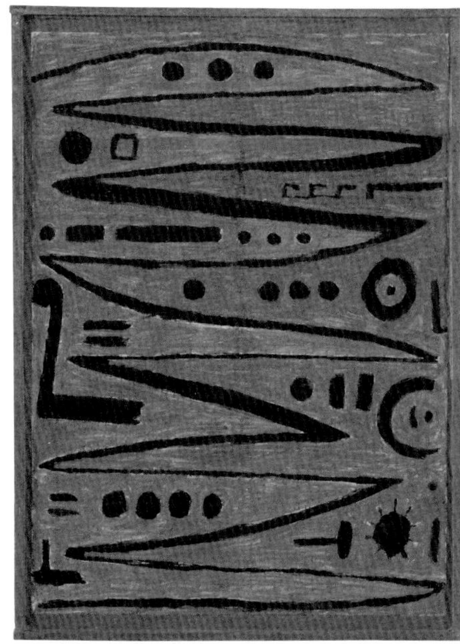

frame is noted in Klee's oeuvre catalogue.[9] Nevertheless, it is likely that these are original frames.[10] They can also be seen in several exhibitions through the mid-1930s (fig. 81).[11] Two paintings in America have been documented with this frame: *Maske Furcht [Mask: Fear]* (1932.286) and *Hoch oder Tief?*. Conversely, while retaining its original frame in Europe through at least 1936, *Die Frucht [The Fruit]* (1932.284) bore a standardized gallery frame by the time of the 1948 Buchholz Gallery exhibition in New York, similar to those seen on several others in the same exhibition (see page 222).

The fourth group consists of frames and support systems that Klee either painted or covered with materials so as to make them integral with the image. *Stilleben (Töpfe, Frucht, Osterei, Gardinen, Etc.) [Still Life (Pots, Fruit, Easter Egg, Curtains Etc.)]* (1927.18, pl. 51), a painting on plaster, has a wooden strip frame painted in colors that correspond to the adjacent areas in the painting. *Heroische Bogenstriche [Heroic Strokes of the Bow]* (1938.1, fig. 82) has perhaps the most integral joining of painting, frame, and color. In this instance Klee covered the strip frame with the same painted blue fabric that lies under the painted paper. This fabric overlaps the face of the frame and folds over onto the sides.

Alterations to Frames and Mounts

In the framing of artworks, the subordination of some elements of artistic intent to individual and institutional aesthetics is particular neither to Klee nor to his American collectors. Rather it is a symptom of multiple changes in ownership and the passage of time, both of which often result in changes to methods of presentation, such as framing, mounting, and matting. For intact original framing and presentation formats, the Paul Klee-Stiftung in the Kunstmuseum Bern is the most representative collection, consisting of works that rarely, if ever, left the sphere of influence of the artist and his family. Outside this unique collection, however, the presentation of Klee's work has been more varied and subject to periodic revision. Dealers, individual owners, and institutional repositories have all made changes for a variety of reasons.

As Klee's works entered American collections through various dealers, some of the eccentricities of Klee's framing choices may have been relinquished for the sake of a more consistent institutional presentation. Given the limited number of archival exhibition photographs and records prior to the 1950s, it is difficult to piece together a complete picture of exactly when such changes might have occurred and what may have prompted them. At The

Phillips Collection in Washington, D.C., for example, most changes took place before the paintings entered the collection. At the Solomon R. Guggenheim Museum in New York, the Metropolitan Museum of Art in New York, and the Norton Simon Museum in Pasadena, California, some works by Klee retain their original frames, and some reflect the aesthetics of their respective institutions or their previous owners.

By modern standards, Klee's works are small in scale. Their highly individualized surfaces and imagery results in a visual weight that is often difficult to balance within a grouping or with the work of other artists hung in close proximity. Therefore, institutions often made an attempt to unify Klee's paintings through framing and mounting. The Buchholz Gallery mounted several well-documented Klee exhibitions, including one in 1940 and one in the spring of 1948, entitled "Paul Klee." Several paintings in the 1940 exhibition received new frames, sometimes even replacing original frames.[12] Although the paintings ranged from 1919 to 1930, they all received the same simple frame, made of light wood with a stepped molding, which appears to be the gallery frame specific to the exhibition. Since several works did retain their original frames in this exhibition, it is not entirely clear what prompted the changes.[13] Again, in the 1948 Buchholz exhibition "Paul Klee," several paintings appeared in frames different from those previously documented.[14] This time the standard frame was made of a plain wide pine molding with a linen liner. At least one of the paintings that had received a gallery frame in 1940, *Bilderbogen [Printed Sheet with Picture]* (1937.133, pl. 93), received this new version in 1948 (see page 222). The standardization of framing

for a group of works by Klee was not unique to American institutions or collectors. Installation photographs from the 1933 exhibition at the Städtisches Museum für Kunst und Kunstgewerbe, Halle, Germany, show a group of Klees in identical frames (fig. 83).

The Klee works currently in the Guggenheim Museum collection entered through a variety of avenues: some were purchases from galleries; some came from Hilla Rebay as purchases, gifts, or estate items; and some were acquired from the Karl Nierendorf estate. In spite of this, all the paintings are currently framed in modern frames. The Guggenheim changed the frames to meet the philosophical and aesthetic installation demands imposed on the collection in 1959 with the opening of the new museum building designed by Frank Lloyd Wright. In a telegram to a lender to the museum's 1967 Klee retrospective, then director Thomas Messer wrote, "because of museum's architectural features would strongly urge you allow removal of their frame and their reframing during the New York show only. Special Guggenheim frames to be made…"[15] *Roter Ballon [Red Balloon]* (1922.179, pl. 18) and *Offenes Buch [Open Book]* (1930.206) had already received standardized white shadow box frames, in 1961 and 1965 respectively, replacing the frames noted in the inventory of assets purchased from the Nierendorf estate made by The Solomon R. Guggenheim Foundation.[16] Based on the simple frame descriptions available in the inventory ledger, it is not clear whether any of the frames that the Guggenheim replaced were original. The silver-leafed strip frames currently on both *In der Strömung Sechs Schwellen [In the Current Six Weirs]* (1929.92, pl. 65) and *Brückenbogen treten aus der Reihe [Arches of the Bridge Stepping Out of Line]*

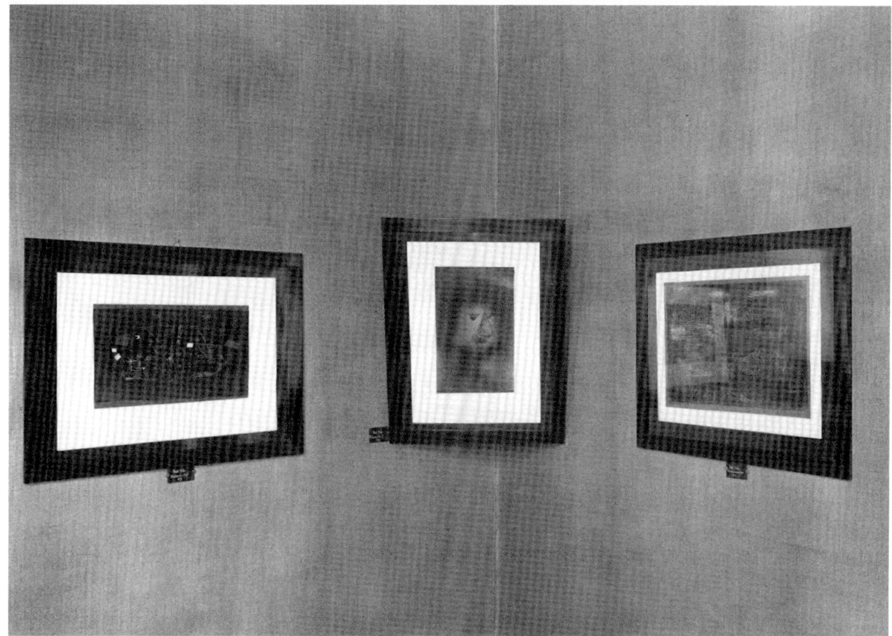

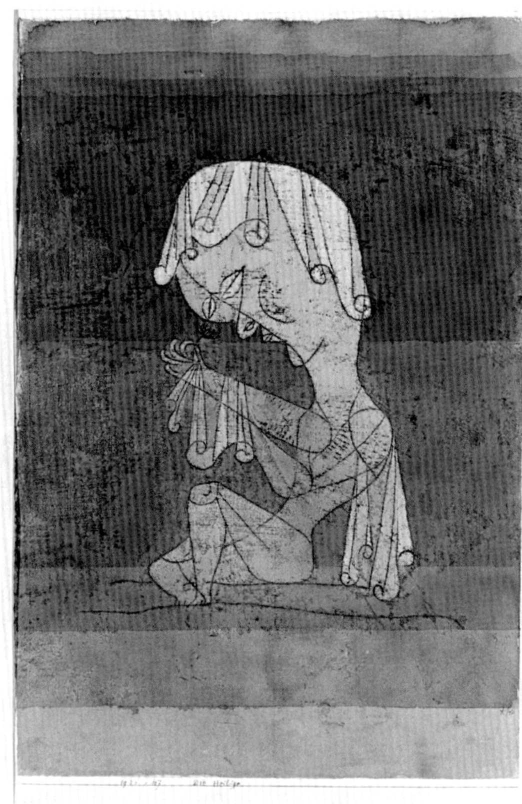

vidual frames may vary subtly, the use of a single style of frame tends to unify the presentation of the works on paper overall, punctuated occasionally by the paintings with an original artist's frame.

In a given work, we can trace modifications not only in framing, but also in mounting through comparisons with archival photographs or by close technical examination. (The mounting always marked the conclusion of the working process for Klee, who never entered an unmounted drawing into the oeuvre catalogue). Klee himself mounted the majority of his works on paper on secondary supports (usually stiff cardstock) from early on in his career.[20] He deliberately chose the dimensions of each mount according to the dimensions of the work rather than using a standard size. In most cases he added an inscription,[21] and from 1912 on he frequently decorated the mount with bands of watercolor or gouache (sometimes also with painted paper strips and metallic foil), which made them an integral part of the works.[22]

Within the group of Klee works bequeathed in 1953 to the Pasadena Art Museum (now the Norton Simon Museum) as part of Galka Scheyer's Blue Four Collection are several works where modifications to the mount, such as cropping and/or toning of the edges, can probably be attributed to Scheyer's hand. We can see evidence for these types of modifications in two works in the exhibition: *Das Tor zum Hades [The Gateway to Hades]* (1921.29, pl. 9) and *Die Heilige [The Saint]* (1921.107, pl. 12). It can be assumed that cropping of a work often went hand in hand with a change to a smaller frame, but it is also plausible that a mount was cropped in order to make worn edges appear cleaner. Toning the edges was another way of visually "improving" their condition—for example, by hiding discoloration in the mount.[23] In *Die Heilige,* adding a more opaque tone over the original earth red on the margins almost entirely concealed the original marginal ink lines (at the top, right, and left edges).[24] An archival photograph shows the condition of the work before the mount was modified (fig. 84).

The mounts of several works that had been in Nierendorf's possession were also modified. After Nierendorf's death in 1947, two curators from the Kunstmuseum Bern in Switzerland were asked to assess the condition of a group of Klee works from his estate.[25] The conclusion of the appraisal was that more than half

(1937.111, pl. 86) reflect the most recent changes and were designed to accommodate a variety of exhibition requirements.[17]

Several Klees acquired by the Guggenheim Foundation from the Nierendorf estate eventually entered the collection of Heinz Berggruen and were subsequently given to the Metropolitan Museum of Art.[18] When original frames existed with the paintings at the time Berggruen obtained the works, as was the case with *Stilleben (Töpfe, Frucht, Osterei, Gardinen, Etc.)* and *Kl. Mädchen Bildnis in Gelb [Small Portrait of a Girl in Yellow]* (1925.149), they were retained. For the majority of the collection, however, which consists of works on paper and their original auxiliary mounts, Berggruen preferred gilded frames with linen liners in the French eighteenth-century style, and the maintenance of this presentation in perpetuity was one of the conditions of Berggruen's bequest to the Metropolitan Museum.[19] While the indi-

of the examined works had been modified in some way. The types of modifications included tinting the mount with watercolor, trimming the mount to the edges of the primary support (at times cutting off the original inscription), and removing the mount. These modifications were considered substantial damages that reduced the value of the works, quite drastically in some instances. In cases where the mount had been completely removed and the original mounting could not be reconstructed, it was assumed that the work itself had been damaged or trimmed, and the work was depreciated thirty percent. In cases where the mount had been trimmed to the edges of the primary support, the work was depreciated fifteen percent.[26] The anti-German sentiment of the time might have prompted an art dealer to remove Klee's original mounts or cut off the artist's inscription: it being more difficult to sell a work with German writing on it.[27]

Conclusions

Over the past twenty-five years, reproductions of Klee's works in exhibition catalogues have increasingly included the original frames in the case of paintings and the complete mounting presentations for the works on paper. This acknowledgment of the work's presentation helps convey the extent to which Klee infused every component of his art with careful thought and his own aesthetic sensibility. While a variety of forces have intervened since to modify a given artwork, including material damage and the presentation requirements of dealers, collectors, and institutions, numerous examples of unaltered Klees have survived. Though the small number of archival installation photographs limits research, it is possible to trace the occurrence of some changes as well as speculate as to the various factors that influenced the current framing of Klee's works in American collections.

NOTES

The authors would like to acknowledge the following for their assistance with the research and preparation of this paper: Susan Davidson, Patricia Favero, Béatrice Ilg, Elizabeth Lunning, Sabine Rewald, and Patrizia Zeppetella. A special thanks is reserved for Stefan Frey, without whom this research would not have been possible.

1. "… and I painted a severely organic piece called 'The Dream' on coarse linen paper with a plaster base. At once I put a white frame around it and hung it." Paul Klee, *The Diaries of Paul Klee, 1898–1918*, ed. Felix Klee (Berkeley, Calif.: University of California Press, 1964), 398, entry 8.19. *Der Traum [The Dream]* (1918.121) is presumably the painting indicated in the diaries. Klee did not note a frame for this entry in his oeuvre catalogue. According to the catalogue raisonné, the original white frame has been lost and the painting's whereabouts are unknown.

2. *Meerschnecken-König [Seasnail King]* (1933.279) retains its original painted and silver-leafed frame, visible in studio photographs.

3. Paul Klee, *Briefe an die Familie*, vol. 1, 1893–1906, ed. Felix Klee (Cologne: DuMont, 1979), 596. We are grateful to Béatrice Ilg, who brought this reference to our attention. See also Nathalie Bäschlin, Béatrice Ilg, and Patrizia Zeppetella, "Die maltechnischen Angaben von Paul Klee," Berner Kunstmitteilungen (September/October 1998): 9–10.

4. These include *Urkunde [Document]* (1933.283), listed in Klee's oeuvre catalogue as framed with "Goldleisten" ("gold strips"); *Blatt-Fisch [Leaf-Fish]* (1937.263) with "Pariser=Rahmen" ("Parisian frame"); and *Kl Herbstlandschaft [Small Autumn Landscape]* (1920.127) which retains its original black lacquer frame, though no frame is noted in Klee's oeuvre catalogue.

5. There is no mention of an original frame for this painting in Klee's oeuvre catalogue. However, the frame in the photograph is significantly different from those of other works that were reframed for this particular exhibition. It is, in fact, unique within the exhibition.

6. Exceptions to this are *Bunte Mahlzeit [Colorful Meal]* (1928.29, pl. 52) and *Fisch Zauber [Fish Magic]* (1925.85, pl. 34), which appear to have their original strip frames with mitered corners. Of these two, an original frame is mentioned only for *Bunte Mahlzeit* in Klee's oeuvre catalogue.

7. The authors would like to thank Patricia Favero for confirming a similar construction for *Ankunft der Gaukler [Arrival of the Jugglers]* (1926.203) and *Im Zeichen der Blüte [Under the Sign of the Flower]* (1937.131) in The Phillips Collection, Washington, D.C. Favero also noted that Klee attached the cardboard of *Im Zeichen der Blüte* to the stretcher prior to painting, while the mounting of *Ankunft der Gaukler* occurred after the painting was completed, indicating that the framing on occasion evolved simultaneously with the painting.

8. Twenty works by Klee, including *Maske Furcht [Mask:Fear]* (1932.286) and *Gartenfigur [Garden Figure]* (1932.282), were included in "Lebendige deutsche Kunst" held at the Galerie Paul Cassirer in Berlin from December 10, 1932, to mid January 1933.

9. The seventeen paintings are: *Maske Furcht, Gartenfigur, Hoch oder Tief?, Polyphonie [Polyphony]* (1932.273), *Ad Parnassum [Ad Parnassum]* (1932.274), *Kleine Felsenstadt [Small Town Among the Rocks]* (1932.276), *Die Frucht [The Fruit]* (1932.284), *Siesta* (1932.329), *Pyramide [Pyramid]* (1932.331), *Büste eines Kindes [Bust of a Child]* (1933.380), *Angst [Fear]* (1934.202, pl. 81), *Engel im Werden [Angel*

in the Making] (1934.204), *Ruhende Sphinx [Sphinx Resting]* (1934.210), *Ent-Seelung [The Soul Departs]* (1934.211), *Der Schöpfer [The Creator]* (1934.213), *Prämierter Apfel [Prizewinning Apple]]* (1934.215), and *Unterwasser-Garten [Underwater Garden]* (1939.746). With the exception of *Maske Furcht* and *Unterwasser-Garten*, all were in the 1935 exhibition at the Kunsthalle Bern, Switzerland.

10. A photograph from Klee's Dessau studio from 1932 shows *Gartenfigur* with this type of frame.

11. Installation photographs documenting paintings in this frame exist for the "International Surrealist Exhibition" at the Burlington Galleries, London, in 1936 and for a 1936 exhibition at the Kunstmuseum Luzern, Lucerne, Switzerland.

12. Following the 1937 "Entartete Kunst [Degenerate Art]" exhibition in Munich, the artworks from that show were stored at the Depot Schloss Niederschönhausen. Several works were photographed individually at that time, including works by Klee. A number of these appeared in the 1940 Buchholz Gallery exhibition without the original frames noted in Klee's oeuvre catalogue, including *Die Pauken-Orgel [The Kettledrum-Organ]* (1930.212) and *Junger Garten (Rhythmen) [Young Garden (Rhythms)]* (1927.25).

13. It is possible that the gallery made the decision to replace the frames based in part on their condition, or an interpretation of their condition, upon their arrival in the United States. In the photograph of *Junger Garten (Rhythmen)* from the Depot Schloss Niederschönhausen, the frame appears to have a very distressed and worn surface.

14. For example, *Die Frucht* is documented in 1936 with its original frame. See figure 81.

15. Telegram, January 1, 1967, Klee Object File, Solomon R. Guggenheim Museum, New York. Susan Davidson researched the history of the framing of several paintings in the Guggenheim Museum's collection and kindly shared this information. Susan Davidson, correspondence with the authors, August 17, 2005.

16. The authors consulted a duplicate copy of the "Inventory of Karl Nierendorf Estate Assets Located at 53 East 57th Street New York City Purchased by the Solomon R. Guggenheim Foundation Consisting of Paintings Art Objects Prints Books and Booklets Furniture, Fixtures, and Equipment and Miscellaneous Items January 27, 1948" located in the Hilla von Rebay Foundation Archives, on deposit to the Solomon R. Guggenheim Museum, New York. The archives contain an inventory of the Karl Nierendorf estate, specifically the assets located at 53 East 57th Street, New York, and purchased by the Guggenheim Foundation. The inventory checklist includes a list of works along with their dimensions, a media description, and a frame description. At the time of the inventory, *Roter Ballon, Offenes Buch*, and *Brückenbogen treten aus der Reihe [Arches of the Bridge Stepping Out of Line]* (1937.111, pl. 86) were all described as having a "wood frame." Of these three works, only *Offenes Buch* has a frame noted in Klee's oeuvre catalogue.

17. Susan Davidson, correspondence with the authors, August 17, 2005.

18. The works listed in the ledger (see note 15), along with the accompanying frame descriptions, are as follows: *Das Pathos der Fruchtbarkeit [The Pathos of Fertility]* (1921.130), "wood frame"; *Das Stuhltier [The Chair Animal]* (1922.45), "wood frame"; *Officinale Flora [Medicinal Flora]* (1924.140), "wood frame"; *Astrologisch-Phantastisches Bildnis [Astrological-Fantastic Portrait]* (1924.159), "gilt frame"; *Figurinensammlung [Collection of Figurines]* (1926.248, pl. 49), "gilt frame"; and

Scene B aus Kairuan (Nach Zeichng. v. 1914) [Episode B from Kairouan (after a drawing of 1914)] (1931.28), "unframed."

19. Sabine Rewald, correspondence with the authors, March 16, 2005.

20. In many instances he also mounted works that were executed on bits of canvas, gauze, jute, or other materials.

21. Usually the artist's signature and the title and year of the work, as well as its oeuvre catalogue number, are indicated on the mount; in some instances a coded key also denotes its value.

22. For a more detailed account of Klee's mounting, see E. Kaiser Schulte, M. Holben Ellis, and A. King, "An Approach to the Conservation Treatment of Paul Klee Drawings," *The Book and Paper Group* 5 (1986): 19–32.

23. This was noted for *Erinnerungsblatt an eine Empfängnis [Remembrance Sheet of a Conception]*. See Vivian Endicott Barnett, *The Blue Four Collection at the Norton Simon Museum* (New Haven, Conn., and London: Yale University Press, 2002), 266.

24. It is possible that the later paint was added in an attempt to visually suppress the appearance of the work as a "work on paper" by toning back the lightness of the mount and concealing the marginal lines that are typical of works on paper.

25. Arnold Rüdlinger and Max Huggler to Rolf Bürgi, March 15, 1948, Zentrum Paul Klee, loan, Archive Bürgi, Bern, Switzerland. These works were paintings on commission that Nierendorf's gallery in New York had returned to the Klee-Society in Bern in 1947 for exchange. Nierendorf died shortly thereafter and the majority of the works have remained in Switzerland since then. We are grateful to Stefan Frey who brought this document to our attention.

26. It is interesting to note that the mount of *Zweier Enge [Constriction Between Two]* (1934.13, which was believed to have been removed by Nierendorf, had actually been removed by Klee himself in 1935 for the transport of the work from Bern to Paris. He reused the mount later for other works. Information provided by Stefan Frey.

27. This notion came to our attention through Kim Sharon and was confirmed by Michael Baumgartner.

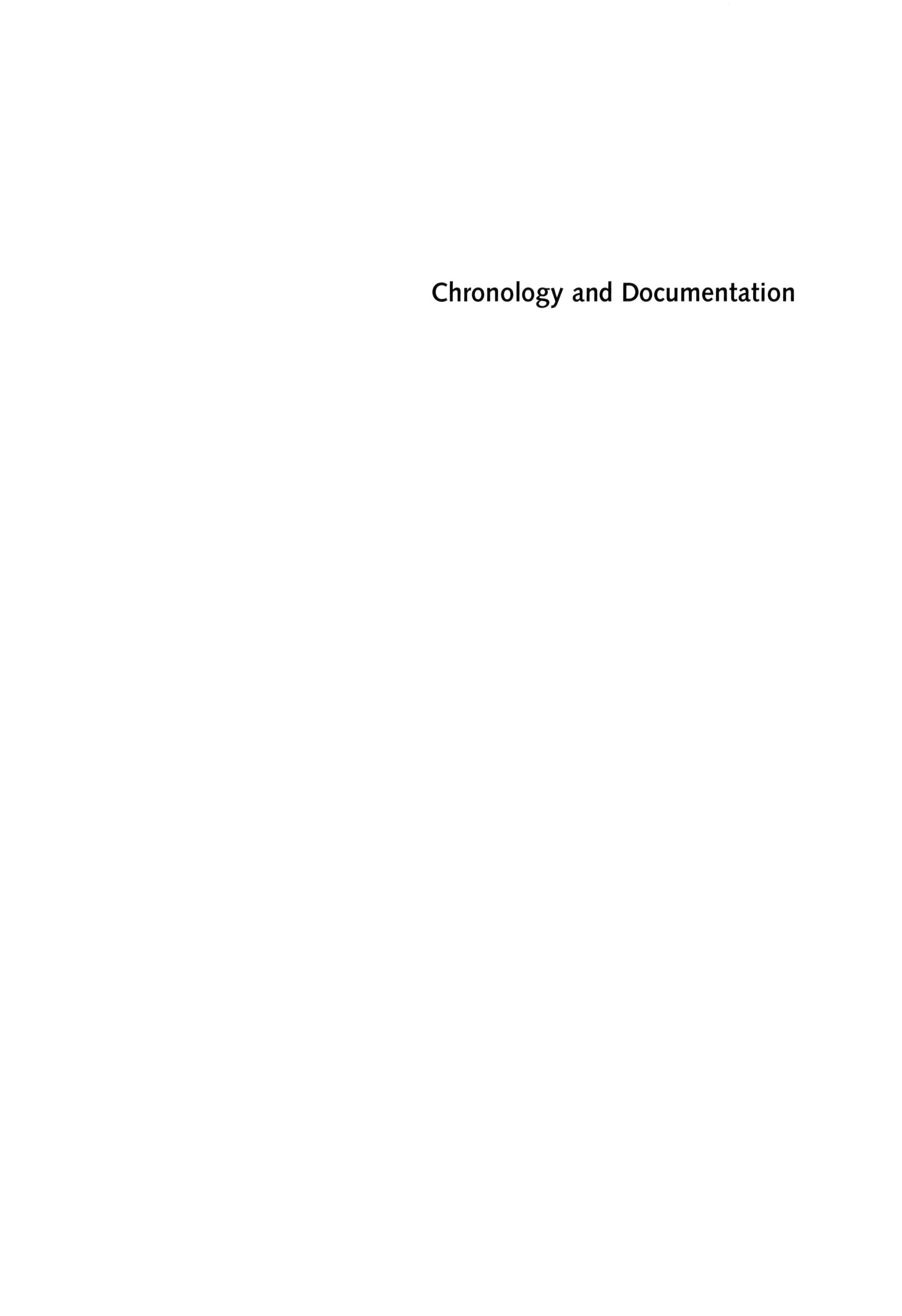

Chronology and Documentation

Klee and America: Chronology of Events

SARAH ECKHARDT

NOTE

This chronology is primarily based on events highlighted in the authors' essays in this volume, as well as on chronologies in *The Blue Four: Feininger, Jawlensky, Kandinsky, and Klee in the New World*, eds. Vivian Endicott Barnett and Josef Helfenstein (Cologne: DuMont; and New Haven, Conn.: Yale University Press, 1997), chronology by Michael Baumgartner and Christina Houstian; *Paul Klee Rediscovered: Works from the Burgi Collection*, eds. Josef Helfenstein and Stefan Frey (London: Merrell, 2000); *Paul Klee: His Life and Work*, ed. Carolyn Lanchner (New York: The Museum of Modern Art, 1987); *Fulfillment in the Late Work* (Basel, Switzerland: Fondation Beyeler, 2003), "Chronology 1931–1941" by Stefan Frey in collaboration with Anke Beck; and *Paul Klee: The Berggruen Klee Collection in the Metropolitan Museum of Art*, Sabine Rewald, ed. (New York: The Metropolitan Museum of Art and Harry Abrams, 1988).

1879   **December 18**: Paul Klee is born in Münchenbuchsee, near Bern, Switzerland, to Ida Marie Frick Klee and Hans Klee. Although his mother is Swiss, Klee receives his father's German nationality.

1880   The Klee family moves to Bern.

1898–1901   Klee studies in Munich.

1906   **September 15**: Klee marries the German pianist Lily Stumpf in Bern.

October: The couple moves to Munich.

1907   **November 30**: Felix Klee is born.

1911   **Spring**: Klee begins compiling a catalogue of his works to date, which he maintains until his death.

Fall: He meets August Macke and Vasily Kandinsky.

1912   **February**: Klee exhibits seventeen works in the second Blaue Reiter exhibition at Galerie Goltz, Munich.

Through several different connections, he meets artists Franz Marc, Alexei Jawlensky, Robert Delauney, and Hans Arp.

1913

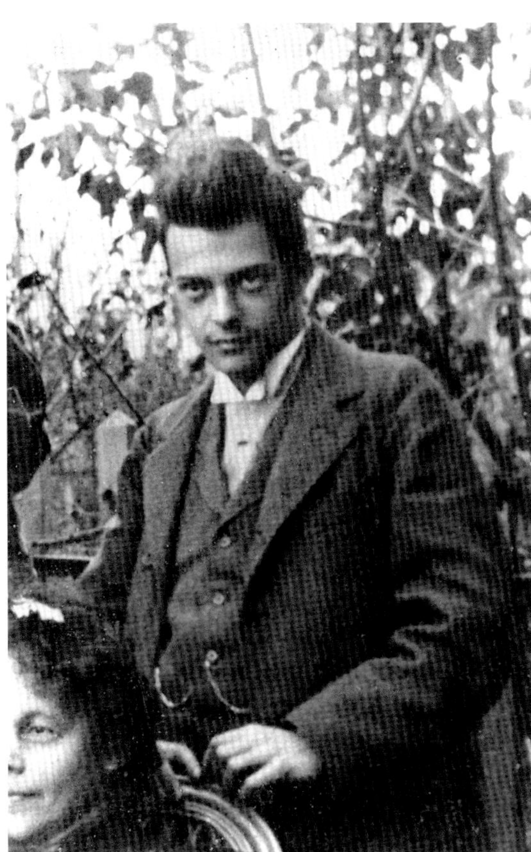

Fig. 85
Paul Klee with Elsie Wächter, 1896.

February 15–March 15: The Armory Show is presented in New York. Officially titled the "International Exhibition of Modern Art," it represents the first large-scale introduction of European avant-garde art to a broad American audience. Although Paul Klee's work is not included in the exhibition, several future Klee collectors buy important pieces of modern art at the exhibition, including Walter and Louise Arensberg as well as Arthur Jerome Eddy.

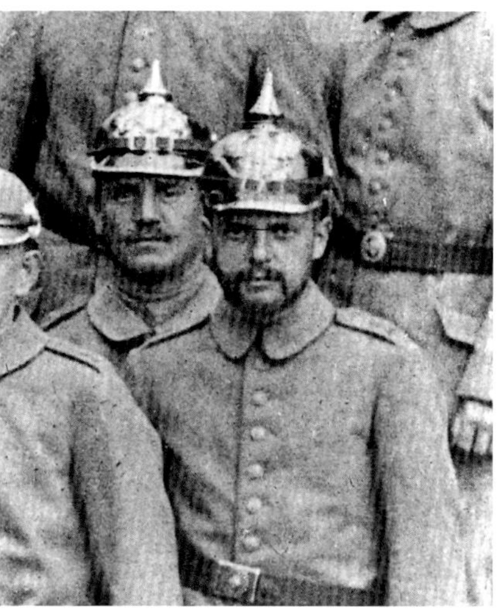

Fig. 86
Paul Klee with his German army unit, Landshut, Germany, 1916.

1914   **April:** Klee travels to Tunisia for two weeks with August Macke and Louis Moilliet. He celebrates this trip as his "breakthrough to color."

May: Klee exhibits in the first exhibition of the Neue Münchner Secession [New Munich Secession].

1916   **March:** Klee and American artist Albert Bloch have a two-person show at Galerie der Sturm, Munich. Klee is drafted into the German army.

1918   **December:** Klee returns home from military duty.

1919   **February:** Officially discharged from the military, Klee signs a three-year contract with the dealer Hans Goltz in Munich.

1920   The German artist Emmy "Galka" Scheyer, who will later become an important promoter of Klee's work in America, meets him in Munich.

May: Hans Goltz's Galerie Neue Kunst in Munich holds the largest exhibition of Klee's work to date with 371 works.

September: The American collector Katherine Dreier (who traveled annually to Germany to visit friends and relatives) buys four of Klee's watercolors and two ink drawings from Galerie Der Sturm in Munich.

October: Walter Gropius invites Klee to teach at the Bauhaus, Weimar.

January: Klee sends twenty-five watercolors to the American collector Arthur Jerome Eddy, who traveled to Germany following the Armory Show.

Klee's work first appears in America when Eddy publishes Klee's watercolor *Das Haus an der Brücke [House by the Brook]* (1911.58) in his influential book *Cubists and Post-Impressionism.*

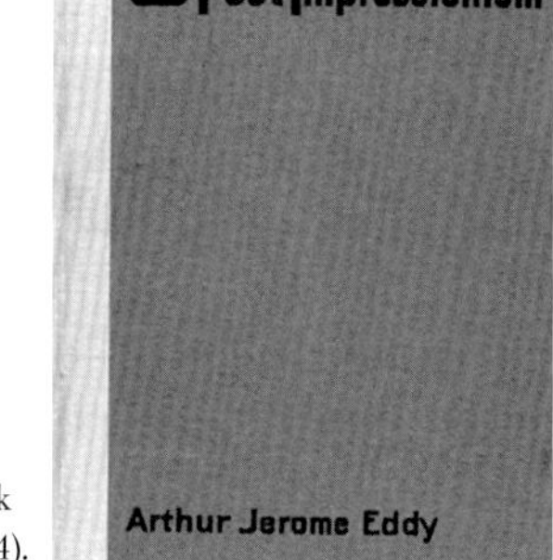

Fig. 87
Cover of Arthur Jerome Eddy's book *Cubists and Post-Impressionism* (1914).

With Marcel Duchamp and Man Ray, Katherine Dreier founds Société Anonyme in New York for the purpose of researching and promoting modern art.

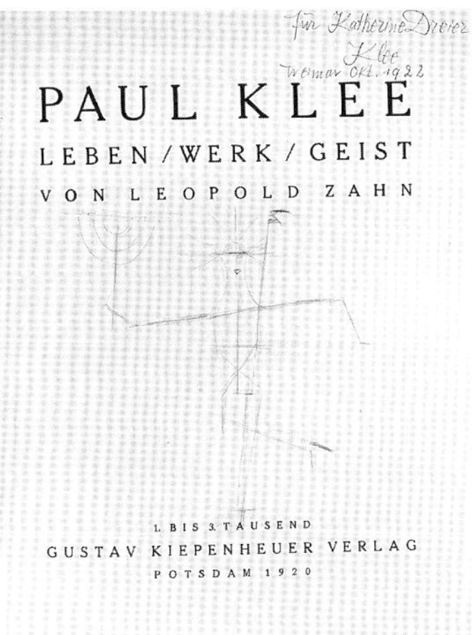

Fig. 88
Cover of Leopold Zahn's book *Paul Klee: Leben/Werk/ Geist* (1920), inscribed by the artist. Yale University Art Gallery, Gift from the Estate of Katherine S. Dreier.

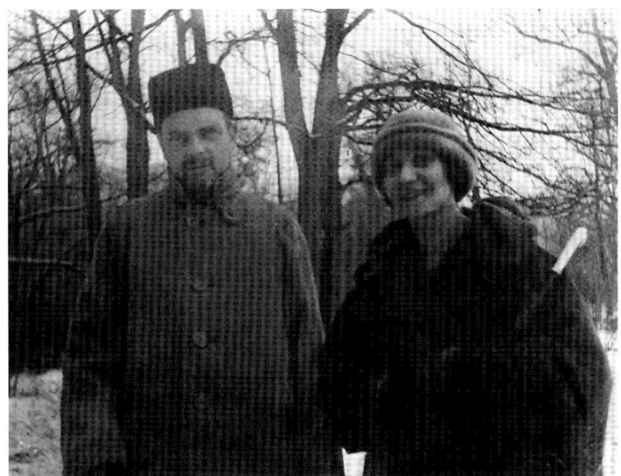

Fig. 89
Paul Klee and Emmy (Galka) Scheyer in Weimar, Germany, 1922.

Leopold Zahn and Hermann von Wedderkop publish the first monographs on Klee: respectively, *Paul Klee: Leben, Werk, Geist [Paul Klee: Life, Work, Spirit]* and *Paul Klee.*

1921   Wilhelm Hausenstein publishes his monograph on Klee: *Kairuan oder eine Geschichte vom Maler Klee und von der Kunst dieses Zeitalters [Kairuan or the Story of the Painter Klee and the Art of His Time].*

January: Klee begins teaching at the Bauhaus, traveling from Munich.

March 15–April 12: Société Anonyme holds a group exhibition in its space on East 47th Street, where works by Klee are shown in America for the first time.

1922   **October:** Katherine Dreier visits Klee and Vasily Kandinsky at the Bauhaus, buying works from them and making plans to hold a one-person show for each.

1923

February: The magazine *Broom* publishes three drawings by Klee, along with five by George Grosz. These are the first reproductions of Klee's work published in America since Arthur Jerome Eddy's book in 1914.

October: Klee's work appears in "Modern German Art," an exhibition at the Anderson Galleries in New York organized by William Valentiner, who will become director of the Detroit Institute of Arts in 1924. It is the first exhibition in America of contemporary German art.

1924   **March 31:** Along with Vasily Kandinsky, Lionel Feininger, and Alexei Jawlensky, Klee signs an agreement to form The Blue Four. The group's founder, Galka Scheyer, intends to represent the group in America through lectures and exhibitions.

January 7–February 7: Under Katherine Dreier's direction, Société Anonyme holds the first one-person Klee exhibition in America at the Heckscher Building on West 57th Street, New York. It consists of twenty-six works.

　　　

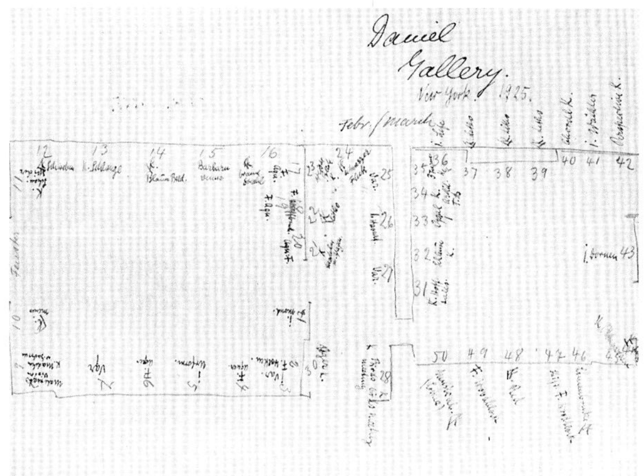

Fig. 91
Floor plan for "The Blue Four" exhibition
at Daniel Gallery, New York, February
20–March 10, 1925.

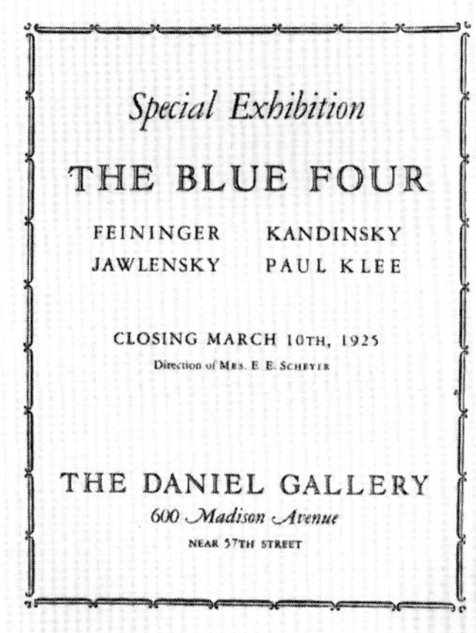

Fig. 92
Announcement for "The Blue Four" exhibition
at Daniel Gallery, New York, February 20–
March 10, 1925.

1924

February: The German gallery owner J. B. Neumann, who
has been showing Klee's work in Berlin since the 1910s,
establishes a gallery in New York.

Summer: Galka Scheyer arrives in New York. She receives
financial support from her brother Erich Scheyer who, with
his wife, Margrit, is a member of the Gesellschaft der Freunde
Junger Kunst [Society of Friends of New Art], founded by
the Klee collector Otto Ralfs in Braunschweig, Germany.

June: Galka Scheyer meets Dreier.

August: Scheyer circulates advertising material about
The Blue Four to around six hundred universities and four
hundred museums in the United States.

October: Scheyer works as an assistant with gallery owner
Neumann.

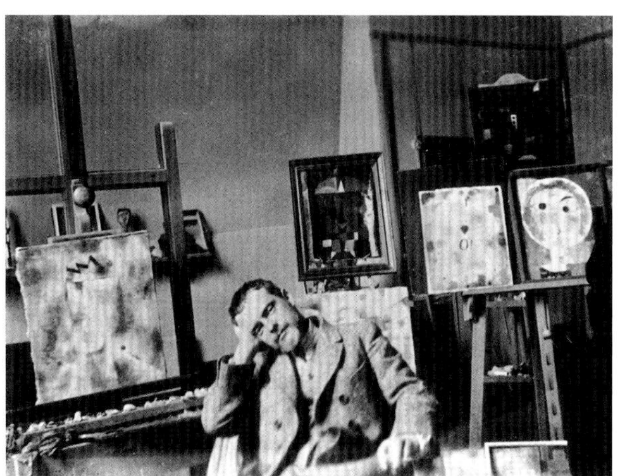

Fig. 90
Paul Klee in his atelier in Weimar, Germany, 1925.

1925　**June:** Klee begins teaching his classes at the Bauhaus and
for the following year commutes between Dessau and
Weimar, alternately spending a week in each.

July: Brunswick collector Otto Ralfs founds the
Klee-Gesellschaft [Klee Society].

October: The Galerie Vavin-Raspail in Paris presents Klee's
first one-person exhibition in France, which includes thirty-
nine works.

November: At Galerie Pierre in Paris, Klee's work appears
in a Surrealist exhibition for the first time.

February 20–March 10: Organized by Galka Scheyer, the
first exhibition of The Blue Four is held at the Daniel
Gallery, New York, with seventeen works by Klee.

August: Scheyer moves to San Francisco.

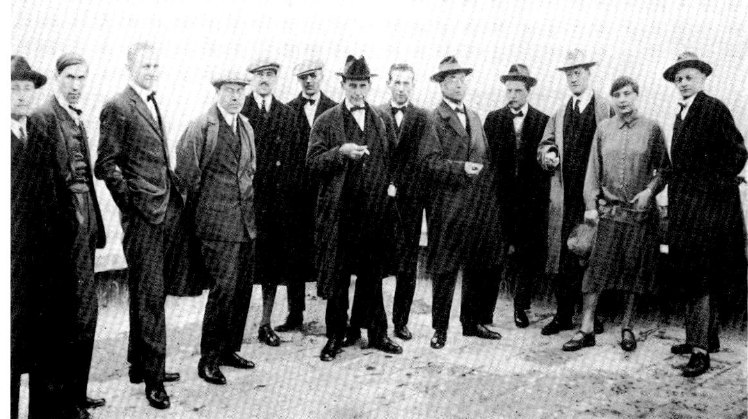

Fig. 93
Faculty of the Bauhaus, Dessau, 1926: Josef Albers, Hinnerk Scheper, Georg Muche, László Moholy-Nagy, Herbert Bayer, Joost Schmidt, Walter Gropius, Marcel Breuer, Vasily Kandinsky, Paul Klee, Lyonel Feininger, Gunta Stölzl, and Oskar Schlemmer.

Klee ends his exclusive contract with Hans Goltz and signs a contract with Alfred Flechtheim, a dealer with galleries in Düsseldorf and Berlin.

The Bauhaus moves to Dessau from Weimar.

Klee's *Pädagogisches Skizzenbuch [Pedagogical Sketchbook]* is published as volume 2 of a series of Bauhaus books published by Walter Gropius and Lázló Moholy-Nagy.

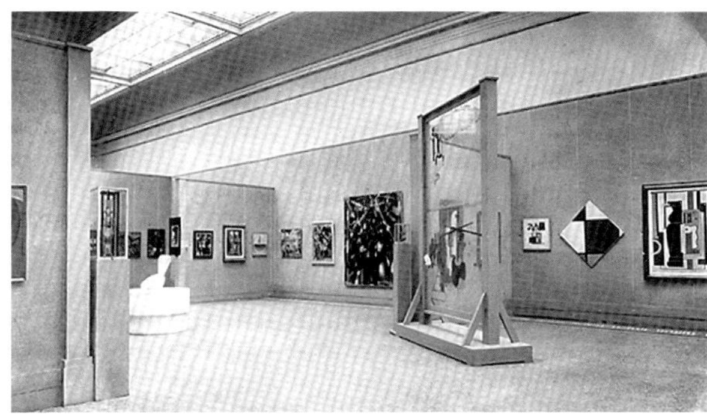

Fig. 94
Installation view, Société Anonyme's "An International Exhibition of Modern Art," Brooklyn Museum, New York, November 1926–January 1927.

1926 **July:** Klee and his family share a two-family home ("Meisterhaus") with Vasily and Nina Kandinsky, designed by Walter Gropius for the professors at the Bauhaus in Dessau.

May 2–31: A Blue Four exhibition is held at the Oakland Art Gallery in California. Galka Scheyer borrows works for the show from the collections of both Katherine Dreier and Arthur Jerome Eddy. The exhibition travels to several other venues, including the Los Angeles Museum.

November: Several works by Klee appear in "An International Exhibition of Modern Art," organized by Dreier that opens at the Brooklyn Museum, New York.

1927 **Early December:** Encouraged by the dealer J. B. Neumann, Alfred H. Barr Jr., the future founding director of The Museum of Modern Art, New York, visits Walter Gropius, Lyonel Feininger, Josef Albers, and Klee at the Bauhaus while he is on an extensive tour of Europe. He travels with Jere Abbott, who will later become his assistant at the museum.

December: A. E. Gallatin, a former member of the Société Anonyme, opens his Gallery of Living Art in New York. Although at this time Gallatin only owns two works by Klee, they are continually on view at his gallery in the company of those by the most important modernist masters.

The Baroness Hilla von Rebay arrives in America. While she is primarily concerned with promoting the work of Vasily Kandinsky and Rudolf Bauer, she is also committed to Klee. She influences Solomon R. Guggenheim, who is forming a collection for a possible museum of modern art, and by the time the Museum of Non-Objective Art (now the Solomon R. Guggenheim Museum) opens in 1939, the collection includes sixteen works by Klee.

1927

Galka Scheyer meets Marjorie Eaton, an artist and actress who buys pictures by Alexei Jawlensky, Vasily Kandinsky, and Klee.

1928

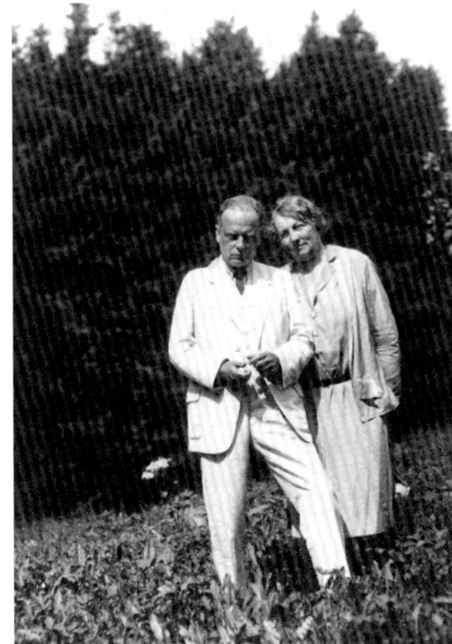

Fig. 95
Paul and Lily Klee in
Lucerne, Switzerland, 1930.

January 1: Galka Scheyer organizes the exhibition "Thirty European Artists" at the Oakland Art Gallery, which includes works by The Blue Four as well as by Ernst Ludwig Kirchner, Emil Nolde, Henri Matisse, and Pablo Picasso, among others.

Scheyer goes back to Germany and returns works she has had on consignment while acquiring new ones. She visits Klee at the Bauhaus.

1929 In honor of Klee's fiftieth birthday, the Galerie Alfred Flechtheim in Berlin and Galerie Neue Kunst Fides in Dresden each show a survey of his work.

Christian Zervos publishes the first non-German monograph on Klee, *Les expositions à Paris et ailleurs. Paul Klee [Paul Klee: The Exhibitions in Paris and Elsewhere]*, with *Cahiers d'Art* in Paris, with an introduction by Will Grohmann.

May: Galka Scheyer moves to Los Angeles.

August: The film director Josef von Sternberg buys works by The Blue Four.

Alfred Barr is appointed director of the newly founded Museum of Modern Art in New York.

1930 **April**: A major Klee exhibition at the Nationalgalerie, Berlin, features fifty-six works from the Otto Ralfs Collection.

July: Hilla Rebay and Solomon R. Guggenheim make a trip to the Bauhaus and purchase their first work by Klee.

March 13–April 2: The exhibition "Paul Klee" is the first one-person show of a living European painter at The Museum of Modern Art, New York. Organized by Alfred Barr in consultation with J. B. Neumann, the exhibition includes sixty-three works from 1919–30.

April: Klee is the most prominently featured artist in the exhibition "Modern German Art" at the Harvard Society for Contemporary Art, Cambridge, Massachusetts.

April–May: Galka Scheyer gets to know the collectors Walter and Louise Arensberg, who are close friends with Marcel Duchamp and played an important role in the New York Dada movement more than a decade earlier. They moved permanently from New York to Hollywood in 1927. They buy eight works by Klee. After making further purchases in the 1930s, the Arensbergs develop the largest collection of Klee works on the West Coast.

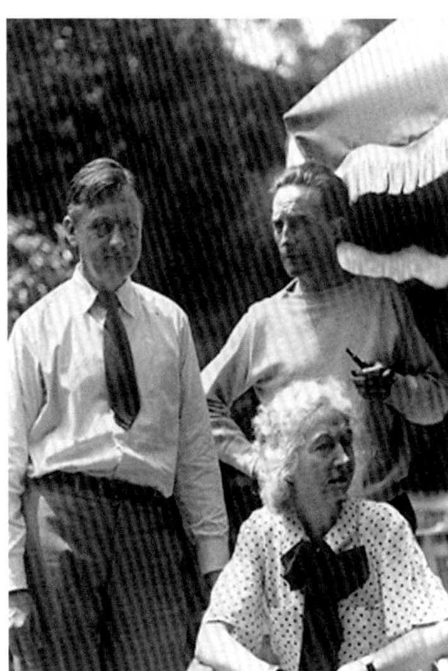

Fig. 96
Walter and Louise
Arensberg with Marcel
Duchamp, Arensberg residence, Los Angeles, 1936.

Albert C. Barnes, an influential collector of modern art, acquires his first three works by Klee: *Ort-Zeichen [Place-Signs]* (1926.151), *Sicilische Landschaft [Sicilian Landscape]* (1924.236), and *Nach einer Scizze aus Zürich [After a Sketch from Zurich]* (1914.123).

1931 Klee resigns his position at the Bauhaus in Dessau. He begins to teach painting in Düsseldorf at the Staatliche

Galka Scheyer meets the artist-couple Diego Rivera and Frida Kahlo in San Francisco.

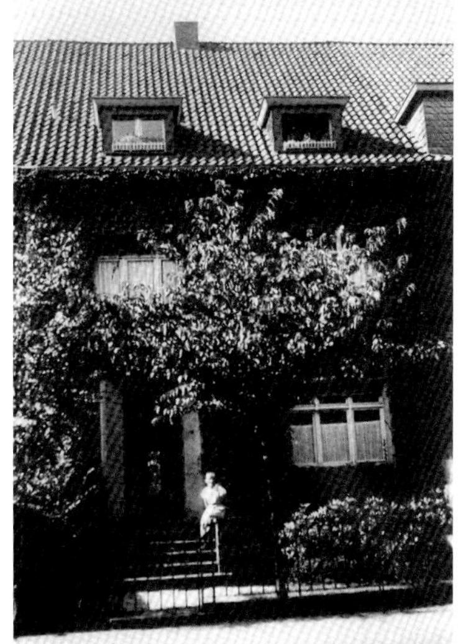

Fig. 97
Klee family residence,
Heinrichstrasse 36,
Düsseldorf, Germany, 1933.

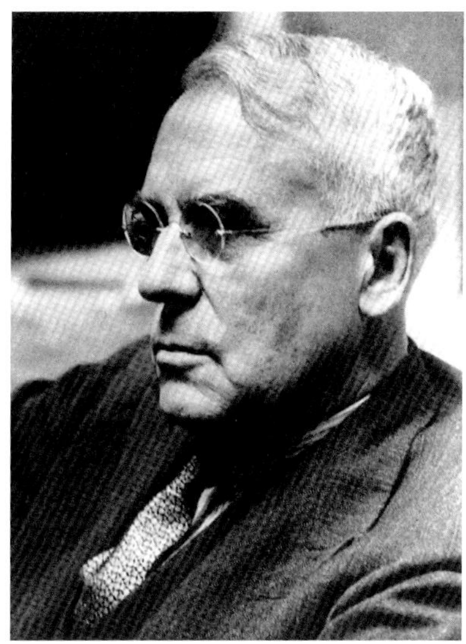

Fig. 99
Dr. Albert C. Barnes,
c. 1935.

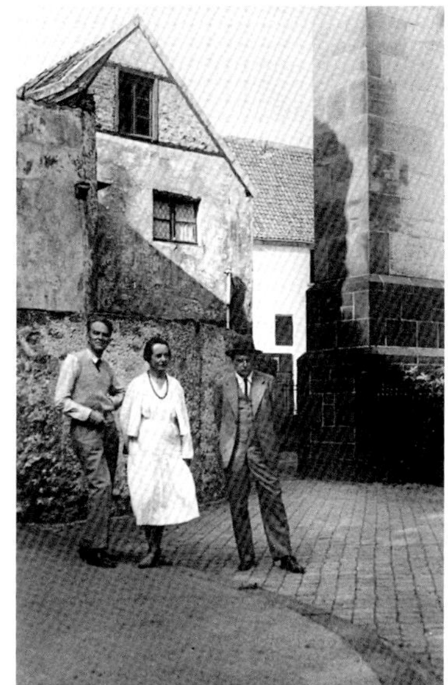

Fig. 98
Will and Eulein Grohmann
with Paul Klee in Wesel,
Germany, 1933.

Kunstakademie [Academy of Art], but he keeps his house
and studio in Dessau, commuting biweekly between the two
cities for the following two years.

The Museum of Modern Art, New York, acquires its first
work by Klee, the print *Seiltänzer [Tightrope Walker]*
(1923.138).

April: Scheyer collaborates with Rivera to organize a Blue
Four exhibition at the California Legion of Honor in San
Francisco.

November 24: The exhibition "Cuatro Azules [Blue Four],"
organized by Scheyer and Rivera, opens at the Biblioteca
National de Mexico in Mexico City. Rivera writes an essay
about Klee for the catalogue.

Two important collectors on the West Coast, Ruth Maitland
and Charlotte Mack, begin purchasing Blue Four works
from Scheyer.

Winter 1931 and Spring 1932: Klee's work circulates in
several important group exhibitions, including the "International Exhibition Illustrating the Most Recent Development in Abstract Art," Société Anonyme, The Buffalo Fine
Arts Academy, New York; "Bauhaus," Harvard Society
for Contemporary Art, Cambridge, Massachusetts; and
"German Painting and Sculpture," The Museum of
Modern Art, New York.

1932   **Fall:** On separate trips, Galka Scheyer and Alfred Barr each
return to Europe and are shocked to witness the radical
transformation of the German art world as Hitler gains power.

April 1–15: An exhibition of The Blue Four is held at the
Arts Club of Chicago with works loaned by Walter and
Louise Arensberg, Galka Scheyer, and Ruth Maitland.

1933   **January 30:** Adolf Hitler becomes Chancellor of Germany.

March: National Socialists search Klee's Dessau apartment.

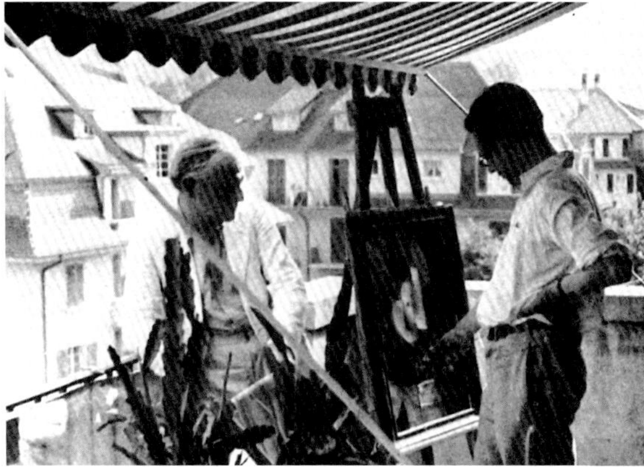

Fig. 100
Paul and Felix Klee on balcony of apartment, Kistlerweg 6, Bern,
Switzerland, 1934.

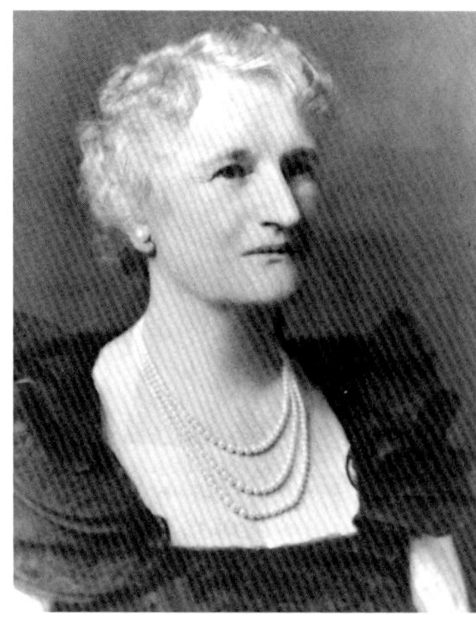

Fig. 101
Abby Aldrich (Mrs. John D.)
Rockefeller Jr., c. 1932.

1933   **April 21**: Klee is suspended from the Düsseldorf academy by the new Nazi-appointed director.

June: Klee sends eighteen paintings and fifty-one colored works on paper to Galka Scheyer in Hollywood.

October: Klee signs an exclusive contract with Daniel Henry Kahnweiler, owner of Galerie Simon in Paris.

December 24: Klee emigrates to Bern.

Josef and Anni Albers emigrate to America, where they become teachers at Black Mountain College in North Carolina. As a colleague and admirer of Klee, Josef Albers often discusses Klee's work with his students, influencing a generation of American painters, including Willem de Kooning and Robert Rauschenberg.

October: An exhibition of The Blue Four, organized by Galka Scheyer, opens at the Los Angeles Museum, with the eighteen paintings and twenty-two of the watercolors Klee sent her the previous June.

1934   **January 1**: Klee's position at the Düsseldorf academy is officially withdrawn.

Spring: The Mayor Gallery in London holds the first exhibition of Klee's work in the United Kingdom.

The Nazis confiscate Will Grohmann's new book on Klee's drawings: *Paul Klee: Handzeichnungen 1921–1930 [Paul Klee: Drawings 1921–1930]*.

Klee's dealer, Daniel Henry Kahnweiler, grants J. B. Neumann exclusive representation of Klee's work in New York for one year.

1935   **February–March**: The Kunsthalle Bern presents a major exhibition of Klee's work from 1919–34, which includes 273 works.

August: Klee becomes seriously ill and is later diagnosed with scleroderma, a progressive disease that will eventually prove fatal.

March: J. B. Neumann opens his first one-person exhibition of Klee's work at his New York gallery, New Art Circle. The exhibition takes place in two parts: paintings from March 2–16 and watercolors from March 18–30.

May: Galka Scheyer begins loaning Blue Four works as props for Hollywood films.

October: Professor Alfred Salmony asks Klee to direct a summer course at Mills College in California; Klee refuses the offer.

Abby Aldrich Rockefeller, a critical supporter of The Museum of Modern Art, New York, donates *Sklaverei [Slavery]* (1925.148) to the museum, its first unique work by Klee.

1936 Due to his illness, Klee is forced to stop working for most of the year.

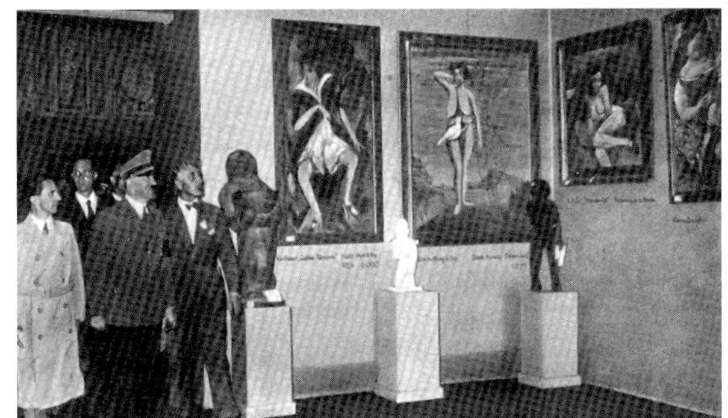

Fig. 103
Adolph Hitler attends the exhibition "Entartete Kunst," Munich, 1937.

1937 Klee's health stabilizes over the year and he resumes work.

July: The traveling exhibition "Entartete Kunst [Degenerate Art]," organized by the Nazis, opens in Munich. It includes seventeen works by Klee.

The Nazis systematically remove modern art from museum collections throughout Germany, including over a hundred works by Klee.

1938

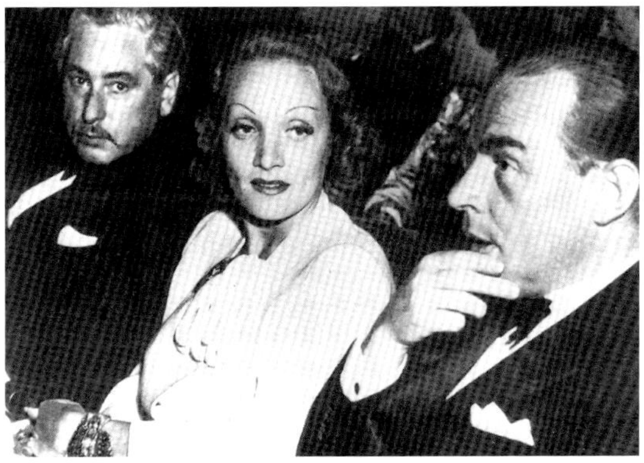

Fig. 102
Director Josef von Sternberg (a Klee collector), actress Marlene Dietrich, and author Erich Maria Remarque, Hotel Eden Roc at the French Riviera, 1939.

From 1935 on, Klee is featured prominently in at least one and often several exhibitions a year in major American cities, including New York, Chicago, San Francisco, and Los Angeles.

January 21–February 11: The Wadsworth Atheneum in Hartford, Connecticut, presents a Klee exhibition that features fifty works on loan from J. B. Neumann.

July: The gallery owner Karl Nierendorf, an associate of Neumann's, moves from Berlin to Los Angeles. He begins to work closely with Galka Scheyer.

Substantial groups of Klee's work are shown at The Museum of Modern Art, New York, in two of the most important surveys of avant-garde art to date: "Cubism and Abstract Art" from March 2–April 17 and "Fantastic Art, Dada, Surrealism" from December 7–January 17, 1937.

January 12–February 26: The exhibition "Paul Klee" at the San Francisco Museum of Art includes sixty-four works on loan from Galka Scheyer.

Karl Nierendorf cancels his plan to open a gallery in California and establishes himself in New York. He helps to organize "Recent Pictures by Paul Klee" at the Howard Putzel Gallery in Los Angeles, and he opens "Three Masters of the Bauhaus: Klee, Kandinsky and Feininger" at his own gallery in New York. Tension grows between Nierendorf and Scheyer, and she tries to renew exclusive contracts with Klee and Vasily Kandinsky; both artists refuse.

Howard Putzel, director of the Stanley Rose Gallery and a close friend of both Walter and Louise Arensberg and Marcel Duchamp, gives Klee a one-person show.

Curt Valentin moves his Buchholz Galerie from Berlin to New York. He becomes a competitor with both Nierendorf and J. B. Neumann.

January: Karl Nierendorf opens his first one-person exhibition of Klee at his New York gallery.

Galka Scheyer ends her contract with Nierendorf.

February: Daniel Henry Kahnweiler grants exclusive American representation of Klee to Nierendorf, though Scheyer retains the right to acquire new works directly from Klee.

March 23–April 23: Curt Valentin opens his first one-person exhibition of Klee's work at the Buchholz Gallery, which includes seventy-five works.

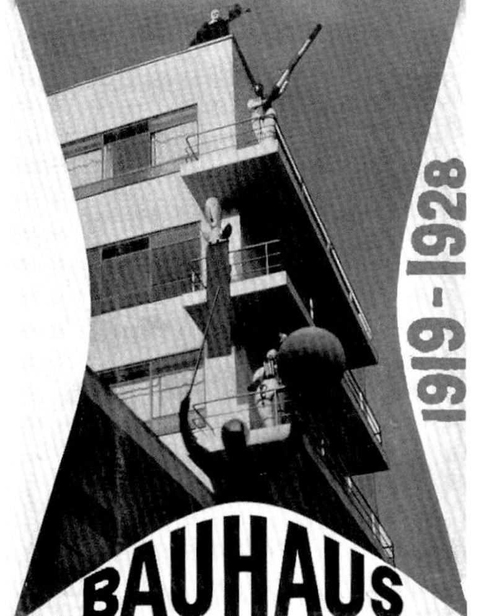

Fig. 104
Cover of the exhibition catalogue *Bauhaus: 1919–1928* (New York: The Museum of Modern Art, 1938).

July: Scheyer befriends Valentin.

The exhibition "Bauhaus, 1919–1928" opens at The Museum of Modern Art, New York. Lyonel Feininger writes Klee a letter from the United States regarding the exhibition and emphasizes Klee's success in America.

Fall: Valentin begins receiving Klee works confiscated from German collections through his Berlin business partner Karl Buchholz, who has received orders from the "Commission for the Utilization of the Products of Degenerate Art" to sell the work for foreign currency; Valentin continues to acquire such works through June 1941.

October–November: The Nierendorf Gallery opens an exhibition of sixty-two works by Klee.

November 1–26: Valentin opens his second one-person Klee exhibition at the Buchholz Gallery with thirty-seven works.

Regularly from 1938 on, gallery owner J. B. Neumann and art dealers Nierendorf and Valentin separately organize exhibitions of Klee's work in New York and other American cities.

1939

June 30: Works of art exhibited in the "Entartete Kunst" exhibition and confiscated from German museums are auctioned at the Galerie Fischer, Lucerne. Curt Valentin offers Galka Scheyer several pictures by Klee, which he bought at the auction.

Despite his illness, Klee produces an enormous number of works.

January–May: Supported by Galka Scheyer, John Cage organizes several exhibitions of The Blue Four in Seattle and Tacoma, Washington.

July: Scheyer and Karl Nierendorf resolve their conflict.

October: Nierendorf opens a permanent Klee room in his gallery.

The United States and Switzerland become the only remaining markets for Klee's work.

The Museum of Modern Art, New York, acquires two Klee works that were confiscated by the Nazis from public collections in Germany: *Die Zwitscher-Maschine [The Twittering Machine]* (1922.151) and *Um den Fisch [Around the Fish]* (1926.124).

1940

February: In honor of Klee's sixtieth birthday, the Kunsthaus Zurich holds a major exhibition of his works from 1935–40. It is the only presentation of Klee's later works that he himself conceived.

Although severely ill, Klee continues working until May 10.

June 29: Klee dies at a hospital in Muralto-Locarno, Switzerland.

Fall: Curt Valentin's Buchholz Gallery, in association with the Marian Willard Gallery, holds a memorial exhibition that includes a hundred works by Klee from 1913–39. The exhibition catalogue includes an introduction by James Johnson Sweeney, which emphasizes the importance of Klee's presence in America.

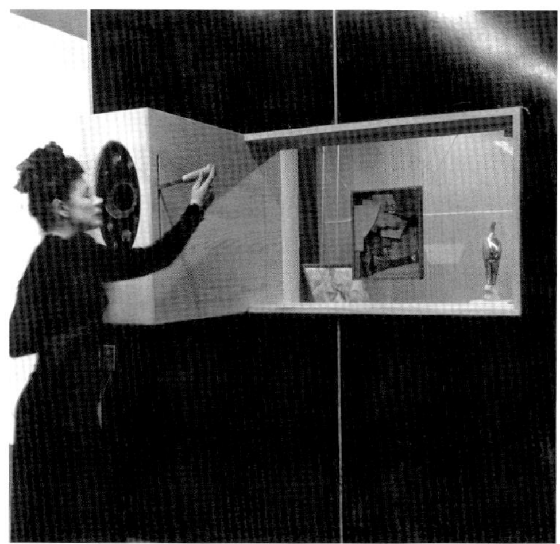

Fig. 105
Buffie Johnson lifts the lever on the shadowbox viewing mechanism containing Paul Klee's *Magic Garden* (1926), Art of This Century, New York, 1942.

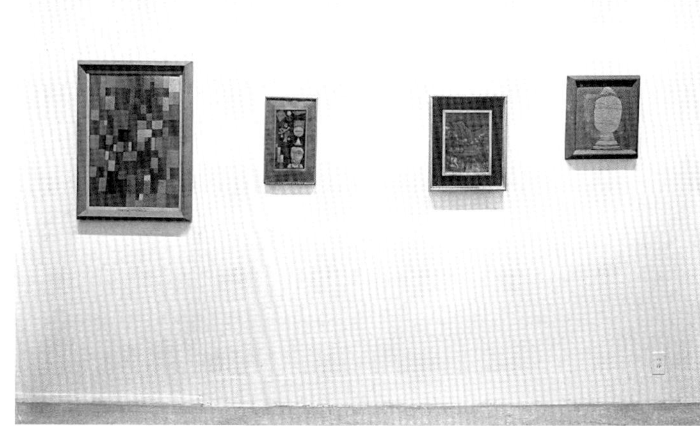

Fig. 106
Installation view of the exhibition "Paul Klee," The Museum of Modern Art, New York, December 20, 1949–February 19, 1950.

1941

April 14–May 5: "Paul Klee Memorial Exhibition" opens at the San Francisco Museum of Art and travels to several venues, including The Museum of Modern Art, New York.

Karl Nierendorf's book *Paul Klee: Paintings, Watercolors 1913 to 1939* is published.

1942

Frederick Kiesler installs his "Klee paternoster" and a shadowbox viewing mechanism at Peggy Guggenheim's Art of This Century gallery. In the first, Klee's works are mounted on an automated conveyor belt that displays each work for ten seconds and in the latter, they are viewed through a lever-operated peephole.

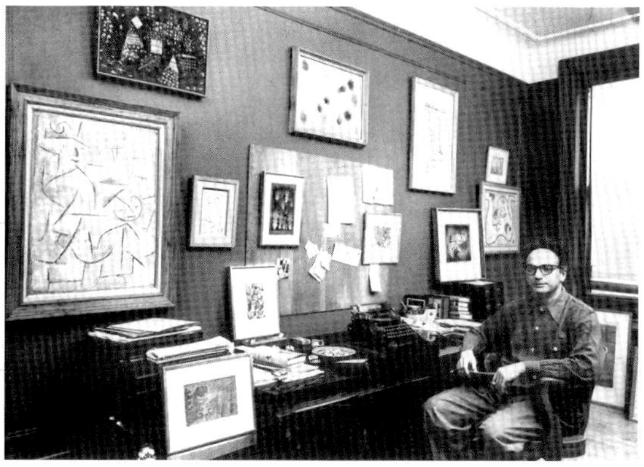

1944

Klee's *Pedagogical Sketchbook* is translated into English for the first time and becomes influential for American artists.

1948

Duncan Phillips, who began collecting Klee's work in 1930, opens a small room dedicated to Klee's paintings in the Phillips Collection. Visitors include members of an important generation of American artists: Kenneth Noland, Morris Louis, Mark Tobey, and Mark Rothko.

Fig. 107
Playwright Clifford Odets in his study with a number of Klee works from his collection, New York, 1950.

1949–1950

December 20, 1949–February 14, 1950: The exhibition "Paintings, Drawings, Prints by Paul Klee," consisting of 202 works, organized by the Klee Foundation, Bern, Switzerland, with additions from American collections, is presented at The Museum of Modern Art, New York. The exhibition travels to the Cincinnati Museum Association, the Detroit Institute of Arts, the Portland Art Museum in Oregon, the City Art Museum of St. Louis, the San Francisco Museum of Art, and The Phillips Collection in Washington, D.C.

This list refrences all known exhibitions of Klee's work that took place in America between 1921 and 2003. Please see the Paul Klee Catalogue Raisonné *for a complete exhibition history.*

This list is based on the Paul Klee Catalogue Raisonné *exhibition bibliography.*

1921

"14th Exhibition, Société Anonyme," Galleries of the Société Anonyme, New York, March 15–April 12.

1923

"22nd Exhibition, Société Anonyme [Graphic Arts]," Galleries of the Société Anonyme, New York, February 5–12.

"Modern German Art," The Anderson Galleries, New York, October 1–20 (nine works).

1924

"Paul Klee: 28th Exhibition of Modern Art," Galleries of the Société Anonyme, New York, January 7–February 7 (twenty-six works).

1925

"The Blue Four," Daniel Gallery, New York, February 20–March 10 (nineteen works).

1926

"Graphic Art of the Blue Four," Paul Elder Gallery, California School of Fine Arts, San Francisco, January 18–23.

"The Blue Four," Oakland Art Gallery, Oakland, California, May 2–31, extended to June 15; traveled to Los Angeles Museum, Los Angeles, October; University of California, Southern Branch, Los Angeles, October; California School of Fine Arts, San Francisco, March 1–20, 1927; Fine Arts Gallery of San Diego, San Diego, April; Portland Art Association, Portland Museum of Art, Portland, Oregon, April; and Spokane Art Association, Grace Campbell Memorial Building, Spokane, Washington, May 15–31 (twenty-one works).

"Painting, Sculpture and Prints," Sesquicentennial International Exposition, Department of Fine Arts, Philadelphia, January 6–December 1.

"Ausstellung von Gemälden jüngerer Künstler aus Deutschland, England, Frankreich und den Vereinigten Staaten [Exhibition of Paintings by Younger Artists from Germany, England, France, and the United States]," Nationalgalerie, Berlin, July 22–August; traveled to Kunsthalle Bern, Bern, Switzerland, September 5–26; Chenil Galleries, London, December; Galerie Bernheim Jeune, Paris, January 1927; and Grand Central Art Galleries, New York, March (three works).

"International Exhibition of Modern Art," assembled by Société Anonyme, Brooklyn Museum, New York, November 19–January 9, 1927; traveled to Anderson Galleries, New York, January 25–February 5; Albright Art Gallery, Buffalo, New York, February 25–March 20; and Art Gallery of Toronto, Toronto (four to seven works).

1927

"48th Exhibition, Société Anonyme," Cosmopolitan Club, New York, March 15, 1927.

"European Modernists," Los Angeles Museum, Los Angeles, April 1927 (seven works).

"The Blue Four," Henry Art Gallery, University of Washington, Seattle, Fall 1927.

1928

"Thirty European Modernists," Oakland Art Gallery, Oakland, California, January 4–29 (six works).

"50th Exhibition, Société Anonyme," Arts Council Gallery at the Barbizon Hotel, New York, February 20–March 10.

"51st Exhibition, Société Anonyme," The Worker's Center, New York, May 7–21.

"52nd Exhibition, Société Anonyme," Women's City Club of New York, October 4–November 1.

"Reproductions Showing the Development of Art During the Past One Hundred Years," The Berkeley Art Museum, Berkeley, California, December 15–January 15, 1929 (two reproductions).

"The Blue Four," Warenhaus Hales, San Francisco; traveled to Oakland, Sacramento, and San Jose, California.

1929

"53rd Exhibition, Société Anonyme," Daniel Galleries, New York, January 7–19.

"The Blue Four," Oakland Art Gallery, Oakland, California, April.

"The Ninth International Exhibition: Watercolors, Pastels, Drawings and Miniatures," The Art Institute of Chicago, Chicago, May 2–June 2 (one work).

Group exhibition, Brummer Galleries, New York, November.

1930

"Loan Exhibition of Modern Drawings and Sculpture, Privately Owned by Chicagoans," The Arts Club of Chicago, Chicago, January 3–17 (two works).

"Exhibition of Modern German Prints," Verein deutscher Buchkünstler [Association of German Book Artists], Art Center, New York, after January 5; traveled to Detroit Institute of Arts, Detroit; museums in Toledo, Ohio, and Cambridge, Massachusetts; and Carnegie Institute, Pittsburgh, May.

"Paul Klee," The Museum of Modern Art, New York, March 13–April 2 (sixty-three works).

"Modern German Art," The Harvard Society for Contemporary Art, Cambridge, Massachusetts, April 18–May 10 (ten works).

"The Blue Four," Braxton Gallery, Hollywood, California, Kandinsky, March 1–15; Jawlensky, March 16–31; Feininger, April 15–30; and Klee, May 1–15 (thirty-eight works).

"The Blue Four," Braxton Gallery, Hollywood, California, after June 1.

"Summer Exhibition: Retrospective," The Museum of Modern Art, New York, June 15–late September (two works).

"Paintings: Paul Klee, Beckmann, Lee Gatch, Hilaire Hiler, Rouault, etc.," New Art Circle, J. B. Neumann, New York, Summer.

"Paintings, Watercolors and Drawings," New Art Circle, J. B. Neumann, New York, August.

"Pictures Lent by the Metropolitan Museum and the Société Anonyme, Inc.," 59th Exhibition, Société Anonyme, Rand School of Social Science, New York, November 10–December 10.

"Modern German Painters," Penthouse S. P. R. Galleries, New York, November 17–December 18.

"The Staatliches [National] Bauhaus, Dessau," The Harvard Society for Contemporary Art, Cambridge, Massachusetts, December 13–January 17, 1931.

1931

"Special Exhibition Arranged in Honor of the Opening of the New Building of the New School," Société Anonyme, New School of Social Research, New York, January 1–February 10.

"62nd Exhibition, Société Anonyme," Rand School of Social Science, New York, January 5–March 16.

"Exhibition of Water Color Paintings, Pastels and Drawings by American and Foreign Artists and Miniatures by the Brooklyn Society of Miniature Painters," Brooklyn Museum, New York, January 23–February 24 (seven works).

"International Exhibition Illustrating the Most Recent Development in Abstract Art," Société Anonyme, The Buffalo Fine Arts Academy, Albright Art Gallery, Buffalo, New York, February 18–March 8 (four works).

Works from the Dessau Bauhaus, Becker Gallery, New York, February.

"Bauhaus, Dessau, Germany," The Arts Club of Chicago, Chicago, March 13–28.

"German Painting and Sculpture," The Museum of Modern Art, New York, March 13–April 26 (five works).

"International Competitive Print Exhibition," The Cleveland Museum of Art, Cleveland, March 18–April 15 (one work).

"The Blue Four," California Palace of the Legion of Honor, San Francisco, Kandinsky and Feininger, April 8–22; Jawlensky and Klee, April 23–May 8 (thirty-one works).

"The Blue Four," Oakland Art Gallery, Oakland, California, August–September 14 (thirty-seven works).

"Living Artists," Pennsylvania Museum of Art, Philadelphia, November 20–January 1, 1932.

"Cuatro Azules [The Blue Four]," Biblioteca Nacional, Mexico City, November 24–December 1.

1932

"The Blue Four," Faulkner Memorial Art Gallery, Santa Barbara, California, March 3–13 (twenty-five works).

"First International Exhibition of Etching and Engraving," Art Institute of Chicago, Chicago, March 24–May 15.

"12th International Exhibition of Watercolors, Pastels, Drawings and Monotypes," Art Institute of Chicago, Chicago, March 31–May 30.

"The Blue Four," The Arts Club of Chicago, Chicago, April 1–15 (thirty-seven works).

"The Blue Four," Wiebolt Hall, University of Chicago, Chicago, April.

"Outdoor Life," New Art Circle, J. B. Neumann, New York, April.

"Modern versus Academic Exhibition," Ilsley Galleries, Los Angeles, September 12–October 1 (two works).

1933

International exhibition, College Art Association, Rockefeller Center, New York, February.

Exhibition of contemporary German watercolors and graphics, International Art Center, Roerich Museum, New York, March 1–27.

"College Art Association, International 1933," The Cleveland Museum of Art, Cleveland, March 8–April 8 (one work).

"A Century of Progress," The Art Institute of Chicago, Chicago, June 1–November 1 (one work).

"England, France, Germany: Water Colors," Smith College Museum of Art, Northampton, Massachusetts, June (one work).

"Summer Exhibition of Painting and Sculpture," The Museum of Modern Art, New York, July 10–September 30.

"The Blue Four," Los Angeles Museum, Los Angeles, October (forty works).

"The Blue Four," University of California, Los Angeles, November.

1934

"The Blue Four," Oakland Art Gallery, Oakland, California, February.

"13th International Exhibition of Watercolors," The Art Institute of Chicago, Chicago, March 29–April 29 (two works).

"International Exhibition of Contemporary Prints: A Century of Progress," The Art Institute of Chicago, Chicago, June 1–November 1 (two works).

Group shows of American and French paintings and German watercolors, Smith College Museum of Art, Northampton, Massachusetts, Summer.

"8 Modes of Modern Painting," College Art Association, Julien Levy Gallery, New York, Fall (one work).

"The Blue Four," Hansen Music Company, Hollywood, California, November 17.

"Modern Works of Art," Fifth Anniversary Exhibition, The Museum of Modern Art, New York, November 20–January 20, 1935 (two works).

1935

"The Blue Four," Oakland Art Gallery, Oakland, California, January.

"8 Modes of Modern Painting," The Cleveland Museum of Art, Cleveland, February 19–March 24 (two works).

"Twelfth Exhibition of Water Colors and Pastels," The Cleveland Museum of Art, Cleveland, February 20–March 24 (three works).

"Paul Klee at Neumann's," New Art Circle, J. B. Neumann, New York, Paintings, March 2–16; Watercolors, March 18–30.

"Summer Exhibition: The Museum Collection and a Private Collection on Loan," The Museum of Modern Art, New York, June 4–September 24.

"From the Collection of Josef von Sternberg," Los Angeles Museum, Exposition Park, Los Angeles, June 16–July 31 (one work).

"Paintings by Paul Klee," Hollywood Gallery of Modern Art, Hollywood, California, after July 31; Oakland Art Gallery, Oakland, California, September 1–29; San Francisco, October(?).

Ausstellung der Société Anonyme [exhibition of Société Anonyme], Black Mountain College, Black Mountain, North Carolina, October–June 1936.

"Wassily Kandinsky, Paul Klee, Max Weber," New Art Circle, J. B. Neumann, New York, November 4–16 (23?).

1936

"The Art of Today," Albright Art Gallery, Buffalo, New York, January 3–31 (one work).

"Paul Klee," Wadsworth Atheneum, Hartford, Connecticut, January 21–February 11 (fifty works).

"The Blue Four," Hanson Music Company, San Francisco, January.

"Exhibition of Twentieth Century Painting," The Society of the Four Arts, Palm Beach, Florida, February 28–March 15.

"Solomon R. Guggenheim Collection of Non-Objective Paintings," Gibbes Memorial Art Gallery, Charleston, South Carolina, March 1–April 12 (one work).

"Cubism and Abstract Art," The Museum of Modern Art, New York, March 2–April 19; traveled to Cincinnati Art Museum, Cincinnati; San Francisco Museum of Modern Art, San Francisco, July 27–August 27; and The Cleveland Museum of Art, Cleveland, January 8–February 7, 1937 (seven works).

Group exhibition, New Art Circle, J. B. Neumann, New York, Summer.

"Modern Water Colors, Drawings and Prints from the Museum of Modern Art and Private Collections," Russel A. Alger House, Detroit Institute of Arts, Detroit, October 12–November 15 (one work).

"Max Beckmann, Paul Klee, Vassily Kandinsky, Georges Rouault," New Art Circle, J. B. Neumann, New York, October.

"Fantastic Art, Dada, Surrealism," The Museum of Modern Art, New York, December 7–January 17, 1937; traveled to San Francisco Museum of Art, San Francisco, August 6–31, 1937 (nine works).

"Museum of Living Art: A. E. Gallatin Collection," New York University, New York, December (two works).

1937

"Paul Klee," San Francisco Museum of Art, San Francisco, January 12–February 26 (sixty-six works).

Group exhibition, New Art Circle, J. B. Neumann, New York, January 25–February 8.

"Solomon R. Guggenheim Collection of Non-Objective Paintings," Philadelphia Art Alliance, Philadelphia, February 8–28.

"Contemporary Art," Nierendorf Gallery, New York, February 13–March 15.

"Thirteenth Exhibition of Water Colors and Pastels," The Cleveland Museum of Art, Cleveland, March 10–April 18 (one work).

"International Water Color Exhibition," The Art Institute of Chicago, Chicago, March 18–May 16 (four works); traveled to The Toledo Museum of Art, Toledo, Ohio, September 5–26 (one work).

"Modern Art," Mills College Art Gallery, Oakland, California, April 11–May 15 (three works).

"German Art," Buchholz Gallery, Curt Valentin, New York, May 10–June 4.

Group exhibition, New Art Circle, J. B. Neumann, New York, May–Summer.

"Selected Exhibition of the Walter P. Chrysler, Jr., Collection," Detroit Institute of Arts, Detroit, October 5–31 (two works).

"Recent Pictures by Paul Klee," Putzel Gallery, Hollywood, California, November 15–December (thirty-nine works).

"Kandinsky, Klee, Feininger: Paintings," Nierendorf Gallery, New York, December 18–31.

"Seventy-Five Selected Prints," Buchholz Gallery, Curt Valentin, late December–January 1938.

"Paul Klee," East River Gallery, Marian Willard, New York.

"Museum of Living Art," A. E. Gallatin Collection, New York University, New York (one work).

1938

"Solomon R. Guggenheim Collection of Non-Objective Paintings," Gibbes Memorial Art Gallery, Charleston, South Carolina, March 7–April 17 (five works).

"Modern German Painting," Columbus Gallery of Modern Art, Columbus, March 8–April 4.

"Paul Klee," Buchholz Gallery, Curt Valentin, New York, March 23–April 23 (seventy-five works).

"Klee, Léger, Kandinsky: Paintings," Nierendorf Gallery, New York, March 28–April 30.

Group exhibition of paintings and watercolors, Katharine Kuh Gallery, Chicago, April 1–30.

"International Water Color Exhibition," The Art Institute of Chicago, Chicago, April 28–May 30 (one work).

"Oils, Watercolors and Prints by Paul Klee," Institute of Arts, The Alger House, Detroit, May 8–June 12.

Exhibition of works by Klee, Kandinsky, and Feininger, Nierendorf Gallery, New York, June 21–July 15.

"Exhibition of 20th Century (Banned) German Art," New Burlington Gallery, London, July; traveled to City Arts Gallery, Leeds, England, early 1939; Milwaukee Art Institute, Milwaukee, June 1–25; City Art Museum, St. Louis, September 1–25; Smith College Museum of Art, Northampton, Massachusetts, October 6–25; William Rockhill Nelson Gallery of Art, Kansas City, through November 25; Albright Art Gallery, Buffalo, New York, December 1–22; San Francisco Museum of Art, San Francisco, February 6–26; The Dayton Art Institute, Dayton, Ohio, March 3–25; and Joslyn Art Museum, Omaha, April 9–19 (four works).

"Oskar Kokoschka: Paintings and Sculptures by Barlach, Beckmann, Braque, Despiau, Klee, Kolbe, Kollwitz, Laurens, Lehmbruck, Maillol, Marcks, Roesch, Sintenis," Buchholz Gallery, Curt Valentin, New York, September 22–October 12.

"International Water Color Exhibition," Detroit Institute of Arts, Detroit, October 4–30 (three works).

"Paul Klee: A Choice Collection of the Master's Work," Nierendorf Galleries, New York, October 24–November (sixty- two works).

"Paul Klee," Buchholz Gallery, Curt Valentin, New York, November 1–26 (thirty-seven works).

"Contemporary Movements in European Painting," The Toledo Museum of Art, Toledo, Ohio, November 6–December 11.

"Three Masters of the Bauhaus: Klee, Kandinsky, Feininger," Nierendorf Gallery, New York, December 10–March 1, 1939.

"Bauhaus 1919–1928," The Museum of Modern Art, New York, December–January 1939.

Works from the John Davenport Collection, San Francisco Museum of Modern Art, San Francisco, late December–February 1939 (one work).

"From Bosch to Klee," New Art Circle, J. B. Neumann, New York.

1939

"Solomon R. Guggenheim Collection of Non-Objective Paintings," Baltimore Museum of Art, Baltimore, January 6–29.

"Modern German Art," Springfield Museum of Fine Arts, Springfield, Massachusetts, January 10–30 (five works).

"Expressionism and Related Movements," The Cleveland Museum of Art, Cleveland, January 25–February 28 (five works).

"Paul Klee," Cornish School, Seattle, January 26–February 9; traveled to Tacoma Art Association, Galleries at the College of Puget Sound, Tacoma, Washington, February 13(?)–27 (twelve works).

Exhibition to commemorate the opening of The Room of Contemporary Art, Albright Art Gallery, Buffalo, New York, January.

"Four Europeans: Feininger, Hofer, Kandinsky, Klee," Nierendorf Gallery, New York, January.

"Contemporary Art," Golden Gate International Exposition, Department of Fine Arts, Division of Contemporary Painting and Sculpture, San Francisco, February 18–December 2 (three works).

"European Master Drawings of the Nineteenth and Twentieth Centuries," Mills College Art Gallery, Oakland, California, February 19–March 29; traveled to Seattle Art Museum, Seattle, April 5–May 7 (five works).

"The Sources of Modern Painting," loan exhibition assembled from American public and private collections by the Institute of Modern Art, Boston, Museum of Fine Arts, Boston, March 2–April 10; traveled to Wildenstein and Co., New York, April 25–May 20 (five works).

"Nature Forms in Art: Paintings," Nierendorf Gallery, New York, March 20–April 18.

"International Water Color Exhibition," The Art Institute of Chicago, Chicago, March 23–May 14 (three works).

"Contrasts," Nierendorf Gallery, New York, March 28–April 8 (one work).

Works by Franz Marc and other German Expressionists, Nierendorf Gallery, New York, c. April 20–May 15.

"Art in Our Time," The Museum of Modern Art, New York, May 8–October (two works).

"Contemporary European Painters & Sculptors," Buchholz Gallery, Curt Valentin, New York, May 9–27 (four works).

"Paul Klee," Neumann-Willard Gallery, New York, May 15–June 10 (twenty-seven works).

"Twentieth Century German Art," Milwaukee Art Institute, Milwaukee, June 1–25; traveled to St. Louis; Kansas City, November; Buffalo, New York, December 1–21; Portland, Oregon; and San Francisco.

"Art of Tomorrow," Solomon R. Guggenheim Collection of Non-Objective Paintings, Solomon R. Guggenheim Foundation, New York, after June 1.

"Collection of Dr. and Mrs. Leslie M. Maitland," Los Angeles Museum, Exposition Park, Los Angeles, July 1–September 20 (three works).

"Contemporary European Art," Buchholz Gallery, Curt Valentin, New York, September 18–October 5 (two works).

"Paul Klee," San Francisco Museum of Art, San Francisco, October 17–30 (forty-five works).

Comprehensive exhibition of abstract painting, Mills College Art Gallery, Oakland, California, October 19–December 3 (three works).

"The 1939 International Exhibition of Paintings," Carnegie Institute, Pittsburgh, October 19–December 10 (one work).

"Contemporary German Art," The Institute of Modern Art, Boston, November 2–December 9 (six works).

"Some New Forms of Beauty 1909–1936, A Selection of the Collection of the Société Anonyme–Museum of Modern Art: 1920," Anniversary Exhibition, The George Walter Vincent Smith Art Gallery, Springfield, Massachusetts, November 9–December 17 (four works).

"Exhibition of Modern Paintings from Cincinnati Collections," Cincinnati Art Museum, Cincinnati, November 10–December 10 (one work).

"Seven Centuries of Painting," California Palace of the Legion of Honor and M. H. de Young Memorial Museum, San Francisco, December 29–January 28, 1940 (one work).

Exhibition of paintings by Klee, Katharine Kuh Gallery, Chicago, December.

1940

"Contemporary Art: Paintings, Watercolors and Sculpture Owned in the San Francisco Bay Region," Fifth Anniversary Exhibition, San Francisco Museum of Art, San Francisco, January 18–February 5 (five works).

"Paul Klee," Germanic Museum, Harvard University, Cambridge, Massachusetts, February 28–March 27 (thirty-seven works).

"Paul Klee: An Exhibition in Honor of the Sixtieth Birthday of the Artist," Nierendorf Gallery, New York, February (forty-four works).

"Paul Klee," Stendahl Art Galleries, Los Angeles, March 11–30.

"Landmarks in Modern German Art," Buchholz Gallery, Curt Valentin, New York, April 2–27 (four works).

"The Nineteenth International Exhibition of Water Colors," The Art Institute of Chicago, Chicago, April 25–May 26 (thirty-two works).

"Documents of Modern Painting from the Collection of J. B. Neumann," New Art Circle, J. B. Neumann, New York, September 23–November 30 (two works).

"Paul Klee," Buchholz Gallery, Curt Valentin, and Willard Gallery, Marian Willard, New York, October 9–November 2 (100 works).

"Seventy-Five Selected Prints," Buchholz Gallery, Curt Valentin, New York, December 9–28.

"Art," Golden Gate International Exposition, Palace of Fine Arts, San Francisco (nine works).

1941

"Paul Klee: Memorial Exhibition," Smith College Museum of Art, Northampton, Massachusetts, January 7–22; traveled to Arts Club of Chicago, Chicago, January 31–February 28; Portland Art Museum, Portland, Oregon, March(?); San Francisco Museum of Art, San Francisco, April 14–May 5; Stendahl Art Galleries, Los Angeles, May 8–18; City Art Museum, St. Louis; Wellesley College, Wellesley, Massachusetts, October 14–November 2; The Museum of Modern Art, New York, June 30–July 27 (Smith College Museum of Art: sixty-four works; traveling venues: eighty-three works).

"Paul Klee," Art Students League of New York, Nierendorf Gallery, New York, January–February (forty-two works).

"The Blue Four," Academy of Arts, Honolulu, early Spring.

"Paul Klee," Nierendorf Gallery, New York, November (forty-one works).

1942

"Fifth Selection of Works by Paul Klee," Nierendorf Gallery, New York, March–June (thirty-seven works).

"Paintings by Paul Klee and Mobiles and Stabiles by Alexander Calder," Cincinnati Art Museum, Cincinnati, April 7–May 3 (forty-three works).

"A Memorial Exhibition of Paintings by Paul Klee," Phillips Memorial Gallery, New York.

1943

"Paul Klee, André Masson & Some Aspects of Ancient and Primitive Sculpture," Buchholz Gallery, Curt Valentin, New York, February 23–March 20 (twenty-seven works).

"Paul Klee," New Art Circle, J. B. Neumann, New York, October 4–30 (twenty-four works).

1944

"Modern Drawings," The Museum of Modern Art, New York, February (nine works).

"Paul Klee: Paintings, Drawings, Prints," The Philadelphia Art Alliance, 2nd Floor Galleries, Philadelphia, March 14–April 9 (ninety-seven works).

"The Blue Four: Feininger, Jawlensky, Kandinsky, Paul Klee," Buchholz Gallery, Curt Valentin, New York, October 31–November 25 (twenty-three works).

1945

"Works by Klee," Nierendorf Gallery, New York, March 8–April 8 (fifty-nine works).

1946

"A New Way to Paul Klee," Denver Art Museum, Denver, March 1–April 13 (sixty-nine works).

"Paul Klee," The Renaissance Society at the University of Chicago, Chicago, June 5–24 (fifty works).

1947

"Paul Klee," Nierendorf Gallery, New York, October (fifty-one works).

"20th Century Abstract Painting and Sculpture," Rhode Island School of Design, Providence, Rhode Island (nine works).

1948

"Paul Klee," Buchholz Gallery, Curt Valentin, New York, April 20–May 15 (forty works).

"Klee: 30 Years of Paintings, Water Colors, Drawings and Lithographs—and in a Klee-like mood, 2000 Years of Coptic, Persian, Chinese, European and Peruvian Textiles," The Modern Institute of Art, Beverly Hills, California, September 3–October 6 (ninety works).

"St. Louis Collections: An Exhibition of 20th Century Art," City Art Museum, St. Louis, September 20–October 25 (six works).

"Fifty Drawings by Paul Klee," Buchholz Gallery, Curt Valentin, New York, October 26–November 13 (fifty works).

1949

"Paintings, Drawings, and Prints by Paul Klee from the Klee Foundation, Berne, Switzerland, with Additions from American Collections," San Francisco Museum of Art, San Francisco, March 24–May 2; traveled to Portland Art Museum, Portland, Oregon, May 16–June 12; Detroit Institute of Arts, Detroit, September 15–October 9; City Art Museum, St. Louis, November 3–December 5; The Phillips Gallery, Washington, D.C., March 4–April 10, 1950; and Cincinnati Art Museum, Cincinnati, April 19–May 24 (202 works).

"20th Century Art from the Louise and Walter Arensberg Collection," The Art Institute of Chicago, Chicago, October 20–December 18 (nineteen works).

1950

"Paul Klee," Buchholz Gallery, Curt Valentin, New York, May 2–27 (sixty works).

"An Exhibit of Thirty Drawings by Paul Klee," Main Street Gallery, Chicago, October 9–November 15 (thirty works).

1951

"Klee: Sixty Unknown Drawings," Buchholz Gallery, Curt Valentin, New York, January 16–February 3 (sixty works).

"Klee, Kandinsky, Feininger," Woman's College Library Gallery, Duke University Arts Council, Durham, North Carolina, February 3–28 (seventeen works).

"Paintings by Paul Klee, 1879–1940," Society of the Four Arts, Palm Beach, Florida, March 9–April 1 (seventy-nine works).

1952

"Paul Klee," New Art Circle, J. B. Neumann, New York, April 13–May 30 (thirty-seven works).

"The Evolution of Painting from 1900 to 1952—Academism, Impressionism, Expressionism, Cubism, Abstraction to Non-Objectivity," Museum of Non-Objective Painting, Solomon R. Guggenheim Foundation, April 29 (thirty works).

1953

"Paul Klee," Curt Valentin Gallery, New York, September 29–October 24 (fifty-seven works).

1954

"Paul Klee: An Exhibition of Paintings and Drawings Commemorating the 75th Anniversary of His Birth," Saidenberg Gallery, New York, March 8–April 26 (forty-nine works).

1955

"Blaue Reiter: Exhibition of Painting and Graphic Works," Busch-Reisinger Museum, Harvard University, Cambridge, Massachusetts, January 21–February 24 (twenty-one works).

"Paul Klee (1879–1940)," Kleemann Galleries, New York, March 5–31 (thirty-five works).

"Paul Klee: Sixty-Six Unknown Drawings," Curt Valentin Gallery, New York, April 11–23 (sixty-six works).

"Works by Paul Klee from the Collection of Mrs. Edward Hulton," Tate Gallery, London, May 4–June 5; traveled to City Art Gallery, York, England, August; and The Arts Club, Chicago, November 8–December 6 (fifty-one works).

"Feininger, Jawlensky, Kandinsky, Paul Klee—The Blue Four: Galka E. Scheyer Collection," Pasadena Art Museum, Pasadena, California, May 27–August 30 (fifty-six works).

"40 Works by Paul Klee from the Collection of F. C. Schang," Minneapolis Institute of Arts, Minneapolis, through August 31 (forty works).

"Paul Klee," Saidenberg Gallery, New York, October 10–November 19.

1956

"15 Modern European Paintings and 16 Drawings by Paul Klee," Feigl Gallery, New York, April 11–May 15 (sixteen works).

"Selections from the Blue Four Galka E. Scheyer Collection Lent by the Pasadena Art Museum," Western Association of Art Museums, Fine Arts Gallery, University of British Columbia, Vancouver, July–August 31; traveled to Seattle Art Museum, Seattle, October 10–November 4; Portland Art Museum, Portland, Oregon; and Colorado Springs Fine Arts Center, Colorado Springs, Colorado, December 28–January 31, 1957 (thirteen works).

1957

"Modern Painting, Drawing and Sculpture: Collected by Louise and Joseph Pulitzer, Jr.," Knoedler and Company, New York, April 9–May 4; traveled to Fogg Art Museum, Harvard University, Cambridge, Massachusetts, May 16–September 15 (six works).

"Paul Klee," Third Biannual Exhibition of Paintings and Drawings, Saidenberg Gallery, New York, November 11–December 14 (forty-seven works).

1958

"Paul Klee: Watercolors and Drawings," World House Galleries, New York, April 22–May 17 (fifty works).

"Modern German Art/Moderne Deutsche Kunst," World House Galleries, New York, October 29–December 10 (nineteen works).

1960

"Paul Klee: Drawings and Watercolors," New Art Center Gallery, New York, January 18–February 20 (thirty-six works).

"The Collection of Frank and Ursula Laurens," Contemporary Arts Center, Cincinnati Art Museum, Cincinnati, February 4–March 6 (forty-six works).

"Paul Klee," World House Galleries, New York, March 8–April 2 (forty-nine works).

"The Colin Collection: Paintings, Watercolors, Drawings and Sculpture," Knoedler Gallery, New York, April 12–May 14 (seven works).

"Paul Klee," Museum of Fine Arts, Houston, April 19–May 22 (thirty-seven works).

"Paul Klee," Santa Barbara Museum of Art, Santa Barbara, California, April (fifty-two works).

"Paul Klee," Brandeis University, Waltham, Massachusetts, May 15–June 15 (thirty-seven works).

"Paul Klee: Private Collection James Gilvarry," Baltimore Museum of Art, Baltimore, June 12–September 4; traveled to Virginia Museum of Fine Arts, Richmond, Virginia, September 16–October 30 (twenty-one works).

1961

"The Maremont Collection," Institute of Design, Illinois Institute of Technology, Crown Hall, Chicago, April 5–30 (twenty-two works).

1962

"Paul Klee: Works from Chicago Collections," Arts Club of Chicago, Chicago, January 16–February 20 (sixty-six works).

"Paul Klee," The Obelisk Gallery, Washington, D.C., March 9–April 6 (sixty-six works).

"Homage to Paul Klee: Exhibition of Paul Klee from the Collection of Felix Klee." E. & A. Silberman Galleries, Inc., New York, April 4–21 (forty-two works).

"Paul Klee: An Exhibition from the Galka E. Scheyer Collection of the Pasadena Art Museum," University Art Gallery, University of California, Berkeley, May 3–27 (forty-two works).

"Paul Klee: Watercolors, Drawings," World House Galleries, New York, May 29–June 23 (twenty-two works).

"Gifts to the Albright Knox Art Gallery from A. Conger Goodyear," Albright Knox Art Gallery, Buffalo, New York, December 14–January 6, 1963 (three works).

1963

"Paul Klee: Exhibition of Paintings and Drawings," Saidenberg Gallery, New York, January 8–February 16 (thirty-nine works).

"20th Century Master Drawings," Solomon R. Guggenheim Museum, New York, November 6–January 5, 1964; traveled to University Gallery, University of Minnesota, Minneapolis, February 3–15; and Fogg Art Museum, Harvard University, Cambridge, Massachusetts, April 6–May 24 (three works).

1964

"Treasures of 20th Century Art from The Maremont Collection," Washington Gallery of Modern Art, Washington, D.C., April 1–May 3 (thirty-one works).

"Paintings, Drawings and Prints by Paul Klee from the James Gilvarry Collection," Krannert Art Museum, College of Fine and Applied Arts, University of Illinois, Champaign, Illinois, September 27–October 25 (thirty-five works).

1965

"Paul Klee," The Museum of Modern Art, New York, circulated 1965–67 (seventy-three works).

1966

"Paul Klee," Herron Museum of Art, Indianapolis, January 1–30 (twenty-six works).

"Works of Art by Bauhaus Faculty," Busch-Reisinger Museum, Harvard University, Cambridge, Massachusetts, November 1–December 16 (fifteen works).

"Klee, Kandinsky, Jawlensky: Works from the Bauhaus Period," School of Art Gallery, Ohio State University, Columbus, November 11–30 (ten works).

1967

"Paul Klee: Drawings," Saidenberg Gallery, New York, February 1–March 25 (thirty-eight works).

"Paul Klee 1879–1940: A Retrospective Exhibition," Solomon R. Guggenheim Museum, New York, February 17–April 30 (192 works).

"Paul Klee 1879–1940: A Retrospective Exhibition," Pasadena Art Museum, Pasadena, California, February 21–April 2; traveled to San Francisco Museum of Art, San Francisco, April 13–May 14; Columbus Gallery of Fine Arts, Columbus, May 25-June 25; The Cleveland Museum of Art, Cleveland, July 5–August 13; William Rockhill Nelson Gallery of Art, Kansas City, September 1–30; Baltimore Museum of Art, Baltimore, October 6–November 19; Washington University Gallery of Art, St. Louis, December 3–January 5, 1968; and Philadelphia Museum of Art, Philadelphia, January 15–February 15 (187 works).

"100 European Paintings & Drawings from the Collection of Mr. and Mrs. Leigh B. Block," National Gallery of Art, Washington, D.C., May 4–June 11; traveled to Los Angeles County Museum of Art, Los Angeles, September 21–November 2 (two works).

"Paul Klee: Oils, Watercolors, Gouaches, Drawings, Prints from the James Gilvarry Collection," The Art Gallery, University of California, Santa Barbara, California, October 5–November 12 (thirty-five works).

1968

"The Sirak Collection," J. B. Speed Art Museum, Louisville, Kentucky, October 22–December 1 (nine works).

1969

"Paul Klee: A Retrospective Exhibition," Saidenberg Gallery, New York, October 14–November 29 (fifty-six works).

1971

"Modern Painting, Drawing & Sculpture Collected by Louise and Joseph Pulitzer, Jr.," vol. 3, Fogg Art Museum, Harvard University, Cambridge, Massachusetts, November 15–January 3, 1972; traveled to Wadsworth Atheneum, Hartford, Connecticut, February 2–March 19, 1972 (one work).

1973

"The Private Collection of Martha Jackson," University of Maryland Art Gallery, Baltimore, June 22–September 30; traveled to Finch College Museum of Art, Chicago, October 16–November 25; and Albright Knox Art Gallery, Buffalo, New York, January 8–February 10, 1974 (one work).

"Paul Klee: Paintings and Watercolors from the Bauhaus Years, 1921–1931," Des Moines Art Center, Des Moines Iowa, September 18–October 28 (sixty-one works).

1976

"Bauhaus Color," High Museum of Art, Atlanta, January 31–March 14; traveled to Museum of Fine Arts, Houston, April 8–May 30; and Fine Arts Gallery of San Diego, San Diego, August 1–September 21 (eighteen works).

1977

"Paul Klee 1879–1940 in the Collection of the Solomon R. Guggenheim Museum," Solomon R. Guggenheim Museum, New York, June 24–September 5; traveled to Musée d'Art Contemporain, Montréal, September 18–October 23; Musée du Quebec, Quebec, November 3–December 4; Milwaukee Art Center, Milwaukee, February 2–March 18, 1978; and Berkeley Art Museum, Berkeley, California, April 11–June 4 (sixty-seven works).

"Paul Klee: The Late Years, 1930–1940," Serge Sabarsky Gallery, New York, Fall 1977 (thirty-four works).

1979

"Paul Klee Centennial: Prints and Transfer Drawings," The Museum of Modern Art, New York, January 8–April 3 (seventy-two works).

"Honoring the Centenary of the Birth of Paul Klee: An Exhibition in Oils, Watercolors, Mixed Media and Drawings by Paul Klee, Dating from 1913 to 1940," Saidenberg Gallery, New York, March 22–May 19 (fifty-four works).

"In Celebration of Paul Klee 1879–1940: Fifty Prints," Stanford University Museum of Art, Stanford, California, September 25–November 4 (fifty works).

"The Spirit of Surrealism," The Cleveland Museum of Art, Cleveland, October 3–November 25 (six works).

"Paul Klee 1879–1940: A Tribute in Celebration of the Artist's Centennial Year," Worthington Gallery, Chicago, October 12–December 1 (twenty-four works).

1980

"The Morton G. Neumann Family Collection: Selected Works," National Gallery of Art, Washington, D.C., August 31–December 31 (seventeen works).

1982

"Kandinsky und München: Begegnungen und Wandlungen, 1896–1914 [Kandinsky and Munich: Meetings and Transformations, 1896–1914]," Solomon R. Guggenheim Museum, New York, January 22–March 21; traveled to San Francisco Museum of Modern Art, San Francisco, April 22–June 20; and Städtische Galerie im Lenbachhaus, Munich, August 18–October 17 (seven works).

1983

"Klee: 1914–1940," Marisa del Re Gallery, New York, April (twenty works).

"The Graphic Legacy of Paul Klee," Bard College, Annandale-on-Hudson, New York, October 23–December 28 (125 works).

"Kandinsky: Russian and Bauhaus Years 1915–1933," Solomon R. Guggenheim Museum, New York, December 9–February 12, 1984; traveled to High Museum of Art, Atlanta, March 15–April 29 (twelve works).

1984

"The Spirit of Modernism—The Tremaine Collection: 20th Century Masters," Wadsworth Atheneum, Hartford, Connecticut, February 26–April 29 (six works).

"Paul Klee from the Guggenheim: The Bauhaus Years," Worcester Art Museum, Worcester, Massachusetts, September 11–February 28, 1985 (thirty-nine works).

"'Primitivism' in 20th Century Art," The Museum of Modern Art, New York, September 19–January 15, 1985; traveled to Detroit Institute of Arts, Detroit, February 27–May 19; and Dallas Museum of Art, Dallas, July 23–September 1 (sixteen works).

"Paul Klee: Selections from the Djerassi Collection," San Francisco Museum of Modern Art, San Francisco, December 9–July 7, 1985 (twenty-three works).

1985

"Drawings from the Collection of Mr. & Mrs. Eugene Victor Thaw," part 2, Pierpont Morgan Library, New York (one work).

1986

"Paul Klee: Figurative Graphics from the Djerassi Collection," San Francisco Museum of Modern Art, San Francisco, January 23–January 4, 1987 (thirty-two works).

1987

"Pattern & Process: Nature and Architecture in the Work of Paul Klee," San Francisco Museum of Modern Art, San Francisco, January 15–November 29 (twenty-six works).

"Paul Klee (1879–1940)," Achim Moeller Fine Art Ltd, New York, February 4–March 14 (twenty-three works).

"Paul Klee," The Museum of Modern Art, New York, February 12–May 5; traveled to The Cleveland Museum of Art, Cleveland, June 24–August 16; and Kunstmuseum Bern, Bern, Switzerland, September 25–January 3, 1988 (296 works).

1988

"From Liotard to Le Corbusier: 200 Years of Swiss Painting, 1730–1930," High Museum of Art, Atlanta, February 9–April 10 (six works).

"The In-Between World of Paul Klee," San Francisco Museum of Modern Art, San Francisco, February 11–July 31 (twenty-seven works).

1989

"Paul Klee: Faces and Figures," San Francisco Museum of Modern Art, San Francisco, June 27–April 15, 1990 (six works).

1990

"Paul Klee: The Bauhaus Years, 1921–1931," San Francisco Museum of Modern Art, San Francisco, May 31–October 21.

1991

"'Degenerated Art': The Fate of the Avant-Garde in Nazi Germany,"
Los Angeles County Museum of Art, Los Angeles, February 17–May 12;
traveled to The Art Institute of Chicago, Chicago, June 23–September 22;
International Gallery, Smithsonian Institution, Washington, D.C.,
October 8–January 12, 1992; and Altes Museum, Berlin, March 4–
May 31 (seven works).

1993

"Paul Klee," Busch-Reisinger Museum, Harvard University,
Cambridge, Massachusetts, April 17–June 13 (thirty-one works).

"Paul Klee at the Guggenheim Museum," Solomon R. Guggenheim
Museum, New York, May 7–September 19 (seventy-seven works).

1994

"A Piece of the Moon World: Paul Klee in Texas Collections,"
The Menil Collection, Houston, March 9–June 5 (thirty-six works).

"The Thaw Collection: Master Drawings and New Acquisitions,"
Pierpont Morgan Library, New York, September 21–January 22, 1995
(one work).

1998

"Paul Klee: Traces of Memory," Jan Krugier Gallery, New York,
May 6– July 23 (seventy-nine works).

1999

"New York Collects: Drawings and Watercolors 1900–1950," Pierpont
Morgan Library, New York, May 20–August 29 (five works).

2000

"Paul Klee: Recent Acquisitions of the Djerassi Collection," San Francisco
Museum of Modern Art, San Francisco, March 18–October 24.

"Paul Klee: Conductor of Color," San Francisco Museum of Modern
Art, San Francisco, November 2–April 3, 2001.

2001

"Paul Klee: Materials and Techniques," San Francisco Museum of
Modern Art, San Francisco, September 13–February 10, 2002.

"Neue Welten, Deutsche und österreichische Kunst, 1890–1940
[New Worlds: German and Austrian Art, 1890–1940]," Neue Galerie,
New York, November 16–February 18, 2002 (five works).

"A Century of Drawing: Work on Paper from Degas to LeWitt,"
National Gallery of Art, Washington, D.C., November 18–July 4, 2002
(four works).

2003

"A Passion for Paul Klee: The Djerassi Collection at San Francisco
Museum of Modern Art," San Francisco Museum of Modern Art,
San Francisco, March 1–June 8.

Selected Bibliography

compiled by SARAH ECKHARDT with CLARE ELLIOTT

Works have been selected from the complete bibliography of the Paul Klee Catalogue Raisonné *based on their relevance to Klee's reception in America.*

1914

Eddy, Arthur Jerome. *Cubists and Post-Impressionists,* 88, 114. Chicago: A. C. McClurg, 1914.

1923

Broom 4, no. 3 (February 1923): 171, 179, 181.

Kramrisch, Stella. "The New Art in Europe." *Vivabharati Quarterly* 1 (April 1923): 69–75.

Medgyes, Ladislas. "Comment." *Broom* 4, no. 3 (February 1923): 212–13.

1924

Cheney, Sheldon. *A Primer of Modern Art.* New York: Horace Liverwright, 1924.

1925

McBride, Henry. "A New Group of Modernists." *The Sun* 21 (February 1925): 21.

1926

Dreier, Katherine S. *Modern Art,* edited by Katherine S. Dreier and Constantin Aladjalov, 86. New York: Société Anonyme and Museum of Modern Art, 1926.

1927

Braun, Hazel Boyer, "Art Comment: The Blue Four in the Fine Arts Gallery." *The San Diego Tribune,* January 15, 1927.

Wilenski, Reginald Howard. *The Modern Movement in Art.* London: Faber & Gwyer, 1927: 239f.

1929

"Germany's Own Estimate of 'The Blue Four.'" *Art Digest* 3 (December 1929): 10.

Neagoc, Peter. "Dreams." *Transition,* no. 18 (November 1929): 64–65.

1930

A.F.C. "Modern Wing of German Art Shown, Harvard Society Sponsors Exhibit in which Post-war Teutonic Painting Is Featured." *Boston Transcript,* April 23, 1930.

"The Art Galleries: One German and a Lot of Americans." *The New Yorker* (March/April 1930).

Barr, Jr., Alfred Hamilton. "Introduction." *Paul Klee.* Exhibition catalogue. New York: Museum of Modern Art, 1930.

Bulliet, Clarence Joseph. *Apples and Madonnas: Emotional Expression in Modern Art,* 55f., 166, 184, 191, 196, 238. New York: Covici Friede, 1930.

Cary, Elisabeth Luther. "Max Weber, Paul Klee, Aristide Maillol and Lehmbruck at Museum of Modern Art." *New York Times,* March 16, 1930.

Coburn, F. W. "Revealing Exhibits Contained in First Showing of German Art in Many Years." *Boston Herald,* April 19, 1930.

Cortissoz, Royal. "Current Exhibits at the Modern Museum and Elsewhere." *New York Herald Tribune,* March 16, 1930.

Kiesler, Frederick. *Contemporary Art Applied to the Store and Its Display,* 25, 27. New York: Bretano's, 1930.

"Modern Museum Shows Weber, Klee, Maillol, Lehmbruch." *Art News* 28 (March 15, 1930): 3, 11f.

Neumann, Israel Ber. "Paul Klee." *Artlover* 3, no. 1 (1930): 3–7.

"Paul Klee and Max Weber, MoMA Features Them in Its Present Exhibition." *New York Sun,* March 15, 1930.

Rivière, G. H. "The Gallery of Living Art at New York University." *Documents* 2, no. 6 (1930): 374.

1931

Barr, Jr., Alfred Hamilton. "Deutsche Kunst in New York." *Museum der Gegenwart* 2 (1931): 1–6.

______. "Die Wirkung der deutschen Ausstellung in New York." *Museum der Gegenwart* 2 (1931): 58–75.

______. "Paul Klee." *Omnibus* (1931): 206–209.

______. "The Pros and the Cons, Alfred H. Barr, Jr., Museum of Modern Art's Director, Replies to Robert McBeth," *New York Times,* March 22, 1931.

"The Bauhaus Exhibit." *Art News* 29 (January 17, 1931): 12.

Heiden, Margaret. "Neue Deutsche Kunst im Detroit Institute of Arts." *Museum der Gegenwart* 2 (1931): 12–22.

Hemingway, Ernest. "A Farewell to Arms." *Omnibus* (1931): 73.

Jewell, Edward Alden. "Art with a Vengeance, New Shows Everywhere at Once—Academy Prize Winners." *New York Times*, March 22, 1931.

Ozenfant, Amedée. *Foundations of Modern Art*, 116-135. London: John Rodker, 1931.

Read, Herbert. *The Meaning of Art*, 145–48. London: Faber & Faber, 1931.

______. "Paul Klee." *The Listener* 25 (March 1931): 509.

Rivera, Diego. "Paul Klee." *Cuatro Azules.* Exhibition catalogue. Mexico City: Biblioteca Nacional, 1931.

1932

Linderman, Verne. "'Blue Four' Art Exhibit Holds an Interest for All Lovers of Art in Faulkner Gallery." *Santa Barbara Morning Press* (March 5, 1932): 509.

1933

Barr, Jr., Alfred Hamilton. "Paul Klee." *Gaceta de Arte* 2 (May 1933): 3.

Gallery of Living Art: A. E. Gallatin Collection. New York: 1933.

Millier, Arthur. "'Blue Four' Art Expresses Feeling Rather than Sight." *Los Angeles Times*, October 15, 1933.

1934

Bloch, Albert. "Kandinsky, Marc, Klee: Criticism and Reminiscence." 1934 Denver lecture typescript. In *Albert Bloch: Ein amerikanischer Blauer Reiter*, 199–205. Exhibition catalogue. Munich: Städtische Galerie im Lenbachhaus, 1997.

Blunt, Anthony. "Doctrinal Advertisement." *The Spectator* (London) (January 31, 1934): 15.

______. "Artists and Materials." *The Spectator* (London) (February 2, 1934): 160.

Cheney, Sheldon. *Expressionism in Art*, 66, 75, 306-308, 345. New York: Liveright, 1934.

Davidson, Morris. *Understanding Modern Art*. New York: Tudor, 1934.

Grigson, Geoffrey. "Paul Klee." *The Bookman* 85 (January 1934): 390f.

"Junk?" *Art Digest* 8 (August 1934): 7.

"The Modernist's Creed: Klee and Picasso." *Scottish Educational Journal* 16 (December 14, 1934).

Read, Herbert. *Art Now: An Introduction to the Theory of Modern Painting and Sculpture*. London, Faber & Faber, 1933.

______. "Paul Klee." *The Listener* 11, no. 262 (January 17, 1934): 108.

Rothschild, Edward F. *The Meaning of Unintelligibility in Modern Art*, 88. Chicago: University of Chicago Press, 1934.

Stokes, Adrian. "Paul Klee." *The Listener* 11 (February 14, 1934).

Sweeney, James Johnson. *Plastic Redirections in 20th Century Painting*, 30, 77, 90. Chicago: University of Chicago Press, 1934.

1935

"Dots and Dashes: Klee's Abstraction Techniques." *Art Digest* 10 (November 1935): 19.

Grohmann, Will. "Klee at Berne." *Axis* 1 (April 1935): 12f.

Jewell, Edward Allen. "Oils by Paul Klee on Exhibition." *New York Times,* March 11, 1935.

M.M. "Paul Klee: Contemporary Art Circle." *Art News* 34 (March 9, 1935): 12.

Morris, George L. K. "The Gallery of Living Art, New York University." *Axis* 1 (November 1935): 9f.

"Sir Michael Sadler's Collection." *Axis* 1 (April 1935): 24–26.

Soby, James Thrall. *After Picasso*, 3f, 80. New York: Dodd, Meade, 1935.

1936

Artlover, J. B. Neumann's Bilderhefte: Anthologie d'un marchand d'art 3, no. 3 (1936): 61.

Artlover, J. B. Neumann's Bilderhefte: Anthologie d'un marchand d'art 3, no. 6 (1936): 92, 94.

Bulliet, Clarence Joseph. *The Significant Moderns and Their Picture*, 172–74. New York: Covici Friede, 1936.

Causton, Bernard. "Art in Germany under the Nazis." *The Studio* 112 (November 1936): 235–47.

Hugnet, Georges. "Dada and Surrealism." *The Bulletin of the Museum of Modern Art* 4 (November/December 1936): 3–31.

Porteus, Hugh Gordon. "A Few Lines." *Axis* 2 (Fall 1936): 13–26.

Read, Herbert, André Breton, Hugh Sykes Davies, Paul Eluard, and Georges Hugnet. *Surrealism,* edited by Herbert Read. London: Faber & Faber, 1936.

Thwaites, J. and M. "Surrealism and Abstraction—The Search for Subjective Form." *Axis* 2 (Summer 1936): 21–28.

1937

Artlover, J. B. Neumann's Bilderhefte: Anthologie d'un marchand d'art 3, no. 6 (1937).

Frankenstein, Alfred. "One Man Show Versatile in Aspects." *San Francisco Chronicle,* January 17, 1937.

Fried, Alexander. "Klee Paintings on View." *San Francisco Examiner,* January 17, 1937.

Gabo, Naum, J. L. Martin, and Ben Nicholson, eds. *Circle: International Survey of Constructive Art.* London: Faber & Faber, 1937.

Hodel, Emilia. "Unusual Work of Paul Klee Displayed Here." *San Francisco News,* January 16, 1937.

Medley, Robert. "Hitler's Art in Munich." *Axis 3* (Winter 1937): 28f.

Thwaites, John Anthony. "Paul Klee and the Object." *Parnassus 9* (November 1937): 9–11, and *Parnassus 9* (December 1937): 7–9, 33f.

1938

"'All degenerate,' said Hitler—but 2,000,000 came to see them!" *Weekly Illustrated* (July 16, 1938).

"Art: Ideas and Illuminations." *Time* 41 (April 11, 1938): 39.

Bayer, Herbert, and Walter and Ilse Gropius, eds. *Bauhaus 1919–1928.* Exhibition catalogue. New York: Museum of Modern Art, 1938.

Burrows, Carlyle. "A German Modern." *New York Herald Tribune,* March 27, 1938.

Coates, Robert M. "The Art Galleries." *The New Yorker* (April 2, 1938).

______. "Paul Klee." *The New Yorker* (November 12, 1938).

"The Eye." *Transition,* no. 27 (April/May 1938): 265.

Genauer, Emily. "Close to the Realists." *New York World-Telegram,* March 26, 1938.

Goldwater, Robert J. *Primitivism in Modern Painting,* 153–61. New York and London: Harper and Brothers, 1938.

Jewell, Edward Allen. "Paul Klee Represented." *New York Times,* March 22, 1938.

______. "Paul Klee Retrospective." *New York Times,* March 27, 1938.

M. D. "Directions in German Painting: Klee, Kandinsky, Feininger." *Art News* 36, no. 15 (January 1938): 14.

______. "Four Current Shows of German and Native Abstractionists." *Art News* 36 (April 9, 1938): 15.

______. "Brilliant Improvisations in Line and Color by Paul Klee." *Art News* 36 (November 5, 1938).

"Paul Klee Shown in Two Exhibitions." *The Springfield (Mass.) Sunday Union and Republican,* November 13, 1938.

Read, Herbert. "Klee: Imagination and Fantasy." *XXe siècle* 1, no. 4 (1938): 31–33.

Thoene, Peter. *Modern German Art,* 58–75. Harmondsworth, England: Penguin Books, 1938.

1939

Bertram, Anthony. *Contemporary Painting in Europe.* New York: The Studio Publications, 1939.

"Exiled German Art." *Direction* 2 (December 1939).

"Exiled Reich Art Put on View Here." *New York Times,* August 8, 1939.

J. L. "The Fantasies of Paul Klee Seen in a Twenty-nine Year Review." *Art News* 37 (May 20, 1939): 12.

1940

Ayre, Robert. "Paul Klee." *The Standard* (Montreal), November 23, 1940.

Baynes, H. G. *Mythology of the Soul: A Research into the Unconscious from Schizophrenic Dreams and Drawings,* 515–17, 563, 607–609, 678f, 705. London: Routledge & Kegan Paul, 1940.

Bulliet, Clarence Joseph. "Bulliet's Artless Comment—Intimate Glimpse of Klee." *Chicago Daily News,* October 26, 1940.

Burrows, Carlyle. "Paul Klee." *New York Herald Tribune,* October 13, 1940.

Breuning, Margaret. *American Journal* (October 13, 1940).

Brown, Milton. "Paul Klee Retrospective." *Parnassus* 12, no. 7 (November 1940): 37.

Coates, Robert M. "A Memorial to Paul Klee." *The New Yorker* (October 12, 1940): 94.

Cortissoz, Royal. "Paul Klee." *New York Herald Tribune,* October 13, 1940.

Craven, Thomas. *Modern Art: The Men, the Movements, the Meaning,* 228. New York: Simon & Schuster, 1940.

Feininger, Julia and Lyonel. "Recollections of Paul Klee." In exhibition catalogue, 7f. New York: Buchholz Gallery, 1940.

"Fish of the Heart." *Time* (October 21, 1940).

Genauer, Emily. "Compositions of the Swiss Surrealists." *New York World-Telegram,* October 12, 1940.

Johnson, D. Rhodes. "The Arts—Here and There." *The Jersey Journal* (Jersey City), October 8, 1940.

J. W. L. "Klee's Symbolism Clear and Thoughtful." *Art News* 38, no. 18 (February 3, 1940).

Lowe, Jeanette. "Of the Mortal Klee: Memorial View of the Wittiest Surrealist." *Art News* 39, no. 2 (October 1940): 12, 15.

Museum of Living Art: A. E. Gallatin Collection. New York: New York University, 1940.

"New York Sees Paul Klee Memorial Show." *Art Digest* 15, no. 2 (October 15, 1940).

"Paul Klee, Artist Banned by Nazis." *New York Times,* July 3, 1940.

"Paul Klee Dies, Paintings Often Shown in US." *New York Herald Tribune,* July 2, 1940.

Sacartoff, Elizabeth. "New Show: Paul Klee Thought Like a Man, Painted Like a Child." *PM* (October 16, 1940).

Sweeney, James Johnson. "Paul Klee." Exhibition catalogue. New York: Buchholz Gallery, 1940.

Todd, Rutheven. "Paul Klee 1879–1940." *Horizon* 2, no. 12 (December 1940): 340–44.

Upton, M. "Memorial to Klee." *New York Sun,* October 12, 1940.

1941

Cheney, Sheldon. *The Story of Modern Art*. New York: Viking, 1941.

Cooper, Douglas. "Paul Klee: A Memorial." *The Listener* 25 (March 13, 1941): 381.

Greenberg, Clement. "On Paul Klee (1879–1940)." *Partisan Review* 8, no. 3 (May/June 1941).

McCausland, Elizabeth. "Paul Klee's Paintings in Memorial Showing." *Parnassus* (1941).

Nierendorf, Karl, ed. *Paul Klee, Paintings, Watercolors 1913 to 1939*, introduction by James Johnson Sweeney. New York: Oxford University Press, 1941.

Schardt, Alois. "Paul Klee." *California Arts and Architecture* 58 (June 1941): 20f, 40.

1942

Frost, Rosamund. "Klee: Pigeons Come Home to Roost." *Art News* 41 (1942): 24f.

Guggenheim, Peggy, ed. *Art Of This Century*. New York: Art Of This Century Gallery, 1942.

1943

"Buchholz Exhibition." *New York World-Telegram,* February 27, 1943.

Connoly, Jean. *The Nation* (March 13, 1943).

Pearson, Ralph M. *Experiencing American Pictures*. New York: Harper & Bros., 1943.

Upton, M. "Buchholz Gallery Showing." *New York Sun*, February 26, 1943.

1944

Greenberg, Clement. *The Nation* (December 9, 1944).

Genauer, Emily. "How the New Art Books Stack Up." *New York World-Telegram,* December 9, 1944.

Jewell, Edward Alden. "The Blue Four." *New York Times,* November 5, 1944.

M. R. "The Blue Four Reunited in New York Show." *Art Digest* (November 15, 1944).

Upton, M. "Things Dealers Are Showing." *New York Sun,* November 11, 1944.

1945

Ironside, Robin. "Paul Klee." *Horizon* 12, no. 72 (December 1945): 413–17.

Jewell, Edward Alden. "Prints by Paul Klee." *New York Times,* February 25, 1945.

"The Prints of Paul Klee." *Art Digest* (November 15, 1945).

Soby, James Thrall. *The Prints of Paul Klee*. New York: C. Valentin, 1945.

1946

Miller, Margaret, ed. *Paul Klee: Statements by the Artist,* with contributions from Alfred H. Barr, Jr., Julia and Lyonel Feininger, and James Johnson Sweeney. New York: Museum of Modern Art, 1946.

Porteous, Hugh Gordon. "Klee and the Antiquities." *World Review* (March 1946): 48–55.

Read, Herbert. "Paul Klee." *The Listener* 35 (January 3, 1946): 20f.

Reynolds, Graham, ed. *Twentieth Century Drawings.* London: Pleiades Books, 1946.

Vaughan, Keith. "At the Klee Exhibition." *New Writing and Daylight* 7, no. 7 (1946): 117–21.

1947

"Klee Fancy Lacks Substance." *New York World-Telegram,* April 27, 1948.

1948

Forge, Andrew. *Klee, 1879–1940.* Vol. 1, introduction by Herbert Read. London: Faber & Faber, 1948.

"Paul Klee and Two Sculptors." *The New Yorker* (May 1, 1948).

Paul Klee on Modern Art, introduction by Herbert Read. London: Faber & Faber, 1948.

1949

Cooper, Douglas, *Paul Klee*. Harmondsworth, England: Penguin Books, 1949.

Ritchie, Andrew C., ed. *Albright Art Gallery: Catalogue of Contemporary Paintings and Sculptures,* 98, 197–212. Buffalo, N.Y.: Buffalo Fine Arts Academy, 1949.

1950

Armitage, Merle, ed. *5 Essays on Klee,* with contributions by Armitage, Clement Greenberg, Howard Devree, Nancy Wilson Ross, and James Johnson Sweeney. New York: Duell, Sloan and Pearce, 1950.

Breuer, Marcel, and Ben Shahn. "Aspects of the Art of Paul Klee." *Museum of Modern Art Bulletin* 17, no. 4 (Summer 1950): 3–9.

Dreier, Katherine S., and Marcel Duchamp. *The Collection of the Société Anonyme: Museum of Modern Art 1920,* 140, 219–23. New Haven, Conn.: Yale University Art Gallery, 1950.

1951

Thwaites, John Anthony. "The Bauhaus Painters and the New Style—Epoch." *The Art Quarterly* (Detroit) 14, no. 1 (Spring 1951): 19–32.

1952

"Paul Klee." In *Collection of F. C. Schang*. South Norwalk, Conn.: PUB, 1952.

1953

Fitzsimmons, James. "The Berne-Locarno Road." *Art Digest* (October 1, 1953).

1954

Forge, Andrew. *Klee, 1879–1940.* Vol. 2. London: Faber & Faber 1954.

The Louise and Walter Arensberg Collection. Philadelphia: Philadelphia Museum of Art, 1954.

1956

Hulton, Nika. *An Approach to Paul Klee.* London: Phoenix House, 1956.

Melville, Robert. "Paul Klee's Architectural Mirages." *The Architectural Review* 120, no. 716 (September 1956): 145–49.

1957

Grohmann, Will. "Paul Klee—A Classic of Modern Painting." *Universitas* 1, no. 2 (1957): 147–52.

Kessler, Charles S. "Science and Mysticism in Paul Klee's 'Around the Fish.'" *Journal of Aesthetics and Art Criticism* 16 (1957): 76–83.

Marsh, Ellen. "Paul Klee and the Art of Children." *College Art Journal* 16, no. 2 (Winter 1957): 132–45.

1959

A Handbook to the Solomon R. Guggenheim Museum Collection. New York: Solomon R. Guggenheim Foundation, 1959.

1960

Johnson, Lincoln. "To the Tightrope Walker." *The Baltimore Museum of Art News* 33, no. 2 (Winter 1960): 9–15.

1962

The Louis E. Stern Collection. Brooklyn, N.Y.: Brooklyn Museum, 1962.

1964

The Louis E. Stern Collection. Philadelphia: Philadelphia Museum of Art, 1964.

1967

Catalogue of European and American Paintings and Sculpture in the Allen Memorial Art Museum. Oberlin, Ohio: Oberlin College, 1967.

The Brooklyn Museum Handbook. Brooklyn, N.Y.: Brooklyn Museum, 1967.

Irwin, David. "Paul Klee." *The Masters*, no. 94 (1967): 2–8.

Smith-Pierce, James. "Pictographs, Ideograms, and Alphabets in the Work of Paul Klee." *Journal of Typographic Research* 1, no. 3 (July 1967): 219–43.

Selections from the Permanent Collection. Poughkeepsie, N.Y.: Vassar College Art Gallery, 1967.

1968

Shapiro, Maurice L. "Klee's 'Twittering Machine.'" *The Art Bulletin* 50 (March 1968): 67–69.

Verdi, Richard. "Musical Influences on the Art of Paul Klee." *Museum Studies* 3 (1968): 81–107.

1970

Catalog of the Permanent Collection of Painting and Sculpture. San Francisco: San Francisco Museum of Art, 1970.

Catalogue of European Paintings in The Minneapolis Institute of Arts. Minneapolis: Institute of Arts, 1970.

Henning, Edward B. "Paul Klee: Carnival in Snow." *The Bulletin of The Cleveland Museum of Art* 62, no. 4 (April 1970): 113–17.

Kedward, H. R. "Modern Man in Search of His Art." *The Social Context of Art,* edited by Jean Creedy, 163–86. London and New York: Tavistock Publications, 1970.

Phillips, Marjorie. *Duncan Phillips and His Collection,* foreword by Laughlin Phillips. Boston: Little, Brown, 1970.

Prak, Nils Luning. "Persistent Schemes: The Quest of a Neutral Form." *Art International* 14, no. 7 (1970): 74–79.

1971

Cummings, Frederick J., and Charles H. Elam, eds. *The Detroit Institute of Arts Illustrated Handbook.* Detroit: Wayne State University Press, 1971.

1972

Geelhaar, Christian. *Paul Klee und das Bauhaus.* Cologne: DuMont, 1972.

Messer, Thomas M. "Paul Klee at the Baltimore Museum of Art." *Baltimore Museum of Art Annual* 4, no. 2 (1972): 70–79.

Three Generations of Twentieth-Century Art: The Sidney and Harriet Janis Collection of the Museum of Modern Art, foreword by Alfred H. Barr, Jr., and introduction by William Rubin. New York: Museum of Modern Art, distributed by New York Graphic Society, 1972.

1973

Teuber, Marianne L. "New Aspects of Paul Klee's Bauhaus Style." In *Paul Klee, Paintings and Watercolors from the Bauhaus Years 1921–1931*, 6–17. Exhibition catalogue. Des Moines: Des Moines Art Center, 1973.

1974

Verdi, Richard. "Paul Klee's 'Fish Magic': An Interpretation." *The Burlington Magazine* 116, no. 852 (March 1974): 147–55.

1975

Kagan, Andrew. "Paul Klee's Influence on American Painting." *Arts Magazine* 49, no. 10 (June 1975): 54–59, and *Arts Magazine* 50, no. 1 (September 1975): 84–90.

Rosenblum, Robert. *Modern Painting and the Northern Romantic Tradition: Friedrich to Rothko.* New York: Harper and Row, 1975: 149–56.

1976

Campbell, Sara, ed. *The Blue Four Galka Scheyer Collection.* Pasadena, Calif.: Norton Simon Museum of Art, 1976.

Catalogue of Drawings and Watercolors in the Allen Memorial Art Museum, Oberlin College, compiled by Wolfgang Stecho. Oberlin, Ohio: Oberlin College, 1976.

European Drawings in the Collection of the Santa Barbara Museum of Art, compiled by Alfred Moir. Santa Barbara, Calif.: Santa Barbara Museum of Art, 1976.

Haxthausen, Charles Werner. "Paul Klee: The Formative Years." 2 vols. Dissertation, Columbia University, 1976.

Pierce, James Smith. "Paul Klee and Primitive Art." Dissertation, New York University, 1976.

Rudenstein, Angelica Zander. *The Guggenheim Museum Collection: Paintings 1880–1945.* Vol. 2: 398–421. New York: Solomon R. Guggenheim Foundation, 1976.

Teuber, Marianne L. "'Blue Night' by Paul Klee." *Vision and Artifact*, edited by Mary Henle, 131–51. New York: Springer, 1976.

1977

Barr, Jr., Alfred Hamilton. *Painting and Sculpture in the Museum of Modern Art 1929–1967.* New York: Museum of Modern Art, 1977.

Legg, Alicia. *Painting and Sculpture in the Museum of Modern Art with Selected Works on Paper; Catalog of the Collection, January 1, 1977.* New York: Museum of Modern Art, 1977.

Werckmeister, Otto Karl. "The Issue of Childhood in the Art of Paul Klee." *Arts Magazine* (1977): 138–51.

1978

Rosenthal, Mark. "Paul Klee's *Tightrope Walker*: An Exercise in Balance." *Arts Magazine* 53, no. 1 (September 1978): 106–11.

1979

Barron, Stephanie. "Two Recent Acquisitions: A Painting by Paul Klee and a Sculpture by Naum Gabo." *Bulletin of Los Angeles County Museum of Art* 25 (1977): 66–79.

Geelhaar, Christian. "Journal intime oder Autobiographie? Über Paul Klees Tagebücher." In *Paul Klee das Frühwerk 1883–1922*, 246–60. Exhibition catalogue. Munich: Städtische Galerie in Lenbachhaus, 1979.

Glaesemer, Jürgen. *Paul Klee, The Colored Works in the Kunstmuseum: Paintings, Colored Sheets, Pictures on Glass, and Sculptures*, translated by Renate Franciscono. Bern, Switzerland: Kornfeld, c.1979.

______. *Paul Klee: Handzeichnungen III, 1937–1940.* Bern, Switzerland: Kunstmuseum Bern, 1979.

Klee, Paul. *Briefe an die Familie 1893–1940*, edited by Felix Klee. 2 vols. Cologne: DuMont, 1979.

The Peggy Guggenheim Collection: Venice. Turin, Italy, 1979.

Selected Works from the Detroit Institute of Arts. Detroit: Detroit Institute of Arts, 1979.

1981

Boltin, Lee. *The Nelson A. Rockefeller Collection: Masterpieces of Modern Art.* New York: Hudson Hills Press, 1981.

Werckmeister, Otto Karl. *Versuche über Paul Klee.* Frankfurt am Main: Syndikat, 1981.

1982

Masterpieces of German Expressionism at the Detroit Institute of Arts, foreword by Horst Uhr. New York: Hudson Hills Press in association with the Detroit Institute of Arts, distributed by Viking Penguin, 1982.

1983

Elderfield, John. *The Modern Drawing: 100 Works on Paper from The Museum of Modern Art.* New York and Boston: Museum of Modern Art, distributed by New York Graphic Society, 1983.

Messer, Thomas M., and Lucy Flint. *Handbook: The Peggy Guggenheim Collection.* New York: Abrams, 1983.

1984

Herbert, Robert L., Eleanor S. Apter, and Elise K. Kenney, eds. *Société Anonyme and the Dreier Bequest at Yale University: A Catalogue Raisonné*. New Haven, Conn., and London: Yale University Press, 1984.

Jordan, Jim M. *Paul Klee and Cubism*. Princeton, N.J.: Princeton University Press, 1984.

Verdi, Richard. *Klee and Nature*. London: A. Zwemmer, 1984.

1985

Rudenstein, Angelica Zander. *Peggy Guggenheim Collection, Venice*. New York: Solomon R. Guggenheim Foundation, 1985.

Werckmeister, Otto Karl. Essay. In *Paul Klee in Exile, 1933–1940*, edited and translated by Tadayasu Sakai, 27–174. Himeji City Museum of Art exhibition catalogue. Tokyo: Fuji Television Gallery, 1985.

1987

Frey, Stefan, and Wolfgang Kersten. *Paul Klees geschäftliche Verbindung zur Galerie Alfred Flechtheim*, 64–91. Exhibition catalogue. Düsseldorf/Münster, Germany: Galerie Alfred Flechtheim, 1987.

Hüneke, Andreas. "Die faschistische Aktion 'Entartete Kunst' 1937 in Halle." In *Schriftenreihe zur Geschichte der Staatlichen Galerie Moritzburg*. Halle, Germany: Staatlichen Galerie Mortizburg, 1987.

Kersten, Wolfgang. *Paul Klee: "Zerstörung der Konstruktion zuliebe?"* Marburg, Germany: Jonas, 1987.

Lanchner, Carolyn. "Klee in America." In *Paul Klee 1879–1940*, 83–111. Exhibition catalogue. New York: Museum of Modern Art; and Boston: Little, Brown, distributed by New York Graphic Society Books, c. 1987.

Maur, Karin von. "Bildersturm in der Staatsgalerie Stuttgart: Mit einer Dokumentation der 1937 beschlagnahmten Gemälde und Skulpturen, Zeichnungen und Druckgraphiken." In *Ausst.kat. Bildzyklen. Zeugnisse verfemter Kunst in Deutschland 1933–45*, 3–68. Stuttgart, Germany: Graphische Sammlung, 1987.

Schiff, Gert. "Klee's Array of Angels." *Art Forum* 25, no. 9 (May 1987): 126–33.

Temkin, Ann. "Klee and the Avant-garde, 1912–1940." In *Paul Klee 1879–1940*, 13–38. Exhibition catalogue. New York: Museum of Modern Art; and Boston: Little, Brown, distributed by New York Graphic Society Books, c. 1987.

Uhr, Horst. *German Drawings and Watercolors (including Austrian and Swiss Works): The Collections of the Detroit Institute of Arts*, 256–75. New York: Hudson Hills Press in association with the Founders Society, Detroit Institute of Arts, distributed by Rizzoli International Publications, 1987.

Werckmeister, Otto Karl. "From Revolution to Exile." In *Paul Klee: His Life and Work*, 39–64. Exhibition catalogue. New York: Museum of Modern Art, 1987.

1988

Ebert, Hans. "Die Verfemung und Verfolgung moderner Künstler und Kunstwerke durch das Naziregime." In *Das Schicksal einer Sammlung: Aufbau und Zerstörung der neuen Abteilung der Nationalgalerie im ehemaligen Kronprinzen-Palais unter den Linden, 1918–1945*, 12–21. Exhibition catalogue. Berlin: Neue Gesellschaft für bildende Kunst, 1988.

Hüneke, Andreas. "Expressionistische Kunst in deutschen Museen bis 1919." In *Das Schicksal einer Sammlung: Aufbau und Zerstörung der neuen Abteilung der Nationalgalerie im ehemaligen Kronprinzen-Palais unter den Linden, 1918–1945*, 8–11. Exhibition catalogue. Berlin: Neue Gesellschaft für bildende Kunst, 1988.

Janda, Annegret. "Die Gemälde und Bildwerke der Expressionisten im ehemaligen Kronprinzen-Palais." In *Das Schicksal einer Sammlung: Aufbau und Zerstörung der neuen Abteilung der Nationalgalerie im ehemaligen Kronprinzen-Palais unter den Linden, 1918–1945*, 22–86. Exhibition catalogue. Berlin: Neue Gesellschaft für bildende Kunst, 1988.

Rewald, Sabine. *Paul Klee: The Berggruen Collection in The Metropolitan Museum of Art*. New York: Metropolitan Museum of Art, 1988.

Tagebücher 1898–1918: Paul Klee Foundation, Kunstmuseum Bern, edited by Wolfgang Kersten. Textkritische Neueedition. Stuttgart, Germany: Hatje, 1988.

1989

Boulez, Pierre. *Le pays fertile: Paul Klee*, edited by Paule Thévenin. Paris: Gallimard, 1989.

Hopfengart, Christine. *Klee: Vom Sonderfall zum Publikumsliebling, Stationen seiner öffentlichen Resonanz in Deutschland 1905–1960*. Mainz, Germany: P. von Zabern, 1989.

Werckmeister, Otto Karl. *The Making of Paul Klee's Career 1914–1920*. Chicago: University of Chicago Press, 1989.

1991

Franciscono, Marcel. *Paul Klee: His Work and Thought*. Chicago: University of Chicago Press, 1991.

Frey, Stefan, and Josef Helfenstein, eds. *Paul Klee: Verzeichnis der Werke des Jahres 1940*. Stuttgart, Germany: Hatje, 1991.

Roberts, Norma J., ed. *Impressionism and European Modernism: The Sirak Collection, Columbus Museum of Art*, 70–91. Columbus: Columbus Museum of Art, distributed by University of Washington Press, 1991.

1994

Paintings from Europe and the Americas in the Philadelphia Museum of Art. Philadelphia: Philadelphia Museum of Art, 1994.

1995

Kersten, Wolfgang, and Osamu Okuda. *Paul Klee: Im Zeichen der Teilung.* Exhibition catalogue. Düsseldorf, Germany: Kunstsammlung Nordrhein-Westfalen, 1995.

1996

Helfenstein, Josef. "The Issue of Childhood in Klee's Late Work." In *Discovering Child Art,* edited by Jonathan Fineberg. Princeton, N.J.: Princeton University Press, 1996.

1997

Barnett, Vivian Endicott. "The Founding of the *Blue Four* and Their Presentation in New York in 1924–1925." In *The Blue Four in the New World,* 15–27. Exhibition catalogue. Bern, Switzerland: Kunstmuseum Bern; Düsseldorf, Germany: Kunstsammlung Nordrhein-Westfahlen; and Cologne: DuMont, 1997.

______. "The Last Years of the *Blue Four, 1933–1945.*" In *The Blue Four in the New World,* 263–72. Exhibition catalogue. Bern, Switzerland: Kunstmuseum Bern; Düsseldorf, Germany: Kunstsammlung Nordrhein-Westfahlen; and Cologne: DuMont, 1997.

Bishop, Janet, Kelly Purcell, and John S. Weber. *Paul Klee: The Djerassi Collection at the San Francisco Museum of Modern Art.* San Francisco: San Francisco Museum of Modern Art, 1997.

Frey, Stefan, "'*Blue Four?* Hardly Anyone in Germany Has Ever Heard of Them'—The *Blue Four* Exhibition at the Galerie Ferdinand Möller, Berlin, in October 1929." In *The Blue Four in the New World,* 247–62. Exhibition catalogue. Bern, Switzerland: Kunstmuseum Bern; Düsseldorf, Germany: Kunstsammlung Nordrhein-Westfahlen; and Cologne: DuMont, 1997.

Helfenstein, Josef. "'The Most Precious and Most Personal of Gifts: Pictures Exchanged between Feininger, Jawlensky, Kandinsky, and Klee." In *The Blue Four in the New World,* 79–135. Exhibition catalogue. Bern, Switzerland: Kunstmuseum Bern; Düsseldorf, Germany: Kunstsammlung Nordrhein-Westfahlen; and Cologne: DuMont, 1997.

Houstian, Christian. "Minister, Kindermädchen, Little Friend: Galka Scheyer and *The Blue Four.*" In *The Blue Four in the New World.* Exhibition catalogue. Bern, Switzerland: Kunstmuseum Bern; Düsseldorf, Germany: Kunstsammlung Nordrhein-Westfahlen; and Cologne: DuMont, 1997.

Müller, Maria. "'It Is a Long Long Road': John Cage and Galka Scheyer." In *The Blue Four in the New World,* 273–78. Exhibition catalogue. Bern, Switzerland: Kunstmuseum Bern; Düsseldorf, Germany: Kunstsammlung Nordrhein-Westfahlen; and Cologne: DuMont, 1997.

Sawelson-Gorse, Naomi. "Narrow Circles and Uneasy Alliances: Galka Scheyer and American Collectors." In *The Blue Four in the New World,* 51–61. Exhibition catalogue. Bern, Switzerland: Kunstmuseum Bern; Düsseldorf, Germany: Kunstsammlung Nordrhein-Westfahlen; and Cologne: DuMont, 1997.

Zaugg, Karin. "*The Blue Four*—Letters." In *The Blue Four in the New World,* 291–321. Exhibition catalogue. Bern, Switzerland: Kunstmuseum Bern; Düsseldorf, Germany: Kunstsammlung Nordrhein-Westfahlen; and Cologne: DuMont, 1997.

1998

Baumgartner, Michael. "Josef Albers und Paul Klee—zwei Lehrerpersönlichkeiten am Bauhaus." In *Josef und Anni Albers: Europa und Amerika. Künstlerpaare-Künstlerfreunde,* 165–86. Exhibition catalogue. Bern: Kunstmuseum Bern; and Cologne: DuMont, 1998.

Rewald, Sabine. "Amerika und Klee." In *Klee aus New York: Hauptwerke der Sammlung Berggruen im Metropolitan Museum of Art,* 26-40. Exhibition catalogue. Berlin: Staatliche Museen zu Berlin, Preussischer Kulturbesitz, 1998.

1999

Kort, Pamela. "Die rebellische Stimme der Kunst." In *Paul Klee: in der Maske des Mythos,* 9–38. Exhibition catalogue. Munich: Haus der Kunst, 1999.

2000

Anger, Jenny. "Der dekorative Klee." In *Paul Klee Kunst und Karriere Beiträge des Internationalen Symposium in Bern,* 238–53. Bern, Switzerland: Stämpfli, 2000.

Bäschlin, Nathalie, Béatrice Ilg, and Patrizia Zeppetella. "Beiträge zur Maltechnik von Paul Klee." In *Paul Klee Kunst und Karriere Beiträge des Internationalen Symposium in Bern,* 173–203. Bern, Switzerland: Stämpfli, 2000.

Bätschmann, Oskar. "Grammatik der Bewegung: Paul Klees Lehre am Bauhaus." In *Paul Klee Kunst und Karriere Beiträge des Internationalen Symposium in Bern,* 107–24. Bern, Switzerland: Stämpfli, 2000.

Baumgartner, Michael. "Klee und seine frühen Sammler." In *Paul Klee Kunst und Karriere Beiträge des Internationalen Symposium in Bern,* 93–106. Bern, Switzerland: Stämpfli, 2000.

Haxthausen, Charles W. "Zwischen Darstellung und Parodie: Klees 'auratische' Bilder." In *Paul Klee Kunst und Karriere Beiträge des Internationalen Symposium in Bern,* 9–26. Bern, Switzerland: Stämpfli, 2000.

Helfenstein, Josef. "'Ein kleines Publikum aus feinen Köpfen': Klees Bidertausch mit befreundeten Künstlern." In *Paul Klee Kunst und Karriere Beiträge des Internationalen Symposium in Bern,* 125–45. Bern, Switzerland: Stämpfli, 2000.

Hopfengart, Christine. "Klee an den deutschen 'Museen der Gegenwart,' 1916–1933." In *Paul Klee Kunst und Karriere Beiträge des Internationalen Symposium in Bern,* 68–92. Bern, Switzerland: Stämpfli, 2000.

Okuda, Osamu. "Erinnerungsblick und Revision: Über den Werkprozess Paul Klees in den Jahren 1919–1923." In *Paul Klee Kunst und Karriere Beiträge des Internationalen Symposium in Bern,* 159–72. Bern, Switzerland: Stämpfli, 2000.

Prange, Regine. "Das utopische Kalligramm: Klees 'Zeichen' und der Surrealismus." In *Paul Klee Kunst und Karriere Beiträge des Internationalen Symposium in Bern,* 204–38. Bern, Switzerland: Stämpfli, 2000.

Rümelin, Christian. "Klee und der Kunsthandel." In *Paul Klee Kunst und Karriere Beiträge des Internationalen Symposium in Bern,* 27–37. Bern, Switzerland: Stämpfli, 2000.

Sladeczek, Eva Wiederkehr. "Der handschriftliche Oeuvre-Katalog von Paul Klee." In *Paul Klee Kunst und Karriere Beiträge des Internationalen Symposium in Bern,* 146–58. Bern, Switzerland: Stämpfli, 2000.

Werckmeister, Otto Karl. "Sozialgeschichte von Klees Karriere." In *Paul Klee Kunst und Karriere Beiträge des Internationalen Symposium in Bern,* 38–67. Bern, Switzerland: Stämpfli, 2000.

2001

Barnett, Vivian Endicott. "The Architect as Art Collector." In *Mies in America.* Exhibition catalogue. New York: Harry N. Abrams, 2001.

2002

Aigner, Carl, ed. *Paul Klee: Masterpieces of the Djerassi Collection.* Exhibition catalogue. San Francisco: San Francisco Museum of Modern Art, 2002.

Barnett, Vivian Endicott. *The Blue Four Collection at the Norton Simon Museum.* New Haven, Conn., and London: Yale University Press, 2002.

2003

Anger, Jenny. *Paul Klee and the Decorative in Modern Art.* Cambridge, England: Cambridge University Press, 2003.

Frey, Stefan, and Andreas Hüneke. "Paul Klee, Kunst und Politik in Deutschland 1933: Eine Chronologie." In *Paul Klee, 1933,* 268–306. Exhibition catalogue. Cologne: König, 2003.

Friedel, Helmut, and Pamela Kort. *Paul Klee, 1933.* Exhibition catalogue. Cologne: König, 2003.

Kort, Pamela. "Paul Klee und die Zeichnungen zur 'nationalsozialistischen Revolution.'" In *Paul Klee, 1933,* 183–216. Exhibition catalogue. Cologne: König, 2003.

Okuda, Osamu. "Versuch über Honoré Daumiers sichtbaren Einfluß auf Paul Klee." In *Paul Klee, 1933,* 228–41. Exhibition catalogue. Cologne: König, 2003.

Werckmeister, Otto Karl. "Körperfigur und Kunstfigur in Klees Zeichnungen von 1933." In *Paul Klee, 1933,* 217–27. Exhibition catalogue. Cologne: König, 2003.

Works in the Exhibition

ALS GOTT SICH MIT DER ERSCHAFFUNG
DER PFLANZEN TRUG, 1913.176 *pl. 1*
[When God Considered the Creation of the Plants]
Pen, brush, wet in wet, and watercolor on paper,
mounted on cardboard
6 x 8½ inches (15 x 21.5 cm)
Worthington Collection, Chicago
CR 1078

GELBES HAUS, 1915.55 *pl. 2*
[Yellow House]
Watercolor on paper, mounted on cardboard
8 x 5⅜ inches (20.3 x 13.8 cm)
Private Collection
CR 1388

TUNESISCHE GÄRTEN, 1919.81 *pl. 3*
[Tunisian Gardens]
Watercolor and pen on paper, mounted on cardboard
9⅜ x 5⅛ inches (23.8 x 13 cm)
Private Collection
CR 2144

SCHULHAUS, 1920.23 *pl. 4*
[Schoolhouse]
Oil on paper, mounted on cardboard and mounted on
stretcher
14½ x 11⅜ inches (37 x 29 cm)
The Art Institute of Chicago
Gift of Mr. and Mrs. Leigh B. Block, 1969.811
CR 2368

HOFFMANNESKE GESCHICHTE, 1921.18 *pl. 10*
[Hoffmannesque Tale]
Oil transfer and watercolor on paper, with watercolor
margin, mounted on cardboard
12¼ x 9½ inches (31.1 x 24.1 cm)
Metropolitan Museum of Art, New York
The Berggruen Klee Collection, 1984.315.26

STADT IM ZWISCHENREICH, 1921.25 *pl. 5*
[City in the Intermediate Realm]
Oil transfer and watercolor on paper, mounted with
glue spots on cardboard
12⅜ x 18⅞ inches (31.3 x 48 cm)
Columbus Museum of Art, Columbus, Ohio
Sirak Collection
CR 2616

DAS TOR ZUM HADES, 1921.29 *pl. 9*
[The Gateway to Hades]
Oil transfer and watercolor on paper, mounted
on cardboard
10¾ x 14⅜ inches (27.3 x 39.2 cm)
Norton Simon Museum, Pasadena, California
The Blue Four Galka Scheyer Collection.
CR 2620

KALTE STADT, 1921.66 *pl. 11*
[Cold City]
Watercolor on paper, mounted on maroon paper
and mounted on cardboard
8¼ x 11⅝ inches (21 x 29.5 cm)
Metropolitan Museum of Art, New York
The Berggruen Klee Collection, 1987.455.8
CR 2657

NOTTURNO FÜR HORN, 1921.91 *pl. 8*
[Nocturne for Horn]
Watercolor and pen on paper, cut and recombined,
bordered with gouache and pen, and mounted on
cardboard
12¾ x 9½ inches (32.3 x 24 cm)
Private Collection
CR 2682

STUFUNG ROT/GRÜN (ROTER ZINNOBER),
1921.102 *pl. 7*
[Gradation, Red–Green (Vermilion)]
Watercolor on paper, with watercolor and pen margin
above and below, mounted on cardboard
9½ x 12¼ inches (24.4 x 31.1 cm)
Pierpont Morgan Library, New York, Thaw Collection
CR 2693

DIE HEILIGE, 1921.107 *pl. 12*
[The Saint]
Watercolor and oil transfer on laid paper, mounted
on thin cardboard
17¾ x 12¼ inches (45.2 x 31.1 cm)
Norton Simon Museum, Pasadena, California
The Blue Four Galka Scheyer Collection
CR 2698

DER ANGLER, 1921.140 *pl. 6*
[The Angler]
Oil transfer and watercolor on paper, with watercolor
and pen margin above and below, mounted on
cardboard
18¾ x 12¼ inches (47.6 x 31.2 cm)
The Museum of Modern Art, New York
John S. Newberry Collection, 64.61
CR 2731

NARR IN CHRISTO, 1922.92 *pl. 13*
[Fool in Christ]
Oil transfer and watercolor on gypsum-primed gauze,
bordered with watercolor and pencil, and mounted on
cardboard
17¾ x 9½ inches (45.1 x 24.1 cm)
Private Collection
CR 2916

KLEINES REGATTABILD, 1922.108 *pl. 17*
[Small Picture of a Regatta]
Pen and watercolor on paper, bordered with water-
color and mounted on cardboard
5¾ x 9 inches (14.6 x 22.8 cm)
The Phillips Collection, Washington, D.C.
Gift from the estate of Katherine S. Dreier, 0998
CR 2932

SCHRECK EINES MÄDCHENS, 1922.131 *pl. 14*
[Fright of a Girl]
Oil transfer and watercolor on paper, bordered with
India ink on paper and mounted on cardboard
11¾ x 8⅝ inches (29.7 x 22 cm)
Solomon R. Guggenheim Museum, New York
48.1172x220
CR 2955

**AGRICULTUR VERSUCHS ANLAGE FÜR
DEN SPÄTHERBST**, 1922.137 *pl. 16*
[Agricultural Research Station for Late Autumn]
Pen and watercolor on paper, lined with pen on
cardboard
7⅜ x 11⅞ inches (18.6 x 30.1 cm)
Colby College Museum of Art, Waterville, Maine
Gift of Jere Abbott
CR 2961

DIE ZWITSCHER-MASCHINE, 1922.151 *pl. 15*
[The Twittering Machine]
Oil transfer and watercolor on paper, bordered with
watercolor and pen, and mounted on cardboard
16¼ x 12 inches (41.3 x 30.5 cm)
The Museum of Modern Art, New York
Mrs. John D. Rockefeller Jr. Purchase Fund, 564.39
CR 2975

ROTER BALLON, 1922.179 *pl. 18*
[Red Balloon]
Oil on chalk-primed muslin, mounted on cardboard
12½ x 12¼ inches (31.7 x 31.1 cm)
Solomon R. Guggenheim Museum, New York
48.1172x524
CR 3003

SCHAUSPIELER ALS FRAU, 1923.49 *pl. 19*
[Actor as a Woman]
Watercolor, ink, and pencil on paper, cut and
re-combined, with one watercolor and pen margin
above and two below, and mounted on cardboard
9 x 9 inches (22.9 x 23 cm)
Norton Simon Museum, Pasadena, California
The Blue Four Galka Scheyer Collection
CR 3142

MÄDCHEN MIT PUPPEN WAGEN, 1923.50 *pl. 20*
[Girl with Doll's Pram]
Oil transfer and watercolor on paper, with added paper
strip in watercolor and watercolor and pen margin
below, mounted on cardboard
15⅜ x 8⅜ inches (39 x 21.3 cm)
The Museum of Modern Art, New York, 13.51
CR 3143

TROPISCHE GARTEN KULTUR, 1923.55 *pl. 23*
[Tropical Garden Plantation]
Oil transfer and watercolor on paper, with watercolor
and pen margin below, mounted on cardboard
7⅜ x 19¼ inches (18.7 x 48.9 cm)
Solomon R. Guggenheim Museum, New York
Gift of Solomon R. Guggenheim, 37.509
CR 3148

ABSTRAKTES TERZETT, 1923.88 *pl. 22*
[Abstract Trio]
Oil transfer (drawing), watercolor, and oil on paper,
with watercolor and pen margin below, mounted on
cardboard
12⅝ x 19¾ inches (32.1 x 50.2 cm)
Metropolitan Museum of Art, New York
The Berggruen Klee Collection, 1984.315.36
CR 3181

SCIZZE IM CHARAKTER EINES TEPPICHS,
1923.142 *pl. 21*
[Sketch in the Manner of a Carpet]
Pen and watercolor on paper, with watercolor and pen
margin above and below, mounted on cardboard
8⅝ x 5¾ inches (22 x 14.7 cm)
Denver Art Museum, Gift of Katherine C. Detre
CR 3236

UNTITLED, 1924.77 *pl. 24*
Watercolor, pen, and pencil on paper, mounted
on cardboard
11⅛ x 12⅜ inches (28.3 x 31.3 cm)
Marion Koogler McNay Art Museum, San Antonio
Mary and Sylvan Lang Collection, 1975.38
CR 3445

VORHANG, 1924.129b *pl. 26*
[Curtain]
Watercolor and tempera on red paste-primed muslin,
bordered with gouache and pen, and mounted on
cardboard
7⅛ x 3⅝ inches (18.1 x 9.2 cm)
Solomon R. Guggenheim Museum, New York
Hilla Rebay Collection, 71.1936 R115
CR 3499

PRINZESSIN VON ARABIEN, 1924.136 *pl. 27*
[Princess of Arabia]
Watercolor and oil glazes on brown paste priming on
cardboard
10 x 7¾ inches (25.5 x 19.7 cm)
The Baltimore Museum of Art
Gift of Blanche Adler, 1930.36.1
CR 3508

PAL, 1924.180 *pl. 36*
Pen and watercolor, wet in wet, and pencil on paper,
mounted on cardboard
3⅞ x 8⅞ inches (10 x 22.6 cm)
Private Collection
CR 3552

MÄRCHENBILD, 1924.185 *pl. 25*
[Fairy Tale Picture]
Watercolor on paper, mounted on silver paper and
mounted on cardboard
15 x 10¾ inches (38.1 x 27.3 cm)
Private Collection
CR 3557

MAZZARÓ, 1924.218 *pl. 29*
Watercolor on black glue priming on paper, with
watercolor margins above and below, mounted on
cardboard
9⅛ x 12 inches (23.3 x 30.5 cm)
Extended loan and promised gift of the Carl Djerassi
Trust I to the San Francisco Museum of Modern Art
CR 3590

SICILISCHE FLORA IM SEPTEMBER, 1924.240
[Sicilian Flora in September] *pl. 30*
Watercolor and pencil on black-primed paper,
mounted on cardboard
8¾ x 11⅜ inches (22.2 x 28.8 cm)
Collection of The Arts Club of Chicago
Bequest of Arthur Heun, 1947
CR 3612

BAUM KULTUR, 1924.245 *pl. 32*
[Tree Culture]
Oil transfer (drawing) and watercolor on paper, with
watercolor and pen margin above and below, mounted
on cardboard
19⅛ x 13¾ inches (48.7 x 34.9 cm)
Solomon R. Guggenheim Museum, New York, 38.511
CR 3617

~~JUGENDLICHER~~ SCHAUSPIELER=MASKE,
1924.252 *pl. 28*
[~~Youth~~ Actor's Mask]
Oil on canvas, mounted on cardboard and nailed
on wooden panel
14½ x 13¼ inches (36.7 x 33.8 cm)
The Museum of Modern Art, New York
The Sidney and Harriet Janis Collection, 616.67
CR 3624

SEGELSCHIFFHAFEN, 1925.45 *pl. 37*
[Harbour for Sailing Ships]
Watercolor brushed and sprayed on paper
12⅝ x 17⅝ inches (32.1 x 44.7 cm)
Courtesy Calder Foundation, New York
CR 3726

FISCH ZAUBER, 1925.85 *pl. 34*
[Fish Magic]
Oil and watercolor on muslin, mounted on cardboard
and mounted on stretcher, with original strip frame
30¼ x 38¾ inches (77 x 98.3 cm)
Philadelphia Museum of Art
The Louise and Walter Arensberg Collection, 1950
CR 3766

**GEISTERZIMMER MIT DER HOHEN TÜRE
(NEUE FASSUNG)**, 1925.102 *pl. 38*
[Ghost Chamber with the High Door
(New Version)]
Oil transfer (drawing) and partly sprayed watercolor
on paper, bordered with gouache and pen and
mounted on cardboard
19⅛ x 11⅝ inches (48.7 x 29.4 cm)
Metropolitan Museum of Art, New York
The Berggruen Klee Collection, 1987.455.16
CR 3783

ORIENTALISCHER LUSTGARTEN, 1925.131 *pl. 31*
[Oriental Pleasure Garden]
Oil on cardboard
15¾ x 20½ inches (40 x 52 cm)
Metropolitan Museum of Art, New York
The Berggruen Klee Collection, 1984.315.41
CR 3812

SKLAVEREI, 1925.148 *pl. 33*
[Slavery]
Oil transfer drawing and watercolor on paper,
mounted on cardboard
10 x 14 inches (25.4 x 35.6 cm)
The Museum of Modern Art, New York
Gift of Abby Aldrich Rockefeller, 96.35
CR 3829

BOCK, 1925.198 *pl. 48*
[Billy-Goat]
Pen and sprayed watercolor on white chalk and tempera-
primed paper, mounted on cardboard
8⅝ x 11 inches (21.8 x 28.1 cm)
Smith College Museum of Art, Northampton,
Massachusetts
Gift of Jere Abbott, 1976:23
CR 3879

HEILIGE INSELN, 1926.6 *pl. 40*
[Sacred Islands]
Watercolor and pen on paper, mounted on cardboard
18½ x 12⅜ inches (47 x 31.5 cm)
The Museum of Modern Art, New York
Gift of Philip Johnson, 457
CR 3952

EULENKOMOEDIE, 1926.48 *pl. 44*
[Owl Comedy]
Partly sprayed watercolor and pen on paper, mounted
on cardboard
12½ x 18½ inches (31.7 x 46.9 cm)
Solomon R. Guggenheim Museum, New York, 39.512
CR 3994

ELEFANT UND LOEWE, 1926.56 *pl. 45*
[Elephant and Lion]
Pen and sprayed watercolor on paper mounted
on cardboard
12 x 18¼ inches (30.5 x 46.3 cm)
Museum of Art, Rhode Island School of Design,
Providence, Gift of Bayard and Harriet K. Ewing
Collection, 1993.105.15
CR 4002

ANMASSUNG, 1926.64 *pl. 43*
[Arrogance]
Ink and partly sprayed watercolor on paper, mounted
on cardboard
8¼ x 8¼ inches (21.1 x 21.1 cm)
Galerie Jan Krugier, Ditesheim & Cie, Geneva
CR 4010

KL. DÜNENBILD, 1926.115 *pl. 42*
[Small Dune Picture]
Oil on black casein ground, mounted on cardboard
12¾ x 9⅛ inches (32.4 x 23.2 cm)
The Menil Collection, Houston
CR 4066

PALAST, TEILWEISE ZERSTÖRT, 1926.119 *pl. 39*
[Palace, Partly Destroyed]
Watercolor on paper, mounted on cardboard
20 x 13 inches (51 x 33 cm)
The Denver Art Museum
The Charles Francis Hendrie Memorial Collection
CR 4070

DORF-CARNAVAL, 1926.135 *pl. 35*
[Village Carnival]
Oil on muslin, mounted on cardboard, with original
painted strip frame
21½ x 17¼ inches (54.6 x 43.8 cm)
Philadelphia Museum of Art
The Louise and Walter Arensberg Collection, 1950
CR 4086

FIGURINENSAMMLUNG, 1926.248 *pl. 49*
[Collection of Figurines]
Oil on canvas, mounted on cardboard
10⅜ x 9⅝ inches (26.4 x 24.4 cm)
Metropolitan Museum of Art, New York
The Berggruen Klee Collection, 1984.315.47
CR 4207

STILLEBEN (TÖPFE, FRUCHT, OSTEREI,
GARDINEN, ETC.), 1927.18 *pl. 51*
[Still Life (Pots, Fruit, Easter Egg, Curtains, Etc.)]
Oil on gypsum, with original strip frame
18⅞ x 25¼ inches (47.9 x 64.1 cm)
Metropolitan Museum of Art, New York
The Berggruen Klee Collection, 1984.315.49
CR 4231

MEGÁNTHEMUM, 1927.177 *pl. 64*
Oil on wood, with original strip frame
28⅞ x 18 inches (73.3 x 45.7 cm)
Frelinghuysen Morris Foundation, Lenox, Massachusetts
CR 4391

NEGRIDE SCHÖNHEIT (PRAECISION), 1927.192
[Negroid Beauty (Precision)] *pl. 47*
Pen on paper, mounted on cardboard
17⅜ x 13 inches (44 x 33 cm)
Extended loan of the Carl Djerassi Trust II
to the San Francisco Museum of Modern Art
CR 4406

PFLANZEN SAMEN, 1927.288 *pl. 46*
[Plant Seeds]
Partly sprayed watercolor and pen on paper, with
gouache and pen margins above and below, mounted
on cardboard
12⅛ x 18⅜ inches (30.8 x 46.7 cm)
Norton Simon Museum, Pasadena, California
The Blue Four Galka Scheyer Collection
CR 4502

ZAUBER KUNST STÜCK, 1927.297 *pl. 54*
[Conjuring Trick]
Oil and watercolor on cardboard, with original painted
strip frame
19⅝ x 16½ inches (49.8 x 41.8 cm)
Philadelphia Museum of Art
The Louise and Walter Arensberg Collection, 1950
CR 4511

STRENGE FELSBILDUNG, 1927.321 *pl. 41*
[Austere Rock Formation]
Pencil on paper, mounted with glue spots on cardboard
8¾ x 13 inches (22.2 x 33 cm)
The Menil Collection, Houston
CR 4535

BUNTE MAHLZEIT, 1928.29 *pl. 52*
[Colorful Meal]
Oil and watercolor on canvas, with original strip frame
31⅞ x 26⅜ inches (81 x 67 cm)
Private Collection, courtesy Neue Galerie New York
CR 4570

NICHT OHNE HERZ, 1928.33 *pl. 56*
[Not without Heart]
Pen on paper, mounted with glue spots on cardboard
12 x 11½ inches (30.5 x 29.2 cm)
Private Collection
CR 4574

SPUKENDE GAUKLER, 1928.42 *pl. 57*
[Haunting Entertainers]
Pen on paper, mounted with glue spots on cardboard
11¾ x 18 inches (29.9 x 45.8 cm)
Courtesy Calder Foundation, New York
CR 4583

MARJAMHAUSEN, 1928.54 *pl. 61*
Watercolor on paper, with watercolor and pen margin
above and below, mounted on cardboard
14⅛ x 8 inches (36 x 20.5 cm)
The Museum of Fine Arts, Houston
Gift of Miss Ima Hogg, 39.111
CR 4595

STILLEBEN MIT TIERSTATUETTE, 1928.158   *pl. 50*
[Still Life with Animal Statuette]
Oil and watercolor on white-primed canvas, bordered
with watercolor and pen, and mounted on cardboard
12⅜ x 12⅝ inches (31.5 x 32 cm)
Private Collection
CR 4700

GABEN FÜR "J.", 1928.212   *pl. 53*
[Gifts for "J."]
Oil on chalk-primed canvas, mounted on wood, with
original painted frame
15¾ x 22 inches (40 x 55.9 cm)
The Museum of Modern Art New York
Gift of James Thrall Soby, 1092.69
CR 4754

MONUMENT IN ARBEIT, 1929.88   *pl. 55*
[Monument Under Construction]
Watercolor on plaster-primed paper, with watercolor and
pen margins above and below, mounted on cardboard
22⅛ x 15¼ inches (56.3 x 38.6 cm)
Collection of Michael and Judy Steinhardt, New York
CR 4844

IN DER STRÖMUNG SECHS SCHWELLEN,
1929.92   *pl. 65*
[In the Current Six Weirs]
Oil and tempera on canvas
16⅝ x 16⅝ inches (42.2 x 42.2 cm)
Solomon R. Guggenheim Museum, New York, 67.1842
CR 4848

JUNGE PFLANZUNG, 1929.98   *pl. 59*
[Young Plantation]
Oil on primed canvas, with original strip frame
17¼ x 20⅝ inches (43.9 x 52.4 cm)
The Phillips Collection, Washington, D.C., 1000
CR 4854

SEL, 1929.128   *pl. 60*
Watercolor and pen on paper, mounted on cardboard
9¼ x 8⅞ inches (23.5 x 22.5 cm)
The Museum of Fine Arts, Houston
Gift of Miss Ima Hogg, 39.110
CR 4884

HEITERE GEBIRGSLANDSCHAFT, 1929.134   *pl. 63*
[Bright Mountain Landscape]
Oil on plywood
17¼ x 24⅞ inches (43.9 x 63.1 cm)
Yale University Art Gallery, New Haven, Connecticut
Katharine Ordway Collection, 1980.12.22
CR 4890

ORPHEUS, 1929.257   *pl. 62*
Watercolor on cotton, mounted on plywood
19¾ x 9½ inches (50.2 x 24.2 cm)
Private Collection
CR 5013

BEBEN, 1929.290   *pl. 58*
[Quake]
Pen and sprayed watercolor on paper, mounted
on cardboard
13 x 8 inches (33 x 20.5 cm)
Collection of the Tobin Foundation for Theatre Arts,
long-term loan to the Marion Koogler McNay Art
Museum, San Antonio, R69.17
CR 5046

DER MANN MIT DEM MUNDWERK, 1930.33
[The Man with the Big Mouth]   *pl. 66*
Oil transfer (drawing) on paper, mounted with glue
spots on cardboard
13 x 16½ inches (33 x 41.9 cm)
The Detroit Institute of Arts
Bequest of John S. Newberry, 65.187
CR 5149

POLYPHONE ARCHITEKTUR, 1930.130   *pl. 70*
[Polyphonic Architecture]
Watercolor and pen on cotton on canvas
16½ x 18⅛ inches (42 x 46 cm)
The Saint Louis Art Museum, Purchase, 9:42
CR 5246

BLÜTEN IN DER NACHT, 1930.207   *pl. 68*
[Flowers in the Night]
Watercolor on paste-primed paper, mounted
on cardboard
9¼ x 12¼ inches (23.5 x 31.2 cm)
San Francisco Museum of Modern Art
Gift of Charlotte Mack
CR 5325

SONNENUNTERGANG, 1930.209   *pl. 72*
[Sunset]
Oil and pencil on primed canvas
18¼ x 27⅝ inches (46.2 x 70.2 cm)
The Art Institute of Chicago
Gift of Mr. and Mrs. Leigh B. Block, 1981.13
CR 5327

PLAN EINER BURG, 1930.218   *pl. 69*
[Plan of a Castle]
Watercolor and pen on paper, mounted on cardboard
15 x 19 inches (38.1 x 48.3 cm)
Collection of Hope Dempsey Hungerford
CR 5337

"ODER DER VERSPOTTETE SPÖTTER," 1930.246
["Or the Mocked Mocker"]   *pl. 67*
Oil on canvas, with original strip frame
17 x 20½ inches (43 x 52 cm)
The Museum of Modern Art, New York
Gift of J. B. Neumann, 1939, 637.39
CR 5365

DAS GANZE DÄMMERND, 1932.4   *pl. 71*
[The Whole Is Dimming]
Watercolor on paper, mounted on cardboard
15¾ x 12⅜ inches (40 x 31.4 cm)
Private Collection
CR 5700

ZWEI BETONTE LAGEN, 1932.6   *pl. 73*
[Two Emphasized Layers]
Watercolor on paper mounted on cardboard
9½ x 12 inches (24.1 x 30.4 cm)
The Menil Collection, Houston
CR 5702

VOR ANKER, 1932.22   *pl. 75*
[At Anchor]
Oil on canvas
34¼ x 36⅝ inches (87 x 93 cm)
Private Collection
CR 5718

KLAERUNG, 1932.66   *pl. 74*
[Clarification]
Oil on canvas
27½ x 37¾ inches (70 x 96 cm)
Metropolitan Museum of Art, New York
The Berggruen Klee Collection, 1984.315.54
CR 5762

ARABISCHES LIED, 1932.283   *pl. 76*
[Arabian Song]
Oil on jute
35⅞ x 25½ inches (91.1 x 64.7 cm)
The Phillips Collection, Washington, D.C., 0990
CR 5979

BLICK DER STILLE, 1932.285 *pl. 82*
[Gaze of Silence]
Oil on jute
21⅞ x 27¾ inches (55.6 x 70.5 cm)
The Menil Collection, Houston
CR 5981

ZWEI KÖPFE, 1932.332 *pl. 80*
[Two Heads]
Oil and pencil on canvas
31¾ x 33⅜ inches (80.8 x 84.7 cm)
Norton Simon Museum, Pasadena, California
The Blue Four Galka Scheyer Collection
CR 6028

ERNEUERUNG DER MANNSZUCHT, 1933.71
[Revival of Manly Discipline] *pl. 77*
Pencil on paper, mounted on cardboard
17 x 12¾ inches (43.2 x 32.4 cm)
Colgate University, The Picker Art Gallery, Hamilton,
New York
Gift of Herbert Mayer, 1966.1.324
CR 6116

MASKE ROTER JUDE, 1933.386 *pl. 78*
[Mask: Red Jew]
Paste paint on paper, mounted on cardboard
12¾ x 8⅛ inches (32.5 x 20.6 cm)
Collection of Michael and Judy Steinhardt, New York
CR 6433

LÖWENMENSCH, 1934.2 *pl. 79*
[Lion Man]
Watercolor on paper
18¾ x 12 inches (47.6 x 30.6 cm)
Fractional and promised gift of the Djerassi Art Trust
to the San Francisco Museum of Modern Art
CR 6540

EINSAME BLÜTE, 1934.5 *pl. 83*
[Lonely Flower]
Watercolor, pen, and pencil on paper
18⅞ x 12⅜ inches (47.8 x 31.5 cm)
Columbus Museum of Art, Columbus, Ohio
Sirak Collection, 1991.001.025
CR 6543

BEULEN BIRNE, 1934.164 *pl. 84*
[Bulgy Pear]
Watercolor and oil on primed paper, with colored
paper strips placed above and below, mounted on
cardboard
8¼ x 8½ inches (21 x 21.6 cm)
Private Collection, New York
CR 6702

ANGST, 1934.202 *pl. 81*
[Fear]
Watercolor on chalk-primed jute
(verso: gouache and wax on jute)
19⅝ x 23⅝ inches (49.9 x 60 cm)
National Gallery of Canada, Ottawa
Purchased 1979
CR 6740

DER WEG INS BLAUE, 1934.203 *pl. 88*
[The Path into the Blue]
Oil on wood
16¼ x 16½ inches (41.3 x 41.9 cm)
The Old Jail Art Center, Albany, Texas
Gift of Bill Bomar, 1991, 91.002
CR 6741

W=GEWEIHTES KIND, 1935.31 *pl. 90*
[W=Consecrated Child]
Oil and watercolor on primed paper, mounted on
cardboard
6⅜ x 9⅜ inches (16 x 23.9 cm)
Albright-Knox Art Gallery, Buffalo, New York, RCA
1940:12
CR 6793

ILFENBURG, 1935.109 *pl. 85*
Watercolor on primed paper, mounted on silver paper
and mounted on cardboard
11⅞ x 10⅜ inches (30.3 x 26.2 cm)
Columbus Museum of Art, Columbus, Ohio
Sirak Collection, 1991.001.028
CR 6871

NEUE HARMONIE, 1936.24 *pl. 89*
[New Harmony]
Oil on canvas
36½ x 26⅛ inches (93 x 66 cm)
Solomon R. Guggenheim Museum, New York
CR6935

HARTE WENDUNGEN, 1937.68 *pl. 87*
[Sharp Turns]
Colored paste on cotton canvas, mounted on cardboard
8½ x 10 inches (21.6 x 25.4 cm)
The Menil Collection, Houston
CR 7004

BRÜCKENBOGEN TRETEN AUS
DER REIHE, 1937.111 *pl. 86*
[Arches of the Bridge Stepping Out of Line]
Charcoal and red chalk on linen, mounted on cardboard
16¾ x 16½ inches (42.6 cm x 42 cm)
Solomon R. Guggenheim Museum, New York
48.1172x59
CR 7047

FRAGMENTE, 1937.132 *pl. 92*
[Fragments]
Oil on jute
21⅝ x 28 inches (55 x 71 cm)
San Francisco Museum of Modern Art
Gift of Wilbur D. May
CR 7068

BILDERBOGEN, 1937.133 *pl. 93*
[Printed Sheet with Picture]
Oil on canvas
23¼ x 22 inches (59 x 56 cm)
The Phillips Collection, Washington, D.C., 0999
CR 7069

BEGINNENDE KÜHLE, 1937.136 *pl. 94*
[Incipient Coolness]
Oil on cardboard, nailed on stretcher
29½ x 20⅞ inches (75 x 53 cm)
Galerie Jan Krugier, Ditesheim & Cie, Geneva
CR 7072

DER WEG ZUR STADTBURG (STÄDTEBILD),
1937.137 *pl. 95*
[The Way to the Citadel (Picture of a City)]
Oil on canvas, mounted on cardboard and nailed on
stretcher, with original strip frame
26⅜ x 22½ inches (67 x 57 cm)
The Phillips Collection, Washington, D.C. , 1001
CR 7073

WANDER-CIRCUS, 1937.139 *pl. 91*
[Traveling Circus]
Oil on canvas
25⅝ x 19⅝ inches (65 x 50 cm)
The Baltimore Museum of Art
Bequest of Saidie A. May, 1951.317
CR 7075

DER MANN DER VERWECHSLUNG, 1939.350
[The Man of Confusion] *pl. 97*
Watercolor and oil on jute
26 x 19⅝ inches (66 x 50 cm)
The Saint Louis Art Museum
Gift of Mr. and Mrs. Joseph Pulitzer, Jr., 410:1952
CR 8055

DAS KRANKE HERZ, 1939.382 *pl. 96*
[The Sick Heart]
Watercolor and paste paint on cardboard, nailed on
stretcher, with original strip frame
16 x 21¼ inches (40.7 x 54 cm)
Private Collection, New York
CR 8087

Index of Selected American Collectors

This list references illustrated works owned by American collectors during the 1920s–1950s. Please see the Paul Klee Catalogue Raisonné *for complete provenance information.*

Works are identified by Catalogue Raisonné *number followed by Klee number. Illustrations are indicated by plate number (pl. 00) or figure number (fig. 00).*

Charlotte Mack

4231	1927.18	*pl. 51*
5325	1930.207	*pl. 68*
6743	1934.205	fig. 80

Ruth Maitland

| 4010 | 1926.64 | *pl. 92* |
| 7068 | 1937.132 | *pl. 43* |

Clifford Odets

| 2616 | 1921.25 | *pl. 5* |
| 3590 | 1924.218 | *pl. 29* |

Katharine Ordway

| 4890 | 1929.134 | *pl. 63* |

Robert and Elodie E. Osborn

| 2657 | 1921.66 | *pl. 11* |

Duncan and Marjorie Phillips

2932	1922.108	*pl. 17*
3009	1922.184	*fig. 54*
4854	1929.98	*pl. 59*
5979	1932.283	*pl. 76*
7069	1937.133	*pl. 93*
7073	1937.137	*pl. 95*

Joseph Pulitzer Jr.

2144	1919.81	*pl. 3*
5718	1932.22	*pl. 75*
8055	1939.350	*pl. 97*

Hilla von Rebay

| 3499 | 1924.129b | *pl. 26* |

Helen and Stanley Resor

| 4570 | 1928.29 | *pl. 51* |

Elmer Rice

| 4002 | 1926.56 | *pl. 45* |

Diego Rivera and Frida Kahlo

| 3552 | 1924.180 | *pl. 36* |

Abby Aldrich Rockefeller

| 3829 | 1925.148 | *pl. 33* |

Nelson Rockefeller

2609	1921.18	*pl. 10*
6740	1934.202	*pl. 81*
7202	1938.1	*fig. 82*

James Thrall Soby

| 4754 | 1928.212 | *pl. 53* |

James Johnson Sweeney

| 4659 | 1928.117 | *fig. 46* |

Mark Tobey

| 5046 | 1929.290 | *pl. 58* |

William Valentiner

1078	1913.176	*pl. 1*
2682	1921.91	*pl. 8*
2693	1921.102	*pl. 7*

Edward Warburg

| 4353 | 1927.140.2 | *fig. 13* |

Andy Warhol

| 4574 | 1928.33 | *pl. 56* |

Billy Wilder

| 6540 | 1934.2 | *pl. 79* |

Photography

Every reasonable attempt has been made to identify owners of copyright. Errors or omissions will be corrected in subsequent editions.

Academy of Motion Pictures Arts and Sciences, Los Angeles, fig. 32

akg-images, Berlin, London, Paris, fig. 77

Albright Knox Art Gallery, Buffalo, New York, pl. 90

Archives of American Art, Smithsonian Institution, Washington, D.C., courtesy of the Chester Dale Papers, 1897–1971 (bulk 1950–1968), photograph by Peter A. Juley, fig. 36

Archives of American Art, Smithsonian Institution, Washington, D.C., J.B. Neumann Papers, 1914–1917, photograph by Helen Blafour-Morrison, fig. 28

Archives of American Art, Smithsonian Institution, Washington, D.C., image provided by Lily Harmon, 1930–1996, photograph by Aaron Siskind, fig. 107

The Art Institute of Chicago, pls. 4, 72; fig. 3

The Arts Club of Chicago, pl. 30

The Baltimore Museum of Art, pls. 27, 91

The Barnes Foundation, Merion, Pennsylvania, figs. 26, 99

Bauhaus Archive, Berlin, fig. 93

The Beinecke Rare Book and Manuscript Library, Yale University, New Haven, Connecticut, fig. 21

Bildarchiv Preussischer Kulturbesitz / Art Resource, New York, figs. 13, 31, 40, 66

Mrs. Albert Bloch, fig. 10

Bogner and Lord, Vienna, fig. 94

Busch-Reisinger Museum, Harvard University, fig. 15

Busch-Reisinger Museum, Harvard University, © Ruth Asawa Lanier, Inc., photograph by Katya Kallsen, fig. 71

Courtesy Calder Foundation, New York, pls. 37, 57; fig. 56

Colby College Museum of Art, Waterville, Maine, pl. 16

Colgate University, The Picker Art Gallery, Hamilton, New York, pl. 77

Columbus Museum of Art, Columbus, Ohio, pls. 5, 83, 85

Denver Art Museum, pls. 21, 39

Detroit Institute of Arts, pl. 66

Joseph Fiore, photograph by Mary Emma Harris, fig. 69

Fondation Beyeler, Riehen/Basel, Switzerland, fig. 53

Frelinghuysen Morris Foundation, Lenox, Massachusetts, pl. 64

Friends of the Schindler House, Los Angeles, gift of Peg Weiss, fig. 37

Galerie Jan Krugier, Ditesheim & Cie, Geneva, pls. 43, 94

Getty Images, Hulton Archive, pages 16 (top), 136

Grohmann Archive, Stuttgart, fig. 98

Hope Dempsey Hungerford, pl. 69

The Josef and Anni Albers Foundation, Bethany, Connecticut, fig. 67

The Josef and Anni Albers Foundation, Bethany, Connecticut, photograph by Tim Nighswander, figs. 63, 68

Kiesler Foundation, Vienna, figs. 58, 105

The Marion Koogler McNay Art Museum, San Antonio, pls. 24, 58

Kunstmuseum Bern, Switzerland, fig. 12

The Menil Collection, Houston, pls. 41, 42, 73, 82, 87

The Metropolitan Museum of Art, New York, pls. 10, 11, 22, 31, 38, 49, 51, 74

Museum of Art, Rhode Island School of Design, Providence, Rhode Island, photograph by Erik Gould, pl. 45

The Museum of Fine Arts, Houston, pls. 60, 61

The Museum of Modern Art / Licensed by SCALA / Art Resource, New York, cover; pls. 6, 15, 20, 28, 33, 40, 53, 67; figs. 14, 22, 30, 41, 48, 74, 78, 82

The Museum of Modern Art / Licensed by Art Resource, New York, Museum of Modern Art Archives, The Margaret S. Barr Papers, fig. 39

The Museum of Modern Art / Licensed by SCALA / Art Resource, New York, photographic archive, figs. 101, 106

The Museum of Modern Art / Licensed by SCALA / Art Resource, New York, photograph by Jay Leyda, gift of the photographer, (65.1941), fig. 27

National Gallery of Canada, Ottawa, pl. 81

National Gallery of Ireland, Dublin, fig. 46

Neue Galerie New York, pl. 52

Courtesy The North Carolina State Archives, Raleigh, North Carolina, fig. 64

Courtesy, The North Carolina State Archives, Raleigh, North Carolina, photograph by Trude Guermonprez, figs. 72, 73

Norton Simon Museum, Pasadena, California, pls. 9, 12, 19, 46, 80; figs. 18, 19, 84, 85, 91, 92; page 96 (bottom)

Offentliche Kunstsammlung, Kunstmuseum Basel, Switzerland, page 70 (left)

The Old Jail Art Center, Albany, Texas, pl. 88

Philadelphia Museum of Art, pls. 34, 35, 54; fig. 25

Philadelphia Museum of Art, photograph by Fred R. Dapprich, frontispiece; figs. 34, 35, 55

Philadelphia Museum of Art archives, photograph by Beatrice Wood, figs. 33, 96

The Phillips Collection, Washington, D.C., pls. 17, 59, 76, 93, 95; figs. 49, 50, 51, 52, 60, 61, 62

Pierpoint Morgan Library, New York, pl. 7

Private Collection, pls. 2., 3, 8, 13, 25, 36, 50, 56, 62, 71, 75, 84, 96; figs. 6, 43; page 137

Private Collection, courtesy Marlborough Fine Art, fig. 23

Private Collection, New York, Private Collection, reproduced in "Arthur Jerome Eddy and His Collection," *Arts Magazine* 61, no. 6 (February 1987): 40, fig. 2

The Saint Louis Art Museum, pls. 70, 97

San Francisco Museum of Art, pls. 29, 47, 68, 79, 92

Miriam Sihvonen, photograph by Vicky McLaine, fig. 70

Smith College Archives, Smith College, Northampton, Massachusetts, fig. 29

Smith College Museum of Art, Northampton, Massachusetts, pl. 48

Solomon R. Guggenheim Foundation, Peggy Guggenheim Collection, Venice, fig. 59

Solomon R. Guggenheim Museum, New York, pls. 14, 18, 23, 26, 32, 44, 65, 86, 89; figs. 24, 44; page 70 (right)

Collection of Michael and Judy Steinhardt, pls. 55, 78

Washington University Gallery of Art, St. Louis, fig. 8

Worthington Collection, Chicago, pl. 1

Yale University Art Gallery, New Haven, Connecticut, pl. 63; fig. 17

Yale University Art Gallery, New Haven, Connecticut, photograph by Joseph Szaszfai, fig. 88

Zentrum Paul Klee, Bern, Switzerland, figs. 4, 9, 16, 38, 47, 54, 79, 80, 83, page 96 (top)

Zentrum Paul Klee, Bern, Switzerland, estate of Konrad Farner, fig. 81

Zentrum Paul Klee, Bern, Switzerland, photograph by Adolph Studly, page 222

Zentrum Paul Klee, Gift of the Klee Family, Bern, Switzerland, figs. 85, 86, 89, 90, 93, 95, 97, 100

Zentrum Paul Klee, Gift of the Klee Family, Bern, Switzerland, photograph by F. Fass, fig. 1

Zentrum Paul Klee, Gift of the Klee Family, Bern, Switzerland, photograph by Felix Klee, figs. 11, 75, 76

Zentrum Paul Klee, Livia Klee Donation, Bern, Switzerland, fig. 7; page 179

Hatje Cantz books are available internationally at selected bookstores and from the following distribution partners:

USA/North America: D.A.P., Distributed Art Publishers, New York, www.artbook.com
UK: Art Books International, London, sales@art-bks.com
Australia: Tower Books, Frenchs Forest (Sydney), towerbks@zipworld.com.au
France: Interart, Paris, commercial@interart.fr
Belgium: Exhibitions International, Leuven, www.exhibitionsinternational.be
Switzerland: Scheidegger, Affoltern am Albis, scheidegger@ava.ch

For Asia, Japan, South America, and Africa, as well as for general questions, please contact Hatje Cantz directly at sales@hatjecantz.de, or visit our homepage www.hatjecantz.com for further information.

Managing Editor: Sarah Eckhardt
Copy Editor: Polly Koch
Editorial Asssitant: Clare Elliott

Design: Don Quaintance, Public Address Design
Design/production assistant: Elizabeth Frizzell

Michael Baumgartner and Osamu Okuda texts, originally written in German, were translated by Russell Stockman.

Typography: Monotype Bulmer (text) and Syntax (display)
Reproductions: Pallino cross media GmbH, Ostfildern-Ruit, Germany
Paper: Galaxi Super Matte
Printing: Dr. Cantz'sche Druckerei, Ostfildern-Ruit, Germany
Binding: Kunst- und Verlagsbuchbinderei GmbH, Leipzig, Germany